A Treasury of the World's

Great Diaries

A Treasury of the World's

Great Diaries

EDITED BY PHILIP DUNAWAY AND MEL EVANS

WITH AN INTRODUCTION BY LOUIS UNTERMEYER

Doubleday & Company, Inc.
Garden City, New York

An Introduction

BY LOUIS UNTERMEYER

Reading the manuscript of this book made me realize that I had forgotten a great experience. I had forgotten how exciting a diary can be. Every other kind of writing—a novel, an interview, a poem, a play—is aimed at publication or performance with (hopefully) a wide and appreciative audience. But the diary is written without consciousness of a public. It is, in fact, the effort to escape the public man (what everybody is most of the time) that compels a person to save his secret life for himself. Only in the privacy of his diary can he write without reticence, rid of the fear of being considered shameless or silly, and free of the postures with which he faces the world. The diary serves as his catharsis, his patient confidant, his father confessor, his other self.

When we read a diary, we are not merely looking over a man's shoulder. We are looking into his inmost mind, his hidden heart: here everything is forthright and without subterfuge. There is no critic to frown, no censor to intimidate; no editor can come between the writer and his uninhibited thoughts. Emotions find their expression without fumbling for the precise word, although the perfect phrase is often achieved. Whatever happens is usually described just after it has occurred—everything is spontaneous, unpremeditated, and completely convincing.

This sense of immediacy gives authority and excitement to every page of this collection. The first diary in the book—Anne Frank's trembling idyl of first love against a background of terror—stirs us and almost overcomes us, its final tragedy accentuated by the utter candor and heart-breaking innocence with which the young girl records the dreams and growing pains of adolescence. As though to point up the kaleidoscopic character of the book, Anne Frank's diary is followed by that of a startlingly different teenager—the self-conscious Marie Bashkirtseff, an outrageous flirt, accomplished artist, and highly articulate woman of the world at fourteen. Still another contrast is the third figure, the nineteen-year-old Lester Ward—not the famous sociologist he was to become, but a shy and ingenuous youth stumbling into sex, a boy whose naïve discoveries seem to have been written between blushes. A few pages later we encounter Ward's opposite, Marie Henri Beyle (Stendhal), who, at the same age as Ward, was already a sexual virtuoso, a *voyeur* who was not afraid to be ribald and not ashamed to appear ridiculous.

On one intimate page after another are sketched a series of vivid personalities who, in revealing their extraordinary selves, picture the everyday (but by no means mundane) life of their times. Never pretending to be historians, they illumine history by way of autobiography. Every reader will find his own favorite diarists, some famous and some obscure, who fulfill this function without being aware of it.

One can only be grateful for a selection which, for the first time, brings together so many unusual and unlikely figures. Here is the laconic Joshua Sears, the nineteenth-century clipper ship captain who carries the tang of northern pine and the tart flavor of New England around the world. And Edmund Temple, a somewhat earlier sailor, whose journal smolders with the scorching heat of the pampas and the violence of primitive Peru. Mark Twain at twenty-six (not the traditionally genial humorist, but an itinerant news-paperman and apprentice author whose first book was still years in the fu-ture) appears here as the doleful recorder of a pestilential voyage almost as macabre as the one described in *The Rime of the Ancient Mariner*—a voyage cursed by cholera and lack of medicine, on a ship that turns first into a hos-pital and then into a charnel house. Lewis Carroll is seen in his two rôles: the pseudonymous creator of *Alice* and the shy mathematician who was a deacon in holy orders. Both sides of the double man are glimpsed as the diarist un-wittingly contrasts Carroll's wayward whimsies with the Reverend Dodgson's prim regard for the proprieties.

In this gallery of self-portraits there are none more pitilessly detailed, more unsparingly frank than those done by women. Alone and rejected George Sand sits through the night pouring out her love and bitterness to herself—and to the departed de Musset. And here is Victoria—not the dour "Widow of Windsor", embodiment of the Victorian Mrs. Grundy, but the nineteen-year-old princess contemplating the throne with a schoolgirl's mind and a match-ing prose style. She reveals her timid self in awe of the magisterial Lord Melbourne, her dogmatic mentor, who warns her against playwrights ("They are not good for much else.") and the danger of dancing quadrilles; she is girlishly agitated by a Russian grand-duke; she falls gushingly in love with her cousin, the German Prince Albert—he of the "beautiful blue eyes, ex-quisite nose, pretty mouth, with delicate moustachios and slight but very slight whiskers, broad in the shoulders and a fine waist"—the paragon to whom, according to protocol, she proposed and whom she worshipped all his life and even more after his death . . . And Dorothy Wordsworth, whose delicate apperceptions are a rewarding study for any writer and whose fixed devotion to her brother (my Beloved) must be a challenge to every Freudian. . . . And Countess Tolstoy, a case history of the intricate interrelationship of love and hate: disgusted with her husband's past, distrustful of his prin-ciples, maniacally jealous of his associates—a woman who loathed the physi-cal act of love, and, though she bore her husband thirteen children, never established a genuine rapport with him during the forty-eight years they lived unhappily together and desperately apart.

The range widens and the contrasts increase as the book shuttles from age to age, from one culture to another. Out of the tenth century comes a strange figure, Ki no Tsurayuki, a Japanese noble and diplomat who, during a diffi-cult time, persuades his companions to calm themselves by composing poetry. Equally strange is Marjory Fleming, the breathless six-year-old who died àt nine, whose childish but exact reportage is only enhanced by her struggles with spelling and punctuation, especially the "commoes" and "simecolings". What reader will not relish the tangled—and slightly reprehensible—affairs of Samuel Sewall, the artful amorist and much-married New England clergyman; or appreciate the frankness of a rogue like Thomas Hearne, gossip and blood brother to the bawdy Elizabethans; or be shocked by the unretouched candid-camera portrait of the aging Queen Elizabeth caught by the outspoken French ambassador, Monsieur de Maisse? I confess that nothing I had read in the *Intimate Journal* of Henri-Frederic Amiel, edited so properly by the sentimental Mrs. Humphrey Ward, prepared me for the curious episode related here: the progress of passion in the otherwise aloof mind of a prudent professor—and its shocking anticlimax.

But the book is by no means all brutal candor and unrelenting introspection. The sober confidences of John Quincy Adams—scientist, scholar, President and son of a President, and, not least, frustrated poet—show us, not a marble effigy of the official man, but a wonderfully lifelike picture of a great mind and a warm fellow creature. The profound serenity of Emerson, the patrician dignity of Washington, the spiritual certainty of the dedicated John Wesley, the fierce integrity of Thoreau—all are extraordinary self-revelations, all become part of this fascinating mosaic of man's mind.

No facet of life is foreign to these indefatigable diarists. In a dozen grouped journals one lives again through the agony of the Civil War: with Mary Boykin Chesnut we watch the gallant hope of the Confederacy dwindle to final despair; John B. Jones, Augustus C. Brown, and Lawrence Van Alstyne report the pitiable, forgotten incidents of patriotism on the battlefield and profiteering on the home front. Here, too, are the visions and vicissitudes of authors from Sir Walter Scott to John Steinbeck, from Edmond de Goncourt to Arnold Bennett, from Katherine Mansfield to Virginia Woolf—two souls so sensitized that they failed to survive the brutality of their times. And always there is that curious and everlasting modernity that lives in all men, in the quaint language and remote incidents preserved by Samuel Pepys and John Evelyn as well as in Dr. Michihiko Hachiya's horrifying description of the bombing of Hiroshima with which the book ends.

Here, in short, is a generous collection of precious documents unlike any other form of literature. Some of the pages are given to self-glorification, some to self-exposure. But whether apologetic or boastful or severely detached, they allow, as Dean Inge remarked of diaries in general, "the repressed self to stretch his legs." And they are truthful. The diarist, writing only to comfort himself, his one reader, and not trying to impress anyone else, is obviously honest—at least as honest as a man can be. How and when his most private papers were discovered, edited, and published is another story. But we who read them today are peculiarly privileged. If we wish, we can, of course, examine the pages with the illicit pleasure of a Peeping Tom, or that of an eavesdropper hoping to overhear something disreputable. But most of these excerpts give us a far deeper pleasure—the rare miracle of participation.

Here, through the magic of the secretly written word, we share a man's lightest fancies and his deepest preoccupations. Here are triumphs and defeats of which the world knows nothing, the unacknowledged truths that emerge when the masks are dropped and the carefully hidden self stands before us undisguised.

A Note by the Editors

Who keeps a diary?

The question might better be phrased: Who does *not* keep a diary? From the evidence it is clear that at some time or other nearly everybody attempts one. Published diaries alone run into the thousands. Libraries bulge with more thousands of manuscripts, and surely there are few families that do not treasure a trunkful of yellowing pages that grandfather left or a clasp-locked legacy from Aunt Ida. And month after month still more journals are discovered, deciphered, edited and published. Who can say how many are even now being written? How many people all over the world—to take an example from the final selection in this volume—how many people in August, 1945, fearfully entered in their diaries, "A bomb has fallen . . ."?

Nobody, we suppose, knows better than we the staggering mass of accumulated diaries. We have recently *read* more than 1200—many of them running to several volumes—and we have *scanned* almost as many more. From this mountain of diaries we have chosen—as generously as space permitted—for scope, for flavour, for variety, and above all, for interest. In all there are nearly a hundred journals represented here. We are keenly aware that many great diaries are not included—simply because there was no room for them—and that we have been able to give only a too-brief sample of the excellence of many others. Even though the book now runs far longer than we had planned, we have still had to eliminate much that we would have preferred to retain.

The rich material hidden away in diaries has been too long neglected. A handful of the most famous are published and read in their entirety. But even the best of them are cluttered with catalogues of unknown people, dreary dinner menus, reviews of forgotten books, accounts of weather, scenery and household trivia. Only the dedicated reader ever discovers beneath all this detail the singularly revealing incident or the sudden insight that make the search worth while. If we have been able to assemble here a few of these great and exciting moments of experience, we will have accomplished at least a little of what should have been done long ago.

The selections here have been limited to diaries written (for the most part) within a few hours of the impact of the experience. All, we feel, were intended at least primarily as private records. That is not to say that all are equally disingenuous: Fanny Burney will pose and chatter to the end of time; Thoreau will listen for the literary overtones of the distant call of the loon.

As nearly as possible the diaries are reproduced in the form in which they were written, preserving whatever eccentricities of spelling and grammar occur in available texts. Nothing has been added except an occasional missing date or an explanatory note in square brackets. Omissions have been marked with points of suspension, thus. . . . A few unwieldy paragraphs have been broken up to make for easier reading. For the same reason the dates of the entries have been put in uniform style throughout.

Grateful acknowledgement is made to authors, agents and publishers, noted elsewhere in the book, for permission to reprint material. The editorial assistance of George de Kay and the stern counsel of Ralph A. Beebe have been valuable from beginning to end. To Lillian Zaret Dunaway and to Pauline Rush Evans we owe special thanks for critical help, for unfailing advice, and for an unfaltering faith that someday the hundreds of volumes of diaries scattered throughout their houses would rise from the floor and return again to their proper shelves.

P.D.–M.E.

New York City
20 February, 1957

Contents

A Treasury of the World's

Great Diaries

1. IN YOUTH IS THE BEGINNING

". . . what have you done to me? What do you want
of me? Where will this lead us? . . ."

Anne Frank

The most famous, and the most heart-rending, of World War II
diaries is that of a little Dutch girl. It was written in secret between her thirteenth and fifteenth years in a hidden apartment
behind a disguised cupboard door leading to a back apartment
in an old Amsterdam house overlooking the Prinsengracht Canal.
Anne Frank (1929–1945) and her family and friends, aided by
courageous Dutch patriots, had found refuge there in crowded,
fear-ridden quarters safe for a time from the relentless efforts of
the Nazi Gestapo to carry away all Jewish families to the consuming gas chambers of German concentration camps.

Throughout Anne Frank's diary the war rumbles on outside.
Implicit in this record are the deathly consequences of letting
a whisper or footstep be heard, or allowing a candle's flame to
shine for even a moment under close-drawn blackout curtains.
But even though the indecencies of the German occupation remain for the most part in the background, heard mostly in shrieks
from the street below, it was impossible to ignore them for more
than the interval of minutes that could precede disaster.

Anne Frank was a child with the clear-eyed innocence of a
child beginning to be sharpened by the newly maturing instincts
of womanhood. She saw, and wrote down, not only the ordeals
of people thrust too closely together, with all the horror and
humiliation the circumstances entailed, but (more important for
her in the unfolding years of early adolescence) the coming of
love and of love's problems, in a world cruelly and strangely shut
in and one not of her choosing. The diary's end has the inevita-
bility of a Greek tragedy.

When Anne's story was dramatized it immediately became one
of the most successful of recent plays. In print it is already a
classic of our time. And so long as diaries are read, a little Dutch

From *Anne Frank: The Diary of a Young Girl*, by Anne Frank. Copyright 1952
by Otto H. Frank. Copyright 1952 by The American Jewish Committee, reprinted
by permission of Doubleday & Company, Inc.

girl's day-to-day annotations of troubled youth in a hostile world will continue to seize the heart.

June 20, 1942.

. . . It's an odd idea for someone like me to keep a diary; not only because I have never done so before, but because it seems to me that neither I—nor for that matter anyone else—will be interested in the unbosomings of a thirteen-year-old schoolgirl. Still, what does that matter? I want to write, but more than that, I want to bring out all kinds of things that lie buried deep in my heart. . . .

July 11.

I expect you will be interested to hear what it feels like to "disappear"; well, all I can say is that I don't know myself yet. I don't think I shall ever feel really at home in this house, but that does not mean that I loathe it here, it is more like being on vacation in a very peculiar boardinghouse. Rather a mad idea, perhaps, but that is how it strikes me. The "Secret Annexe" is an ideal hiding place. . . .

I am looking for Tuesday when the Van Daans arrive; it will be much more fun and not so quiet. It is the silence that frightens me so in the evenings and at night. I wish like anything that one of our protectors could sleep here at night. I can't tell you how oppressive it is *never* to be able to go outdoors, also I'm very afraid that we shall be discovered and be shot. That is not exactly a pleasant prospect. . . .

August 14.

. . . At nine-thirty in the morning (we were still having breakfast) Peter arrived, the Van Daans' son, not sixteen yet, a rather soft, shy, gawky youth; can't expect much from his company. . . .

January 5, 1944.

Yesterday I read an article about blushing by Sis Heyster. This article might have been addressed to me personally. Although I don't blush very easily, the other things in it certainly all fit me. She writes roughly something like this—that a girl in the years of puberty becomes quiet within and begins to think about the wonders that are happening to her body. . . .

I think what is happening to me is so wonderful, and not only what can be seen on my body, but all that is taking place inside. I never discuss myself or any of these things with anybody; that is why I have to talk to myself about them.

Each time I have a period—and that has only been three times—I have the feeling that in spite of all the pain, unpleasantness, and nastiness, I have a sweet secret, and that is why, although it is nothing but a nuisance to me in a way, I always long for the time that I shall feel that secret within me again.

Sis Heyster also writes that girls of this age don't feel quite certain of themselves, and discover that they themselves are individuals with ideas, thoughts, and habits. After I came here, when I was just fourteen, I began to think about myself sooner than most girls, and to know that I am a "person." Sometimes, when I lie in bed at night, I have a terrible desire to feel my breasts and to listen to the quiet rhythmic beat of my heart.

I already had these kinds of feelings subconsciously before I came here, because I remember that once when I slept with a girl friend I had a strong desire to kiss her, and that I did do so. I could not help being terribly inquisitive over her body, for she had always kept it hidden from me. I asked her whether, as a proof of our friendship, we should feel one another's breasts, but she refused. I go into ecstasies every time I see the naked figure of a woman, such as Venus, for example. It strikes me as so wonderful and exquisite that I have difficulty in stopping the tears rolling down my cheeks.

If only I had a girl friend!

January 6.

My longing to talk to someone became so intense that somehow or other I took it into my head to choose Peter.

Sometimes . . . I tried to think of an excuse to stay in his room and get him talking, without it being too noticeable, and my chance came yesterday. Peter has a mania for crossword puzzles at the moment and hardly does anything else. I helped him with them and we soon sat opposite each other at his little table, he on the chair and me on the divan.

It gave me a queer feeling each time I looked into his deep blue eyes, and . . . I noticed his shy manner and it made me feel very gentle; I couldn't refrain from meeting those dark eyes again and again, and with my whole heart I almost beseeched him: oh, tell me, what is going on inside you, oh, can't you look beyond this ridiculous chatter?

But the evening passed and nothing happened, except that I told him about blushing—naturally not what I have written, but just so that he would become more sure of himself as he grew older.

When I lay in bed and thought over the whole situation, I found it far from encouraging. . . .

January 7.

. . . I saw my face in the mirror and it looks quite different. My eyes look so clear and deep, my cheeks are pink—which they haven't been for weeks—my mouth is much softer; I look as if I am happy, and yet there is something so sad in my expression and my smile slips away from my lips as soon as it has come. I'm not happy. . . .

Once, when we spoke about sex, Daddy told me that I couldn't possibly understand the longing yet; I always knew that I did understand it and now I understand it fully. . . .

February 12.

The sun is shining, the sky is a deep blue, there is a lovely breeze and I'm longing—so longing—for everything. To talk, for freedom, for friends, to be alone. And I do so long . . . to cry! I feel as if I'm going to burst, and I know that it would get better with crying; but I can't, I'm restless. I go from one room to the other, breathe through the crack of a closed window. . . .

I feel that spring is awakening, I feel it in my whole body and soul. It is an effort to behave normally, I feel utterly confused, don't know what to read, what to write, what to do, I only know that I am longing . . . !

February 13.

Since Saturday a lot has changed for me. It came about like this. I longed —and am still longing—but . . . now something has happened, which has made it a little, just a little, less.

To my great joy—I will be quite honest about it—already this morning I noticed that Peter kept looking at me all the time. Not in the ordinary way, I don't know how, I just can't explain. . . .

I made a special effort not to look at him too much, because whenever I did, he kept on looking too and then—yes, then—it gave me a lovely feeling inside, but which I mustn't feel too often. . . .

February 18.

Whenever I go upstairs now I keep on hoping that I shall see "him." Because my life now has an object, and I have something to look forward to, everything has become more pleasant.

At least the object of my feelings is always there. . . . Don't think I'm in love, because I'm not, but I do have the feeling all the time that something fine can grow up between us, something that gives confidence and friendship. If I get half a chance, I go up to him now. It's not like it used to be when he didn't know how to begin. . . .

February 19.

. . . The morning was quiet. I helped a bit upstairs, but I didn't have more than a few fleeting words with "him." At half past two . . . I went . . . to sit at the desk and read or write. It was not long before it all became too much for me, my head drooped on to my arm, and I sobbed my heart out. The tears streamed down my cheeks and I felt desperately unhappy. Oh, if only "he" had come to comfort me. It was four o'clock by the time I went upstairs again. . . .

Suddenly I felt the tears coming back and I hurried to the lavatory, quickly grabbing a pocket mirror as I passed. There I sat then, fully dressed, while the tears made dark spots on the red of my apron, and I felt very wretched.

This is what was going through my mind. Oh, I'll never reach Peter like this. Who knows, perhaps he doesn't like me at all and doesn't need anyone to confide in. Perhaps he only thinks about me in a casual sort of way. I shall have to go on alone once more, without friendship and without Peter. Perhaps soon I'll be without hope, without comfort, or anything to look forward to again. Oh, if I could nestle my head against his shoulder and not feel so hopelessly alone and deserted! . . .

February 23.

It's lovely weather outside and . . . nearly every morning I go to the attic where Peter works to blow the stuffy air out of my lungs. From my favorite spot on the floor I look up at the blue sky and the bare chestnut tree, on whose branches little raindrops shine, appearing like silver, and at the seagulls and the other birds as they glide on the wind.

He stood with his head against a thick beam, and I sat down. We breathed the fresh air, looked outside, and both felt that the spell should not be broken by words. We remained like this for a long time. . . .

February 27.

From early in the morning till late at night, I really do hardly anything else but think of Peter. I sleep with his image before my eyes, dream about him and he is still looking at me when I awake.

I have a strong feeling that Peter and I are really not so different as we would appear to be, and I will tell you why. We both lack a mother. His is too superficial, loves flirting and doesn't trouble much about what he thinks. Mine does bother about me, but lacks sensitiveness, real motherliness.

Peter and I both wrestle with our inner feelings, we are still uncertain and are really too sensitive to be roughly treated. . . .

But how and when will we finally reach each other? I don't know quite how long my common sense will keep this longing under control.

February 28.

It is becoming a bad dream—in daytime as well as at night. I see him nearly all the time and can't get at him, I mustn't show anything, must remain gay while I'm really in despair. . . .

March 3.

. . . I'm just like someone in love, who can only talk about her darling. And Peter really is a darling. When shall I be able to tell him so? Naturally, only if he thinks I'm a darling too. But I'm quite capable of looking after myself, and he knows that very well. And he likes his tranquillity, so I have no idea how much he likes me. In any case, we are getting to know each other a bit. I wish we dared to tell each other much more already. Who knows, the time may come sooner than I think! . . .

March 4.

. . . Mrs. Van Daan quite approves when I go and talk to him, but she asked today teasingly, "Can I really trust you two up there together?"

"Of course," I protested, "really you quite insult me!"

From morn till night I look forward to seeing Peter.

March 6.

. . . Oh, Peter, if only I could help you, if only you would let me! Together we could drive away your loneliness and mine!

I think a lot, but I don't say much. I am happy if I see him and if the sun shines when I'm with him. . . .

Who will be the first to discover and break through this armor? . . .

March 7.

If I think now of my life in 1942, it all seems so unreal. It was quite a different Anne who enjoyed that heavenly existence from the Anne who has grown wise within these walls. Yes, it was a heavenly life. Boy friends at every turn, about twenty friends and acquaintances of my own age, the darling of nearly all the teachers, spoiled from top to toe by Mummy and Daddy, lots of sweets, enough pocket money, what more could one want? . . .

What is left of this girl? . . . One period of my life is over forever. The carefree schooldays are gone, never to return. . . .

The sunny life at home, then coming here in 1942, the sudden change. . . .

The first half of 1943: my fits of crying, the loneliness, how I slowly began to see all my faults and shortcomings, which are so great and which seemed much greater then. . . .

Things improved slightly in the second half of the year, I became a young woman and was treated more like a grownup. I started to think, and write stories, and . . . wanted to change in accordance with my own desires. . . .

At the beginning of the New Year: the second great change . . . I discovered my longing, not for a girl friend, but for a boy friend. I also discovered my inward happiness and my defensive armor of superficiality and gaiety. In due time I quieted down and discovered my boundless desire for all that is beautiful and good.

And in the evening, when I lie in bed and end my prayers with the words, "I thank you, God, for all that is good and dear and beautiful," I am filled with joy. Then I think about "the good" of going into hiding, of my health and with my whole being of the "dearness" of Peter, of that which is still embryonic and impressionable and which we neither of us dare to name or touch, of that which will come sometime; love, the future, happiness and of "the beauty" which exists in the world; the world, nature, beauty and all, all that is exquisite and fine.

I don't think then of all the misery, but of the beauty that still remains. . . .

Oh, it is so terribly difficult never to say anything to Peter, but I know that the first to begin must be he; there's so much I want to say and do, I've lived it all in my dreams, it is so hard to find that yet another day has gone by, and none of it comes true! . . . I do live in crazy times and under still crazier circumstances.

But, still, the brightest spot of all is that at least I can write down my thoughts and feelings, otherwise I would be absolutely stifled! I wonder what Peter thinks about all these things? I keep hoping that I can talk about it to him one day. . . .

Can he possibly be the first and only one to have looked through my concrete armor? And will it take him long to get there? . . .

March 17.

. . . Although I'm only fourteen, I know quite well what I want, I know who is right and who is wrong, I have my opinions, my own ideas and principles, and although it may sound pretty mad from an adolescent, I feel more of a person than a child, I feel quite independent of anyone.

I know that I can discuss things and argue better than Mummy, I know I'm not so prejudiced, I don't exaggerate so much, I am more precise and adroit and because of this—you may laugh—I feel superior to her over a great many things. If I love anyone, above all I must have admiration for them, admiration and respect. Everything would be all right if only I had Peter, for I do admire him in many ways. He is such a nice, good-looking boy!

March 19.

Yesterday was a great day for me. . . . After the dishes were done, I stood by the window in his parents' room awhile for the look of things, but it wasn't long before I went to Peter. He was standing on the left side of the open window, I went and stood on the right side, and we talked. It was much easier to talk beside the open window in semidarkness than in bright light, and I believe Peter felt the same.

We told each other so much, so very very much, that I can't repeat it all, but it was lovely; the most wonderful evening I have ever had in the "Secret Annexe." . . .

I have the feeling now that Peter and I share a secret. If he looks at me with those eyes that laugh and wink, then it's just as if a little light goes on inside me. I hope it will remain like this. . . .

March 22.

. . . We may have a real great love in the "Secret Annexe." Don't worry, I'm not thinking of marrying him. I don't know what he will be like when he grows up, nor do I know whether we should ever love each other enough to marry. I know now that Peter loves me, but just how I myself don't know yet. Whether he only wants a great friend, or whether I attract him as a girl or as a sister, I can't yet discover. . . .

March 23.

. . . I often go upstairs after supper nowadays and take a breath of the fresh evening air. I like it up there, sitting on a chair beside him and looking outside.

Van Daan and Dussel make very feeble remarks when I disappear into his room; "Anne's second home," they call it, or "Is it suitable for young gentlemen to receive young girls in semidarkness?" . . . Peter says it's nothing but envy on the part of the grownups, because we are young and we don't pay much attention to their spitefulness. . . .

I hear a lot from all sides about the sudden friendship. We don't take much notice of all this parental chatter, their remarks are so feeble. Have the two sets of parents forgotten their own youth? It seems like it, at least they seem to take us seriously, if we make a joke, and laugh at us when we are serious.

March 28.

. . . Mummy has more or less forbidden me to go upstairs so often . . . thinks that Peter is in love with me; quite frankly, I only wish he were, then we'd be quits and really be able to get to know each other. She also says that he keeps on looking at me. Now, I suppose that's true, but still I can't help it if he looks at my dimples and we wink at each other occasionally, can I?

I'm in a very difficult position. Mummy is against me and I'm against her, Daddy closes his eyes and tries not to see the silent battle between us. Mummy is sad, because she does really love me, while I'm not in the least bit sad, because I don't think she understands. And Peter—I don't want to give Peter up, he's such a darling. I admire him so; it can grow into something beautiful between us; why do the "old 'uns" have to poke their noses in all the time? Luckily I'm quite used to hiding my feelings and I manage extremely well not to let them see how mad I am about him. Will he ever say anything? . . . They don't understand us; won't they ever grasp that we are happy, just sitting together and not saying a word. They don't understand what has driven us together like this. Oh, when will all these difficulties be overcome? And yet it is good to overcome them, because then the end will be all the more wonderful. . . .

March 31.

. . . The chatter about Peter and me has calmed down a bit now. We are very good friends, are together a lot and discuss every imaginable subject. It is awfully nice never to have to keep a check on myself as I would have to with other boys, whenever we get on to precarious ground. We were talking, for instance, about blood and via that subject we began talking about menstruation. He thinks we women are pretty tough. Why on earth? My life here has improved, greatly improved. God has not left me alone and will not leave me alone.

April 1.

And yet everything is still so difficult; I expect you can guess what I mean, can't you? I am so longing for a kiss, the kiss that is so long in coming. I wonder if all the time he still regards me as a friend? Am I nothing more?

You know and I know that I am strong, that I can carry most of my burdens alone. I have never been used to sharing my troubles with anyone, I have never clung to my mother, but now I would so love to lay my head on "his" shoulder just once and remain still. . . .

Wouldn't he long for it too? Is it that he is just too shy to acknowledge his love? Why does he want me with him so often? Oh, why doesn't he speak?

I'd better stop, I must be quiet, I shall remain strong and with a bit of patience the other will come too, but—and that is the worst of it—it looks just as if I'm running after him; *I* am always the one who goes upstairs, *he* doesn't come to me.

But that is just because of the rooms, and he is sure to understand the difficulty.

Oh, yes, and there's more he'll understand.

April 4.

. . . Peter filled my days—nothing but Peter, dreams and thoughts until Saturday, when I felt so utterly miserable; oh, it was terrible. I was holding back my tears all the while I was with Peter, then laughed with Van Daan over lemon punch, was cheerful and excited, but the moment I was alone I knew that I would have to cry my heart out. So, clad in my nightdress, I let myself go and slipped down onto the floor. First I said my long prayer very earnestly, then I cried with my head on my arms, my knees bent up, on the bare floor, completely folded up. One large sob brought me back to earth again, and I quelled my tears because I didn't want them to hear anything in the next room. Then I began trying to talk some courage into myself. I could only say: "I must, I must, I must . . ." Completely stiff from the unnatural position, I fell against the side of the bed and fought on, until I climbed into bed again just before half past ten. . . .

April 11.

. . . I am becoming still more independent of my parents, young as I am, I face life with more courage than Mummy; my feeling for justice is immovable, and truer than hers. I know what I want, I have a goal, an opinion, I have a religion and love. Let me be myself and then I am satisfied. I know that I'm a woman, a woman with inward strength and plenty of courage.

If God lets me live, I shall attain more than Mummy ever has done, I shall not remain insignificant, I shall work in the world and for mankind! . . .

April 14.

. . . I am sentimental sometimes, I know that, but there is occasion to be sentimental here at times, when Peter and I are sitting somewhere together on a hard, wooden crate in the midst of masses of rubbish and dust, our arms around each other's shoulders, and very close, he with one of my curls in his hand; when the birds sing outside and you see the trees changing to green, the sun invites one to be out in the open air, when the sky is so blue, then—oh, then, I wish for so much! . . .

April 16. Sunday morning, just before eleven o'clock.

Remember yesterday's date, for it is a very important day in my life. Surely it is a great day for every girl when she receives her first kiss? . . .

Yesterday evening at eight o'clock I was sitting with Peter on his divan, it wasn't long before his arm went round me. "Let's move up a bit," I said, "then I don't bump my head against the cupboard." He moved up, almost into the corner, I laid my arm under his and across his back, and he just about buried me, because his arm was hanging on my shoulder.

Now we've sat like this on other occasions, but never so close together as yesterday. He held me firmly against him, my left shoulder against his chest; already my heart began to beat faster, but we had not finished yet. He didn't rest until my head was on his shoulder and his against it. When I sat upright again after about five minutes, he soon took my head in his hands and laid it against him once more. Oh, it was so lovely, I couldn't talk much, the joy was too great. He stroked my cheek and arm a bit awkwardly, played with my curls and our heads lay touching most of the time. . . .

How it came about so suddenly, I don't know, but before we went downstairs he kissed me, through my hair, half on my left cheek, half on my ear; I tore downstairs without looking round, and am simply longing for today!

April 17.

Do you think that Daddy and Mummy would approve of my sitting and kissing a boy on a divan—a boy of seventeen and a half and a girl of just under fifteen? I don't really think they would, but I must rely on myself over this. It is so quiet and peaceful to lie in his arms and to dream, it is so thrilling to feel his cheek against mine, it is so lovely to know that there is someone waiting for me. But there is indeed a big "but," because will Peter be content to leave it at this? I haven't forgotten his promise already, but . . . he *is* a boy! . . .

Oh, Anne, how scandalous! But honestly, I don't think it is; we are shut up here, shut away from the world, in fear and anxiety, especially just lately. Why, then, should we who love each other remain apart? Why should we wait until we've reached a suitable age? Why should we bother?

I have taken it upon myself to look after myself; he would never want to cause me sorrow or pain. Why shouldn't I follow the way my heart leads me, if it makes us both happy? . . .

April 18.

. . . Yesterday . . . I explained everything about girls to him and didn't hesitate to discuss the most intimate things. The evening ended by each giving the other a kiss, just about beside my mouth, it's really a lovely feeling.

Perhaps I'll take my diary up there sometime, to go more deeply into things for once. I don't get any satisfaction out of lying in each other's arms day in, day out, and would so like to feel that he's the same.

We are having a superb spring after our long, lingering winter; April is really glorious, not too hot and not too cold, with little showers now and then. Our chestnut tree is already quite greenish and you can even see little blooms here and there.

April 19.

Is there anything more beautiful in the world than to sit before an open window and enjoy nature, to listen to the birds singing, feel the sun on your cheeks and have a darling boy in your arms? It is so soothing and peaceful to feel his arms around me, to know that he is close by and yet to remain silent, it can't be bad, for this tranquillity is good. Oh, never to be disturbed again. . . .

April 28.

. . . Yesterday . . . we were, as usual, sitting on the divan, our arms around each other's waists. Then suddenly the ordinary Anne slipped away and a second Anne took her place, a second Anne who is not reckless and jocular, but one who just wants to love and be gentle.

I sat pressed closely against him and felt a wave of emotion come over me, tears sprang into my eyes, the left one trickled onto his dungarees, the right one ran down my nose and also fell onto his dungarees. Did he notice? He made no move or sign to show that he did. I wonder if he feels the same as I do? He hardly said a word. Does he know that he has two Annes before him? These questions must remain unanswered.

At half past eight I stood up and went to the window, where we always say good-by. I was still trembling, I was still Anne number two. He came towards me, I flung my arms around his neck and gave him a kiss on his left cheek, and was about to kiss the other cheek, when my lips met his and we pressed them together. In a whirl we were clasped in each other's arms, again and again, never to leave off. Oh, Peter does so need tenderness. For the first time in his life he has discovered a girl, has seen for the first time that even the most irritating girls have another side to them, that they have hearts and can be different when you are alone with them. For the first time in his life he has given of himself and, having never had a boy or girl friend in his life before, shown his real self. Now we have found each other. For that matter, I didn't know him either, like him having never had a trusted friend, and this is what it has come to. . . .

Once more there is a question which gives me no peace: "Is it right? Is it right that I should have yielded so soon, that I am so ardent, just as ardent and eager as Peter himself? May I, a girl, let myself go to this extent?" There is but *one* answer: "I have longed so much and for so long—I am so lonely—and now I have found consolation."

In the mornings we just behave in an ordinary way, in the afternoons more or less so (except just occasionally); but in the evenings the suppressed longings of the whole day, the happiness and the blissful memories of all the previous occasions come to the surface and we only think of each other. Every evening, after the last kiss, I would like to dash away, not to look into his eyes any more—away, away, alone in the darkness.

And what do I have to face, when I reach the bottom of the staircase? Bright lights, questions, and laughter; I have to swallow it all and not show a thing. My heart still feels too much; I can't get over a shock such as I received yesterday all at once. The Anne who is gentle shows herself too little anyway and, therefore, will not allow herself to be suddenly driven into the background. Peter has touched my emotions more deeply than anyone has ever done before—except in my dreams. Peter has taken possession of me and turned me inside out; surely it goes without saying that anyone would require a rest and a little while to recover from such an upheaval?

Oh Peter, what have you done to me? What do you want of me? Where will this lead us? . . .

Am I only fourteen? Am I really still a silly little schoolgirl? Am I really so inexperienced about everything? I have more experience than most; I have been through things that hardly anyone of my age has undergone. I am afraid of myself, I am afraid that in my longing I am giving myself too quickly. How, later on, can it ever go right with other boys? Oh, it is so difficult, always battling with one's heart and reason; in its own time, each will speak, but do I know for certain that I have chosen the right time?

May 2.

. . . I went off with Daddy to get some water; and while we were on the stairs I said, "Daddy, I expect you've gathered that when we're together Peter and I don't sit miles apart. Do you think it's wrong?" Daddy didn't reply immediately, then said, "No, I don't think it's wrong, but you must be careful, Anne, you're in such a confined space here." When we went upstairs, he said something else on the same lines. On Sunday morning he called me to him and said, "Anne, I have thought more about what you said." I felt scared already. "It's not really very right—here in this house; I thought that you were just pals. Is Peter in love?"

"Oh, of course not," I replied.

"You know that I understand both of you, but you must be the one to hold back. Don't go upstairs so often, don't encourage him more than you can help. It is the man who is always the active one in these things; the woman can hold him back. It is quite different under normal circumstances, when you are free, you see other boys and girls, you can get away sometimes, play games and do all kinds of other things; but here, if you're together a lot, and you want to get away, you can't; you see each other every hour of the day—in fact, all the time. Be careful, Anne, and don't take it too seriously!" . . .

Daddy doesn't want me to go upstairs so much in the evenings now, but I don't want that. Not only because I like being with Peter; I have told him that I trust him. I do trust him and I want to show him that I do, which can't happen if I stay downstairs through lack of trust.

No, I'm going! . . .

May 3.

. . . I am young and I possess many buried qualities; I am young and strong and am living a great adventure; I am still in the midst of it and can't grumble the whole day long. I have been given a lot, a happy nature, a great deal of cheerfulness and strength. Every day I feel that I am developing inwardly, that the liberation is drawing nearer and how beautiful nature is, how good the people are about me, how interesting this adventure is! Why, then, should I be in despair?

May 5.

Daddy is not pleased with me; he thought that after our talk on Sunday I automatically wouldn't go upstairs every evening. He doesn't want any "necking," a word I can't bear. It was bad enough talking about it, why must he make it so unpleasant now? . . .

May 7.

. . . I'm not alone any more; he loves me. I love him, I have my books, my storybook and my diary, I'm not so frightfully ugly, not utterly stupid, have a cheerful temperament and want to have a good character!

May 19.

. . . All goes well with Peter and me. The poor boy seems to need a little love even more than I do. He blushes every evening when he gets his goodnight kiss and simply begs for another. . . .

After my laborious conquest I've got the situation a bit more in hand now, but I don't think my love has cooled off. He's a darling, but I soon closed up my inner self from him. If he wants to force the lock again he'll have to work a good deal harder than before!

May 26.

. . . This evening at eight o'clock I had to go to the downstairs lavatory all alone; there was no one down there, as everyone was listening to the radio; I wanted to be brave, but it was difficult. I always feel much safer here upstairs than alone downstairs in that large, silent house; alone with the mysterious muffled noises from upstairs and the tooting of motor horns in the street. I have to hurry for I start to quiver if I begin thinking about the situation.

Again and again I ask myself, would it not have been better for us all if we had not gone into hiding, and if we were dead now and not going through all this misery, especially as we shouldn't be running our protectors into danger any more. But we all recoil from these thoughts too, for we still love life; we haven't yet forgotten the voice of nature, we still hope, hope about everything. I hope something will happen soon now, shooting if need be—nothing can crush us *more* than this restlessness. Let the end come, even if it is hard; then at least we shall know whether we are finally going to win through or go under.

June 13.

Another birthday has gone by, so now I'm fifteen. . . .

June 14.

. . . I often accuse myself to such an extent that I simply long for a word of comfort, for someone who could give me sound advice and also draw out some of my real self; but, alas, I keep on looking, but I haven't found anyone yet.

I know that . . . Peter loves me not as a lover but as a friend and grows more affectionate every day. But what is the mysterious something that holds us both back? I don't understand it myself. Sometimes I think that my terrible longing for him was exaggerated, yet that's really not it, because if I don't go up to see him for two days, then I long for him more desperately than ever before. Peter is good and he's a darling, but still there's no denying that there's a lot about him that disappoints me. . . . Why should he keep his innermost self to himself and why am I never allowed there? By nature he is more closed-up than I am, I agree, but I know—and from my own experience —that at some time or other even the most uncommunicative people long just as much, if not more, to find someone in whom they can confide.

Both Peter and I have spent our most meditative years in the "Secret Annexe." We often discuss the future, the past, and the present, but, as I've already said, I still seem to miss the real thing and yet I know that it's there.

July 15.

. . . How is it that Daddy was never any support to me in my struggle, why did he completely miss the mark when he wanted to offer me a helping hand? Daddy tried the wrong methods, he always talked to me as a child who was going through difficult phases. It sounds crazy, because Daddy's the only one who has always taken me into his confidence, and no one but Daddy has given me the feeling that I'm sensible. But there's one thing he's omitted: you see, he hasn't realized that for me the fight to get on top was more important than all else. I didn't want to hear about "symptoms of your age," or "other girls," or "it wears off by itself"; I didn't want to be treated as a girl-like-all-others, but as Anne-on-her-own-merits. . . .

Yet this was not my greatest disappointment; no, I ponder far more over Peter than Daddy. I know very well that I conquered him instead of he conquering me. I created an image of him in my mind, pictured him as a quiet, sensitive, lovable boy, who needed affection and friendship. I needed a living person to whom I could pour out my heart; I wanted a friend who'd help to put me on the right road. I achieved what I wanted, and slowly but surely, I drew him towards me. Finally, when I had made him feel friendly, it automatically developed into an intimacy which, on second thought, I don't think I ought to have allowed.

We talked about the most private things, and yet up till now we have never touched on those things that filled, and still fill, my heart and soul. I still don't know quite what to make of Peter, is he superficial, or does he still feel shy, even of me? But dropping that, I committed one error in my desire to make a real friendship: I switched over and tried to get at him by developing it into a more intimate relation, whereas I should have explored all other possibilities. He longs to be loved and I can see that he's beginning to be more and more in love with me. He gets satisfaction out of our meetings, whereas they just have the effect of making me want to try it out with him again. And yet I don't seem able to touch on the subjects that I'm so longing to bring out into the daylight. . . .

It's really a wonder that I haven't dropped all my ideals, because they seem so absurd and impossible to carry out. Yet I keep them, because in spite of everything I still believe that people are really good at heart. I simply can't build up my hopes on a foundation consisting of confusion, misery, and death. I see the world gradually being turned into a wilderness, I hear the ever approaching thunder, which will destroy us too, I can feel the sufferings of millions and yet, if I look up into the heavens, I think that it will all come right, that this cruelty too will end. . . .

[A few days after this entry, the Nazis raided the "Secret Annexe" and Anne, Peter and all the other occupants, were taken away to concentration camps. Anne's father alone survived. In March 1945, three months before her sixteenth birthday and two months before the liberation of Holland, Anne died in the concentration camp at Bergen-Belsen.]

"Four years . . . change a man greatly . . ."

Marie Bashkirtseff

On publication few journals have been showered with such
prompt indignation as greeted the diary of Marie Bashkirtseff
(1860–1884). She was denounced as a libertine, a disgrace to
young womanhood, a precocious and spoiled child likely to cor-
rupt her elders. And some of those who did not find fault with
the frankness of her confessions of love, professed that they were,
nevertheless, nauseating, selfish, written with crude, arrogant
egotism. "What a horrid little pig she was!" said one critic. Still
the story of her love affairs, and her flirtations, made her something of a heroine in enlightened circles during the gay, but not
yet altogether emancipated, nineties.

The subject of all this uproar was a Russian artist and writer,
born of wealthy and noble parents, a girl who as a child showed
signs of great promise. Before she reached her 'teens she read the
Latin poets in the original and could speak and write in four
modern languages. A gifted musician, she was especially talented
as a singer, but at the age of seventeen she abandoned music to
establish herself as a painter in Paris where her work almost immediately won recognition and awards. Her canvases still hang
in the Luxembourg Gallery. Meanwhile she travelled widely and
became prominent in the world of society and fashion, numbering
among her devoted friends some of the famous literary and political figures of Europe. And then she died lingeringly of tuberculosis, having crowded into twenty-four years more than many
achieve at three times her age.

From the age of thirteen Marie Bashkirtseff was conscientious
about keeping the diary that later was to enrage her contemporaries. It is a journal of loves—and of unrequited ambition, in
which the flutterings of her heart share equal space with a consuming and inordinate desire for fame and recognition. She was,
indeed, a young flirt, and it is in that context we see her here,
complete with the urge for sentimental hand-touchings, tender

From *The Journal of a Young Artist,* by Maria Bashkirtseff, translated by Mary J.
Serrano. Copyright, 1919, by E. P. Dutton & Co., Inc.; renewal, 1947, by Harold G.
Villard.

glances and, though still a child, self-consciously aware of each
gesture of amorous import.

January, 1873.

. . . God grant that the Duke of H—— may be mine! I will love him and
make him happy! I will be happy too. I will do good to the poor. It is a sin
to think that one can purchase the favor of God by good works, but I know
not how otherwise to express myself.

I love the Duke of H——, but I cannot tell him that I love him; and even
if I were to tell him so, he would pay no attention to it. When he was here
I had some object in going out, in dressing myself, but now!—I used to go
to the terrace in hope of seeing him for even a single instant, at a distance.
My God, assuage my grief! . . .

March 14.

This morning I heard a noise of carriages in the Rue de France; I looked
out and saw the Duke of H—— driving with four horses on the Promenade.
. . . No one bears himself as he does; he has the air of a king. . . .

I shall be happy with my husband, for I will not neglect myself. . . . I
cannot understand how a man and woman can love each other tenderly, and
endeavor to please each other unceasingly, and then neglect themselves after
marriage. . . . Why not retain always something of coquetry with one's husband, and treat him as a stranger whom one desires to please? Is it because
one need not conceal one's love, because it is not a crime to love, and because
marriage has received God's benediction? Is it because that which is not forbidden possesses no value in our eyes, and that one can find pleasure only
in secret and forbidden things? This ought not to be. . . .

April 30.

. . . I should be so happy if the Duke would only take notice of me, and
I would bless God. . . . I must either be the Duchess of H——, and that is
what I most desire . . . or become famous on the stage. . . .

May 6.

. . . Yesterday I prayed to God, and when I came to the part where I
asked him that I might know the Duke, that God would grant me this happiness, I shed tears. Three times already has God listened to me and granted
my prayer: the first time when I asked him for a set of croquet. . . .

June 9.

. . . I am to have a horse. Did anyone ever see a little girl like me with
a race-horse? I shall make a *furore*. What colors shall my jockey wear? Gray

and parti-colored? No, green and pale rose. A horse for me! How happy I
am! . . .

October 17.

I was playing on the piano when the newspapers were brought in . . .
and the first words on which my eyes fell related to the marriage of the Duke
of H——. The paper did not fall from my hands; on the contrary, it remained
tight in my grasp. I had not the strength to stand. . . . O Divine Charity!
what have I read! My God, what have I read! . . . . And I have to take a
Latin lesson! Oh, torture! . . .

August 18, 1874.

Today has been spent in admiring me. Mama admired me, and the Princess G. admired me. The Princess is always saying that I look either like
Mama or like her daughter; and that is the greatest compliment she could
pay me. One never thinks better of others than of one's own. The fact is that
I am really pretty. The picture on the ceiling of the great salon of the Ducal
Palace at Venice, by Paul Veronese, represents Venus as a tall woman, blonde
and fresh-colored. I resemble that picture.

August 24.

I begin now to live, and to try to realize my dreams of becoming famous.
I am already known to many people. I look at myself in the glass, and I find
that I am beautiful. I am beautiful; what more do I want? Can I not accomplish anything with that? My God, in giving me the little beauty I possess (I say little through modesty) you have already given me too much.
O my God! I feel myself to be beautiful; it seems to me that I shall succeed
in all that I undertake. Everything smiles upon me, and I am happy, happy,
happy!

The noise of Paris, this hotel, as large as a city, with people always walking, talking, reading, smoking, looking, confuses me. I love Paris, and it makes
my heart beat with emotion to be here. I want to live faster, faster, faster!

September 5.

. . . And when the moon shines, leaving a silvery track upon the waters
that looks like an enormous fish with diamond scales, and I am seated at
my window, peaceful and alone, a mirror and two wax tapers in front, I ask
for nothing more, and I bow down in thankfulness before God. Oh, no, what
I desire to express will not be understood because it has not been experienced. No, it is not that! It is that I grow desperate every time I try to express
what I feel! It is as when one is in a nightmare and has not the strength to
cry out!

. . . What does it matter to others? Others will never understand it, since
it is not they, but I, who have felt it. I alone understand and remember. And

then, men are not worth the trouble of trying to make them understand. Every one feels for himself, as I do. I should like to see others feel as I feel, through my means; but that would be impossible; to do so they must be *I*. My child, my child, leave all this alone; you lose yourself in subtleties of thought.

October 1, 1875.

God has not done what I asked Him to do; I am resigned; (not at all, I am only waiting). Oh, how tiresome it is to wait, to do nothing but wait! . . . I despise men profoundly and from conviction. I expect nothing good from them. . . . Those who are good are stupid, and those who are intelligent are either too false or too self-conceited. . . . The day will doubtless come when I shall think I have found a man, but if so, I shall deceive myself woefully. I can very well foresee that day; I shall then be blind. I say this now while I can see clearly. But in that case why live; since there is nothing but meanness and wickedness in the world? Why? Because I am reconciled to the knowledge that this is so; because, whatever people may say, life is very beautiful. . . .

Is it not strange to hear me reason in this way? Yes, but this manner of reasoning in a young creature like me is but another proof of how bad the world is; it must be thoroughly saturated with wickedness to have so saddened me in so short a time. I am only fifteen.

April 5, 1876.

. . . For a vain creature like me it is best to devote one's self entirely to painting, because that is imperishable.

I shall be neither a poet nor a philosopher nor a *savante*. I can be nothing more than a singer and a painter. But that is always something. And then I want to be talked of by everybody, which is the principal thing. Stern moralists, do not shrug your shoulders and censure me with an affected indifference for worldly things because I speak in this way. If you were more just you would confess that you yourselves are the same at heart!

October 5, 1877.

"Did you do that [painting] by yourself?" M. Julian asked me on entering the studio today.

"Yes, Monsieur."

I grew red as if I had told a falsehood.

"Well, I am satisfied with it, very well satisfied with it." . . .

In the studio all distinctions disappear. One has neither name nor family; one is no longer the daughter of one's mother, one is one's self—an individual —and one has before one art, and nothing else. One feels so happy, so free, so proud!

At last I am what I have so long wished to be. I have wished for it so long that I scarcely believe it now to be true.

Apropos, whom do you think I saw in the *Champs Élysées* today?

None other than the Duke of H—— occupying a *fiacre* all by himself.

The handsome, vigorous young man with yellow locks and a delicate mustache now looks like a big Englishman; his face is very red, and he has little red whiskers that grow from the tip of the ear to the middle of the cheek.

Four years, however, change a man greatly; at the end of half an hour I had ceased to think of him.

Sic transit gloria Ducis.

*"We had a lovely time . . . on the
shoemaker's bench. . . ."*

Lester Frank Ward

Lester Frank Ward (1841–1913) was a distinguished scientist, a
paleontologist and an internationally famous pioneer in sociology
who shared honors with such men as Sumner, Spencer and
Comte. But there is little hint of the professor and scientist of
the future in this ingenuous picture of a youth discovering
himself.

Ward was born in Joliet, Illinois, the tenth son of a millwright.
For years the family wandered about the country, pursued by
hardship and poverty, but while he was still in his 'teens, Lester
came to Pennsylvania to help his brother run a wagon hub factory
—a business which soon failed.

Ward was an omnivorous, self-educated scholar who taught
himself the fundamentals of Latin, German and Greek. At nineteen he was teaching in a one-room country school. That same
year he began to keep a diary—in French. Ostensibly, the entries
were intended to serve as exercises in composition, but it is likely
that the diarist was at least as interested in excluding eavesdrop-
pers as he was in perfecting his French.

In one sense at least, the language must have seemed appropriate to young Ward. Hardly had he begun the diary when he
fell in love—intensely, miserably, happily in love for the first time.

July 8, 1860.

In undertaking a journal of events which concern me, I shall record a few
of the most interesting things which have transpired since the fourth of this
month. . . . My spirit has been for almost two months the lowest it has ever
been in my life, on account of the profound disappointment in the love which
I had acquired for a girl, so pretty but so false. I sent her a letter that day,
telling her that I wish only to see her once more and to receive only one
more letter from her. I . . . bought two strings for my violin, which I enjoy
very much.

From *Young Ward's Diary*, by Lester Frank Ward, edited by Bernhard J. Stern.
Copyright 1935 by Bernhard J. Stern.

July 9.

I cultivated the corn this morning . . . a little annoyed with the horse's not keeping to the row . . . gathered and bound the sheaves. When night came . . . my heart was very light regarding the girl ["the girl" was Lizzie Vought] whom I loved, and whom I no longer esteem. But everyone has gone to bed, and I must wash my feet before going myself.

July 11.

. . . I went to the post office to look for the promised letter from the girl, but did not find it, so I came to the conclusion that I never wished to see her again. My heart is light. I was almost sick cutting the corn all this morning. My girl, I am going to abandon you eternally, you whom I have loved so deeply! It will kill me, but let me perish.

August 19.

Hearing mention of an Episcopal meeting at six o'clock in the evening I decided to attend it. . . . The girl was there. . . . We returned in the evening . . . arrived at the door, I entered with her, she lit a lamp and we sat down together talking, but . . . I could no longer keep my place. Leaning forward I received her sweet and tender form in my arms and in an instant her face was covered with kisses . . . and there we bathed ourselves in the passion of love until the crowing of the cocks announced that it was day.

August 26.

I have just finished the history of De Soto, the great discoverer of the Mississippi. It is a very interesting as well as edifying book. The love aroused between the girl and myself in our last meeting has not yet vanished. . . .

September 22.

Monday I went to town, and that evening I went to see the girl with the excuse that I wished to borrow some oil. . . . I could not sit long with her without feeling my trapped heart dart forth. . . . We had considerable difficulty with the lamp, which finally went out at the critical moment when it started to rain so that I could not go home. Taking her by the hand I attempted to find the door but in the shadows we stumbled over a shoemaker's bench, and embracing her I sat down with her on the bench, where we remained about an hour, embracing, caressing, hugging and kissing. O bliss! O love! O passion pure, sweet, and profound! . . .

September 30.

. . . Went to Towanda last evening. I bought material for a waistcoat and some for a shirt, mailed my letter to the girl and got a shave and a hair-cut.

I sold my old watch to the jeweler for 80 cents. Lent 47 cents to Fred and we came back. I had ($1.26) a dollar and twenty-six cents in silver. I returned with ($1.14) a dollar and fourteen cents. I spent 22+18=40 cents, received 80 cents, lent 47. $1.26+.80−.47+.18+ .22+.04 (tot.) =$1.14. I have $1.14. . . .

October 7.

. . . Sometimes I am so stirred by love for my girl that I become almost mad; on such occasions my heart seems to rise into my throat; everything which passes me I embrace. . . .

October 11.

. . . I went to the post office this evening expecting a letter from the girl, but it wasn't there. Why has she not written? I am in great suspense. Is she angry with me for what I wrote her? . . .

October 21.

I went to church Sunday night last, and . . . to the girl's. I did not plan to remain more than two hours, but O, the charms of love! . . . "I love you," she said, kissing me on the mouth, "I love this mouth, I love these dear eyes, I love this head" and . . . about three o'clock we were sleepy. Arranging three chairs and the old shoemaker's bench in line, she sat down in the middle chair. I sat in the chair near the end of the bench, and stretching myself on the bench put my head in her gentle lap. She put her little feet on the remaining chair and we were settled. Have I ever been so happy? We lay with our faces together. I unfastened my shirt and put her tender little hands on my bare breast, and there we counted the beatings of our hearts like the whisperings of angels. . . . With what tenderness and humility she said, "I am afraid I am doing something I shouldn't in putting my hands on your bare breast." I loved her for that! Dear, dear little one. As we lay in this position the cocks crowed and the old man got up, but happily I escaped to the workshop. . . .

November 6.

I husked corn today and yesterday. It returned me 48 bushels. Today is the great day—election day. I hope that Mr. Lincoln will be elected. I did not go to church once on the sabbath day, but . . . went to the sweet girl's . . . and sat down together to talk and kiss and embrace and bathe in love. We had a lovely time as before on the shoemaker's bench. . . . It was four-thirty when we heard her father jump out of bed. Gathering up my things very promptly and snatching a farewell kiss I left my sweet darling. I tried to be very careful on arriving not to let them know I had not remained all night and was at this moment getting up, but I did not succeed.

December 3.

One day has gone of my first school [which he had been hired to teach for $16 a month]. At last I have begun to make money through the use of my talents. . . .

December 12.

I had some trouble [with his pupil] George King this morning. I did not want to whip him. . . . Played the violin a little. Evening. No trouble this afternoon. Ruth Osmun has lost her arithmetic and has not seen it for several days.

December 28.

I got a whip this morning, but I hope I shall have no occasion to use it.

January 4, 1861.

. . . I had to punish Edward Davenport and Ruth Osmun a little.

February 3.

I left yesterday morning with old Bill and the sleigh at half after eight. Went to the girl's, whom I took with me and we went to Camptown . . . arrived at her house at six, going very slowly part of the time because of the rain, which was falling, and partly because of the hills and the bad road, and partly because we wished to kiss one another. . . .

February 9.

It was very cold yesterday morning, 14 degrees below. Friday evening the girl and I had a very sweet time. I kissed her on her soft breasts, and took too many liberties with her sweet person, and we are going to stop. It is a very fascinating practice and fills us with very sweet, tender and familiar sentiments, and consequently makes us happy. But the difficulty is that we might become so addicted in that direction that we might go too deep and possibly confound ourselves by the standards of virtue. . . .

February 14.

Being lost among the Greek roots yesterday, I actually forgot to write in my journal. The river is very high, the highest it has ever been. . . .

February 24.

Friday evening I went to my darling's. . . . We commenced to feel that we were very ardent lovers, and, becoming very much upset at what we had done we began to weep and beg and embrace and kiss the tears from one another's wet cheeks. Her father growled a little, and I am determined not to go back before the end of two weeks. . . .

March 3.

. . . I spent most of my time today in studying Hollick's *Physiology.* I wish that I dared take it to the girl's and read it with her. But no. . . .

March 14.

. . . Love. O sweet passion! I spent this morning with Hollick's *Physiology.* . . .

March 15.

I have been busy reading the *Physiology* all day. . . .

March 18.

Two days of inexpressible happiness have passed since I last wrote in my journal. . . . After supper came trouble. My heart was full . . . almost to overflowing. . . . Closely held in loving arms we lay, embraced, and kissed all night (not going to bed until five in the morning). We have never acted in such a way before. All that we did I shall not tell here, but it was all very sweet and loving and nothing infamous. When we got up . . . we went for a walk. We went the whole length of the road past the school house and about a half-mile into the woods. There we sat down on stones and spoke of love and future happiness. But the worst of all was this. I had forgotten and brought the *Physiology* by Hollick in my satchel, and by the circumstance that I did not let her open it she had suspected the fact, for I had informed her that I had such a book in my letters. She had begged me to bring it on our walk, to which I finally agreed. While we were sitting there she asked me to read her a little from the book. I tried, but failed entirely. I could not either give it nor read it to her. I wished to show it to her, and accordingly went into the woods to cut canes for us, and left the book with her. How much of it she read I do not know, but she liked it. After that we became more familiar. . . .

May 7.

. . . I burn with the wish to be her husband and live in her arms. I left her among kisses and sweet emotions of love Sunday morning, leaving also with her Hollick's *Physiology* which she in her purity and virtue took with much hesitation.

June 10.

. . . Her mother went away after supper and my sweet girl and I were alone in each other's loving arms. She reads the Latin marvellously. We played checkers, and she plays better than I. . . .

June 17.

. . . Tomorrow is my birthday and I shall be twenty years old.

July 8.

. . . Saturday I helped my girl's brother work in the corn and to manure it. Sunday I stayed with my sweet girl all day. We love each other with a very pure and perfect love and we hope very much to get married. I hoed some turnips this morning and it rained at noon. . . .

July 9.

. . . I have a fife which is from my sweet girl, and I play a little on it. I have commenced the algebra and I am in the divided numbers. I am a little tired. I burn with the desire to be married. . . .

September 10.

I have just done a terrible thing. It will cost me sixty cents because I broke a thermometer. It puts me in horrible misery. I shall have no money after this. Where I can borrow a little money I do not know. Everything else is all right. But I must hope.

September 18.

. . . Sometimes my heart is full of sweet feelings for my sweet darling and loving lover. I burn with the desire to press her to my breast. I have just discovered a rip in one of my boots. They will go soon, but they have lasted well, better than any other pair I have ever had in my life. I must buy another pair.

October 19.

I have solved three very difficult examples in algebra, learned my Greek lesson, read about two chapters of history and wrote a love-note to my lovely little one.

October 22.

I have just read Shakespeare's poem "Venus and Adonis." It is very amorous and exciting to the passions at first, but the last part is a little more tender, so that I wept while reading it. Saturday I went to John's and talked a little while in the corn-field and secured an order to have my boots mended. . . .

October 25.

. . . Our lips touched and we entered Paradise together. . . . That evening and night we tasted the joys of love and happiness which only belong to a married life. . . .

November 10.

. . . Friday evening I had a very happy time at my girl's house not going to bed until one in the morning. She had a bad cold. Saturday morning tried to have my boots mended without success. . . .

November 19.

. . . Crossed the river and soon arrived at my girl's. There I stayed until Monday noon, having a very happy and joyful time. Sunday at eleven we went to church and listened to the most beautiful sermon I have ever heard. What profound and even redoubtable truths! Monday morning I mended my boots. . . .

December 1.

. . . Saturated my boots with grease this morning, and kissed my darling a thousand times. She becomes more dear to me every day. . . .

December 12.

I have just punished (whipped) three pupils. John McCracken, William Dunn and Marie Dunn. . . .

December 16.

I had a little trouble today. As I was slapping Philip Dunn my palm by chance touched his nose and made it bleed. Then John Bush told me that the parents did not wish me to punish their children in this manner. I did not say much, but enough to make them understand I should do what I wished. . . .

December 18.

Last Monday my pupils were very difficult to keep quiet, and consequently I punished them considerably. Among others Hattie Clark, who lied to me and made a picture on the blackboard, I whipped with my palm too savagely. . . .

January 6, 1862.

. . . After having whipped William Dunn because he ran away from school, I left for my little one's. . . .

January 7.

. . . Went to Towanda, where I procured many things, as follows: a little material for a shirt (five yards at 16 cents a yard), a pair of gloves for 25 cents, 25 sheets of paper at 20 cents, a pencil-holder, 10 cents, two linen handkerchiefs, 25 cents, a bottle of ink, 5 cents, 2 shawl pins at 16 cents, a yard of bleached muslin at 8, besides thread and buttons. . . . I have now in my purse seven dollars and thirty-three cents. . . . Last evening I whipped Dayton Ennes because when I excused him to go home he went to the canal to play.

February 4.

I planned to whip Bartley this evening, but while I was getting the switches he ran away. No matter! He shall suffer the more, that is all. . . .

May 4.

Today the girl and I walked . . . along the stream, enjoying ourselves thoroughly. Last evening . . . what happy hours of love! I forgot to say that I bought a box of blacking last Monday morning ($.06). My heart burns with pure love, so that I cannot write. New Orleans is taken.

May 16.

. . . Yesterday afternoon the whole school was present at an exhibition of an artist in glass ($.05). It was very fine. His name is Owen. I burn with the wish to kiss my darling. I forgot to say that last Friday I bought twelve sheets of paper ($.12), and that same evening as I was passing the shop, I paid for the carrying of my *Tribune* ($.26). Also I lent a dollar to my girl. ($1.00).

July 14.

. . . Saturday evening I set out for my girl's, and we had a fine conversation, not going to bed until three o'clock. Sunday, after we had read some Latin, we took a long walk on the "State Road" and gathered and ate a great many berries, getting back at about three o'clock in the afternoon. I stayed very comfortably with her until it became dark, and leaving her with a million sweet kisses returned here, bringing the violin and my old boots, which I have been wearing today. . . .

August 13.

. . . Monday evening I got hold of John's horse and carriage and came back here to take my girl up the mountain to pick berries Tuesday morning. Finding no one to accompany us, we set out alone. Quite near Mr. Elliott's the rim of one of the wheels broke, and I had to go back to the city and wake up a blacksmith. After an hour and a half, I was once more ready to set out. We arrived on top of the mountain about noon. Consequently we were obliged to spend the night on the mountain. We had a sweet time. Wednesday morning our horse got loose while we were picking a few berries before breakfast. What a condition! Alone on the mountain without a horse. Despair . . . at first. I looked all day without finding him. Finally I persuaded a man to take us in the back of his wagon to the foot of the mountain, where I engaged a horse to bring us here again, where we arrived at daybreak. Thursday . . . before we came back I broke the pole of the carriage. Friday morning . . . back to the mountain and find the horse. I found him. Saturday I spent the day learning about the war. I determined to enroll and thus finish this week full of events.

This week has not been any less full of important circumstances, but now I must go to bed with my wife.

August 14.

. . . Went to church to hear an Episcopal discourse by Mr. Brush. Not very good. Monday morning I went to Towanda to buy some kerosene oil and . . . again I resolved to go to war. On my return I found Ed Own who had already enrolled, and as I came here with him in his carriage, I found occasion to write my name among the brave men of Pennsylvania . . . joined the company, and Tuesday we all went to Towanda to elect officers. Put Spalding is captain. Every man who can is going to war, and everything is very exciting. But one more event . . . Wednesday, August 13, 1862, I had to register my marriage! What? I, married? True enough. My heart's darling whom I have loved so long, so constantly, so frantically, is mine! We are keeping it a secret, but it has been guessed but not yet discovered. How sweet it is to sleep with her! I paid $3.00 fee. . . .

". . . I am so afraid I shall get to be
like every-one else."

Julia Newberry

Walter Loomis Newberry, Chicago banker, merchant prince and exemplar of the Gilded Age, died in 1868 leaving behind a vast fortune, a bequest to found a great library, and a grief-stricken fourteen-year-old daughter, Julia Newberry (1854–1876). A few months later the girl began to keep a diary. Several years elapsed before Mrs. O'Leary's cow kicked over the lantern and doomed much of Chicago's recent jerry-built past to flame and ash. Meanwhile as a bobby-soxer of that halcyon day, Julia took note of the way it felt to be a young heiress: the foods she ate, the novels she read, the boys she appraised and found wanting through thick lashes, eyes delicately averted.

Julia Newberry loved Chicago. Though most of her remaining years were to be spent in Europe, her *patrie* was rarely out of mind. It meant little to this child of grace that only thirty-six years had passed since Chicago had taken itself seriously enough to become incorporated as a town. Hers was real and present luxury and the consequent sophistication afforded by her father's wealth. She was intrigued by the attentions of a dashing general, sorely tempted to go riding with an eligible youth behind a be-ribboned horse hitched to a "swell drag," and altogether enchanted by a tower studio built just for her, complete with a "genuine skylight" and a lock on the door.

Julia read improving books, languished whole days away in bed after the accepted manner of *jeune filles,* and contemplated a European trip with some misgivings, fearful that an old-fashioned continent would be lacking in Chicago amenities. She has left us a misspelled and plaintive record of a poor young rich girl, sharp-eyed and elegantly bustled, who almost a century ago was beginning to reach outward from a moneyed and fabulous childhood towards the fascinating, but as yet unfathomed, process of growing up.

Reprinted from *Julia Newberry's Diary,* by Julia Newberry. By permission of W. W. Norton & Company, Inc. Copyright 1933 by W. W. Norton & Company, Inc.

June 6, 1869. Home. Chicago, U.S.A. In the Library. Sunday.

Europe is a dream . . . while hotels, bad eating, & sea-sickness, are things of the past. I know that it wont last but a few months, nevertheless I am home, yes actually at home. Here I am in the old house, where I was born, & where I wish I could always live; it is the dearest place on earth to me, & worth all London Paris & New York put together; Sister & Mother may talk, & say what they like, still I shall persist in my opinion, that there is no place equal to Chicago, & no place like home. . . . Our breakfast of pigeons, fried potatoes & corn-bread tasted deliciously, as did also my favorite dinner; roast-beef, asparagrass, & strawberries. . . .

July 4.

. . . I wonder if the knowledge that we acquire here, will be useful to us in our futur state? Certainly reading, writing, drawing, painting & playing on the piano wont do us any good; once there was a man who committed suicide because he was tired of buttoning & unbuttoning his clothes; I think it was quite natural, & rather a bright idea of his. . . .

August 17.

. . . Yesterday Sister & I went fishing, & we caught ninety four fish in all. Fifty-four Shiners which we threw away, with quantities of sunfish & perch. Then we trolled, & caught two pickerel, that is Sister did, & I pulled one nearly into the boat, & then oh *malheur* it got away. We had a very good boatman who talked bad grammar pretty freely. Coming back I headed the procession & walked into the hotel with this immense string of fish. Everybody stopped to exclaim & enquire where we had *bought* them. A lady & gentleman had sunburned themselves all day & had not caught a single fish. . . .

September 5.

I'm tired to death of having company. Julia Douw . . . is as good, quiet, & prim as ever, if she does wear trains. But oh! what a strain on the nerves to entertain her; we had to keep going, morning, noon & night. There is nothing I hate as much as driving in the country, & she was very fond of it, & we had to drive all the time. I know she liked to go sketching but Sister insisted that she didn't & so we had to go rowing, & bowling, & everything else. . . . We played croquet. The Pierrepont boys play very well, & I beat them completely; that was one comfort, but that we must needs go rowing, & though I was not well Sister made me go, & I caught a terrible cold, & was sick in bed for three days. Bertha left the same day as Julia did, & all the swell people besides. Mr Bosworth is the queerest specimen; he is a youth, (at first I thought he was the biggest snip I ever laid eyes on) about twenty three or four, & . . . generally he parts his hair directly in the middle, & combs it down very low over his forehead. He has the very longest nose, & altogether the most comical face I ever saw. His eyes are good, dark grey with long lashes & he makes the most of them. He is very clever, amusing, & funny, he is over a great deal & Mother is rather nervous. . . .

November 22.

. . . Mr Peaboddy is dead, Père Hyacinthe is in America, Napoleon is sick, & Italy has an heir to the throne. —I am reading the 'Illiad', 'Shelly', 'Keats', 'Coleridge', 'Chatterton', 'Héloise et Abélard', 'travels in Spain', & painting whenever I have strength. I have had various presents since my sickness; old wine, flowers cut & uncut, cream from the country, pears from Gen. Hooker, horses heads, books etc; people have been very kind. . . .

November 22.

The days roll on, one is just like another. I wake between ten and eleven, feeling dull & heavy, & with a bad taste in my mouth. I put on my dressing gown, & have a little breakfast which I dont relish. I lounge round till one or two, when they make me drive out, bundled up like an Egyptian mummey. We go to the Park & then come home, take our dinner, & go to bed. And oh I am very sick and miserable.

December 27. New York. Brevoort House.

This is the last night I shall ever be fifteen; tomorrow I shall be sixteen & when once a person is sixteen, though they are still very young, they can never be called, 'child'. . . . I have grown old the last year. I feel it, though the idea may be exagerated by my feeling so blue tonight, perhaps I had better stop writing, for it is nearly mid-night. . . .

March 16, 1870. St Augustine, Florida.

. . . I made Jack Foster's acquaintance when I first arrived, but he has been away a good deal. He is very homely, & wears shockingly old fashioned clothes, checked pantaloons for instance. —On the other hand, his blood is blue, his connections splendid, his manners excellent; he is polite, kind, attentive, jolly, amusing, & 23. What is more, he has never said or done anything that jarred me in the least. We had a very nice time together at the tableaux, & he was very attentive. After that I saw him occasionally, & about three weeks ago, he made me a present of a beautiful little alligator, about eight inches long, & just the right size.

March 21.

The alligator died last night, a most untimely death, & from no apparent cause; I feel dreadfully about it, & especially so, because I did not paint his picture as I might have done. . . .

April 20. New York. Brevoort House.

Monday Sister and I took dinner at the Lows. . . . I like the Low's house immensely, it is so elegant, & not a bit stiff. Gussie showed me his room, (the first one belonging to a young man that I had ever seen.) It was a perfect gem; crowded with knick-knacks & pretty things, & the walls covered with pictures. And then it was in such *perfect* order; I should have thought it belonged to some lovely young lady. Seth's room was larger, with more light, & less fancy; he showed me his books, of which he is very proud. After dinner Gussie & Hattie played duetts, & Jay Pierrepont came in & had the sulks. . . .

May 9. Home in Chicago.

We arrived here Friday the 28th of April, & I stayed the first night at the Sherman House, & then came directly over here. I was amazed & delighted with the house, which has been almost entirely rebuilt since last summer at the gentle cost of $60,000. Every one says it is the handsomest house in Chicago, & every one in town, including many strangers, have been to see it. I am writing in what (to me) is the most perfect room I ever was in, My Studio. It fronts South & East, with the most beautiful view of the lake, & the most delicious window, so wide & deep. It is irregular in shape also, & just the right size, with a genuine skylight, & private stair-case leading down into my dressing-room. There are two bookcases, & the loveliest closet; indeed it is just perfection. My real room down stairs is splendid, but I like the Studio best; down stairs I shall have to keep it in order, but here the door can be eternally locked if I choose, & no one can enter without permission. I dont believe there is another girl in the United States, or even in the world that has a real studio room built for *her;* it nearly breaks my heart to think of leaving it all & going to Europe again, & I am so afraid I shall get to be like every-one else, & not want to come home, getting so accustomed to the life over there, that I shall care for nothing else. I like Chicago so much, so much better than any other place, & we have such a beautiful home, & it is all associated with Papa, & now to go & leave it all! If I only keep on liking it just as well, why then when I am an old maid I can always live here, & even *if* I *should* marry, my husband will have to live here, & there is one comfort in that, for then my children would live here too, & it would all go down in the family, it is too dreadful to think of strangers ever living here. The handsomest thing in the house is the hall, wainscoated, & finished beautifully in hard wood, & a clear sweep through the house, with a vestibule at either end. The library & dining room are very large, & beautiful rooms, while the "Butler's Pantry" is too charming. And as regards bath-rooms, light, heat, there is nothing to desire. The window glass is splendid & cost alone $3,000. . . .

We had a dashing call from Gen. Phil Sheridan the other night; he is distingue, but frightfully ugly. (perhaps not frightfully, but still anything but handsome.) He is very short, (shorter than I.) *very* broad; & his eyes are only long narrow holes. His head is most extraordiry shape. It is sunk between his shoulders & his mouth is covered with a large moustache. He has a nice foot, & good manners, an irish accent, & . . . has a good deal of the "General" about him, though he is very modest, & well-bred; he is very complimentary to ladies, & evidently is a great admirer of female beauty. He made me a great many sweet speeches, none of which were very original.

June 2.

I have just been skimming Disraeli's last novel "Lothaire" & it is simply horrid! If I were a great Statesman & had nothing better to do than to write such trash! I would give up. His plebian adoration of the English Aristocracy is disgusting. . . .

I have not read but one novel since we arrived, which I think is doing pretty well. I have been reading "Lamb", Tuckerman's book on American Artists, "Young's Night Thoughts", "Chemistry", "Pickwick", & the book of "Genisis", which are all very interesting. Some of Disraeli's "Curiosities of literature", with biographys of "Mrs Sigourney", "Ristori", "Theodosia Burr", "Mad. Necker", "Lady Anne Lindsey", "Maximilian" & others. I really am not well enough to read anything *deep*. A number of "lives of the Old Masters" I liked best of all. Scott's "Lord of the Iles" is charming.

June 20.

. . . The only young gentlemen in this big town, who merit the slightest consideration at the present moment, are the two Mr Whitehouse (Frank and William). I meet them driving often, & William who has a very "swell drag" has repeatedly asked me to go driving with him, & poor me, though I want to go ever so much, I always refuse, because I dont think it is quite proper to go driving with young gentlemen.

11 o'clock in bed! And yet all most all the girls here & elsewhere do it! I am always glad afterwards that I stood firm, though at the time it is very hard! . . .

June 22.

Tomorrow I am going to leave my beloved Chicago for another long while, years perhaps! I am not well here, & I think it is my bounden duty to go away, & not get any sicker! . . . When we shall come back, is more than I know; I hope and trust I shall not be entirely weaned from my own home, & prefer Europe to anything else, on the earth or under it.

". . . I must acquire worldly experience
to be able to choose my pleasures."

Marie Henri Beyle (Stendhal)

From a fifth-floor attic chamber in an obscure Paris street came in
close succession two of the great novels of the nineteenth century,
and indeed of all time. Little noticed as these books were then,
few novelists have since written without profit from the example
set for them a century or more ago.

Up the five long, wearisome flights of stairs sat the author, an
ex-soldier, reluctant diplomat, café wit, impoverished man of
fortune, bored traveller, and would-be great lover who, from a
score of literary aliases, chose to sign himself "Stendhal." The
man who wrote *The Red and the Black* (1831) and *The Char-
terhouse of Parma* (1839) long had made a brave and foppish
show. Born Marie Henri Beyle (1783–1842) of an ancient and
rich family of Grenoble in south-eastern France, he went abroad
(when his purse was full) with a sophisticated man-about-town
swagger. A very plump, middle-aged dandy he was, possessed of
a red face, tousled red wig and whiskers dyed to match, a fat
green cigar cocked in his mouth, high hat tilted over one ear,
pinched waistcoat and white flannel trousers cut after the advanced English fashion, a jaunty cane, and an air of heedless,
dissipated nonchalance.

Behind the mask lived another person. Stendhal's life spanned
the portentous years between the French Revolution and the ascent of Queen Victoria. In the stirring era of Napoleon, who
was a particular hero of his, he had marched as a professional
soldier in the disastrous campaign against Russia and, on a June
day in 1815, saw still another ignominious defeat for France at
Waterloo. Stendhal was unhappy and ill at ease in the face of
post-war reaction, out of sympathy with his times, disillusioned
with his own achievements (a few slim books of travel sketches
and lives of composers), and disheartened by the hypocrisy of
his tricolour-waving contemporaries. Alone, with an extraordinary psychological understanding far in advance of his day,

Stendhal gathered his strength, squeezed dry what he had laid up from life, and wrote the novels which have served as models for Mann, Gide, Proust, Joyce and scores of others.

It happened, fortunately for him (and for those who have come after), that in his youth Stendhal kept a diary. Shy as a lover, he had taken pains to examine that special passion and wrote down in almost clinical detail and not without a flourish of egotism, all his yearnings and his conquests. When at middle age Stendhal came to write his great novels he refreshed his recollection from the gleanings of those impressionable years when he had tried as a fledgling writer to tell the truth not only about his experiences but also about himself. Stendhal's youth bursts forth from the two thousand pages or so of his early journal, as clear-eyed and naïve he sets forth to investigate and report upon unexplored life . . .

April 18, 1801.

I'm undertaking to write the history of my life day by day. I don't know whether I'll have the fortitude to carry out this plan . . . because I'm making it a rule not to stand on ceremony and never to erase. . . .

May 27.

I took twenty-five grains of ipecacuanha and one of antimonic tartar, which only made me vomit once, and feebly. I'm reading Caesar's *Campaigns*. . . .

May 30.

. . . I haven't anyone to advise me, no friend, I'm weakened by my long spell of fever; yet I'm full of determination, convinced that through audacity and perseverance I shall end up by being General Michaud's aide-de-camp. Then I shall owe this success, like all the others, to myself alone. . . .

June 6.

The medicine succeeded fairly well; I seem to have less fever. I shaved myself. I'm starting again on my sabre lessons tomorrow. . . .

July 12.

. . . Let us put the present to good use, for our minutes are numbered. The hour I've spent fretting has nonetheless brought me that much nearer death. Let us work, for work is the father of pleasure, but let us never fret. Let us reflect sanely before deciding on our course; once our decision is taken we ought never to change our minds. With a steadfast heart, anything can be attained. Give us talent; the day will come when I'll regret the time I've wasted. . . . My mind, which is constantly occupied, always drives me to seek instruction which may justify my hopes. As soon as there is an opportunity to improve myself and have a good time, I need to remind myself that I must acquire worldly experience to be able to choose my pleasures. After that, how can I be surprised to be awkward with women, not to succeed with them . . . ?

December 10.

. . . To inspire in a woman a high opinion of one's learning is a sure means of gaining one's end. Heroes have intervals of fear, poltroons moments of bravery, and virtuous women moments of weakness. It's a great art to be capable of discerning and benefitting from these moments.

February 7, 1802.

. . . Felix Faure . . . told us he didn't attach any value to possessing a woman, that what he could understand the least was why a man should keep a woman. Faure has an unresponsive character and no mistake. . . .

August 27.

I saw Mme. Rebuffel at seven o'clock in the evening. I found M. Rebuffel there, and he greeted me with the greatest kindness. He went out, I went to bed with [her]. . . .

April 14, 1804.

. . . I talked with M. Salmon about his system concerning women; I urged him to publish it. He said no, but I believe he has made up his mind and the book is possibly already written. He holds that the Italian woman is the primitive woman; by modifying her in various ways, you get the French woman, the German woman, etc. He believes that woman's whole character consists of *an insatiable desire to please,* and that it's consequently impossible to overpraise them. He's seen miracles wrought by praise. A woman said of a man whose face was almost hideous, "What a monster! He's an eyesore." The monster praised her, succeeded in pleasing her and ended by sleeping with her. He believes that men are more sensitive than women, that a man or a woman always puts feeling into the first love affair. I feel that he's made me bolder with A.

August 3.

Curiosity plays an important role in love. I, to whom drawing has given the habit of seeking the nude beneath the clothes and of picturing it to myself distinctly, am consequently less susceptible to love than another person might be.

November 17.

. . . A Grenoble girl said to Penet, "Once you've had it, you can't get along without it," which confirms the maxim of Jean-Jacques: "Refuse everything to the senses unless you wish to be led to the ultimate weakness."

January 21, 1805.

. . . All your thoughts serve to work you up to the erethism of passion, your whole body is taut. When that happens, if the subject be love, your thoughts engaged in making you taut, are unable to leave room for the promises of happiness given you by the face, the manner and the words of your mistress. The habit of seeing whores leads to that. A man's imagination gets excited each time he holds one of them in his arms while picturing a woman who has more appeal for him. I discuss her beauty, I say, "Her eyes are dark for such-and-such a reason, because they're the most beautiful, etc. She resembles Angelina Pietagrua. While I'm trying to recall where the resemblance lies, and, *so to speak, to build the uprights of the arch,* I'm *far from being conscious of the impression she'd give me if seen from the exterior.* And yet this impression is the whole pleasure of passion.

November 8.

. . . This morning we got up at half-past eight and filled a black half bottle with wine. I took it, I went to the pastry cook's next door to Casati's, where I bought two cold thrushes, a lark and two little pies, one with jam and the other with cream. We reached the Montfuront fields by going across some private properties. We had a delicious lunch under a tree, enjoying that rustic and poetic happiness I've so often imagined, particularly at Saint-Vincent. Under the tree we left some bread and almost a whole pie, which we scattered about for the happiness of the birds. . . . We rested at R in a charming spot . . . our feet in the sun and our heads in the shade of the trunk of a large poplar. She told me that I looked as though I was dying to do that; it was true, but that wasn't all I desired. I'd have liked a few more transports on her part—or, more exactly, a few transports. . . .

March 2, 1806.

. . . A dinner for sixty-five people at three tables. I spoke a minute to Mme. ——, the mother of Pauline and Félicité, feeling Pauline's backside and Félicité's thighs; it would have been perfect if I'd my thigh against that of Colette, the third daughter, as I had during dinner. Mme. Tivollier continues to greet me in a very friendly fashion. I used to think that a year and a great talent would be necessary in order to have her. Perhaps I could have her without either in two months.

March 30.

. . . [At dinner] Mme. Filip, on my right, got drunk on white wine; prattle without imagination or gaiety. . . . We left, Mme. Filip taking my arm. All along the way, she witlessly bothered the buxom Mme. Decrai, whom I gave a slap on the backside which she repulsed with genuine dignity. I had held

Mme. Filip's thighs all through dinner; her drunkenness and her horrible ugliness, which literally made her a market woman, so disgusted me that yesterday, Sunday, I had no desire to go to see her. I no longer recapture, except in moments as fleeting and rare as lightning flashes, the delightful sentiments I used to be given by a rainstorm, a fog, etc. when I was in the land of chimeras about women. . . . We arrived pretty much soaked at Mme. Filip's. She . . . stretched out on a day bed in her yellow salon, to which her indolent daughter finally found the key. She *belched*, which completed my disgust with her. A voluptuous face and sighs, the latter running up and down the chromatic scale; these sighs were particularly voluptuous when she was inhaling punk smoke. . . .

July 4, 1807.

At Frau von Lefzau's. Boredom. What kind of face should you put on in society when you are bored or sick? A person is quite right to say, *Audaces fortuna juvat;* with all due respect, what subterfuges are necessary in order to pinch Fräulein von Oeynhausen's thighs! From sheer boredom, I did so yesterday with success. I even touched the spot where the ebony must start to shade the lily. But I'm afraid that Frau von Strombeck, who was filling the functions of a mother, noticed it and was angry. All in all, as Mirabeau said, I've had enough of Brunswick.

July 6.

. . . Heerdt's good nature. His anecdotes, which he tells well for this country, win over Strombeck completely. He's frankly and openly in love with Minette, he follows her everywhere and all the time, talks to her incessantly and very often at ten paces from the others, most often in French, in a serious, ponderous way and without grace. . . . An ass, said Lichtemberg, is a horse translated into Dutch. . . . The open manner in which Herr von Heerdt courts Minette would be the height of indecency, ridicule and rudeness in France. But then, Strombeck told me as we were returning that, of all the women in his family (very large), he didn't believe there was one who had made her husband a cuckold. His strange proposal to his sister-in-law, Frau von Knisted, whose family is going to die out through lack of male heirs and all the property to revert to the sovereigns, received with haughtiness, but, "Don't ever speak to me of it again." . . . During one of his voyages, Φ leaned on his shoulder while sleeping or pretending to sleep; a jolt threw her a little on him, he squeezed her, she moved over to the other side of the carriage. He doesn't believe her to be unseduceable, but he believes that she would kill herself on the morrow of her crime. It's perhaps his pride that makes him believe in this sequel, he loved her passionately. . . .

On the other hand, a married man convicted of adultery can be sentenced by the courts to ten years in prison. The law has fallen into desuetude, but it still keeps this matter from being treated lightly. It's a long way from being, like in France, a quality that one can scarcely deny in front of a husband without insulting him. A few years ago, a woman told her husband, a man of the Court here, that she'd made him a cuckold; like a fool, he went and told the duke about it, the man who made him a cuckold was obliged to tender his resignation from all his employments and to leave the country within twenty-four hours as the result of the duke's threat to apply the laws. I've said elsewhere that the majority of the men marry for love. They aren't cuckolds, but what wives they have! Chunks of wood, clods destitute of vitality. . . .

I came back to Der Grüne Jäger . . . went to bed with the host's daughter for the first time, and began writing this at four o'clock. She's the first German woman I've seen who was totally exhausted after sex. I made her passionate by caresses; she was very afraid.

I'm gradually learning my trade. . . .

March 25, 1808.

For me. An efficacious remedy for love: eat peas. Tested today, March 25, after going for a very pleasant horseback ride and feeling a strong desire for the little girl who lives near the Bevern Palace. . . .

February 4 and 5, 1809.

The whole day of the 4th was livened up by the thought of going in the evening to see the girl of the Vaudeville, whom I endowed with a thousand charms. I went to her house at five o'clock, she'd just gone out. . . . At noon today, the 5th, I found Elisa in bed, I got in; fine thighs, but a face that looks stupid and lives up to its promise; twenty-four livres.

August 10, 1811.

. . . During one of my trips (to Raincy), I found THE LITTLE π [Pulchérie Le Brun]. . . . I talked to her for want of something better to do. She hasn't much in the way of breasts and wit, TWO GREAT WANTS! Likewise for want of something better to do, I took a few liberties, there wasn't any resistance. So yesterday, not knowing what to do with myself, I got in my cabriolet and showed up at Villemomble. There were a lot of people there; I went out on the terrace, the little girl followed me, I took her arm and put mine around her a bit; later, in the salon, her knees and thighs. Her eyes thanked me by their look of love, outside that it was innocence itself. But on the terrace, I became conscious of a great truth. Novelty is a great source of pleasure, you must give yourself up to it. I was sure of sleeping in the evening with the pretty Angéline, but I can only do anything with her now by making an effort, and by thinking of another woman. . . .

September 2.

Before going to bed, I spent a long time watching the room of a woman across from whom I sat at supper and who looked quite possessable. Her door was ajar, and I had some hope of catching a glimpse of a thigh or breast. A woman who'd have no effect on me if she were in my bed, gives me a delightful sensation when seen unexpectedly, then she's natural, *I'm not occupied with my role,* and I'm entirely given over to sensation. My love affairs have always been a bit disturbed by my concern with being agreeable; in other words, being occupied with a role. In these circumstances you can't be thoroughly natural. It's not impossible to become bored in the presence of a mistress, you can't let her see your boredom; you'd lose her. But, for me, love would be a far keener pleasure if, like Signor Lechi for instance, when I'm with my mistress, I thought of nothing else. . . . All this is sorry business, but, I'm only twenty-eight; I hope it will pass as I grow older. . . .

"... some families have had a sorry time of it."

John Halliday

Like Thomas Carlyle, another proud and doughty rebel, John Halliday (1815–1906) was born amidst the fogs of Scotch Puritanism in the Border Country village of Ecclefechan where grey houses straggle along the main highway to England, a little short of the Highlands and in sight of a less exacting theology.

Bred in hardship, reared in a simple frugal life in which unyielding Calvinism was opposed to indomitable independence of spirit, the cobbler Halliday met his match in Anne Kilner, a gentleman's daughter from below the border.

A landholder, it was said that William Kilner had never worked a day in his life, except to read the Riot Act. In one sense, however, Lord Kilner (a "laird" he was really, and not a Lord) was a Leveler, and this was in his love for music. He was the cellist as well as the patron of an excellent string quartet, and as such he was bound to admit beneath his roof even a cobbler, if that cobbler happened to be the best violinist within fifty miles, as well as the finest maker of stringed instruments in the shire.

And it was these qualities, doubtless, which enabled him to win the hand of the gentleman's daughter.

Life was hard for shoemaker Halliday, with a rapidly growing family to feed, and America beckoned. And so, with the high silk hat which he had worn to the coronation of Queen Victoria, with a trunkful of books, with a violin, a violin cello and a bass viol—all of his own craftmanship—and also with wife and children, he sailed, in August, 1855 for the rich land across the sea. He came first to Canada, then finally, as a farmer, to Pipestone, Minnesota, famous for the quarries where the Indian peace pipes were made.

He died in comfort at the age of ninety-one, surrounded by grandchildren, dozing over his Robert Burns.

Halliday's diary is filled with the salt and tang of the early days of emigration to the United States. One trembles, as he does, when children die at sea, when a child is born out of wedlock, when rations, on a sailing ship becalmed for days and weeks, dwin-

From *The Journal of John Halliday.* Used by permission of Warrington Winters.

dle alarmingly. And one shares his delight at the sight of the new land— "It is a beautiful place. . . ."

August 28, 1855.

Calm foggy morning but very cold. Making no way. So it has been since we started [from Liverpool], no sooner we get a fair wind than a few hours suffice to blow it out. A nice breeze has again started us on our way. We are in Lat 40′ Lon 45′–20″, and as cold as ever I felt it in December. . . . At noon all the second cabin passengers were ordered to take their beds on deck and the berths underwent the same process as those below rendering the place much sweeter. Another row among the sailors which required the captain and both mates to suppress. We are now on the banks of Newfoundland and the captain says we are greatly favoured, with clear weather being a rare circumstance. It is owing to the north wind. Another child committed to the deep. We lose our breeze at 8 p.m. Nothing done all night.

August 29.

A beautiful morning for landmen but too quiet for us who are all anxious for a glimpse of terra firma. Many of the passengers who could not eat the oatmeal or biscuits on any account are beginning to alter their tale. And should we be kept here for another fortnight I am of the opinion that the flavour and quality of the ships provisions will have greatly improved. 11 Oclock very hot. The temperature here seems to be very variable, yesterday we could scarcely keep heat walking. Today we can hardly keep cool sitting. Had a look through the Quadrant and a lesson from the captain as to the mode of using it. He also shewed me the manner of working out the observation which is done in very few figures. We are in Lat 46′ 12″ having just made 18 miles south since yesterday. Heartless work. Today we have done next to nothing. The invalids from seasickness are improving.

August 30.

Awoke at 4 Oclock by the mate dancing his Hornpipe right overhead. One of the comforts of sea life, only a board between your head and the feet of the sailors who are obliged to be on duty all night and the rougher the sea the more work they have got to do. Very wet but a fair wind 12½ miles per hour and what is better in the proper course. In the afternoon the wind shifted into all the 4 qrs. but seemed to like none as well as the west and fixed there again about 7 p.m. . . .

August 31.

Strong wind dead a head with a heavy sea. Our course is Northwest obliged to steer south a good prospect of reaching Quebec in that direction must submit to the will of Heaven. . . . Had a hunt for lice last night but found none. Very thankful for they are become very common. A few mornings ago one of the Germans or Dutch came on deck pulled off his undergarment and commenced hunting. The sport was excellent, the game proving most abundant. The second mate noticed him and calling to the party who was washing decks (an operation performed by means of a pump hose and pipe out of which the water is ejected with great force) ordered him to turn his pipe on the huntsman, no sooner said than done, and the cold water proved most effectual causing both huntsman and game to disappear as if by magic. Today one of the grey ones was discovered on a lads coat. One of the passengers desired him to go down and take it off, the captain who was present ordered him to take off his coat and to do it gently. This was done and then he ordered him to heave it overboard repeating the word 5 or 6 times causing much laughter increasing it by adding that it was large enough to bait a codfish hook. So that with one thing and another the time passes swiftly away with those in health among which thanks be to an all merciful God are me and mine.

September 1.

Fancy yourself lashed to a weigh beam feet to one end head to the other fancy the beam kept continually up and down, and you will have a pretty clear picture of our condition during the whole of last night, add to this the full consciousness that this fine ride is all given gratis, that is that you are not advancing an inch on your journey and you must confess that our position is a most enviable one. Not withstanding we would all sleep well were it not for the tremendous noise caused at times by the tumbling about of boxes, rolling of bottles, tin cans etc etc. The captain informed me that we had gained the enormous distance of 5 miles during the last 36 hours. . . . This is provision day and we are comforted with the announcement that the sugar is done our butter is nearly done our ham is nearly done and we still 1000 miles from the end of our journey. Glorious position. All in good health and spirits though. As soon as [young son] Wm made his appearance on deck this morning the captain laid hold of his cap saying now the cap's mine I have seen land, Wm said no not till I'm on't. The captain thought he had cut his teeth early. We have done next to nothing all day the wind is however nearly gone and we have the consolation of knowing that it cannot blow from a more unfavourable quarter. Another child has just died in the Stearage.

September 3.

A strong hot west wind. Consequently right ahead. Tossed and tumbled about all day making nothing of it, all night the same. The sailors are of opinion that we have got a Jonas on board. It is indeed strange that out of 31 days we should only have had 2 days of favourable wind. The children are both complaining. Hot and feverish. We had a very sleepless night.

September 4.

. . . Our water is becoming scarce and . . . the children are no better very flushed in the face and hot. Gave them each a pill. 4 Oclock Mary much better and up Wm still in bed bowels a good deal disordered. Afraid of dioerhea. 24 hours of fair wind would take us to the mouth of the St. Lawrence pity we can't have it. The wind has shifted a little in our favour and as usual fallen to a very gentle breeze if breeze it can be called. Passed very close to a felled tree. Another row with the second mate and sailors. A quiet evening.

September 5.

. . . Cape Breton is in view. The spirits of all on board seem revived. The children are much better Mary particularly. Wm is still hot in his skin and coughs but has been a great deal on deck. We are very thankful for this is a strange place for a sick person and some families have had a sorry time of it particularly in the Stearage, when I went dwn to it this morning for water the stench was dreadful and the dirt about ½ inch deep many of the passengers being of such filthy habits as to make water on the floor. All the efforts of the captain and officers to improve them are unavailing. On Monday the ship made a very heavy lurch upsetting their *"Nosegays"* alias *Chamber pots* and the stench that came up would have poisoned a pole cat. . . . Last night more robberies were committed. The sailors are still blamed.

September 6.

A heavy sea tossed us up and down all night. And it continues to blow hard. A fishing boat has just crossed our bow the sea dashing over it every few minutes. Had the weather been favourable we would have got some cod. But it was to rough to come alongside. . . . A number of whales about but we could only see them blowing. The children still complain it seems to be cold and indeed there is no wonder since the cold is most intense. I pity the inhabitants of Cape Breton. We have tacked and are making for a small Island on the north of Cape Breton, called St. Pauls.

September 7.

Astonished on going on deck to find St. Pauls still a head of us having only gained 1 mile during the whole of the night. . . . Just 5 weeks today since we left Liverpool. O for a good breeze from the Southeast . . . and we are now Stearing through the narrows with the Studding sails sett.

September 8.

. . . The doctor who is a rime customer and much troubled with the disease called laziness is much afraid of ships fever and says it is already in the Stearage. I would have been alarmed had he not prophesied measales, scarlatina, small pox etc, as soon as we were in the fogs of Newfoundland none of which has happened as yet. God be thanked for his kindness to us. . . .

September 9.

. . . Saw the black back of a whale a great monster it was. Began to
weary yesterday for the first time. The children are beginning to feel the
effects of confinement.

September 10.

The wind arose about 12 Oclock last night blowing very hard. . . . We
were obliged to change positions in bed 4 times before morning. For it is
anything but comfortable to be awaked with your feet considerably higher
than your head. In fact as though . . . laid on the roof of a house feet to the
rigging and head to the eaves. . . . Provisions and water are getting scarce
and the sailors who swear at anything and everything are beginning to swear
about the want of food. The Doctor told me this morning that they had only
cabin provisions for two days. Another child died this morning making the
sixth in all. . . .

September 11.

A beautiful morning the Gulph as smooth as a mirror the sky as pure and
the air as clear as imagination can conceive. . . . Another lovely child died
today of inflammation of the lungs. Typhus has at last made its appearance
among us and we are all more than ever anxious to reach our destination.
. . . 7 Oclock p.m. meet a ship from Quebec bound to Bristol. The Pilot
had not left her and we took him on board. . . . It seems (though strangely
to a contemplative mind) that this circumstance has raised the spirits of all
on board, as though a Pilot could change the wind.

September 12.

Whether the Pilot has power to change the wind or not I will not pretend
to determine. But certain it is that it has changed, and continued to blow
thogh lightly in our favour all day. The Pilot says we shall be alongside
Grouse Island tomorrow night with this wind and we are all praying that it
may continue as things are really growing very threatening. There is a very
pretty child just opposite our berth apparently dying, it is the first serious
case in the second cabin. The doctor calls it cholera and many people are
much alarmed, though from the symptoms I cannot agree with him. Provisions are getting scarce all our ham and butter is done and the last of our
preserves was finished yesterday but sugar is the most precious article. . . .
The ships supply run out a fortnight ago and those who could not afford to
purchase it from passengers have had a sorry time of it. We bought some
salt beef of the captain which did not belie its name being as salt as brine
and as tough as leather. But it must be confessed that dry biscuit and sugar-
less tea are not the most savoury articles of food, but we are all alike and
even the captain has been buying sugar of one of the passengers who laid
in a good stock at Liverpool. The children though still suffering from colds

are in better spirits and as we are now getting into a warmer climate I hope through the blessing of God that they will be preserved to us. We are now fairly in the [St. Lawrence] river a magnificent river it is. . . . Were such a river to run through England it would leave very small parings in the widest of it and across from Whitehaven to Durham it would require to borrow a good deal from the German ocean. A proof of the greatness of the country we are approaching. . . .

September 14.

A fine run all night up early to clean and pack up for removal from prison. A splendid morning far exceeding all my ideas of the American climate. I have often read of Italian skies but if they excel these they must be blue glorious indeed. When I went on deck the change of scene seemed perfectly magical. The river had narrowed greatly was as smooth as glass and the banks on each side was literally covered with houses all white with small patches of clearings. . . . Among all the beauties of the place and they are not a few I missed the green fields of England the general colour being that of dark pine. And the clearings have all the appearance of stubble fields. But the inhabitants here about don't live by agriculture but by fishing and hunting. We were obliged to anchor as we had no wind and the stream would have carried us down. We are only twelve miles from Grouse Island where the doctor says we shall have to remain a few days on account of the fever that is among us. Weighed anchor at 4 p.m. the tide coming up in our favour and we are again moving though slowly towards our destination. Thanks be to God we are all well again. The eighth child died today. 9 Oclock dropt anchor opposite Grouse Island, the quarintine ground.

September 15.

An anxious morning the officers from the Island came on board about 8 a.m. and condemned us. So we shall be obliged to go on quarantine though only for 2 or 3 days but the arrangements seem as bad or worse than those on board ship. . . . We were completely mystified it was provision day and none were served out. The captain could not tell whether we would be provided for or not. Many had nothing to eat and nothing to purchase with. Consequently there case was anything but enviable. The steamboat was to come from Quebec at 2 Oclock and take us off it was 4 before it arrived and a considerable delay occurred after it did arrive so that darkness found us on a strange land with seemingly no one to direct us where to go. My mate a Scotchman agreed that I should go on shore and look after his family and goods and he would remain on board, and I had to hunt about for a house [at the quarantine detention island] . . . one of the long wooden sheds fitted up with berths like a ship. I found one at last but the door was locked and as the officer was at a meal the hungry cattle must wait till his highness had finished. This event actually took place in about half an hour, the shed door was thrown open and we were ushered into it in total darkness and in this pleasant condition we must a remained had we not been able to buy candles . . . and when we inquired if there were any provender for hungry bellies he said there was plenty of food in the store for money and that we could please ourselves whether we eat or starved. Wherever we go *money* is our *friend*. After all our providing before leaving home it has cost us a sovereign on board ship and here and not done yet. Government take great credit to themselves for the protection they give to passengers. But if worse used before the law was enacted than now there case must have been a pitiful one. One of the second passengers child died during the night, the complaint that has been so fatal among young children is inflammation of the lungs.

September 16.

. . . It is a beautiful place. . . .

" . . . I told them my motive . . . "

John Woolman

An itinerant preacher and humanitarian, John Woolman (1720–1772) has been called the Quaker Thomas à Kempis. He was born in a Quaker community in southwestern New Jersey near Mount Holly. Here as a youth he worked as a baker's helper and learned the tailoring trade. By the time he was twenty-one he was well on the way to prosperity as tailor, storekeeper and nurseryman. But his piety would not permit him to be content with business success. He opened a school for poor children and at twenty-three became a minister. The rest of his life was largely devoted to spreading the ethical and social ideals of the Friends.

From Massachusetts to Virginia and westward across Pennsylvania he preached in taverns, courthouses, boats, log cabins and meeting houses, wherever he could find an audience. Particularly he was concerned to point out the evils of slavery, and the shameful mistreatment of Negroes. He was the first of the great American abolitionists. He refused to draw up wills that bequeathed slaves as property, and persuaded many fellow Quakers to give up slaveholding. In 1760 he petitioned the Rhode Island Legislature to forbid the slave trade altogether. He stirred a ferment in man's mind and conscience that continued for a hundred years and lingers still.

Meanwhile he did not neglect the cause of other minorities, or the welfare of the poor. He denounced the taking of the Indians' lands without payment and their exploitation by greedy merchants. And he urged society's responsibility toward its less fortunate members.

From his thirty-sixth year until his death Woolman kept a diary remarkable for its grace of language and spirit, its expressions of charity and devotion. This gentle, roving preacher moved unafraid where few dared follow. Here, for example, with the quiet confidence of the devoted man of God, he tells of the beginning of a dangerous mission to the Indians at a time when the frontier

From *Journal of John Woolman*, in *The London Book of English Prose*, selected and ordered by Herbert Read and Bonamy Dobreé, published by The Macmillan Company.

was still bubbling with tension after years of massacres and re-taliatory raids.

June 10, 1763.

Set out early in the morning and crossed the Western Branch of Deleware called the Great Lehie, near Fort Allen, the water being high we went over in a Canow. Here we met an Indian and had some friendly conversation with him, & gave him some BisKet, and he having killed a deer, gave the Indians with us some of it. Then after travelling some miles we met Several Indian men and women with a Cow and Horse & some household goods, who were lately come from their dwelling at Wioming, and going to Settle in another place. We made them some small presents, and some of them understanding English, I told them my motive in comeing into their Country, with which they appeared Satisfied: and one of our guides talking a while with an Antient woman concerning us, The poor old woman came to my companion and me and took her leave of us with an Appearance of Sincere affection. So going on we pitched our Tent near the banks of the Same River, having laboured hard in crossing some of those Mountains called the Blue Ridge, and by the roughness of the Stones, and the cavities between them, and the steepness of ye hills, it appeared dangerous: but we were preserved in Safety through the kindness of him whose works in these Mountainous Deserts appeared awfull, toward whom my heart was turned during this days Travel.

Near our Tent on the sides of large Trees peeled for that purpose, were various Representations of men going to, and returning from the wars, and of Some killed in Battle, this being a path heretofore used by warriors. And as I walked about viewing those Indian histories, which were painted mostly in red but some with black, and thinking on the Innumerable Affliction which the proud, fierce Spirit produceth in the world; Thinking of the Toyls and fatigues of warriors, traveling over Mountains and Deserts, Thinking on their miseries & Distresses when wounded far from home by their Enemies, and of their bruises and great weariness in Chaseing one another over the Rocks and Mountains, and of their restless, unquiet state of mind who live in this Spirit, and of the hatred which mutually grows up in the minds of the Children of those Nations Engaged in war with each other: The desire to cherish the Spirit of Love and peace amongst these people, arose very fresh in me.

This was the first night . . . in the woods, and being wet travelling in the rain, the ground & our Tent wet, and the bushes wet which we proposed to lay under, our Blankets also, all looked discouraging; but I believed that it was the Lord who had thus far brought me forward, and that he would dispose of me as He Saw good, and therein I felt easie. So we kindled a fire with out Tent door open to it, and with Some bushes next the ground, and then Blankets, we made our Bed, and lying down got some sleep. . . .

" . . . trivial matters . . . not proper
to be Related by a Female pen . . ."

Sarah Kemble Knight

When a thirty-eight year old Boston schoolmistress venture-somely set out for New York on horseback in the autumn of 1704, she and her family and friends must have felt many misgivings. For Sarah Kemble Knight (1666–1727), or Madame Knight as she was called, left behind the urbane society and sophistication of Boston to strike forth into a Connecticut and New York wilderness, tracked by tomahawk-bearing Indians and inhabited by colonists considered only slightly less savage. The rude and uncouth habits and customs of those who had settled this uncivilized frontier fascinated her, and her sharp eyes missed little as she rode along. When night found Madame Knight lodged at a wayside inn, she put down a faithful account of the day's sights in her famous *Private Journal.* She was a shrewd, intelligent woman, and her distaste for what she saw and heard did not keep her from compiling as valuable a reckoning of that time and place as any that survives.

Madame Knight's father was a Boston shopkeeper and she herself later kept a shop. (No wonder she was interested in how Connecticut merchants sold "ribinen for hatbands.") Her husband was a ship captain and during his long absences at sea and after his death she found it necessary to find means of supporting herself. Besides keeping her shop she mastered shorthand so that she could become a court reporter, and she also conducted a boarding house. She is better remembered, however, for her school in Boston, where, it is said, Benjamin Franklin and Cotton Mather were pupils.

The purpose of Madame Knight's trip, which took five months to complete, was to aid in settling a relative's estate. Little is known about what befell her afterwards, except that she must have concluded that Connecticut really wasn't quite so bad a place as she had pictured it, for some years later she returned and set herself up as an innkeeper there near the town of New London.

From *The Private Journal on a Journey from Boston to New York,* by Sarah Kemble Knight. Bruce Rogers.

October 7, 1704.

. . . Arrived at New Haven, where I was received with all Posible Respects and civility. Here I . . . Inform'd myselfe of the manners and customs of the place. . . . They are Govern'd by the same Laws as wee in Boston, (or little differing) thr'out this whole Colony of Connecticot, And much the same way of Church Government, and many of them good, Sociable people, and I hope Religious too: but a little too much Independent in their principalls, and, as I have been told, were formerly in their Zeal very Riggid in their Administrations towards such as their Lawes made Offenders, even to a harmless Kiss or Innocent merriment among Young people. Whipping being a frequent and counted an easy Punishment. . . .

The Youth divert themselves by Shooting at the Target, as they call it, (but it very much resembles a pillory), where hee that hitts neerest the white has some yards of Red Ribbin presented him wch being tied to his hattband, the two ends streeming down his back, he is Led away in Triumph, wth great applause, as the winners of the Olympiack Games. They generally marry very young: the males oftener as I am told under twentie than above; they generally make public wedings, and have a way something singular (as they say) in some of them, *viz.* Just before Joyning hands the Bridegroom quitts the place, who is soon followed by the Bridesmen, and as it were, dragg'd back to duty—being the reverse to ye former practice among us, to steal his Bride.

There are great plenty of Oysters all along by the sea side, as farr as I Rode in the Collony, and those very good. And they Generally lived very well and comfortably in their famelies. . . . There are every where in the Towns as I passed, a Number of Indians the Natives of the Country, and are the most salvage of all the salvages of that kind that I had ever Seen: little or no care taken (as I heard upon enquiry) to make them otherwise. They . . . marry many wives and at pleasure put them away, and on the least dislike or fickle humour, on either side, saying *stand away* to one another is a sufficient Divorce. And indeed those uncomely *Stand aways* are too much in Vougue among the English in this (Indulgent Colony) as their Records plentifully prove, and that on very trivial matters, of which some have been told me, but are not proper to be Related by a Female pen, tho some of that foolish sex have had too large a share in the story. . . .

They mourn for their Dead by blackening their faces, and cutting their hair, after an Awkerd and frightfull manner; But can't bear You should mention the names of their dead Relations to them: they trade most for Rum, for wch they^d hazzard their very lives; and the English fit them Generally as well, by seasoning it plentifully with water. . . .

Being at a merchants house, in comes a tall country fellow, wth his alfogeos full of Tobacco; for they seldom Loose their Cudd, but keep Chewing and Spitting as long as they'r eyes are open—he advanc't to the midle of the Room, makes an Awkward Nodd, and spitting a Large deal of aromatick Tincture, he gave a scrape with his shovel like shoo, leaving a small shovel of dirt on the floor, made a full stop, Hugging his own pretty Body with his hands under his arms, Stood staring rown'd him, like a Catt let out of a Baskett.

At last . . . said: have You any Ribinen for Hatbands to sell I pray? The Questions and Answers about the pay being past, the Ribin is bro't and opened. Bumpkin simpers, cryes its confounded Gay I vow; and beckning to the door, in comes Jone Tawdry, dropping about 50 curtsees, and stands by him: hee shows her the Ribin. *Law you*, sais shee, *its right Gent*, do You, take it, *tis dreadfull pretty*. Then she enquires, *have You any hood silk I pray?* wch being brought and bought, Have You any *thred silk to sew it with* says shee, wch being accomodated wth they Departed. They Generaly stand after they come in a great while speachless and sometimes dont say a word till they are askt what they want, which I impute to the Awe they stand in of the merchants, who they are constantly almost Indebted too; and must take what they bring without Liberty to choose for themselves; but they serve them as well, making the merchants stay long enough for their pay.

We may Observe here the great necessity and bennefitt both of Education and Conversation; for these people have as Large a portion of mother witt, and sometimes a Larger, than those who have bin brought up in Citties; But for want of emprovements, Render themselves almost Ridiculos, as above. I should be glad if they would leave such follies, and am sure all that Love Clean Houses (at least) would be glad on't too. . . .

Their Cheif Red Letter day is St. Election, wch is annualy Observed according to Charter, to choose their Goven^r: a blessing they can never be thankfull enough for, as they will find, if ever it be their hard fortune to loose it. . . .

December 6.

The Cittie of New York is a pleasant, well compacted place, situated on a Commodius River wch is a fine harbour for shipping. The Buildings Brick Generaly, very stately and high . . . of divers Coullers and laid in Checkers, being glazed look very agreeable. The inside of them are neat to admiration, the wooden work, for only the walls are plasterd, and the Sumers and Gist are plained and kept very white scowr'd as so is all the partitions if made of Bords . . . Chimney Corners like ours, and they and the hearths were laid wth the finest tile that I ever see, and the stair cases laid all with white tile which is ever clean, and so are the walls of the Kitchen wch had a Brick floor. . . .

They are Generaly of the Church of England and have a New England Gentleman for their minister, and a very fine church set out with all Customary requisites. There are also a Dutch and Divers Conventicles as they call them, *viz.* Baptist, Quakers, &c. They are not strict in keeping the Sabbath as in Boston and other places where I had bin, but seem to deal with great exactness as farr as I see or Deall with. They are sociable to one anotjer and Curteos and Civill to strangers and fare well in their houses. The English go very fasheonable in their dress. But the Dutch, especially the middling sort, differ from our women, in their habitt go loose, were French muches wch are like a Capp and a head band in one, leaving their ears bare, which are sett out wth Jewells of a large size and many in number. And their fingers hoop't with Rings, some with large stones in them of many Coullers as were their pendants in their ears, which You should see very old women wear as well as Young.

They have Vendues very frequently and make their Earnings very well by them, for they treat with good Liquor Liberally, and the Customers Drink as Liberally and Generally pay for't as well, by paying for that which they Bidd up Briskly for, after the sack has gone plentifully about, tho' sometimes good penny worths are got there. Their Diversions in the Winter is Riding Sleys about three or four Miles out of Town, where they have Houses of entertainment at a place called the Bowery. . . .

". . . an admirable act of providence . . ."

Jacques Marquette

Jacques Marquette (1637–1675), sometimes called Père Marquette, was born at Laon, France, and at seventeen became a Jesuit. He spent twelve years preparing to be a missionary before he went to Canada to minister to the Indians. There several more years were spent in further study. He struggled to learn the Indian languages, especially those of the Hurons and the Iroquois among whom he was assigned to work. But there was still more to learn, for wilderness missionaries had to master Indian customs, crafts, religious beliefs, methods of warfare and food habits —even the art of bartering for things to eat and fur robes to keep out the cold.

After demonstrating his ability, Marquette was sent to found the Mission of St. Ignace in the Mackinac Strait between Lake Huron and Lake Michigan. It was here that he received reports from the natives of a great river that ran southward through the country of the Illinois. When this information reached him, the French Governor chose Louis Joliet to lead an expedition to search for the river. Joliet was a Canadian fur-trapper and trader and an experienced explorer who later was appointed royal hydrographer.

On May 17, 1673, the expedition set out in two birch bark canoes along unknown waters leading to strange lands. Five *voyageurs* came along to do the paddling. For food they took only a little Indian corn and some smoked meat. In addition, they carried a good store of tobacco for trading purposes.

Just one month later, Marquette quietly notes in his journal: "We safely entered Missisipi on the 17th of June, with a Joy that I cannot Express"—an entry it is impossible to read without a tingle of the excitement he must have felt that day.

The voyage took five months in all, and on his return Marquette immediately began preparations to establish a mission among the Illinois in the newly found river country. But weakened by several attacks of dysentery during the first trip, he fell ill again on the

Reprinted by permission of The Vanguard Press from *The Jesuit Relations and Allied Documents*, edited by Edna Kenton. Copyright, 1954, by The Vanguard Press.

second expedition and died at the age of 38 of a "bloody flux" in a lonely forest lean-to near what is now Ludington, Michigan. He was mourned by Indians and fellow priests alike, for he had won deep respect for his saintliness and good works. His Superior, the head of Jesuit missions in Canada, said of him that his gentleness "rendered him beloved by all, and made him all things to all men."

June, 1673.

. . . Arrived on The 7th of June. Here we are at Maskoutens [a village of the Algonquins on the shore of Lake Michigan, discovered by Jean Nicolet in 1634, near Green Bay, Wisconsin]. This Word may, in Algonquin, mean, "the fire Nation,"—which, indeed, is the name given to this tribe. Here is the limit of the discoveries which the french have made, For they have not yet gone any further.

This Village Consists of three Nations who have gathered there—Miamis, Maskoutens, and Kikabous. The former are the most civil, the most liberal and the most shapely. They wear two long locks over their ears, which give them a pleasing appearance. They are regarded as warriors, and rarely undertake expeditions without being successful. . . . The Maskoutens and Kikabous are ruder, and seem peasants in comparison with the other. As Bark for making Cabins is scarce in this country They use Rushes; these serve Them for making walls and Roofs, but do not afford them much protection against the winds, and still less against the rains when they fall abundantly. The Advantage of Cabins of this kind is, that they make packages of Them, and easily transport them wherever they wish, while they are hunting. . . .

No sooner had we arrived than we, Monsieur Jollyet and I, assembled the elders together; and he told them that he was sent by Monsieur Our Governor to discover New countries, while I was sent by God to Illumine them . . . needed two guides to show us the way; and We gave them a present, by it asking them to grant us the guides. To this they very Civilly consented; and they also spoke to us by means of a present, consisting of a Mat to serve us as a bed during the whole of our voyage.

On the following day, the tenth of June, two Miamis who were given us as guides embarked with us, in the sight of a great crowd, who could not sufficiently express their astonishment at the sight of seven frenchmen, alone in two Canoes, daring to undertake so extraordinary and so hazardous an Expedition.

We knew that, at three leagues from Maskoutens, was a River, which discharged into the Missisipi . . . the road broken by so many swamps and small lakes that it is easy to lose one's way . . . so full of wild oats that it is difficult to find the Channel. For this reason we greatly needed our two guides, who safely Conducted us to a portage of 2,700 paces, and helped us to transport our Canoes to enter That river; after which they returned home, leaving us alone in this Unknown country, in the hands of providence.

Thus we left the Waters flowing to Quebec, 4 or 500 Leagues from here, to float on Those that weould thenceforward Take us through strange lands . . . and, after mutually encouraging one another, we entered our Canoes.

The River on which we embarked is called Meskousing [i.e., the Wisconsin; the voyagers had accomplished the Fox River portage through Lake Winnebago]. It is very wide . . . full of Islands Covered with Vines. On the banks one sees fertile land, diversified with woods, prairies and Hills . . . many deer and a large number of cattle. . . . After proceeding 40 leagues on This same route, we arrived at the mouth of our River, and, at 42 and a half degrees of latitude, We safely entered Missisipi on the 17th of June, with a Joy that I cannot Express.

Here we are, then, on this so renowned River. . . . We saw only deer and cattle, bustards and Swans without wings, because they drop Their plumage in This country. From time to time, we came upon monstrous fish, one of which struck our Canoe with such violence that I Thought that it was a great tree, about to break the Canoe to pieces. On another occasion, we saw on The water a monster with the head of a tiger, a sharp nose Like That of a wildcat, with whiskers and straight, Erect ears; the head was grey and the neck quite black; but We saw no more creatures of this sort. When we cast our nets into the water we caught a Sturgeon, and a very extraordinary Kind of fish. It resembles the trout, with This difference, that its mouth is larger. Near its nose—which is smaller, as are also the eyes—is a large Bone shaped like a woman's busk, three fingers wide and a cubit long, at the end of which is a disk as Wide As one's hand. . . .

When we reached the parallel of 41 degrees 28 minutes, following The same direction, we found that Turkeys had taken the place of game; and the pisikious, or wild cattle, That of the other animals. We call them "wild cattle," because they are very similar to our domestic cattle. They are not longer, but are nearly as large again, and more Corpulent. When Our people killed one, three persons had much difficulty in moving it. The head is very large; The forehead is flat, and a foot and a half Wide between the Horns, which are exactly like Those of our oxen, but black and much larger. Under the Neck They have a Sort of large dewlap, which hangs down; and on the back is a rather high hump. The whole of the head, The Neck, and a portion of the Shoulders, are Covered with a thick Mane Like That of horses; It forms a crest a foot long, which makes them hideous, and falling over the eyes, Prevents them from seeing what is before Them. The remainder of the Body is covered with a heavy coat of curly hair, almost Like That of our sheep, but much stronger and Thicker . . . moreover, they are very fierce; and not a year passes without their killing some savages. . . .

We continued to advance, but, As we knew not whither we were going,—for we had proceeded over One hundred leagues without discovering anything except animals and birds,—we kept well on our guard. On this account, we make only a small fire on land, toward evening, to cook our meals; and after supper, we remove Ourselves as far from it as possible, and pass the night in our Canoes, which we anchor in the river at some distance from the shore. This does not prevent us from always posting one of the party as a sentinel, for fear of surprise. . . .

July.

After a month's Navigation, while descending Missisipi from the 42nd to the 34th degree, and beyond, and after preaching the Gospel as well as I could to the Nations that I met, we start on the 17th of July from the village of the akensea [Arkansas], to retrace our steps. We therefore reascend the Missisipi which gives us much trouble in breasting its Currents. It is true that . . . had this voyage resulted in the salvation of even one soul I would consider all my troubles well rewarded, and I have reason to presume that such is the case for . . . while we were embarking, a dying child was brought to me at The water's edge, and I baptized it shortly before it died, through an admirable act of providence for the salvation of that Innocent soul.

"Universal independence is an almighty idea . . ."

Davy Crockett

Like Paul Bunyan and Pecos Bill, Davy Crockett (1786–1836) has become an American myth, and his life forms a colorful early chapter in the country's folklore. "I'm that same David Crockett," he is supposed to have said, "fresh from the backwoods, half-horse, half-alligator, a little touched with the snapping turtle; can wade the Mississippi, leap the Ohio, ride upon a streak of lightning, and slip without a scratch down a honey locust; can whip my weight in wild cats—and if any gentleman pleases, for a ten dollar bill, he may throw in a panther. . . ."

Some of the legends that grew up around the man were probably of Crockett's own making, for he seems to have been one of the first politicians to understand the vote-getting magic of a palatable mixture of demagoguery, eccentric speech and dress, appeals to ignorance, eulogies of whiskey and branch water, and racy rural humor. Five generations of imitators have found the formula still potent.

There is good reason to believe, however, that in a larger sense Crockett, the vote-winning buffoon, the betting, poker-playing, horse-swapping, stump-speaking, seducing, swearing, backwoods coonskin hero, was the deliberate creation of astute Whig politicians who saw that he was just what they needed to ensure success in the struggle to undermine the hated Andrew Jackson in the south and west where his political strength lay.

But behind the myth was a man—a man born in Limestone, Tennessee, a poor frontier squatter whose only education was what he painfully acquired by his own efforts as he struggled to make a living by hunting and trapping. While still young he served under Jackson in the brutal campaigns against the Creek Indians, and became a Colonel in the State militia. Back home, as his horizons widened, he sought his first public office. It was virtually thrust upon him. He advanced rapidly from justice of the peace to magistrate and from there moved on to two terms in the Tennessee Legislature and two terms in Congress. For a time Crockett even aspired to nomination for the Presidency. His con-

From *The Life of Davy Crockett by Himself*, by Davy Crockett. The New American Library. 1955.

stituents, though, apparently saw more clearly than did he what
was going on in Washington. They brought his political career to
an abrupt end by failing to re-elect him.

Bitter and disillusioned at this turn of events, Crockett declared that he would never again return to his native state and
went off to Texas to join the forces that were fighting for independence from Mexico. He was one of the brave company of men
that defended the Alamo against the Mexican Army. His diary
record of the last ten days of the siege was found after his death.

February 19, 1836. San Antonio.

. . . We are all in high spirits, though we are rather short of provisions, for
men who have appetites that could digest anything but oppression; but no
matter, we have a prospect of soon getting our bellies full of fighting, and
that is victuals and drink to a patriot any day. We had a little sort of convivial party last evening: just about a dozen of us set to work, most patriotically, to see whether we could not get rid of that curse of the land, whisky,
and we made considerable progress; but my poor friend, Thimblerig, got
sewed up just about as tight as the eyelet-hole in a lady's corset, and a little
tighter too, I reckon; for when he went to bed he called for a bootjack,
which was brought to him, and he bent down on his hands and knees, and
very gravely pulled off his hat with it, for the darned critter was so thoroughly
swiped that he didn't know his head from his heels. But this wasn't all the
folly he committed; he pulled off his coat and laid it on the bed, and then
hung himself over the back of a chair. . . . Seeing the poor fellow completely
used up, I carried him to bed. . . .

February 22.

The Mexicans, about sixteen hundred strong, with their President Santa
Anna at their head, aided by Generals Almonte, Cos, Sesma, and Castrillon,
are within two leagues of Bexar. . . . Some of the scouts came in, and bring
reports that Santa Anna has been endeavoring to excite the Indians to hostili-
ties against the Texians, but so far without effect. The Comanches, in particular, entertain such hatred for the Mexicans, and at the same time hold them
in such contempt, that they would rather turn their tomahawks against them,
and drive them from the land, than lend a helping hand. We are up and
doing, and as lively as Dutch cheese in the dog-days. . . .

February 23.

Early this morning the enemy came in sight, marching in regular order,
and displaying their strength to the greatest advantage, in order to strike us
with terror. But that was no go; they'll find that they have to do with men
who will never lay down their arms as long as they can stand on their legs.
We held a short council of war, and finding that we should be completely
surrounded, and overwhelmed by numbers, if we remained in the town, we
concluded to withdraw to the fortress of Alamo, and defend it to the last

extremity. We accordingly filed off, in good order, having some days before placed all the surplus provisions, arms, and ammunition in the fortress. We have had a large national flag made; it is composed of thirteen stripes, red and white, alternately, on a blue ground, with a large white star, of five points, in the centre, and between the points the letters TEXAS. As soon as all our little band, about one hundred and fifty in number, had entered and secured the fortress in the best possible manner, we set about raising our flag on the battlements. . . .

The enemy marched into Bexar, and took possession of the town, a blood-red flag flying at their head, to indicate that we need not expect quarters if we should fall into their clutches. In the afternoon a messenger was sent from the enemy to Colonel Travis, demanding an unconditional and absolute surrender of the garrison, threatening to put every man to the sword in case of refusal. The only answer he received was a cannon shot, so the messenger left us with a flea in his ear, and the Mexicans commenced firing grenades at us, but without doing any mischief. . . .

February 24.

Very early this morning the enemy commenced a new battery on the banks of the river, about three hundred and fifty yards from the fort, and by afternoon they amused themselves by firing at us from that quarter. Our Indian scout came in this evening, and with him a reinforcement of thirty men from Gonzales, who are just in the nick of time to reap a harvest of glory; but there is some prospect of sweating blood before we gather it in. . . .

February 25.

The firing commenced early this morning, but the Mexicans are poor engineers, for we haven't lost a single man, and our outworks have sustained no injury. Our sharpshooters have brought down a considerable number of stragglers at a long shot. . . . The enemy have been busy during the night, and have thrown up two batteries on the opposite side of the river. The battalion of Matamoras is posted there, and cavalry occupy the hills in the east and on the road to Gonzales. They are determined to surround us, and cut us off from reinforcement, or the possibility of escape by a sortie. Well, there's one thing they cannot prevent; we'll still go ahead, and sell our lives at a high price.

February 26.

Colonel Bowie has been taken sick from over-exertion and exposure. He did not leave his bed today until twelve o'clock. He is worth a dozen common men in a situation like ours. . . .

February 27.

The cannonading began early this morning, and ten bombs were thrown into the fort, but fortunately exploded without doing any mischief. So far it has been a sort of tempest in a tea-pot, not unlike a pitched battle in the Hall of Congress, where the parties array their forces, make fearful demonstrations on both sides, then fire away with loud-sounding speeches, which contain about as much meaning as the report of a howitzer charged with a blank cartridge. Provisions are becoming scarce, and the enemy are endeavoring to cut off our water. If they attempt to stop our grog in that manner, let them look out, for we shall become too wrathy for our shirts to hold us. We are not prepared to submit to an excise of that nature, and they'll find it out. This discovery has created considerable excitement in the fort.

February 28.

Last night our hunters brought in some corn, and had a brush with a scout from the enemy beyond gun-shot of the fort. They put the scout to flight, and got in without injury. They bring accounts that the settlers are flying in all quarters, in dismay, leaving their possessions to the mercy of the ruthless invader, who is literally engaged in a war of extermination more brutal than the untutored savage of the desert could be guilty of. Slaughter is indiscriminate, sparing neither sex, age, nor condition. Buildings have been burnt down, farms laid waste, and Santa Anna appears determined to verify his threat, and convert the blooming paradise into a howling wilderness. For just one fair crack at that rascal, even at a hundred yards' distance, I would bargain to break my Betsey, and never pull trigger again. My name's not Crockett if I wouldn't get glory enough to appease my stomach for the remainder of my life. . . .

The enemy, somewhat emboldened, draws nigher to the fort. So much the better. There was a move in General Sesma's division toward evening.

February 29.

Before daybreak, we saw General Sesma leave his camp with a large body of cavalry and infantry, and move off in the direction of Goliad. We think that he must have received news of Colonel Fanning's coming to our relief. We are all in high spirits at the prospect of being able to give the rascals a fair shake on the plain. This business of being shut up makes a man wolfish. I had a little sport this morning before breakfast. The enemy had planted a piece of ordnance within gun-shot of the fort during the night, and the first thing in the morning they commenced a brisk cannonade, point blank, against the spot where I was snoring. I turned out pretty smart and mounted the rampart. The gun was charged again, a fellow stepped forth to touch her off, but before he could apply the match, I let him have it, and he keeled over. A second stepped up, snatched the match from the hand of the dying man . . . the next instant the Mexican was stretched on the earth beside the first. A third came up to the cannon, my companion handed me another gun, and I fixed him off in like manner. A fourth, then a fifth, seized the match, who both met with the same fate, and then the whole party gave it up as a bad job, and hurried off to the camp, leaving the cannon ready charged where they had planted it. I came down, took my bitters, and went to breakfast. Thimblerig told me that the place from which I had been firing was one of the snuggest stands in the whole fort, for he never failed picking off two or three stragglers before breakfast, when perched up there. . . .

March 1.

The enemy's forces have been increasing in numbers daily, notwithstanding they have already lost about three hundred men in the several assaults they have made upon us. I neglected to mention in the proper place, that when the enemy came in sight we had but three bushels of corn in the garrison, but have since found eighty bushels in a deserted house. Colonel Bowie's illness still continues, but he manages to crawl from his bed every day, that his comrades may see him. His presence alone is a tower of strength. The enemy becomes more daring as his numbers increase.

March 2.

This day the delegates meet in general convention at the town of Washington, to frame our [Texan] Declaration of Independence. That the sacred instrument may never be trampled on by the children of those who have freely shed their blood to establish it, is the sincere wish of David Crockett. Universal independence is an almighty idea, far too extensive for some brains to comprehend. . . .

March 3.

We have given over all hopes of receiving assistance from Goliad or Refugio. Colonel Travis harangued the garrison, and concluded by exhorting them, in case the enemy should carry the fort, to fight to the last gasp, and render their victory even more serious to them than to us. This was followed by three cheers.

March 4.

Shells have been falling into the fort like hail during the day, but without effect. . . .

March 5.

Pop, pop, pop! Bom, bom, bom! throughout the day. No time for memorandums now. Go ahead! Liberty and independence forever!

[Here ends Colonel David Crockett's manuscript. Before the sun set again he was dead, as were all of his comrades of the Alamo.]

". . . it was just hell and high water all the time . . ."

Andrew Gordon

Twenty years before the last mile of the transcontinental railway was completed in 1869, the "Great Migration" to the western frontier was well under way along the Santa Fe, Oregon and
California Trails. Lured onward by the discovery of gold in California, and by the promise of rich farming lands in the Northwest
that were free for the taking, straggling ox-driven caravans of
covered wagons dragged across the two thousand miles or so of
prairie and desert that separated the mid-continent from the rich
new coastal lands.

Missouri was the traditional starting point for the long, dusty
odyssey, and it was from St. Joseph, on April 30, 1849, that a
train of fifteen wagons started for California, laden with household
possessions and sixty-one persons besides: three women, six children, and fifty-two men, among them young Andrew Gordon who
had come from Memphis, Tennessee to join the party.

The land-hungry and the gold-hungry had to conquer hundreds of miles of sand and sagebrush and months of privation before they reached their goal—and, too often, their disillusionment.
The trails, although already much traversed, were by no means
highways unless such a word can be used for belts of land a hundred miles wide, where directions often had to be read from stars
or compass. Brightly painted wagons bleached in the blazing sun;
gay, many-hued canvas tops turned grey in the fog of dust that
rose to choke drivers and passengers. Rough patches covered gaping holes torn in the canvas by raging wind storms or the arrows
of unfriendly Indians. Wire, prayers, and ingenuity held creaking,
battered wagons together.

The weather was given to extremes of heat and cold, and there
were torrents of rain. Wide rivers were made doubly perilous by
floods. Sometimes there were shortages of water, too, for man and
beast, and then the last drops in the water casks had to be ra-
tioned. Fuel was hard to find, and hard to kindle with pocket
flints. There was no way to replace worn-out shoes, clothing
weathered to shreds. Food ran low. Animals grew scrawny and

From *The Way Our People Lived*, by William E. Woodward. Copyright, 1944, by
E. P. Dutton & Co., Inc.

weak, ill-nourished on sparse dry grass. Bleached bones and rude crosses along the trail recorded the toll of deaths from starvation, cholera and dysentery. Gnats, sand and deer flies swarmed ceaselessly. Buzzards overhead predicted, and hopefully waited for, disaster, while the night howls of coyotes drove sleep away.

Somehow, after five or six months of struggle and hardship, the indomitable spirit of these pioneers brought some of them through. One of them, Andrew Gordon, asked himself in his diary the question that thousands must have asked, "Are we crazy?"

April 30, 1849.

We got off this morning, clear cool day. We bought two mules yesterday—not to pull the wagons, for the oxen do that, but for two of us to ride. The other two ride on the wagon. . . . I always thought the prairies were flat as a floor, but not so; they have a sort of wavy look, like the sea with billows. . . .

May 7.

There is no wood to be had to build a fire, and we have to depend on dried buffalo chips. That means that the cook and one other at least for every wagon must range the prairie—sometimes for miles—looking for the droppings of buffalos. . . . I had no idea of this before I came on this expedition, or I would have thought twice again before leaving home. Everybody values dried buffalo chips almost as highly as precious gems. . . .

May 8.

We met two wagons coming back from the Promised Land today. The men with them looked pretty well down in the mouth. . . . They stopped and we had a long powwow. We gave them some liquor and grub. They had not been to California—never got there. It seemed that the Humboldt Desert had almost ruined them, and they turned back. Two of their men died of cholera; they had three left, and these survivors had hollow eyes and caved-in cheeks, and looked as if they were about done for. Three of their oxen had died—two of them of thirst, and the other one just could not walk any further. He laid down on the prairie and they had to shoot him. They had three oxen left, but they pulled the wagon easily, for it was almost empty.

They had painted on the white cover of the wagon the words, "Going for Gold." It was not funny, but sad.

They said the prairie is easy going, but when you get into the rough country it was just hell and high water all the time. Also beware of the Indians when we are further along. . . .

May 29.

What a day this has been! We crossed the South Platte, and were in a nervous strain all day for fear that we would lose a man or a wagon. The stream is three thousand feet wide, but it is not deep; not more than three feet deep except in a few places. But the current is as swift as a mill race and there are unexpected beds of quicksand. Upon our arrival on the south side of the river about noon we found a lot of other trains or "caravans" waiting to cross. About fifty wagons in all. We went at it cautiously, a wagon at a time, with Cullen and two other men riding by the wagon, prepared to help. Our party came through all right, except for the water getting into the wagon and ruining about a third of our flour. . . .

June 12.

As the trail gets rougher we encounter piles of things that people have thrown away to lighten their loads. This was a day of scenes of abandoned property; stoves, blacksmith tools, mattresses, cooking utensils, and provisions of every kind strung along the road. There was also an abandoned wagon with broken axles. We have been seeing dead animals from the first day, but today we saw three dead mules and an ox lying by the side of the road. . . .

July 12.

. . . I wish I could never hear the word *lousy* again. I am willing to bet that Tommy Plunkett uses it fifty times a day, but he is no worse than the others. It is "lousy" this and "lousy" that. The rain is lousy, the trail is lousy, the bacon is lousy, some of the drivers are lousy, and Gus Thorpe, losing in the card game, has just said that he has had a lousy deal.

Sometimes I think that I am going on a long journey with a traveling insane asylum, and that I am crazy myself. The thought of California—still far away —makes me want to puke. . . .

August 20.

I hardly know whether I am alive or dead. All day in a blazing heat, with the air so hot that in moving my hand through it I feel as if I were thrusting it into the hot air over a bed of coals. The oxen stagger along, with their tongues hanging out. I mean our six oxen do, but the beasts of some of the other wagons have simply laid down to die. In such cases we cannot wait; we cut them from their traces and leave them lying there.

Our barrel of water helps. The river water can be drunk when it is flowing —in small quantities—but is dangerous (I may say deadly) after it stands a while. Why, I cannot say. . . .

Everybody is going around half-naked on account of the heat. Even old Mrs. Goudy [an octogenarian]. She shed her outer garments and appeared in her petticoat. "I'm going around in my shimmy tail," she called out, "and it's cooler." Later on, when we stopped for nooning, and to eat a little, I saw her grandson throwing buckets of river water over her. He threw it over while she wore her under clothes, so the old gal must have been soaking wet for hours. . . .

I heard one man threaten to kill his partner today because his partner was laughing at him trying to take off his shirt which was a tight fit and was stuck to his body by sweat.

It is difficult to make much progress in the deep, soft sand. It is like fine dust. The cattle are in it up to their knees and we are constantly called on to put our shoulders to the wheel and help push the wagons out. But not for our own shebang, for our cattle are pulling only a light load now. . . .

September 24.

We got to San Francisco yesterday, and have been on the go ever since. . . . This town was built for 800 people and now it has 10,000. We stayed last night at the Parker House, which is called a hotel, but I would call it a shanty. It is small, having room for about a dozen people, if all the space is used. Last night four men slept in the small room we occupied on bunks put up one above the other. We paid ten dollars apiece. That means the proprietor got forty dollars for the rent of that room for one night. . . . Are we crazy?

"Oh! Babylon! . . ."

Edward Ely

About one hundred years ago, Edward Ely (1827–1858) a young physician of Bucks County, Pennsylvania, found that his health was failing. He and his advisers prescribed a long sea voyage, the favorite nineteenth century remedy for an obscure illness, and shortly thereafter Ely signed on as ship's doctor of the schooner *Delia Maria* bound from New York to San Francisco. Thus began years of intermittent wandering which carried the young doctor half-way around the world and ended only with his death eight years later in Bombay where he held the post of United States Consul.

Ely reached California in time to see the Gold Rush at its frenzied height. Leaving his ship he journeyed inland with increasing astonishment and apprehension. At Placerville, in the mountains above Sacramento, he plumbed what seemed to him the very depths of gold-lust and depravity. Here is Ely's picture of the panners sweating out the precious nuggets, dreaming of wealth beyond measure, living in the world's richest squalor—and here is his record of what happened to much of the glittering dust washed from the earth with such pain.

October 12, 1851. Placerville, California.

Yes, sure enough I am now upon that far famed ground which had so recently acquired a golden name throughout the world, "the Gold Region of California." Placerville is the center of a very rich neighborhood, rich I mean in minerals and precious metals, but wild, mountainous and barren in appearance. We arrived here last evening at about ten or eleven o'clock from Sacramento which we left at five in the morning in a large stagecoach drawn by six horses. . . . We reached the town of Colona on the South Fork of the American River just at sunset and here we saw the first diggings. . . . There were more than a hundred men employed here, and a rougher wilder or dirtier set I never saw. Thinks I to myself . . . if these men were to return to the states in their present garb they would excite a greater sensation than

From *The Wanderings of Edward Ely*, A Mid-Century Seafarer's Diary. Edited by Anthony and Allison Sirna. Copyright 1954 by Anthony and Allison Sirna, reprinted by permission of Hastings House Publishers, Inc.

a menagerie of wild animals. Their clothes are of coarse material, ragged and of one uniform color, that of dirt; their hats slouch down over their faces which are almost the color of their clothes, and their beards are long and matted. They scarcely look at you as you pass along, so bent are they upon their engrossing tasks. Poor devils, your toil is spent in search of a useless bauble, your hours are lost in the acquirement of the earth's most unsubstantial production, and your lives are wearing away in misery to yourselves, in absence from your home and friends, and in total neglect of every precept and conjunction of your maker.

. . . At Colona . . . the stage agent sent us forward the remaining distance in a light carriage with two remaining horses. It was a beautiful moonlight night and as we had long exchanged the level plains and scattering oaks for the high mountains and towering forest of pines and firs, the scenery was most romantically wild. About half the distance between the two towns, we broke the hind wheel of the wagon and although it still supported us yet we dreaded that at every rock or at every hill it would go down. . . . At length we came in sight of Placerville, and had just passed the "gallows tree" (so named from its having been the instrument of several lynch executions) and were descending the last hill when down came the wheel pitching us out in the dust and spilling all our baggage in the road. . . .

October 22.

. . . It has been ten days since I first arrived at this place and since that time I have traversed the whole of the region of which it is the center. In the afternoon of my last date, our party started off with knapsacks, arms and brandy bottles . . . to a locality called Coon Hollow, and having been told that it was four miles we expected to make it before sunset. The distance must have been double what we were told however, for the darkness of the night surprised us in the deep forest and the coyotes commenced their serenade to the moon now hid in fleecy clouds, without a cabin, a light, or even a road to be seen. To go forward was impossible, and . . . we spread our blankets beneath huge pine trees. . . .

We arose early in the morning and feeling the calls of a hungry stomach rather sensibly we made haste to pursue our journey. Upon gaining the end of the mountain we were upon Coon Hollow with its log huts, dirt heaps and noisy brook, opened immediately at our feet.

Going to the only place in the digging where "Prospectors" could be accommodated we were soon making a hearty breakfast off a piece of salt pork, some sea biscuit and a cup of what they called tea without any milk or sugar. This is good fare here, and if a man can get that, he is master of all the necessaries, as well as luxuries of California. Those who travel about from place to place, either looking at the count or hunting richer diggings are called by the miners "Prospectors." This class is very numerous and it is a frequent occurrence to meet a solitary man in the mountains with his little mule loaded with his blankets, pickaxe, shovel and wash basin with perhaps a few necessary cooking utensils, while he is armed to the teeth, and both toiling onward. . . . The diggings at Coon Hollow were very rich and the miners are throwing out vast heaps of dirt, in readiness for the rainy season which will set in about the middle of November. Gold cannot be separated from sand and dirt without the aid of water and in the dry season it is too far to convey the dirt to the water with the few and clumsy vehicles that are yet here. . . .

The dust is the only currency here, and every man has his small try scales to weigh it out. An ounce is worth $16, one dollar is half a dracham, and a half dollar is fifteen grains. Below half a dollar the Californian never goes and I might say that there is nothing in the diggings that has a less price than fifteen grains of gold. In Placerville however, there are plenty of coin and plenty of means of getting rid of it too. Everything is very dear here, and there is no end to spending money. Indeed you never think of opening your mouth here without putting your hand in your pocket.

I . . . certainly do thank providence that I have thus far passed through so many dangers and hardships and exposures, without harm, but I do not know that I am more comfortable here than under the pine trees of the mountains or on the banks of the rock bound rivers. We have slept almost every night in the open air, and have sometimes occupied many hours in descending a ravine or in creeping along a precipice, in constant danger of a break-neck tumble, or of a deadly bite of a rattlesnake. We have also been passing through a wood where the grizzly bears were numerous and where a few days ago a poor fellow was torn to pieces by them and his companion, scalped and torn in the most shocking manner. We have encountered many parties of fierce looking Comanches, and even lit our campfire in sight of their own, without ever having received harm or ill, with the single exception of poor Clark's losing one of his boots, which he had left at a little distance from him and which the thieving coyotes stole. . . .

In every village of this golden country we have from one to a hundred houses dedicated to the purpose of gambling. . . . Nevertheless humble the appearances of these places, I have seen hundreds of thousands of dollars of dust change owners here in as short a time as the more refined hells of the cities. Here the banker sits with his cards in his hands, his table loaded with gold, his pistols before him, and his knife in his bosom. . . . All hours are alike to them. There is even another type of business driven on here quite as profitable to the managers, and quite as demoralizing to the community as gambling. I mean prostitution. There is a house here owned by a young woman from New Orleans, who has succeeded in bringing to this retired spot about a dozen Sandwich Island girls and although she has not been in the place one year, she must be worth a hundred thousand dollars. It could scarcely be otherwise considering the high price of everything in California, and more especially where there is a monopoly. To speak plainly one night's enjoyment of the society of the charming mistress of the house, costs the man the moderate sum of one hundred dollars, and the same indulgence with the girls, fifty dollars.

Oh! Babylon! . . .

"Everything looks Blue to me."

George C. Duffield

The ranchers of Texas faced a problem in the middle years of the last century. Texans could not possibly use all of their beef production even when prime steers were offered for as little as $10 a head. Meanwhile, in the newly opening areas to the north, settlers clamored for meat and were willing to pay well for it.

The difficulty was that railroads had not yet penetrated to the cattle country and there seemed to be no way to bring the beef and the beef-hungry together. Then someone, about 1858 it was, had the idea of driving longhorns overland to the far-off booming markets. Fanning outward from Texas ranges, mile-long lines of cattle soon were treading the trails that led to Colorado and Illinois and points between—two thousand or more longhorns at a time trudging northward like an army on the march.

George C. Duffield, a typical early trail driver, describes in his diary, the tribulations of the four-month trek from mid-Texas to the borders of Iowa. Not surprisingly, his is a tale of woe.

More was involved, it turned out, than merely nudging the steers onward. Food and water for the stock were necessary but not always easy to come by. At any moment, night or day, a stampede might be set off by a clap of thunder or deliberately provoked by cunning Indians and cattle thieves. It sometimes took days to round up the scattered animals, with always some lost beyond retrieving.

Deadly arrows, torrential rains, treacherous rivers—all took their toll of the drovers and the driven. Provisions ran low or were exhausted. During storms often it was necessary to stay in the saddle day and night to keep herds together. When a chance to sleep did come, there was little comfort in a rain-soaked bedroll spread on bare, wet earth.

It is 1866. The cattle straggle along the trail into the distance. The "long drive" is under way . . .

April 29, 1866.

. . . Started in evening from Salt Creek & travelled 5 miles to Alexanders gap between Colorado & Brazos.

From *The Iowa State Journal of Science.* Volume 14, No. 2, January, 1940.

April 30.

All well in my herd. Travelled through Pansgath & to Bennett Creek   18 miles.

May 1.

. . . Big Stampede   lost 200 head of cattle.

May 2.

Spent the day hunting & found but 25 Head   it has been raining for three days   these are dark days for me.

May 3.

day Spent in hunting cattle   found 23   hard rain and wind   lots of trouble.

May 4.

Continued the hunt   found 40 head   day pleasant   Sun shone once more. Heard that the other Herd has stampeded & lost over 200.

May 5.

Cloudy damp Morning   rode 16 miles & back to see the other Boys found them in trouble with cattle all scattered over the country.

May 8.

All 3 heards are up & ready to travel off together for the first time   traveled 6 miles   rain pouring down in torrents & here we are on the banks of a creek with 10 or 12 ft water & raising   crossed at 4 Oclock & crossed into the Basque Bottom   found it 20 ft. deep   Ran my Horse into a ditch & got my knee badly sprained— 15 Miles

May 9.

Still dark & gloomy   River up   everything looks *Blue* to me   no crossing to day   cattle behaved well.

May 12.

Lay around camp   visited River & went Bathing.

May 13.

Big Thunder Storm last night   Stampede lost 100 Beeves   hunted all day found 50 all tired. Everything discouraging.

May 14.

Concluded to cross Brazos   swam our cattle & Horses & built Raft & Rafted our provisions & blanket &c over   Swam River with rope & then hauled wagon over   Lost Most of our Kitchen furniture such as camp Kittles Coffee Pots Cups Plates Canteens &c &c.

May 15.

back at River bringing up wagon Hunting Oxen & other *lost* property. Rain poured down for one Hour. It does nothing but rain   got all our *traps* together that was not lost & thought we were ready for off   dark rainy night cattle all left us & in morning not one Beef to be seen.

May 16.

Hunt Beeves is the word— all Hands discouraged & are determined to go   200 Beeves out & nothing to eat.

May 17.

No Breakfast   pack & off is the order. all Hands gave the Brazos one good harty dam & started for Buchanan   travelled 10 miles & camped   found 50 Beeves   nothing to eat.

May 22.

This day has been spent in crossing the West Trinity & a hard & long to be remembered day to me   we swam our cattle & Horses   I swam it 5 times   upset our wagon in River & lost Many of our cooking utensils again drove 3 miles & camped.

May 23.

Travelled 10 Miles over a beautiful Prairie country such as I expected to see before I came here   stopped for dinner on Henrietta Creek & then on to Elisabeth Town & creek & stopped for the night—Hard rain that night & cattle behaved very bad—ran all night—was on my Horse the whole night & it raining hard.

May 31.

Swimming cattle is the order. We worked all day in the River & at dusk got the last Beefe over— & am now out of Texas— This day will long be remembered by me— There was one of our party Drowned to day (Mr. Carr) & several narrow escapes & I among the no.

June 1.

Stampede last night among 6 droves & a general mix up and loss of Beeves. Hunt Cattle again   Men all tired & want to leave. am in the Indian country am annoyed by them   believe they scare the Cattle to get pay to collect them— Spent the day in separating Beeves & Hunting— Two men and Bunch Beeves lost—Many Men in trouble. Horses all give out & Men refused to do anything.

June 5.

Oh! what a night—Thunder Lightning & rain—we followed our Beeves *all* night as they wandered about—put them on the road at day break   found 90 Beeves of an other mans Herd   travelled 18 Miles over the worst road I ever saw & come to Boggy Depot & crossed 4 Rivers   It is well Known by that name   We hauled cattle out of the Mud with oxen half the day.

June 8.

travelled 4 Miles & camped for the day to wait for 12 Beeves that is in another Heard. this is another gloomey evening & I tremble for the result of this night— Thunder & rain all night   was in the saddle until day light am almost dead for sleep.

June 12.

Hard Rain & Wind   Big stampede & here we are among the Indians with 150 head of Cattle gone   hunted all day & the Rain pouring down with but poor success   Dark days are these to me   Nothing but Bread & Coffee Hands all Growling & Swearing— every thing wet & cold   Beeves gone   rode all day & gathered all but 35   Mixed with 8 other Herds   Last Night 5000 Beeves stampeded at this place & a general mix up was the result.

June 14.

Last night there was a terrible storm   Rain poured in torrents *all* night & up to 12 M today   our Beeves left us in the night but for *once* on the whole trip we found them *all* together near camp at day break. *all* the other droves as far as I can hear are scattered to the four winds   our Other Herd was all gone. We are not 25 miles from Ark River & it is Very High   we are water bound by two creeks & but Beef and Flour to eat. am not Home-sick but Heart sick.

July 9.

Still cloudy   followed a man that drove off one of My Beeves & got him. . . .

July 25.

We left the Beefe Road & started due west across the wide Prairie in the Indian Nation to try to go around Kansas & strike Iowa. I have 490 Beeves travelled about 11 Miles.

August 26.

Traveled 3 Miles which took us out of Potawatomie nation into Nimehah Co & through the Town of America   are within 28 Miles of Nebraska.   think there is some hope of reaching Iowa yet. Grass Poor   saw a Meeting House yesterday.

August 28.

. . . Think I see a showing to get home some day yet have travelled 2 miles since dinner & have stopped to let the cattle graze   while I set her writing I can see over into Nebraska & expect to get there in one hour from this time— (did so).

September 1.

Moved the herd up to within 5 miles of Nebraska City— & went to Town took a good look over into Iowa   got my dinner & . . . returned to camp prospects of more rain   This is a fine country without timber.

". . . O for a cot in some wilderness."

Captain Joshua Sears

From Salem, Boston and other bustling ports of New England
a hundred years ago the long, sleek clipper ships slipped forth to
race through green seas to whatever far, outlandish places gave
promise of profitable trade to the early comer. Shaped for speed,
with three raking masts, full rigging and extra sails that could be
unfurled when the wind was right, these were the fastest sailing
vessels ever built, capable of ranging three hundred or more miles
a day. Their holds were stowed with precious, fragrant cargoes
whose very names have the ring of poetry: Sumatra pepper;
hemp, indigo; China tea and Indian opium; gums copal, arabic
and tragacanth; coffee, sandalwood and tortoise shells; grinning,
gilded heathen idols; sea horses and saltpeter; coal, teakwood,
clove buds, cinnamon, elephant tusks; wine, rum, goatskins, ca-
nella bark and mace. And also, alas, sometimes Africans seized
on the way homeward for the trade in slaves.

Captains and crews of the clippers, confined for months in
close quarters and subsisting on wormy rations, soon exhausted
whatever glamour there was in running the trade winds close-
hauled with full canvas set, fumbling out their course with as-
trolabe and ill-drawn charts, buffeted by wind and heavy seas at
both the capes, blown off course by monsoons and becalmed
when there was no wind at all to press the sails. Still, brine was in
the blood of these seafarers, and always they shipped out again.

Joshua Sears was typical of the clipper captains, a salty hard-
bitten New Englander who drove ships and men to the limit of
their endurance. And, typically, he had his softer side. Here he is,
lonely, with a loneliness that can be known only by those who
have spent years at sea, dreaming of a snug Cape Cod cottage,
wife, fire, and a pail of freshly dug clams. Yet, for all his protes-
tations, one may suspect that when he has retired from the sea
he will daily search the waters off East Dennis at the Cape with
his brass-bound telescope, and dream and talk restlessly through
his remaining years of the spice islands that lie beckoning beyond
the horizon.

From *Shipmasters of Cape Cod,* edited by H. C. Kittredge. Reprinted by permission of and arrangement with Houghton Mifflin Company, the authorized publishers.

April 6, 1857. San Francisco to Singapore.

. . . At 8 P.M. took in Top Gall sails and outer jib. Midnight split the upper main Topsail, unbent it and bent another. . . . Ship going like a mad horse.

September 5.

That heavy swell keeps running from the West. Patience, Patience,— Put your trust in God. Distance run 66 miles.

September 6.

. . . Slow getting along— Thy ways, O Lord, are inscrutable.

September 9.

. . . The Lord is my Shepherd; He'll guide me safe through. I wish there was someone else to share this weather with me; Misery loves company.

September 13.

. . . O for a cot in some wilderness.

September 20.

This is certainly very tedious, but I trust it is all for the best—J. Sears. Thy ways, O Lord, are past finding out.

September 25.

Dead calm all this day; Current set the ship 20 miles due East. I have never had such hard luck before. I feel almost discouraged. Think some of going down the China Sea if I ever get out of this calm place.

September 26.

Commences calm, dead calm . . . latter part moderate and ends dead calm. Oh how disconsolate I do feel. Next voyage I will go down the China Sea and face all the Typhoons that blows.

March 9, 1858. Akyab to Falmouth.

. . . The whole Ocean as far as the eye can see is one complete Mirror; not one breath of air the blue waves do curl—nor make the ship go either.

March 10.

Oh for a home in some vast wilderness, where the waves of the Ocean will trouble me no more.

March 16.

Ship going 8 knots . . . the fullest ship that ever was built will go as fast as that.

April 14.

We have got a staggering breeze from the North East. The old ship is going twelve knots and tearing the water up some, I tell you . . . The ship is so cranky that I never think of taking in skysails until the lee plankshear goes under water.

April 25.

Last Tuesday I commenced, with the assistance of one of the sailors that is a bit of Jack Knife Carpenter, to make a turning lathe . . . and it is a capital one. . . . One of the boys turns the crank, and it goes like lightning. Yesterday I turned some belaying pins and a lot of door knobs. . . . I expect I could turn a little baby all but the legs and some other little fixings that it would want to make it perfect.

May 23.

. . . We had four or five vessels in company last week, and they all sail as fast as we do, and some of them outsail us. I don't know what is the matter with the old ship. One ugly looking Portuguese brig kept company three days, the darndest looking dugout that I ever saw. I have been almost angry enough to sink the old ship sometimes.

May 30.

I am lonely, lonesome, disconsolate and low-spirited and have got the blues the worst kind—Oh for a cot in some vast wilderness, but on Cape Cod will do. . . . I shall be forty-one years old—time to hang up my harp.

September. Cardiff to Ceylon.

. . . She ran for four days, 268, 265, 280, 272 miles, which I call pretty good going, drawing 21 feet, 3 inches of water. Ask Levi Howes [a rival Cape Cod skipper] if he has got a ship that will beat that and carry 15,000 tons of coal too. Oh for a cot down by the sea-side where we could dig clams.

December 19.

. . . I hope and pray night and day that I shall have orders in Galle to go to Calcutta and load for home. If I have to go to China, I really believe that I shall lay right down in the furrow and let them plough me under.

December 16, 1859. Hong Kong.

. . . I have never seen the need of a wife before so much as I have this voyage. But it will certainly take six months to get me tame enough to live with one.

"Guns, pistols, hams and sabres;
rum, brandy, powder and shot . . ."

Edmund Temple

Of Edmund Temple the reference books say next to nothing.
He is scarcely less reticent himself, this "Knight of the Royal and
Distinguished Order of Charles III." At the beginning of his journal, copied here from the crumbling, yellowing pages of the 1833
edition, he merely notes that "one of the nine hundred and ninety-
nine speculations of the all-speculating year 1825, was the 'Potosi, La Paz and Peruvian Mining Association'; the object of
which was to work the far-famed mines of Potosi, and sundry
others in Peru." Temple became the Association's secretary at Potosi, although "I must blush to confess it, I was in a state of the
most profound ignorance." The fate of the Potosi enterprise is as
obscure as the rest of the story, but it can safely be assumed that,
like almost all the other ventures after gold and silver of the time,
it ended in failure.

Though almost nothing is known of his life, Temple himself
has provided an astonishingly vivid self-portrait in his journal.
He comes alive in the events and sights he chooses to note down,
in the patience and good humour with which he meets unexpected
adversities, in his sympathetic understanding of strange people,
in his selection of the felicitous phrase and the significant detail.

But Temple does more than reveal himself. He takes us on an
extraordinary journey and lets us (almost makes us) share with
him experiences that have seldom been recorded—the first sight
of a slave ship, gallops across wild pampas in the burning heat,
a method for making summer boots ("take a horse, cut off his
hind legs . . .") and other strange things from a remote and vanished world.

October 23, 1825.

In the morning-watch, we passed close to the eastward of the Cap Verd Islands, which it is scarcely possible to view without a thought upon the scenes
of human wretchedness which have there been exhibited. The sun, too, shone

From *Travels in Various Parts of Peru*, Vol. 1, by Edmund Temple. E. L. Cary &
A. Hart. Philadelphia 1833.

with intense heat, as if to excite by sympathy our utmost compassion for the sufferings of thousands of our fellow-creatures, who have here pined in indescribable misery under its scorching rays, crowded in the pestilential holds of slave ships that at one time frequented the harbours of these islands.

When the slave trade flourished, the Cap Verd Islands had the sad celebrity of being the principal rendezvous of slave ships to and from the coast of Africa. A perpetual mart existed there, to which slave-merchants from all parts resorted to make their purchases; and to this day, something of the same kind exists in the Island of St. Jago, which has been declared a *"free port."* There a slave ship may take refuge, and remain secure from the cruisers of those nations which have abolished the trade, and which make prizes of slave ships when they can catch them elsewhere.

A slave ship, with its cargo of four or five hundred wretched victims (*stowed in bulk*), is a valuable prize for a man-of-war to fall in with; for, besides the ship itself becoming the property of the captors, the British government pay a handsome sum for every slave found on board. And what value shall we set upon the heartfelt gratification which a British officer and his crew must experience, when they have relieved from the dreadful tortures of suffocation, and restored to the light of day, to fresh air and to liberty, five hundred human beings gasping for existence, which, even if prolonged, is expected at best to terminate in the drudgery of brutes!

October 30.

It seemed as if the flood-gates above had been opened, and all the waters there concentrated, poured down upon us. To call these inundations by the European term "rain" would be . . . far from conveying any idea of what they actually are . . . in a ten-gun brig, rolling, pitching, heaving, and setting, in the midst of the Atlantic ocean, upwards of two thousand six hundred miles from home, and nearly the same distance from the port of our destination . . . the ocean itself turned topsy-turvy.

November 5.

We are now running at the rate of eight and nine knots upon a bow-line; shoals of flying-fish are skimming around the vessel in every direction. . . . At six-bells, in the morning watch, we generally emerge from our wooden cells; whether refreshed or not by the night's repose depends in a great degree upon the motion of the vessel, the creaking of the guns, masts, and bulkheads, but more upon the state of the thermometer, which is materially influenced by the hatches being placed on or off, as the weather admits.

After performing our ablutions in about a pint of fresh water, economically served out by the steward, we . . . stroll up and down the deck, in conversation upon the weather, as it *was,* and *is,* and *is to be;* we then examine the log, and calculate the distance run since yesterday at noon, and often the distance still to be run before we eat fresh beef at Buenos Ayres. At two bells we all descend rather hastily. . . . When seated at breakfast, each, to his taste, butters a smoking hot roll, which, if not so light as a French roll, is certainly not so heavy as a nine-pound shot. The table is covered with luxuries: here, the remains of a cold roast duck; there, the bones of what was once a fowl; at the head, a noble dish of salt fish, mashed in a mortar and seasoned with onions; at the foot, the liver and lights of a pig or sheep recently killed; in the middle, a dish of fried salt tripe and broiled fat pork; with other little dainties equally exquisite, which, if not all served up on the same day, appear in rotation, according to the studied arrangement of our steward. Tea, or coffee, or both, may be had on asking for, but latterly there is no milk; because in the first place, the old goat, which for a time yielded us a scanty supply of that luxury, was drained to death, poor wretch! and its starved carcass thrown overboard in the Bay of Biscay; in the second place, our patent milk soon failed us, as out of eighteen cases, with which we were provided, only five, upon opening, proved fit for use. This patent milk is common milk preserved by a particular process, and tastes like boiled milk a little burnt, but not unpleasant when mixed with tea. It is put up in tin cases hermetically sealed; and will no doubt be improved upon, for if one case can be preserved sweet and good for many months, so may a thousand by the same process.

After breakfast, we again lounge upon deck, and look out for flying-fish, or skip-jacks, or dolphins; if none appear to detain us, we go below, and take our accustomed seats round the cabin table, where each commences an occupation suited to his disposition, which generally terminates in an easy nap.

A journal is sure to be seen, with the journalist poring over it, anxiously thinking, rethinking, and drawing canals from a bottle of ink. . . . Another amuses himself with a flute, for which instrument one of our companions suddenly acquired a most ungovernable passion.

. . . Announcement of dinner is received with a delightful emotion, and . . . every exertion is made to strew the dinner upon the table before the sound is out of the bell. I have said *"to strew"* upon the table, because I consider it a prettier word than scatter; but far be it from me to insinuate thereby, irregularity or disorder in the arrangement; for although the business is managed in that off-hand sailor-like manner which despises the rigid rules of formality, it cannot at the same time be termed *disorder*. . . . I have seen three puddings placed at one side of the table on board the *Frolic*, with only a saucer of pickled onions or of pickled samphire to separate them, and I never remarked that they excited the least alarm, or uneasiness, either in the mind or in the countenance of our host, or any of his guests. . . .

Bottled porter and bottled stout, a few degrees above temperate, froth round the chattering board. Madeira, very good indeed; sherry, very bad indeed; port . . . very fair claret and occasionally champagne, are all at the discretion of the guests, together with gin, rum, brandy, and tamarind-water. . . . When the cloth is removed, a plate of dried figs, another of dried raisins, and a third of dried almonds, are placed upon the table. . . .

Again upon deck . . . one may, perhaps, seat himself comfortably upon the breech of a carronade to study his Spanish grammar; another disposes himself still more comfortably to sleep; a third hauls in the fishing-line, which is generally towing astern, to catch what it can. . . .

At seven-bells in the last dog-watch, tea is announced, when those who wish to steam themselves for half an hour, descend to do so. Shortly after this alimentary operation, sighs and yawns proclaim the approaching hour for bed, and before two-bells are struck in the first watch, some are already "turned in" and fast secured in the spells of sleep. Others may prefer remaining upon deck, listening to the sailor's song, sometimes droll and merry, sometimes dismally pathetic; or, it may be, reclining over the gangway, idly gazing on the sparkling lustre of the moon, as it dances on the gently rippled waves, or in thoughtful remembrance of those far away. . . .

November 21.

Last night the gale considerably increased, and before daylight this morning the boatswain's hoarse voice was heard summoning all hands to send down top-gallant yards, to strike top-gallant masts, and reef and furl the necessary sails, which is called *"making all snug"*; but, woe is me! what a sea! and what a ship! and what a berth! for *snugness!*

November 26.

Rode out the gale perfectly safe, and at three o'clock this morning the wind came round to a favourable point, when we weighed anchor, [the land of Argentina having been sighted] and made all sail up the stupendous, but wholly uninteresting river Plate. . . .

In the course of the day, the rigging of the ship, from top to bottom, was literally covered with long fine cobwebs that had been blown off the shore, having attached to them their insect manufacturers, who dispersed themselves in thousands over our decks. We saw upon the distant hills along the coast immense herds of cattle. . . .

November 30.

. . . At eleven o'clock at night we anchored, *at last,* in the wild open roads of Buenos Ayres, about eight miles distant from the town; but were it not that we could discover, at day-light, the domes of cathedrals, the steeples of churches, and the long white ranges of buildings, we might still imagine ourselves in the midst of the ocean, for so low and flat is the land that none could be seen from our deck. Here terminates a voyage of exactly nine weeks. . . .

December 2.

. . . I was conveyed full gallop to Faunch's Hotel . . . considered the principal hotel in the city, out of compliment, I suppose, to the proprietors, who are English; but there is nothing whatever in the whole straggling building, within doors or without, that can induce an English traveller to fancy himself in an English hotel. My bed-room, selected as one of the very best in the house, was not many degrees more capacious than my berth on board the *Frolic.* My bed was certainly good enough for any body, being composed of a hard straw mattress and clean sheets, which were all I desired. . . . I felt considerable inconvenience in finding no more space than just sufficient to contain my portmanteaus, over one of which I was always obliged to stand astride when in the room. The door opened abruptly into the yard or court, as is usual in this country, where all rooms have free communication with the street; in short, the habitation was what in England is called an "out-house," which might be considered a very convenient place for keeping coals, or where a sportsman might probably tie up his dogs. . . . The walls and floor of this apartment were nearly covered with . . . a colony of ants, which had their settlement in one of the beams of the roof, and having several roads to it, they were spread in divisions of millions over the room, but always preserved the nicest order and regularity in their ranks. Day and night their industry was unceasing, and I suppose of too much interest to themselves to admit of their interference with others, for I never found the least inconvenience from them, but often much amusement in observing their curious labours. . . .

An Englishman, taking up one of the public papers for the first time, cannot but experience very strange sensations upon seeing men, women, and children, advertised for sale amongst horses, cattle, Burton ale, fresh butter, and goods of all sorts; and, like horses, warranted sound and free from vice. . . . I copied the following:

> "To be sold, a female servant, sound and free from vice;
> 300 dollars. Inquire at this office."

I have frequently seen in the "Farmer's Journal" a cow with her first calf advertised for sale, but I never saw till now an advertisement like the following:

> "To be sold a young Mulatta, sound and without vice,
> with her first child, and four months' milk. Inquire at the house
> of foundlings."

December 28.

Heat excessive, which makes one of the preparations for our journey across the *Pampas* very laborious, that of stowing our baggage-carts, two of which we have purchased. These are capacious, rude, uncouth-looking vehicles, with cane sides, and roof covered with hides, the body balanced upon two prodigiously high wheels, for the convenience of passing through rivers. We have also purchased for our own conveyance a long coach, called here a *galera*, the seats running sideways, and the door at the end. . . . The carriage we brought from England was found totally unfit for the roads of this country. . . . Guns, pistols, hams, and sabres; rum, brandy, powder and shot; chronometers, sausages, thermometers, barometers, and biscuits; telescopes, books, pens, ink, and sugar; a change of linen, razors, soap, lemons, and oranges; after the most ingenious packing, and to say nothing of the contents of our own pockets, left but very scanty room for ourselves, and when each had settled into his place, there was just room, and no more, to give Carlo a berth on a Cheshire cheese.

According to the custom here of posting, each horse is ridden by a postilion; and as each of our vehicles required four horses, we were under the necessity of hiring nine *peones* for the journey . . . also hired a *capataz* who superintends the *peones*, manages the concerns of the journey, and is supposed to possess ingenuity sufficient to repair the frequent damages that occur; for which purpose the requisite tools are provided, and amongst them, spades, shovels, and pickaxes. . . .

In the cool of the evening, after the moon had risen, we left Buenos Ayres, a formidable cavalcade; the *galera* taking the lead, the two baggage carts following, and the *capataz* bringing up the rear; our twelve horses, nearly as wild as the twelve postilions who mounted them . . . uncombed, dishevelled locks—the once black hat of many dinted shape, pitched some how or other on the head—the rent garment of a species of frieze—the bare leg, indifferent to a squeeze between the horses—the spur (a most unmerciful instrument of punishment in this country) attached to the naked heel—the devil-may-care kind of way in which they galloped us through ruts, over stones, and round sharp corners—the flourish of the whip above the head—the wild shriek to encourage the horses to go faster . . . altogether awakened reflections in my mind that occupied me very happily until we stopped at La Figura. . . .

December 31.

. . . Got no farther than Areco, one post of six leagues, where the repairs of our baggage carts again compelled us to pass a day. . . . In the evening we were sadly tormented by divers kinds of insects; they did not, however, prevent our *peones* from making a hearty supper, for these ten men devoured nearly two sheep at that meal. The sheep were full grown, of common size, and cost three shillings each. Killing, skinning, roasting, and eating did not exceed thirty-five minutes. They were devoured, as is customary here, without bread, or vegetables of any kind. . . .

January 1, 1826.

This new year we commenced early, for at three o'clock we were already upon our journey. The morning was delightful. . . . As the day advanced the heat became dreadful, and two of our horses died upon the road from its effects, aided, no doubt, by the murderous spurs of the riders, which are used with an indifference towards the animal truly shocking. . . .

I discovered a bullock that had fallen into a deep pit of water, out of which it struggled in vain to extricate itself. I immediately hastened . . . to acquaint the post-master, who was proprietor of the soil for many miles round. He was sitting under a shed, smoking a cigar, with not fewer than a dozen of his *peones* lying on the ground around him, indulging in the *siesta,* all of whom I expected he would have instantly roused to rescue the bullock when I delivered my breathless account of its fate; but, to my surprise . . . "I suppose," said he, with infinite composure, "it wanted to cool itself." "But," cried I, with infinite warmth, "will it not be drowned?" "*Quien sabe!*" rejoined he. . . .

In the middle of the night, when all our senses were lulled in sleep, a sudden gust of wind carried off counterpanes, sheets, and sundry pieces of wearing apparel, before the owners had time to secure them, or indeed before they could imagine what had happened. . . . Here was to be seen a person, with legerdemain agility, bundling up his bed and bed clothes, but in so violent a hurry as to impede the accomplishment of his object. . . . There goes Mr. Scriviner in pursuit of his hat, and although right before the wind, with all sail spread full to the gale, he makes but little way, because particles of thistles *an' sic like,* form a very unsteady footing for bare feet, and because a broad-brimmed straw hat has decidedly the advantage in such a chase. . . .

January 13.

Arrived at Chacarilla, the first post, six leagues from Cordova, where the host and hostess . . . obligingly warned us against sleeping within their house, in consequence of the danger to be apprehended from *vinchucas,* a species of Brobdignag bug, which infests most houses in this country during the hot weather; their bite is extremely severe, and if rubbed or scratched, from which it is difficult to forbear, occasions very serious inflammation. In size and appearance, these insects resemble the common beetle, but are much more active . . . in search of blood. . . .

January 15.

This day we have travelled but twelve leagues, in consequence of the extreme difficulty of the way, for . . . the rumbling tumbling we have endured in our *galera,* in its bounces over roots and broken branches of trees, into ruts and through thickets, is admitted by us all to have been the most violent exercise we ever underwent . . . four Christians, such as we are, one dog, two paroquets, (saved from being put into a pie at one of the post houses), boxes, packages, books, guns, pistols, biscuits, cheese and ham, have been jostled, pounded and compounded, pitched, and tossed, and crossed, throughout the day's journey, with all the celerity of a juggler's balls. . . .

January 22.

. . . It is impossible to describe what we suffered this day from the heat . . . the thermometer in the carriage stood at 104°. . . .

January 23.

. . . This evening, after dinner, as we went out to sit half naked at the door in the street, according to the custom of the country, to enjoy the cool air . . . we were astonished at seeing the atmosphere in a state resembling a thick mist moving rapidly over us, but which we soon discovered to be locusts. . . . For upwards of an hour we sat gazing at them with increased astonishment, and when the sun set, as far as the eye could reach we perceived no diminution of their numbers. On they went in their ominous flight, seeking some devoted region where to repose, every fruit, flower, and vegetable of which, in a few hours, they would utterly consume. . . .

February 1.

. . . I have lately supplied myself with a pair of light summer boots . . . had without the necessity of employing either boot or shoemaker, for there is not a single seam, or a single stitch used in their construction; leg, foot, sole, being all of one piece, and fitting admirably. . . . Here is the receipt.— Take a horse, cut off his hind legs considerably above the hocks; pull the skin down over the hoofs, just as if you were pulling off a stocking; when off, scrape the hair from the skin with a sharp knife, and remove every particle of flesh that may have adhered to the inside; hang the skins to dry, and in the process of drying draw them two or three times on your legs, that they may take their shape, form and figure. The upper part becomes the mouth of the boot; the round projecting part of the hock, the heel; the foot terminates above the hoof, where it is cut to the required length. The whole operation may be performed, and the boots ready for use, in the course of a week. The people here do not even sew up the end of the foot, but allow the great toes to project for the convenience of the stirrup, which is made so small as only just to admit them, and they occasionally support the whole weight of the body. . . .

February 9.

Bread, milk, and eggs, were supplied in abundance for our breakfast, and our dinner was quite as good, I believe, as any cook in the province was capable of dressing, but such as "pampered menials" in England would scarcely condescend to sit down to. A large silver dish full of a glutinous composition of bread, vegetables, hog's lard, and the cook knows what besides, called *sópa*, invariably occupied the centre of the table; a fowl torn to pieces and fried with grease, several lumps of beef transfixed upon a long stick, which served as the spit for roasting, young ears of Indian corn boiled (a delicious vegetable,) were the daily dishes of our dinner. Our liquor, I admit, was in abundance, for the *well*, supplied by a copious spring, was situated within five yards of the door of our apartment. . . .

February 13.

. . . About ten leagues from Trancas, where we stopped to change horses, we found . . . a woman of the place was busily employed in making a Franciscan friar's dress for her son, two years old; he had been unwell, and during his illness, the mother vowed to Saint Francis, that if he would have the goodness to restore her son to health, she would make him a friar of his order. . . . In Spain and Portugal, I have seen children of all ages dressed as nuns, monks, or friars of this kind. Their appearance to strangers is truly ridiculous, but I doubt if even their patron saints could view a number of nuns and friars, from five to ten years of age, playing at leap-frog or other gambols, without being very much amused.

February 15.

Just as night commenced, we reached the house of a private gentleman, Don José Torres, who was sitting with his wife and seven children under a shed, or a sort of verandah, in front of his house. We requested permission to remain for the night, which was granted with a readiness and frankness that proved we were heartily welcome. . . . Here is no calling for chambermaids to prepare a room, no disturbing the housekeeper from her tea to air a pair of sheets, no demand upon the butler for a bottle, nor upon the cook for any extra exercise of his art, nor upon coachmen and grooms to take care of carriages and horses. The traveller alights at the door of a house, which he enters . . . says, "with your permission, *señores,* I shall stop here for the night" . . . points to a spot, either inside or outside the house, according to the state of the weather, where he wishes his *muchacho* (servant) to spread his saddle-cloths; these being three or four fold, are sufficiently large to lie upon, and, with his saddle under his head and poncho or cloak over him, complete the bed. . . .

Within very little more than half an hour after our arrival . . . our *peones* had killed, roasted and devoured three-full grown goats. Our own supper consisted of a kid, two fowls, good bread, and bad cheese, served up in large silver dishes, with forks, spoons, drinking-cups and candlesticks of the same metal. . . . Don José is a gentleman of large landed property, and of the first respectability in the province, but has nothing in his dress or appearance indicative of it, still less in his habitations and family. . . . Dirty, half-naked children, and dirtier slaves, male and female, were all of one party; there was nothing by which a stranger, unaccustomed to the manners of the country, could distinguish birth, or rank, or education.

General Paroissien, who becomes passionately fond of other people's children, after covering a boy of four years old with kisses, and sharing with it alternately a mouthful from his spoon or fork, called for some water to wash . . . the child's face, and certainly improved it very much, even in the opinion of the mother; who said, that "for some days past the weather had been too cold and damp for using water with any degree of comfort, and that, for her part, she never had the courage to wash herself on a cold day."

March 7.

This morning I had a trifling misunderstanding with the *patrona* on the subject of making tea, for I had provided myself with that refreshing herb. . . . She carefully drained off the water, and served up the leaves upon a plate, when she considered them sufficiently boiled. . . .

March 15.

With three-pennyworth of very good potatoes and a little salt, I this night made an excellent supper, and, notwithstanding interruption from a passing thunder storm, I slept soundly in the open air till four o'clock in the morning.

March 19.

Before one hour after midnight, I was on the last stage of my journey; a fine, frosty starlight morning enlivening the spirits, which were already elated by the near approach to [Potosi, in Peru] the place where I was about to establish a home. . . . Forty miles upon a bad road (my mule assured me it was full forty-five) is a wearisome distance before breakfast for either man or beast; and mine, every mile I now advanced, gave indubitable evidence of exhausted strength; yet . . . in ten minutes more I was at the post house in the centre of it. . . . After throwing some barley to my poor mule, I sallied forth with my letters of introduction in search of a dinner; for, although I had not breakfasted, dinner hour had arrived, and there being no tavern in Potosi wherein to obtain one, I was obliged to *sponge*. . . . I believe that, before the sun had withdrawn his last ray from the summit of the mountain of Potosi, I might have been numbered among the happy on earth. . . .

". . . we are in sore distress, in desperate straits . . ."

Mark Twain

In August, 1866, Mark Twain (1835–1910), returned to San Francisco from a trip to Hawaii made as a newspaper correspondent. He found that the city where he had spent two years as a journalist had lost its glamour for him. "In prison again," he notes in the last page of his Hawaii diary, "and all the wide sense of freedom gone. The city seems so cramped and so dreary with toil and anxiety. God help me, I wish I were at sea again."

At twenty-six a full life already lay behind him. His boyhood had been spent in Hannibal, Missouri, the scene of *Tom Sawyer* and *Huckleberry Finn*. He had become a river pilot (*Life on the Mississippi*). It was from "mark twain," the call of the leadsman when his weighted line measured the depth of two fathoms, that Samuel L. Clemens later took his pen name. He had learned to set type and wandered across the continent from one coast to the other as a tramp printer. In western frontier towns he had been reporter, prospector, miner and fortune-seeker (*Roughing It*). In San Francisco, he wrote for eastern newspapers, sending off his copy by pony express, and tried his hand at lecturing and humorous pieces. He had been away from home five and a half years.

Though his celebrated books were yet unwritten, hints of them were beginning to appear in the journals and notebooks that Mark Twain kept for nearly fifty years of his life. It was in one of those journals, too, that he wrote down the account of the grim voyage he restlessly embarked on within a few months of his return from Hawaii. He was at sea again, as he had wished, but on a pestilence-stricken ship twenty-seven days out from New York, medicines exhausted, and a daily round of heart-catching burials in shark-filled waters . . .

December 15, 1866.

Sailed from San Francisco . . . at noon . . . [and at] night a tempest—the greatest seen on this coast for many years. . . .

From *Mark Twain's Notebook*, Prepared for Publication with Comments by Albert Bigelow Paine. Copyright, 1935, The Mark Twain Company. Reprinted by permission of Harper & Brothers.

A sea that broke over the ship about midnight carried away 20 ft. of the bulwarks forward. The forward cabin was drenched with water and the steerage fairly flooded—a case of claret floated into a stateroom in the forward cabin. . . . They prepared the boats for emergency. Old ship captain of 28 years' experience said he had never seen the equal of this storm. . . .

December 16.

This is a long, long night. I occupy lower berth and read and smoke by ship's lantern, borrowed from the steward. . . . I don't know what time it is—my watch is run down—I think it is 7 bells in the 3rd watch but I am not certain . . . the wind may have blown away one tap of the bell—we hear it very faintly up here, anyway.

December 20.

At noon, 5 days out from San Francisco abreast a high stretch of land at foot of Magdalena Bay. Capt. came and said: "Come out here . . . I want to show you something"—Took the marine glass—Whaleship at anchor under the bluffs—one listed and hoisting vast mass of blubber aboard. Capt. said: "Now tonight they'll try it out on deck and it will look like a whole ship on fire. The first time I ever saw it was in '50s—I came along here just after dark—saw a ship on fire, apparently—I didn't know the country—didn't dare to go in there with the ship, so I sent a boat crew and said, 'Pull for your lives d'n you, and tell the captain I'll lay here for a week and send him all the assistance I can and then carry his people to San Francisco.' Well, we laid to, and waited and waited—all the passengers on deck and anxious for boat to come back and report,—but . . . no boat—every passenger gave up and went below except one old woman, she stuck it out and never took her eyes off the fire.

"By and by, at 12:30, back the boat come, and I and the old woman crowded to the lee rail to see and hear it all—couldn't see any extra men. The officer of the boat stepped on deck and lifted his hat and says: 'The captain of the ship sends great gratification . . . but he ain't in trouble, but quite the reverse—is full of oil and ready to up anchor tomorrow and is giving his crew a big blow-out on deck and is illuminating. Sends his good wishes for success, and hopes you will accept this boat-load of A-1 sea turtles.' The old woman leaned over the rail and shaded her eyes from the lantern, and she saw them varmints flapping their flippers about in the boat and she says 'For the land's sake, I sot here and sot here all this blessed night calculating to see a whole boatload of sorrowful roasted corpses and now it ain't nothin' after all but a lot of nasty turtles.'"

January 2, 1867.

Two cases of cholera reported in the steerage today. . . . 7 P.M. Neither of the sick men quite dead yet—the ship has stopped her wheels. . . . One of the sick men is bad . . . buried overboard at a little past 10 P.M. Midnight, another patient at the point of death. They are filling him up with brandy. 2 bells—the man is dead. 4 bells—he is cast overboard—expedition is the word in these crowded steerages.

January 3.

Our tropic drink: ¾ lb. of sugar, 1½ lbs. of ice, 1 doz. limes, 1 lemon, 1 orange, half a bottle of brandy. Put in a ¾ gallon ice pitcher and fill up with water.

. . . A captain who came aboard at Grey Town, where in 3 years he had worn out his constitution and destroyed his health, lingered until 10 this morning and then died and was shoved overboard half an hour afterward, sewed up in a blanket with 6 lbs. of iron. He leaves a wife at Rochester, New York. This makes the 4th death on shipboard since we left Francisco. . . .

January 5.

We are to put in at Key West, Florida, today for coal, for ballast—so they say—but rather for medicines, perhaps—the physic locker is about pumped dry. 7 cases sickness yesterday . . . half a dozen on the sick list today. . . . Shape has been walking the deck in stocking feet getting wet—exposing himself—is going to die. The disease has gotten into the second cabin at last and one case in first cabin. . . . 10 A.M. The Episcopal clergyman Rev. Mr. Fackler is taken—bad diarrhea and griping . . . Shape dead—fifth death . . . only sick about 12 hrs. . . . Verily the ship is fast becoming a floating hospital herself—not an hour passes but brings its fresh sensation, its new disaster —its melancholy tidings. When I think of poor Shape and the preacher, both so well when I saw them yesterday evening, I realize that I myself may be dead tomorrow. Since the last two hours all laughter, all levity, has ceased in the ship—a settled gloom is upon the faces of the passengers.

4 P.M. The unfortunate minister is dying—he has bidden us all good-bye and now lies barely breathing. . . . The passengers are fearfully exercised, and well they may be, poor devils, for we are about to see our fifth death in five days, and the sixth of the voyage. The surgeon, a most excellent young man. . . . Discovering that he was a Mason, I took him aside and asked him a plain statement for myself *alone*, and told him I thought I was man enough to stand the truth, in its worse form. He then said that the disease was *cholera* and of the most virulent type—that he had done all a man could do, but *he had no medicines* to work with. . . .

5 P.M. That bolt-head broke day before yesterday and we lost 2 hours. It broke again yesterday and we lost 3 or 4 hours. It broke again this afternoon, and again we lay like a log on the water (head wind) for 3 or 4 hours more. These things distress the passengers beyond measure. They are scared about the epidemic, and so impatient to get along—and now they have lost confidence in the ship and fear she may break again in the rough weather that is to come . . . say that we are out of luck and that it is a doomed voyage. It appears, though it is kept from the passengers, that there are seven or eight patients in the hospital down below. . . .

Some misgivings, some distress as to whether the authorities of Key West will let our pestilence-stricken ship land there—but the captain says we are in sore distress, in desperate straits, and we must land; we will land in spite of orders, cannon or anything else—we cannot go on in this way. If we do land, some of our people are going to leave—among them the doctor, who is afraid of the crazy machinery.

Sea in storm—caps crawling and squirming like white worms in the midst of ink. . . .

January 7. Key West.

21 passengers left the ship here, scared. Some of them gave dinner and berth tickets to remaining friends in the steerage. I am glad they are gone, d'n them. . . . 18 invalids yesterday and 13 today—only 2 really dangerous —one of them was getting along handsomely, but got drunk and took a relapse. . . .

January 10.

26 days out from San Francisco today—at noon we shall be off Cape Hatteras and less than 400 miles south of N.Y.—a day and a half's run. . . . 8 sick, 5 diarrhea, 3 convalescent—2 better. . . .

January 11.

7 P.M. Been in bed all day to keep warm—fearfully cold. We are off Barnegat—passed a pilot boat a while ago. We shall get to N.Y. before morning. . . . 2 bells. P. Peterson has just died, "dropsy"—the Highland lightship and several other lights at entrance to N.Y. harbor in full view. This is the 8th death this voyage. Bury him ashore, as we are now on soundings.

January 12.

Arrived today, 27½ days out.

3. THE MANY CHAMBERS OF THE HEART

*". . . how much of neglect, carelessness and sin
have I to remember!"*

Lewis Carroll

Charles Lutwidge Dodgson (1832–1898) spent his life as a lecturer in mathematics at Christ Church College, Oxford. He taught the fundamentals of that science to several thousands of young men, was ordained a deacon in 1861, wrote *An Elementary Treatise on Determinants, Euclid and His Modern Rivals* and a number of other works. Among those others were *Alice In Wonderland* and *Through the Looking Glass*.

This gentlest of men, this painfully shy and reticent Lewis Carroll—the pen name by which he is remembered—lived diffidently and methodically in a well-ordered academic world. He experimented in the new art of photography, walked in the country and boated on Oxford's rivers, delighted in the company of children. Fortunately for posterity, Carroll often had as his companions the four young children of Dean Liddell—Harry (about nine), Lorina (about six), Edith (about two), and Alice, *The Alice* (about four), when he first met them at the Deanery. His journal records the adventures of an innocent and logical mind, and tells how it happened that an obscure mathematician now sits among the immortals because of a make-believe rabbit that disappeared down a magical hole into wonderland.

April 25, 1856.

Went over with Southey in the afternoon to the Deanery, to try to take a photograph of the Cathedral: both attempts proved failures. The three little girls were in the garden most of the time, and we became excellent friends: we tried to group them in the foreground of the picture, but they were not patient sitters. I mark this day with a white stone.

From *The Diaries of Lewis Carroll*, edited by Roger Lancelyn Green. Copyright 1954 by Oxford University Press, Inc. Reprinted by permission of Oxford University Press, Inc., Mr. Green, Cassell & Co., and the Dodgson executors.

June 3.

Spent the morning at the Deanery, photographing the children. . . .
Afterwards Frank and I, with Harry Liddell, went down to Sandford in a gig.
We rowed with sculls down, with Harry as stroke, and he steered back.

June 5.

From 4.30 to 7 Frank and I made a boating excursion with Harry and Ina:
the latter, much to my surprise, having got permission from the Dean to
come. We went down to the island, and made a kind of picnic there, taking
biscuits with us, and buying ginger beer and lemonade there. Harry as before
rowed stroke most of the way, and fortunately, considering the wild spirits
of the children, we got home without accidents, having attracted by our remarkable crew a good deal of attention from almost everyone we met. Mark
this day, annalist, not only with a white stone, but as altogether '*Dies
mirabilis*'.

October 22.

Fell in with Harry and Ina Liddell down in the meadow, and took them
up to see my book of photographs. . . .

November 10.

Clear sun—went to the Deanery to take portraits at 2, but the light failed,
and I only got one of Harry. I spent an hour or so afterwards with the children and the governess, up in the schoolroom, making them paper boats,
etc. . . .

November 14.

Was at the Deanery in the morning taking pictures, and went again in the
afternoon by Harry's request to take him and Ina. However I found that Mrs.
Liddell had said they were not to be taken till all can be taken in a group.
This may be meant as a hint that I have intruded on the premises long
enough: I am quite of the same opinion myself, and, partly for this reason,
partly because I cannot afford to waste any more time on portraits at such
a bad season of the year, I have resolved not to go again for the present, nor
at all without invitation, except just to pack up the things and bring them
back.

December 18.

Called at the Deanery and took Harry a Christmas Box, a mechanical
tortoise: (I gave Ina one the other day, *Mrs. Rutherford's Children*). . . .

December 31.

. . . 11.30 p.m. Now at the close of the Old Year, let me review the past and take counsel with myself for the future. I must with sorrow confess that my bad habits are almost unchanged. I am afraid lately I have been even more irregular than ever, and more averse to exertion. . . . As to the future: —I may lay down as absolute necessities *Divinity Reading* and *Mathematical Reading.* I trust to do something this vacation, but most of the Long Vacation must be devoted to work. . . . (I hope to make good progress in Photography in the Easter Vacation: it is my one recreation, and I think should be done well.)

I do trust most sincerely to amend myself in those respects in which the past year has exhibited the most grievous shortcomings, and I trust and pray that the most merciful God may aid me in this and all other good undertakings.—Midnight is past: bless the New Year, oh heavenly Father, for thy dear Son Jesus Christ's sake!

January 29, 1857.

Arranged with Miss Prickett [the governess at the Deanery] for Harry Liddell to come to me three days a week to learn sums.

February 5.

. . . Walking in the afternoon I fell in with Ina Liddell and the governess, and returned with them to the Deanery, where I spent about an hour with the young party in the schoolroom. Miss Prickett showed me a letter the other day from Mrs. Reeves (Mrs. Liddell's mother) in which she expressed great alarm at Harry's learning 'mathematics' with me! She fears the effect of overwork on the brain. As far as I can judge, there is nothing to fear at present on that score, and I sent a message to that effect.

February 8.

Went to Chapel in surplice for the first time since 14th of October, 1855. I read the second lesson in the afternoon. Harry ran up to me afterwards to tell me 'You've got your white gown on, and you *read in the Church.*'

May 5.

. . . I went to the Deanery in the afternoon, partly to give little Alice a birthday present [she became five the day before], and stayed for tea. . . .

May 17.

Took Harry Liddell to chapel, and afterwards walked back with the children to the Deanery. I find to my great surprise that my notice of them is construed by some men into attentions to the governess, Miss Prickett. . . .

Though for my own part I should give little importance to the existence of so groundless a rumour, it would be inconsiderate to the governess to give any further occasion for remarks of the sort. For this reason I shall avoid taking any public notice of the children in future, unless any occasion should arise when such an interpretation is impossible.

May 27.

Took Harry down to see the races in the evening. We went on to the barge for a short time, but I did not like staying long as some of the men were very undesirable acquaintances for him.

June 2.

. . . Spent the morning at the Deanery. . . . Harry was away, but the two dear little girls, Ina and Alice, were with me all the morning. To try the lens, I took a picture of myself, for which Ina took off the cap, and of course considered it all her doing! Southey came for a short time in the afternoon to help with the pictures, and before 5 I had got everything packed up and returned with the camera. I mark this day with a white stone.

June 26.

Spent the day at the Deanery, photographing, with very slender success. Though I was disappointed in missing this last opportunity of getting good pictures of the party, it was notwithstanding one of the pleasantest days I have ever spent there. I had Alice and Edith with me till 12; then Harry and Ina till the early dinner at 2, which I joined; and all four children for the afternoon. The photographing was accordingly plentifully interspersed with swinging, backgammon, etc. I mark this day most specially with a white stone.

November 18.

Called at the Deanery in the afternoon to wish them goodbye. It took a long time to get to the end of the adieus of the dear, loving little children; and I spent more than an hour there instead of about a quarter as I had intended. The party leave here on Friday morning [for Madeira].

[Two manuscript volumes of Carroll's diaries have disappeared—unfortunately those from the spring of 1858 until early 1862, when Carroll's long friendship with the Liddell children was ripening into the intimacy from which "Alice in Wonderland" came. Little Edith had become almost eight, while Ina was twelve. There were two younger sisters now, Rhoda and Violet; Harry, the eldest child, had been sent away to school. The surviving diaries resume shortly after Alice's tenth birthday, May 4, 1862.]

May 26, 1862.

Went down the river with Southey (who has lately returned to England, and is going abroad again very soon) taking Ina, Alice and Edith with us: we only went to Iffley—even then it was hard work rowing up again, the stream is so strong. Afterwards we went in and had a game of croquet with them in the Deanery garden.

June 17.

Expedition to Nuneham. Duckworth (of Trinity) and Ina, Alice and Edith came with us. We set out about 12.30 and got to Nuneham about 2: dined there, then walked in the park and set off for home about 4.30. About a mile above Nuneham heavy rain came on, and after bearing it a short time I settled that we had better leave the boat and walk: three miles of this drenched us all pretty well. I went on first with the children, as they could walk much faster than Elizabeth, and took them to the only house I knew in Sandford, Mrs. Broughton's, where Ranken lodges. I left them with her to get their clothes dried, and went off to find a vehicle, but none was to be had there, so on the others arriving, Duckworth and I walked on to Iffley, whence we sent them a fly. We all had tea in my rooms about 8.30, after which I took the children home. . . .

July 4.

. . . Duckworth and I made an expedition *up* the river to Godstow with the three Liddells: we had tea on the bank there, and did not reach Christ Church again till quarter past eight, when we took them on to my rooms to see my collection of microphotographs, and restored them to the Deanery just before nine. [Opposite this entry there is a note dated February 10, 1863]: On which occasion I told them the fairy-tale of *Alice's Adventures Underground*, which I undertook to write out for Alice, and which is now finished (as to the text) though the pictures are not yet nearly done.

August 1.

As the Dean's children are still here . . . went over to see if they could come on the river today or tomorrow, and remained a short time, for me to write the names in the books for crests, etc. which I have given to Alice and Edith, and to hear them play their trio and sing. . . .

August 6.

. . . Took the three Liddells up to Godstow, where we had tea; we tried the game of 'the Ural Mountains' on the way, but it did not prove very successful, and I had to go on with my interminable fairy-tale of *Alice's Adventures*. We got back soon after eight, and had supper in my rooms, the children coming over for a short time. A very enjoyable expedition—the last,

I should think, to which Ina is likely to be allowed to come—her fourteenth time.

August 8.

In the morning happened to cross the quadrangle as the two flies from the Deanery were driving out, and so got a last sight of my young friends.

November 13.

Walked with Liddon. On returning to Christ Church I found Ina, Alice and Edith in the quadrangle, and had a little talk with them—a rare event of late. Began writing the fairy-tale for Alice, which I told them July 4, going to Godstow—I hope to finish it by Christmas.

November 21.

Was surprised by a message from Mrs. Liddell asking whether the children should come over to me, or if I would go to them. No other alternative being offered, I chose the latter, and found that Alice and Edith had originated the idea, that I might put their crests into their books for them. With that and a game of parlour croquet, I had a very pleasant two hours with them. . . .

March 10, 1863.

Called at the Deanery to arrange about our expedition tonight, and to borrow a Natural History to help in illustrating *Alice's Adventures.* Afterwards Edwin and I went into the Broad Walk to see the three Deanery children plant three trees along the Cherwell in memory of the day. . . . After Hall we went to the Deanery for the children, and set out. We soon lost the others, and Alice and I with Edwin, took the round of all the principal streets in about two hours, bringing her home by half past nine. . . . It was delightful to see the thorough abandonment with which Alice enjoyed the whole thing. The Wedding Day of the Prince of Wales I mark with a white stone.

March 13.

Went into the Broad Walk soon after 11, and met Alice and Edith with Miss Prickett, and had a very pleasant two hours' walking with them round the meadow. I began a poem the other day in which I mean to embody something about Alice, (if I can at all please myself by any description of her) and which I mean to call 'Life's Pleasance'. I think of preparing a simpler version of the first two books of Euclid this term.

[The verses were printed at the beginning of *Through The Looking Glass— and what Alice Found There:*

Child of the pure unclouded brow
   And dreaming eyes of wonder!
Though time be fleet, and I and thou
   And half a life asunder,
Thy loving smile will surely hail
The love-gift of a fairy-tale.

I have not seen thy sunny face,
   Nor heard thy silver laughter:
No thought of me shall find a place
   In thy young life's hereafter—
Enough that now thou wilt not fail
   To listen to my fairy-tale.

A tale begun in other days,
   When summer suns were glowing—
A simple chime, that served to time
   The rhythm of our rowing—
Whose echoes live in memory yet,
Though envious years would say "forget."

Come, hearken then, ere voice of dread,
   With bitter tidings laden,
Shall summon to unwelcome bed
   A melancholy maiden!
We are but older children, dear,
Who fret to find our bedtime near.

Without, the frost, the blinding snow,
   The storm-wind's moody madness—
Within, the firelight's ruddy glow,
   And childhood's nest of gladness.
The magic words shall hold thee fast:
Thou shalt not heed the raving blast.

And, though the shadow of a sigh
   May tremble through the story,
For "happy summer days" gone by,
   And vanish'd summer glory—
It shall not touch, with breath of bale,
The pleasance of our fairy-tale.]

April 17.

   Harry Liddell came to ask me to go with them down the river: Miss Prickett came (by Mrs. Liddell's wish) with them. (I quite think that Ina is now so tall as to look odd without an escort.)

April 21.

I went to see Alice, who is laid up with a sprained leg, and stayed about an hour with her and Rhoda.

June 25.

About 10 o'clock Alice and Edith came over to my rooms to fetch me over to arrange about an expedition to Nuneham. It ended in our going down at 3. . . . We had tea under the trees at Nuneham, after which the rest drove home in the carriage (which met them in the park), while Ina, Alice, Edith and I (*mirabile dictu!*) walked down to Abingdon-road Station, and so home by railway: a pleasant expedition, with a *very* pleasant conclusion. . . .

December 31.

Here, at the close of another year, how much of neglect, carelessness, and sin have I to remember! I had hoped, during the year, to have made a beginning in parochial work, to have thrown off habits of evil, to have advanced in my work at Christ Church. How little, next to nothing, has been done of all this! Now I have a fresh year before me: once more let me set myself to do something worthy of life 'before I go hence, and be no more seen'. . . .

April 5, 1864.

Heard from Tenniel that he consents to draw the pictures for *Alice's Adventures Underground.* . . .

May 6.

Walked on the other side of the river, and met Ina, Alice and Edith, with Miss Prickett: we inspected the new 'grandstand' intended for spectators of the boat-races. Went down to the races, and saw Christ Church bump Magdalene. . . . Sent to the Press a batch of MS. from the first chapter of *Alice's Adventures.*

May 12.

During these last few days I have applied in vain for leave to take the children on the river, i.e., Alice, Edith and Rhoda: but Mrs. Liddell will not let *any* come in future—rather superfluous caution.

May 11, 1865.

Met Alice and Miss Prickett in the quadrangle: Alice seems changed a great deal, and hardly for the better—probably going through the usual awkward stage of transition [Alice was now thirteen].

August 2.

. . . The total cost [of printing *Alice* in final form] will be:

Drawing pictures	138
Cutting	142
Printing (by Clay)	240
Binding and advertising (say)	80
	£600

i.e. 6/– a copy on the 2000. If I make £500 by sale, this will be a loss of £100, and the loss on the first 2000 will probably be £100, leaving me £200 out of pocket. But if a second 2000 could be sold it would cost £300, and bring in £500, thus squaring accounts and any further sale would be a gain, but that I can hardly hope for.

[About 180,000 copies of *Alice* were actually sold before Carroll's death in 1898; the total sales now have to be counted in the millions of copies.]

"I was a little in love . . ."

Queen Victoria

The name of Queen Victoria (1819–1901) calls up an image of a cross-looking, austere, obstinate, prim old lady who for more than sixty years dominated her era, recast England's hearty past, shaped it to conform to the lines of her own homely tastes, and finally gave the century its label: the Victorian age.

There might be little more to the picture, despite the surmises of perceptive biographers, had not the thirteen-year-old princess, probably as an exercise set by her governess, begun the habit of keeping a diary. She continued this daily task through more than a hundred thick volumes of journals that ended only with her death seven decades later.

From even the expurgated portions of the diaries which have been published, a somewhat different view of Victoria emerges, tantalizing in its intimate, if incomplete, glimpses of the life the sovereign led beyond the façade of reticence her position imposed upon her.

Not that Victoria's indiscretions were ever more than verbal, unlike the episodes we might have savoured in the journal her distant predecessor, Elizabeth I., was too prudent to write down. The last century's mentor of propriety reveals herself first as a naïve young girl, unworldly, with more artless enthusiasm than intellectual gifts, at ease with the domestic skills rather than in the realm of books and ideas. She had been called suddenly from a secluded childhood by a series of unexpected deaths to succeed, at 18, her uncle William IV. as monarch of the earth's greatest empire.

Simple and sincere, from the beginning she was sure of her own will and she never doubted her destiny. But she turned readily for guidance to a succession of devoted ministers, among them Lord Melbourne, Lord Beaconsfield (Disraeli), Lord Salisbury. With Lord Melbourne, her first Prime Minister, she was particularly impressed. He combined the rôles of father and gallant to teach her politics and bring her reports of the world beyond the palace gates. Lytton Strachey, in his lively life of Victoria, says:

From *The Girlhood of Queen Victoria*, edited by Viscount Esher, 1912; reprinted by permission of Longmans, Green & Co., Inc.

"Upon every page [of the diaries] Lord M. is present, Lord M. is speaking, Lord M. is being amusing, instructive, delightful and affectionate at once, while Victoria drinks in the honeyed words, laughs till she shows her gums, tries hard to remember and runs off as soon as she is left alone to put it all down." He even served as a guide and confidant when the young queen, just out of her 'teens, felt the first stirrings of romantic interest in the consort of *his* choice, Victoria's dashing cousin, Prince Albert of Saxe-Coburg-Gotha, he of the "exquisite nose, and such a pretty mouth with delicate moustachios."

"It was with some emotion that I beheld Albert . . ." But let Victoria herself tell how the tender passion moved a young queen's heart.

September 1, 1838.

Spoke of my going to Bushey and Bagshot which I disliked; of my hating morning visits; of the habit I had when a little girl and visited my aunts, of praising everything, in order to get it, which made Lord Melbourne laugh very much. . . .

September 2.

. . . At a ¼ to 8 we 13 dined. Lord Melbourne led me in. . . . Spoke with him of various things; of my tight *sleeves* which he admired; of some excellent red deer we had at dinner; of being able to manage animals by feeding. Lord M. said, "You can do anything almost by feeding, from a man to a goat or a deer," which made us laugh much. . . .

September 4.

. . . I said I liked French books; he observed, "They write shortly and clearly, and very concise. . . . The English books," he continued, "are so very long; they are apt to be prosing, and one gets to read without attending, and not to know what it's all about," which is most true. He added that long books alarm one. I said that I couldn't understand the German books; Lord M. mentioned . . . "They are apt to be misty and obscure, the Germans—and cloudy," he said laughing. Spoke of my disliking Ancient History; of my having read many dull books; of my having disliked learning formerly, and particularly Latin, and being naughty at that, and at my Bible lessons; Lord M. said it was a good thing to know a little Latin, on account of the construction of English; Greek he thinks unnecessary for a woman, as there are very many other things more necessary.

September 8.

. . . We rode round Virginia Water. As I was galloping homewards, before we came to the Long Walk, on the grass and not very fast . . . something frightened Uxbridge . . . so much that I came *off;* I fell on one side sitting, not a bit hurt or put out or frightened, but astonished and amused. . . . Uncle talked much, and praised me for my behaviour during my *feat* of falling! Lord Melbourne said most kindly and anxiously, "Are you *really* not the worse?" He repeated this twice. We spoke of how it happened; he said he didn't *see* me fall, but *heard* me fall. . . .

September 22.

Spoke for some time of church-going; and . . . George III., Lord M. believes, never went twice . . . wasn't at all for all those Puritanical notions. . . . Lord M. said it wasn't well to puzzle myself with controversies, but read the simple truths; the Psalms he thinks very difficult to understand, and he thinks very probably *not* rightly translated.

October 13.

. . . Lord M. said the expense of fires in this Castle must be very great, for that there must be "several 100 fires"; lighting and warming are the great expenses. . . . Lord Ashley [spoke of] . . . a remonstrance from Queen Elizabeth's Maids of Honour, which had been found amongst some old papers; which showed the uncouthness of those times; they lived all in one room, which was separated from the gentlemen by a partition which didn't reach to the Ceiling, and they begged it might be made to reach the Ceiling, as the gentlemen climbed up and looked over the other side. This made us all laugh very much. . . .

November 21.

I forgot to say that Lord Conyngham's 2 youngest children, Cecilia, 7, and Francis, who they generally call Peacock and sometimes Franky, 5, arrived here yesterday, and I saw them when I came home from riding. Peacock is a beautiful boy, with long black hair; Cecilia has fine eyes but is not otherwise pretty. . . . Went into the Gallery and played with the children for an hour . . . charming, delightful children, quite at home with me and treated me quite like a playfellow, which pleased me much; played at ball with them, and then I sat in the window-seat and looked at picture books of animals with them, and told them the names of the animals. They would hardly let me go.

December 23.

Read in *Eugene Aram* [by Bulwer Lytton] for some time while my hair was doing, and finished it; beautifully written and fearfully interesting as it is, I am glad I have finished it, for I never feel quite at ease or at home when I am reading a Novel. . . .

January 1, 1839.

Got up at 9. Most fervently do I beseech Almighty God to preserve me and all those most dear to me safely through this year, and to grant that all may go on as it has hitherto done, and to make me daily more fit for my station. . . . Talked of my getting on in *Oliver Twist;* of the descriptions of "squalid vice" in it; of the accounts of starvation in the Workhouses and Schools, Mr. Dickens gives in his books. Lord M. says, in many schools they give children the worst things to eat, and bad beer, to save expense; told him Mamma admonished me for reading light books. . . .

January 3.

. . . Lord Alfred brought in his dog; she is a fine large black dog, half Newfoundland, half retriever, called *Diver,* but also sometimes *Mrs. Bumps;* she's a dear affectionate gentle creature and took a great liking to me and lay near me. . . .

January 20.

After dinner Lord Melbourne came up to me and said, "I've seen Sir James Clark this morning; he's very anxious about this vaccination [against small-pox]." Lord M. then talked for some time about this, urging me to have it done; I resisted. "You'll have it done," he said; if it doesn't take, why then you're safe; and if it does, it can do no harm." . . . Said to Lord M. I should resist about this Vaccination; "Oh! no, you'll do it," he said kindly; I said No, and that no one could force me to it; he agreed in that, but strongly urged it and said earnestly, "*Do.*" "Think if you were to have it [the disease]; think of the responsibility, of the scrape you'd get them into; of the scrape you'd get us all into." . . .

February 14.

At 20 m. to 3 I rode out . . . and came home at ½ p. 5. . . . We saw no less than *4 trains* pass close to us, and had to wait for one where we have to cross the rail-road; once we were lost. . . .

February 20.

. . . Talked of teaching the poor people to cook, and all those sorts of things, and Lord M. said Plato could never bear that sort of useful knowl-edge. . . . "You'll never teach English people to cook," said Lord M., and he added, "Walter Scott said, 'Why do you bother the poor? leave them alone'." . . .

March 13.

. . . I couldn't get my gloves on, and Lord M. said, "It's those consumed rings; I never could bear them." I said I was fond of them, and that it im-proved an ugly hand. "Makes it worse," he replied; I said I didn't wear them of a morning; "*Much* better," he said. . . .

March 18.

. . . Talked of the Sovereign's great power over the marriages of his relations, being great tyranny in my opinion, but Lord M. said, "No, quite
right, it's much better." Of its being better in my opinion that they should
not be allowed to marry a subject, as they got so mixed up else. . . .

April 10.

Talked of . . . Augusta, who I said was to go out everywhere, like any
other girl; Lord M. said that it was the first time a Princess of England did
such a thing. "I don't think the King (George III.) would have liked that,"
said Lord M. "If she goes out like any other girl, she runs the risk like other
girls of forming attachments," which is very true and very awkward. "She
may take a liking to somebody whom she couldn't marry," he added. . . .

April 15.

Talked of some people, and Lord Melbourne said, "An Italian and an
English makes the finest animal in the world; it's the mixture of nations that
makes the finest specimens of the human race." . . .

April 18.

Lord M. then said, "Now, Ma'am for this other matter." I felt terrified.
. . . Well, I mustered up courage, and said that my Uncle's great wish—was
—that I should marry my Cousin Albert. . . . He said, "Cousins are not very
good things," and "Those Coburgs are not popular abroad; the Russians hate
them." I then said, who was there else? . . . I said I dreaded the thought
of marrying; that I was so accustomed to have my own way, that I thought
it was 10 to 1 that I shouldn't agree with any body. Lord M. said, "Oh! but
you would have it still." . . .

May 24.

This day I *go out of my* TEENS and become 20! It sounds so strange to
me! . . .

May 27.

It was a most beautiful, bright day, yet the 1st impression, I know not
why—beautiful as it looked and green and bright—is always a triste one. I
saw the Grand-Duke [later Czar Alexander II. of Russia] arrive at 20 m. to
7; he bowed up to my window. At a ¼ to 8 we dined. . . . The Grand-Duke
led me in and . . . I really am quite in love with the Grand-Duke; he is a
dear, delightful young man. At about a little after 10, we went into the red
drawing-room, (next the dining room), where . . . dancing began. I danced
1st a quadrille with the Grand-Duke, then followed a Valse, during which

ime I sat down; then a quadrille which I danced with Prince Henry; then
again a Valse followed; and I danced after this a quadrille with M. de
Tolstoy; this was followed again by a Valse (of course I and also the Grand-
Duke sitting down during the Valse); and then I danced a quadrille with
Lord Clarence Paget. . . . At a little after 12 we went into the dining-room
or supper; after supper they danced a Mazurka for ½ an hour, I should think
nearly; the Grand-Duke asked me to take a turn, which I did (never having
done it before) and which is very pleasant; the Grand-Duke is so very strong,
that in running round, you must follow quickly, and after that you are
whisked round like in a Valse, which is very pleasant. I also had a turn
with Prince Henry; I then danced a quadrille with Patkul, which was followed by a Valse. After this we danced (what I had never even seen before)
the *"Grossvater"* or *"Rerraut,"* and which is excessively amusing; I danced
with the Grand-Duke, and we had such fun and laughter; Patkul and the
Countess Potoska led the way. It begins with a solemn walk round the room,
which also follows each figure; one figure, in which the lady and gentleman
run down holding their pocket-handkerchief by each end, and letting the
ladies on one side go under it, and the gentlemen jump over it, is too funny.
I never enjoyed myself more. We were all so merry; I got to bed by a ¼ to 3,
but could not sleep till 5.

May 28.

The Grand-Duke talked of his very fine reception here, and said he . . .
never would forget these days here, which I'm sure *I* shall never also, for
I really love this amiable and dear young man, who has such a sweet smile.
I talked to Lord Melbourne of . . . Countess Potoska. . . . He observed
upon the great length of the petticoats, which he said gave a suspicion that
the feet and the ankles are not quite right. He said, "I don't like blue gowns;
it's an unlucky colour; no girl ever marries who wears a blue gown."

May 29.

. . . The Grand-Duke took my hand and pressed it warmly; he looked pale
and his voice faltered as . . . he said how deeply grateful he felt for all the
kindness he met with . . . pressed and kissed my hand, and I kissed his
cheek; upon which he kissed mine (cheek) in a very warm affectionate manner, and we again warmly shook hands. . . . I felt so sad to take leave of
his dear amiable young man, whom I really think (talking jokingly) I was
a little in love with, and certainly attached to; he is so frank, so really young
and merry, has such a nice open countenance with a sweet smile, and such
a manly fine figure and appearance. . . .

May 30.

They played the Grand-Duke's and my favourite quadrilles . . . which
made me quite melancholy, as it put me so in mind of all, and I felt sadly the
change . . . and of it being so seldom that I had young people of my own
rank with me . . . and that now I was so *very very* sorry at his going. . . .

I said a young person like me must *sometimes* have young people to laugh
with. "Nothing so natural," replied Lord M. with tears in his eyes; and I
said that I had *that* so seldom. . . .

August 9.

The Band played some of my favourite Quadrilles during dinner, which
I said made me quite frantic when I heard them. "Those Quadrilles are dangerous," said Lord M., if they produce that effect on you." . . .

October 10.

At ½ p. 7 I went to the top of the staircase and received my 2 dear cousins
Ernest and Albert—whom I found grown and changed, and embellished. It
was with some emotion that I beheld Albert who is *beautiful*. I embraced
them both and took them to Mamma. . . .

October 11.

. . . Albert really is quite charming, and so excessively handsome, such
beautiful blue eyes, an exquisite nose, and such a pretty mouth with delicate
moustachios and slight but very slight whiskers; a beautiful figure, broad in
the shoulders and a fine waist. At about ½ p. 10 dancing began. I danced
5 quadrilles . . . it is quite a pleasure to look at Albert when he gallops
and valses, he does it so beautifully, holds himself so well with that beautiful
figure of his. . . .

October 13.

. . . I sat on the sofa with dearest Albert; Lord Melbourne sitting near me
Ernest playing at chess. . . . I played 2 games at Tactics with dear Albert
and 2 at Fox and Geese. Stayed up till 20 m. p. 11. A delightful evening.

October 14.

. . . At 1 came Lord Melbourne. . . . Talked of my Cousins' having gone
out shooting. After a little pause I said to Lord M., that I had made up
my mind (about marrying dearest Albert). —"You have?" he said; "well then
about the time?" Not for a year, I thought; which he said was too long. . .
"I think it is a very good thing, and you'll be much more comfortable; for a
woman cannot stand alone for long, in whatever situation she is." . . . Then
I asked, if I hadn't better tell Albert of my decision soon, in which Lord M
agreed. How? I asked, for that in general such things were done the other
way,—which made Lord M. laugh. . . .

October 15.

. . . At about ½ p. 12 I sent for Albert; he came to the Closet where I was
alone, and after a few minutes I said to him, that I thought he must be aware

why I wished them to come here,—and that it would make me *too happy* if he would consent to what I wished (to marry me). We embraced each other, and he was *so* kind, *so* affectionate. I told him I was quite unworthy of him,—he . . . was so kind, and seemed so happy, that I really felt it was the happiest brightest moment in my life. I told him it was a great sacrifice,— which he wouldn't allow; I then told him of the necessity of keeping it a secret . . . and also that it was to be as early as the beginning of February. . . .

October 19.

. . . My dearest Albert came to me at 10 m. to 12 and stayed with me till 20 m. p. 1. Such a pleasant happy time. He looked over my shoulder and watched me writing to the Duchess of Northumberland, and to the Duchess of Sutherland; and he scraped out some mistakes I had made. I told him I felt so grateful to him and would do everything to make him happy. I gave him a ring with the date of the ever dear to me *15th* engraved in it. I also gave him a little seal I used to wear. I asked if he would let me have a little of his dear hair. . . .

November 10.

. . . I sat on the sofa with Albert and we played at that game of letters, out of which you are to make words, and we had great fun about them. . . .

November 13.

. . . Serjeant Talfourd . . . Lord M. didn't quite like. "He writes plays," he said, "and I don't think a man who writes plays is ever good for much else; and he is a great friend of Wordsworth's." . . .

January 1, 1840.

. . . Talked of the danger for us of an alliance between France and Russia, when the former might say Russia might take Constantinople, and Russia would let France go up to the Rhine; on the other hand, Lord M. said, France dreaded an alliance between England and Russia, when *we* might let Russia take Constantinople, and they let us take Egypt and Syria. The *only* country sincerely *friendly* to England, Lord M. says, is Austria. Stayed up till 20 m. p. 11. I feel *most grateful* for all the blessings I have received in the past year, the acquaintance and love of dearest Albert! I only implore Providence to protect me and those most dear to me in *this* and many succeeding years, and to grant that the *true* and *good* cause may prosper for *this year* and *many* years to come, under the guidance of my kind Lord Melbourne!

January 13.

I asked if on the Wedding day, as I should *not drive* in full state, and Albemarle said he did not make a point of going with me, I should take Mamma with me. "Yes, I think so," said Lord M. "I think it would be a very right thing to do on that day." . . .

January 22.

. . . Talked of various things, and German being so difficult. "So everybody says," Lord M. said. "Is it possible to be so difficult?" "Oughtn't to know more than one language," he continued. "You can't *speak* one purely if you know a great many,—you mix them. They say you needn't know more than Latin and French"; Greek, Lady Lyttelton mentioned. "There's no necessity for it," he said; its being difficult; "a very copious language," he replied. I observed learning much as I did at once, prevented one from learning anything very well, and bewildered one. "That's very true what you say," Lord M. said, "that's the fault now, they teach too much at once." Talked of teaching being a dreadful thing, the poor children being more eager to learn than the higher classes, and Lady Lyttelton saying the Irish children were so very much quicker in learning than the English. "It's that quickness that leads to that disregard of truth," Lord M. said, "for when you ask them anything, they don't think of what you *say*, but of what they think will *please* you. He told me at dinner that he was having a new *full-dress* coat made, for the *great* occasion, which was "like building a 74-gun ship" in point of trouble and work, and that he had had the man with him in the morning, trying it on and pinning and stitching. . . .

After this some new *Assam* tea. . . . "The advantage of Monarchy is unity," Lord M. said, "which is a *little* spoilt by 2 people,—but that must be contended against." "I've no doubt," he continued, "that is what kept Queen Elizabeth from marrying; but you mustn't think I advocate that; I think that's not right, it's unnatural, and nothing's right that's unnatural." . . .

February 7.

. . . We were seated as usual, Lord Melbourne sitting near me. Talked of Bull-dogs; of the Marriage Ceremony; my being a little agitated and nervous; "Most natural," Lord M. replied warmly; "how could it be otherwise?" Lord M. was so warm, so kind, and so affectionate, the whole evening, and so much touched in speaking of me and my affairs. Talked of my former resolution of never marrying. "Depend upon it, it's right to marry," he said earnestly; "if ever there was a situation that formed an exception, it was yours; it's in human nature, it's natural to marry; the other is a very unnatural state of things; it's a great *change*—it has its inconveniences; everybody does their best, and depend upon it you've done well; difficulties may arise from it," as they do of course from everything. . . .

February 9.

Received a beautiful Prayer-book from Mamma; breakfasted at 10. Wrote to Lord M. Dearest Albert came in . . . looking so well, with a little of his blue ribbon showing. He brought me 4 beautiful old Fans. At 12 I went down to Prayers with my beloved Albert . . . a very fine sermon . . . over at 5 m. p. 1. Talked of dearest Albert's being agitated. "That's very natural," Lord M. said, "I don't wonder at it." . . . I couldn't believe what was to happen next day, I said. At a ¼ to 6 my beloved Albert came to me and stayed till 20 m. to 7. We read over the Marriage Service together and tried how to manage the *ring*. Wrote my journal. At 8 we dined. . . . Albert led me in . . . my last unmarried evening, which made me feel so odd. I sat on the sofa with dearest Albert, Lord Melbourne sitting near me. Talked of . . . guessing words; the Lord's Prayer being almost entirely composed of Saxon words, all but 4; of the Cathedral at Canterbury and Bishop Chichley being buried there.

February 10.

Got up at a ¼ to 9—well, and having slept well; and breakfasted at ½ p. 9. Mamma came before and brought me a Nosegay of orange flowers. . . . Wrote my journal, and to Lord M. Had my hair dressed and the wreath of orange flowers put on. Saw Albert for the *last* time *alone*, as my *Bridegroom*. Dressed. . . .

At ½ p. 12 I set off, dearest Albert having gone before. I wore a white satin gown with a very deep flounce of Honiton lace, imitation of old. I wore my Turkish diamond necklace and earrings, and Albert's beautiful sapphire brooch. Mamma and the Duchess of Sutherland went in the carriage with me. . . . When I arrived at St. James's, I went into the dressing-room where my 12 young Train-bearers were, dressed all in white with white roses, which had a beautiful effect. Here I waited a little till dearest Albert's Procession had moved into the Chapel. I then went with my Train-bearers and ladies into the Throne-room, where the Procession formed; Lord Melbourne in his fine new dress-coat, bearing the Sword of State. . . . Queen Anne's room was full of people, ranged on seats one higher than the other, as also in the Guard room, and by the Staircase,—all very friendly; the Procession looked beautiful going downstairs. Part of the Colour Court was also covered in and full of people who were very civil. The Flourish of Trumpets ceased as I entered the Chapel, and the organ began to play, which had a beautiful effect. At the Altar, to my right, stood Albert. . . . The Ceremony was very imposing, and fine and simple, and I think OUGHT to make an everlasting impression on every one who promises at the Altar to *keep* what he or she promises. Dearest Albert repeated everything distinctly. I felt so happy when the ring was put on, and by Albert. As soon as the Service was over . . . I gave all the Train-bearers as a brooch a small *eagle* of turquoise. I then returned to Buckingham Palace alone with Albert; they cheered us most warmly and heartily; the crowd was immense. . . . I went and sat on the sofa in my dressing-room with Albert . . . then we went downstairs where all the

Company was assembled and went into the dining-room—dearest Albert leading me in, and my Train being borne by 3 Pages, Cowell, little Wemyss, and dear little Byng. . . . Albert and I drank a glass of wine with Lord Melbourne, who seemed much affected by the whole. I talked to all after the breakfast, and to Lord Melbourne, whose fine coat I praised. . . . I went upstairs and undressed and put on a white silk gown trimmed with swansdown, and a bonnet with orange flowers. Albert went downstairs and undressed. . . . Dearest Albert came up and fetched me downstairs, where we took leave of Mamma and drove off at near 4; I and Albert alone.

"The fire flutters, and the watch ticks. I hear nothing
else save the breathing of my Beloved . . ."

Dorothy Wordsworth

Lingering in the shadows cast by the towering figures of William Wordsworth and Samuel Taylor Coleridge, her genius and fervid personality forced to turn inward by the restraints imposed on women of her time and by her involvement in a strange triangle of love, Dorothy Wordsworth (1771–1855), still remains an enigma. Further, as her biographer, Ernest de Selincourt, points out, she is noteworthy for another reason; she is "probably the most remarkable and the most distinguished of English writers who never wrote a line for the general public." She composed only private letters and journals which were not published until many years after her death. Of the journals, the most revealing is the *Grasmere Journal,* portions of which are given here.

Dorothy Wordsworth's literary gifts, insight and keenness of observation found vicarious expression in the works of her two "beloved" idols, William and Samuel. She served them as Muse, collaborator, critic, captive audience and amanuensis. She discovered so much source material for them that at times their poems seem rhymed versions of her prose. Her brother said that "she gave me eyes . . . ears . . . love, and thought and joy." And, linking together the three of them, he acknowledged that "S. T. C. and my beloved sister are the two beings to whom my intellect is most indebted."

Dorothy became William's intimate companion and housekeeper at secluded Dove Cottage near Lake Grasmere in the English Lake country shortly before 1800 when this journal opens. Brief absences aside, both spent the remainder of their lives together by the lake; both died there, and the burial place of Wordsworth, his sister, wife and children can still be seen in the Grasmere churchyard. When Dorothy made her first, untidy, hurriedly scrawled diary entry she was twenty-nine, her brother thirty, Coleridge twenty-eight.

Coleridge, with whom Dorothy was desperately in love, already had a wife; he wandered unsatisfactorily in and out of her

From *Journals of Dorothy Wordsworth,* edited by E. de Selincourt. The Macmillan Company 1941. Reprinted by permission of Macmillan and Co., Ltd. and the Trustees of Dove Cottage, Grasmere.

life until he finally disappeared in a fog of opium. Wordsworth had his own serious emotional conflicts. He and Dorothy clung together in a devotion that was abnormal, at least, in its intensity. The troubled depths of the attachment between brother and sister began to emerge late in 1802 when William married Mary Hutchinson, their childhood friend. Perhaps because normal outlets were lacking for the fires that burned within her, from that time forward Dorothy's disturbance increased until it culminated in a nervous breakdown from which she did not recover. She subsequently became insane.

Thomas De Quincey, a Grasmere neighbor, described Dorothy Wordsworth as having skin that was unusually dark, gypsy-like colouring, wild startling eyes, and a manner extremely shy that could never quite conceal a seething agitation. The bride of genius if not of man, she tried her best to conform to what society expected of her. With all her good intentions she nevertheless managed to shock people in one way or another. At home, where she was safe from gossiping tongues, she nursed William, Samuel and herself through the constant indispositions of mind and body to which poets are prone, devoted precious hours to mending and baking, sat up late to read novels and books of travel by the fire, went out before bed to see if moon and stars had messages for her. In her diary, kept as the mood struck her, Dorothy transcribed the real life of real people (including the somewhat unlikely inhabitants of Dove Cottage) applying principles expressed in the poems William and Samuel were then writing. As one turns the pages, he cannot help wondering which came first, William's lyrical ballad or Dorothy's diary embryo?

June 1, 1800. Dove Cottage, Grasmere.

Rain in the night—a sweet mild morning. Read Ballads; went to church. . . . After tea, went to Ambleside, round the lakes—a very fine warm evening. I lay upon the steep of Loughrigg, my heart dissolved in what I saw, when I was not startled but re-called from my reverie by a noise as of a child paddling without shoes. I looked up and saw a lamb close to me. It approached nearer and nearer, as if to examine me, and stood a long time. I did not move. At last it ran past me, and went bleating along the pathway, seeming to be seeking its mother. I saw a hare on the high road. . . .

July 31.

All the morning I was busy copying poems. Gathered peas, and in the afternoon Coleridge came, very hot. . . . The men went to bathe, and we afterwards sailed down to Loughrigg. Read poems on the water, and let the boat take its own course. We walked a long time upon Loughrigg. I returned in the grey twilight. The moon just setting as we reached home.

September 1.

. . . Coleridge obliged to go to bed after tea. John and I followed Wm.
up the hill, and then returned to go to Mr. Simpson's. We borrowed some
bottles for bottling rum. The evening somewhat frosty and grey, but very
pleasant. I broiled Coleridge a mutton chop which he ate in bed. Wm. was
gone to bed. I chatted with John and Coleridge till near 12.

September 14.

Made bread. A sore thumb from a cut. A lovely day. Read Boswell in the
house in the morning, and after dinner under the bright yellow leaves of the
orchard. The pear trees a bright yellow. The apple trees green still. A sweet
lovely afternoon. . . .

October 31.

W. and I did not rise till 1 o'clock. W. very sick and very ill. . . . A very
fine moonlight night— The moon shone like herrings in the water.

November 10, 1801.

Poor C. left us. . . . a sweet day for his ride. Every sight and every sound
reminded me of him—dear, dear fellow, of his many walks to us by day and
night, of all dear things. I was melancholy, and could not talk, but at last I
eased my heart by weeping—nervous blubbering, says William. It is not so. O!
how many, many reasons have I to be anxious for him.

November 11.

Baked bread and giblet pie—put books in order—mended stockings. Put
aside dearest C.'s letters, and now at about 7 o'clock we are all sitting by a
nice fire. Wm. with his book and a candle. . . .

December 12.

A fine frosty morning— Snow upon the ground. I made bread and pies.
We walked. . . . The snow hid all the grass, and all signs of vegetation, and
the . . . hips very beautiful, and so good! ! and, dear Coleridge! I ate twenty
for thee, when I was by myself. . . . We played at cards—sate up late. The
moon shone upon . . . the white fields, [the] glittering roof of Thomas Ash-
burner's house, the dark yew tree, the white fields gay and beautiful. Wm. lay
with his curtains open that he might see it.

December 14.

Wm. and Mary walked to Ambleside in the morning to buy mousetraps.
Mary fell and hurt her wrist. I accompanied them to the top of the hill—

clear and frosty. I wrote to Coleridge a very long letter while they were absent. Sate by the fire in the evening reading.

December 21.

Mary walked to Ambleside for letters. It was a wearisome walk, for the snow lay deep upon the roads and it was beginning to thaw. I stayed at home and clapped the small linen. Wm. sate beside me, and read [his] *The Pedlar*. He was in good spirits, and full of hope of what he should do with it. . . . Coleridge's were melancholy letters, he had been very ill in his bowels. We were made very unhappy. . . . In the afternoon Mary and I ironed, afterwards she packed her clothes up, and I mended Wm.'s stockings while he was reading. . . .

December 22.

Still thaw. I washed my head. Wm. and I went to Rydale for letters . . . stopped a long time in going to watch a little bird with a salmon-coloured breast, a white cross or T upon its wings, and a brownish back with faint stripes. It was pecking the scattered dung upon the road. . . . As we came up the White Moss, we met an old man, who I saw was a beggar by his two bags hanging over his shoulder; but from a half laziness, half indifference, and a wanting to *try* him, if he would speak, I let him pass. He said nothing, and my heart smote me. I turned back, and said, "You are begging?" "Ay," says he. I gave him a halfpenny. . . .

December 25.

Christmas Day. A very bad day. . . . We received a letter from Coleridge . . . poorly but better—his letter made us uneasy about him. I was glad I was not by myself when I received it.

December 28.

. . . We all went weary to bed—my bowels very bad.

January 24, 1802.

We went into the orchard as soon as breakfast was over. Laid out the situation for our new room, and sauntered a while. We had Mr. Clarkson's turkey for dinner; the night before we had boiled the gizzard and some mutton, and made a nice piece of cookery for Wm.'s supper. We walked in the morning, I wrote to Coleridge. After dinner I lay down till tea time— I rose refreshed and better. Wm. could not beat away sleep when I was gone. We went late to bed.

January 27.

. . . We had ate up the cold turkey before we walked so we cooked no dinner. Sate a while by the fire. . . . The bees were humming about the hive. William raked a few stones off the garden, his first garden labour this year; I cut the shrubs. When we returned from Frank's, Wm. wasted his mind in the Magazines. . . . Then we sate by the fire, and were happy, only our tender thoughts became painful. Went to bed at ½ past 11.

January 29.

Wm. was very unwell. Worn out with his bad night's rest. He went to bed —I read to him, to endeavour to make him sleep. Then I came into the other room, and read the first book of *Paradise Lost*. . . . It was a mild afternoon—there was an unusual softness in the prospects as we went, a rich yellow upon the fields, and a soft grave purple on the waters. When we returned many stars were out, the clouds were moveless, in the sky soft purple, the Lake of Rydale calm, Jupiter behind, Jupiter at least *we* call him, but William says we always call the largest star Jupiter. When we came home we both wrote to C. I was stupefied.

March 4.

Before we had quite finished breakfast Calvert's man brought the horses for Wm. We had a deal to do, to shave, pens to make, poems to put in order for writing, to settle the dress, pack up etc., and the man came before the pens were made, and he was obliged to leave me with only two. Since he has left me at half-past 11 (it is now 2) I have been putting the drawers into order, laid by his clothes which we had thrown here and there and everywhere, filed two months' newspapers and got my dinner, 2 boiled eggs and 2 apple tarts. . . . Now for my walk. I *will* be busy. I *will* look well, and be well when he comes back to me. O the Darling! Here is one of his bitten apples. I can hardly find in my heart to throw it into the fire. I must wash myself, then off. I walked around the two Lakes, crossed the stepping-stones at Rydale foot. Sate down where we always sit. I was full of thoughts about my darling. Blessings on him. . . .

March 14.

William had slept badly—he got up at nine o'clock, but before he rose he had finished *The Beggar Boys*, and while we were at breakfast that is (for I had breakfasted) he, with his basin of broth before him untouched, and a little plate of bread and butter, he wrote the Poem to a Butterfly! He ate not a morsel, nor put on his stockings, but sate with his shirt neck unbuttoned, and his waistcoat open while he did it. The thought first came upon him as we were talking about the pleasure we both always feel at the sight of a butterfly. I told him that I used to chase them a little, but that I was afraid of brushing the dust off their wings, and did not catch them. He told me how they used to kill all the white ones when he went to school because they were Frenchmen. . . . We dined and then Wm. went to bed. I lay upon the fur gown before the fire, but I could not sleep—I lay there a long time. It is now halfpast 5—I am going to write letters—I began to write to Mrs. Rawson. William rose without having slept—we sate comfortably by the fire till he began to alter *The Butterfly,* and tired himself—he went to bed tired.

March 17.

William went up into the orchard and finished the Poem. . . . Mr. O. met us and I went to their house—he offered me manure for the garden. I went and sate with W. and walked backwards and forwards in the orchard till dinner time. He read me his poem. I broiled beefsteaks. After dinner we made a pillow of my shoulder—I read to him and my Beloved slept. . . . A sweet evening as it had been a sweet day, a grey evening, and I walked quietly along the side of Rydale Lake with quiet thoughts—the hills and the lake were still—the Owls had not begun to hoot, and the little birds had given over singing. . . .

March 18.

A very fine morning. The . . . rocks glittered in the sunshine, the crows and the ravens were busy, and the thrushes and little birds sang. I went through the fields, and sate ½ an hour afraid to pass a cow. The cow looked at me, and I looked at the cow, and whenever I stirred the cow gave over eating. . . .

March 23.

A mild morning. William worked at *The Cuckow* poem. I sewed beside him. After dinner he slept, I read German, and, at the closing-in of day, went to sit in the orchard—he came to me, and walked backwards and forwards. We talked about C. . . . It is about 10 o'clock, a quiet night. The fire flutters, and the watch ticks. I hear nothing else save the breathing of my Beloved, and he now and then pushes his book forward, and turns over a leaf. . . .

March 27.

A divine morning. At breakfast William wrote part of an ode. Mr. Olliff sent the dung and Wm. went to work in the garden. We sate all day in the orchard.

April 7.

Wm.'s birthday. . . . It rained a little but a fine day. Broth to supper, and went soon to bed.

April 12.

Had the mantua-maker. The ground covered with snow. Walked to T. Wilkinson's and sent for letters. The woman brought me one from William

and Mary. It was a sharp windy night. Thomas Wilkinson came with me to
Barton, and questioned me like a catechizer all the way. Every question was
like the snapping of a little thread about my heart—I was so full of thought
about my half-read letter and other things. I was glad when he left me.
Then I had time to look at the moon while I was thinking over my own
thoughts. . . .

May 4.

   . . . William and C. repeated and read verses. I drank a little brandy
and water, and was in Heaven. . . .

May 31.

   . . . My tooth broke today. They will soon be gone. Let that pass, I shall
be beloved—I want no more.

June 10.

   . . . Coleridge came in with a sack full of books, etc., and a branch of
mountain ash. He had been attacked by a cow. He came over by Grisdale.
A furious wind. . . .

October 4.

   . . . My brother William was married to Mary Hutchinson. I slept a good
deal of the night, and rose fresh and well in the morning. At a little after 8
o'clock I saw them go down the avenue towards the church. William had
parted from me upstairs. When they were absent my dear little Sara prepared the breakfast. I kept myself as quiet as I could, but when I saw the
two men running up the walk, coming to tell us it was over, I could stand it
no longer, and threw myself on the bed, where I lay in stillness, neither
hearing or seeing anything till Sara came upstairs to me, and said "They are
coming." This forced me from the bed where I lay, and I moved, I knew
not how, straight forward, faster than my strength could carry me, till I met
my beloved William, and fell upon his bosom. . . .

December 24. Christmas eve.

   William is now sitting by me, at ½ past 10 o'clock. I have been beside
him ever since tea running the heel of a stocking, repeating some of his
sonnets to him, listening to his own repeating, reading some of Milton's, and
the *Allegro* and *Penseroso*. It is a quiet keen frost. Mary is in the parlour
below attending to the baking of cakes. . . . It is to-day Christmas Day,
Saturday, 25th December 1802. I am thirty-one years of age. It is a dull,
frosty day. . . .

". . . There's something the matter with Lyova."

Countess Tolstoy

The Tolstoys were a diary-writing family. Among the most indefatigable at this pursuit were Count Leo Tolstoy (1828–1910), his eldest daughter Countess Tatiana (1864–   ), and his wife, Countess Sophie (1844–1919). These diaries have one thing in common. No matter who wrote them they are all largely concerned with Tolstoy himself. It is sometimes difficult to get these startlingly different images to coincide, or even to recognize them as being likenesses of the same person, but that is perhaps because no more baffling and inconsistent human being ever lived.

Tolstoy's first thirty years or so were largely given to gambling, drunken carousing, and the fleshly debauchery that led Sophie to say, when she had seen his early diaries, "The *whole* of my husband's past is so dreadful that I don't think I will ever be able to accept it." There was an interval at school where for the most part he disdained learning and professed to look on culture as the enemy of happiness. There was an interval in the army when he took part in repressive campaigns against the people of the Caucasus and commanded a gun battery during the siege of Sebastopol in the Crimean War. Toward the end of this period he began to write and his books were immediately successful.

Then came the middle years. In 1862 he married Sophie Behrs, daughter of a fashionable Moscow physician. With his eighteen-year-old bride, little more than half his age, he retired to Yasnaya Polyana, his family estate and birthplace several hundred miles south of Moscow, there to become paterfamilias (Sophie gave birth to thirteen children within the next twenty-six years) and to write prodigiously. Short stories, criticism, books of autobiography and philosophy poured forth, while day-by-day he slowly brought closer to completion two of the greatest novels of all time, *War and Peace* (1866) and *Anna Karenina* (1875).

In his last thirty-five years, Tolstoy became increasingly preoccupied with social and religious causes. He identified himself with the struggles of the peasants to better their condition. He evolved a half-mystical, half-primitive Christian creed that substi-

From *The Diary of Tolstoy's Wife* 1860–1891, translated by Alexander Werth. Payson & Clarke Ltd. Reprinted by permission of the translator.

tuted for the teachings and rites of the Orthodox Church a simplified belief in love for all men and non-resistance to evil. His new
religion grew into something of a cult that was followed for a time
with fanaticism in many parts of the world, and the long-haired,
white-bearded, venerable founder was thought of as its high
priest.

While the young man who had delighted to sport with dancing
girls was transforming himself into a family man, then a great
novelist, and finally into a prophet and saint, his young wife
looked on her whirling dervish of a husband (who went about
his luxurious estate in serf's costume denouncing vodka and planning to set up a distillery there to make it), with a mixture of be-
wilderment, heartbreak and dismay. She was deeply, intensely in
love. She sought love or, failing that, affection in return. This he
seemed totally unable to give her. There *was* something the matter with Lyova.

Here Sophie's long agony begins—only a few weeks after her
marriage.

October 8, 1862.

A diary once again . . . which I gave up when I got married. I used to take
to writing whenever I felt depressed and I am probably doing it now for
the same reason. I have been feeling frightened ever since yesterday when
he told me he did not believe in my love. . . . Ever since my early girlhood
I have dreamed of a man *as a whole,* a new and *pure* man whom I would
love. Those were childish dreams, but I still find it hard to give up the idea
of loving a man who would always be with me, whose slightest thought and
feeling I would know, who would love no one but me, and who, like myself,
and unlike all other people, would not need *to sow his wild oats* before
becoming good and sound. . . .

The *whole* of my husband's past is so dreadful that I don't think I will ever
be able to accept it. Unless, of course, I acquire some new interest in life,
such as children, whom I want terribly, for they alone will give me a *sound*
future and will enable me to see things in a pure light, without his past,
without all the filth which I still see in him, and which makes me so unhappy.

He . . . likes to torture me and to see me weep because he has no faith
in me. He would like me to have gone through as much evil as himself, so
that I might more fully appreciate the good. It instinctively annoys him that
I should have gained happiness so easily, without reflection, without previous
suffering. I am going to be strong enough not to weep. I don't want him to
see that I suffer; let him believe that I am always happy. . . .

October 9.

We had a heart-to-heart talk yesterday, and I am feeling more at ease,
even happier. We had such a fine ride to-day, and yet I still feel oppressed.
I had some depressing dreams last night, and, though I don't remember them

very clearly, my heart is heavy. . . . Something seems to be hanging over me; it seems to me that I shall soon die. This is strange, now that I have a husband. I listen to him sleeping, and I am frightened to be left alone. He won't let me go near him, which is sad; physical things disgust him.*

October 11.

. . . He grows colder and colder every day, while I go on loving him more and more. His coldness will soon become unbearable. He is too candid to deceive me. . . . I am afraid to show him how sad I am; such silly melancholy always annoys husbands. I sometimes try to console myself with the thought that it will pass and that everything will yet be right, but now I feel that it will not pass and that things will only go from bad to worse. Father writes to me: "Your husband loves you passionately." Yes, he did love me *passionately,* but passion dies, and no one except myself can understand that he was attracted to me without loving me. . . . All that I once possessed has gone: my energy to work, my joy in life, my household talents. Now I only want to sit here all day long doing nothing and thinking of all kinds of sad things. I wanted to work, and I couldn't; what's the good of putting on a silly bonnet which merely gives me a headache? I want to play the piano, but it's awkward upstairs, for it'll be heard all over the house, and the piano down here is too bad. . . . What good am I in this world?

November 13.

. . . One can't live on love alone; and I am so stupid that I can do nothing but think of him. He is unwell, and I begin to believe that he will die, and that is enough to make me miserable for three hours. When he is cheerful, it makes me so glad, and I am only afraid lest his happy mood pass. When he is away or working, I always think of him, listening for his footsteps; and when he is here, I keep watching his face. . . . It isn't hard to find

---

[*Thirty years later her daughter wrote in her diary:

14th January, 1891.

. . . Meditated on married life and congratulated myself I am not married. First, I am glad to be a girl still, and not to have gone through that terrible shame which every married woman has to bear, and which I have understood so clearly from what Mamma related, saying that the morning after her marriage she was so ashamed that she did not want to leave the bedroom, but hid her face in the pillows and cried. I am proud not to have been through that and never wish to. I am surprised that it should happen the very first night; if it has to be, one ought first to accustom one's wife to that intimacy, which, moreover, must seem savage and unpleasant; and that, the first step in conjugal life should be that which brings the most trying and most painful injury to the spirit. . . .
The Tolstoy Home. Diaries of Tatiana Sukhotin-Tolstoy. Columbia University Press, New York. 1951.]

work, but before doing anything one has to create some enthusiasm for breeding hens, tinkling the piano, and reading a lot of silly books and a few very good ones, or pickling cucumbers and what not. All this will come in time, when I forget my lazy old life and get used to the country. I don't want to get into the common rut and be bored; but I shan't be. I wish my husband had a greater influence over me. It's strange that I should love him so much and yet feel his influence so little. There are some lucid moments when I realise everything and realise what a fine world this is to live in, and how many pleasant duties depend upon me; but the mood passes and I forget everything. I . . . haven't prayed for a long time. In the old days, I enjoyed even the external side of religion. I would often, on the quiet, light the wax candle in front of the ikon, adorn it with flowers, lock the door, and kneel before it for an hour or more. Now it all seems stupid and ludicrous, and yet I find pleasure in remembering it. . . .

November 23.

. . . If I am no good to him, if I am merely a doll, a *wife,* and not a *human being*—then it is all useless and I don't want to carry on this existence. Of course I am idle, but I am not idle by nature; I simply haven't yet discovered what I can do here. He is angry and impatient. Oh, but never mind! I am feeling free and happy to-day, and, although he was very gloomy, he didn't touch me. I know he is brilliant, poetic, and intelligent, full of *power,* but it annoys me that he should look at everything from a gloomy angle. I sometimes want to break loose from his somewhat sombre influence, to ignore it—but I can't. . . . In future I shall go out or drive somewhere whenever I feel bored. Sometimes, when I go out, I suddenly feel so free. At other times I begin to imagine him worried and searching for me, and this depresses me so much that I come back home.

He was so gloomy that I nearly wept. He won't speak to me. It is terrible to live with him. . . . I'll go and play the piano again. He is in his bath just now; he's a stranger to me to-day.

December 6.

Some day I shall kill myself with jealousy. . . . I kept looking at his daggers and rifles with the greatest joy. One jerk—it's so easy. So long as there is no child. And there she is, a few yards from here. It drives me mad! I shall go out for a drive. I may meet her at any moment. So that's how he loved her! If only I could burn his diary and his whole past! . . . I have read the beginnings of some of his books, and each time he speaks of love and women I begin to feel disgusted and depressed and want to burn all, all that he has written. May I never be reminded of his past! . . . If I could kill him and then make another man exactly like him, I should do it joyfully.

January 9, 1863.

. . . It is agony to watch his face and his kind look, which I love so much, but which I have been avoiding ever since last night. How can I ever cause him such annoyance? I kept wondering how I could cover up my guilt—cover up is a silly word—I mean, how could I become more fit for him. I cannot love him any more than I do, because I love him to the uttermost limit, with all my soul, and I have no other thought in my mind, no other desire—nothing at all, beyond my love for him. . . . I was in a particularly bad temper yesterday; I quite surpassed myself. . . . what have I done? . . . what if he grows cold to me? Oh, God! I am so mean and unworthy, and this mental pettiness weighs heavily on me. . . .

January 11.

. . . There are days when I love him almost morbidly. This is one of these days. It is always when I feel guilty. It hurts me to look at him, to listen to him; I feel like a devil in the presence of saints. When I can do anything to please him and to make him love me as before, our relations will again become more simple and straightforward. . . . I used to love him boldly, with self-assertion, but now I thank him, and God, for every kind word he utters, every caress, every lenient, gentle look. Now I just live for all this, waiting for his kindness, and it is all I need. I used to be full of pride at the thought of the child inside me, but that is merely fate and a law of nature. There's no consolation in this, either . . . I love him terribly, and nothing matters except him.

January 17.

. . . It is difficult to live together without quarrelling, but, all the same, I shan't quarrel, for L. is quite right in saying that a quarrel between husband and wife makes a *cut* which never heals. My greatest misfortune is my jealousy. We must both watch this very carefully. He doesn't always want to take me with him; a hat and crinoline, all this gets on his nerves, and yet I always feel so lonely when he is away. I'm afraid of clinging to him; if only he would always feel the need for my company, since my longing to see him grows stronger every day. I have waited and waited for him, and now I have sat down again to write. . . . It is past 2 o'clock, and he still hasn't arrived. . . .

April 8.

. . . There's something the matter with Lyova. He seems to have become insincere and unnatural. Or is it merely his headaches? What's the matter with him? What does he want? I'd do anything he wanted, if only I could. He is away now, but I'm already frightened in case he comes back in a bad temper and something annoys him. I love him terribly, I know it, for I could tolerate anything from him, if ever there were anything to tolerate.

April 28.

Lyova is either old or unhappy. I wonder if really nothing has any interest for him, beyond money, his estate, and his distillery. Except when he eats or sleeps or sits in silence, he spends his time roaming about the estate, all alone. I am bored at always being left alone. He expresses his love for me by automatically kissing my hand. . . .

April 29.

. . . Lyova is breaking away from me more and more. The physical side of love matters a great deal to him. That's dreadful—for it's exactly the other way round with me. . . .

May 8.

. . . I simply don't exist, so far as Lyova is concerned. I feel I am distasteful to him, and my only aim now is to leave him alone and to cut him out of my life as far as possible. I can bring him no joy of any kind so long as I am pregnant. How sad to discover that a wife can only learn during her pregnancy whether or not her husband really loves her. He is down among the beehives. I would give anything to be with him, and yet I'm not going, for I have terrible palpitations, and it is uncomfortable to sit there, and a thunderstorm is coming on, and I have a headache, and I'm bored—I want to weep. . . .

May 9.

He promised to be here at 12, and now it is 2 o'clock. I wonder if anything has happened? Why does he torture me like this? It's a pity to chase even a friendly dog away. My mother's fate was rather like mine during the first year of her marriage. It was even worse for her, for while Lyova is merely busy on the estate, Father used to drive out, visiting patients and gambling. But, like her, I am ill and pregnant, and feel lonely and abandoned. . . . After all, you can't spend all day *in perfect solitude*, sewing and playing the piano, and gradually coming to the conclusion that you've got to stick where you are, even though your husband cares nothing for you. . . .

May 22.

. . . I must treasure *his* love. It lingers on, but very feebly; or perhaps it has ceased altogether. That is terrible, and I always keep thinking of it. I have been ill ever since yesterday. I am afraid of a miscarriage, and yet the pain in my belly gives me pleasure. It was the same in my childhood. Although Mother would forgive me for some misdeed, I wouldn't forgive myself and pinch my hand and prick it with a needle as a punishment. Though the pain becomes unbearable, I endure it with an intense feeling of pleasure. This is the right time for putting love to the test. When good weather and good health come back, life will become more orderly. I will take pride in the house, in the baby, and —— [two words expurgated] will come back, too— that's disgusting. . . . As for my own life, it is all gone; it is nothing but a remembrance of the love I had for him and of the thought that he may love me yet. I'm a fool to have believed it and to have prepared so much suffering for myself. Everything seems too miserable. The clock strikes mournfully, the dog is sad, Dushka is so unhappy, and the two old women are both so miserable, and everything is dead. And if Lyova—

June 7.

I love him madly; this emotion has taken such a powerful hold on me He . . . loves me now—I think I can feel it. I wonder if this doesn't mean an early death for me. It will be sad and terrible to leave him. Every day I feel that I love him more than ever before. Nothing exists for me except him and his concerns.

July 17.

It's all over now; the child [Sergei] is born. My suffering is at an end, and I am gradually entering into life again. . . .

July 23.

I have now been married for ten months. I lose courage terribly. I automatically look for support, as the child looks for the breast. I am all doubled up with pain. Lyova is helpless. He can't run the estate for anything—it isn't in his line. He is too restless. He still isn't satisfied with what he's got; I know what he wants, but he shan't have it. Everything is so cheerless. I am used to his caresses, like a dog—but he has grown cold. I believe that such moods do occur. But it seems to happen too often. *Patience. . . .*

July 31.

. . . But patience! At any rate, I can always bless our past. I have loved him deeply, and feel grateful to him for everything. . . . *These past nine months are about the worst in my life*—to say nothing of the tenth one. . . .

August 3.

. . . What a weakness on his part not to be able to be patient until I am better. I suffer and endure ten times as much as he. I wanted to write all this because I was in a temper. It has started raining, and I'm afraid he will catch a cold. I am no longer angry; I love him—may God bless him. . . .

September 10.

I am a little sad that my youth is gone, a little envious, and very bored. All the pain and suffering of my life lies within these four walls; when I am outside I feel blissfully happy, and lighthearted, and so contented with my family life. Again the moon is shining and the nights are so warm and gentle, but they don't seem to belong to me. . . . Lyova's look pursues me wherever I go. At the piano yesterday, it made me shudder. What were his thoughts just then? I had never seen such an expression in his eyes before. Was he remembering anything about the past? Jealousy? He loves—

September 22.

It'll be a year to-morrow since we were married. Then I looked forward to happiness, now I anticipate unhappiness. I had thought that all this about going to the war [the Polish revolt] was a joke, but there seems to be something in it. It's most puzzling. . . . They get married, and like it, and produce a number of children, and then—drop it all and go off to fight. I ought to hope now that my child will die, for I will never survive him. I haven't much faith in all this patriotism and *enthusiasme* in a man of thirty-five. Are not children the same *patrie*, the same Russia? But no! he is quite prepared to drop them because it's fine to gallop across the battlefield and revel in the romance of war and listen to the whistling of bullets! . . . Why did I ever get married to him? . . . What did he need my love for? . . . Now he wants a change. He is tired of this life. He shan't have any more children; I shan't give him any more, so that he can desert them. Just listen to the despot: "I want to do it, and don't you dare say a word." All the worse for me having to wait and languish. It will be the same in the end, anyway. And the worse of it is that I still love him. It breaks my heart. . . .

*"I had often wondered what I would do when I
loosened the reins on myself."*

Wanda Gág

Wanda Gág (1893–1946), artist and author, is widely known
for the many children's stories that she wrote and illustrated,
among them *Millions of Cats* (1928). Less well known is another child's story she has told, her own. It is an account of her
youth and art-student days in Minnesota, kept in thirty-one
closely scribbled notebooks dated 1908 to 1917.

In her journal Wanda Gág tells the story of her emigrant family's struggle to survive poverty when her mother, herself, and
seven other young children were left at her father's death with
twelve hundred dollars of insurance and an allowance of eight
dollars a month from the county. The tale is told against a background of the gropings of an adolescent girl toward maturity
and her attempts to educate herself and achieve fulfillment as an
artist and a woman.

Somehow, with miracles of economy, the family managed to
carry on, making two thousand dollars or so stretch over six
years. But for Wanda Gág the darkest hours never dimmed her
dream of becoming an artist.

The passages from her diary given here begin in 1914, when
with some of the problems of her family grown less acute, generous friends made it possible for her to enroll in the Minneapolis
School of Art. There, however, a new problem arose, one of a very
personal sort. Girl met boy. Adolf Dehn, later to become the famous etcher, was then a classmate of twenty-three. The diarist
was twenty-one. Generally held beliefs about the goings-on of
young art students may or may not prepare the reader for what
happens next.

December 11, 1914.

Monday I came over to Minneapolis. I went over to Art School directly. . . .

January 5, 1915.

. . . Mr. Dehn (one of the boys at school) . . . is German, brilliant, and has much charm. . . .

January 23.

We had no school Thursday afternoon, for we are moving to the new Museum. Thursday evening we had a Farewell Spread at our old quarters and there were toasts bad and good and clever. In this case the clever toasts were also *good*. After the spread we danced. Mr. MacDonald [a fellow student] taught me the Pose Waltz. As we finished it he said, "You want to get Dehn to dance too, he's sort of timid about starting." I said, "Allright." Mr. MacDonald said, "Hey, Dehn!" and as Mr. Dehn turned around I said, "I'm going to teach you to dance, whether you want to or not." He kept saying he didn't know the first thing about it, that he had never danced before in his life, and that he would be very awkward. We went into the Art Gallery where I taught him a Hesitation. He learned it very easily, and as soon as he had proper control of his steps we floated into the Antique room. He seemed to enjoy it very much and would have liked to dance the dance over and over again for an hour or so, but I thought he would appreciate it more if I would make him wait for a while. Besides I wanted to dance with other people. . . . I had a happy time. Mr. Dehn was very thankful to me for teaching him the dances—so thankful, in fact, that he saw me home. . . . Pretty soon I shall grow tired of him, I think; altho he is very nice indeed, and is original and a man with big possibilities. . . .

February 15.

. . . There is a new exhibition at the Museum now, and Thursday morning I skipped Anatomy lecture and went up to the gallery all by myself. I was met in the hall by Mr. Dehn who asked me to come into the Antique room with him to criticize his drawing. I did so but it was fully an hour before I left that room, for we wandered from one subject to another and it really seemed that we would never get thru unburdening our minds. I knew that Mr. Dehn had the most virtuous intentions of finishing his cast-drawing so I gradually moved towards the door, he following all the time, and both of us talking just as fast as our tongues could wag. I went out of the door and he followed, and before we knew it we were stationed outside the door discussing religion and other things. It was almost four when I started for home. . . . I spent a miserable Sunday. It was half-raining, half-sunny outside. I felt dumpy, my drawing mood had left me, my diary was filled (and as it was Sunday I could not get a new one) and I wasn't even artistically inclined enough to plan my spring wardrobe. I read Milton for a while and then, in sheer desperation, I tried to write a letter. . . .

February 24.

. . . He doesn't look any more like an Adolph [as Dehn spelled his name then] than I do. I think his name ought to be George. . . .

March 10.

. . . Mr. Dehn and I have many views in common. His face looked very interesting today. . . .

March 15.

Sunday afternoon I received a telephone call. "Is this Whistler?" said the voice, "this is John Ruskin." I said, "Yes this is James Abbott McNeill Whistler." "Would you let John Ruskin take you somewhere tonight?" "Why yes, I'll let him," I said. "Where are we going?" "Why I thought you'd enjoy it more if it came as a surprise," said Mr. Dehn.

He arrived at a quarter after seven. "We're going to church," he said. . . . After church we went to have some ice-cream and we discussed among other things, Mr. Dehn's plans for the next two years or so. He will have to earn his way thru school, and we exchanged ideas as to what would be the best thing for him to do. He also suggested that I go fishing with him sometime this summer. He thinks it would be interesting to see me fish. . . .

April 25.

. . . It has been a queer day. I have been designing a dress and listening to good singing and dreaming myself into one or two of Anderson's Fairy Tales in German and going off into trances and telling myself that I shall grow tired of Mr. Dehn if he comes to see me four evenings a week. I don't care if that sentence is long and unbalanced. I don't care, I don't care, I don't care.

May 31.

Tonight I am rather a jumble of emotions again. And I don't know exactly why either. Of course Mr. Dehn is gone, and I am just beginning to realize it now. I think if Stella [her sister] were not here I should cry a little. . . . Because I really like him very much. Of course there is nothing sentimental about my attitude towards him, and unless I am very much mistaken his attitude towards me is also only friendly. . . .

Yesterday we walked to Lake of the Isles . . . but we said very little. Not that there was scarcity of material. There was altogether too much to say. I could not say, of course, that I thought he had been very nice to me, and that—oh well. . . . Sometimes I think I am very imprudent to let myself care for him, because he is such a pieface anyway. Sometimes I think he is a poet first and a man second, and although I admire his unsusceptibility—being a woman I resent it.

I am very unsusceptible too, I suppose. But not nearly as much as it seems. I am very severe with myself. Perhaps I am almost a prude in that respect. I scarcely allow a man to touch me. If our hands meet accidentally I draw mine away, almost unconsciously because it has become a habit. And yet, sometimes I have all I can do to keep myself in this self-adjusted strait-jacket. For at times I find myself thinking recklessly and blindly, "What does it matter? There is so much love being given and taken in the world. Why should I guard mine so rigidly?" I would so love to run my hands thru people's hair sometimes or give someone a little, little caress. You see I am very conventional about these things. Or perhaps I should say, "I am extremely reserved." But I can't help that. Principles are principles you know. Yet, as I have said, sometimes I feel very much like saying, "Principles go hang." I am not such a cold, flapping fish as I may seem.

July 1.

Yesterday they told me that a man had called twice for me during the afternoon and at about 6 o'clock I received a telephone call. . . . Mr. Dehn of course. . . . We talked a long while and he said he'd come at 7 p.m. to see me. Which he did accordingly. He was obviously glad to see me. So was I glad to see him. He looked at my new sketches and then we took a walk. To Loring Park as of old. We kept up a bantering sort of conversation for a while and then he suggested that we stop talking nonsense. So we talked Socialism. . . . After he had left me I saw him across the street kicking at things dejectedly. I was comparatively reckless myself, but in another way. I allowed him to grasp me by the arm as he switched me over to the other side of the sidewalk. Which is a good deal for me. I even let him hold me by both arms for a moment when he showed me something in a window. He was standing a little behind, with each hand on one of my arms just a little above the elbow. Last night was one of those nights when I almost felt like letting "principles" go hang.

I am reserving the Fourth for Mr. Dehn, altho I do not know whether he will ask me to spend it with him or not. It is too silly for me to call him Mr. Dehn. He calls me Wanda, almost ever since we have known each other, and it is simply because he doesn't look like an Adolph that I refrain from calling him so.

I have not enough outlets for Myself. The things which are churning about within me are too persistent to admit of the slow progress of coming out thru one channel, be it literature, music or anything else. I am going to the library to get some books on aesthetic dancing. Dancing will help some.

July 7.

. . . We went out to Lake Minnetonka. I was very peevish when we started out, and . . . the fact that two feather-headed couples were walking before us may have been responsible for part of my disgust. They would fool around, grabbing each other's hands or managing to touch each other as if by accident, and it irritated me. Of course I know it is as old as the world is old, but just that afternoon I couldn't bear to think of such a thing as physical attraction. There are times when I hope violently that I am never physically attractive. I nearly always wish that, but sometimes I wish it so much more vehemently than at other times. Not that I would despise a girl for allowing a man to take little liberties—I suppose it isn't her fault that she is so primitively constructed. But that day it did seem so irritatingly *"animalisch."* As I sat there I was filled with revolt at the thought of any man except a relative touching me. I don't know what I would be like if I were a man. If my feelings would be the same as they are now, I certainly would be able to have good morals. . . .

February 18, 1916.

. . . Last night Adolph called on me again. I was rambling on, telling him all the news, but when I would happen to look up I would find him looking at me intently. This was a trifle disconcerting and I would always run on hastily with my talk. At about nine we went to a movie. I knew I would be cold and reserved that night. And I was. I gathered all my little prudishnesses about me and there I sat as cold and cruel as you please. This is silly but it's true; he had had his hair cut again and that was responsible, to a small extent, for my attitude. His intent looks may have had something to do with it. It was obvious that he hadn't come to the movie for the movie's sake. He wished to talk and he wished to have me talk. "Say something," he said.

He spoke again about my treating him as a "nameless creature." I told him he was justified in objecting to the way I omitted his name in speaking to or of him, that it was foolish of me to do so, and that I was sorry to be hurting him so. . . . Towards the end of the movie we said nothing at all. I slipped into my wraps very silently and we walked for blocks and blocks without talking. It was not till we got to Twelfth Street that he talked at all. . . . He had evidently been doing some tall thinking, for he said, slowly but without hesitation, "Well, I suppose I ought to tell you what my attitude towards you is."

My heart quaked within me, and I didn't know whether I ought to let him go on or not. He continued to talk but I don't remember what it was. The next thing I remember is that I heard him saying, "But the truth is, Wanda, I'm in love with you."

I knew neither what to do nor what to say. I said, "Oh you aren't!"

He said, "Perhaps I shouldn't have told you this, and I really didn't intend to say it for a long time to come, but it just seemed that that was the only thing that was left for me to do." . . . It made me awfully nervous and worried—the whole thing. The next day at school we acted just as usual, thank goodness.

March 1.

. . . Adolph continues to come—and I continue to treat him namelessly. It is so hard to all of a sudden call him Adolph. . . .

March 30.

. . . Last Thursday Adolph and I went to a movie. I had been having an awful toothache. I was worn out and weak and had a headache. I said I was weak. And I was listless. Adolph's hand touched my arm and I hadn't the strength to remove it. I was on the point of taking his hand and laying it back on the arm of the seat where it belonged, and saying, "It is better so." But I didn't. Sometimes one just doesn't, that's all. . . .

April. Undated.

. . . Friday Adolph came over to see me. He brought a "Vanity Fair" and the "Masses." I sat in the big chair and he beside me, and a number of times as I was looking thru "Vanity Fair" he would catch my hand. But I fought against it every time and told him to be good. I said "I'm a little disappointed in you. I thought that *you* at least would be able to resist temptation." "But it's a legitimate temptation," he said. "Isn't it legitimate?" "I don't know," I replied. Goodnight, perhaps it wouldn't be so bad. I had always supposed it to be very harmful, to the man at least, but judging from things I have heard people say lately it may not be as bad as I thought. . . . Why do folks have to fall in love with me so long before I am ready for it? . . .

May. Undated.

. . . A few weeks ago Adolph and I went for a walk out to Fair Oaks. Adolph actually tried to embrace me but I fought hard. Oh dear, if it had been only a matter of disliking it I should not have objected so strenuously. Oh Wanda, Wanda, where is your cold and prudish outlook upon the world? . . .

May 21.

. . . He and I walked over to the little park. . . . I don't know whether I couldn't get out of it or whether I gave in, but I let Adolph play with my hands. Yes I did, *yes I did.* . . . I don't blame him for it. And I think even I may be forgiven for submitting. I like him very much. Oh this is all so new to me and I can't quite grasp it, but sometimes even I, strong fighter that I am, seem to be powerless to gather my prudishness about me and remain cold and icy.

Sunday evening I went with him to get some library books which I was to return for him the next day, as he was leaving in the morning. He was almost provokingly good all the time. On the way home we sat down in the little park for a while, and a little later he said rather quietly, "Wanda, may I kiss you?"

I said "No," and sprang from the bench. "Well, I won't," he said in the same almost quiet tone. I said, "I have a record to keep up." "A record?"

"Yes I have never allowed it and won't allow it." "Never?" "Well, perhaps in about 4 or 5 years." I told him it would break my heart if anyone should ever break my record without my permission. When we shook hands I said, "Be nice and good this summer." . . . I went upstairs and told Lucile [a friend and fellow student] all. I didn't want to tell her about his request for a kiss but it was too heavy and I couldn't go to sleep, so I had to. I cried a little too. . . .

June 30. New Ulm.

I have been at home for about two weeks. I have been missing Adolph a good deal and have become very home-sick for the company of men in general. . . . Tomorrow morning at 4.15 a.m. Paula [a friend] and I are going to Waterville to visit Adolph and his sister . . . Viola. . . .

July 15

. . . He is very, very brown. We rowed home via two lakes and a nice shallow winding river. Adolph has a nice cozy *homey* home and a nice, nice family. My regard for him flew up a couple of pegs on account of these. In fact after seeing him at home, I liked him better day after day.

One day he and I went over into the pasture to read a book on Anarchism and Socialism. We read it too, but got very little out of it. For one thing it was written in an exceedingly involved manner, and for another thing he seemed to be much more interested in me than in the book. He made it very uncomfortable for me because he wanted always to sit rather near to me and I, to get out of the way, had to be moving about continually and most of the time I had to sit one-sidedly—I mean, bent to one side in order to get out of his way. Finally I declared I would go home, and got up. He begged me to come back but I refused. "I'll be good," he promised like a little boy, "you can sit on one side and I'll sit way over here." So I sat down again. Usually at this stage he is filled with remorse over what he calls his foolishness. . . . Saturday . . . was one of those peaceful moonlit nights. I could not bear to go in, especially since this was to be my last night on the lake for a long time to come. The rest wished to go in—I don't see how they could—so I said I'd stay and go with Adolph to return the boat. . . . Well, after the others left we rowed for a while. It was an ideal night and silence would have gone capitally with it, but Adolph kept looking at me with such appalling seriousness that I became uneasy. "Say something," I said in desperation. But he declared he couldn't. . . . A number of times I suggested that we get out of the boat but he wanted to put it off as long as possible. We finally got out and started to walk home. "May I put my arm around you?" he asked. I did not resist, so he did. I think I may be forgiven for not having resisted. I don't think anybody but the pruniest, primmest, dried-upest, old-maidest prude would have had the strength to do so. I might have had the strength but I certainly didn't have the desire. Besides I saw no definite reason why I should object. There is just as much of a possibility of my being in love with him as there is of my not being so, and I certainly would have to know—before I could tell absolutely how I felt about it—

whether I could stand that sort of thing from him. I seemed to have no difficulty in standing it.

There was a long puddle which had to be crossed by way of unsteady stones. Adolph took my hand to help me and when, after we had crossed it, our little fingers were still interlocked I made no move to alter the arrangement. I had often wondered what I *would* do when I loosened the reins on myself. I find that my demonstrations are very mild. I curled my fingers around his hand and bent his fingers, one by one. I could see that he was glad about it and that he regretted we were so near home. I am not a bit sorry I did it either.

Then he drew me over to the pump. "May I kiss your hand, Wanda? Just once?" he asked. I said, "No," at first but then I let him take it. I don't care, I think it wasn't very bad.

The next morning we went home. Adolph had given me one of his graduation pictures. I must say I felt somewhat sentimental looking at it.

March 21. 1917.

. . . Adolph and I sent some drawings to the New York Art Students' League Competition. . . .

April 12.

And now I have done it. I knew it would come but didn't think it would happen so soon. I gave to Adolph my first kiss. Down in the unromantic sewing room (which we use to paint in) surrounded by temperas, brushes and our new poster. It was all on account of the war. The United States has been drawn into the conflict and there is much talk of conscription and people are very much alarmed. And of course I am becoming much worried for fear that Adolph may have to go. . . . He kept on asking and altho I wanted to very much, I didn't quite know whether I ought to. And then I thought of the war and of how he might be here only a short while and of how nice he was and how I liked *Himself* as shown in his drawing, and then I gave it. I should say there were three of them but he insists that it was one, with interruptions.

I had often wondered just what the "first kiss" would be like. I did not feel the thrill one reads about. I should say that the memory is more thrilly than the actual thing itself. There was a faint and almost indefinable feeling, tho, which was connected with the thought that this was the only "first kiss" I could ever give or take and that I was experiencing it now for the first and last time. And right after that, with my head on his rough woolen coat, I shed a few tears about it. I meant to go right up and tell Lucile but I haven't told her yet. I feel and act strangely after it and I wonder whether she has noticed it.

April. Undated.

Adolph and I have each been awarded a scholarship at the Art Students' League in New York! We are two out of twelve of the entire United States, and I believe this is the first time that this honor has been conferred on any member of our school. . . . Adolph . . . may not even be able to take advantage of the Scholarship. I have spent so much time and energy worrying about this. It interferes with my sleep and it just makes me sick to think of the war. It has driven away my appetite too. Last week I weighed 99 lbs. (with my clothes on). I am trying hard to have an appetite and I am virtuously swallowing Scott's Emulsion. . . .

September. Undated.

. . . Adolph . . . and I start out for New York Wednesday evening.

4. A TOUCH OF TORTURE—SELF-APPLIED

"What exhausts the man nourishes the woman . . ."

Henri-Frederic Amiel

A retiring Swiss professor of aesthetics and of moral philosophy at the Geneva Academy, Henri-Frederic Amiel (1821–1881), left behind him several volumes of stuffy poetry, the usual learned papers, and to the amazement of his executors, almost 17,000 pages of an intimate journal so vast in scope that only fragments of it have been published.

Amiel's sentimental morality, first excerpted for readers of English by the Victorian novelist Mrs. Humphry Ward, was much to the taste of the time, but the prudery of seventy-five years ago retouched the picture. More recent searchers in this immense gallery of words uncovered suppressed entries, among them the remarkable story of his strange affair with the young woman he calls "X" or "Philine".

Amiel's story of his timid, yet bold, search for a love to which he might be able at last to surrender more than his mind is a fascinating one in its frank details of how these things were managed a century ago. More important is the candour and depth of self-analysis involved in this contribution to the psychology of love.

But here departs a 39-year-old professor of philosophy, pen in hand, to investigate the phenomenon of passion . . .

April 2, 1859.

Might this be the answer of Providence? Is this love that seeks me out the offered cure, the needed strength, the solution awaited? The anonymous writer of March 13 and 16 (whom I was not able to reach through a notice in one of our papers of March 25) has written to me again. . . .

April 8.

The affair is resumed. . . . She has prudence in her tenacity and courage in her feminine discretion. I am put off till Monday; we shall see. . . .

From *Philine,* by Henri-Frederic Amiel, reprinted by permission of Constable and Company Limited. Published in the U.S. by Houghton Mifflin Company.

April 11.

The projected meeting has taken place. . . . The mysterious unknown seemed to me charming through her veil; she had all the calm and assurance that I lacked. . . . I am never at grips with reality, never serious, aroused, willing, possessing. Hence my moral impotence. My claws are clipped, my fangs filed off, my mane shorn: the lion is only a bow-wow. Desire and will characterize males; I seem to have lost my sex. . . .

April 14.

. . . The inner demon possessed me once more. Oh! misery, and misery of the vilest, the lure of voluptuousness, and a voluptuousness without ardour; ugly dreams, bad night. . . .

April 26.

Letter from X; she has taken fright; nevertheless we must see each other again. . . .

June 3.

Yesterday a walk from eight to ten in the evening with X. . . . Accompaniment of nightingales and frogs. Night quite dark. We did not meet anybody. She paints flowers, she draws landscapes, she speaks German and English, she has read much, she writes well, she opens the depths of her heart to me. . . . But memory and foresight restrained me, and I believe also generosity. I remained a simple comrade.

July 4.

. . . To-day a twilight and evening walk with X. As it is the last one for a long time . . . I wondered if I were not a ninny. But I remained faithful to my rôle of a Puritan. . . .

July 9.

. . . Everything ends to-day, occupations, labours, hopes. I have been deeply moved all day. I had hoped that I should become a man and that I had found my Dame de Warens [of whom Rousseau wrote in his *Confessions*]. It has come to nothing. Calm, slightly egotistical prudence has carried the day against affection. . . . One is cautious before everything, one calculates calmly, and one risks only one's foliage, not one's flower. . . . I remain with the curiosity of the senses unsatisfied, and my virile backwardness retains all its absurdity. No matter! A solution is always soothing, and this evening, while drinking my solitary mug of beer at the Nusser *brasserie*, and here at night without a light, I have rejoiced long and loud, like a man who has had a narrow escape. . . .

uly 11.

To take away the attraction of mystery, to destroy the charm of the unknown, to free myself from the excesses of the imagination, the uneasiness of curiosity, and the provocation of dreams by directly attacking the feminine reality is, I think, what I wanted to accomplish last week. . . . It no longer seems to me that a woman, a wife, would be very grateful to me for an absolute continence in which she would not believe, and that it was absurd to pay so dearly for a ridiculous situation, that of being her pupil and not her monitor in the initiation of Venus. I told myself . . . that my ignorance in such matters was harmful and perhaps stupid for a writer and teacher. In short, I was ashamed of my virginity, which gave me neither physical peace nor moral force . . . but the barrier remains. . . . My mad impulse stops short before what is right. . . .

September 25, 1860.

Woe to him who arouses sleeping dogs or the torpid imagination! . . . Venus has haunted me as if I were a young man, and a gnawing curiosity concerning sensual pleasure has tickled my imagination, as it did Saint Anthony's. It seems to me that the more discreet, continent, scrupulous I am in practical matters, the more licentious reading tempts me. My ignorance of living women makes me blush less when, in the company of the erotics, I feel myself a man, young and passionate, capable of the sports of Aphrodite and the transports of the senses. Ashamed of my actual innocence, and almost proud to discard it in spirit, it happens with me as with women who suffer from over-modesty; I take my revenge inwardly; I feed myself on forbidden pleasures in the secrecy of solitary reading. . . . I have had neither wife, nor mistress, nor passion, nor affair; I have especially avoided sensual pleasure and let the golden age pass; have I not been a fool? Such is the thought that besieges the celibate of thirty-nine, in his solitary room, on his sleepless pillow. . . .

September 28.

. . . Theoretically, I have greatly diminished my timid ignorance and my missish embarrassments. I no longer experience the same bashful confusion at allusions or on reading or hearing voluptuous tales; the modesty of my ears and eyes has become much less susceptible; feminine caresses and kisses have finally emboldened me a little and made me less of a simpleton. But practically I am not yet a man; I still belong to the confraternity of dreamers, seminarists, white monks. Now this is a stupid position to occupy at my age; or if old maids are bores, old virgins of the male sex are perhaps laughable. . . . I must, therefore, take the bull by the horns, no matter how great my repugnance, at the first opportunity. If you have remained puerile, futile, foolish, it is partly because of this long infancy. If you are often tempted by books of gallantry and erotic poetry, it is because you have not given nature its due. If you wish to become somewhat more serious and virile you must marry, and before marriage you must clear up this matter in order to avoid a frightful disappointment. Odd counsel, perhaps, for your birth day. . . .

September 30.

Yesterday, meditated on my mother tongue, on the Comic and the Mar vellous, the three subjects that tempt me most for this winter. Then called on Str. A glass of Danzig brandy with golden flecks in it warmed me, then a solitary walk in the moonlight brought my mind back to the forbidden sub jects. . . .

October 5.

. . . A bad night. Went to bed at half-past one in the morning. Lilith persecutes me. Temptations. Rhymed a Priapean poem: "Bacchante and Satyr." . . . As in the legends of the Middle Ages, my demon and my good angel are playing at dice for my soul and drag me now in one direction, now in the other. . . .

October 6.

. . . What am I to call the experience of this evening? Was it disappoint ing, was it intoxicating? Neither the one nor the other. For the first time I have received a woman's favours, and frankly, compared to what the imagi nation assumes or expects, they are a small matter. It was like a bucket of cold water. . . . At bottom I am stupefied at the relative insignificance of this pleasure over which they make such a stir. . . . It is thus that I begin my life as a mature man almost on the anniversary of my birth. . . .

October 7.

. . . X is pretty and well made, and yet I said to myself: "Is that all!" . . . Listened to a sermon by Naef at Saint-Pierre (moderate and serious).— Walk with Prof. Ch.—visited the exposition of fruits and vegetables at the Electoral Palace. Dined with Car. with the Ams. of Pré l'Évêque and my cousins Cav. and B.— The Midolle album. Conversation about Athens and Paris. Called on the Blv. Two games of bowls. Talked about early marriages and the ascendancy of man over woman, etc. Supped with A.—Showed a few sleight-of-hand tricks to the young pupils, Gengine, Machinka. Met X this morning on La Treille, all smiles and graciousness. What exhausts the man nourishes the woman. . . .

"I feel, that is all. I love."

George Sand

Maurice Dupin, musician, retired army officer and descendant of the illegitimate offspring of French and Saxon kings, was playing a country dance the night of July 1, 1804 when his pregnant wife of one month, Sophie Delaborde, daughter of a bird-fancier, excused herself and went out into the garden. The first cries of an infant were heard a few minutes later, and someone said of the future George Sand (1804–1876) "She will be lucky—she was born among the roses to the sound of music."

Thus began the remarkable life of a woman whose pen-name came to symbolize the emancipation of women from the restrictions imposed by society and oppressive French marriage laws which barred divorce. In the 110 volumes of her collected works she repeatedly urged the need for a new morality in which it would be possible to follow the promptings of the heart. She practiced what she preached.

The darling of General Murat at three, she was dolled out in complete military regalia to delight him; she was reared after Rousseau-ean precepts yet spent years in a convent and managed to acquire proficiency in Latin, the modern tongues, and some of the philosophers; she married a baron and left him when his indiscretions with drink and her maids became intolerable; she supported herself in a Paris attic by painting scenes on screens and snuffboxes. When she discovered her gift for writing, she became the *protégée* of the critic Sainte-Beuve and the intimate of the novelist Jules Sandeau. Other literary-musical-amatory relationships followed with the poet Alfred de Musset, a Venetian doctor, a religious philosopher, and the composers Liszt and Chopin.

George Sand was an early convert to socialism, dabbled briefly in the politics of the 1848 revolution, mothered, nursed and embraced a succession of men of genius, and all the while, every night, sat down at her desk at ten o'clock. In the hours before dawn she wrote the novels that influenced such contemporaries as Turgeniev, Dostoievski, Thackeray, Dickens and Hardy, and at-

From *The Intimate Journal of George Sand,* edited and translated by Marie Jenney Howe. Copyright 1929 by Marie Jenney Howe, reprinted by permission of The John Day Co.

tracted to her the English disciple who called herself George
Eliot.

George Sand's diary entries of her passing loves seem always
to be written as by a woman scorned. In them there is no more
moving episode than that which relates the last moments of the
year she and Alfred de Musset spent together. It was love at first
sight. Algernon Swinburne dryly observed: "Alfred was a terrible
flirt and George did not behave as a perfect gentleman." After
their separation, George Sand wrote these lines in her journal late
at night as she waited for her lover to return, sitting by the last
coals of the fire in her tiny apartment in the Quai Malaquais,
high above the Seine. Musset's possessions were scattered around
the room, and a small square of window glass framed the Cathedral of Notre-Dame . . .

November, 1834. Paris.

You do not love me. You do not love me any more. I cannot blind myself
to the truth. Last evening while we were together I was feeling very ill. As
soon as you noticed it you went away. No doubt it was right to leave me
because you were tired last night. But to-day, not one word. You have not
even sent to inquire about me. I hoped for you, waited for you, minute by
minute, from eleven in the morning until midnight. What a day! Every ring
of the bell made me leap to my feet. Thank God I have heart disease. If only
I could die! You love me with your senses more than ever before. And I, you
I have never loved anyone, I have never loved you, in this way. But I love
you also with my whole being—and you do not even feel friendship for me
I wrote to you early this evening. You have not answered my note. The
told my messenger you had gone out; yet you did not come to see me for
even five minutes. . . .

November 25. Tuesday evening.

. . . Will my despair ever leave me? It grows stronger day by day. The
heart that used to be open to mine is now wholly closed to me.—Oh, this
terror of loneliness! Sometimes I am tempted to go to his house and pull on
his door bell until the cord breaks. Sometimes I imagine myself lying down
outside his door waiting for him to come out. I would like to fall at his feet—
no, not at his feet, that would be madness—but I would like to throw myself
into his arms and cry out, "Why do you deny your love for me? You do love
me!"

Yes, you still love me, but you are ashamed of it. You love me and it
makes you suffer. You pity me too much not to love me.

Alfred, you know that I love you, that I cannot love anyone but you. Kiss
me, do not argue, say sweet things to me, caress me, because you do find
me attractive, in spite of my short hair [she had cut off her hair and sent it
to him], in spite of the wrinkles that have come on my cheeks during these
last few days. And then, when you are exhausted with emotion and feel

irritation returning, treat me badly, send me away, but not with those dreadful words, *the last time.*

I will suffer as much as you wish, but let me go to you sometimes, if only once a week, for the sake of the tears, the kisses, which bring me back to life. . . .

He is wrong. Is he not wrong, my God, wrong to leave me now when my soul is purified and, for the first time, my strong will has lost its power? Is it my will that is broken? I do not know and I am content to remain ignorant. What do I care about their theories and social principles! I feel, that is all. I love. The force of my love would carry me to the ends of the earth. But no one wants it! . . .

Am I not thirty years old and in full possession of all my powers? Yes, God in heaven, I feel that I am. I am still able to make a man happy and proud if he is willing to help me. I need a steady arm to uphold me, a heart without vanity to receive and sustain me. If I had ever found such a man I should not be where I am now. But these masterful men are like gnarled oaks whose exterior is repellent.

And you, poet, lovely flower, your fragrance intoxicated me, poisoned me. When I tried to draw near, you dissolved into air before my lips could touch you. You are like those blossomy shrubs of India and China that bend with the slightest wind. From their frail stems we never obtain strong beams with which to build homes. We taste their nectar, we grow heady with their perfume, under their influence we fall asleep and die. . . .

Friday.

. . . Yes, dear friend, I love. In vain do I summon anger to my aid. I love, I shall die of it, unless God works a miracle to save me. . . .

Midnight. I cannot work. Oh, loneliness, loneliness! I can neither write nor pray. Sainte-Beuve says I need distraction. With whom? What do all these people amount to? When they have talked for an hour about things I don't care about, they disappear. They are merely shadows that come and go. I remain alone, alone forever. I want to kill myself. And who has the right to prevent me? . . .

Saturday midnight.

. . . Wretched man, why is it that you cannot love me? According to logic, according to man's justice, no doubt this is right. But you . . . are leaving me in the most beautiful mood of my life, in the phase of my love that is most real, most passionate, and most replete with suffering! You have broken a woman's pride. You have thrown her at your feet. Does this mean nothing to you? . . . If I left Paris they would only say that I had lost my head, and . . . give all those beautiful women the right to say that I disguise myself as a man in order to go to your room at night and crawl on my knees to you. . . .

Last night I dreamed that he was beside me, that he embraced me. I awoke swooning with joy. . . . I cannot suffer like this! And all for nothing. I am thirty years old, I am still beautiful—at least I should regain my looks if I could stop crying. . . . I do not want to die. I want to love. I want to be young again, I want to live! But all these warm impulses have fallen into ashes. . . . For ten weeks I have died day by day, and now I am dying minute by minute. It is too long an agony. Cruel child, why did you love me after having hated me? What mystery fulfills itself in you each week? Why this crescendo of displeasure, disgust, aversion, fury, cold and contemptuous raillery, and then, suddenly, these tears, this sweetness? Torment of my life! Disastrous love! I would give every experience I have lived through for one day of your ineffable love. But never more. . . .

Thursday morning.

Claustration, asceticism, mortification, exalt the senses. Why should I exalt mine by dangerous solitude—I who am unconscious of the senses while living, as I do, in the midst of men? . . . As soon as I can make some more money I shall start housekeeping again and eat at home. Then every evening I shall give a small dinner to two or three friends, as I used to do. I shall work hard. I shall go out more. I must distract myself, strengthen myself against despair. After I have led this sane and honest life long enough to prove that I can maintain it, I shall go, O my love, to ask you to shake my hand. I shall not torment you with jealousies and persecutions. I realize that when one no longer loves, one no longer loves. But I must have your friendship. I need it in order to endure the love in my own heart and prevent it from killing me. . . .

Never again, blue eyes, will you gaze at me. Lovely head, never again shall I see you press against me, veiled in sweet languor. Warm, supple body, never again will you hover over me. . . . O my tears, tears of my heart, sign this page, and may his own tears some day find your traces near his name.

"I am really like a lost sheep . . ."

Franz Kafka

The diary of Franz Kafka (1883–1924) is a peephole into a tiny room. The room is in Prague, illumined at night by lights from the hall of his father's apartment, by trolley lights passing below. Within, a genius tosses on a narrow bed, irritated by lumpy pillows and disconsolate thoughts, darkly brooding on love, marriage, death and art, trembling with the fevers and weakness of a tuberculosis-ridden body, kept awake by the surgings of an unruly mind ranging the dimensions of sense and madness. A hacking cough shakes the thin figure as he writes, sometimes all the night through, the manuscripts of *The Castle, The Trial,* or *Amerika,* among the most extraordinary books of modern times.

Franz Kafka was born in Prague, the eldest of six children. His father was a prosperous Austrian businessman who never ceased to be puzzled by his odd, ugly-duckling son. He clumsily sought to express affection for the youth, and as clumsily the affection was returned. But there was a never-surmounted chasm between them. It grew and grew and nourished a neurosis that emerged in one form or another in much that the novelist wrote.

The lonely, anxious, depressed child became Kafka the man. He was precocious and sensitive, but perfected a pose as horseman, swimmer, and oarsman. At his parent's urging he studied law and then gave it up after obtaining his doctorate in jurisprudence for a post in the civil service where the hours were short and responsibilities few, leaving him ample time to write. His first fiction was published when he was 26.

Kafka fell in love and for years was at the point of marriage, vacillating and uncertain. Finally the engagement was broken off. His disease having taken a turn for the worse, he tried one self-prescribed cure after another. Then he cut his ties with his family and went off to live in Berlin where he was nursed by a devoted mistress until the German inflation set in, leaving him with little food and no coal to heat his miserable lodgings. By 1924 his health had failed so badly that he reluctantly went home to

From *The Diaries of Franz Kafka,* 1910–1913 edited by Max Brod. Copyright 1948 by Schocken Books, Inc. Reprinted by permission of Schocken Books, Inc. and Martin Secker & Warburg, Ltd.

Prague. There, in great pain from his wracked lungs and throat, he died on June 3, 1924.

Through the years of searching, of fleeting assurance and of lasting doubt, Kafka kept journals so candid and revealing that he asked they be burnt after his death. The friend to whom he entrusted this mission felt they were too valuable to destroy. And so, for anyone who cares to put his eye to the peephole, there has been preserved this remarkable view of the torment and anguish of genius in gestation.

December 15, 1910.

. . . This condition is new—I have had similar ones, but never one like this. It is as if I were made of stone, as if I were my own tombstone, there is no loophole for doubt or for faith, for love or repugnance, for courage or anxiety, in particular or in general, only a vague hope lives on, but no better than the inscriptions on tombstones. Almost every word I write jars against the next, I hear the consonants rub leadenly against each other and the vowels sing an accompaniment. . . . My doubts stand in a circle around every word, I see them before I see the word, but what then! I do not see the word at all, I invent it. Of course, that wouldn't be the greatest misfortune, only I ought to be able to invent words capable of blowing the odor of corpses in a direction other than straight into mine and the reader's face. . . .

December 16.

I won't give up the diary again. I must hold on here, it is the only place I can. . . .

December 22.

Today I do not even dare to reproach myself. Shouted into this empty day, it would have a disgusting echo.

December 26.

. . . Being alone has a power over me that never fails. My interior dissolves (for the time being only superficially) and is ready to release what lies deeper. A slight ordering of my interior begins to take place and I need nothing more, for disorder is the worst thing in small talents.

December 27.

My strength no longer suffices for another sentence. Yes, if it were a question of words, if it were sufficient to set down one word and one could turn away in the calm consciousness of having entirely filled this word with oneself. . . .

September 26, 1911.

The artist Kubin recommends Regulin as a laxative, a powdered seaweed that swells up in the bowels, shakes them up, is thus effective mechanically in contrast to the unhealthy chemical effect of other laxatives which just tear through the excrement and leave it hanging on the walls of the bowels.

He . . . [told] stories about an artist's pension in Munich where painters and veterinaries lived (the latters' school was in the neighborhood) and where they acted in such a debauched way that the windows of the house across the way, from which a good view could be had, were rented out. . . . A manufacturer of fraudulent antiques who got the worn effect by means of buckshot and who said of a table: Now we must drink coffee on it three more times, then it can be shipped off to the Innsbruck Museum. . . .

September 30.

The girl in the adjoining room yesterday. I lay on the sofa and, on the point of dozing off, heard her voice. She seemed to me in my mind to be overdressed not only because of the clothes she wore, but also because of the entire room; only her shapely, naked, round, strong, dark shoulders which I had seen in the bath prevailed against her clothes. For a moment she seemed to me to be steaming and to be filling the whole room with her vapors. Then she stood up in her ash-gray-colored bodice that stood off from her body so far at the bottom that one could sit down on it and after a fashion ride along.

October 2.

Sleepless night. The third in a row. I fall asleep soundly, but after an hour I wake up, as though I had laid my head in the wrong hole. I am completely awake, have the feeling that I have not slept at all or only under a thin skin, have before me anew the labor of falling asleep and feel myself rejected by sleep. And for the rest of the night, until about five, thus it remains, so that indeed I sleep but at the same time vivid dreams keep me awake. I sleep alongside myself, so to speak, while I myself must struggle with dreams. About five the last trace of sleep is exhausted, I just dream, which is more exhausting than wakefulness. In short, I spend the whole night in that state in which a healthy person finds himself for a short time before really falling asleep. When I awaken, all the dreams are gathered about me, but I am careful not to reflect on them. Toward morning I sigh into the pillow, because for this night all hope is gone. I think of those nights at the end of which I was raised out of a deep sleep and awoke as though I had been folded in a nut. . . .

October 3.

The same sort of night, but fell asleep with even more difficulty. While falling asleep a vertically moving pain in my head over the bridge of the nose, as though from a wrinkle too sharply pressed into my forehead. To make myself as heavy as possible, which I consider good for falling asleep, I had crossed my arms and laid my hands on my shoulders, so that I lay there like a soldier with his pack. Again it was the power of my dreams, shining forth into wakefulness even before I fell asleep, which did not let me sleep. . . .

October 9.

If I reach my fortieth year, then I'll probably marry an old maid with protruding upper teeth left a little exposed by the upper lip. The upper front teeth of Miss K., who was in Paris and London, slant toward each other a little like legs which are quickly crossed at the knees. I'll hardly reach my fortieth birthday, however; the frequent tension over the left half of my skull, for example, speaks against it—it feels like an inner leprosy which, when I only observe it and disregard its unpleasantness makes the same impression on me as the skull cross-sections in textbooks, or as an almost painless dissection of the living body where the knife—a little coolingly, carefully, often stopping and going back, sometimes lying still—splits still thinner the paper-thin integument close to the functioning parts of the brain.

Last night's dream . . . brothels . . . whores . . . one . . . I fingered her legs and then for a long time pressed the upper parts of her thighs in regular rhythm. My pleasure in this was so great that I wondered that for this entertainment, which was after all really the most beautiful kind, one still had to pay nothing. I was convinced that I (and I alone) deceived the world. Then the whore, without moving her legs, raised the upper part of her body and turned her back to me, which to my horror was covered with large sealing-wax-red circles with paling edges, and red splashes scattered among them. I now noticed that her whole body was full of them, that I was pushing my thumb to her thighs in just such spots and that there were these little red particles—as though from a crumbled seal—on my fingers too. . . .

October 17.

I finish nothing because I have no time and it presses so within me. If the whole day were free and this morning restlessness could mount within me until midday and wear itself out by evening, then I could sleep. This way, however, there is left for this restlessness only an evening twilight hour at most, it gets somewhat stronger, is then suppressed, and uselessly and injuriously undermines the night for me. Shall I be able to bear it long? And is there any purpose in bearing it, shall I, then, be given time? . . .

October 20.

. . . I am probably sick, since yesterday my body has been itching all over. In the afternoon my face was so hot and blotched that I was afraid the assistant giving me a haircut, who could see me and my reflected image all the time, would recognize that I had a serious disease. Also the connection between stomach and mouth is partly disturbed, a lid the size of a gulden moves up or down, or stays down below from where it exerts an expanding effect of light pressure that spreads upward over my chest. . . .

October 24.

. . . For a long time now I have been complaining that I am always ill, but never have any definite illness that would compel me to go to bed. This wish certainly goes back chiefly to the fact that I know how comforting Mother can be when, for example, she comes from the lighted living room into the twilight of the sick room, or in the evening, when the day begins to change monotonously into night . . . causes the day, already so late, to begin again and rouses the invalid to help her in this. I should wish that for myself once more, because then I should be weak, therefore . . . enjoy every childish pleasure with age's keener capacity for gratification. . . .

October 30.

This craving that I almost always have, when for once I feel my stomach is healthy, to heap up in me notions of terrible deeds of daring with food. I especially satisfy this craving in front of pork butchers. If I see a sausage that is labeled as an old, hard sausage, I bite into it in my imagination with all my teeth and swallow quickly, regularly and thoughtlessly, like a machine. The despair that this act, even in the imagination, has as its immediate result, increases my haste. I shove the long slabs of rib meat unbitten into my mouth, and then pull them out again from behind, tearing through stomach and intestines. I eat dirty delicatessen stores completely empty. Cram myself with herrings, pickles and all the bad, old, sharp foods. Bonbons are poured into me like hail from their tin boxes. I enjoy in this way not only my healthy condition but also a suffering that is without pain and can pass at once. . . .

November 2.

This morning, for the first time in a long time, the joy again of imagining a knife twisted in my heart.

November 5.

. . . I want to write, with a constant trembling on my forehead. I sit in my room in the very headquarters of the uproar of the entire house. I hear all the doors close, because of their noise only the footsteps of those running between them are spared me, I hear even the slamming of the oven door in the kitchen. My father bursts through the doors of my room and passes through in his dragging dressing gown, the ashes are scraped out of the stove in the next room, Valli asks, shouting into the indefinite through the anteroom as though through a Paris street, whether Father's hat has been brushed yet, a hushing that claims to be friendly to me raises the shout of an answering voice. The house door is unlatched and screeches as though from a catarrhal throat, then opens wider with the brief singing of a woman's voice and closes with a dull manly jerk that sounds most inconsiderate. My father is gone, now begins the more delicate, more distracted, more hopeless noise led by the voices of the two canaries. I had already thought of it before, but with the canaries it comes back to me again, that I might open the door a narrow crack, crawl into the next room like a snake and in that way, on the floor, beg my sisters and their governess for quiet. . . .

November 7.

. . . To the adult there comes the childish conviction that nothing can happen to a child who is with its parents . . . and that if you think about it, real troubles are not to be met with so close to the earth but only at the height of an adult's face. . . .

November 11.

As soon as I become aware in any way that I leave abuses undisturbed which it was really intended that I should correct (for example, the extremely satisfied, but from my point of view dismal life of my married sister), I lose all sensation in my arm muscles for a moment. . . .

November 14.

. . . In the afternoon while falling asleep. As though the solid skullcap encircling the insensitive cranium had moved more deeply inward and left a part of the brain exposed to the free play of light and muscles.

To awaken on a cold autumn morning full of yellowish light. To force your way through the half-shut window and while still in front of the panes, before you fall, to hover, arms extended, belly arched, legs curved backward, like the figures on the bows of ships in old times.

Before falling asleep.

It seems so dreadful to be a bachelor, to become an old man struggling to keep one's dignity while begging for an invitation whenever one wants to spend an evening in company, having to carry one's meal home in one's hand, unable to expect anyone with a lazy sense of calm confidence, able only with difficulty and vexation to give a gift to someone, having to say good night at the front door, never being able to run up a stairway beside one's wife, to lie still and have only the solace of the view from one's window when one can sit up, to have only side doors in one's room leading into other people's living rooms, to feel estranged from one's family, with whom one can keep on close terms only by marriage, first by the marriage of one's parents, then, when the effect of that has worn off, by one's own, having to admire other people's children and not even being allowed to go on saying: "I have none myself," never to feel oneself grow older since there is no family growing up around one. . . .

November 16.

This noon, before falling asleep, but I did not fall asleep, the upper part of the body of a wax woman lay on top of me. Her face was bent back over mine, her left forearm pressed against my breast.

No sleep for three nights. . . .

November 21.

My former governess, the one with the black-and-yellow face, with the square nose and a wart on her cheek which used to delight me so, was at our house today for the second time recently to see me. The first time I wasn't home, this time I wanted to be left in peace and to sleep and had them tell her I was out. Why did she bring me up so badly, after all I was obedient, she herself is saying so now to the cook and the governess in the anteroom, I was good and had a quiet disposition. Why didn't she use this to my advantage and prepare a better future for me? She is a married woman or a widow, has children, has a lively way of speaking that doesn't let me sleep, thinks I am a tall, healthy gentleman at the beautiful age of twenty-eight who likes to remember his youth and in general knows what to do with himself. Now, however, I lie here on the sofa, kicked out of the world, on the lookout for the sleep that refuses to come and will only graze me when it does, my joints ache with fatigue, my dried-up body trembles toward its own destruction in turmoils of which I dare not become fully conscious, in my head are astonishing convulsions. And there stand the three women before my door, one praises me as I was, two as I am. The cook says I shall go straight—she means without any detour—to heaven. Thus it shall be. . . .

It is certain that a major obstacle to my progress is my physical condition. Nothing can be accomplished with such a body. I shall have to get used to its perpetual balking. As a result of the last few nights spent in wild dreams but with scarcely a few snatches of sleep, I was so incoherent this morning, felt nothing but my forehead, saw a halfway bearable condition only far beyond my present one, and in sheer readiness to die would have been glad simply to have curled up in a ball on the cement floor of the corridor with the documents in my hand. My body is too long for its weakness, it hasn't the least bit of fat to engender a blessed warmth, to preserve an inner fire, no fat on which the spirit could occasionally nourish itself beyond its daily need without damage to the whole. How shall the weak heart that lately has troubled me so often be able to pound the blood through all the length of these legs. It would be labor enough to the knees, and from there it can only spill with a senile strength into the cold lower parts of my legs. But now it is already needed up above again, it is being waited for, while it is wasting itself down below. Everything is pulled apart throughout the length of my body. What could it accomplish then, when it perhaps wouldn't have enough strength for what I want to achieve even if it were shorter and more compact. . . .

November 24.

Honesty of evil thoughts. Yesterday evening I felt especially miserable. My stomach was upset again. I had written with difficulty. . . . I had no defense this evening against such thoughts except to say to myself: "It is now that you come, evil thoughts, now, because I am weak and have an upset stomach. You pick this time for me to think you. You have waited for your advantage. Shame on you. Come some other time, when I am stronger. Don't exploit my condition in this way." And, in fact, without even waiting for other proofs, they yielded, scattered slowly and did not again disturb me during the rest of my walk, which was, naturally, not too happy. They apparently forgot, however, that if they were to respect all my evil moments, they would seldom get their chance.

December 3.

. . . The unhappiness of the bachelor, whether seeming or actual, is so easily guessed at by the world around him that he will curse his decision, at least if he has remained a bachelor because of the delight he takes in secrecy. He walks around with his coat buttoned, his hands in the upper pockets of his jacket, his arms akimbo, his hat pulled down over his eyes, a false smile that has become natural to him is supposed to shield his mouth as his glasses do his eyes, his trousers are tighter than seem proper for his thin legs . . . and when he dies the coffin is exactly right for him.

December 13.

Because of fatigue did not write and lay now on the sofa in the warm room and now on the one in the cold room, with sick legs and disgusting dreams. A dog lay on my body, one paw near my face. I woke up because of it but was still afraid for a little while to open my eyes and look at it. . . .

December 26.

. . . It is unpleasant to listen to Father talk with incessant insinuations about the good fortune of people today and especially of his children, about the sufferings he had to endure in his youth. No one denies that for years, as a result of insufficient winter clothing, he had open sores on his legs, that he often went hungry, that when he was only ten he had to push a cart through the villages, even in winter and very early in the morning—but, and this is something he will not understand, these facts, taken together with the further fact that I have not gone through all this, by no means lead to the conclusion that I have been happier than he, that he may pride himself on these sores on his legs, which is something he assumes and asserts from the very beginning, that I cannot appreciate his past sufferings, and that, finally, just because I have not gone through the same sufferings I must be endlessly grateful to him. How gladly I would listen if he would talk on about his youth and parents, but to hear all this in a boastful and quarrelsome tone is torment. Over and over again he claps his hands together: "Who can understand that today! What do the children know! . . ."

My feeling when I write something that is wrong might be depicted as follows: In front of two holes in the ground a man is waiting for something to appear that can rise up only out of the hole on his right. But while this hole remains covered over by a dimly visible lid, one thing after another rises up out of the hole on his left, keeps trying to attract his attention, and in the end succeeds. . . .

January 3, 1912.

. . . When it became clear in my organism that writing was the most productive direction for my being to take, everything rushed in that direction and left empty all those abilities which were directed toward the joys of sex, eating, drinking, philosophical reflection and above all music. I atrophied in all these directions. This was necessary because the totality of my strengths was so slight that only collectively could they even halfway serve the purpose of my writing. . . . I shouldn't complain that I can't put up with a sweetheart, that I understand almost exactly as much of love as I do of music and . . . that on New Year's Eve I dined on parsnips and spinach, washed down with a glass of Ceres. . . . My development is now complete and, so far as I can see, there is nothing left to sacrifice . . . my face will finally be able to age in a natural way.

September 23.

. . . *The Judgment* I wrote at one sitting during the night of the 22nd-23rd, from ten o'clock at night to six o'clock in the morning. I was hardly able to pull my legs out from under the desk, they had got so stiff from sitting. The fearful strain and joy, how the story developed before me, as if I were advancing over water. Several times during this night I heaved my own weight on my back. How everything can be said, how for everything, for the strangest fancies, there waits a great fire in which they perish and rise up again. How it turned blue outside the window. A wagon rolled by. Two men walked across the bridge. At two I looked at the clock for the last time. As the maid walked through the anteroom for the first time I wrote the last sentence. Turning out the light and the light of day. The slight pains around my heart. The weariness that disappeared in the middle of the night. The trembling entrance into my sisters' room. Reading aloud . . . stretching in the presence of the maid and saying, "I've been writing until now." The appearance of the undisturbed bed, as though it had just been brought in. The conviction verified that . . . only *in this way* can writing be done, only with such coherence, with such a complete opening out of the body and the soul. . . .

May 4, 1913.

Always the image of a pork butcher's broad knife that quickly and with mechanical regularity chops into me from the side and cuts off very thin slices which fly off almost like shavings because of the speed of the action. . . .

July 21.

Summary of all the arguments for and against my marriage:

1. Inability to endure life alone . . . the demands of my own person, the attacks of time and old age, the vague pressure of the desire to write, sleeplessness, the nearness of insanity. . . .

2. Everything immediately gives me pause . . . the sight of the nightshirts on my parents' beds, laid out for the night . . . afraid again.

3. I must be alone a great deal. What I accomplished was only the result of being alone.

4. I hate everything that does not relate to literature, conversations bore me (even if they relate to literature), to visit people bores me, the sorrows and joys of my relatives bore me to my soul. Conversations take the importance, the seriousness, the truth out of everything I think.

5. The fear of the connection, of passing into the other. Then I'll never be alone again.

6. In the past, especially, the person I am in the company of my sisters has been . . . fearless, powerful, surprising, moved as I otherwise am only when I write. If through the intermediation of my wife I could be like that in the presence of everyone! But then would it not be at the expense of my writing? Not that, not that!

7. Alone, I could perhaps some day really give up my job. Married, it will never be possible. . . .

Miserable creature that I am!

November 18.

I will write again, but how many doubts have I meanwhile had about my writing. At bottom I am an incapable, ignorant person who, if he had not been compelled—without any effort on his own part and scarcely aware of the compulsion—to go to school, would be fit only to crouch in a kennel, to leap out when food is offered him and to leap back when he has swallowed it. . . .

November 19.

. . . I am more uncertain than I ever was, I feel only the power of life. And I am senselessly empty. I am really like a lost sheep in the night and in the mountains, or like a sheep which is running after this sheep. . . .

". . . my heart and head have stood
many a crash . . ."

Lord Byron

Lord Byron (1788–1824) was born in London of an ancient family that traced its origins to Norman times. His father was Captain John ("Mad Jack") Byron, gambler and spendthrift, who ran through his first wife's fortune and the money brought him by a Scotch heiress, Catherine Gordon, who was his second wife and the poet's mother. As a boy of ten he became the sixth Baron Byron and the successor to vast estates, among them palatial Newstead Abbey in Sherwood Forest.

Byron was educated at Harrow and Trinity College, Cambridge, where despite an annual allowance of £500, a servant and a horse, he ran up debts of £10,000 before he was twenty-one. His life became one of dissipation and sensual indulgence.

Byron's macabre gestures (he spent hours musing on a tombstone and served his friends wine poured from a human skull) and his fondness for mystification and robust humour concealed his seriousness of purpose and eagerness for learning. His quick, retentive mind laid up in a few years a vast store of knowledge. Despite a crippled leg he actively engaged in swimming, cricket, fencing, boxing, riding and sailing.

Byron's first poems appeared while he was still in college. They were savagely attacked in the *Edinburgh Review,* and this led Byron to a scathing rejoinder, "English Bards and Scotch Reviewers," published when he was twenty-one. Leaving behind the stir in London caused by this effective polemic, Byron travelled for several years in Mediterranean countries. He swam the Hellespont, conquering that mile of choppy water in little more than an hour. More important, he wrote "Childe Harold's Pilgrimage." Its publication in the spring of 1812, after his return to London, made Byron famous and sought after overnight; he found himself a literary celebrity at the time this diary opens. Shortly before, he had written bitterly to a friend of his despair for the future. "My whole life," he said, "has been at variance with propriety, not to say decency; my circumstances are become involved; my friends are dead or estranged, and my existence a dreary void."

There were no dreary voids henceforth for Byron, although he never did succeed in meeting accepted standards of propriety. Because of many indiscreet love affairs, family and friends pressed him to marry Anne Milbank, hoping this would steady him. The marriage was unsuccessful and soon ended in separation. The charge was made that his relationship with his half-sister, Augusta, had not been a proper one. After the failure of his marriage in 1816, he went to live abroad and never returned. He had a beloved daughter, Allegra, by his mistress Jane Clairmont, and established a permanent liaison with another mistress, Teresa, the Countess Guiccioli. Shelley was his fellow expatriate in Italy; it was in Byron's boat that the poet drowned when it sank in the Gulf of Spezia.

Byron's poetry was eagerly read, not only in England (where whole editions were often sold out in a single day) but in many other countries as well. Three dozen translations of "Manfred" alone were made. His last years were spent aiding the cause of Italian and Greek independence. He gave generously both time and money, and developed a flair for revolutionary conspiracy, plot and counterplot. He died in Greece at Missolonghi of a fever contracted while drilling troops he had secretly raised to resist the Turkish invasion.

Those who knew Byron thought him strikingly handsome. He was of middle height, strongly built, a little plump, with a small head curled over with dark brown hair. His eyes were a light grey, his face was pale. He was painfully self-conscious about the shortened and twisted leg that made him walk with a limp.

Byron talked well, and when he was in the mood he bubbled with exuberant speech. Something of this spilled out onto the pages of his diary. His entries have a wonderful spontaneity. They seem lively transcripts of whatever was on the top of his mind at the moment, hastily scribbled down without pause for second thought.

November 14, 1813.

If this had begun ten years ago, and faithfully kept! ! !—heigho! there are too many things I wish never to have remembered, as it is. Well,—I have had my share of what are called the pleasures of this life, and have seen more of the European and Asiatic world than I have made a good use of. They say "Virtue is its own reward",—it certainly should be paid well for its trouble. At five-and-twenty, when the better part of life is over, one should be *something;*—and what am I? nothing but five-and-twenty—and the odd months. What have I seen? The same man all over the world,—ay, and woman too. . . .

November 16.

To-day received Lord Jersey's invitation to Middleton—to travel sixty miles to meet Madame De Stael! I once travelled three thousand to get among silent people; and this same lady writes octavos and *talks* folios. I have read her books—like most of them, and delight in the last; so I won't hear it, as well as read. . . .

November 17.

I have dined regularly to-day, for the first time since Sunday last—this being Sabbath, too. All the rest, tea and dry biscuits—six *per diem*. I wish to God I had not dined now!—It kills me with heaviness, stupor, and horrible dreams; and yet it was but a pint of Bucellas, and fish. Meat I never touch,—nor much vegetable diet. I wish I were in the country, to take exercise,—instead of being obliged to *cool* by abstinence, in lieu of it. I should not so much mind a little accession of flesh—my bones can well bear it. But the worst is, the devil always came with it,—till I starved him out,—and I will *not* be the slave of *any* appetite. If I do err, it shall be my heart, at least, that heralds the way. Oh, my head—how it aches?—the horrors of digestion! I wonder how Buonaparte's dinner agrees with him? . . .

Tuesday morning. Undated.

I awoke from a dream!—well! and have not others dreamed? —Such a dream!—but she did not overtake me. I wish the dead would rest, however. Ugh! how my blood chilled,—and I could not wake—and—and—heigho! . . .

No letters to-day;—so much the better,—there are no answers. I must not dream again;—it spoils even reality. I will go out of doors, and see what the fog will do for me. Jackson has been here; the boxing world much as usual; —but the club increases. I shall dine at Crib's tomorrow. I like energy—even animal energy—of all kinds; and I have need of both mental and corporeal. I have not dined out, nor, indeed, *at all*, lately: have heard no music—have seen nobody. . . .

November 24. 12, Mezza Notte.

Just returned from dinner with Jackson (the Emperor of Pugilism) and another of the select, at Crib's the champion's. I drank more than I like, and have brought away some three bottles of very fair claret—for I have no head-ache. We had Tom Crib up after dinner;—very facetious, though somewhat prolix. . . . Tom has been a sailor—a coal-heaver—and some other genteel profession, before he took to the cestus. Tom has been in action at sea, and is now only three-and-thirty. A great man! has a wife and a mistress, and conversations well—bating some sad omissions and misapplications of the aspirate. Tom is an old friend of mine; I have seen some of his best battles in my nonage. He is now a publican, and, I fear, a sinner;—for Mrs. Crib is on alimony, and Tom's daughter lives with the champion. *This* Tom told me,—Tom, having an opinion of my morals, passed her off as a legal spouse. Talking of her, he said, "she was the truest of women"—from which I immediately inferred she could *not* be his wife, and so it turned out. . . .

November 26.

. . . I have been thinking lately a good deal of Mary Duff. How very odd that I should have been so utterly, devotedly fond of that girl, at an age when I could neither feel passion, nor know the meaning of the word. . . . We were both the merest children. I had and have been attached fifty times since that period; yet I recollect all we said to each other, all our caresses, her features, my restlessness, sleeplessness . . . our walks, and the happiness of sitting by Mary, in the children's apartment, at their house not far from the Plain-stanes at Aberdeen, while her lesser sister Helen played with the doll, and we sat gravely making love, in our way.

How the deuce did all this occur so early? I certainly had no sexual ideas for years afterwards; and yet my misery, my love for that girl were so violent, that I sometimes doubt if I have ever been really attached since. . . .

November 30.

. . . Sunday, I dined with the Lord Holland in St. James's Square. Large party . . . stuffed myself with sturgeon, and exceeded in champagne and wine in general but not to confusion of head. When I *do* dine, I gorge like an Arab or a Boa snake, on fish and vegetables, but no meat. I am always better, however, on my tea and biscuit than any other regimen, and even *that* sparingly.

Why does Lady H. always have that damned screen between the whole room and the fire? I, who bear cold no better than an antelope, and never yet found a sun quite *done* to my taste, was absolutely petrified, and could not even shiver. All the rest, too, looked as if they were just unpacked, like salmon from an ice-basket, and set down to table for that day only. When she retired, I watched their looks as I dismissed the screen, and every cheek thawed, and every nose reddened with the anticipated glow. . . .

December 1.

. . . I shall soon be six-and-twenty (January 22d, 1814). Is there any thing in the future that can possibly console us for not being always *twenty-five*? . . . Dallas's nephew (son to the American Attorney-general) is arrived in this country, and tells Dallas that my rhymes are very popular in the United States. These are the first tidings that have ever sounded like *Fame* to my ears—to be redde on the banks of the Ohio! . . .

Last night I supped with Lewis; and, as usual, though I never exceeded in solids nor fluids, have been half dead ever since. My stomach is entirely destroyed by long abstinence, and the rest will probably follow. Let it—I only wish the *pain* over. The "leap in the dark" is the least to be dreaded. . . .

December 6.

. . . This journal is a relief. When I am tired—as I generally am—out comes this, and down goes every thing. But I can't read it over; and God knows what contradictions it may contain. If I am sincere with myself (but I fear one lies more to one's self than to any one else), every page should confute, refute, and utterly abjure its predecessor. . . . That confounded supper at Lewis's has spoiled my digestion and my philanthropy. I have no more charity than a cruet of vinegar. Would I were an ostrich, and dieted on fire-irons—or any thing that my gizzard could get the better of. . . . Redde a good deal, but desultorily. My head is crammed with the most useless lumber. It is odd that when I do read, I can only bear the chicken broth of—*any* *thing* but Novels. It is many a year since I looked into one. . . . I shall now smoke two cigars, and get me to bed. The cigars don't keep well here. They get as old as a *donna di quaranti anni* in the sun of Africa. The Havannah are the best;—but neither are so pleasant as a hooka or chiboque. The Turkish tobacco is mild and their horses entire—two things as they should be.

I am so far obliged to this Journal, that it preserves me from verse, at least from keeping it. I have just thrown a poem into the fire (which it has re-lighted to my great comfort), and have smoked out of my head the plan of another. I wish I could as easily get rid of thinking, or, at least, the confusion of thought.

December 7.

Went to bed, and slept dreamlessly, but not refreshingly. Awoke, and up an hour before being called; but dawdled three hours in dressing. When one subtracts from life infancy (which is vegetation),—sleep, eating, and swilling—buttoning and unbuttoning—how much remains of downright existence? The summer of a dormouse. Redde the papers and *tea*-ed and soda-watered, and found out that the fire was badly lighted. . . .

December 10.

I am ennuyé beyond my usual tense of that yawning verb, which I am always conjugating; and I don't find that society much mends the matter. I am too lazy to shoot myself—and it would annoy Augusta. . . .

December 14, 15, 16.

Much done, but nothing to record. It is quite enough to set down my thoughts,—my actions will rarely bear retrospection.

December 17, 18.

. . . Went to my box at Covent Garden to-night; and my delicacy felt a little shocked at seeing S * * *'s mistress (who, to my certain knowledge, was actually educated, from her birth, for her profession) sitting with her mother, "a three-piled b——d, b——d-Major to the Army," in a private box opposite. I felt rather indignant; but casting my eyes round the house in the next box to me, and the next, and the next, were the most distinguished old and young Babylonians of quality;—so I burst out a laughing. It was really odd; Lady * * divorced—Lady * * and her daughter, Lady * *, both divorceable—Mrs. * *, in the next the like and still nearer * * * * * *! What an assemblage to me, who know all their histories. It was as if the house had been divided between your public and your understood courtesans;— but the intriguantes much outnumbered the regular mercenaries. On the other side were only Polly and her mother, and, next box to her, three of inferior note. Now, where lay the difference between her and mamma, and Lady * * and daughter? except that the two last may enter Carleton and any other house, and the two first are limited to the opera and b—— house. How I do delight in observing life as it really is!—and myself, after all, the worst of any. . . .

Redde some Italian, and wrote two sonnets on * * *. I never wrote but one sonnet before, and that was not in earnest, and many years ago, as an exercise—and I will never write another. They are the most puling, petrifying, stupidly platonic compositions. I detest the Petrarch so much, that I would not be the man even to have obtained his Laura, which the metaphysical, whining dotard never could.

January 16, 1814.

. . . I am getting rather into admiration of [Lady Catherine Annesley]. . . . A wife would be my salvation. I am sure the wives of my acquaintances have hitherto done me little good. Catherine is beautiful, but very young, and, I think, a fool. . . . That she won't love me is very probable, nor shall I love her. But, on my system, and the modern system in general, that don't signify. The business (if it came to business) would probably be arranged between papa and me. She would have her own way; I am good-humoured to women, and docile; and, if I did not fall in love with her, which I should try to prevent, we should be a very comfortable couple. As to conduct, that she must look to. But if I love, I shall be jealous;—and for that reason I will not be in love. Though . . . I should like to have somebody now and then to yawn with one. . . .

February 18.

. . . Had a note from Lady Melbourne, who says, it is said I am "much out of spirits." I wonder if I really am or not? I have certainly enough of "that perilous stuff which weighs upon the heart," and it is better they should believe it to be the result of these attacks than of the real cause; but—ay, ay, always but to the end of the chapter. . . . I am now six-and-twenty; my passions have had enough to cool them; my affections more than enough to wither them—and yet—and yet—always yet and but—"Excellent well, you are a fishmonger—get thee to a nunnery." . . .

Midnight. Began a letter which I threw into the fire. Redde—but to little

purpose . . . smoked cigars. Napoleon!—this week will decide his fate. All
seems against him; but I believe and hope he will win—at least beat back
the invaders. What right have we to prescribe sovereigns to France? Oh for
a Republic! . . . I wonder how the deuce any body could make such a world;
for what purpose dandies, for instance, were ordained—and kings—and fellows of colleges—and women of "a certain age"—and many men of any age—
and myself, most of all! . . .

February 19.

. . . Went to Waite's. Teeth are all right and white; but he says that I
grind them in my sleep and chip the edges. That same sleep is no friend of
mine, though I court him sometimes for half the twenty-four.

February 27.

Here I am, alone, instead of dining at Lord H.'s, where I was asked,—but
not inclined to go anywhere. Hobhouse says I am growing a *loup garou,*—
a solitary hobgoblin. True;—"I am myself alone." . . . If I could always read,
I should never feel the want of society. . . . Heigho! I would I were in mine
island!—I am not well; and yet I look in good health. At times I fear, "I am
not in my perfect mind";—and yet my heart and head have stood many a
crash, and what should ail them now? They prey upon themselves, and I
am sick—sick—"Prithee, undo this button—why should a cat, a rat, a dog have
life—and *thou* no life at all?" Six-and-twenty years as they call them. . . .

March 17.

. . . What the devil had I to do with scribbling? It is too late to inquire,
and all regret is useless. But, an it were to do again,—I should write again, I
suppose. Such is human nature, at least my share of it;—though I shall think
better of myself, if I have sense to stop now. If I have a wife, and that wife
has a son—by any body—I will bring up mine heir in the most anti-poetical
way—make him a lawyer, or a pirate, or—any thing. But, if he writes, too, I
shall be sure he is none of mine, and cut him off with a Bank token. Must
write a letter—three o'clock.

April 8.

Out of town six days. On my return, found my poor little pagod, Napoleon,
pushed off his pedestal;—the thieves are in Paris. It is his own fault. Like
Milo, he would rend the oak; but it closed again, and now the beasts—lion,
bear, down to the dirtiest jackal—may all tear him. . . .

April 9.

I mark this day!
Napoleon Buonaparte has abdicated the throne of the world. . . . I don't
know—but I think *I*, even *I* (an insect compared with this creature), have

set my life on casts not a millionth part of this man's. But, after all, a crown may not be worth dying for. . . .

April 10.

I do not know that I am happiest when alone; but this I am sure of, that I never am long in the society even of *her* I love, (God knows too well, and the devil probably too,) without a yearning for the company of my lamp and my utterly confused and tumbled-over library. . . . To-day I have boxed an hour—written an ode to Napoleon Buonaparte—copied it—eaten six biscuits—drunk four bottles of soda water—redde away the rest of my time. . . .

April 19.

There is ice at both poles, north and south—all extremes are the same—misery belongs to the highest and the lowest only, to the emperor and the beggar, when unsixpenced and unthroned. There is, to be sure, a damned insipid medium—an equinoctial line—no one knows where, except upon maps and measurement.

> "And all our *yesterdays* have lighted fools
> The way to dusty death."

I will keep no further journal of that same hesternal torchlight; and, to prevent me from returning, like a dog, to the vomit of memory, I tear out the remaining leaves of this volume, and write in *Ipecacuanha*,—"that the Bourbons are restored! ! !"—"Hang up philosophy." To be sure, I have long despised myself and man, but I never spat in the face of my species before—"O fool! I shall go mad."

"And here was I, photographer, 'sportsman',
and blazing jackass . . ."

John Barrymore

Youngest of the Royal Family of the theatre, John Barrymore (1882–1942) grew up a handsome, undisciplined youth in a roistering world of pyrotechnic pride, temperament and tradition. After a brief Bohemian attempt at painting and cartooning, he reluctantly entered the theatre in 1909. Within ten years he was the most distinguished tragic actor in America. In 1922—when he had reached the pinnacle of his career in *Hamlet,* perhaps the most eloquent and flawless performance of the century—he collapsed in nervous and mental exhaustion.

Profligate of talent and time and energy, tortured by his own Hamlet-like weaknesses, Barrymore turned to Hollywood and lived out the remnants of a brilliant stage career in theatrical heroics, bitter mockery, and a pathetic burlesque of his own extraordinary talents.

But behind the elaborate masks he wore in public there sometimes could be seen glimpses of the agony which not even the talents of a Barrymore could hide. At intervals throughout his life there flared desperate attempts to recapture his own being, to escape the self-destruction he had contrived. Here is Barrymore as Barrymore—his most tragic rôle.

December 27, 1925.

Got away ten p.m. from Wilmington [on the eighty-foot cabin cruiser *The Gypsy,* bound for the southern tip of the Mexican peninsula of Lower California]. . . .

December 31. Leammon's Lagoon, Cerros Island.

Got home at dusk, to find big boat absolutely on her *ear.* Walking the deck was like an Alpine ascension. Speared a shark on the way in while walking in shallow water. Terribly hungry, ate dinner of lamb sandwiches and coffee, as Chef couldn't get into icebox on account of list. Sitting on floor, using wing of table off which to eat. . . . I must say sailors are amazing, and their point of view is peculiarly akin to my own. New Year's Eve meant nothing whatever in their lives. Any more than it does in mine. I have always been subconsciously embarrassed by the "function" of Christmas and New Years. The spirit of "loving kindness," that is presumed to come to a head like a boil once a year. . . . I wonder if there is any more pathetic evidence of the fatuity and childishness of mankind than the "New Year's Resolution"? . . . Must get up for geese at 3.30 a.m.

January 1, 1926.

Got off at four a.m. in dinghy, trailing skiff. Moon and stars still up. Lovely time of morning. Landed with skiff. Dawn came up beautifully about five. Couldn't get near geese. . . . Came back to *Gypsy* at ten a.m. Got stuck again about one p.m. Nothing to do but wait till tide gets us off. Saw huge turtle, went out and speared it, proving efficacy of small harpoon-like device. Pierced shell and held turtle for twenty minutes while getting it to boat. Made some very good shots with Mauser 30. Crazy about her, very powerful, beautiful mechanism. German sailors on board handled her like Pygmalion did Galatea, before she came to! . . . Crabbed, spending night on island, as intended doing. Bed awfully early.

January 3.

Funny little community of about six huts; must be as gay as the devil as a steady diet! Took moving pictures of pelicans, tame as possible, did everything but come on board to get fish. Pulled out about two p.m. Dined on turtle, fried, tasted like rabbit, very good. At night pretty rough, about a hundred small squid flew on deck, some going as high as pilot house. One I was holding, small one, bit me hard. Can imagine what honest to God devilfish must be like. . . .

January 4.

Saw whale being cut beside big boat. Officials out of Gilbert and Sullivan came on board. Usual drink, bunk, and cigars. Left like two Spanish grandees in preposterous little rowboat with two large flags. . . . Wireless government operator on board, *bel-homme,* with oily black mustache and meticulous English, very exhausting to listen to, as every word was like having a child, but he seemed so pleased with it one had to let him go!

Reading Pepys *Diary.* Not particularly pleased with it, although expected to be. Ran across delightful line in another book, a quotation from Renan. He says: "The man who has time enough to keep a private diary has never understood the immensity of the Universe." Am inclined to agree with him. . . . The devastating Mexican wireless operator, with the military hat, said that on the night of December thirty-first there was a dance, a fiesta at the school-house, at which thirty "charming girls" participated. I'd loved to have

seen them! There are about eighteen houses [in Magdalena], but the owners
do what they can to help the census, one lady having twenty sons! One
would like to know the husband's point of view, if he has any left! Bed early,
nine o'clock.

January 5.

Read book by one Ronald Firbank of whom I have never heard. Got it in
hectic quest for "reading matter" day before leaving Los Angeles. It is called
The Flower Beneath the Foot. . . . The first couple of lines, when judged
by the sort of railway-station perusal one inflicts on a volume in a book-shop,
with a taxicab and its mounting clock waiting outside, seemed amusing if
ultra-sophisticated. But I was completely unprepared for the epicene riot, the
super-civilized, arrant merry-go-round of all-around sportingness, this Beards-
leyesque duck indulges in! . . . It makes one feel blazingly and happily relaxed in the atmosphere of normality—fish, guns, California, et al.—after the
pale, liver-colored but pungent memories of Paris, Venice, God knows where,
Deauville, Chamonix . . . when one in the desperation of loneliness climbed
Mt. Blanc, with a taciturn and preposterous little person, whose passion was
mountain peaks, which he collected with his large nose pointed consistently
to the ground, the rocks and the snow; till the summit, when, after a short
rest, he went down the same way! Amazing! Exhausted as I was, and bewildered by my own trance-like pilgrimage, with an aspirin tablet rattling
'round in my stomach, and nothing else, I could still realize the beauty of a
dimension that I was never to see again, and knew it! But this small, archaic,
black-avised ass, with his Alpine button for which he risked his amoeba-like
life, scaled one blazing pinnacle of beauty after another, where the sun rises
underneath one and casts gigantic shadows of Celestial purple up over the
eye-splitting brilliance of the snow, like giant diamonds gone mad, or on a
bat with the spectrum. Reading that exotic pustule of a book, on this open
swinging sea, brought back the pathetic jackass-years of absurdity in Europe,
of my trying to make life with B. or her with me! This West of hicks and sun-
sets, if properly used, may be a spiritual bath that will mean never living
against one's own center again!

January 6.

Went on shore in extraordinary primitive dug-out boat "manned" by same
type of childish opera bouffe crew as have already encountered. Entirely unprepared for positive enchantment of place itself. Rode official's horse.
Buttercup-colored, like D'Artagnan's, with large retention of early beauty. In
the town itself [at Cape St. Lucas] one saw the most decorative, provocative,
enchanting little damned horses I have ever looked at, bred here. . . . George
Tomato, on hearing my name, after having asked it point-blank, slightly impressed although greatly bewildered by my peculiar exterior—khaki pants
full of old fish and older gravy, and Nat Wills beard—took me to his house
and introduced me to his wife, a native of the place itself. . . . Mounted
Rosinante, and ambled at peace with the world toward the setting sun and
the beach. Our purchases: five boxes of fresh tomatoes, an indigenous cheese,

some jerked venison, and several bottles of oddities to drink, on pack-mules trailing behind. . . .

January 7.

. . . We had brought, by the Grace of God, the moving-picture camera. Directly in front of us whales were spouting, many of them, and showing occasional black domes above the water. At last, not over a hundred yards in front of us, a whale shot up straight out of the sea, and flopped on its back with a gigantic burst of spray—then right back to wave its long black, shiny flukes in the air. Over and over again this happened as we crept nearer, if a launch can creep! The Cap taking pictures all the time. . . . The cove we are anchored in is peaceful and silent, with strange, fantastic, jagged rocks rearing out of the sea like gnomes' castles, one sinuous, slender one, like a cyclops' forefinger, with a pelican's nest perched rakishly on the top of it. The very end of California, bleak and beautiful, like a sword-point breaking through the scabbard of the hills in back. . . . *Nota bene!* As an evidence that I am getting either very pure or very dull, I forgot entirely to remark that the whales mentioned were in amorous dalliance when photographed (if anything so enviably and titanically active comes under the head of dalliance!) but be that as it may, we eavesdropped, and I trust, for the stimulus of one's old age, recorded the largest mammals *in flagrante delicto*. A memorable day.

January 8.

O day of days! O song of songs! O Jesus, Mary and Joseph, and all points going south! Today I caught my first unbelievable Marlin swordfish, landing him in thirty minutes. Weight one hundred and eighty-five pounds. Seven and one-half feet long, seventeen inches deep, measured properly. . . .

January 9.

Early to bed, looking at the billions of stars that make the strange soft black sky look almost over-dressed to anyone who has had the damnable misfortune to have lived in sophisticated communities. . . . What in the name of God I have been doing in this maelstrom of fourteen years I cannot imagine. It has been like some strange form of bombastic levitation. I seem finally to have been permitted to be loosened, and light on the sand, instead of on a spike! like Sinbad dropped from the Roc! . . . Maybe some lobsters have escaped from the lobster-pot with scratches that heal, with their actual organs unimpaired! Impervious or crustacean, I don't know which, but something, *something* terribly young, terribly strong and vital, and fairly lost as yet, is inside. It is looking at and snorting tiny, whimsical, and frightfully needful exhortations to that big evening star, that I've never noticed before till this time . . . it only seemed to start to get big, not so very long ago!

January 11.

Clementine [his small monkey] put her long, little, black, leathery fore-finger in the ink and showed me how to write! I'm afraid it will take her some time. She is at the moment flirting with me shamelessly from the bath-tub spigots where she is tied for the night. As I am blissfully in bed after a lazy day in the sun, as I write this at seven p.m. the bathroom door is open to keep her company. . . . The reassuring thing about Clementine is that one knows *definitely* that she is fond of one, as she proves it so extraordinarily and unequivocally! She clutches one with her little black hands and buries her little white soft nose . . . in one's neck and won't let go. . . . Outside through the porthole, there is heard the intermittent lap of the waves on the beach, like lace in the utter stillness, punctuated by little happy grunts from Clementine, who is going to sleep with her finger in her mouth.

January 12.

. . . Got a mammoth strike rounding the rocks on the way home. Played him in the dusk, but he tore loose the jig I was using, a makeshift combina-tion of rags and feathers, that thank God I lost in a few minutes. I should have known better than to troll again at that hour; but the Cap, who is jejune, said, in the voice the pudding used to Alice, "Go ahead." So against my better judgment I did, and, Wham! almost at once, almost to a certainty a shark, and at that hour. I played the bastard till seven o'clock and cut him loose when I felt the double line on the reel, particularly as there were hints from the gallant Captain, whose soul at the moment was with a succulent dish called *Chepine,* a fish-chowder one of the sailors made for supper to-night.

January 13.

Mac is the tallest person I've almost ever seen . . . an *excellent* cook. He drapes his slim and sinuous person, half in the galley and half in the "saloon" while I eat. We talk about food, and various matters, some approaching profundity, some not coming within a mile of it. He is a cheery and equable elongation, pallid, chinless, and very nice indeed. He started to grow a mus-tache but thought better of it, why, I cannot imagine—has gone ashore for the evening (I have never written a sentence more like Henry James!) leav-ing me—(Good God I'm still *at it*) with a glass of anisette, *excellent,* too, at my elbow, and this manuscript! which I hope I am writing in English. One of the sailors caught a diverting looking fish today over the side. It has a bright yellow tail and spots all over it. It is called the Quarantine Fish. I think it is a dramatic critic, except that it has no horn glasses.

January 18.

This afternoon went on to the point. Heavy surf, difficult to land, took cameras. . . . Decided to climb over high rocks and get to caves that way.

Had, on the whole, what would come under the head of a diverting experience. Got three-quarters of the way up with heavy Graflex camera tied around neck, hanging down back, weighing needless to say a ton by that time. "Bruno," the German sailor, who, it turned out later, used to be a "steeplejack," gave out, not being on *his* vacation; and went back, and he cameraless! Got to a place about ninety feet up (like Mt. Blanc, the first day). It seemed impossible to go either one way or the other, up or back. . . . The pieces of rock I tried tentatively broke off like plaster; the entire damned thing being formed of some kind of sandy granite, and as old as the hills first formed by volcanic eruptions from the sea. And here was I, photographer, "sportsman," and blazing jackass, spread like some heraldic lizard on the lonesomest rock in the Pacific Ocean, with nothing between me and dissolution, in an extremely unpleasant and jellified form, but a gradually atrophying big toe. One thought of prayer came, one must confess, but . . . I couldn't expect any reasonable God to imagine I had any respect for His sense of fitness, if I flung Him a strangled prayer under such conditions, having been in the habit of doing so, so very *little*. I *have* done it, and always tried to be fairly on the level in the performance. I don't remember ever quite indulging in that deliciously naive rhapsody of Louis XI's "Just *one* more *little* murder, dear, dear God—and we'll call it square!" Meanwhile, as I was beginning to sink, something had to be done. I noticed a tiny jutting edge of that filthy fakey rock—that looked as solid as the one Peter built his church on—and that fell to smithereens the moment one actually depended on it, about level with my waist.

If I could get poor old George Toe into *that,* I'd be nearer by a couple of feet to a beautiful saddle-like resting place that would be either the last thing I would objectively see on this odd planet, or a memory transcribed in this nautical *Book of Hours.* I placed the sweating palms and the prehensile fingers on the bland and bulbous forehead of that poxed and passive peak, and heaved. The only thing in God's world that stood at that moment between Papa and Infinity was that *one* effort, and it had to be done. I remember distinctly, as I was doing it, being rather grateful that I was far less like a human being at that moment than I was like a monkey with a dash of octopus—otherwise I never would have survived.

I got, not the toe, but the *knee* in that blessed but painfully temporary sanctuary, and hung. Something, rock or sweat, I don't know which, *gave* slightly, and one felt a sensation not so much of fright as extraordinary lightness and breathlessness—like levitation. . . . Precisely what muscles and movements *made* that ledge—I naturally cannot tell. . . . All I know is that there I was, safe for the moment, with that damned camera, like an albatross, the symbol of a preposterous but plausible profession, heavy, heavy, round my neck. . . . I stood up, by that time inured to acrobatics, on the knife-blade of Chaos, and took some photographs of it. Inasmuch as it had pretty nearly put me on the blink, it seemed reasonable that the camera should be utilized before we both were amalgamated into one unctuous mass of ground glass and movie actor at the memorable (for twenty minutes: the first edition headline: "Distinguished Tragedian Falls to Death while Walking Cliff in Drunken Stupor!") juncture of some Mexican crevasse.

Meanwhile, to add to the "gaiety of nations" (I never knew till last night,

by the way, reading Boswell, where that particular expression originated)
t was getting much rougher below. I put the black things one tears out
(when one remembers it!) after a picture is taken, in a niche in the rocks—
nore out of bravado combating nausea than anything else, and scratched
with my fishing knife a "J" for jackass as deeply as I could in the scabrous
rock. I then prepared—without gusto—to descend. Bruno had evolved the
idea of throwing me a leaded line, by means of which I could unburden
myself of the child, "Graflex." After repeated efforts, all well-meant, he finally
scraped the cerebellum with one desperate heave, on which the jaded in-
cumbent lashed [it]. . . . Then there was some haggard shouting anent
throwing me up a rope; but I made a mental reservation that this would not
only be slightly degrading but it would also be unfeasible. So I decided nobly
to come down as I came up. . . . Anyway, that's that. It's taken a deal of
footage in the telling. It will be amusing to read maybe in the years, as a
photograph however badly taken and exposed, of certain sensation. It will
also be bound to be relaxing to read any literary endeavor of one's own when
one isn't used to the medium. It will be a little, I imagine, like "Lasca, down
by the Rio Grande," recited after dinner at an otherwise inoffensive party,
by the younger son, who is a champion quoit thrower.

January 19.

[At Mazatlán] I wandered entirely unprepared into what seemed a vision
of the past—a high, cool, scrupulous bar, presided over by angels in white,
real bartenders with linen coats, affable exterior, everything. Two excellent
English cock-fighting prints on the wall and the inevitable stoutish nude lady
stepping over a brook, whose name used to be legion in the old days. I stood
hat in hand in the sanctified twilight of that spacious and cleanly haven, like
a good Catholic would in a cathedral on his return from arid and heathen
ports; and, after the proper genuflexion, ordered a glass of beer. It was hotter
than blazes outside, real tropical, depleting heat. Here, within that exquisitely
appointed grot, all was peace and zephyrous coolness. The beer arrived—
draft beer—in a tall, thin, clean crystal of Grecian proportions, with a creamy
bead on it. I tasted it. . . . The planets seemed to pause a moment in their
circling to breathe a benediction on that Mexican brewer's head. . . . Then
the universe went on its wonted way again. Hot Dog! But that *was* a glass
of beer!

5. DECIPHERED FROM A FADING SCRIPT

"What must the trout have thought . . ."

Ki no Tsurayuki

One of the oldest of diaries, perhaps the oldest of all that survive, is that of Ki no Tsurayuki (?–946), Japanese nobleman, poet and diplomat who was governor of the province of Tosa on Shikoku Island, just south of Hiroshima, from 930 to 935. In his *Tosa Nikki,* or Tosa Diary, he tells of his homeward journey by sea to Kyoto at the end of his governorship.

The vessel in which Ki no Tsurayuki embarked was probably a large, hollowed-out log, some forty feet long and five feet in width, propelled by oars with the aid of a single crude paper sail. It took 55 days for his craft to go 200 miles, in a voyage then considered difficult and hazardous through seas swept by unfavourable winds, prowled by pirates, ranged by unfriendly fates and furies.

The diarist is esteemed by his countrymen as a writer of major importance. An anthology of poetry he helped to compile is still read. His own writings are cherished as felicitous examples of the ancient Japanese style. Even those who must read him in translation can scarcely fail to savour his dry wit, engaging self-deprecation, and ready acceptance of days happily becalmed with good company, good food, and good drink.

The Tosa Diary is written in the third person, as were most diaries in all countries until four or five centuries later. (The first diarist to venture boldly on the use of the pronoun "I" remains obscure.) The translator has put within quotation marks some of the author's oblique references to himself, but the narration scarcely requires such an aid.

Tsurayuki can be seen, as in an ancient tapestry with colours still vivid after the passage of nine hundred years, an intrepid seafarer setting forth through strange, threatening and unfathomed waters, alert to the sounds, sights and smells they hold for him—and ready, this sensitive voyager, with brush and ink, to write it all down for those snugly at home in following centuries.

From *The Tosa Diary*, by Ki no Tsurayuki, translated by William N. Porter. Reprinted by permission of The Clarendon Press, Oxford.

January 28, 935.

One year on the twenty-first day of the twelfth month "a certain personage" left home at the Hour of the Dog (8.0 p.m.) which was the beginning of this modest record. He had just completed the usual period of four or five years as Governor of a Province; everything had been wound up, documents, &c., had been handed over, and now he was about to go down to the place of embarkation; for he was to travel on shipboard. All sorts of people, both friends and strangers, came to see him off, including many who had served him faithfully during the past years, and who sorrowed at the thought of losing him that day. There was endless bustle and confusion; and so with one thing and another the night drew on.

January 29.

He prayed for a calm voyage to the Land of Izumi. . . . Upper, middle, and lower classes all drank too heavily. . . .

January 30.

A certain man, called Yagi no Yasunori . . . openly made him a farewell present. Perhaps he had not made a very good Governor; but still, the country-folk usually on an occasion like this just said good-bye, and then disappeared; and here was a kind heart which was not ashamed to come back again. This word of praise for him is not due to the present he brought!

January 31.

The Chief Priest made him a farewell present; and accordingly everybody, high and low, got . . . intoxicated. . . .

February 1.

A written invitation arrived from Government House, asking him to go and call. He accordingly went to call; and, what with one thing and another all day and all night passed away pleasantly, till at last the day broke.

February 2.

Still at Government House, where the entertainment grew boisterous; the host and even the servants became uproarious. With loud voices Chinese poems were declaimed. . . .

February 4.

They set out rowing from Urato and made for Ōminato, where Yamaguchi no Chiminé, the son of a former Governor, came with *saké* and good things to eat, which he put aboard the boat. There will be plenty to eat and drink during the voyage!

February 6.

Still they remained at the same place. The *byakusan* [food gift] had been placed for safe-keeping during the night in the ship's cabin; but the wind which is usual at this time of year got up and blew it all into the sea. They had nothing left to drink, no potatoes, no seaweed and no rice-cakes; the neighbourhood could supply nothing of this kind, and so their wants could not be satisfied. They could do nothing more than suck the head of a trout. What must the trout have thought of everybody sucking it in turn! . . .

February 8.

In the same place. I wonder if the wind and waves had a tender feeling for him, as they seemed to wish to delay him for some time? He certainly had no tender feeling for them!

February 14.

They set out from Ōminato the first thing in the morning and rowed on. . . . Those who remained upon the sea-shore grew further and further away, and they in their turn could no longer see those in the boat; from the shore they could not speak to the ship, and if the ship called to them, it was all in vain. . . . After this they passed the pine forest of Uta. I know not how many pine trees there were there, nor for how many thousand years they had lived. The ripples lapped against the foot of each, and amid the branches of each the storks flitted about. . . . As he could no longer distinguish east from west, he left all thought about the weather to the steersman. Those of the men who were unused to the sea began to feel gloomy and pensive, while the women laid their heads upon the bottom of the boat and cried aloud. . . .

February 20.

This day no rice and bean gruel was cooked, and, as it was an unlucky day, they crawled slowly along, much to his regret. To-day the voyage had already lasted more than twenty days, and they were but as so many days wasted. . . .

February 23.

They were still at the same spot. As long as the sea remains rough they will never get there. This stopping-place was very beautiful, whether looked at from afar or close at hand; but under the present conditions they all too weary to take any pleasure in it. In order to pass the time, as it was hopeless to expect the boat to start, the men composed classical verses, &c., together. . . .

February 26.

The boat set forth about the Hour of the Hare (6.0 a.m.). Many other boats started as well, and the sight seemed to him like autumn leaves scattered upon the sea, although it was spring time. There was no breath of wind—no doubt in answer to their prayers for haze—and the sun was shining brightly as they set out rowing. . . . Some birds called blackbirds were clustered upon the cliffs, and at the foot of these cliffs the waves were breaking into foam. The steersman remarked, "Under the blackbirds the white waves are breaking!" These words, whatever they might be worth, sounded remarkable, and, as he had never met a man like that before, he was much struck with them. At these words and while still travelling on, he who was "the passenger" noticed the waves and remembered that the pirates had threatened to take revenge upon him, when once he had left the Province; all his hair turned white, when the waves once more became rough. Seventy or eighty years are what one must expect at sea! . . .

March 2.

The ship's officers said the north wind was unfavourable, so the boat did not start. There were many reports going about that the pirates were actually in pursuit!

March 3.

Can this really be true? As they say the pirates are in chase, the boat is not to start before midnight, and offerings are to be made while rowing. The steersman accordingly offered prayer-papers, and, as they fluttered away to the east, he prayed, "Graciously allow our gallant ship to be rowed with all speed in the direction taken by these prayer-papers." . . .

March 4.

The wind blew, the waves were rough, and the boat could not start. They were all complaining dreadfully; so the men, to cheer up their hearts, composed a Chinese poem. . . .

March 7.

The wind and rain had stopped; and so, hearing that the pirates never travel by night, the boat set out to cross the Awa Channel at midnight. . . .

March 8.

Rain fell in the morning, and stopped only at the Hour of the Horse (noon). Passing through the Sea of Izumi, they rowed on. Just as yesterday no wind-tossed waves were visible at sea. They passed the pine forest on Black Head. The name of the headland was black, the colour of its pines green, the breakers upon the shore white as snow, and the tint of its shells pink. . . . "The passenger" spoke lamenting that (the voyage) had lasted into this month, and for the many hardships they had endured, to which the others agreed. Out of the fullness of his heart he recited this: "Though the days in spring grow as long as is the rope used to tow our boat, forty days we've spent,—maybe fifty days upon the sea." People who hear this will say to themselves that this kind of stuff is very poor. But "the passenger" produced it with a good deal of difficulty and thought it pretty good; so they should stop whispering such cruel things about it. But suddenly the wind and waves got up, and so they had to stop talking.

March 17.

There was something wrong and they did not go forward.

March 23.

. . . As he went up to the Capital, he saw in the shops the little boxes painted with pictures and the rice-cakes twisted into the shape of conch shells just the same as ever. . . . After this, on the road to the Capital, many people, and not necessarily his own relations entertained him at Shimasaka. . . . On reaching his home and entering his door, the moon was so bright that he could see the state of things at a glance. Needless to say the whole place was hopelessly overgrown and ragged, even more than he had been told! . . . Well, that evening he determined he would not speak about it in a loud tone of voice; and, though he felt very angry, he had to make some sort of acknowledgement. Then, again, the ground had sunk and was full of water, as if it was a pond. There was a pine tree close by, and it had overgrown in five or six years, as if in a thousand years; half its branches were dead, and the young growing ones all in confusion. Almost everything was the same, and everybody offered him their sympathy. He recalled especially how his little daughter had been born in that house, in its beloved interior; how sad it was that [because of her death] she had not returned with them! The sailors and others were talking loudly as they embraced their children, and just then his grief was more than he could bear. . . . His sorrows which he can never forget, are more than he can ever express. Well, well,—this must be torn up at once.

"—Some of these ffoolerys are requisite . . ."

Celia Fiennes

Just nine years before Sarah Kemble Knight began her horseback journey through the New England countryside, Celia Fiennes climbed into a sidesaddle and set out in 1695 to wander through Old England. Both were sharply observant and keenly interested in whatever was noteworthy about the places to which their horses trotted them; both often deplored what they discovered ("I was much pleased wth my supper," says Celia Fiennes of a night spent in Cornwall, "tho' not with the Customs of the Country wch is a universall smoking, both men, women and children have all their pipes of tobacco in their mouths and soe sit round the fire smoaking wch was not delightfull to me . . ."); both had the courage to defy conventions that kept other members of their sex from venturing out to see the world for themselves.

But here resemblance lessens. Madame Knight was of humble origin while Madame Fiennes was a member of one of England's ancient noble families. She was the sister of the third Viscount Saye and Sele; her ancestor, Lord Saye, Treasurer of Henry VI., was the first court official Jack Cade beheaded in the rebellion of 1450. Her social position opened all doors to her, even those of the moated castles of William and Mary whose intimate fittings she describes with relish.

Celia Fiennes had a mission. She sought to persuade her contemporaries that there were as interesting sights to be seen in their own country as any to be found on the continent where it was then the fashion to travel. To prove her point she journeyed on horseback as many as 1,500 miles in a single summer, compiling as she went along a sort of running guide book interspersed with reports of road and weather conditions and a shrewd, tart commentary on the follies of man. Her diary was written from day to day as she rode along. However, as with many of the diaries of the time, her entries were not dated.

Celia Fiennes' account of English life at the end of the seventeenth century, in itself quaint and delightful, provides important information about many things of which there is no other record.

From *The Minde's Delight,* published by The Cayme Press.

She was a good reporter, if not skilled as an author. Aware of this, she warns: "As most I converse with knows both the ffreedom & Easyness I speak & write as well as my defect in all, so they will not expect exactness or politeness in this book, tho' such Embellishments might have adorned the descriptions and suited the nicer taste."

Summer, 1695. Undated.

Drawing Room of State, Windsor.

The Cannopy & throne & ye part behind is all green velvet Richly Embroyder'd with silver & Gold, of high Emboss'd work. . . . The Cannopy was so rich and curled up & in some places so ffull it Looked very Glorious, & was newly made to give audience to the Ffrench Embassadour to shew ye Grandeur & Magnificence of the British Monarch—some of these ffoolerys are requisite sometymes to Create admiration & regard to keep up the state of a kingdom and nation.

Lord Exeter's House, near Stamford.

Very fine paint in pictures, but they were all without Garments or very little, that was the only fault, the immodesty of ye Pictures, Especially in My Lord's Appartment.

Wilton.

A Grottoe is att ye end of the garden just ye middle off ye house—its garnished with many fine ffigures of ye Goddesses, and about 2 yards off the doore is severall pipes in a line that with a sluice spoutts water up to wett the strangers—in the middle roome is a round table and a large Pipe in the midst, on which they put a Crown or Gun or a branch, and yt spouts the water through ye Carvings and poynts all round ye roome at ye Artists pleasure to wet ye Company—there are figures at Each corner of ye roome that Can weep water on the beholders and by a straight pipe on ye table they force up ye water into ye hollow carving of ye rooff like a Crown or Coronet to appearance but is hollow within to retaine ye water fforced into it in great quantetyes yt disperses in ye hollow Cavity over ye roome and descends in a Shower of raine all about ye roome—on each side is two little roomes which by the turning their wires ye water runnes in ye rockes—you see and hear it and also it is so contrived in one roome yt it makes ye melody of Nightingerlls and all sorts of birds wch engages ye Curiosity of ye Strangers to go in to see, but at ye Entrance off each room is a line of pipes that appear not till by a Sluce moved—it washes ye spectators designed for diversion.

Hampton Court.

Thence into a Dressing-roome hung with Divers Coulld flowered sattin, chaires and stooles the same, ffine fflower'd muslin window curtaines, A fine

Little high screen burnt jappan of 4 Leaves, another Chimney screen wth 4 leaves of the stone work in ffigures—indian. Out of this was ye Queens Closet just over Prince Georges but y^t was Locked. The other side was a little waiting roome to Just such marble seates of Easem^t wth the sluces of water as that below was in the Queen's bed Chamber. . . .

The Bath [in Somerset].

The third bath is called the Cross bath wch is some thing bigger than the former and not so hot; the Cross in the middle has seates round it for ye Gentlemen to sitt, and round the walls are Arches wth seates for the Ladyes, all stone and the seate is stone and if you thinke the seate is too Low they raise it with a Coushon as they call it, another stone, but indeed the water bears you up that ye seate seemes as easy as a down Coushon. Before the Arch the Ladyes use to have a laced toilet hung up on the top of the Arch and so to shelter their heads even to the water if they please. You Generally sit up to the Neck in water, this Cross bath is much the Coolest and it is used mostly in ye heate of summer; there are Gallery's round ye top that ye Company that does not Bathe that day walkes in and lookes over into ye bath on their acquaintance and company—there are such a number of Guides to each bath of women to waite on ye ladyes, and of men to wait on the Gentlemen, and they keepe their due distance. There is a serjeant belonging to ye baths that all the bathing tyme walkes in galleryes and takes notice order is observed and punishes ye rude, and most people of fashion send to him when they begin to bathe, then he takes particular Care of them and Complements you every morning wch deserves its reward at ye end of the Season. . . . The Ladyes goes into the bath with Garments made of a fine yellow canvas, which is stiff and made large with great sleeves like a parsons gown; the water fills it up so that its borne off that your shape is not seen, it does not cling close as other linning, which Lookes sadly in the poorer sort that go in their own linning. The Gentlemen have drawers and wastcoates of the same sort of canvas, this is the best linning, for the bath water will change any other yellow . . . the pump is in one of these galleryes at ye King's bath which ye Company drinks of, its very hot and tastes like ye water y^t boyles Eggs, has such a smell, but ye nearer ye pumpe you drinke it, ye hotter and less offencive and more spiriteous. . . .

> ## "*Personal charms are as nothing if the hart is not good & virtuous . . .*"

Marjory Fleming

Among those who lived at 1 North Charlotte Street, Edinburgh, in the winter of 1808, were two kittens, two turtle doves, one hawk, six canaries, two green linnets, one thrush, one dog named "Help" and one plump little girl, minus a baby tooth or two, named Marjory Fleming (1803–1811). She was just six years old. When the birds and animals could spare her attention she occupied herself by putting down an account of the day's happenings in the ruled pages of her copybooks. The habit of diary-keeping, thus begun, continued until the end of her life—unhappily, only three years away. What she wrote in the 154 pages she filled in those years promises to last as long as diaries are read. Since the manuscript was accidentally discovered among family papers a century ago, Marjory has won fame and a host of admirers, among them Scott, Stevenson and Swinburne. She is the youngest person to have her biography included in the many thick volumes of the *Dictionary of National Biography*, the youngest writer to receive mention in textbooks of English literature and the encyclopedias, the youngest—well, Marjory's distinctions are numerous, and she herself was unique.

The daughter of James Fleming and his wife, Isabella Rae, Marjory was born in Kircaldy, a town on the northern shore of Scotland's Firth of Forth. She was a precocious child, taught to read at an early age, and apparently allowed to range at will through whatever books caught her fancy. She devoured *Tom Jones, Mother Goose,* Isaac Newton and the lurid tales of crime contained in *The Newgate Calendar*. Hints of this odd curriculum for a child of six or seven can be found in her diary, sandwiched between her own thoughts and the echoed words of adults around her.

Family tradition tells that she had a close acquaintance with one adult in particular. She is pictured as spending much time on Sir Walter Scott's knee reciting Shakespeare, and gravely teaching him nursery and counting-out rhymes which he pro-

From *The Complete Marjory Fleming*, edited by Frank Sidgwick. Reprinted by permission of Sidgwick & Jackson, Ltd.

fessed to find difficult to learn. ("Wonery, twoery, tickery, seven; alibi, crackaby, ten and eleven; pin, pan, musky dan . . ."). Plausibility is lent the story by her own admission, impossible to deny, that she was a "loveress" of men.

John Brown, a mid-nineteenth century Edinburgh physician and author of the much-loved children's book *Rab and His Friends,* was the first to print her diary. Unfortunately, he accompanied it with a commentary thick-smeared with sticky sentiment. It turned Mark Twain's stomach when he read it, but he was one of many who were quick to see a delightful child under the gluey overcoating. "She was made out of thunder-storm and sunshine," Twain wrote, "and not even her little perfunctory pieties and shop-made holinesses could squelch her spirits or put out her fires for long. Under pressure of a pestering sense of duty she heaves a shovelful of trade godliness into her journals every little while, but it does not offend, for none of it is her own . . ."

Marjory is remembered as a poet as well as a diarist. Her elegy on the death of three bubbly-jocks (turkeys, in Scots vernacular) is one of her triumphs:

> Three turkeys fair their last have breathed,
> And now this world forever leaved;
> Their father, and their mother too,
> They sigh and weep as well as you;
> Indeed, the rats their bones have cranched,
> Into eternity theire launched.
> A direful death indeed they had,
> As wad put any parent mad;
> But she was more than usual calm,
> She did not give a single dam.

The portions of Marjory Fleming's diary given here open at Braehead, a country village near Edinburgh, where the six-year-old Marjory was visiting and shed her tears for these deceased bubbly-jocks. They are reproduced, line for line, exactly as they were written, from a facsimile of the manuscripts. Isabella, sometimes Isa, is her cousin, companion and tutor in "simecolings" and "commoes."

Shortly after Marjory's last entry she fell ill with measles, and died, not yet nine years old, of a more severe illness that followed.

1810. Summer. Braehead, Scotland.

*. . . The Day of my existence here has been delightful & enchanting. On Saturday I expected no less than three well made Bucks the names of whom is here advertised M*r*. Geo Crakey and W*m* Keith and J*n* Keith, the first is the funniest of every one of them Mr. Crakey & I walked to Crakyhall han*

by hand in Innocence and
matitation sweet thinking
on the kind love which
flows in our tenderhearted
mind which is overflow-
ing with majestick pleasure
nobody was ever so polite
to me in the hole state
of my existence.
Mr Craky you must
know is a great Buck &
pretty goodlooking

I am at Ravelston
enjoying natures fresh air
the birds are singing
sweetly the calf doth
frisk and play and
nature shows her glorious
face. the sun shines
through the trees, it is delightful.

July 12.

I confess that I have been
more like a little young
Devil then a creature for
when Isabella went up
the stairs to teach me religion and my multi-
plication and to be good
and all my other lessons
I stamped with my feet
and threw my new hat
which she made on the
ground and was sulky an
was dreadfuly passionate
but she never whiped me
but gently said Marjory
go into another room and
think what a great crime
you are committing
letting your temper
git the better of you
but I went so sulkely that
the Devil got the better of me. . . .
Yesterday I behave extremely
ill in Gods most holy church

for I would never attand myself nor let Isabella attand
which was a great crime for
she often tells me that when
to or three are geathered together God is in the midst of
them and it was the very
same Divel that tempted
Job that tempted me I am
sure but he resisted satan
though he had boils and
many many other mis-
fortunes which I have es-
caped.—
I am now going to tell you
about the horible and wretched
plaege that my multiplication
gives me you cant concieve it—
the most Devilish thing is 8 times 8
& 7 times 7 it is what nature itselfe
cant endure. . . .

I will walk to Craky-hall wich puts
me In mind
that I walked to that delightfull
place with a delightfull
young man beloved by all his
friends and espacialy by
me his loveress but I must not
talk any longer about hin
for Isa said it is not
proper for to speak of gentalman
but I will never forget him
I hope that at 12 or 13 years old
I will be as learned as Miss Isa
and Nancy Keith for many
girls have not the advan-
tage I have and I am very very
glad that satan has not geven me boils and many other
Misfortunes, in the holy bible these
words are written that the
Devel goes about like a roaring
lyon in search of his pray
but the lord lets us escape from
him but we sometimes do
not strive with this au-
full spirit.
To Day I pronunced a

word which should never
come out of a ladys lips it was
that I caled John a Impu-
dent Bitch and Isabella afterwards
told me that I should never say
it. . . . What I think
made me in so bad a homo-
ur is I got 1 or 2 cups of that
bad bad sina tea to Day

Last night I behaved extremely ill and threw my
work in the stairs and
would not pick it up
which was very wrong
indeed; and all that
William could do I would
not go out of the room
till he himself put me out and I
roared like a bull and would
not go to bed though
Isabella bid me go
which was very wrong. . . .

Ravelston is a fine place
because I got balm wine
and many other dainties
and it is extremely pleasant
to me by the company of swine
geese cocks &c and they are the delight of my heart.
I was at a race to Day &
liked it very much but we missed
one of the starts which was very
provoaking indeed but I cannot help it so I must not complain lord Mongumorys
horse gained it but I am clat-
tering so I will turn the subject
to another think;—but no I
must git my spelling first
I acknowledge that this page is
far from being well written
Isabella teaches me my
lessons from ten till two every
day and I wonder she is
not tired to death with me
for my part I would
be quite Impatient if I
had a child to teach. . . .

This is Saturday, & I
am very glad of it, be-
cause I have play
half of the Day, & I get
mony too, but alas I
owe Isabella 4 pence
for I am finned 2 pence
whenever I bite my nails
Isa is teaching me
to make Simecolings nots
of interrigations peorids & commoes &c; . . .

Now I am quite
happy for I am going
tomorrow to a delightfull
place, Braehead by name,
belonging to Mrs Crra-
ford, where their is ducks
cocks hens bublyjocks 2 dogs
2 cats & swine. & which is
delightful; I think
it is shoking to think
that the dog & cat
should bear them &
they are drowned after all
I would rather have
a man dog then a
women dog because they
do not bear like women
dogs, it is a hard case
it is shoking;—
I came here as
I thought to enjoy na-
tures delightful breath
it is sweeter than
a fial of rose Oil
but Alas my hopes
are dissoopinted, it is always spitring but then
I often get a blink
& than I am hap-
py. . . .

I am going to turn
over a new life &
am going to be a very
good girl & be obedient
to Isa Keith,
here there is planty of

goosberys which makes
my teath watter;
Yesterday there was campony
Mr & Mrs Bonner
& Mr Philip Caddle
who paid no little attention
to me he took my hand
and led me down
stairs & shook my
hand cordialy. . . .

Love I think is in the fasion for
every body is marring there
is a new novel published nam-
ed selfcontroul a very good
maxam forsooth Yesterday
a marrade man named Mr
John Balfour Esqe offered
to kiss me, & offered to marry
me though the man was es-
pused, & his wife was present, &
said he must ask her per-
mision but he did not I
think he was ashamed or con-
founded before 3 gentelman
Mr Jobson & two Mr Kings. . . .

The Mercandile Afares
are in a perilious situ-
ation, sickness & a delicate
frame I have not &
I do not know what
it is but Ah me perhaps
I shall have it, Grandure
reagns in London & in
Edinburgh there are a great
many balls & routs but
none here.—The childish
distempers are very
frequent just now. . . .

The weather is very mild
& serene & not like winter
A sailor called here to say
farewell, it must be dread-
full to leave his native country
where he might get a wife

or perhaps me, for I love
him very much & wth
all my heart, but O I
forgot Isabella forbid me to
speak about love.—A great
many bals & routs are geven
this winter & the last winter
too. . . . love is a very
papithatick thing as well as
troubelsom & tiresome but O
Isabella forbid me to speak
about it.—General Grame
has defeted the Franch the Franch
prisoners have made a tumbling
and my cosin says it is very
neat I heard that they made night-
caps of there blankets and bows to
make them smart and shewy
My cosins are sober and well behaved
and very gentele and meak.—I
study writing & counting & deferent
accomplishments. . . .
This is a very windy stor-
my day and looks as if it was
going to snow or rain but it is
only my opinion which is
not always correct. . . .
I think the price of a pine-
apple is yery dear for I here
it is a whole bright goulden
geinie
that might have sustained a
poor family a whole week and
more. . . .
Isabella this morning taught me
some Franch words one of which
is bon suar the interpretation
is good morning.—I like sermons
better than lectures.—Joy depends
on thou O virtue!.—Tom Jones &
Greys Elegey in a country Church
yard are both excelent & much
spoke of by both sex particularly
by the men. Personal charms
are as nothing if the hart is
not good & virtuous. . . .

". . . a letter, a keg of prunes, a Rosary . . ."

The Jesuit Fathers

The Society of Jesus, whose members are commonly called Jesuits, is the largest religious order of the Catholic Church. It was founded in 1534 by St. Ignatius of Loyola and one of its chief concerns has always been the establishment of foreign missions. Bound together by vows of poverty, chastity and soldierly obedience to higher authority, Jesuits have no home; traditionally the whole world has been their parish.

In the days when the frontiers of the world were being rapidly pushed back, Jesuit missionaries and educators hastened to each newly opened land to do battle for the minds and souls of those subjugated or subdued by advancing generals and trains of settlers that followed. While not always in favor either within the Church or without, there were able explorers among the Jesuits, (Marquette and Clavigero, for example), brave martyrs, and brilliant students of the sciences who did much to advance knowledge of astronomy, geology, botany and geography.

Canada, at first called New France, was opened to settlement under French rule at the beginning of the seventeenth century, and the first mission of the Jesuits was stationed in Acadia in 1611. Not long afterwards a residence and general headquarters was set up in Quebec. The "black robes," as the Indians called the Jesuit fathers, were especially successful in their missions to the Huron and Iroquois tribes; they boldly ranged ever farther westward into the depths of the American continent.

Meanwhile it seemed desirable to record what was taking place inside the Jesuit enclave of Quebec. To meet this need the superior of the order began to keep a journal. In it he put down a private reckoning of daily happenings at the residence during the years between 1645 and 1668. It was a convenient way to make note of occurrences that might otherwise be forgotten when the time came to submit reports to the provincial of the order across the sea. This detailed journal, of which only a tiny portion can be sampled here, brings glimpses, still fresh, zestful and vivid, of

Reprinted by permission of The Vanguard Press from *The Jesuit Relations and Allied Documents*, edited by Edna Kenton. Copyright, 1954, by The Vanguard Press.

a religious way of life three centuries ago. Careful count is taken
of candlesticks, gifts given and received, pigeons, masses and other
matters of housekeeping concern. One can almost see the per-
plexed author shaking his head over administrative problems;
what to do about the too elaborately dressed bread a parishioner
brought for the service, a flute out of tune, a cow that trampled
the corn, an alarming want of consecrated ground in which to lay
the dead.

The manuscript of the Jesuit journal, written with a firm hand
in ink that is beginning to fade a little after so many years, was
lost for a time when the last of the original Canadian Jesuit fathers died in 1800. Found again, it is now preserved among the
precious treasures of Laval University in Quebec.

November, 1645. Quebec.

On the 27th, Marriage of the daughter of Monsieur Couillar to The son of
Jean Guion; there were two violins, for the 1st time.

December.

On the 3rd the Ursulines sent dinner to the house, a perfect banquet indeed. . . . Began to make bread at the house,—not only because that made
for us at the warehouse oven was not good, but because we wished to use
the corn of the land, which they did not use at the warehouse. . . .

Ceremonies at the feast of Christmas. The 1st stroke of the midnight mass
rang at eleven o'clock, the 2nd, a little before the half-hour; and then they
began to sing two airs—*Venez, mon Dieu,* etc., and *Chantons noe,* etc. Monsieur de la ferté sang the bass; St. martin Played the violin; there was also
a german flute, which proved to be out of tune when they came to the
Church. We had finished a little before midnight; they nevertheless sang the
Te Deum, and a little later a cannon shot was fired as the Signal of midnight, when mass began.

There were four candles in the Church in small iron candlesticks in the
form of a Bracket, and that is enough. There were, besides, two great kettles
full of fire, furnished by the warehouse in order to warm the chapel; they
were kindled beforehand, on the bridge. Directions had been given to remove them after mass, but that having been neglected, the fire caught in the
night on the floor under one of the kettles, in which there were not enough
ashes at the bottom . . . toward 5 o'clock in the morning, above our hall or
refectory, and kitchen, in which was pierre gontier, our Cook—who, perceiving
this, immediately went up and, without other noise, put out the fire. . . .

January, 1646.

New-year's gifts. They Saluted Monsieur the Governor,—to wit, the soldiery
with their arquebuses; *Item,* the Habitans in a body. He forestalled us, and
was here at 7 o'clock to greet all our fathers. I went to greet him after high
mass; (another time we must anticipate him). Monsieur giffar also came to

see us, and the nuns sent letters early in the morning, to offer their Compliments. The Ursulines also sent many beautiful New-year's gifts, with tapers, rosaries, etc.; and, toward the dinner, two handsome pieces of pastry. I sent them two Images . . . gave Monsieur Giffar a book . . . to Monsieur bourdon a galilean telescope in which there was a compass; and to others, reliquaries, Rosaries, etc. We gave a Crucifix to the woman who washes the Church linen, 4 handkerchiefs to the wife of Abraham, and to him a bottle of brandy; two handkerchiefs to robert hache and then two more that he asked for. . . . Monsieur the Governor sent 3 capons and 6 pigeons . . . Monsieur Giffar gave a bottle of hippocras; the hospital mothers a cake and 6 wax Candles; and the next day they sent a fine dinner. . . .

Innovations regarding the consecrated bread. On the Sunday before Septuagesima, Madame Marsolet, having to prepare bread for consecration, desired to present it with the greatest possible display; she had it furnished with a toilet,—a crown of gauze or linen puffs around it. She wished to add candles, and quarter-écus at the Tapers, but seeing that we were not willing to allow her this, she nevertheless had it carried with the toilet and the Crown of puffs. However, before consecrating it, I had all that removed . . . fearing lest this change might occasion Jealousy and Vanity.

February, 1646.

On the 12th, while returning from the benediction at the hospital, I met two Hurons coming from three rivers, who reported the news *of the death of father Anne de noüe.* He started from 3 rivers to go to richelieu, to spiritually assist the garrison, on the 30th of January in company with two soldiers and a Huron. They lay down for the night, 6 leagues above 3 rivers; but the Father left them after midnight, in order to send people to meet them and relieve them of their sledge; and he set forth *by the light of the moon.* But the sky became overcast, and it began to snow. His companions follow him by the trail of his snowshoes, and at last they find him, 4 leagues above richelieu,—kneeling in a hollow of the snow, with his arms crossed and his eyes raised to Heaven, his hat and snowshoes near him.

April.

The 1st Day was easter, which was very beautiful.

The Ursuline mothers of the Incarnation employed nearly the whole of Lent in painting two pieces of Architecture to match the Tabernacle of the parish church; Monsieur bourdon painted some steps.

The savages returned from the chase . . . and came back quite rich and burdened. . . .

July.

On the 4th, two Abnaquiois Captains come to Monsieur the governor, to beg him to make arrangements for a black gown to go to the Abnaquiois, to Instruct them. Monsieur the governor sent them back to me, and I put them off till Autumn, in order to take time to consider the matter. They were given a bag of Indian corn for a Parting Gift, some tobacco, some fish, etc.; and we gave them a feast, and also one to the principal persons of Sillery.

On the 8th, a little savage girl named Charité, aged 5½, died at the Ursulines'; she was interred at the french Cemetary, where her father was buried. She was borne thither by 4 domestics of the Ursulines, with 4 others bearing torches, and 2 french girls and two savage girls holding the corners of the pall.

The savages of Sillery kill a cow of Monsieur Nicolas, which had been in their corn; she was valued at 75 livres. The savages were summoned by Monsieur the governor, to do Justice in this matter, and he ordered them that they should pay 6 Beavers, which was done,—with the assurance that when they should complain, Justice would be done for them for the damage which the cows might have wrought in their corn.

September.

. . . [There came] a Young gentleman from the house of Courtené, who had been converted at la rochelle and had subsequently made a vow to go to the Hurons. But it proved that he was *only a swindler,* who . . . learning that news from france was on the way, in consequence of information that had been given about him, he fled; He played a thousand tricks here, and finally avowed, or lied, that he was *a benedictine religious,*—a professed, for several years,—and that he was a subdeacon; and it was affirmed here that he *had entered, at Alençon, a monastery of benedictine nuns,* where he had heard the confession of a dying nun. He affected to wish to remain, and was enraged because they had written about him that he was a bastard; but those who had seen him in England whispered to him to be quiet; and he then went away. He cheated us by more than 200 livres, which we advanced for him.

January–February, 1647.

. . . [At the New Year] the Hospital nuns sent a letter by Monsieur de St. Sauveur, and two boxes of Lemon-peel by a man. The Ursulines sent a letter, a keg of prunes, a Rosary and a paper Image. There were sent us, by Monsieur the governor, 4 capons, two bustards, and 8 young pigeons; by others, some 10 or 12 pieces of other poultry. On the 2nd . . . we sent to Sillery a bustard and four capons. To the Ursulines, a picture of St. Joseph; 7 or 8 pairs of Savage shoes to our servants. . . .

On the 7th, the Hospital nuns regaled us magnificently.

On the 27th of February, there was a ballet at the warehouse; it was the wednesday in shrovetide. Not one of our fathers or brethren was present; also none of the sisters of the hospital and the Ursulines.

About this time one of our cows with calf was drowned in the St. Charles river; she broke through the ice.

Toward the end of the month, Noel, Jean baptiste, and other savages of Sillery returned from the chase; the fear of the yroquois caused them to hasten.

This month, all the Timber for our house was brought over the snow by our oxen.

January, 1649.

On the 19th occurred the first execution by the hand of the hangman, in the case of a Creature of 15 or 16 years, a thief. At the same time they accused Monsieur Abraham of having violated her; he was imprisoned for this. . . .

The winter's Work was to pile sand for building, and wood for heating.

May.

Return of the Shallops from 3 rivers and Montreal, where famine was found on all sides. We succored the people down here, in the matter of seed and food, with 16 casks of wheat sent from 3 rivers, and several puncheons of peas and Indian corn; and furthermore by the grist of the mill, making in all more than 40 casks of grain.

July, 1665.

On the 16th, Captain poulet arrived, with Monsieur bourdon, 12 Horses, 8 girls, and others. . . .

September.

The 14th. The Ship called la Justice arrived, with more than 100 sick in all. Most of them were placed in the hospital, some in the sick-ward, and some in the Church. Many of them died.

October.

. . . The 2nd. The ship from Normandy arrived, with 82 girls and women —among others, 50 from a charitable institution in Paris, where they have been very well taught. *Item,* 130 laboring men, all in good health; an excellent cargo for the company, and at good prices. . . .

Thomas Hearne

Antiquarian and librarian, Thomas Hearne (1678–1735) is known to scholars as the editor of many English chronicles and classical works. His voluminous diary, written in 148 notebooks, is in a lighter vein. It was his habit to carry one of these notebooks always in his pocket so that he could enter at once anything he heard or saw that interested him. In his taste for recording scandal and curious happenings he in many ways anticipated the gossip columnists of the present day.

Hearne was born at Littlefield Green, Berkshire, the son of a parish clerk in humble circumstances. When his quickness at learning became evident a wealthy neighbour paid for his schooling. At Oxford he received his degree, became a keeper in the famous Bodleian Library there, and was appointed to other college posts. These he had to resign as a nonjuror (one who refused to swear allegiance to the King). He continued to live in Oxford, spending the remainder of his life editing the dozens of works that bear his name.

Thomas Hearne's diaries remained long unpublished after his death, but their liveliness and savour have not lessened with the passing years. He has left a compendium of rogues, male and female; strange cures for bothersome ailments; shameful escapades; and the singular episode of studious Lord Colerane and his estranged wife.

March 30, 1712.

A certain barbarous Sect of People arose lately in London who distinguish themselves by the Name of Mohocks. There are great Numbers of them, & their Custom is to make themselves Drunk and in the Nightime go about the Streets in great Droves & to abuse after a most inhumane Manner all Persons they meet, by beating down their Noses, pricking the fleshy Parts of their Bodys with their swords, not sparing even the Women, whom they usually set upon their Heads & commit such Indecencies towards them as are not to be mention'd; nor indeed shall I descend to any other particulars about these Brutish People, against whom there is a Proclamation issu'd with the

From *The Minde's Delight,* published by The Cayme Press.

Tender of a considerable Reward for Discovery of any of them. Divers have been taken up, & Strict Watches are kept every Night. They are found to be young, lewd, debauch'd Sparks, all of the Whiggish Gang, & the Whiggs are now so much asham'd of this great Scandal (provided Whiggs can be asham'd) that they publickly give out there have been no such People, nor no such Inhumanities committed, thereby indeavouring to perswade People out of their Senses. But this is only one Instance of their abominable Lying, &c.

September 20, 1720.

Yesterday was a great Foot-race at Woodstock, for 1400 libs. between a running Footman of the D. of Wharton's and a running Footman of Mr. Diston's of Woodstock, round the 4 Mile course. Mr. Diston's Man, being about 25 years of Age (& the Duke's about 45) got it with ease, out-distancing the Duke's near half a Mile. They both ran naked, there being not the least scrap of anything to cover them, not so much as Shoes or Pumps, wch was look'd upon deservedly as ye Height of Impudence, & the greatest Affront to the Ladies, of wch there was a very great Number.

October 19.

Meeting to-day with an old Man of Oxford, of very good understanding, he told me of a very great cure upon one very much afflicted with the King's Evil. He was advis'd to eat a very great Quantity of black Cherrys, wch accordingly he did, grew well, and living very many Years after. He told me another Story of a Person that had a strange Cancer, wch was cured by having mole Skins clapt upon the Place. He told me of a Woman at Wolvercote strangely afflicted with the Dropsy, wch was cured by smoking abundance of Tobacco, & eating an immoderate Quantity of Hazel Nutts. He is a Man of good Credit. So I listened the more.

July 23, 1721.

Yesterday a Man was whipp'd at the Cart's Tail from Cairfax to East Gate in Oxford. He was a perfect Stranger, & some time since came into Brazen-Nose Coll. Common Room, & into some Chambers of the same College, uninvited and against all People's Wills, took up the Glass, & propos'd & drank the Healths of K. James, the D. of Ormond, &c., on purpose to trepan Gentlemen; upon w^ch, complaint being made to the V. Chanc., he was apprehended, & committed to the Castle, & being try'd this Assizes, he was sentenc'd to be whipt, & 'tis found that he is a Rogue that goes about to ensnare Men.

August 15, 1723.

Browne Willis, of Whaddon Hall in Bucks, Esq., being in Oxford told me last Night . . . he hath heard it several times said in the Packington Family that Queen Elizabeth lay with one of the Packingtons, a lusty, jolly, tall, proper Man. She happened to see him accidentally at a Meeting where she was, & desired, at breaking up, that he might stay, & an Apartment was provided for him. He was carried to bed. A Lady was brought to bed to him in the dark, & carry'd off again before light, wch he had good reason to think to be the Queen. He said Queen Elizabeth had two daughters.

1725. Undated.

John Wilmot, the frolicksome Earl of Rochester . . . used sometimes, with others of his Companions, to run naked, and particularly they did so once in Woodstocke Park, upon a Sunday in the Aftrenoon, exspecting that several of the female Sex would have been Spectators, but not one appear'd. The Man that stript them, & pull'd off their Shirts, kept the Shirts & did not deliver them any more, going off with them before they finish'd the Race. . . . Once the wild Earl of Rochester, and some of his Companions, a little way from Woodstock, meeting in a morning with a fine young Maid going with butter to Market, they bought all the butter of her, & paid her for it, & afterwards stuck it up against a Tree, wch the Maid perceiving, after they were gone, she went & took it off, thinking it a pity that it should be quite spoil'd. They observ'd her, &, riding after her, soon overtook her, &, as a punishment, set her upon her head, & clapt the Butter upon her Breech.

July 30, 1725.

Last night, between five and six of the Clock, was buried . . . my Lady Tyrrell. . . . This Lady had been some Years ago a very gay Woman, insomuch that she used to say that my Lord Hillesborough, who had been, & so he is still, a very handsome man, had two hundred Graces in his Lips. This Lord Hillesborough is one of those wanton, immodest Gentlemen that, a year or two ago, us'd to ride naked, & make strange work with young Women, and others, of wch we had accounts in the publick Prints, 'till at last a Carter happened to whip some of them, as they were thus naked, at a place in Buckinghamshire, after wch we heard no more of their Pranks. She was fourty six Years of Age. The Servants mightily lament her, as having, they say, lost the best of Mistresses.

November 30, 1726.

One Mrs. Anne Toff, Wife of William Toff, Clothworker, of the town of Godliman, within 3 miles of Guilford in Surrey, was deliver'd of 9 Creatures, resembling Rabbits, at several times in the Month of October last, and since that she hath been delivered of 8 more, in all seventeen. All Papers are full of this, as are also many Private Letters, and 'tis so well attested by several Chirurgeons, Physicians, and others (among wch is Mr. John Howard, Chirurgeon and Man-Midwife in Guildford, who deliver'd her, Woman Midwifes being, after one Rabbit came from her, afraid to proceed), that no doubt is made about the Truth of the Fact.

December 29, 1726.

An Apothecary near Cairfax had a Daughter that lately put on Men's

Apparel, and endeavoured to act the Part of a Man. She hath rambled in that condition about the Country, and hath courted young Women, and been married as if she were a Man. She is a bold, wild young Creature. . . .

1726. Undated.

On Wednesday last died, in St. Peter's Parish . . . one Madam Best. . . . Her maiden Name was Gracious Crooke, & she made a great noise formerly in Oxford before she married, when she lived in St. Aldate's Parish, where she kept Blackamores, Monkeys, & Dogs, & was reported to lye with them. She was carryed out of Town yesterday, in order to be buried at Kensington, her husband not mourning, to whom, it seems, she has left nothing.

June 7, 1731.

Lord Colerane married the daughter, a fine Woman, of Mr. Hanger . . . but they have not lived together many years; I know not for what reason. Lord Colrane is a very sober, studious, religious Gentleman. He hath no child. He reads Prayers in his own House constantly night and morning, and . . . he was so studious that when his Lady and he lived together, he would (as he lay in bed with her) have one come up to him at midnight and read Greek to him.

". . . what can I do for the cause of God and man . . ."

John Quincy Adams

A frosty, irascible little man with a high, shrill voice and a biting pen spent an hour or more a day from youth to old age keeping a remarkable record of his own life and the lives of those around him. His diary is such an extraordinary document that had he done nothing else he would still be remembered.

But John Quincy Adams (1767–1848) was one of the busiest men of his age. He was a President of the United States and the son of a President, member of Congress for twenty years, Secretary of State, diplomat, poet, scientist, scholar, lawyer, abolitionist, author of the Monroe Doctrine and friend and intimate of the greatest figures of his time.

It is difficult to measure the stature of Adams. Philip Hone, himself a man of great accomplishments, said of Adams, "No man knows so much or so accurately. He has probed deeply into the arcana of all the sciences, understands and can explain all subjects, from the solar system down to the construction of a toothpick. He has the Holy Scriptures at his fingers' ends, knows every line of Shakespeare, can recite Homer in the original Greek . . . knows all about Jack the Giant Killer." Hone, marvelling, relates how Adams held forth to him and Daniel Webster for an hour over the breakfast table on dancing girls and harem capers.

Adams continued his daily entries even when he was forced to tie the pen to his tired, shaking fingers. When at last he abandoned his journal, he had written an extraordinary chronicle of a many-sided genius, a moving record of one of the finest minds America has ever produced.

October 21, 1803.

At eleven this morning I took my seat in the Senate. . . . There was little business done. . . .

From *The Diary of John Quincy Adams 1791–1845*, edited by Allan Nevins, copyright 1928, 1951 by Charles Scribner's Sons, 1956 by Allan Nevins. Reprinted by permission of the publishers.

November 7.

. . . The Senate . . . adjourned early, until Thursday, to give time for the workmen to repair the ceiling, which is ruinous. Another motive, not mentioned, might be that the annual horse races of the city are held this week. . . .

November 16.

The races at length are finished, and the Senate really met this day. . . .

November 23.

[President Jefferson at dinner] observed that both French and Spanish ought to be made primary objects of acquisition in all the educations of our young men. As to Spanish, it was so easy that he had learned it, with the help of a Don Quixote lent him by Mr. Cabot, and a grammar, in the course of a passage to Europe, on which he was but nineteen days at sea. But Mr. Jefferson tells large stories. . . .

January 11, 1805.

. . . [Jefferson's] itch for telling prodigies . . . is unabated. Speaking of the cold, he said he had seen Fahrenheit's thermometer, *in Paris*, at twenty degrees below zero, and that, not for a single day, but that for six weeks together it stood *thereabouts.* "Never once in the whole time," said he, "so high as zero, which is *fifty* degrees below the freezing point." These were his own words. He knows better than all this; but he loves to excite wonder. Fahrenheit's thermometer never since Mr. Jefferson existed was at twenty degrees below zero in Paris. It was never for six weeks together so low as twenty degrees below zero. Nor is Fahrenheit's zero fifty degrees below freezing point. . . .

January 15.

. . . [In taking part in a Senate debate] on this occasion, as on almost every other, I felt most sensibly my deficiency as an extemporaneous speaker. In tracing this deficiency to its source, I find it arising from a cause that is irreparable. No efforts, no application on my part can ever remove it. It is slowness of comprehension—an incapacity to grasp the whole compass of a subject in the mind at once with such an arrangement as leaves a proper impression of the detail—and incapacity to form ideas properly precise and definite with the rapidity necessary to give them uninterrupted utterance. My manner, therefore, is slow, hesitating, and often much confused. Sometimes, from inability to furnish the words to finish a thought commenced, I begin a sentence with propriety and end it with nonsense. Sometimes, after carrying through an idea of peculiar force to its last stage, the want of a proper word at the close drives me to use one which throws the whole into a burlesque. And sometimes the most important details of argument escape my mind at the moment when I want them, though ever ready to present them before and after.

. . . At dinner [with President Jefferson] there was, as usual, a dissertation upon wines; not very edifying. . . . Dr. Mitchell mentioned Mr. Fulton's steamboat as an invention of great importance. To which Mr. Jefferson, assenting, added, "and I think his torpedoes a valuable invention too." . . . Conversation was very various, of chemistry, of geography, and of natural philosophy; of oils, grasses, beasts, birds, petrifactions, and incrustations; Pike and Humboldt, Lewis and Barlow, and a long train of et cetera—for the Doctor knows a little of everything, and is communicative of what he knows—which makes me delight in his company. . . . On the whole, it was one of the most agreeable dinners I have had at Mr. Jefferson's.

July 11, 1808.

I enter this day upon my forty-second year. I employed it from early in the morning until the dusk of evening assiduously writing at my lecture and reading. The day was dull and rainy until towards night, when the sky cleared and the sun with "farewell sweet" made its appearance. I walked nearly an hour in the Mall. The return of my birthday is one of the seasons which call upon me for reflection. In the course of the last year I have been called by my duties as a citizen and man to act and to suffer more than at any former period of my life. To my duties I have steadfastly adhered. The course I pursued has drawn upon me much obloquy, and the change of parties in the State, with an accumulated personal malignity borne me, both on my father's [President Samuel Adams] and my own account, by those who rule the State, produced in the first instance the election of a Senator to fill my place after the third of March next. . . .

September 7, 1820.

. . . A letter from M. M. Noah, editor of the New York *Advocate* . . . like all the editors of newspapers in this country who have any talent, an author to be let. There is not one of them whose friendship is worth buying, nor one whose enmity is not formidable. They are a sort of assassins who sit with loaded blunderbusses at the corner of streets and fire them off for hire or for sport at any passenger whom they select. . . .

October 22.

. . . A shopkeeper by the name of Holmead dropped yesterday from his pocket, in the street, a cheque upon one of the banks for a hundred dollars, and a hundred and fifty dollars in bank-bills. A mulatto boy of fourteen or fifteen years of age found the cheque, and not knowing how to read, took it to a shop to enquire what it was. He was then called upon for the bank-bills, and denying that he had found them, was tortured, thumb-screwed, and hung by the neck (so this man says) to extort confession from him. . . .

This is a sample of the treatment of colored people under criminal charges or suspicions here [in the Capital].

November 18.

Members of Congress, visitors at the office [Adams was then Secretary of State in the Monroe administration], occupied again all the hours of business. This rapid and continual change of persons and of subjects calling for attention that has such an effect upon the memory that the proverbial defect of that quality may be accounted for without supposing it intentional or pretended. Every man comes with a story, demand, or solicitation of his own; almost every one comes to ask favors. No sooner has one left the office than another enters. I have often attempted to keep a minute of the names of the persons who come from day to day, but without success. I have not time to write the name of one who retires before another comes in. . . . The sun goes down upon business uncompleted.

December 25.

Christmas Day. No attendance at the office. I gave the day to relaxation, and, with a view to make an experiment upon the taste of the younger part of our present family, after breakfast I read aloud Pope's *Messiah*, a poem suited to the day, and of which my own admiration was great at an earlier age than that of my son Charles, the youngest person now in my family. Not one of them, excepting George, appeared to take the slightest interest in it; nor is there one of them who has any relish for literature. Charles has a great fondness for books, and a meditative mind, but neither disposition nor aptitude for public speaking or correct reading. Charles must teach himself all that he learns. He will learn nothing from others. Literature has been the charm of my life, and, could I have carved out my own fortunes, to literature would my whole life have been devoted. I have been a lawyer for bread, and a statesman at the call of my country. . . . The summit of my ambition would have been by some great work of literature to have done honor to my age and country, and to have lived in the gratitude of future ages. This consummation of happiness has been denied me.

July 11, 1823.

And I commence upon my fifty-seventh year. Swam with Antoine an hour in the Potomac. We started for the bridge, but after swimming about half an hour, I perceived by reference to a house upon the shore, beyond which we were to pass that we had ascended very little above where we had left our clothes, and that the current of the tide was insensibly carrying us into the middle of the river. . . . We had been an hour and five minutes in the water, without touching ground, and before turning back I began to find myself weary.

September 20. Quincy, Massachusetts.

I walked in the burying-yard, and viewed the granite tombstones erected over the graves of my ancestors . . . four generations, of whom very little more is known than is recorded upon these stones. There are three succeeding generations of us now living. Pass another century, and we shall all be mouldering in the same dust, or resolved into the same elements. Who then of our posterity shall visit this yard? And what shall he read engraved upon the stones?*

February 9, 1825.

May the blessing of God rest upon the event of this day!—the second Wednesday in February, when the election of a President of the United States for the term of four years, from the 4th of March next, was consummated. . . . On opening and counting the votes in joint meeting of the two Houses, the House of Representatives immediately proceeded to the vote by ballot from the three highest candidates, when John Quincy Adams received the votes of thirteen, Andrew Jackson of seven, and William H. Crawford of four States. The election was thus completed, very unexpectedly, by a single ballot. . . .

April 30.

Since my removal to the Presidential mansion I rise about five; read two chapters of Scott's Bible and Commentary, and the corresponding Commentary of Hewlett; then the morning newspapers, and public papers from the several departments; write seldom, and not enough; breakfast an hour, from nine to ten; then have a succession of visitors, upon business, in search of place, solicitors for donations, or from mere curiosity, from eleven till between four and five o'clock. The heads of departments of course occupy much of this time. Between four and six I take a walk of three or four miles. Dine from about half past five to seven, and from dark till about eleven I generally pass the evening in my chamber, signing land-grants or blank patents, in the interval of which, for the last ten days, I have brought up three months of arrears in my diary index. About eleven I retire to bed. My evenings are

---

* [When the century contemplated by Adams had passed, a biographer of the family began his account with these words: ". . . In America there is one family, and only one, that generation after generation has consistently and without interruption made contributions of the highest order to our history and civilization. . . . That a farmer's son should become a President is, happily, no strange phenomenon in the great democracy, but it is strange indeed, that *his* descendants for five generations, by public service in the highest of offices or by intellectual contributions, should remain leaders of the nation which their ancestor so conspicuously helped to found. . . ." *The Adams Family,* James Truslow Adams, Little, Brown and Company, Boston, 1930.]

not so free from interruption as I had hoped and expected they would be.

May 31.

. . . The bathing season has come, and the heat of summer, which renders it necessary to transpose my hours of exercise from the afternoon, before dinner, to the morning, before breakfast. This I have done for the last three days, taking two morning hours for bathing and swimming in the Potomac. My diary has been more steadily kept up, yet not without negligent interruption. . . .

June 13.

I attempted to cross the river with Antoine in a small canoe, with a view to swim across it to come back . . . at the shore near Van Ness's poplars; but in crossing the Tiber to the point, my son John, who was with us, thought the boat dangerous, and instead of going with us, went and undressed at the rock, to swim and meet us in midway of the river as we should be returning. I thought the boat safe enough, or rather persisted in going without paying due attention to its condition; gave my watch to my son; made a bundle of my coat and waist-coat to take in the boat with me; put off my shoes, and was paddled by Antoine, who had stripped himself entirely naked. Before we had got half across the river, the boat had leaked itself half full, and then we found there was nothing on board to scoop up the water and throw it over. Just at that critical moment a fresh breeze from the northwest blew down the river as from the nose of a bellows. In five minutes' time it made a little tempest, and set the boat to dancing till the river came in at the sides. I jumped overboard, and Antoine did the same, and lost hold of the boat, which filled with water and drifted away. We were as near as possible to the middle of the river, and swam to the opposite shore. Antoine, who was naked, reached it with little difficulty. I had much more, and, while struggling for life and gasping for breath, had ample leisure to reflect upon my own indiscretion. My principal difficulty was in the loose sleeves of my shirt, which filled with water and hung like two fifty-six pound weights upon my arms. I had also my hat, which I soon gave, however, to Antoine. After reaching the shore, I took off my shirt and pantaloons, wrung them out, and gave them to Antoine to go and look out for our clothes, or for a person to send to the house for others, and for the carriage to come and fetch me. Soon after he had gone, my son John joined me, having swum wholly across the river, expecting to meet us returning with the boat. Antoine crossed the bridge, sent a man to my house for the carriage, made some search for the drifted boat and bundles, and found his own hat with his shirt and braces in it, and one of my shoes. He also brought over the bridge my son's clothes with my watch and umbrella, which I had left with him. While Antoine was gone, John and I were wading and swimming up and down on the other shore, or sitting naked basking on the bank at the margin of the river. John walked over the bridge home. The carriage came, and took me and Antoine home, half dressed. I lost an old summer coat, white waistcoat, two napkins, two white handkerchiefs, and one shoe. Antoine lost his watch, jacket, waistcoat, pantaloons, and shoes. The boat was also lost. . . .

July 22.

I walked as usual to my ordinary bathing-place, and came to the rock where I leave my clothes a few minutes before sunrise. I found several persons there, besides . . . a boat with four men in it, and a drag-net . . . which was going in search of a dead body. I enquired if any one had been drowned, and the man told me it was old Mr. Shoemaker, a clerk in the post-office. . . . I stripped and went into the river. I had not been more than ten minutes swimming, when . . . the body floated immediately opposite the rock, less than one hundred yards from the shore, at the very edge of the channel, and where there could not be seven feet deep of water. . . . There was nothing terrible or offensive in the sight, but I returned home musing . . . uncertainly whether I ought to renounce altogether my practice of swimming in the river.

July 6, 1826.

Governor Barbour brought information of the decease of Mr. Jefferson at Monticello on the 4th inst., at ten minutes past one in the afternoon—a strange and very striking coincidence. . . .

July 9.

. . . Mr. Merrill told me that he had come this morning out from Baltimore, and was informed there that my father died on the 4th of this month about five o'clock in the afternoon . . . the ninety-first year of his life—a life illustrious in the annals of his country and the world . . . the time, the manner, the coincidence with the decease of Jefferson, are visible and palpable. . . .

March 20, 1827.

. . . This morning, before breakfast, into a sonnet. . . .

June 23, 1828.

For the benefit of my health I began this day to combine the river bath and the [horse-back] ride. Rode to the rock near the bridge. Swam about ten minutes and then rode again around the Capital Square home. . . . Mrs. Adams is winding silk from several hundred silkworms that she has been rearing, and I am engaged in a long correspondence with my son Charles, and now much involved in giving him an analysis of Cicero's *Oration for Roscius of Ameria.*

July 4.

Independence Day. Chesapeake and Ohio Canal commenced. Between seven and eight this morning . . . a procession was formed, preceded by a band of music, to the wharf, where we embarked in the steamboat *Surprise;* followed by two others, we proceeded to . . . the spot selected for breaking the ground. . . . It happened that at the first stroke of the spade it met immediately under the surface a large stump of a tree; after repeating the stroke three or four times without making any impression, I threw off my coat, and, resuming the spade, raised a shovelful of the earth, at which a general shout burst forth. . . . The marshals of the day escorted me home on horseback, came in and took a glass of wine, and took leave with thanks for their attentions. The day was uncommonly cool for the season, with a fresh breeze, and towards evening there was a gentle shower. The exertion of speaking in the open air made me hoarse, and with the anxiety, more oppressive than it should have been, to get well through the day, exhausted and fatigued me so . . . as has happened to me whenever I have had a part to perform in the presence of multitudes, I got through awkwardly, but without gross and palpable failure. The incident that chiefly relieved me was the obstacle of the stump, which met and resisted the spade, and my casting off my coat to overcome the resistance. It struck the eye and fancy of the spectators more than all the flowers of rhetoric in my speech, and diverted their attention from the stammering and hesitation of a deficient memory.

July 27.

With my son John, my nephew, and Antoine, I crossed the river in our canoe and swam a quarter of an hour on the other side; but . . . I found myself so fatigued that I called the boat to me, and clung to her till she was rowed to the shore . . . annoyed with leeches and ticks at the landing. The decline of my health is in nothing so closely brought to my conviction as in my inability to swim more than fifteen or twenty minutes without tiring. This was the day of most overpowering heat that we have had this season.

December 3.

A continual stream of visitors . . . and they had but one topic of conversation—the loss of this day's election [for the Presidency, to Andrew Jackson]. . . . The sun of my political life sets in the deepest gloom. But that of my country shines unclouded.

May 13, 1830.

Mr. Poinsett, our late Minister to Mexico, . . . told me he was going immediately home to South Carolina, even at this season of the year to see if he could, by good advice, calm the excitement. . . . South Carolina has been potioned and philtered and back-scourged, like an old lecher, into a frenzy of excitement, and has now a prospect of coming into physical collision with

he Government of the Union [over, among other issues, that of slave-hold-
ng]. As the Government is now administered, there is every prospect that her
ullies will succeed, to the sacrifice of the interest of all the rest of the Union,
s the bullies of Georgia have succeeded in the project of extirpating the
ndians, by the sacrifice of the public faith of the Union and of all our treaties
vith them.

August 18.

I this day finished the reading of the Bible, which I began about the 1st
of May last year . . . not so profitable to me as it ought to have been. Among
he decays of age which I cannot dissemble to myself is a falling off of the
liscipline of the mind. . . .

December 24.

Our house is a hospital of invalids. My cough continues, varying in its
ymptoms, but no better. A hoarse sore throat every night. Lungs loaded
vith phlegm every morning. I consulted Huntt, and he advised trash which
vill tease me and leave me just where I am—rye mush and milk for break-
ast, a plaster on the breast; Seidlitz powders, and no suppers. I do not sup.
The rest is about as effective as the bread and cheese of Molière's *Médecin
Malgré Lui.*

January 11, 1831.

. . . Read about fifty pages of the first volume of Jefferson's *Memoirs.* . . .
There are no confessions. He tells nothing but what redounds to his own
redit . . . always in the right. This is not uncommon to writers of their own
ives. Dr. Franklin was more candid. . . .

January 12.

I finished the memoir of Jefferson's life, which terminates . . . when he
rrived at New York to take upon him the office of Secretary of State. There it
nds; and there, as a work of much interest to the present and future ages,
t should have begun . . . then that all the good and all the evil parts of his
haracter were brought into action. His ardent passion for liberty and the
ights of man; his patriotism; the depth and compass of his understanding;
he extent and variety of his knowledge, and the enviable faculty of applying
t to his own purposes; the perpetual watchfulness of public opinion, and the
liability of principle and temper with which he accommodated to it his own
lesigns and opinions; all these were in ceaseless operation during those twenty
ears; and with them were combined a rare mixture of infidel philosophy
nd epicurean morals, of burning ambition and of stoical self-control, of deep
luplicity and of generous sensibility, between which two qualities, and a
reacherous and inventive memory, his conduct towards his rivals and op-
onents appears one tissue of inconsistency. His treatment of Washington, of
Knox, of my father, of Hamilton, of Bayard, who made him President of the

United States, and, lastly, of me, is marked with features of perfidy worthy
of Tiberius Caesar or Louis the Eleventh of France . . . that in deceiving
others he seems to have begun by deceiving himself.

January 27.

. . . Mr. Jefferson's love of liberty was sincere and ardent—not confined
to himself, like that of most of his fellow slave-holders. He was above that
execrable sophistry of the South Carolina nullifiers, which would make of
slavery the corner-stone to the temple of liberty. He saw the gross inconsist
ency between the principles of the Declaration of Independence and the fact
of Negro slavery, and he could not, or would not, prostitute the faculties of
his mind to the vindication of that slavery which from his soul he abhorred
Mr. Jefferson had not the spirit of martyrdom. He would have introduced a
flaming denunciation of slavery into the Declaration of Independence, but
the discretion of his colleagues struck it out. . . . And in his memoirs he
leaves a posthumous warning to the planters that they must at no distant
day emancipate their slaves, or that worse will follow; but he withheld the
publication of his prophecy till he should himself be in the grave.

January 31.

. . . I frequent no society, and, with the exception of my daily walks, we
are confined within the walls of our house as if it were a ship at sea. I spend
about six hours of the day in writing—diary, arrears of index, and letters. . . .
I enjoy a degree of tranquillity such as I never before experienced; interrupted
only by . . . the consciousness that it must speedily be changed for a return
to all the cares, mortifications, and complexities of ungracious public life [he
had been elected to the House of Representatives].

March 8.

It is a doctrine of the medical faculty that bodily exercise to be salutary
should be taken with a vacant mind; such is the precept of Mr. Jefferson.
. . . At certain seasons, however, the propensity becomes too strong for me
I walk and muse and pour forth premeditated verse. . . . I am accredited
as one of the smallest poets of my country. Very short fugitive pieces are the
only rhymes I have ever committed to the press . . . one short poem . . .
one translation, the thirteenth satire of Juvenal. . . .

August 9, 1833.

Cold and cloudy day, clearing off towards evening. In the multitudinous
whimseys of a disabled mind and body, the thick-coming fancies often occur
to me that the events which effect my life and adventures are specially
shaped to disappoint my purposes. My whole life has been a succession of
disappointments. I can scarcely recollect a single instance of success to anything I ever undertook. Yet, with fervent gratitude to God, I confess that

ny life has been equally marked by great and signal successes which I
either aimed at nor anticipated.

October 17.

The state of my health, I fear, is irretrievable. The summer is gone, and
have done nothing of what I had intended. My time is now absorbed—
. In the mornings, minutes of Thomson's translation of the Septuagint Bible.
. In teaching my granddaughter to read; a task to which I devote from
two to three hours of every day. 3. In the exercise of my garden and nursery,
n average of two hours more. 4. My diary, one hour. 5. Correspondence,
two hours. 6. Miscellaneous reading, two hours. There are twelve: seven in
ed, three at and after meals, and two wasted, I know not how. This wasted
ime I have found by constant experience to be as indispensable as sleep. It
annot be employed in reading, nor even in thinking upon any serious subject.
t must be wasted on trifles—doing nothing. The string of the bow must be
lackened, and the bow itself laid aside.

August 14, 1835.

The accounts of the riots in Baltimore continue. In the State of Mississippi
nobs are hanging up blacks suspected of insurgency, and whites suspected
f abetting them. . . . One can scarcely forsee to what it will lead.

July 11, 1836.

With praise and prayer to God, and a solemn sense of my earthly condition,
nd hopes of a better world, I enter upon the seventieth year of my pil-
rimage. . . .

November 22, 1837.

. . . The most atrocious case of rioting which ever disgraced this country
appened on the night of the 7th of this month at Alton, in the State of
llinois, where a man by the name of Lovejoy, one of the leading abolitionists
f the time, has been striving to establish a newspaper. Three times he had
nported printing-presses in the place, and three times they had been de-
royed by mobs, and once or twice the offices in which they were placed.
he fourth time the press was imported and deposited in a merchant's ware-
ouse. The mob assembled in the night, surrounded the warehouse, and de-
nanded that the press should be delivered up to them. It was refused. They
ssailed the house with musketry, forced their way into it, set fire to the roof
f the building, shot Lovejoy dead, wounded several others, till the press was
elivered up to them, which they broke in pieces and threw into the river.
. . This Lovejoy wrote me a letter last January, which I answered in April.
le was a man of strong religious, conscientious feeling, deeply indignant at
hat he deemed the vices and crimes of the age. Such men are often fated
) be martyrs; and he has fallen a martyr to the cause of human freedom.

May 27, 1838.

. . . The neglect of public worship in this city is an increasing evil, and the indifference to all religion throughout the whole country portends no good. There is in the clergy of all the Christian denominations a time-serving, cringing, subservient morality, as wide from the spirit of the Gospel as it is from the intrepid assertion and vindication of truth. The counterfeit character of a very large portion of the Christian ministry of this country is disclosed in the dissensions growing up in all the Protestant churches on the subject of slavery. The abolitionists assume as the first principle of all their movements that slavery is sin. Their opponents, halting between the alternative of denying directly this position and of admitting the duty binding upon them to bear their own testimony against it, are prevaricating with their own consciences, and taxing their learning and ingenuity to prove that the Bible sanctions slavery; that Abraham, Isaac, and Paul were slave-holders; and that St. Paul is the apostle of man-stealers, because he sent Onesimus back to his master Philemon. These preachers of the Gospel might just as well call our extermination of the Indians an obedience to Divine commands because Jehovah commanded the children of Israel to exterminate the Canaanitish nations. . . .

February 16, 1840.

Mr. Meehan, the Librarian of Congress, yesterday told me that in the violent storm of the night before last one arm of the emblematical statue of America in the pediment over the entrance-door of the House of Representatives—my design, so beautifully executed by Persico—had been blown away, and came down with a tremendous crash. . . . But he was mistaken as to the statue mutilated. It is not the figure of America, but that of Justice, which has lost her right arm nearly to the elbow . . . painfully significant of the Hall within, where Justice has emphatically lost her right arm.

April 17.

A dark-colored mulatto man, named Joseph Cartwright, a preacher of a colored Methodist church, came this morning with a subscription book to raise $450 to purchase the freedom of his three grandchildren—two girls and one boy, all under three or four years of age. He told me that he had been upwards of twenty years in purchasing his own freedom and that of his three sons; that after this, Henry Johnson, late a member of the House of Representatives from Louisiana, had bought his son's wife and her three children, with many other slaves, to carry them away to Louisiana; that after the purchase he had been prevailed upon to consent . . . that this Joseph Cartwright should purchase them for $1,025. He had actually purchased and paid for the mother, and was now endeavouring to raise $450 for the three children. There were in the subscription book certificates of two white Methodist ministers, Hamilton and Cookman, to the respectability of this man—a preacher of the gospel! What a horrible exemplification of slavery!

March 29, 1841.

I am yet to revise for publication my argument [before the Supreme Court] in the case of the *Amistad* Africans [Adams in large part was responsible for the liberation of a number of Negroes who sought their freedom in a revolt while being transported on the schooner *Amistad* from Cuba to slavery under Spanish rule]; and, in merely glancing over the slave-papers sent me by Mr. Fox, I find impulses of duty upon my own conscience which I cannot resist, while on the other hand are the magnitude, the danger, the insurmountable burden of labor to be encountered in the undertaking to touch upon the slave-trade. No one else will undertake it; no one but a spirit unconquerable by man, woman or fiend can undertake it but with the heart of martyrdom. The world, the flesh, and all the devils in hell are arrayed against any man who now in this North American Union shall dare to join the standard of Almighty God to put down the African slave-trade; and what can I, upon the verge of my seventy-fourth birthday, with a shaking hand, a darkening eye, a drowsy brain, and with all my faculties dropping from me one by one, as the teeth are dropping from my head—what can I do for the cause of God and man, for the progress of human emancipation, for the suppression of the African slave-trade? Yet my conscience presses me on; let me but die upon the breach.

April 4.

At thirty minutes past midnight, this morning of Palm Sunday, the 4th of April, 1841, died William Henry Harrison, precisely one calendar month President of the United States after his inauguration. . . . It makes the Vice-President of the United States, John Tyler of Virignia, Acting President of the Union for four years less one month. Tyler is a political sectarian, of the slave-driving, Virginian, Jeffersonian school, principled against all improvement, with all the interests and passions and vices of slavery rooted in his moral and political constitution—with talents not above mediocrity, and a spirit incapable of expansion to the dimensions of the station upon which he has been cast by . . . the agency of chance. . . . This . . . brings to the test that provision of the Constitution which places in the Executive chair a man never thought of for it by anybody. This day was in every sense gloomy—rain the whole day.

June 17, 1843.

This was the day of the great celebration of the completion of the monument on Bunker Hill; and never since the existence of the three hills was there such a concourse of strangers upon their sides. . . . What a name in the annals of mankind is Bunker Hill! what a day was the 17th of June, 1775! And what a burlesque upon them both is an oration upon them by Daniel Webster, and a pilgrimage of slave-drivers, to desecrate the solemnity by their presence! . . . Now with the ideal associations of the thundering cannon, which I heard, and the smoke of burning Charlestown, which I saw, on

that awful day, combined with this pyramid of Quincy granite, and Daniel
Webster spouting, and John Tyler . . . how could I have witnessed this all
at once, without an unbecoming burst of indignation, or of laughter? Daniel
Webster is a heartless traitor to the cause of human freedom; John Tyler is
a slave-monger. What have these to do with the Quincy granite pyramid
on the brow of Bunker Hill? What have these to do with a dinner in Faneuil
Hall, but to swill like swine, and grunt about the rights of man?

I stayed at home, and visited my seedling trees, and heard the cannonades
of the rising, the meridian, and the setting sun, and answered a letter. . . .

March 25, 1844.

I approach the term when my daily journal must cease from physical
disability to keep it up. I have now struggled . . . while mind and body have
been wearing away under the daily, silent, but unremitting erosion of time.
I rose this morning at four, and with smarting, bloodshot eye and shivering
hand, still sat down and wrote to fill up the chasm of the closing days of the
last week; but my stern chase after Time is, to borrow a simile from Tom
Paine, like the race of a man with a wooden leg after a horse.

"This silence . . . the room Jesus told us to
enter into when we pray."

Thomas Merton

There are few if any precedents for the journal published by
Thomas Merton (1915–   ), now Father M. Louis, after five
years in the Trappist monastery of Gethsemani, Kentucky. The
withdrawal into a spiritual and mystic world has rarely been described from the inside, and the Trappist life of prayer, penance,
study and labor has never had so eloquent an advocate.

Merton was born in France, the son of an English painter. His
mother was an American Quaker. He grew up in France and
was educated at the universities of Cambridge and Columbia,
where he taught briefly. He wrote poetry, was a book reviewer,
and worked in a Catholic Settlement House in Harlem before he
became a Catholic in 1935. Six years later he entered the Gethsemani monastery and subsequently was ordained a priest.

The spiritual pilgrimage that preceded this step is described in
his autobiographical *The Seven Storey Mountain* (1941). His
journal continues that narrative.

In a Trappist monastery there is no speech. The life is physically hard, and ordinarily monks work every day in the field. They
sleep short hours on straw and boards and their fare is plain.
Gethsemani, a huge, hundred-year-old building, lies in a Kentucky valley that is hot in summer and cold in winter. Monks assigned to the night vigils chant the Psalms throughout all the
dark hours; Mass is said each morning at four. All are sworn to
five vows: poverty, chastity, obedience, stability, and conversion
of manners.

Against this background, postulant Merton, later novice, still
later priest, tells his story. . . .

December 10, 1946. Advent.

It is five years since I came to the monastery. It is the same kind of day,

From *The Sign of Jonas* by Thomas Merton, copyright, 1953, by the Abbey of
Our Lady of Gethsemani. Reprinted by permission of Harcourt, Brace and Company, Inc.

overcast. But now it is raining. I wish I knew how to begin to be grateful to God and to Our Lady for bringing me here.

There was a long interval after afternoon work. It was good to be in the big quiet church. The church is dark, these winter afternoons.

January 27, 1947.

This week I am serving Father Abbot's Mass. He says Mass in the back sacristy, when the conventual Mass is going on in the church. You can hear the choir, indistinctly, through the two closed doors. On the other side, outside, down the hill at the mill this morning the brothers were filing the teeth of the big buzz-saw. In choir the monks were singing *Justus ut Palma florebit*, in the Mass for the Feast of Saint John Chrysostom. And outside the saw rang under the grating file. The sounds of prayer and of distant work mingle well. There, on the altar, in the midst of these various discrete sounds of homage, in the midst of the order ruled by love for Him, the Lord of all things said nothing, but filled the room with peace. . . .

February 8.

. . . It is really cold, for the first time this winter. The other night the holy water was frozen in the fonts of our dormitory cells when we went up to go to bed. But by the time we got up at two o'clock it had started to melt, because of the presence of so many monks in one room, with all the windows closed.

February 17. Shrove Tuesday.

. . . Yesterday morning I made my will. You always make a will before solemn vows, getting rid of everything, as if you were about to die. It sounds more dramatic than it really is. As a matter of fact, as soon as I had renounced all earthly things, I was called into Father Abbot's room and he presented me with a contract with Harcourt, Brace for the publication of *The Seven Storey Mountain*. So after making my will I put my living signature on this contract. The royalties of the dead author will go to the monastery. Meanwhile, I spent the afternoon writing business letters and making all kinds of mistakes. . . .

. . . Now it is three days before I go on retreat for my final vows.

The wardrobe keeper went up to the attic and brought down the suitcase that came into the monastery with me five years ago. It is in our dormitory cell. I am supposed to check over the clothes to see that everything is there, before formally renouncing that blue woolen sweater, those four striped sports shirts, those tweeds and the dark blue suit I was wearing. The whole job took about half a minute. But the suitcase remains in the cell. It still looks shiny and new and has a blue and white Cuba Mail Line label on it, with the letter M. It still has the rich new smell which, as I remember, impressed me when I first unpacked it at a hotel in Florida. It is almost impossible to believe that that was seven years ago. . . .

March 20.

So yesterday I made my solemn vows.

I do not feel much like writing about it.

This does not mean that I am not happy about profession. But I am happy in a way that does not want to talk. One thing I will say: that the stamp of grace is on the memory of yesterday. And by that I mean that I am left with a sense of deep union with all the other monks. I do not know what I expected to feel after my profession. But afterwards I was left with a profoundly clean conviction that I had done the right thing and that I had given myself as best I could to God. And beyond that the nearest thing to sensible consolation was a deep and warm realization that I was immersed in my community. I am part of Gethsemani. I belong to the family. . . .

April 4. Good Friday.

I had a pious thought, but I am not going to write it down.

It is raining. The best place to hide, this afternoon, was in church. It rained hard and you could hear the rain beating all over the long roof.

I had a thought about the Psalter, too—but I will not put that down either. The thoughts that come to me are stupid.

Father Renatus and I helped Father Prior dismantle the baldachin that was used in the processions of the Blessed Sacrament. . . . Father Renatus is one of the holiest monks in the house and one of the most impractical. He is thin, angelic, and Polish, and talks in his sleep—in Polish. He is awkward and shy and intensely zealous. I am very fond of him. Together we started fumbling with the screws and strings that hold the baldachin together. For a long time we could not seem to make anything come undone. Then, suddenly, all the poles and parts began to fall to the floor with a great clatter.

A guest of the monastery, a big fat man, was half-kneeling, half-sitting at the benches and I looked at him out of the corner of my eye to see if he jumped. But he was very placid. He did not jump. Speaking of guests, I am reminded that the man whose feet I washed at the *Mandatum* definitely did not need the dollar I placed in his hands, with liturgical kisses. On the whole, both Father Renatus and I were very proud to have been asked to take apart the baldachin. It made us feel as though we were really efficient after all.

Yesterday, when I was thurifer, I had a sore knee and had my bows and genuflections all mixed. Father Abdon . . . and I went about incensing first one abbot then another. There were four abbots in the house, including Dom Gildas. Father Abdon forgot Dom Gildas and I gave him a nudge and we spun around again and hastened to the presbytery step and Father Abdon started praying out loud, which is, with him, a sign of panic.

April 20. Good Shepherd Sunday. Day of Recollection.

It is a day of recollection. That means we are supposed to be thinking about ourselves. It seems as though a year had passed since my solemn profession. But it is only a month. The more I think of my vows the happier I am. For there is only one thing left to live for: the love of God. There is only one unhappiness: not to love God. That is why I wish I did not find my soul so full of movement, and shadows and cross-currents of dry wind that stir up the dust of my human desires. Everywhere I turn I find the stuff I write sticking to me like flypaper.

April 25. Feast of Saint Mark.

Litany after Prime today. The weather has been very bad: cold and rainy, and we have hardly planted anything yet.

Typewriter broken. And now the infinite God has to compete, for possession of my mind, with the image of a beautiful new typewriter with French accents on it. . . .

Monks (myself included) get very restless in Chapter as soon as anything controversial is introduced. We seem to find argument oppressive beyond measure. The reason is, of course, that no one can answer back. After years of being unable to talk back, a Cistercian is apt to be nauseated by the mere suggestion of controversy. When a conference is really argumentative the atmosphere gets to be so tense that the monks cannot even seek solace by falling asleep. When it is all over they file out in silent dejection, dispersing, running outdoors on every side to find solitude and fresh air. . .

April 28.

On and off since Easter I have been playing a new game called insomnia It goes like this: You lie down in your dormitory cell and listen to first one monk and then another monk begin to snore without, however, going to sleep yourself. Then you count the quarter hours by the tower clock and console yourself with an exact knowledge of the amount of sleep you are missing. The fun does not really begin until you get up at 2 A.M. and try to keep awake in choir. All day long you wander around the monastery bumping into the walls.

Insomnia can become a form of contemplation. You just lie there, inert, helpless, alone, in the dark, and let yourself be crushed by the inscrutable tyranny of time. The plank bed becomes an altar and you lie there without trying to understand any longer in what sense you can be called a sacrifice. Outside in the world, where it is night, perhaps there is someone who suddenly sees that something he has done is horrible. He is most unexpectedly sorry and finds himself able to pray. . . .

May 29.

I am trying to tone down The Seven Storey Mountain. When I wrote it three years ago, I don't know what audience I might have been thinking of I suppose I just put down what was in me, under the eyes of God Who knows what is in me. But not everything that I remember will please—or help—everyone who may happen to read the book. Now I have suddenly thought of all the different kinds of people who may some day read it: men

iding on the Long Island Railroad, nuns in Irish convents, my relatives, secu-
ar priests, communists . . . and young girls in boarding schools, whom the
ensors are afraid to scandalize.

May 31. Ember Saturday.

. . . The sun is bright. Catbirds sing with crazy versatility above my head
n the tree. Fasting is easy in nice weather.

August 31.

Another August has ended and we will never see it again. It was hot and
stuffy all day, but although it did not rain, after Vespers the air was cooler
and the sky had brushed up to look something like September. O frightening
and beautiful month with Saint Giles standing in your door to be the patron
of those who are afraid. Soon we will fight the fields of corn.

We have the biggest retreat of the year. There are eighty-two or more in
the guest house that was built for fifty. One of them is an old man with a
magnificent white beard and a big curled mustache. He must be one of the
wonders of Kentucky and I am overwhelmed with awe whenever he appears.

Waiting in the empty guest house dining-room, amid the smells of hot
soup and fresh pie, while the brothers bring more wagons of food from the
kitchen I lean in the window-sill and read snatches of Paul Claudel's prose. I
like his prose more than his verse. Especially a long prose poem about rain,
somewhere in Japan. Someone ought to write a whole book full of things like
that.

October 12. Sunday.

All the hills and woods are red and brown and copper, and the sky is clear,
with one or two very small clouds. A buzzard comes by and investigates me,
but I am not dead yet. This whole landscape of woods and hills is getting to
be saturated with my prayers and with the Psalms and with the books I read
out here under the trees, looking over the wall, not at the world but at our
forest, our solitude. . . .

November 23.

By God's mercy I have found someone in the monastery who is willing
and able to help me produce something acceptable as a souvenir for the
Centenary. This providential helper is Brother Theodoret, the baker, who is
also an artist and an architect. He has plenty of time to do things while he
is waiting for the dough to rise, and so he has a drawing-board in the bakery,
on which he draws up plans for new monasteries. . . . He has ideas. And
he does not believe that God can be glorified by the solidified molasses which
some people call religious art. Once in a while we have to talk to one another, but it is worth it. . . .

August 13, 1948.

. . . Yesterday I had to go in to Louisville. It was the first time I was ou
of the monastery in seven years. I had to go in to act as interpreter for Don
Gabriel Sortais, the Vicar General, who has come to make a Visitation, and
who was called in to the Good Shepherd convent because their Mother Gen
eral from Angers was there and wanted him to talk to the community and
then hear her confession. The sisters received us in a cool library with a lo
of armchairs and carpets. The place was cool because all the buildings wer
surrounded by big shade trees and on the whole the convent is a pleasan
one—and very big. Big police dog, a laundry, brick houses, porches. So he
told them, in French, to love their vocations, and I translated his message
into English. I think they were happy. One sister held the black hat I had
been wearing in her hand while I drank a glass of ginger ale and ate a cookie
and was too shy to look at any of the sisters.

September 7. Vigil of Our Lady's Nativity.

The laybrother novices with pneumatic drills and sledge hammers are
pounding and battering at the foundations of this wing under the Scriptorium
to make a hole big enough to get a new heating plant into the cellar. The
place sounds and smells like New York.

October 10. Sunday.

Sooner or later the world must burn, and all things in it—all the books, the
cloister together with the brothel, Fra Angelico together with the Lucky
Strike ads which I haven't seen for seven years because I don't remember
seeing one in Louisville. Sooner or later it will all be consumed by fire and
nobody will be left—for by that time the last man in the universe will have
discovered the bomb capable of destroying the universe and will have been
unable to resist the temptation to throw the thing and get it over with.

And here I sit writing a diary.

But . . . love, love, love, in the cloister and in the choir and out there in
the presence of the forest and the hills where all the colors are changing, and
under the steeple whose topmost cross has been painted with yellow traffic
paint by Brother Processus who swung up there for days in the sky with his
angel holding on to him. (He upset a bucket of paint and I could see it
flying upside down on the end of a rope, and the paint turned to spray be
fore it was half way down, and a drop fell on our Psalter and there were
little yellow spots all over the stones and the bushes of the cemetery where
today I saw a hawk.)

December 14.

The most precious thing I had today was an hour of silence out behind
the church. It has been warm and damp and the knobs are hidden in mist
It started to rain a little and I came in but the laybrother novices were

practicing part-singing in the choir novitiate and were singing better than the choir novices who were practicing Gregorian chant in the professed singing room. By that time I discovered that it wasn't really raining after all and so I escaped to my silence and stood out there all alone, drugged and happy, with a book under my arm.

Tomorrow: revolution. Self-shaving is to be introduced at Gethsemani for the first time in a century. Father Prior is going to give out brushes and safety razors and small bars of soap and (o horror!) mirrors. Father Abbot has received a letter of instructions from Our Lady of the Valley telling all about how to shave. We are supposed to shave twice a week. Such effeminacy! We shall rake and hack at our own miserable chins; in the end this is going to be more penitential—but faster than the communal electric shave: we won't have to sit around waiting our turn.

Apparently this is what they do in Europe. Dom Gabriel was shocked to see us so hairy. . . .

May 29, 1949.

. . . Friday I said that Mass I had promised to Our Lady of Cobre. I had been told one got so mixed up in the rubrics that the first Mass was no fun. I did not find that to be true at all. On the contrary, I felt as if I had been saying Mass all my life, and the liturgical text of the Votive Mass of our dearest Lady in this season became immensely rich. It was at Saint Anne's altar and the church was full of sun (after Chapter) and there was no one else saying Mass nearby so I could really *speak* it. Then there was a beautiful chalice Dan Walsh brought down, and I had an amice and corporal and purificator and even a finger towel, all of which came from some colored boys and girls in a Catholic High School in Mobile, Alabama; and I had a cincture given by a sister in a hospital in St. Louis. If I had tried to say all the names of all the people I wanted to remember at the *Memento* I would have stood there until dinner time: but I had kept forming intentions for them all days beforehand, so that they would all be included when the time came. Even then I took time to remember all those that God wanted me explicitly to remember over again at that moment.

So I gave Communion to Nanny and to Dan Walsh and Bob Lax and Ed Rice and Bob Giroux, who wore his U.S. Navy jacket, and to Tom Flanagan who came with Ed, and Rod Mudge who came with Dan and to McCauliffe who wrote here about poetry. But I couldn't give Communion to Jay Laughlin or to Seymour. And after the Mass I had plenty of time to make a good thanksgiving by myself at Our Lady of Victories altar and after that I went out and talked, or rather Someone talked through me. It was a marvelous morning under the tree that Father Mauritius once marked *Gingko Biloba*, though all the botanical signs are now gone.

July 11.

We have a new mechanical monster on the place called a D-4 Traxcavator which is enormous and rushes at the earth with a wide-open maw and devours everything in sight. It roars terribly, especially when it is hungry. It has been given to the laybrother novices. They feed it every day and you can't hear yourself think in the monastery while the brute is at table. It is yellow and has a face like a drawbridge and is marked all over with signs saying it comes from the Whayne supply company in Louisville, but really, as I know from secret information, it was born on a raft in Memphis, Tennessee. There, the hippopotamus abounds: which this instrument greatly resembles.

Also we have bought fans. They are exhaust fans. You make a hole in the building and put the fans there and they draw all the hot air out of the dormitory. Nobody knows what happens after that. My guess is that the hot air that went out through the fan is then replaced by the hot air that comes in through the windows. The fans are not yet running because the laybrother novices have not yet made the holes in the building. However, they have begun. They have a scaffold up on the roof of the infirmary and they have been blasting at the gable of that wing with jack-hammers, and two frail novices who are very young were posted down on the ground floor near the doorways with artistic signs which read "Falling Bricks." At first one of them was standing at the precise spot where all the falling bricks would land on his head. He was saying the rosary in an attitude of perfect abandonment. Afterwards he got a stool and moved inside the cloister and propped up the sign in his lap and took to reading the immortal masterpiece of Father Garrigou-Lagrange, *Christian Perfection and Contemplation.*

November 24.

. . . It was raining and there was a wind. I went out to the wagon shed. You could still see the hills in the distance, not too much rain for that—many black clouds, low and torn, like smoke from a disaster, flying angrily over the wide open ruin of the old horsebarn, where I now love to walk alone. On sunny days it does not have this Castle of Otranto look about it. Today, first I was full of a melody that might have been related to something in Stravinsky's "Firebird" which I have nevertheless forgotten. This was mostly my own and I sang it to God, along with angels. Then the melody went away and I sat on a stone.

December 27. Feast of Saint John.

Yesterday Father Cellarer lent me the jeep. I did not ask for it, he just lent it to me out of the goodness of his heart, so that I would be able to go out to the woods on the other side of the knobs. I had never driven a car before. Once or twice at Saint Bonaventure's I took lessons. Father Roman tried to teach me to drive a little broken-down Chevvie he had there. Yesterday I took the jeep and started off gaily all by myself to the woods. It had been raining heavily. All the roads were deep in mud. It took me some time to discover the front-wheel drive. I skidded into ditches and got out again, I went through creeks, I got stuck in the mud, I bumped into trees and once, when I was on the main road, I stalled trying to get out of the front-wheel drive and ended up sideways in the middle of the road with a car coming down the hill straight at me. Thank heaven I am still alive. At the

moment I didn't seem to care if I lived or died. I drove the jeep madly into
the forest in a rosy fog of confusion and delight. We romped over trestles
and I sang "O Mary I love you," went splashing through puddles a foot
deep, rushed madly into the underbrush and backed out again.

Finally I got the thing back to the monastery covered with mud from stem
to stern. I stood in choir at Vespers, dizzy with the thought: "I have been
driving a jeep."

Father Cellarer just made me a sign that I must never, never, under any
circumstances, take the jeep out again. . . .

December, 1950. Feast of Saint Lucy.

I remember Gray Street, Louisville. A black carnival mask with broken
elastic lying in the dirty snow in front of one of those ancient ornate houses.
Gray Street must look nice in spring when the sun comes shining through
the sycamores. . . .

I am aware of silence all around me in the country as of a world that is
closed to men. They live in it and yet its door is closed to them. This silence,
it is everywhere. It is the room Jesus told us to enter into when we pray.

"All the thoughts of a turtle are turtle."

Ralph Waldo Emerson

One day in 1881 the train from Boston to Concord was a little late. On the railway station platform the usual loungers were jostled aside by an assembly of people. There were little girls in short white dresses with broad bows of silk. Town dignitaries walked up and down in striped trousers and beaver hats. Brass instruments gleamed under the arms of bandsmen. A boy was posted to wave a handkerchief signal to one who waited in a church tower.

"On this green bank, by this soft stream, we set to-day a votive stone. . . ." Then the train crept in. A tall, slender man emerged, bald, a black coat thrown over his old shoulders. Ralph Waldo Emerson (1803–1882), Concord's most noted son, had come home. (Friends had raised a sum of money to pay for a trip to Europe, and to rebuild his house which had burnt down the year before.) He was escorted to a waiting carriage, the band played, the church bells tolled, there were huzzas, school children marched before him and pelted him with roses as he was driven under a triumphal arch covered with leaves and flowers.

What did Emerson see of this scene, what did he think of this belated adulation? He made no note of it, for his dimmed sight had made him give up writing the journals he had kept for 55 years since he was a schoolboy of 16. Did he remember that here at Concord, not so many years before, he had been hissed off a platform for denouncing that form of man's inhumanity to man called slavery? Did he remember, a lifetime of years ago, how he had felt, rising in the dawn of the grim Concord winter, a boy of eight, to chop wood (conjugating irregular Latin verbs in his head, all the while) to stoke the stove on which his mother would transform a bit of cod or a handful of grain into breakfast for the five hungry boys left fatherless at the death of her clergyman husband, sixth of the generations of Emersons to devote their life to the church?

Emerson carried on the family tradition, but not for long. Backward at reading (his father noted) when he was sent to

From *The Heart of Emerson's Journals,* edited by Bliss Perry, reprinted by permission of and arrangement with Houghton Mifflin Company, the authorized publishers.

school at the age of two, his education was taken in hand by his
aunt Mary Moody Emerson. He was a shy boy with a winning
smile, quick to listen and slow to learn. His tutor gave him much
for all that she was queer, prone to speak of the worms that
would ultimately consume her spare body. A dwarf, she lived in
a shroud she had sewn herself, wore it as a nightgown, and to
the perturbation of Concord rode in it up and down the town on
horseback. Yet only Plato taught him more than odd Aunt Mary.
At fourteen his name was entered in the Freshman class at Harvard and four years later he took his degree. Apt in divinity, he
preached for a time in the Unitarian church until his dissenting
views proved too unsettling even for indulgent congregations.
After that he became a writer and lecturer. His talks, published
as "essays" won him popularity and his books found many buyers.
He spoke up and down and across the continent. His hearers were
more excited, quite often, by the appearance of this unfrocked
New England radical, who had become something of a celebrity,
than by what he said, although in his low voice he sometimes
said bold things.

Emerson knew, and spoke well of, such disturbing people as
Karl Marx, John Brown and Walt Whitman. After John Brown
had spent an evening at his house, for example, Emerson concluded that the Fugitive Slave Bill was "a filthy enactment . . .
I will not obey it, by God." He told his audiences his views and
wrote of them. Disgusted with the materialism of his times he
baited his audience with his own sanity. As Vernon Louis Par-
rington noted, "for a generation he was the conscience of America,
a pricker of inflated balloons, a gauger of the national brag and
cant and humbug. With keen insight he put his finger on the
mean and selfish and the great and . . . few of his judgments on
men and measures have suffered reversal in the court of final jurisdiction."

Meanwhile, Emerson kept a diary, and left this precious (and
little-read) heritage to his country. When every poem and essay
he ever wrote has been forgotten, men still will be washing gold
from the ten printed volumes of it. The few pages given here
necessarily fail to do justice to the man.

February 25, 1827. St. Augustine, Florida.

I attended mass in the Catholic Church. The mass is in Latin and the sermon
in English, and the audience, who are Spaniards, understand neither. The
services have been recently interrupted by the imprisonment of the (clergyman) worthy father for debt in the Castle of St. Marks.

February 27.

A fortnight since I attended a meeting of the Bible Society. The Treasurer
of this institution is Marshal of the district, and by a somewhat unfortunate

arrangement had appointed a special meeting of the Society, and a slave-auction, at the same time and place, one being in Government house, and the other in the adjoining yard. One ear therefore heard the glad tidings of great joy, whilst the other was regaled with "Going, gentlemen, going!" And almost without changing our position we might aid in sending the Scriptures into Africa, or bid for "four children without the mother" who had been kidnapped therefrom.

May 19, 1828. Alexandria, Virginia.

Mr. Adams went out a swimming the other day into the Potomac, and went near to a boat which was coming down the river. Some rude black-guards were in it, who, not knowing the character of the swimmer, amused themselves with laughing at his bald head as it poppled up and down in the water, and, as they drew nearer, threatened to crack open his round pate if he came nigh them. The President of the United States was, I believe, compelled to waive the point of honour and seek a more retired bathing place.

January 20, 1832. Boston.

Don't trust children with edge tools. Don't trust man, great God, with more power than he has, until he has learned to use that a little better. What a hell should we make of the world if we could do what we would! Put a button on the foil till the young fencers have learned not to put each other's eyes out.

1833. Undated.

The old jail in Cambridge was immediately back of Mrs. Kneeland's house. The inmates of the prison were very bad neighbors and used to take delight in pestering Mrs. Kneeland with foul names and profane language. Professor Hedge took great pains to get the nuisance removed, and at last the old jail was pulled down. Someone congratulated Mrs. K. upon the happy deliverance, but found her quite sad at the loss of her stimulus. "She kind o' missed 'em," she said.

April 11, 1834.

Went yesterday to Cambridge and spent most of the day at Mount Auburn; got my luncheon at Fresh Pond, and went back again to the woods. After much wandering . . . seeing many things, four snakes gliding up and down a hollow for no purpose that I could see—not to eat, not for love, but only gliding. . . .

March 23, 1835.

There is no greater lie than a voluptuous book like Boccaccio. For it represents the pleasures of appetite, which only at rare intervals, a few times in a life-time, are intense, and to whose acme continence is essential, as frequent, habitual, and belonging to the incontinent. . . .

February 8, 1836.

Women have less accurate measure of time than men. There is a clock in Adam: none in Eve.

April 22, 1837.

Cold April; hard times; men breaking who ought not to break; banks bullied into the bolstering of desperate speculators; all the newspapers a chorus of owls.

November 25.

I do not like to see a sword at a man's side. If it threatens man, it threatens me. A company of soldiers is an offensive spectacle.

June 8, 1838.

A man must have aunts and cousins, must buy carrots and turnips, must have barn and woodshed, must go to market and to the blacksmith's shop, must saunter and sleep and be inferior and silly.

August 18.

Dr. Ripley prays for rain with great explicitness on Sunday, and on Monday the showers fell. When I spoke of the speed with which his prayers were answered, the good man looked modest.

June 4, 1840.

Waldo says, "The flowers talk when the wind blows over them." My little boy grows thin in the hot summer, and runs all to eyes and eyelashes.

June 24.

Montaigne. The language of the street is always strong. What can describe the folly and emptiness of scolding like the word *jawing?* I feel too the force of the double negative, though clean contrary to our grammar rules. And I confess to some pleasure from the stinging rhetoric of a rattling oath in the mouth of truckmen and teamsters. How laconic and brisk it is. . . . Cut these words and they would bleed; they are vascular and alive; they walk and run. Moreover they who speak them have this elegancy, that they do not trip in their speech. It is a shower of bullets, whilst Cambridge men and Yale men correct themselves and begin again at every half sentence. . . .

June 24.

Now for five years I have been indulged by the gracious Heaven in my long holiday in this gracious house of mine, entertaining and entertained by so many worthy and gifted friends, and all this time poor Nancy Burton, the mad-woman has been screaming herself hoarse at the Poor-house across the brook and I still hear her whenever I open my window.

September 16.

A sleeping child gives me the impression of a traveller in a very far country.

October 24.

What a pity that we cannot curse and swear in good society! Cannot the stinging dialect of the sailors be domesticated? It is the best rhetoric, and for a hundred occasions those forbidden words are the only good ones. . . .

June, 1842.

I hear with pleasure that a young girl in the midst of rich, decorous Unitarian friends in Boston is well-nigh persuaded to join the Roman Catholic Church. Her friends, who are also my friends, lamented to me the growth of this inclination. But I told them that I think she is to be greatly congratulated on the event. She has lived in great poverty of events. In form and years a woman, she is still a child, having had no experiences, and although of a fine, liberal, susceptible, expanding nature, has never yet found any worthy object of attention; has not been in love, not been called out by any taste, except lately by music, and sadly wants adequate objects. In this church, perhaps, she shall find what she needs, in a power to call out the slumbering religious sentiment. . . . If the offices of the church attracted her, if its beautiful forms and humane spirit drew her, if St. Augustine and St. Bernard, Jesus and Madonna, cathedral music and masses, then go, for thy dear heart's sake, but do not go out of this icehouse of Unitarianism, all external, into an icehouse again of external. At all events, I charged her to pay no regard to dissenters, but to suck that orange thoroughly.

September, 1842.

How slowly, how slowly we learn that witchcraft and ghostcraft, palmistry and magic, and all the other so-called superstitions, which, with so much police, boastful skepticism, and scientific committees, we had finally dismissed to the moon as nonsense, are really no nonsense at all, but subtle and valid influences, always starting up, mowing, muttering in our path, and shading our day.

October. Undated.

The sannup and the squaw do not get drunk at the same time. They take turns in keeping sober, and husband and wife should never be low-spirited at the same time, but each should be able to cheer the other.

November 11.

Time is the little grey man who takes out of his breast-pocket first a pocket-book, then a Dolland telescope, then a Turkey carpet, then four saddled and bridled nags and a sumptuous canvas tent. . . . I was a little chubby boy trundling a hoop in Chauncy Place, and spouting poetry from Scott and Campbell at the Latin School. But Time, the little grey man, has taken out of his vest-pocket a great, awkward house (in a corner of which I sit down and write of him), some acres of land, several full-grown and several very young persons, and seated them close beside me; then he has taken that chubbiness and that hoop quite away (to be sure he has left the declamation and the poetry), and here left a long, lean person threatening to be a little grey man, like himself.

November 26.

This old Bible, if you pitch it out of the window with a fork, it comes bounce back again.

January 7, 1843. Baltimore.

Here to-day from Philadelphia. The railroad, which was but a toy coach the other day, is now a dowdy, lumbering country wagon. . . . The Americans take to the little contrivance as if it were the cradle in which they were born.

February 7. New York.

Dreamlike travelling on the railroad. The towns through which I pass between Philadelphia and New York make no distinct impression. They are like pictures on a wall. The more, that you can read all the way in the car a French novel.

February 7.

Webster['s] . . . external advantages are very rare and admirable; his noble and majestic frame, his breadth and projection of brows, his coal-black hair, his great cinderous eyes, his perfect self-possession, and the rich and well-modulated thunder of his voice (to which I used to listen, sometimes, abstracting myself from his sense merely for the luxury of such noble expressions of sound). . . . The faults that shade his character are not such as to hurt his popularity. . . . It is sometimes complained of him that he is a man of pleasure, and all his chosen friends are easy epicures and debauchees. But this is after Talleyrand's taste, who said of his foolish wife that he found nonsense very refreshing: so Webster, after he has been pumping his brains in the courts and the Senate, is, no doubt, heartily glad to get among cronies and gossips where he can stretch himself at his ease and drink his mulled wine. They also quote as his *three rules* of living: (1) Never to pay any debt that can by any possibility be avoided; (2) Never to do anything to-day that can be put off till tomorrow; (3) Never to do anything himself which he can get anybody else to do for him. . . . He has misused the opportunity of making himself the darling of the American world in all coming time by abstaining from putting himself at the head of the Antislavery interest, by standing for New England and for man against the bullying and barbarism of the South.

February 8.

Mr. Adams chose wisely and according to his constitution, when, on leaving the Presidency, he went into Congress. He is no literary old gentleman, but a bruiser, and loves the mêlée. When they talk about his age and venerableness and nearness to the grave, he knows better; he is like one of those old cardinals, who, as quick as he is chosen Pope, throws away his crutches and his crookedness, and is as straight as a boy.

May 7.

Yesterday, English visitors, and I waited all day when they should go. If we could establish the rule that each man was a guest in his own house, and when we had shown our visitors the passages of the house, the way to fire, bread, and water, and thus made them as much at home as the inhabitant, did then leave them to the accidents of intercourse, and went about our ordinary business, a guest would no longer be formidable.

May, 1846. Undated.

If I were a member of the Massachusetts legislature, I should propose to exempt all colored citizens from taxation because of the inability of the government to protect them by passport out of its territory. It does not give the value for which they pay the tax.

May 23.

Cotton thread holds the union together; unites John C. Calhoun and Abbott Lawrence. Patriotism for holidays and summer evenings, with music and rockets, but cotton thread is the Union.

February, 1847. Undated.

Health, South wind, books, old trees, a boat, a friend.

May 6, 1848. Paris.

In Paris, my furnished lodgings, a very comfortable suite of rooms (15 *Rue des petits Augustins*) on the second floor cost me ninety francs a month, or three francs a day. . . . The expenses of living for a day, at my rate, are six francs fifteen sous, or seven francs. . . . I looked in all the shop windows for toys this afternoon and they are very many and gay, but the only one of all which I really wish to buy is very cheap; yet I cannot buy it, namely, their speech.

May 6.

The boulevards have lost all their fine trees, which were all cut down for the barricades in February. At the end of a year we shall take account, and see if the Revolution was worth the trees.

September, 1850. Undated.

Macaulay's History is full of low merits; it is like English manufactures of all kinds, neat, convenient, portable, saleable, made on purpose for the Harpers to print a hundred thousand copies of. So far can Birmingham go.

May, 1851. Undated.

Bad Times [the enactment of the Fugitive Slave Law]. We wake up with painful auguring, and, after exploring a little to know the cause, find it is the odious news in each day's paper, the infamy that has fallen upon Massachusetts and until the Government is assured that once for all it cannot and shall not be executed here. All I have and all I can do shall be given in opposition to execution of the law. . . . The word *liberty* in the mouth of Mr. Webster sounds like the word *love* in the mouth of a courtezan. . . . Mr. Choate, whose talent consists in a fine choice of words which he can hang indiscriminately on any offender, has pushed the privilege of his profession so far as to ask, "What would the Puritans of 1620 say to the trashy sentimentalism of modern reformers?" And thus the stern old fathers of Massachusetts who, Mr. Choate knows, would have died at the stake before soiling themselves with this damnation, are made to repudiate the "trashy sentimentalism" of the Ten Commandments. The joke is too impudent. . . . Mr. Webster has deliberately taken out his name from all the files of honour in which he had enrolled it,—from all association with liberal, virtuous, and philanthropic men, and read his recantation on his knees at Richmond and Charleston. . . .

The Union! Oh, yes, I prized that, other things being equal; but what is the Union to a man self-condemned with all sense of self-respect and religion become bitter ironies, and liberty the ghastly nothing which Mr. Webster means by that word? . . .

Mr. Everett, a man supposed aware of his own meaning, advises pathetically a reverence for the Union . . . Does he mean that we shall lay hands on a man who has escaped from slavery to the soil of Massachusetts, and so has done more for freedom than ten thousand orations, and tie him up and call in the marshal, and say, "I am an orator for freedom; a great many fine sentences have I turned,—none has turned finer, except Mr. Webster,—in favor of plebian strength against aristocracy; and, as my last and finest sentence of all, to show the young men of the land who have bought my book and clapped my sentences and copied them in their memory, how much I mean by them, Mr. Marshal, here is a black man of my own age, and who does not know a great deal of Demosthenes, but who means what he says, whom we will now handcuff and commit to the custody of this very worthy gentleman who has come on from Georgia in search of him; I have no doubt he has much to say to him that is interesting, as the way is long. I don't care if I give them—here are copies of my Concord and Lexington and Plymouth and Bunker Hill addresses to beguile their journey from Boston to the plantation whipping-post." . . . Union is a delectable thing, and so is wealth, and so is life, but they may all cost too much, if they cost honour.

July 6, 1852.

The head of Washington hangs in my dining-room for a few days past, and I cannot keep my eyes off it. It has a certain Appalachian strength, as if it were truly the first-fruits of America, and expressed the Country. The heavy, leaden eyes turn on you, as the eyes of an ox in a pasture. And the mouth has gravity and depth of quiet, as if this MAN had absorbed all the serenity of America, and left none for his restless, rickety, hysterical countrymen.

September 5, 1855.

All the thoughts of a turtle are turtle.

"I told her, God knew me better . . ."

John Wesley

John Wesley (1703–1791), the founder of Methodism, spent his long and active life in developing and preaching the evangelical concepts of Christianity which grew into a world-wide religious movement. The son of a Church of England clergyman, he became his father's curate after attending Oxford, and remained an Anglican priest all his life. As a young man, he went to Georgia as a missionary to the Indians. His experiences there and in England after his return from America led him to establish the first "methodist" society.

In the face of years of bitter opposition and physical violence, he persisted in preaching his doctrines of salvation through Christ whenever and wherever he could. In all he delivered some 40,000 sermons in his travels of 250,000 miles up and down the British Isles, mostly by horseback. He worked as a printer and became a hymnwriter (he published 23 collections) to spread his gospel. Yet this gentle, indomitable man, still found time to compile a dictionary, write educational treatises, histories, theological works, make translations from Greek, Latin and Hebrew, and edit the religious works of others.

Until he was physically unable to write any longer, at the age of 87, Wesley made careful journal entries of his daily life and of its triumphs and difficulties. One of the most detailed of all existing diaries, Wesley's journal ranks high among the literary achievements of the eighteenth century. It mirrors not only his age but his fertile, seeking mind. Most of all, it is an inspiring and lively account of courage and faith.

May 28, 1738.

I waked in peace, but not in joy. In the same even, quiet state I was until the evening, when I was roughly attacked in a large company as an enthusiast, a seducer, and a setter-forth of new doctrines. By the blessing of God, I was not moved to anger, but after a calm and short reply went away. . . .

From *John Wesley's Journal,* as abridged by Nehemiah Curnock. Reprinted by permission of Philosophical Library.

June 4. Sunday.

Was indeed a feast-day. For from the time of my rising till past one in the afternoon, I was praying, reading the Scriptures, singing praise, or calling sinners to repentance. All these days I scarce remember to have opened the Testament, but upon some great and precious promise. And I saw more than ever, that the gospel is in truth but one great promise, from the beginning of it to the end.

November 19.

. . . I was greatly troubled in dreams; and about eleven o'clock, waked in an unaccountable consternation, without being able to sleep again. About that time (as I found in the morning), one who had been designed to be my pupil, but was not, came into the porter's lodge (where several persons were sitting), with a pistol in his hand. He presented this, as in sport, first at one, and then at another. He then attempted twice or thrice to shoot himself, but it would not go off. Upon his laying it down, one took it up, and blew out the priming. He was very angry, went and got fresh prime, came in again, sat down, beat the flint with his key, and about twelve, pulling off his hat and wig, said he would die like a gentleman, and shot himself through the head.

March 31, 1739.

In the evening I reached Bristol, and met Mr Whitefield there. I could scarce reconcile myself at first to this strange way of preaching in the fields, of which he set me an example on Sunday; having been all my life (till very lately) so tenacious of every point relating to decency and order, that I should have thought the saving of souls almost a sin, if it had not been done in a church.

June 5.

. . . The street was full of people, hurrying to and fro, and speaking great words. But when any of them asked, "Which is he?" and I replied, "I am he," they were immediately silent. Several ladies following me into Mr Merchant's house, the servant told me there were some wanted to speak to me. I went to them, and said, "I believe, ladies, the maid mistook; you only wanted to look at me." I added, "I do not expect that the rich and great should want either to speak with me, or to hear me; for I speak the plain truth,—a thing you hear little of, and do not desire to hear." A few more words passed between us, and I retired.

July 17.

I rode to Bradford, five miles from Bath, whither . . . I went to a gentleman in the town, who had . . . wished me good luck in the name of the

Lord. But it was past. I found him now quite cold. He began disputing on several heads; and at last told me plainly, one of our own college had informed him they always took me to be a little crack-brained at Oxford.

September 27.

. . . At six, came to Turner's Hall, which holds (by computation) two thousand persons. The press both within and without was very great. In the beginning of the expounding, there being a large vault beneath, the main beam which supported the floor broke. The floor immediately sunk, which occasioned much noise and confusion among the people. But, two or three days before, a man had filled the vault with hogsheads of tobacco. So that the floor, after sinking a foot or two, rested upon them, and I went on without interruption.

October 23.

. . . I was exceedingly pressed to go back to a young woman in Kingswood. (The fact I nakedly relate, and leave every man to his own judgment of it.) I went. She was nineteen or twenty years old; but it seems, could not write or read. I found her on the bed, two or three persons holding her. It was a terrible sight. Anguish, horror, and despair, above all description, appeared in her pale face. The thousand distortions of her whole body showed how the dogs of hell were gnawing her heart. The shrieks intermixed were scarce to be endured. But her stony eyes could not weep. She screamed out, as soon as words could find their way, "I am damned, damned; lost for ever! Six days ago you might have helped me. But it is past. I am the devil's now. I have given myself to him. His I am. Him I must serve. I must go to hell. I will be his. I will serve him. I will go with him to hell. I cannot be saved. I must, I will, I will be damned!" She then began praying to the devil. . . . "Stony hearts, break! [she broke out again]. I am a warning to you. Break, break, poor stony hearts! Will you not break? What can be done more for stony hearts? I am damned, that you may be saved. Now break, now break, poor stony hearts! You need not be damned, though I must." She then fixed her eyes on the corner of the ceiling, and said, "There he is; ay, there he is! Come, good devil, come! Take me away. You said you would dash my brains out; come, do it quickly. I am yours. I will be yours. Come just now. Take me away." We interrupted her by calling again upon God: on which . . . another young woman began to roar out as loud as she had done. . . . We continued in prayer till past eleven; when God in a moment spoke peace into the soul, first of the first tormented, and then of the other.

January 30, 1740.

One came to me, by whom I used to profit much. But her conversation was now too high for me: it was far above, out of my sight. My soul is sick of this sublime divinity. Let me think and speak as a little child! Let my religion be plain, artless, simple! Meekness, temperance, patience, faith, and love, be these my highest gifts: and let the highest words wherein I teach them, be those I learn from the Book of God!

March 19, 1742.

I rode once more to Pensford, at the earnest request of several serious people. The place where they desired me to preach was a little green spot, near the town. But I had no sooner begun, than a great company of rabble, hired (as we afterwards found) for that purpose, came furiously upon us, bringing a bull, which they had been baiting, and now strove to drive in among the people. But the beast was wiser than his drivers; and continually ran either on one side of us, or the other, while we quietly sang praise to God, and prayed for about an hour. The poor wretches, finding themselves disappointed, at length seized upon the bull, now weak and tired, after having been so long torn and beaten both by dogs and men; and, by main strength, partly dragged, and partly thrust, him in among the people. When they had forced their way to the little table on which I stood, they strove several times to throw it down, by thrusting the helpless beast against it; who, of himself, stirred no more than a log of wood. I once or twice put aside his head with my hand, that the blood might not drop upon my clothes; intending to go on, as soon as the hurry should be a little over. But the table falling down, some of our friends caught me in their arms, and carried me right away on their shoulders; while the rabble wreaked their vengeance on the table, which they tore bit from bit. We went a little way off, where I finished my discourse. . . .

September 12.

I was desired to preach in an open place, commonly called the Great Gardens, lying between Whitechapel and Coverlet Fields, where I found a vast multitude gathered together. Many of the beasts of the people laboured much to disturb those who were of a better mind. They . . . threw whole showers of stones, one of which struck me just between the eyes; but I felt no pain at all; and when I had wiped away the blood, went on testifying with a loud voice. . . .

December 29.

. . . Took horse for Tanfield. More than once I was only not blown off my horse. However, at three I reached the Leigh, and explained to a multitude of people the salvation which is through faith. Afterwards I met the society in a large upper room, which rocked to and fro with the violence of the storm. But all was calm within; and we rejoiced together. . . .

September 16, 1743.

In the evening as I was preaching at St Ives, Satan began to fight for his kingdom. The mob of the town burst into the room, and created much disturbance; roaring and striking those that stood in their way, as though

Legion himself possessed them. I would fain have persuaded our people to
stand still; but the zeal of some, and the fear of others, had no ears: so that
finding the uproar increase, I went into the midst, and brought the head of
the mob up with me to the desk. I received but one blow on the side of the
head; after which we reasoned the case, till he grew milder and milder. . . .

October 20.

I rode to Wednesbury. At twelve I preached in a ground near the middle
of the town . . . and no creature offered to molest us, either going or coming;
but the Lord fought for us, and we held our peace. I was writing at Francis
Ward's, in the afternoon, when the cry arose that the mob had beset the
house. We prayed that God would disperse them; and it was so: one went
this way, and another that; so that, in half an hour, not a man was left. I
told our brethren, "Now is the time for us to go"; but they pressed me exceedingly to stay. So that I might not offend them, I sat down, though I
foresaw what would follow. Before five the mob surrounded the house again
in greater numbers than ever. . . . As soon as I was in the midst of them,
I called for a chair; and standing up, asked, "What do any of you want with
me?" Some said, "We want you to go with us to the justice" . . . on which
I went before, and two or three hundred followed; the rest returning whence
they came.

The night came on before we had walked a mile, together with heavy
rain. However, on we went to Bentley Hall, two miles from Wednesbury.
One or two ran before, to tell Mr Lane they had brought Mr Wesley before
his Worship. . . . A servant told them Mr Lane was in bed. His son followed, and asked what was the matter. One replied, "Why, an't please you,
they sing psalms all day; nay, and make folks rise at five in the morning.
And what would your Worship advise us to do?" "To go home," said Mr
Lane, "and be quiet."

November 2.

The following advertisement was published: ". . . By the Edinburgh Company of Comedians . . . will be acted a . . . Farce, called TRICK UPON
TRICK, or METHODISM DISPLAYED."

It was believed there could not be less than fifteen hundred people, some
hundreds of whom sat on rows of seats built upon the stage. Soon after the
comedians had begun the first act of the play, on a sudden all those seats
fell down at once, the supporters of them breaking like a rotten stick. The
people were thrown one upon another, about five foot forward, but not one
of them hurt. After a short time, the rest of the spectators were quiet and
the actors went on. In the middle of the second act, all the shilling seats gave
a crack, and sunk several inches down. A great noise and shrieking followed,
and as many as could readily get to the door went out, and returned no
more. Notwithstanding this, when the noise was over, the actors went on with
the play. In the beginning of the third act the entire stage suddenly sunk
about six inches: the players retired with great precipitation; yet in a while
they began again. At the latter end of the third act, all the sixpenny seats,

without any kind of notice, fell to the ground. There was now a cry on every side. . . . Two or three hundred remaining still in the hall, Mr Este (who was to act the Methodist) came upon the stage and told them, for all this he was resolved the farce should be acted. While he was speaking, the stage sunk six inches more; on which he ran back in the utmost confusion, and the people as fast as they could out of the door, none staying to look behind him.

Which most is surprising—that these players acted this farce the next week, or that some hundreds of people came again to see it?

January 21, 1745.

. . . All this summer, our brethren in the west had as hot service as those in the north of England: the war against the Methodists, so called, being everywhere carried on with far more vigour than that against the Spaniards. I had accounts of this from all parts.

July 6, 1746.

After talking largely with both the men and women leaders, we agreed it would prevent great expense, as well of health as of time and money, if the poorer people of our society could be persuaded to leave off drinking of tea. We resolved ourselves to begin and set the example. I expected some difficulty in breaking off a custom of six-and-twenty years' standing. And, accordingly, the three first days, my head ached, more or less, all day long, and I was half-asleep from morning to night. The third day, on *Wednesday*, in the afternoon, my memory failed, almost entirely. In the evening I sought my remedy in prayer. . . .

May 21, 1747.

I called at Thirsk; but finding the town full of holiday folks, drinking, cursing, swearing, and cock-fighting, I did not stop at all, but rode on. . . .

October 16.

I went with two or three friends, to see what are called the electrical experiments. How must these also confound those poor half-thinkers, who will believe nothing but what they can comprehend! Who can comprehend, how fire lives in water, and passes through it more freely than through air? How flame issues out of my finger, real flame, such as sets fire to spirits of wine? How these, and many more as strange phenomena, arise from the turning round a glass globe? It is all mystery. . . .

February 2, 1751.

. . . Clearly convinced that I ought to marry. For many years I remained single because I believed I could be more useful in a single, than in a married state. And I praise God, who enabled me to do so. I now as fully believed, that in my present circumstances, I might be more useful in a married state; into which, upon this clear conviction, and by the advice of my friends, I entered a few days later.

February 3, 1753.

I visited one in the Marshalsea Prison; a nursery of all manner of wickedness. Oh, shame to man, that there should be such a place, such a picture of hell, upon earth! And shame to those who bear the name of Christ, that there should be any prison at all in Christendom!

December 23, 1755.

I was in the robe-chamber, adjoining to the House of Lords, when the King put on his robes. His brow was much furrowed with age, and quite clouded with care. And is this all the world can give even to a king, all the grandeur it can afford? A blanket of ermine around his shoulders, so heavy and cumbersome he can scarce move under it! An huge heap of borrowed hair, with a few plates of gold and glittering stones upon his head! Alas, what a bauble is human greatness!

September 9, 1756.

I settled my temporal business. It is now about eighteen years since I began writing and printing books; and how much in that time have I gained by printing? Why, on summing up my accounts, I found that on March 1, 1756 (the day I left London last), I had gained by printing and preaching together, a debt of twelve hundred and thirty-six pounds.

November 9.

Having procured an apparatus on purpose, I ordered several persons to be electrified, who were ill of various disorders; some of whom found an immediate, some a gradual cure. From this time I appointed, first some hours in every week, and afterwards an hour in every day, wherein any that desired it, might try the virtue of this surprising medicine. Two or three years after, our patients were so numerous that we were obliged to divide them: so part were electrified in Southwark, part at the Foundery, others near St Paul's, and the rest near the Seven Dials: the same method we have taken ever since; and to this day, while hundreds, perhaps thousands, have received unspeakable good, I have not known one man, woman, or child, who has received any hurt thereby: so that when I hear any talk of the danger of being electrified (especially if they are medical men who talk so), I cannot but impute it to great want either of sense or modesty. . . .

January 16, 1760.

One came to me, as she said, with a message from the Lord, to tell me, I was laying up treasures on earth, taking my ease, and minding only my eating and drinking. I told her, God knew me better; and if He had sent her, He would have sent her with a more proper message.

December 18, 1765.

Riding through the borough, all my mare's feet flew up, and she fell with my leg under her. A gentleman stepping out, lifted me up and helped me into his shop. I was exceeding sick, but was presently relieved by a little hartshorn and water. After resting a few minutes, I took a coach; but when I was cold, found myself much worse; being bruised on my right arm, my breast, my knee, leg, and ankle, which swelled exceedingly. However, I went on to Shoreham; where, by applying treacle twice a day, all the soreness was removed. . . .

September 19, 1769.

. . . I preached . . . on White's Hill, near Bradford, in the evening. . . . A gentleman in the town desired me to preach at his door. The beasts of the people were tolerably quiet till I had nearly finished my sermon. They then lifted up their voice, especially one, called a gentleman, who had filled his pocket with rotten eggs: but a young man coming unawares, clapped his hands on each side, and mashed them all at once. In an instant he was perfume all over; though it was not so sweet as balsam.

February 23, 1770.

I was desired to hear Mr Leoni sing at the Jewish synagogue. . . . The place itself is so solemn, that it might strike an awe upon those who have any thought of God.

February 28.

I sat down to read and seriously consider some of the writings of Baron Swedenborg. I began with huge prejudice in his favour, knowing him to be a pious man, one of a strong understanding, of much learning, and one who thoroughly believed himself. But I could not hold out long. Any one of his visions puts his real character out of doubt. He is one of the most ingenious, lively, entertaining madmen, that ever set pen to paper. But his waking dreams are so wild, so far remote both from Scripture and common-sense, that one might as easily swallow the stories of *Tom Thumb* or *Jack the Giant-Killer*.

July 21, 1773.

We had our quarterly meeting in London; at which I was surprised to find, that our income does not yet answer our expense. We were again near two hundred pounds bad. My private account I find still worse. I have laboured as much as many writers; and all my labour has gained me, in seventy years, a debt of five or six hundred pounds.

June 28, 1774.

This being my birthday, the first day of my seventy-second year, I was considering, How is this, that I find just the same strength as I did thirty years ago? That my sight is considerably better now, and my nerves firmer, than they were then? That I have none of the infirmities of old age, and have lost several I had in my youth? The grand cause is, the good pleasure of God, who doeth whatsoever pleaseth Him. The chief means are: 1. My constantly rising at four, for about fifty years. 2. My generally preaching at five in the morning; one of the most healthy exercises in the world. 3. My never travelling less, by sea or land, than four thousand five hundred miles in a year.

January 25, 1781.

I spent an agreeable hour at a concert of my nephews. But I was a little out of my element among lords and ladies. I love plain music and plain company best.

December 18, 1783.

I spent two hours with that great man, Dr Johnson, who is sinking into the grave by a gentle decay.

August 26, 1784.

On the road I read over Voltaire's memoirs of himself. Certainly never was a more consummate coxcomb! But even his character is less horrid than that of his royal hero! Surely so unnatural a brute never disgraced a throne before.

June 28, 1788.

I this day enter on my eighty-fifth year. . . . It is true I am not so agile as I was in times past. I do not run or walk so fast as I did; my sight is a little decayed; my left eye is grown dim, and hardly serves me to read; I have daily some pain in the ball of my right eye, as also in my right temple (occasioned by a blow received some months since), and in my right shoulder and arm, which I impute partly to a sprain and partly to the rheumatism. I find likewise some decay in my memory, with regard to names and things lately past; but not at all with regard to what I have read or heard twenty, forty, or sixty years ago; neither do I find any decay in my hearing, smell, taste, or appetite (though I want but a third part of the food I did once); nor do I feel any such thing as weariness, either in travelling or preaching: and I am not conscious of any decay in writing sermons. . . .

January 1, 1790.

I am now an old man, decayed from head to foot. My eyes are dim; my right hand shakes much; my mouth is hot and dry every morning; I have a lingering fever almost every day; my motion is weak and slow. However, blessed be God, I do not slack my labour; I can preach and write still.

7. WAR—WITHOUT HOPE, WITHOUT VICTORY

When Walt Whitman worked during the Civil War as a volunteer nurse in Washington hospitals, he often brought his patients gifts paid for with money sent by friends. No presents he distributed were more eagerly received by the convalescent soldiers than pocket-size blank books in which they could write diaries.

This is not surprising, for more Americans kept diaries during these five years of war than ever before or since. It was a time when each man, whether soldier in the field, or one who stayed at home to watch fearfully and wait, seemed to feel the need to keep an account of his own personal involvement. Basic human emotions were stirred by an issue so great that none could escape it, none could ignore the searching challenges to security and conviction. From such stimuli diaries have always come; great trials and conflicts nourish them. Emerson noted in his journal in February, 1863: "The human mind cannot be burned, nor bayonetted, nor wounded, nor missing."

The Civil War was a conflict largely fought by youths, and many of the most moving diaries are the stark accounts of the brutal impact of battle on these boys. Each of them saw his own war, but in general their stories followed the same pattern of disillusionment as ideals of heroism and glory faded in the actuality of mud, short rations, night marches and cannon balls.

But during the years agony hung over the land war was not all fighting. Those behind the lines, particularly in the South, had the problem of finding such food and shelter as could be obtained with the almost worthless currency flooding from Confederate presses; concern that slaves kept long in bondage might turn against their masters; fear of pillage and abuse from invading troops; manifold misgivings, regrets and anxieties.

There follow portions of a dozen war time diaries chosen from hundreds that have been preserved. The first, that of Mary Boykin Chesnut, is the longest and affords the broadest view. It spans in frank and informal detail the time between two ominous bursts of gunfire—the shelling of Fort Sumter on April 12, 1861 and the shots fired by the assassin, John Wilkes Booth.

The other diaries are glimpses of the larger spectacle, vignettes of experience observed from varying vantage points of temperament and geography. Some of the diarists are famous, some obscure. The excerpts tell of the itch of boys to go to war; the *awkward transition from civilian to soldier; the crudeness of sur-gery in the field; hardships at home and at the front; hunger and privation; the plight of prisoners—all the many and varied episodes of triumph and defeat.*

Here, then, with a dash of humour sometimes lightening the tears, is the living account of one war—a war which ended nearly a century ago and yet remains perhaps the most vividly real epi-sode in all American history.

". . . What is the matter? Enough! I will write no more."

Mary Boykin Chesnut

Among the best of all American diaries, and certainly the best of those kept during the Civil War, is that written by Mary Boykin Chesnut (1823–1886). It has wit, taste, style, and remarkably skillful reporting. But most of all, it is distinguished by its deep understanding and breadth of vision.

Mrs. Chesnut belonged to one of the "first families" of the South. She was the daughter of Stephen Decatur Miller, Governor of South Carolina, her native state. She married General James Chesnut, Jr., a former United States Senator, the son of Colonel James Chesnut, a rich planter who in 1860 was approaching ninety, a deaf, dim-sighted and anachronistic patriarch. The younger Chesnut took an active part in the war; he played a key role in the attack on Fort Sumter, served as President Jefferson Davis' military aide, and commanded troops in the field.

The Chesnuts spent much time in the capitals of the Confederacy at Montgomery and Richmond, but at intervals they returned to the family home, Mulberry Plantation, near Camden, South Carolina. Though Mrs. Chesnut found life dull there and her husband's parents difficult to live with, she took some pleasure in its elegant splendour. Her descriptions are flower-scented reminders of the idyllic luxury of the "old South"—yet in her view it was a scene already clouded by a gathering pall.

Well-informed, well-read, articulate, with a first-hand knowledge of Europe and its languages, Mrs. Chesnut also knew her own country, North and South, and the people, enslaved or great, who lived in it. As a diarist she was able to detach herself long enough from her close friendship with the Davises, the Lees, and the dashing generals of the Confederacy to write of them as human beings not without faults, and of the weaknesses as well as the virtues of the Southern cause.

In some 400,000 words of manuscript journal which she copied into about fifty notebooks, she took note of whatever she saw

From *A Diary from Dixie,* by Mary Boykin Chesnut, reprinted by permission of and arrangement with Houghton Mifflin Company, the authorized publishers.

and heard—gossip, scandal, deeds brave or ignoble, and of ways of life, both gay and sad, just beyond the cannon's range.

February 15, 1861.

I came to Charleston on November 7th and then went to Florida to see my mother. On the train, just before we reached Fernandina, a woman called out: "That settles the hash!" Tanny touched me on the shoulder and said: "Lincoln's elected." "How do you know?" "The man over there has a telegram." Someone cried: "Now that the black radical Republicans have the power I suppose they will [John] Brown us all."

I have always kept a journal, with notes and dates and a line of poetry or prose, but from today forward I will write more. . . .

We go now to Montgomery, the capital of the Confederacy.

February 19. Montgomery, Alabama.

The brand new Confederacy is making or remodelling its Constitution. . . . Everywhere political intrigue is as rife as in Washington. . . . I do not allow myself vain regrets or sad forebodings. This Southern Confederacy must be supported now by calm determination and cool brains. We have risked all, and we must play our best, for the stake is life or death.

March 4.

. . . I have seen a Negro woman sold upon the block at auction. I was walking. The woman on the block overtopped the crowd. I felt faint, seasick. The creature looked so like my good little Nancy. She was a bright mulatto, with a pleasant face. She was magnificently gotten up in silks and satins. . . . My very soul sickened. It was too dreadful. I tried to reason. . . .

March 5.

We stood on the balcony to see our Confederate Flag go up. Roar of cannon. Miss Sanders complained, and so did Captain Ingraham, of the deadness of the mob. "It was utterly spiritless," she said. "No cheering, or so little; no enthusiasm." Captain Ingraham suggested: "Gentlemen are apt to be quiet. This was a thoughtful crowd. The true mob element with us just now is hoeing corn." And yet, it is uncomfortable that the idea has gone abroad that we have no joy, no pride in this thing. The Band was playing "Massa's in the Cold, Cold Ground." . . .

March 14.

. . . Mrs. Scott was describing Lincoln, who is of the cleverest Yankee type. She said: "Awfully ugly, even grotesque in appearance. The kind who are always at corner stores sitting on boxes, whittling sticks, and telling stories as funny as they are vulgar." Here I interposed to sigh: "But Douglas said one day to Mr. Chesnut 'Lincoln is the hardest fellow to handle I have ever encountered yet.'" Mr. Scott is from California. He said: "Lincoln is an utterly American specimen, coarse, rough and strong. A good-natured, kindly creature, and as pleasant tempered as he is clever. And if this country can be joked and laughed out of its rights, he is the kind-hearted fellow to do it. Now if there be a war and it pinches the Yankee pocket, instead of filling it—" . . .

I wonder if it be a sin to think slavery a curse to any land. Men and women are punished when their masters and mistresses are brutes, not when they do wrong. Under slavery, we live surrounded by prostitutes, yet an abandoned woman is sent out of any decent house. Who thinks any worse of a Negro or mulatto woman for being a thing we can't name? God forgive us, but ours is a monstrous system, a wrong and an iniquity! Like the patriarchs of old, our men live all in one house with their wives and their concubines; and the mulattoes one sees in every family partly resemble the white children. Any lady is ready to tell you who is the father of all the mulatto children in everybody's household but her own. Those, she seems to think, drop from the clouds. My disgust sometimes is boiling over. Thank God for my country women, but alas for the men! They are probably no worse than men everywhere, but the lower their mistresses, the more degraded they must be.

March 31. Charleston, South Carolina.

My 38th birthday, but I am too old now to dwell in public on that unimportant circumstance. . . .

"Of the fullness of the heart the mouth speaketh," says the Psalmist, but it is not so here. Our hearts are in doleful dumps, and yet we are as gay, as madly jolly as the sailors who break into the strong room when the ship is going down. First came our great agony. We were out alone. We longed for some of our big brothers to come out and help us. Well, they are out; but now it is Fort Sumter and that ill-advised Anderson [commander of U.S. forces at the fort]. There stands Fort Sumter, and thereby hangs peace or war. . . .

April 4.

. . . A ship was fired into yesterday and went back to sea. Is that the first shot? How can one settle down to anything? One's heart is in one's mouth all the time. Any minute, the cannon may open on us, the fleet come in.

April 6.

. . . Things are happening so fast. My husband has been made an aide-de-camp of General Beauregard. Three hours ago we were quietly packing to go home. The Convention had adjourned. Now he tells me the attack upon Fort Sumter may begin tonight.

It depends upon Anderson. . . . Ammunition wagons rumbling along the streets all night. Anderson burning blue lights; signs and signals for the fleet outside, I suppose. . . . Governor Means had found a sword and a red sash and brought them for Colonel Chesnut, who has gone to demand the surrender of Fort Sumter.

And now, patience! We must wait. . . .

April 12.

Anderson will not capitulate!

Yesterday was the merriest, maddest dinner we have had yet. Men were more audaciously wise and witty. We had an unspoken foreboding it was to be our last pleasant meeting. . . .

I do not pretend to go to sleep. How can I? If Anderson does not accept terms at four o'clock, the orders are he shall be fired upon. I count four by St. Michael's chimes, and I begin to hope. At half past four, the heavy booming of a cannon! I sprang out of bed and on my knees, prostrate, I prayed as I never prayed before.

There was a sound of stir all over the house, a pattering of feet in the corridor. All seemed hurrying one way. I put on my double-gown and a shawl and went to the house top. The shells were bursting. In the dark I heard a man say: "Waste of ammunition!" I knew my husband was rowing about in a boat somewhere in that dark bay, and that the shells were roofing it over, bursting toward the Fort. . . . Who could tell what each volley accomplished of death and destruction.

The women were wild, there on the house top. Prayers from the women and imprecations from the men; and then a shell would light up the scene. Tonight, they say, the forces are to attempt to land. . . .

Last night—or this morning, truly—up on the house top, I was so weak and weary I sat down on something that looked like a black stool. "Get up, you foolish woman! Your dress is on fire," cried a man; and he put me out. It was a chimney, and the sparks caught my clothes; but my fire had been extinguished before it broke out into a regular blaze.

Do you know, after all that noise, and our tears and prayers, nobody has been hurt. Sound and fury signifying nothing! A delusion and a snare! . . .

April 13.

. . . How gay we were last night. Reaction after the dread of all the slaughter we thought those dreadful cannons were making such a noise in doing. Not even a battery the worse for wear. Fort Sumter has been on fire. He has not yet silenced any of our guns, or so the aids—still with swords and red sashes by way of uniform—tell us. But the sound of those guns makes regular meals impossible. None of us go to table, but tea trays pervade the corridors going everywhere. Some of the anxious hearts lie on their beds and moan in solitary misery. Mrs. Wigfall and I solace ourselves with tea in my room. These women have all a satisfying faith. "God is on our side," they cry. When we are shut in, we, Mrs. Wigfall and I, ask: "Why?" Answer: "Of course. He hates the Yankees! You'll think that well of Him."

Not by one word or look can we detect any change in the demeanor of these Negro servants. Lawrence sits at our door, as sleepy and as respectful and as profoundly indifferent. So are they all. They carry it too far. You could not tell that they even hear the awful noise that is going on in the bay, though it is dinning in their ears night and day. And people talk before them as if they were chairs and tables, and they make no sign. Are they . . . wiser than we are, silent and strong, biding their time? . . .

April 15.

I did not know that one could live such days of excitement. They called: "Come out! There is a crowd coming." A mob, indeed; but it was headed by Colonels Chesnut and Manning. The crowd was shouting and showing these two as messengers of good news whom they were escorting to Beauregard's Headquarters. Fort Sumter had surrendered! Those up on the house top shouted to us: "The Fort is on fire." . . .

June 28. Richmond, Virginia.

. . . In Mrs. Davis's drawing-room last night, the President took a seat by me on the sofa where I sat. He talked for nearly an hour. He laughed at our faith in our own prowess. We are like the British; we think every Southerner equal to three Yankees at least, but we will have to be equivalent to a dozen now. . . . There was a sad refrain running through it all. For one thing, either way, he thinks it will be a long war. That floored me at once. It has been too long for me already. He said only fools doubted the courage of the Yankees, or their willingness to fight when they saw fit. And now we have stung their pride, we have roused them till they will fight like devils. . . .

July 4.

. . . Noise of drums, tramp of marching regiments all day long, rattling of artillery wagons, bands of music, friends from every quarter coming in. We ought to be miserable and anxious, and yet these are pleasant days. Perhaps we are unnaturally exhilarated and excited. . . .

A young Carolinian with queer ideas of a joke rode his horse through the barroom of this hotel. How he scattered people and things right and left! Captain Ingraham was incensed at the bad conduct of his young countryman. "He was intoxicated, of course," said Captain Ingraham. "But he was a splendid rider." . . .

July 7. White Sulphur Springs, Virginia.

. . . We are always picking up some good thing of the rough Illinoisian's saying. Lincoln objects to some man: "Oh, he is too *interruptious*." That is a horrid style of man or woman. The Interruptious! I know the thing, but had no name for it before.

July 13. Richmond, Virginia.

. . . Yesterday as we left the cars we had a glimpse of war. It was the saddest sight; the memory of it is hard to shake off. Sick soldiers, not wounded. There were quite two hundred lying about as best they might on the platform. . . .

Now every day we grow weaker and they stronger, so we had better give a telling blow at once. Already we begin to cry out for more ammunition, and already the blockade is beginning to shut it all out. . . . I did not know there was such a "bitter cry" left in me; but I wept my heart away today when my husband went off. Things do look so black. . . .

July 24.

. . . They brought me a Yankee soldier's portfolio from the battlefield. One might shed a few tears over some of the letters. Women—wives and mothers—are the same everywhere. . . .

July 27.

. . . There are so many wonderful tales here about everybody. One about that strange looking man, Clingman, I thought funny enough. Dancing is a serious business with him. Some young lady spoke to him while he was dancing with her. "Pray withhold all remarks," he said, "it puts me out. I cannot do two things at once." . . .

Here is one of Mr. Chesnut's anecdotes of the Manassas. He had in his pocket a small paper of morphine. He put it there to relieve pain. . . . A man was howling with pain on the outskirts of the battlefield. He was, by the way, the only one Mr. Chesnut heard that made any outcry that day, be their wounds as grievous as they might. This man proved to be only a case of pain in the stomach. Him Mr. Chesnut relieved with the opiate, and passed on rapidly where he was sent. Later in the day he saw a man lying under a tree who begged for water. He wore the Federal uniform. As Mr. Chesnut carried him the water, he asked where he was from. The man refused to answer. "Poor fellow, you have no cause to care about all that now. You can't hurt me and God knows I would not harm you. What else do you want?" "Straighten my legs. They are doubled up under me." The legs were smashed. Mr. Chesnut gave him some morphine to let him know at least a few moments of peace. He said to me: "This is my first battle. I hope my heart will not grow harder."

August 5.

. . . Dr. Gibbes is a bird of ill omen. Today he tells me eight of our men have died at the Charlottesville Hospital. It seems sickness is more redoubtable in an army than the enemy's guns. There are 1100 there *hors de combat,* and virulent typhoid fever among them. They want money, clothes, nurses; so I am writing right and left calling for help from the sister societies at home. The good and patriotic women at home are easily stirred to this work. . . .

August 23.

. . . Went to the St. Charles. Horrors upon horrors again. Want of organization, long rows of men dead and dying; awful smiles and awful sights. A boy from home had sent for me. He was lying on a cot, ill of fever. Next him a man died in convulsions while we stood there. I was making arrangements with a nurse, hiring him to take care of this lad. I do not remember any more, for I fainted. . . .

August 27.

I do not know when I have seen a woman without knitting in her hand. "Socks for the soldiers" is the cry. One poor man said he had dozens of socks and but one shirt. He preferred more shirts and fewer socks. It gives a quaint look, the twinkling of needles, and the everlasting sock dangling. . . .

I hate slavery. You say there are no more fallen women on a plantation than in London, in proportion to numbers; but what do you say to this? A magnate who runs a hideous black harem with its consequences under the same roof with his lovely white wife, and his beautiful and accomplished daughters? He holds his head as high and poses as the model of all human virtues to these poor women whom God and the laws have given him. From the height of his awful majesty, he scolds and thunders at them, as if he never did wrong in his life. Fancy such a man finding his daughter reading "Don Juan." "You with that immoral book!" And he orders her out of his sight. You see, Mrs. Stowe did not hit the sorest spot. She makes Legree a bachelor. . . .

September 9. Camden, South Carolina.

Mulberry. Home again. . . . The mother of that poor lad I went to see die at the tobacco factory in Richmond met me. She says he is the same boy sent to Miss Henrietta's school. . . . Now they are raising money to bring his body home. Too late. A little of it would have made him comfortable, and maybe saved his life. When I think of the filth and squalor in which I found him, his clothes unchanged for weeks, an atmosphere of horror on every side, wounded men parked in rows like sardines in a box. No wonder I fainted! But now we are efficient at last, and have money to bring home the body! Oh, in this world, if we could only know in time! . . .

November 30.

. . . My sleeping apartment is large and airy, with windows opening on the lawn east and south. In those deep window seats, idly looking out, I spend much time. A part of the yard which was once a deer park has the appearance of the primeval forest; the forest trees have been unmolested and are now of immense size. In the spring, the air is laden with perfumes, violets, jasmine, crabapple blossoms, roses. Araby the blest was never sweeter in perfume. And there hangs here as on every Southern landscape the saddest pall. There are browsing on the lawn, where Kentucky bluegrass flourishes, Devon cows and sheep, horses, mares and colts. It helps to enliven it. . . .

From my window high (I sit here in the library alone a great deal), I see carriages approach. Colonel Chesnut drives a pair of thoroughbreds, mahogany bays with shining coats and arching necks. It is a pleasure to see Scip drive them up. Tiptop and Princess are their names. Mrs. Chesnut has her carriage horses and a huge family coach for herself, which she never uses. The young ladies have a barouche and their own riding horses. We have a pair, for my carriage; and my husband has several saddle horses. There are always families of the children or grandchildren of the house visiting here, with carriage and horses, nurses and children. The house is crammed from garret to cellar without intermission. As I sit here writing, I see half a dozen carriages under the shade of the trees, coachmen on their boxes, talking, laughing. Some are "hookling," they call it. They have a bone hook something like a crochet needle, and they hook themselves woolen gloves. Some are reading hymn books or pretending to do so. The small footmen are playing marbles under the trees. A pleasant, empty, easy-going life, if one's heart is at ease. But people are not like pigs; they cannot be put up and fattened. So here I pine and fret. . . .

December 13.

Charleston is in flames, one part of the city utterly destroyed. On the night of the eleventh, we had here a furious windstorm. We rather enjoyed it, in the interest of the Yankee Fleet outside of the Bar there. As the blast howled, we said: "How now, blockaders?" When the telegram came today, I was too much shocked to speak. Suffering, death and destitution on every side. In all this confusion they might attack us. What then! . . .

December 22.

Anniversary of secession. The reality is not as dreadful as the anticipation. I have not seen half as much as I dreaded of fire and sword, bad as it is. . . .

January 11, 1862.

. . . Colonel Chesnut is so quiet and comfortable. He has forgotten the war. He is busy making another will, telling each Negro to whom he intends to leave him or her—as if there were no Yankees. Some startling shock will come and wake us up again. Yet even this, this cold beneficence, seizes my praise, when I reflect on those who sigh with sympathy for the wretched, yet shun them, nursing their delicious solitude in slothful loves and dainty sympathies. . . .

February 11. Columbia, South Carolina.

. . . Confederate affairs are in a blue way. Roanoke taken, Fort Henry on the Tennessee open to them, and we fear for the Mississippi River too. We have evacuated Romney—wherever that is. New armies and new fleets are swarming and threatening everywhere. We ought to have as good a conceit of ourselves as they have of us, and to be willing to do as much to save ourselves from a nauseous Union with them as they are willing to do by way of revengeful coercion in forcing us back. England's eye is scornful and scoffing as she turns it on our miseries. I have nervous chills every day. Bad news is killing me. . . .

March 11.

. . . Cotton is five cents a pound and labor of no value at all; it commands no price whatever. People gladly hire out their Negroes to have them fed and clothed, which latter cannot be done. Cotton Osnaburg at thirty-seven and a half cents a yard leaves no chance to clothe them. Langdon was for martial law and making the bloodsuckers disgorge their ill-gotten gains. We, poor fools, who are patriotically ruining ourselves, will see our children in the gutter while treacherous dogs of millionaires go rolling by in their coaches—coaches that were acquired by taking advantage of our necessities. . . .

March 19.

He who runs may read. Conscription means that we are in a tight place. This war was a volunteer business. Tomorrow conscription begins—the last resort. . . . Conscription has waked the Rip Van Winkles. The streets of Columbia were never so crowded with men. To fight and to be made to fight are different things.

To my small wits, whenever people were persistent, united, and rose in their might, no general, however great, succeeded in subjugating them. Have we not swamps, forests, rivers, mountains—every natural barrier? . . .

April 27.

New Orleans is gone, and with it the Confederacy! Are we not cut in two? The Mississippi ruins us if it is lost. The Confederacy is done to death by the politicians. Those wretched creatures, the Congress, could never rise to the greatness of the occasion. They seem to think they were in a neighbourhood squabble about precedence. The soldiers have done their duty. All honor to the army. But statesmen, busy bees about their own places or their personal honour, are too busy to see the enemy at a distance. . . .

April 29.

The news from New Orleans is fatal to us. Met Mr. Weston. He wanted to know where he could find a place of safety for two hundred Negroes. I looked in his face to see if he were in earnest, then to see if he were sane. He said there were a certain set of two hundred Negroes that had grown to be a nuisance. Apparently all the white men of the family had felt bound to stay at home to take care of them. There are, apparently, people who still believe Negroes to be property. They are like Noah's neighbours, who insisted that the deluge would only be a little shower after all. . . .

May 24.

. . . Here in Columbia, the family dinners are the specialty. . . . They have everything of the best. Silver, glass, china, table linen, damask, etc. The planters live "within themselves" as they call it; from the plantations come mutton, beef, poultry, cream, butter, eggs, fruits and vegetables. It is easy to live here, with a cook who has been sent to the best eating house in Charleston to be trained. Old Mrs. Chesnut's Romeo was apprenticed at Jones's, in town. I do not know where Mrs. Preston's [cook] got his degrees, but he deserves a medal. . . .

June 9.

. . . When we read of the battles in India, in Italy, in the Crimea, what did we care? It was only an interesting topic, like any other, to look for in the paper. Now, you hear of a battle with a thrill and a shudder. It has come home to us. Half the people that we know in the world are under the enemy's guns. A telegram comes to you and you leave it on your lap. You are pale with fright. You handle it, or dread to touch it, as you would a rattlesnake, or worse; for a snake could only strike you. How many, many of your friends or loved ones this scrap of paper may tell you have gone to their death.

When you meet people, sad and sorrowful is the greeting. They press your hand, and tears stand in their eyes or roll down their cheeks as they happen to have more or less self-control. They have brothers, fathers, or sons as the case may be in the battle; and this thing now seems never to stop. . . .

June 11.

. . . I know how it feels to die. I have felt it again and again. For instance, someone calls out: "Albert Sidney Johnston is killed." My heart stands still. I feel no more. For so many seconds, so many minutes—I know not how long— I am utterly without sensation of any kind, dead. Then there is that great throb, that keen agony of physical pain. The works are wound up again, the ticking of the clock begins anew, and I take up the burden of life once more. Someday it will stop too long, or my feeble heart will be too worn out to make that awakening jar, and all will be over. I do not think that when the end comes that there will be any difference, except the miracle of the new life throb. Good news is just as bad. "Hurrah—Stonewall has saved us!" Pleasure that is almost pain! . . .

June 12.

. . . After all this, I tried to read "Uncle Tom" and could not. It is too sickening. A man sent his little son to beat a human being tied to a tree. It is as bad as Squeers beating Smike. Flesh and blood revolts. You must skip that, it is too bad, like the pulling out of eyeballs in Lear. . . .

November 30, 1863. Richmond, Virginia.

Anxiety pervades. Lee is fighting Meade, Bragg falling back before Grant, Longstreet—the soldiers call him Peter the Slow—sitting down before Knoxville. . . .

December 14.

. . . We went to the White House and they gave us tea. The President said he had been on the way to our house, coming with all the Davis family to see me, but the children became so troublesome that they turned back. Just then little Joe rushed in and insisted on saying his prayers at his father's knee, then and there. He was in his night clothes. . . . At dinner, Mr. Hunter said: "The parsons tell us every Sunday that the Lord is on our side. I wish, however, he would show his preference for us a little more plainly than he has been doing lately."

January 1, 1864.

God help my country! I think we are like the sailors who break into the spirits closet when they find out the ship must sink. There seems to be for the first time a resolute determination to enjoy the brief hour, and never look beyond the day.

I now have no hope. "Have you any of old Mr. Chesnut's brandy here still? It is a good thing never to look beyond the hour. Lawrence, take this key, look in such a place for a decanter . . .".

. . . One more year of Stonewall would have saved us. Chickamauga is the only battle we have gained since Stonewall died; and no results, as usual. Stonewall was not killed by a Yankee. He was shot by his own men. Now that is hard. . . .

General Edward Johnston says he got Grant a place because he could not bear to see an old army man driving a wagon. That was when he found him out west. Grant had been put out of the army for habitual drunkenness. He is their best man, a bull-headed Suwarrow. He don't care a snap if his men fall like the leaves. He fights to win, that chap; he is not distracted by a thousand side issues; he does not see them. He sees only in a straight line. Like Louis Napoleon, from a battle in the gutter he goes straight up.

And like Lincoln, we have ceased to carp at him because he is a rough clown, no gentleman, etc. You never hear now of his nasty fun, but only of his wisdom. It doesn't take much soap and water to wash the hands that hold the rod of empire. They once talked of Lincoln's drunkenness, too. Now, since Vicksburg, they have not a word to say against Grant's habits. He has the disagreeable habit of not retreating before our irresistible veterans! . . .

The last night of the old year sent me a cup of strong, good coffee. I drank two cups and so did not sleep a wink. Like a fool I passed my whole life in review, and bitter memories maddened me. . . .

January 11.

. . . General Preston told us of the impression of the first dead Confederate soldiers' faces, grim in death, lying stark and stiff, made upon him at Shiloh: cold, staring open-eyed. They were all hard frozen, these dead bodies. . . . Everybody who comes in brings a little bad news, not much in itself; but the cumulative effect is depressing indeed.

January 31.

Mrs. Davis gave her "Luncheon to Ladies" on Saturday. Many more persons were there than at any of those luncheons which have gone before. We had gumbo, ducks and olives, *suprême de volaille*, chickens in jelly, oysters, lettuce salad, chocolate cream, jelly cake, claret cup, champagne, etc. . . .

Today, for a pair of forlorn shoes, I gave eighty-five dollars. . . . Mr. Pettigrew says: "You take your money to market in the market basket, and bring home what you buy in your pocketbook."

March 24.

. . . Yesterday we went to the Capitol grounds to see our returned prisoners. . . . Poor fellows! They cheered with all their might, and I wept for sympathy. Their enthusiasm moved me deeply. Oh, these men were so forlorn, so dried up, so shrunken. There was such a strange look in the eyes of some; others were so restless and wild looking; others again had placidly vacant faces, as if they had been dead to the world for years. A poor woman was too much for me. She was hunting for her son. He had been expected back with this batch of prisoners. She said he was taken prisoner at Gettysburg. She kept going in and out among them with a basket of provisions she had brought for him to eat. It was too pitiful. . . .

May 27. Camden, South Carolina.

I hate these constant attacks on Jeff Davis. Old hard-common-sense-Lincoln, the essence of a cute Yankee, says "don't swap horses crossing a stream." In battering down our administration, these people are destroying our last hope of success. In all this beautiful sunshine, in the stillness and shade of these long hours in this piazza, memories haunt me. I see that funeral procession as it wound among those tall monuments up that hillside, and the James River tumbling about below, over rocks and around islands; and I see the dominant figure of that poor old grey-haired man, standing bare-headed, straight as an arrow, clear against the sky, beside the open grave of his son. She stood back, in her heavy black wrappings, and her tall figure drooped. The memory of the flowers, the children, the procession as it moved—these come and go—but these two dark, sorrow-stricken figures rise before me now. I remember that night with no sound but the heavy tramp of his feet over-head, the curtains flapping in the wind, the gas flaring. I was numb, stupid, half dead with grief and terror. . . . Who will they kill next, of that devoted household? . . .

Judge Withers says: "Jeff Davis drinks!" "No, he is an austere man, quiet, grave, devoted to his work, and without a vice in the world." "Oh, if he don't drink then, I dare say he takes opium, for his brain is obfuscated!" Words are wasted on them. They have made Jeff Davis the scapegoat. For their sins, he is tied to the altar. We made the altar, or the burning bush, or whatever that goat has to come out of.

It is impossible to sleep here because it is so solemn and still. The moon-light shines in my window, sad and white; and the wind, the soft south wind, comes over a bank of violets, lilacs, roses, and orange blossoms with magnolia blossoms thrown in. . . .

I was telling them today of a woman who came to Mrs. Davis in Rich-mond, hoping to get her help. She wanted her husband's pardon. He was a deserter. The woman was shabbily dressed, chalk-white and with a pinched face. . . . The army had to pass so near her. Her poor little Susie had just died, and the boy was ailing; food was so scarce and so bad. They all had chills, and she was so miserable. The Negroes had all gone to the Yankees. There was nobody to cut wood, and it was so cold. "The army was coming so near. I wrote, and I wrote: 'If you want to see the baby alive, come! If they won't let you, come anyhow!' So you see, if he is a deserter, I did it. For they would not let him come. Only colonels and generals can get fur-loughs now. He only intended to stay one day, but we coaxed and begged him, and then he stayed and stayed; and he was afraid to go back afterwards. He did not mean to be a coward, nor to desert, so instead of going back to his regiment, he went on the gunboats on the river, to serve there. . . . They are going to shoot him. But it was I who did it. I would not let him alone. Don't you see?"

Mrs. Davis went to the President. She was gone ever so long. . . . Then Mrs. Davis came in, smiling. "Here it is, all that you want." The creature stood straight up; then she fell down on the sofa, sobbing as if soul and body would come asunder. So I fled, blind with tears. . . .

June 2.

. . . I paid today, for two pounds of tea, forty pounds of coffee, and sixty pounds of sugar, $800.

July 26. Columbia, South Carolina.

. . . When I remember all the true-hearted, the light-hearted, the gay and gallant boys who have come laughing and singing and dancing across my way in the three years past! I have looked into their brave young eyes, and helped them as I could, and then seen them no more forever. They lie stark and cold, dead upon the battlefield or mouldering away in hospitals or prisons. I think if I dared consider the long array of those bright youths and loyal men who have gone to their death almost before my very eyes, my heart might break too. Is anything worth it? This fearful sacrifice, this awful penalty we pay for war? . . .

August 19.

Began my regular attendance in the Wayside Hospital. . . . They were awfully smashed-up objects of misery, wounded, maimed, diseased. I was really upset and came home ill. This kind of thing unnerves me quite. As I came into my room I stood there on the bare floor and made Ellen undress me and take every thread I had on and throw them all into a washtub out of doors. She had a bath ready for me and a dressing-gown. . . .

September 2.

Atlanta is gone. Well that agony is over. Like David, when the child was dead, I will get up from my knees, will wash my face and comb my hair. There is no hope, but we will try to have no fear. . . .

November 6.

. . . Sherman in Atlanta has left Thomas to take care of Hood. Hood has thirty thousand men. Thomas forty thousand now and as many more as he wants. He has only to ring the bell and call for more. Grant can get all he wants, both for himself and for Thomas. All the world is open to them; we are shut up in a Bastille. We are at sea—and our boat has sprung a leak!

December 19.

The deep waters are closing over us; and we in this house are like the outsiders at the time of the Flood. We eat, drink, laugh, dance, in lightness of heart!

February 16, 1865. Lincolnton, North Carolina.

My ideas of those last days in Columbia are confused. . . . Sherman was at Orangeburg, barely a day's journey from Columbia, and he left a track as blackened as a fire in the prairies. So my time had come too. My husband urged me to go home. . . . Then a Miss Patterson called, a refugee from Tennessee. She had been in a country overrun by Yankee invaders, and she described so graphically all the horrors to be endured by those subjected to fire and sword and rapine and plunder that I was fairly scared, and I determined to come here. . . . Here in Lincolnton I am broken-hearted, an exile. Such a place. Bare floors. For a featherbed, a pine table and two chairs, I pay $30.00 a day. Such sheets! . . .

February 22.

. . . Charleston and Wilmington are surrendered. I have no further use for a newspaper. I never want to see another one as long as I live. . . .
Shame, disgrace, beggary, all at once. They are hard to bear.
Grand Smash!
Rain! Rain outside! Inside, naught but drowning floods of tears. I could not bear it, so I rushed down in that rain storm to the Martins'. He met me at the door. "Madame, Columbia is burned to the ground." I bowed my head and sobbed aloud. . . .

February 25.

. . . I gave today fifty dollars for a small wooden bucket which in better days, or in metallic currency, was worth twenty-five cents.
I heard a Columbia Hospital tale of an Irish nurse smothering a man who was booked to die, because she wanted his bed for a man whose life could be saved. Millions of soldier's clothes were left in Columbia which could have been brought here, instead of the old chairs and tables we see piled everywhere. The last people who came away say the streets were lined with commissary stores, ready to be removed—if Sherman had waited a day or two longer.

March 1.

. . . Ellen and I are shut up here by the rain, rain, everlasting rain. As our money is worthless, are we to starve? Heavens; how grateful I was today when Miss McLean sent me a piece of chicken! . . . The Fants . . . piously wishing they had some sacred ashes to put on their foreheads, for Ash Wednesday. So we lack even ashes. I have no wood to burn, and cannot afford sackcloth to wail in. We are below the luxury of woe and sackcloth and ashes. Only blockaders can do the thing in that style!

March 5.

Is the sea drying up? It is going up into mist and coming down on us in this water spout, the rain. It raineth every day, and the weather represents our tearful despair on a large scale. It is also Lent; quite convenient, for we have nothing to eat, so we fast and pray and go draggling to church like drowned rats, to be preached at. . . .
How kind my friends were on this my fête day. Mrs. Rutledge sent me a plate of biscuits, Mrs. Munroe sent nearly enough for an entire dinner, Miss

McLean sent in a cake for dessert, and Ellen cooked and served up the materials so happily at hand, very nicely indeed. My heart was too full to eat, but I was quiet and calm and at least spared my husband the trial of a broken voice or tears. As he stood at the window with his back to the room, he said: "Where are they now; my old blind father, and my sister? Day and night, I see her leading him out from under his own roof tree before they burn the house. That picture pursues me persistently." . . .

Now he has gone. With despair in my heart, I left that railroad station. Allan Greene walked home with me. I met his wife and his four ragged little boys, a day or so ago. She is the neatest, the primmest, the softest of women; her voice is like the gentle cooing of a dove. In her dulcet accents she murmured, without the slightest excitement of manner: "You see me! I am going around like a raging lion, seeking what I may devour." A man she had introduced as a faraway cousin of her stepfather interposed. "She talks that way because they would not take Cousin Sarah's money. But one of the storekeepers paid for Cousin Sarah's something-to-eat in yarn!" Mr. Chesnut gave me his last cent. It was a sad parting . . . but I forced myself to listen to Allan, and to say: "Yes, yarn is our circulating medium. It is the current coin of the realm. At a factory here, Mrs. Glover traded off a Negro woman for yarn. The woman wanted to go there as a factory hand, it suited all round." "That's nothing. Yesterday a Negro man was sold for a keg of nails."

General Chesnut said many people were light-hearted at the ruin of the great slave owners. He quoted someone: "They will have no Negroes now to lord it over! They can swell and peacock about and tyrannize now over only a small parcel of women and children, those only who are their very own family." . . .

March 8.

. . . Mrs. Glover, to prove to us the plenty that reigned here in peaceful times, described an "Infair" which she attended here in the early years of the war. An "Infair" means a table standing for days against all comers. At this one, they began to dine at two o'clock in the day, and dined on continuously. As soon as one relay were glutted, another came. Table or tables were constantly replenished. There were two tables in separate rooms; one for beef, bacon, turkeys, fowls, all meats and vegetables and the other for sweets. Everybody fared alike and all fared sumptuously. Without haste, without rest, on flowed the crowd of eaters. Mrs. Glover heard ravenous soldiers aver with delight that they had dined three times that day, and that the last dinner was as good as the first. . . .

March 15.

Lawrence says Miss Chesnut is very proud of her presence of mind and her cool self-possession in the presence of the enemy. She lost, after all, only two bottles of champagne, two of her brother's gold-headed canes, and her brother's horses—including Claudia, the brood mare that he valued beyond price—and her own carriage. A fly-brush boy called Battis, whose occupation in life was to stand behind the table and with his peacock feathers brush the flies. . . .

March 21. Chester, South Carolina.

Another flitting. . . .

March 27.

Today, Stephen D. Lee's corps marched through. The camp songs of the men were a heartbreak, so sad and so stirring. I sat down as women have done before and wept. Oh the bitterness of such weeping! There they go, the gay and gallant few; the last gathering of the flower of Southern manhood. They march with as airy a tread as if they still believed the world was all on their side, and that there were no Yankee bullets for the unwary. . . .

April 3.

. . . For the kitchen and Ellen's comfort, I wanted a pine table and a kitchen chair. A woman sold me a chair today for three thousand Confederate dollars. . . .

April 7.

Richmond has fallen, and I have no heart to write about it. Grant broke through our lines, Sherman cut through them, Stoneman is this side of Danville. They are too many for us. Everything is lost in Richmond, even our archives. Blue-black is our horizon. . . . With this storm of woe impending, we snatched a moment of reckless gayety. Major and Mrs. Hamilton, Captain Barnwell and Captain Ogden, patriots supposed to be sunk in gloomy despondency, came and we played cards, and the stories told were so amusing. I confess I laughed to the point of tears! I knew trouble was all around us, but we put it out and kept it out, let it bang on the door as it would. . . .

April 19.

. . . Just now Mr. Clay dashed up stairs, pale as a sheet. "General Lee has capitulated." I saw the news reflected in Mary Darby's face before I heard him. She staggered to the table, sat down, and wept aloud. Mr. Clay's eyes were not dry. Quite beside herself, Mary shrieked: "Now we belong to Negroes and Yankees." . . .

April 22.

This yellow Confederate quire of paper, blotted by my journal, has been buried three days with the silver sugar dish, the teapot, milk jug, and a few spoons and forks that follow my fortunes. With these valuables was Hood's silver cup, which was partly crushed when he was wounded at Chickamauga. It has been a wild three days, aids galloping around with messages, Yankees hanging over us like the sword of Damocles. We sat up at Mrs. Bedon's, dressed, without once going to bed for forty-eight hours and we were aweary.

Colonel Cadwallader Jones came with a dispatch, sealed and secret. It was for General Chesnut. I opened it. Lincoln, Old Abe Lincoln, killed, murdered! Seward wounded! Why? By whom? It is simply maddening. I sent off messenger after messenger for General Chesnut. I have not the faintest idea where he is, but I know this foul murder will bring down worse miseries on us. . . .

Now look out for bands of marauders, black and white; lawless disbanded soldiers, from both armies.

An armistice, they say, is agreed on.

I take stock, as the shopkeepers say. We have heavy debts for the support of Negroes during the war, and before; but to think of Camden for life, that is worse than the galleys for me. . . .

May 2. Camden, South Carolina.

I am writing from the roadside below Blackstock's, *en route* to Camden. Since we left Chester, solitude; nothing but tall blackened chimneys to show that any man has ever trod this road before us. This is Sherman's track! It is hard not to curse him. . . .

May 4.

From Chester to Winnsboro, we did not see one living thing, man, woman or animal. . . . The blooming of the gardens had a funereal effect. Nature is so luxuriant here; she soon covers the ravages of savages. The last frost occurred the seventh of March, so that accounts for the wonderful advance of vegetation. It seems providential to these starving people; so much that is edible has grown in two months. At Winnsboro, to my amazement, the young people had a May Day amidst the smoking ruins. Irrepressible youth! . . .

May 16.

We are scattered, stunned, the remnant of heart left alive in us filled with brotherly hate. We sit and wait until the drunken tailor who rules the United States of America issues a proclamation and defines our anomalous position. . . .

June 4.

. . . President Davis is in a dungeon, and in chains. Men watch him day and night. . . . Our turn next, maybe. Not among the Negroes does fear dwell now, nor uncertainty, nor anxiety. It dwells here, haunting us, tracking us, running like an accursed discord through all the music tones of our existence.

August 2.

. . . . What is the matter? Enough! I will write no more! [*Here the diary ends.*]

"I do hate to see women cry."

Theodore Upson

The bombardment of Fort Sumter in Charleston Harbour ceased
with its evacuation on April 14, 1861, but the sound of the
thirteen-inch mortar shells the Confederate batteries poured on
the fort echoed through the Northern states. The next day, in
Washington, President Lincoln called for 75,000 volunteers.
When news of the Rebel attack began to reach farms and villages
it had an electrifying and rallying effect, especially in border areas
where there had been little sentiment for war, and especially
among the young.

Young Theodore Upson, born just seventeen years before, tells
in his diary what happened when the first word came to the Indiana farm where he lived with his parents. His father aged and
saddened at the news, his mother and grandmother cried. But
Theodore, like many another youth, wanted to go off to battle.
He enlisted in the Indiana Volunteers, fought with Sherman's
army at Vicksburg, and marched with him to the sea. The end of
the war found him a seasoned veteran, aged twenty-two.

April, 1861. Undated.

Father and I were husking out some corn. We could not finish before it
wintered up. When William Cory came across the field (he had been down
after the Mail) he was excited and said, "Jonathan the Rebs have fired upon
and taken Fort Sumpter." Father got white and couldn't say a word. William said, "The President will soon fix them. He has called for 75,000 men
and is going to blocade their ports, and just as soon as those fellows find out
that the North means business they will get down off their high horse."

Father said little. We did not finish the corn and drove to the barn. Father
left me to unload and put out the team and went to the house. After I had
finished I went in to dinner. Mother said, "What is the matter with Father?"
He had gone right upstairs. I told her what we had heard. She went to him.
After a while they came down. Father looked ten years older. We sat down
to the table. Grandma wanted to know what was the trouble. Father told her

From *With Sherman to the Sea*, by Theodore Upson, edited by Oscar Osburn
Winther. Reprinted by permission of the Louisiana State University Press.

and she began to cry. "Oh my poor children in the South! . . . Oh to think that I should have lived to see the day when Brother should rise against Brother." She and Mother were crying and I lit out for the barn. I do hate to see women cry.

We had another meeting at the school house last night; we are raising money to take care of the families of those who enlist. A good many gave money, others subscribed. The Hulper boys have enlisted and Steve Lampman and some others. I said I would go but they laughed at me and said they wanted men not boys for this job; that it would all be over soon; that those fellows down South are big bluffers and would rather talk than fight. I am not so sure about that. I know the Hale boys would fight with their fists at any rate and I believe they would fight with guns too if needs be. I remember how Charlie would get on our Dick and ride on a galop across our south field cutting mullin heads with his wooden sword playing they were Indians or Mexicans (his father was in the Mexican War), and he looked fine. To be sure there was no danger but I feel pretty certain he could fight. May be it won't be such a picnic as some say it will. There has been a fight down in Virginia at Big Bethel. Al Beecher's Nephew was in it and wrote to his Uncle and he read the letter in his store. I could not make out which side whipped but from the papers I think the Rebels had the best of it. Mother had a letter from the Hales. Charlie and his Father are in their army and Dayton wanted to go but was too young. I wonder if I were in our army and they should meet me would they shoot me. I suppose they would.

". . . and there were no more Bibles . . ."

Charles E. Davis

War is not a solitary pursuit. All soldiers' diaries are records of shared happenings, and the best are often those that reflect group experiences in their greatest breadth. Who the note-taker is, is less important than the secretarial service he furnishes his fellows. When numbers of men live and work and fight together, the highly personal experience and reaction can be grossly misleading.

A special virtue of Charles E. Davis' diary is that it has many authors, for this regimental historian combined his own observations with those of his companions. Here are the farm boys and city apprentices being transformed into soldiers. Davis writes of the Thirteenth Massachusetts Volunteers, but his notes are generally true of all of the raw recruits from both North and South during the early months of the war. Perhaps no conflict was ever waged by forces so largely made up of amateurs. At the beginning of the war the Rebels had no army, and the Union army had only 16,000 officers and men, and only a handful of these had any combat experience. In the newly raised armies there were very few old hands.

With the good humor characteristic of volunteers everywhere and in every war, Davis tells of issues of clothing and other items and of what happened to them, of strange foods that appeared at mess time, of the code word that passed along the marching ranks when a pretty girl came in sight, and of the juicy returns earned by stockholders in the "Joint Stock Frying Pan Company."

August 1, 1861. Hagerstown, Maryland.

After tents were pitched some of the men turned in and went to sleep, though the novelty of the thing was too great for most of us, who straggled back to town. During the day one of the boys brought in a Virginia paper in which it was stated that one "Southerner could lick five Northern mudsills." It was not so very comfortable to feel that we were to be killed off in blocks of five. Nothing was said to us on the 16th of July, the date of our muster-in, about this wholesale slaughter. . . .

From *Three Years in the Army*, by Charles E. Davis. Published by Estes & Lauriat, Boston, 1894.

Some time during the night an alarm was sounded by the beating of the "long roll," and we were ordered into line to drive the terrible foe, who was thought, even then, to be in our midst. Immediately everything was excitement and confusion. We can afford to laugh now, but then it was terribly serious. . . . When it was discovered, as it shortly was, that all this excitement was caused by a pig who strolled into camp and was mistaken by the officer of the guard for the rebel army, many of us were imbued with a courage we hardly felt before. . . . About sunset we struck tents and marched to Boonesboro', fourteen miles . . . were led into an empty corral, lately occupied by mules, to bivouac for the night.

Ordinarily a mule-yard would not be considered a desirable place in which to spend the night, but it was midnight, and we were weary with marching, and worn out with excitement and loss of sleep . . . so that this old mule-yard, as far as we could see it, appeared the most delightful place in the world. . . .

August 3.

A very hot day. Shortly after breakfast we left for Pleasant Valley, sixteen miles, where we arrived in the afternoon, and where we bivouacked for the night. A good many of the men were overcome by the heat, and . . . the size of the knapsack was too heavy for men unused to carrying such a weight. It must be reduced, and there were no more Bibles. . . .

August 23.

While at Sandy Hook we received the hats and uniform coats issued to us by the State, and which were forwarded by express. The coat was much too heavy, with the thermometer in the eighties. It was made with long skirts, and when fitting the wearer was not a bad-appearing garment; but as very few of them did fit, our personal appearance was not improved. They were made large in front, to meet an abnormal expansion of chest. Until we grew to them, it was a handy place to stow some of the contents of our knapsack. The hats were neither useful nor ornamental . . . made of black felt, high-crowned, with a wide rim turned up on one side, and fastened to the crown was a brass eagle containing the figure 13. Now it so happened that the person who selected the sizes was under the impression that every man from Massachusetts had a head like Daniel Webster—a mistake that caused us much trouble, inasmuch as newspapers were in great demand to lessen the diameter of the crown. Those of us who failed to procure newspapers made use of our ears to prevent its falling on our shoulders. . . . They mysteriously disappeared. . . .

September 13.

. . . It was at Darnestown that we were first made acquainted with an article of food called "desiccated" vegetables . . . made in to large, round cakes about two inches thick. When cooked, it tasted like herb tea. From the flow of language which followed, we suspected it contained powerful stimulating properties. . . .

March 12, 1862.

The rattle of drums and the sweet singing of birds announced that morn was here. The army was to move on Winchester at once, so we hastily cooked our coffee, and as quickly as possible ate our breakfast. There was no time to spare as orders . . . were received for the Thirteenth to take the advance of the column as skirmishers. Winchester was four miles away, occupied by 25,000 troops under Stonewall Jackson. . . . It was very warm, and the march a hard one, because the line was irregularly obstructed. . . . We saw those dreaded earthworks a long time before we reached them, and wondered at the enemy's silence, but . . . whatever the boys felt there was no faltering or wavering . . . and with a yell and a rush we bounded over them to find, after all our fears and anticipations, they were empty. We were soon formed in line, and marched, in columns of companies, into town, being the first Union regiment that entered Winchester. We felt proud enough at our bloodless victory . . . we marched down the main street, the band playing patriotic airs, while the people scanned our appearance to see what a Yankee looked like. Some who were prepared to scoff could get no farther than "How fat they are!" . . .

July 22.

In passing through towns and villages, and even on the high-roads, we naturally attracted a good deal of attention. . . . The remarks we heard from the bystanders as we marched along often became by-words in the regiment. We were no exception to the generality of mankind, of liking to see a pretty face, even if it did belong to a woman of "secesh" sentiments. When the boys at the head of the column discovered a pretty girl, if she was on the right side of the road, "*guide right*" would be passed along the line; and "*guide left*" if on the left side of the road . . .

August 9.

The last place to look for a stock company would be among a regiment of soldiers. After being deprived of camp kettles, mess pans, etc., each man was obliged to do his own cooking . . . in his tin dipper, which held about a pint. Whether it was coffee, beans, pork, or anything depending on the services of a fire to make it palatable, it was accomplished by the aid of the dipper only. Therefore any utensil like a frying-pan was of incalculable service in preparing a meal. There were so few of these in the regiment, that only men of large means, men who could raise a dollar thirty days after a paymaster's visit, could afford such a luxury.

In one instance the difficulty was overcome by the formation of a joint-stock company, composed of five stockholders, each paying the sum of twenty cents toward the purchase of a frying-pan, which cost the sum of one dollar. The par value of each share was therefore twenty cents. It was understood that each stockholder should take his turn at carrying the frying-pan when on a march, which responsibility entitled him to its first use in halting for the night. While in camp, it passed from one to the other each day in order of turn. It was frequently loaned for a consideration, thereby affording means for an occasional dividend among the stockholders. The stock advanced in value until it reached as high as forty cents per share, so that a stockholder in the "Joint Stock Frying Pan Company" was looked upon as a man of consequence. Being treated with kindness and civility by his comrades, life assumed a roseate hue to the shareholders in this great company, in spite of their deprivations. It was flattering to hear one's self mentioned in terms of praise by some impecunious comrade who wished to occupy one side of it while you were cooking. . . .

"Where are those damned Secesh women?"

Sarah Morgan Dawson

When Sarah Morgan began her diary in 1862—in many respects a diary as revealing as that of Mary Boykin Chesnut—she was barely twenty-one. But unlike Mrs. Chesnut, she came of a family of townspeople with little direct stake in the maintenance of slavery and the plantation economy. This may account for the independence of viewpoint in her well-written diary, the work of one almost wholly self-educated.

Sarah Morgan's father, a judge, died shortly before her diary opens. A brother, also a judge, lived in New Orleans and was opposed to Secession. Another brother had recently been killed in a duel. Three other brothers were away fighting for the Confederacy. Young Sarah found herself the mainstay of a family of frightened women—three sisters (one of whom had her five children with her) and her weakened mother. They lived in constant apprehension, but with bravery and boldness she succeeded in shepherding her flock through the difficult days following the occupation of Baton Rouge by Federal forces in May, 1862. Later she was to marry Francis Warrington Dawson, English journalist, who had joined Lee's army.

Notable episodes in Sarah Morgan's diary are those describing the burning of baled cotton to keep it from falling into the hands of the advancing Union army, and the plundering of her house by undisciplined Northern soldiers. Looting and sacking was a problem faced by both sides during the war, and it was condoned by neither. Nevertheless, the diarist, contemplating the wanton, senseless destruction of her family's property, could have taken little satisfaction from the knowledge that some of those responsible had been caught and punished.

April 26, 1862. Baton Rouge, Louisiana.

We went this morning to see the cotton burning—a sight never before witnessed and probably never again to be seen. Wagons, drays—everything that

From *A Confederate Girl's Diary,* by Sarah Morgan Dawson edited by Warrington Dawson. Permission to reprint granted by Paul R. Reynolds & Son.

an be driven or rolled—were loaded with the bales and taken a few squares back to burn on the commons. Negroes were running around, cutting them open, piling them up, and setting them afire. All were as busy as though their salvation depended on disappointing the Yankees. Later, Charlie sent for us to come to the river and see him fire a flatboat loaded with the precious material for which the Yankees are risking their bodies and souls. Up and down the levee, as far as we could see, Negroes were rolling it down to the brink of the river where they would set the bales afire and push them in to float burning down the tide. Each sent up its wreath of smoke and looked like a tiny steamer puffing away. Only I doubt that from the source to the mouth of the river there are as many boats afloat on the Mississippi. The flatboat was piled with as many bales as it could hold without sinking. Most of them were cut open, while Negroes staved in the heads of barrels of alcohol, whisky, etc., and dashed bucketfuls over the cotton. Others built up little chimneys of pine every few feet, lined with pine knots and loose cotton, to burn more quickly. There, piled the length of the whole levee, or burning in the river, lay the work of thousands of Negroes for more than a year past. It had come from every side. Men stood by who owned the cotton that was burning or waiting to burn. They either helped or looked on cheerfully. Charlie owned but sixteen bales—a matter of some fifteen hundred dollars; but he was the head man of the whole affair and burned his own as well as the property of others. A single barrel of whisky that was thrown on the cotton cost the man who gave it one hundred and twenty-five dollars. (It shows what a nation in earnest is capable of doing.) Only two men got on the flatboat with Charlie when it was ready. It was towed to the middle of the river, set afire in every place, and then they jumped into a little skiff fastened in front and rowed to land. The cotton floated down the Mississippi one sheet of living flame, even in the sunlight. It would have been grand at night. But then we will have fun watching it this evening anyway. . . .

August 13.

I am in despair. Miss Jones, who has just made her escape from town, brings a most dreadful account. She with seventy-five others, took refuge at Doctor Enders', more than a mile and a half below town, at Hall's. It was there we sent the two trunks containing Father's papers and our clothing and silver. Hearing that guerrillas had been there, the Yankees went down, shelled the house in the night, turning all those women and children out, who barely escaped with their clothing, and let the soldiers loose on it. They destroyed everything they could lay their hands on, if it could not be carried off; broke open armoires, trunks, sacked the house, and left it one scene of devastation and ruin. They even stole Miss Jones's braid. She got here with nothing but the clothes she wore.

This is a dreadful blow to me. Yesterday I thought myself beggared when I heard that our house was probably burnt, remembering all the clothing, books, furniture, etc., that it contained; but I consoled myself with the recollection of a large trunk packed in the most scientific style, containing quantities of nightgowns, skirts, chemises, dresses, cloaks—in short, our very best—which was in safety. Winter had no terrors when I thought of the nice warm clothes; I only wished I had a few of the organdy dresses I had packed up before wearing. And now? It is all gone, Father's law papers, without which we are beggars, and clothing! Nothing left!

August 25.

About twelve at night. Sleep is impossible after all I have heard; so . . . I have lighted my candle and take to this to induce drowsiness. Just after supper . . . I heard a well-known voice . . . and with a cry of surprise, I was hugging Miriam until she was breathless. Such a forlorn creature! so dirty, tired, and fatigued as to be hardly recognizable. We thrust her into a chair and made her speak. . . . She says when she entered the [Morgan] house she burst into tears at the desolation. It was one scene of ruin. Libraries emptied, china smashed, sideboards split open with axes, three cedar chests cut open, plundered, and set up on end; her desk lay open with all her letters and notes well thumbed and scattered around, while Will's last letter to her was open on the floor, with the Yankee stamp of dirty fingers. Mother's portrait, half cut from its frame, stood on the floor. . . .

Upstairs was the finest fun. Mother's beautiful mahogany armoire, whose single door was an extremely fine mirror, was entered by crashing through the glass, when it was emptied of every article and the shelves half split and half thrust back crooked. Letters, labeled by the boys private, were strewn over the floor; they opened every armoire and drawer, collected every rag to be found, and littered the whole house with them, until the wonder was where so many rags had been found. Father's armoire was relieved of everything, Gibbes's handsome Damascus sword with the silver scabbard included. All his clothes, George's, Hal's, Jimmy's, were appropriated. They entered my room, broke that fine mirror for sport, pulled down the rods from the bed, and with them pulverized my toilet set, taking also all Lydia's china ornaments I had packed in the washstand. The debris filled my basin and ornamented by bed. My desk was broken open. Over it were spread all my letters and private papers, a diary I kept when twelve years old, and sundry tokens of dried roses, etc., which must have been very funny, they all being labeled with the donor's name and the occasion. Fool! how I writhe when I think of all they saw; the invitations to buggy rides, concerts, "compliments of," etc.! Lilly's sewing machine had disappeared, but as Mother's was too heavy to move, they merely smashed the needles.

In the pillaging of the armoires they seized a pink flounced muslin of Miriam's, which one officer placed on the end of a bayonet and paraded round with, followed by the others who slashed it with their swords, crying: "I have stuck the damned Secesh! That's the time I cut her!" and continued the sport until the rags could no longer be pierced. One seized my bonnet, with which he decked himself, and ran in the streets. Indeed, all who found such rushed frantically around town, by way of frolicking, with the things on their heads. They say no frenzy could surpass it. Another snatched one of my calico dresses and a pair of vases that Mother had when she was married, and was about to decamp when a Mrs. Jones jerked them away and carried them to her boardinghouse, and returned them to Mother the other day. Blessed be Heaven! I have a calico dress! Our clothes were used for the vilest purposes and spread in every corner, at least those few that were not stolen. . . .

The servants say they broke into the house crying: "Where are those damned Secesh women? We know they are hid in here, and we'll make them dance for hiding from federal officers!" And they could not be convinced that we were not there until they had searched the very garret. Wonder what they would have done? . . .

". . . I said—by Jove, I die like a soldier . . ."

Oliver Wendell Holmes, Jr.

Son of the well-known physician, essayist, and poet ("Old
Ironsides," "The Wonderful One-Hoss Shay"), Oliver Wendell
Holmes, Jr., (1841–1935) was born in Boston where his father, an
active emancipationist, divided his time between literature and
medicine. The younger Holmes came to share his father's early
interest in law, poetry and the anti-slavery cause. On his graduation from Harvard he was commissioned First Lieutenant in the
20th Regiment of Massachusetts Volunteers. He first saw action
on October 21, 1861 when the Union Forces were routed in an
attack on the Confederate position at Ball's Bluff above Washington and across the Potomac on the Virginia shore.

Holmes was seriously wounded that afternoon; he was later
wounded again at Antietam and Chancellorsville. Nevertheless,
after intervals of convalescence, he fought on with his Regiment
until he was mustered out in July, 1864.

But before his burial at Arlington, seventy-one more years of
activity remained for the young student-soldier. He returned to
Harvard to take his law degree, taught in the Harvard Law
School, edited "The American Law Review" and legal commen-
taries, and wrote *The Common Law* which, after three generations, is still considered a classic in legal literature. He served as
a justice of the Massachusetts Supreme Court for ten years. Beginning in 1902 he was Associate Justice of the United States
Supreme Court for thirty years until his retirement at ninety, by
then honoured as one of the four or five greatest American jurists
of all time.

The law reports enshrine Holmes' great decisions upholding,
often as a minority spokesman, the liberties of his countrymen.
Perhaps the principles he cherished were especially meaningful
for him because as a youth, he had fought to preserve them and
still bore the scars left by the bullet fired through his neck at
Antietam, the bullet that pierced his heel at Chancellorsville, and

the lung-riddling bullets he received at Ball's Bluff in circumstances he describes in this recently discovered portion of his wartime journal.

)ctober, 1861. Undated.

. . At Ball's Bluff, Tremlett's boy George told me, I was hit at 4½ P.M., *the eavy firing having begun about an hour before, by the watch*—I felt as if horse had kicked me and went over—1st Serg^t Smith grabbed me and ugged me to the rear a little way & opened my shirt and ecce! the two holes n my breasts & the bullet, which he gave me—George says he squeezed it rom the right opening—Well—I remember the sickening feeling of water in ny face—I was quite faint—and seeing poor Serg^t Merchant lying near—shot hrough the head and covered with blood—and then the thinking begun— (Meanwhile hardly able to think—at least, coherently)—Shot through the ungs? Lets see—and I spit—Yes—already the blood was in my mouth. At nce my thoughts jumped to "Children of the New Forest" (by Marryatt) vhich I was fond of reading as a little boy, and in which the father of one of the heroines is shot through the lungs by a robber—I remember he died vith terrible haemorrhages & great agony—What should I do? Just then I emembered and felt in my waist coat pocket—Yes there it was—a little bottle of laudanum which I had brought along—But I won't take it yet; no ee a doctor first—It may not be as bad as it looks—At any rate wait till the ʲain begins—

When I had got to the bottom of the Bluff the ferry boat, (the scow,) ʲad just started with a load—but there was a small boat there—Then I hought "Now wouldn't Sir Philip Sydney have that other feller put into the ʲoat first?" But the question as the form in which it occurred shows, came rom a *mind* still bent on a becoming and consistent carrying out of its ideals of conduct—not from the unhesitating instinct of a still predominant & heroic *vill*—I am not sure whether I propounded the question but I let myself be ʲut aboard.

I never have been able to account for the fact that bullets struck in the ʲank of the island over our heads as we were crossing—Well; the next question was how to get me from the ferry to the hospital—this I solved by another early recollection—the "Armchair"—Two men crossed their hands in ʲuch a way that I could sit on 'em & put my arms round their necks— & so they carried me—The little house was filled so I was taken into the large ʲuilding which served as a general hospital; and I remember the coup d'oeuil ʲn which I closed my eyes which I had felt on seeing poor Merchant—Men ying round on the floor—the spectacle wasn't familiar then—a red blanket vith an arm lying on it in a pool of blood—it seems as if instinct told me it vas John Putnam's (then Capt. Comdg. Co H)—and near the entrance a ʲurgeon calmly grasping a man's finger and cutting it off—both standing— vhile the victim contemplated the operation with a very grievous mug. Well ʲresently old Hayward approached and inspected me—"How does it look, Doctor, shall I recover? Tell me the truth for I really want to know"— (It seemed then and does now as if I was perfectly rational but Whittier ʲays that when he saw me later I was very light headed—) Hayward in his

deliberate way—"We-ell, you *may* recover—Gen. Shields did"—Shields! I'c
thought of him before and got small comfort from that—we all thought tha
night that I had a couple of bullets in my lungs—& I bled from them (at the
mouth) very freely—"That means the chances are against me, don't it?"
"Ye-es, the chances are against you"—Meanwhile he picked something from
the left opening—I thought it was bone till he told me it was a bit of flannel—
again I felt for the laudanum and again determined to wait till pain or sink
ing strength warned me of the end being near—I didn't feel sure there was
no chance—and watching myself did not feel the hand of death upon me
beyond a hope—my strength seemed to hold out too well.

After this my recollection of events is confused—I remember poor Willy
Putnam's groans—and his refusal to let the Dr. operate on him, saying he
knew the wound was mortal and it would only be more pain for nothing—
I remember hobnobbing with the man who lay near me, and when to my
astonishment John O'Sullivan (Whit's & my serv^t) appeared telling him to
help my neighbor too, and feeling very heroic after that speech—(By the
way Hayward had turned me on my breast & this may have helped a good
deal of the wound to heal almost by first intention)—I remember being very
sleepy—(some enlisted man has since told me he gave me some coffee and
my face flushed and I went right off—) & presently a Doctor of (Baxter's?)
Fire Zouaves coming in with much noise & bluster, and oh, troops were cross
ing to the Virginia side, and we were going to lick, and Heaven knows wha
not—I called him and gave him my address and told him (or meant & tried
to) if I died to write home & tell 'em I'd done my duty—I was very anxious
they should know that—and then I imparted to him my laudanum scheme
—this he dissuaded and gave me a dose of some opiate—he said it wasn'
laudanum, but I guess that was a white lie—and when I slumbered I be
lieve he prigged the bottle. . . .

When I thought I was dying the reflection that the majority vote of the
civilized world declared that with my opinions I was *en route* for Hell came
up with painful distinctness—Perhaps the first impulse was tremulous—bu
then I said—by Jove, I die like a soldier anyhow—I was shot in the breas
doing my duty up to the hub—afraid? No, I am proud—then I thought
couldn't be guilty of a deathbed recantation—father and I had talked o
that and were agreed that it generally meant nothing but a cowardly giving
way to fear. . . .

Later I only can recall, in a general way, being in a general way, being car
ried across the Island in a blanket—lying on the shore comatose, being
ferried across to the M^d shore with some hitch (we came mighty near being
upset I heard afterwards)—swearing terrifically as I've said—and finally afte
being put in the hold of a canal boat and the hatches or scuttle or whateve
you call it tumbling in and nearly all but smashing me & one or two other
into sudden death, that I muzzed away the time till we got to Edwards
Ferry . . . taken from the Canal boat and put into one of the two wheeled
ambulances . . . Captain Dreher was my companion—shot through the head
and insensible, but breathing heavily—The Ambulance was broken—the hors
baulked, and the man didn't know how to drive—whenever we came to a
hill, & there were several, there we stopped, head downward, till some o
the men along the road gave us a boost & started our horse forward again—

suffered much in mind—for what with the rough riding & my momentary expectations of being upset I hardly thought to reach camp alive . . . Dreher —a ghastly spectacle—Two black cavities seemed all that was left for eyes— his whiskers & beard matted with blood which still poured black, from his mouth—and a most horrible stench—

The Hospital Steward—a cockeyed Dutchman who afterwards stuck me certain shekels for his services—looked at my wound and conjectured the true state of affairs—bound me round with an infernal bandage (which Hayward cut as soon as he saw,) having first rammed plugs of lint into the holes, and then left me uncomfortable but still exceedingly joyful, for he had told me I should live—I could have hugged him for that—After this—whiskey—light-headedness—laudanum. . . .

*"They had crawled . . . slowly away . . . and
lain down by the roadside to die."*

John Beatty

Colonel John Beatty, later a Brigadier-General, commanded a brigade of Ohio volunteers through many of the western campaigns.
After the war he became banker, politician and Congressman.
September 20, 1863, however, found him in command of a Union
brigade under General Rosencrans at the Battle of Chickamauga,
near a town at the Tennessee border south of Chattanooga. It
was a critical moment in the war. Success in this area would
have locked the Confederate armies within the coastal states and
opened a way to Georgia and the Carolinas.

The day was Sunday. It was foggy, and there was great confusion in the field. The Rebels suddenly broke through the Union
lines, forcing a disordered withdrawal toward Rossville and Chattanooga. Two months were to pass before this defeat could be
retrieved in the decisive Union victory at Missionary Ridge.

John Beatty's account of the agony at Chickamauga is less important as history than for its evocation of the sights and sounds
of battle. Here are the realities of battle and defeat—the roar and
thunder of musket and artillery; the groans of the wounded lying
neglected by the wayside; hungry horses and men sharing a
few precious ears of corn; a little boy weeping away his last
hours. . . .

September 20, 1863.

. . . The thunder, as of a thousand anvils, still goes on in our front. Men
fall around us like leaves in autumn. Thomas, Garfield, Wood and others are
in consultation below the hill just in rear of Harker. The approaching troops
are said to be ours, and we feel a throb of exultation. Before they arrive
we ascertain that the division is Steedman's; and finally, as they come up
I recognize my old friend Colonel Mitchell, of the 113th. They go into action
on our right, and as they press forward the roar of the musketry redoubles

From *Memoirs of a Volunteer*, by John Beatty. Reprinted by permission of W. W.
Norton & Company, Inc.

the battle seems to be working off in that direction . . . I find that disorganized bodies of men are coming rapidly from the left, in regiments, companies, squads and singly. I meet General Wood and ask if I shall not halt and reorganize them. He tells me to do so; but I find the task impossible. They do not recognize me as their commander, and most of them will not obey my orders. Some few, indeed, I manage to hold together; but the great mass drift by me to the woods in the rear. The dead are lying everywhere; the wounded are continually passing to the rear; the thunder of the guns and roll of musketry are unceasing and unabated until nightfall. Then the fury of the battle gradually dies away, and finally we have a silence, broken only by a cheer here and there along the enemy's line. . . .

Near eight o'clock in the evening I ascertained, from General Wood, that the army had been ordered to fall back to Rossville. . . .

The march to Rossville was a melancholy one. All long the road, for miles, wounded men were lying. They had crawled or hobbled slowly away from the fury of the battle, become exhausted, and lain down by the roadside to die. Some were calling the names and numbers of their regiments, but many had become too weak to do this; by midnight the column had passed by. What must have been their agony, mental and physical, as they lay in the dreary woods, sensible that there was no one to comfort or to care for them and that in a few hours more their career on earth would be ended!

At a little brook, which crossed the road, Wilson and I stopped to water our horses. The remains of a fire, which some soldiers had kindled, were raked together, and laying a couple of ears of corn on the coals for our own use, we gave the remainder of what we had in our pockets to the poor beasts; they had also fasted since early morning.

How many terrible scenes of the day's battle recur to us as we ride on in the darkness! We see again the soldier whose bowels were protruding, and hear him cry, "Jesus, have mercy on my soul!" . . .

A Confederate boy, who should have been at home with his mother and whose leg had been fearfully torn by a minnie ball, hailed me as I was galloping by early in the day. He was bleeding to death and crying bitterly. I gave him my handkerchief and shouted back to him as I hurried on: "Bind up the leg tight!"

The adjutant of the rebel General Adams called to me as I passed him. He wanted help, but I could not help him—could not even help our own poor boys who lay bleeding near him. . . .

At this hour of the night (eleven to twelve o'clock) the army is simply a mob. There appears to be neither organization nor discipline. . . . Were a division of the enemy to pounce down upon us between this and morning, I fear the Army of the Cumberland would be blotted out.

September 21.

Early this morning the army was again got into order. . . . My brigade was posted on a high ridge, east of Rossville and near it. About 10 A.M. it was attacked by a brigade of mounted infantry. . . . After a sharp fight of half an hour . . . the enemy was repulsed, and retired leaving his dead and a portion of his wounded on the field. Of his dead, one officer and eight men were left within a few rods of our line. One little boy, so badly wounded they could not carry him off, said, with tears and sobs, "They have run off and left me in the woods to die." I directed the boys to carry him into our lines and care for him.

"My daughter's cat is staggering today . . ."

John Beauchamp Jones

John Beauchamp Jones, a Southern writer, frankly sought and obtained a position in the War Department of the Confederacy, with a view to making literary capital out of the war through the books he hoped to write later. To serve his purpose he kept a day-to-day diary in which he entered information to which he had official access, supplementing it by personal observations.

As with others who lived in Richmond in the last months before its fall, his most pressing problems were those of increasing hunger and the decreasing value of Confederate currency. Supplies of food grew ever smaller, while presses turned out ever larger numbers of paper bills. Volunteers with scissors had to be called to cut the notes apart and tie them into bundles. At the end, the string used had greater value than what it bound.

The war tale of hunger, as ancient as that of the first prehistoric town under siege, still has the power to stagger—as it staggered a cat, a clerk named Jones, and those who still read the two thick volumes of Jones' printed diary.

October 1, 1862. Richmond, Virginia.

How shall we subsist this winter? There is not a supply of wood or coal in the city—and it is said that there are not adequate means of transporting it hither. Flour at sixteen dollars per barrel and bacon at seventy-five cents a pound threaten a famine. . . . The newspapers are printed on half sheets—and I think the publishers make money; the extras (published almost every day) are sold to the newsboys for ten cents and often sold by them for twenty-five cents. These are mere slips of paper, seldom containing more than a column . . . mostly made up from the Northern papers, brought hither by persons running the blockade. . . . We often get the first accounts of battles at a distance in this way, as our generals and our government are famed for a prudential reticence. . . .

From *A Rebel War Clerk's Diary at the Confederate States Capitol*, by John Beauchamp Jones. J. B. Lippincott, 1866.

October 6.

. . . I expect the arrival of my family from Raleigh, N.C. We have procured for them one pound of sugar, eighty cents; four loaves of bread, as large as my fist, twenty cents each; and we have a little coffee, which is selling at two dollars and a half per pound. In the morning some one must go to market, else there will be short-commons. Washing is two dollars and a half per dozen pieces. Common soap is worth seventy-five cents per pound. . . .

November 21.

Common shirting cotton and Yankee calico that used to sell at twelve and a half cents per yard is now a dollar seventy-five! What a temptation for the Northern manufacturers! . . .

December 1.

God speed the day of peace! Our patriotism is mainly in the army and among the ladies of the South. The avarice and cupidity of the men at home, could only be excelled by the ravenous wolves; and most of our sufferings are fully deserved. Where a people will not have mercy on one another, how can they expect mercy? . . . A portion of the people look like vagabonds. We see men and women and children in the streets in dingy and dilapidated clothes; and some seem gaunt and pale with hunger—the speculators, and thieving quartermasters and commissaries only, looking sleek and comfortable. . . .

February 11, 1863.

Some idea may be formed of the scarcity of food in this city from the fact that, while my youngest daughter was in the kitchen to-day, a young rat came out of its hole and seemed to beg for something to eat; she held out some bread, which it ate from her hand, and seemed grateful. Several others soon appeared and were as tame as kittens. Perhaps we shall have to eat them! . . .

March 30.

The gaunt form of wretched famine still approaches with rapid strides. Meal is now selling at twelve dollars per bushel and potatoes at sixteen. Meats have almost disappeared from the market, and none but the opulent can afford to pay three dollars and a half per pound for butter. . . .

October 22.

A poor woman yesterday applied to a merchant in Carey Street to purchase a barrel of flour. The price he demanded was $70. "My God!" exclaimed she, "how can I pay such prices? I have seven children; what shall I do?" "I don't know, madam," said he coolly, "unless you eat your children." Such is the power of cupidity—it transforms men into demons. . . .

March 18, 1864.

My daughter's cat is staggering to-day, for want of animal food. Sometimes I fancy I stagger myself. . . .

"For such an awkward fellow, I'm pretty sure-footed."

John Milton Hay

Through the whole war period John Hay (1838–1905) was a private secretary to Abraham Lincoln, the man who towered above the Civil War itself, and also above the wars within the war, the copperheads, the greedy and the doubting, the sulky or arrogant generals under his command.

John Hay, of Salem, Indiana, rose to enjoy a measure of fame of his own as statesman and author after the war. The young man of twenty-three who served the President, later became Ambassador to Great Britain, and Secretary of State, under McKinley and Roosevelt. He was responsible for the "Open Door" policy in China and negotiated the treaty that provided for the construction of the Panama Canal and established American domination of the Caribbean. He wrote the famous *Pike County Ballads* (1871) and other books, and with John Nicolay, the vast, ten-volume *Abraham Lincoln, A History*. He married the daughter of a wealthy Cleveland banker. Despite all that he achieved and wrote of afterwards, his five years at Lincoln's side remained the most rewarding.

Hay was often an astute observer, and his suspicion that General George B. McClellan's discourtesy toward Lincoln one night late in 1861 was a "portent of evil to come" was unfortunately confirmed. In 1863 McClellan was the candidate opposing Lincoln. It was a bitter campaign and there were tense moments before the results made it apparent that Lincoln would be re-elected by an overwhelming electoral vote (212 to 21). Hay takes the reader back to that 1864 election eve, to a dark, rainy night in Washington. Lincoln, calmer than his companions as the returns came in, told an anecdote, and awkwardly passed round the oysters at midnight supper. Then he went home to bed. A military band marched up to the White House and under his window played "a small hifalute."

Reprinted by permission of Dodd, Mead & Company from *Lincoln and the Civil War in the Diaries and Letters of John Hay*, selected and with an introduction by Tyler Dennett. Copyright © 1939 by Dodd, Mead & Company, Inc.

November 13, 1861.

I wish to record what I consider a portent of evil to come. The President [Lincoln], Governor Seward, and I, went over to McClellan's house tonight. The servant at the door said the General . . . would soon return. We went in, and after we had waited about an hour, McC. came in and without paying any particular attention to the porter, who told him the President was waiting to see him, went up stairs, passing the door of the room where the President and Secretary of State were seated. They waited about half-an-hour, and sent once more a servant to tell the General they were there, and the answer coolly came that the General had gone to bed. I merely record this unparalleled insolence of epaulettes without comment. It is the first indication I have yet seen of the threatened supremacy of the military authorities. Coming home I spoke to the President about the matter but he seemed not to have noticed it specially, saying it was better at this time not to be making points of etiquette & personal dignity.

July 18, 1863.

Today we spent 6 hours deciding on Court Martials, the President, Judge Holt, & I. I was amused at the eagerness with which the President caught at any fact which would justify him in saving the life of a condemned soldier. He was only merciless in cases where meanness or cruelty were shown. Cases of cowardice he was specially averse to punishing with death. He said it would frighten the poor devils too terribly, to shoot them. On the case of a soldier who had once deserted & reinlisted he indorsed, "Let him fight instead of shooting him." . . .

September 29.

. . . Today came to the Executive Mansion an assembly of cold-water men & cold-water women to make a temperance speech at the Tycoon & receive a response . . . looking blue & thin in the keen autumnal air. . . . Three blue-skinned damsels did Love, Purity, & Fidelity in Red, White & Blue gowns. A few invalid soldiers stumped along in the dismal procession. They made a long speech at the Tycoon in which they called Intemperance the cause of our defeats. He could not see it, as the rebels drink more & worse whisky than we do. . . .

November 8, 1864.

The house [White House] has been still and almost deserted today. Everybody in Washington, not at home voting, seems ashamed of it and stays away from the President. . . . He said, "It is a little singular that I, who am not a vindictive man, should have always been before the people for election in canvasses marked for their bitterness. . . ." During the afternoon few despatches were received. At night, at 7 o'clock we started over to the War Department to spend the evening. . . . The night was rainy, steamy and dark. We splashed through the grounds to the side door . . . where a soaked and smoking sentinel was standing in his own vapor with his huddled-up frame covered with a rubber cloak. Inside a half-dozen idle orderlies, up-stairs the clerks of the telegraph. As the President entered they handed him a despatch from Forney claiming ten thousand Union majority in Philadelphia. "Forney is a little excitable." Another comes from Felton, Baltimore giving us "15,000 in the city, 5,000 in the state. All Hail, Free Maryland." That is superb. A message . . . claiming Boston by 5,000. . . . Eckert came in shaking the rain from his cloak, with trousers very disreputably muddy. We sternly demanded an explanation. He had slipped, he said & tumbled prone, crossing the street. He had done it watching a fellow-being ahead and chuckling at his uncertain footing.

Which reminded the Tycoon, of course. The President said, "For such an awkward fellow, I am pretty sure-footed. It used to take a pretty dextrous man to throw me. I remember, the evening of the day in 1858, that decided the contest for the Senate between Mr. Douglas and myself, was something like this, dark, rainy and gloomy. I had been reading the returns, and had ascertained that we had lost the Legislature and started to go home. The path had been worn hog-back & was slippery. My foot slipped from under me, knocking the other one out of the way, but I recovered myself & lit square, and I said to myself, 'It's a slip and not a fall.'"

The President sent over the first fruits to Mrs. Lincoln. He said, "She is more anxious than I." . . . Despatches kept coming in all the evening showing a splendid triumph in Indiana, showing steady, small gains all over Pennsylvania, enough to give a fair majority this time on the home vote. . . . Towards midnight we had supper, provided by Eckert. The President went awkwardly and hospitably to work shoveling out the fried oysters. He was most agreeable and genial all the evening in fact. . . . Capt. Thomas came up with a band about half-past two, and made some music and a small hifalute. The President answered from the window with rather unusual dignity and effect & we came home. . . . [W. H. Lamon] took a glass of whiskey and then, refusing my offer of a bed, went out & rolling himself up in his cloak, lay down at the President's door; passing the night in that attitude of touching and dumb fidelity, with a small arsenal of pistols and bowie knives around him. In the morning he went away leaving my blankets at my door, before I or the President were awake.

> *"Heaven forbid that I should ever again
> witness such a sight!"*

Augustus C. Brown

It is only fair to warn the squeamish reader, likely to pale at the thought of blood and agony, not to read the entry that Captain Augustus C. Brown, commander of a New York Heavy Artillery battalion, made in his diary the night of May 10, 1864.

He tells of the wounded he saw being brought to a field hospital behind the lines during the Battle of the Wilderness. The particular battle isn't important; it could have been many another. It is a brief and horrible glimpse of mangled, suffering men.

But worse is yet to come. Brown is reminded of what he had observed at a field hospital a few days before. Suddenly the later scene becomes tolerable by comparison. Stretcher-bearers arrange their burdens as on a conveyor belt, the endless dis-assembly line begins to move. . . . War, as Sherman told young ears, "is all hell."

May 10, 1864.

Ambulances and army wagons with two tiers of flooring, loaded with wounded and drawn by four and six mule teams, pass along the plank, or rather corduroy road to Fredericksburg [from the Battle of the Wilderness], the teamsters lashing their teams to keep up with the train, and the wounded screaming with pain as the wagons go jolting over the corduroy. Many of the wounds are full of maggots. I saw one man with an arm off at the shoulder, with maggots half an inch long crawling in the sloughing flesh, and several poor fellows were holding stumps of legs and arms straight up in the air so as to ease the pain the rough road and the heartless drivers subjected them to. These men had been suffering in temporary field-hospitals, as no opportunity had been afforded to send them to the rear. . . .

And this reminds me of a scene I witnessed a day or two since which seemed to me to cap the climax of the horrors of war. Passing along a little in the rear of the lines when a battle was raging in which my battalion was not engaged, I came upon a field-hospital to which the stretcher-bearers were bringing the men wounded in the conflict. Under three large "tent flies,"

From *Diary of a Line Officer,* by Augustus C. Brown.

the center one the largest of all, stood three heavy wooden tables, around which were grouped a number of surgeons and their assistants, the former bare-headed and clad in long linen dusters reaching nearly to the ground, which were covered with blood from top to bottom and had the arms cut off or rolled to the shoulders. The stretcher-bearers deposited their ghastly freight side by side in a winrow on the ground in front of the table under the first tent fly. Here a number of assistants took charge of the poor fellows, and as some of them lifted a man on to the first table others moved up the winrow so that no time or space should be lost. Then some of the surgeons administered an anaesthetic to the groaning and writhing patient, exposed his wound and passed him to the center table. There the surgeons who were operating made a hasty examination and determined what was to be done and did it, and more often than not, in a very few moments an arm or a leg or some other portion of the subject's anatomy was flung out upon a pile of similar fragments behind the hospital, which was then more than six feet wide and three feet high, and what remained of the man was passed on to the third table, where other surgeons finished the bandaging, resuscitated him and posted him off with others in an ambulance. Heaven forbid that I should ever again witness such a sight!

*"All day, as the sad moments rolled on,
were they passing . . ."*

Dolly Sumner Lunt

After General Sherman captured Atlanta he obtained General Grant's permission to march on through Georgia to the Atlantic Coast. That famous march began on November 15th, 1864. Four days later his army, 60,000 strong, passed a plantation near Covington, Georgia, presided over by a former school teacher, born in New England, the widow of a planter. Sherman's troops lived on the country and at Widow Lunt's they made a rich haul. Her cry of anguish at the sight of her depleted food hoard, her "pickles of various kinds—both in vinegar and brine," gone to be swallowed down nasty Yankee gullets, leaves one midway between a chuckle and a tear. Had Sherman been taxed with this pickle-stealing (and worse), he doubtless would have repeated what he told General Halleck of Grant's staff: "If the people raise a howl against my barbarity and cruelty, I will answer that war is war, and not popularity seeking. If they want peace, they and their relatives must stop the war."

November 19, 1864.

Slept in my clothes last night, as I heard that the Yankees went to neighbor Montgomery's on Thursday night at one o'clock, searched his house, drank his wine and took his money and valuables. As we were not disturbed, I walked after breakfast, with Sadai, up to Mr. Joe Perry's, my nearest neighbor, where the Yankees were yesterday. . . . Happening to turn and look behind, as we stood there, I saw some blue-coats coming down the hill. . . . I hastened back to my frightened servants and told them that they had better hide, and then went back to the gate to claim protection and a guard. But like demons they rush in! My yards are full. To my smoke-house, my dairy, pantry, kitchen and cellar, like famished wolves they come, breaking locks and whatever is in their way. The thousand pounds of meat in my smoke-house is gone in a twinkling, my flour, my meat, my lard, butter, eggs, pickles of various kinds—both in vinegar and brine—wine, jars, and jugs are all gone. My eighteen fat turkeys, my hens, chickens, and fowls, my young pigs, are shot down in my yard and hunted as if they were rebels themselves. . . . I saw driven, first, old Dutch, my dear old buggy horse, who has carried my beloved husband so many miles, and who would so quietly wait at the block for him to mount and dismount, and who at last drew him to his grave; then came old Mary, my brood mare, who for years had been too old and stiff for work, with her three-year-old colt, my two-year-old mule, and her last little baby colt. . . .

Sherman himself and a greater portion of his army passed my house that day. All day, as the sad moments rolled on, were they passing not only in front of my house, but from behind; they tore down my garden palings, made a road through my back-yard and lot field, driving their stock and riding through, tearing down my fences and desolating my home—wantonly doing it when there was no necessity for it. . . .

As night drew its sable curtains around us, the heavens from every point were lit up with flames from burning buildings. Dinnerless and supperless as we were, it was nothing in comparison with the fear of being driven out homeless to the dreary woods. Nothing to eat! I could give my guard no supper, so he left us. . . . A colonel from Vermont left me two men, but they were Dutch, and I could not understand one word they said. . . . The two guards came into my room and laid themselves by my fire for the night. I could not close my eyes, but kept walking to and fro, watching the fires in the distance and dreading the approaching day, which, I feared, as they had not all passed, would be but a continuation of horrors.

*"A pack of wolves never acted
more ravenous and bloodthirsty."*

Lawrence Van Alstyne

The great victories of Grant and Sherman in the East were balanced by temporary setbacks in the West. The war was not yet won along the banks of the Mississippi. The Battle of Sabine Crossing, vividly described in an enlisted man's diary, was a bitter tonic for Union over-confidence.

Lawrence Van Alstyne, the diarist, was a youth when the Civil War began. He promptly enlisted in a regiment of New York volunteers, and after the usual brief period of training fought in the Missouri-Mississippi campaigns which had been hurriedly mounted to contain the Confederacy. His story is the classic one of hunger and hardship, of valour and the stinging humiliation of retreat. But Van Alstyne did more than chronicle the misfortunes of a campaign. Through the smoke and confusion of battle this soldier from the ranks portrayed the scene of battle with the skill of a novelist—much the way that Stephen Crane later did in his immortal *The Red Badge of Courage.*

September 17, 1862. Camp Millington, near Baltimore, Maryland.

. . . We are in a field of 100 acres, as near as I can judge, on the side of a hill, near the top. The ground is newly seeded and wets up quickly, as such ground usually does. We sleep in pairs, and a blanket spread on the ground is our bed while another spread over us is our covering. A narrow strip of muslin, drawn over a pole about three feet from the ground, open at both ends, the wind and the rain, if it does rain, beating in upon us, and water running under and about us; this, with all manner of bugs and creeping things crawling over us, and all the while great hungry mosquitoes biting every uncovered inch of us, is not an overdrawn picture of that part of a soldier's life, set apart for the rest and repose necessary to enable him to endure several hours of right down hard work at drill, in a hot sun with heavy woollen clothes on, every button of which must be tight-buttoned, and by

From *Diary of an Enlisted Man*, by Lawrence Van Alstyne. Tuttle Morehouse & Taylor Co. 1910.

the time the officers are tired watching us, we come back to camp wet through with perspiration and too tired to make another move.

Before morning our wet clothes chill us to the marrow of our bones, and why we live and apparently thrive under it, is something I cannot understand. But we do, and the next day are ready for more of it. Very few even take cold. It is part of the contract, and while we grumble and growl among ourselves, we don't really mean it, for we are learning what we will be glad to know at some future time.

. . . Some get mad and cuss the cooks, and the whole war department, but that is usually when our stomachs are full. When we are hungry we swallow anything that comes and are thankful for it. The cook's house is simply a portion of the field we are in. A couple of crotches hold up a pole on which the camp kettles are hung, they are all alike. The camp kettles are large sheet-iron pails, one larger than the other so one can be put inside the other when moving. If we have meat and potatoes, meat is put in one, and potatoes in the other. The one that gets cooked first is emptied into mess pans, which are large sheet-iron pans with flaring sides, so one can be packed in another. Then the coffee is put in the empty kettle and boiled. The bread is cut into thick slices, and the breakfast call sounds. We grab our plates and cups, and wait for no second invitation. We each get a piece of meat and a potato, a chunk of bread and a cup of coffee with a spoonful of brown sugar in it. Milk and butter we buy, or go without. We settle down, generally in groups, and the meal is soon over. Then we wash our dishes, and put them back in our haversacks. We make quick work of washing dishes. We save a piece of bread for the last, with which we wipe up everything, and then eat the dish rag. Dinner and breakfast are alike, only sometimes the meat and potatoes are cut up and cooked together, which makes a really delicious stew. Supper is the same, minus the meat and potatoes.

The cooks are men detailed from the ranks for that purpose. Every one smokes or chews tobacco here, so we find no fault because the cooks do both. Boxes or barrels are used as kitchen tables, and are used for seats between meals. The meat and bread are cut on them, and if a scrap is left on the table the flies go right at it and we have so many the less to crawl over us. They are never washed, but are sometimes scraped off and made to look real clean. I never yet saw the cooks wash their hands, but presume they do when they go to the brook for water.

May 18, 1864. Sabine Crossing, Louisiana.

The rear guard was just coming in sight this morning when we heard firing at the rear. Soon aides came riding down the line . . . raced across the bridge and in a little while troops were hurrying back across the bridge from the front.

It beat all how soon the scene changed. The firing in the rear kept increasing and grew plainer to hear. . . . Unless the bridge was attacked we had only to look on, and it was a sight worth a lifetime to see. The ground, except where worn down by the passing army, was covered with weeds and bushes, which hid the skirmish line from our view until they rose up and fired almost in each others' faces. Smoke soon hid the battleground. There

was no wind and the smoke rose up like a cloud instead of spreading. . . .
By noon it was plain to see that the fight was ours, for the smoke cloud went
faster and the firing grew less. By 4 P.M. it was over and the troops began
recrossing toward the front.

The surgeons had their shop under a big tree near the bridge. I heard one
of them say to another that he had never seen so few slight wounds among
so many. Most of those that were hit were either killed outright or mortally
wounded. Only a few legs or arms were cut off. The saddest sight I saw was
the killing of a boy, son of a colonel somebody, whose name or regiment I
could not get. I had often seen the boy while at Alexandria and wondered
why such a child should be in such a place. He rode a handsome bay pony
and wore the infantry uniform, even to a little sword. When the fight began
he was somewhere in the advance, and came riding back at the head of his
regiment by his father. They went into the cloud of smoke and in a few minutes a man came leading the pony back with the little fellow stretched across
the saddle, his hands and feet hanging down on either side. . . .

May 19.

Our dead were picked up and brought to the bayou where they were laid
in rows on the ground. Those that were identified were buried in separate
graves, and the others put crosswise in a wide ditch, with blankets spread
under and over them. Our loss was estimated at 500 and that of the Rebs at
800. That must mean killed and wounded, for no such number was buried.
The rebel dead were buried in the field, I suppose, for none of them were
brought in.

Later. A couple of our men are sick and Dr. Warren called in another
doctor to look at them. They called it smallpox, and the men were put in a
wagon and carted off right away. When the team came back the driver said
they were put in the first house they came to, and a man who has had the
disease was left to give them medicine. By night everything but the rear
guard was across the bridge, and we had orders to be ready to march. We
settled down to get some sleep if we could, but the long roll soon sounded
and we sprang to our places. No enemy appearing, we built fires and made
coffee, and then sat round nodding our sleepy heads until 4 o'clock in the
morning.

May 20.

By 4 A.M. the troops were across and the pontoons loaded. We marched
at quick time and at 6 o'clock were at Simmsport, where we stopped for a
breakfast of hard-tack and coffee. . . . Simmsport is on the Atchafalaya
River, and the same Colonel who planned the dam at Alexandria had built
a bridge of boats for us to cross over. Twenty-four steamboats were lashed
together side by side, and reached from shore to shore. Across the bows of
these the artillery, cavalry and wagons were passing in a continuous stream,
and infantry was crossing through and among them as best they could. Other
boats were busy ferrying the troops, and such getting across a river I never
saw. . . .

And so the whole day went, first starting and then stopping again, but expecting every minute to set out for good. The time we were waiting, if all put together, would have given us a good rest, and the marching we did would have been good exercise. But as it was, we had a hard day of it. It was pitch dark when we finally started. We came to woods and the darkness could be felt. The train got stalled in the narrow road and then another wait. I was so dead sleepy that twice I fell flat on the ground as I was walking along. The fall woke me up each time and I kept going some way. Men had given out and were sleeping all along beside the road like dead men. Daylight never seemed so long coming. We got through the woods and could see much better. My naps as we walked along, and the falls I had in consequence of them, helped me to drive off the dreadful drowsiness and by daylight I was wide awake.

May 21.

When daylight came we were passing the mouth of the Atchafalaya and were again on the banks of the Red River. About sunrise we halted. Lieutenant Moody and I sat down and began to figure up how long we had been awake, when we both tumbled over on the ground and were fast asleep. The next thing I knew Moody was shaking me and asking if I was hurt. His face was bloody and I supposed he had been shot. But we soon found that a horse had run over us, his hoofs striking between our heads and scraping the skin off Moody's forehead as he picked them up.

We soon started again, and at 8 o'clock stopped for breakfast, after which we took a livelier gait than ever. The day was hot. The horses and mules showed the strain as well as the men, and it was impossible to rouse them from the deathlike sleep that had overtaken them. There was nothing to do but pull them out of the road and leave them, for every horse and vehicle was loaded with all it could carry. No stop was made for dinner. On we went, and by 6 o'clock the men were lying all along by the roadsides. Teams gave out and were left panting, their sides showing how cruelly they had been whipped to get the very last effort out of them. My feet were blistered, I knew by the feeling, though I had no time to see or attend to them. The pain each step gave me was, I think, the only thing that kept me awake and going. About sundown we passed a little village and turned from the road across the country . . . there were some cattle, and a drove of them was gathered and driven along for our supper. . . .

At 9 P.M. we reached the Mississippi at Morgan's Bend or Morganzia. The cattle had been shot and were lying as they fell. It was everyone for himself. Chunks were cut out and were being eaten before the animal was done kicking. A pack of wolves never acted more ravenous and bloodthirsty. I managed to get my hand between the ribs of one and hold of the liver. I couldn't pull my hand out without straightening the fingers and so got only shreds, but I kept it up until I had taken the edge off my appetite and then lay over on my back and was sound asleep. I suppose a hundred men stepped over me and maybe on me, but nothing disturbed my slumbers. I slept like a dead man.

"The night was dark, cloudy, and damp . . ."

Gideon Welles

Good Friday, 1865, was an auspicious day in Washington. The Union Jack had been hoisted again that morning over Fort Sumter. There was still rejoicing over Lee's surrender to Grant five days before, and a triumphant message from Sherman was expected at any moment. At the morning cabinet meeting the President was in a happy, confident mood.

Secretary of the Navy Gideon Welles (1802–1878) entered the day's events in his diary and went to bed early that night. A salty, incorruptible Connecticut newspaper publisher and politician, Welles was one of Lincoln's earliest supporters and throughout the war remained one of his most capable and trusted associates. He built the Union Navy into a formidable force, but perhaps he was of greatest service to Lincoln by giving him his stern honesty and shrewd, often biting, appraisals of men with whom the President had to deal. Now that the future seemed assured, Welles permitted himself a rare moment of relaxation from the cares of his office.

But there was to be no rest for Gideon Welles that night of April 14, 1865. He was hardly asleep when a shout in the street summoned him from nightgown and nightcap to witness the final tragedy of the war. . . .

April 15, 1865.

I had retired to bed about half-past ten on the evening of the 14th of April, and was just getting to sleep when Mrs. Welles, my wife, said some one was at our door. Sitting up in bed, I heard a voice twice call to John, my son, whose sleeping-room was on the second floor directly over the front entrance. I arose at once and raised a window, when my messenger, James Smith, called to me that Mr. Lincoln, the President, had been shot, and said Secretary Seward and his son, Assistant Secretary Frederick Seward, were assassinated. James was very much alarmed and excited. . . . I immediately dressed myself, and, against the earnest remonstrance and appeals of my wife, went

From *The Diary of Gideon Wells*, by Gideon Welles, reprinted by permission of and arrangement with Houghton Mifflin Company, the authorized publishers.

directly to Mr. Seward's, whose residence was on the east side of the square, mine being on the north. James accompanied me. As we were crossing 15th Street, I saw four or five men in earnest consultation, standing under the lamp on the corner by St. John's Church. Before I had got half across the street, the lamp was suddenly extinguished and the knot of persons rapidly dispersed. For a moment, and but a moment I was disconcerted to find myself in darkness, but recollecting that it was late and about time for the moon to rise, I proceeded on, not having lost five steps, merely making a pause without stopping. Hurrying forward into 15th Street, I found it pretty full of people, especially so near the residence of Secretary Seward, where there were many soldiers as well as citizens already gathered.

Entering the house, I found the lower hall and office full of persons, and among them most of the foreign legations, all anxiously inquiring what truth there was in the horrible rumors afloat. I replied that my object was to ascertain the facts. Proceeding through the hall to the stairs, I found one, and I think two, of the servants there holding the crowd in check. The servants were frightened and appeared relieved to see me. I hastily asked what truth there was in the story that an assassin or assassins had entered the house and assaulted the Secretary. They said it was true, and that Mr. Frederick was also badly injured. . . . The bed was saturated with blood. The Secretary was lying on his back, the upper part of his head covered by a cloth, which extended down over his eyes. His mouth was open, the lower jaw dropping down. . . . We almost immediately withdrew and went into the adjoining front room, where lay Frederick Seward. His eyes were open but he did not move them, nor a limb, nor did he speak. Doctor White, who was in attendance, told me he was unconscious and more dangerously injured than his father.

As we descended the stairs, I asked Stanton what he had heard in regard to the President that was reliable. He said the President was shot at Ford's Theatre, that he had seen a man who was present and witnessed the occurrence. . . . The President had been carried across the street from the theatre, to the house of a Mr. Peterson. We entered by ascending a flight of steps above the basement and passing through a long hall to the rear, where the President lay extended on a bed, breathing heavily. Several surgeons were present, at least six, I should think more. Among them I was glad to observe Dr. Hall, who . . . [told me] the President was dead to all intents, although he might live three hours or perhaps longer.

The giant sufferer lay extended diagonally across the bed, which was not long enough for him. He had been stripped of his clothes. His large arms, which were occasionally exposed, were of a size which one would scarce have expected from his spare appearance. His slow, full respiration lifted the clothes with each breath that he took. His features were calm and striking, I had never seen them appear to better advantage than for the first hour, perhaps, that I was there. After that, his right eye began to swell and that part of his face became discolored.

. . . A double guard was stationed at the door and on the sidewalk, to repress the crowd, which was of course highly excited and anxious. The room was small and over-crowded. The surgeons and members of the Cabinet were as many as should have been in the room, but there were many more, and the hall and other rooms in the front or main house were full. One of these rooms was occupied by Mrs. Lincoln and her attendants. . . . About once an hour Mrs. Lincoln would repair to the bedside of her dying husband and with lamentation and tears remain until overcome by emotion.

(April 15.) A door which opened upon a porch or gallery, and also the windows, were kept open for fresh air. The night was dark, cloudy, and damp, and about six it began to rain. I remained in the room until then without sitting or leaving it, when, there being a vacant chair which some one left at the foot of the bed, I occupied it for nearly two hours, listening to the heavy groans, and witnessing the wasting life of the good and great man who was expiring before me.

About 6 A.M. I experienced a feeling of faintness and for the first time after entering the room, a little past eleven, I left it and the house, and took a short walk in the open air. It was a dark and gloomy morning, and rain set in before I returned to the house. . . . Large groups of people were gathered every few rods, all anxious and solicitous. Some one or more from each group stepped forward as I passed, to inquire into the condition of the President, and to ask if there was no hope. Intense grief was on every countenance when I replied that the President could survive but a short time. The colored people especially—and there were at this time more of them, perhaps, than of whites—were overwhelmed with grief. . . .

A little before seven, I went into the room where the dying President was rapidly drawing near the closing moments. His wife soon after made her last visit to him. The death-struggle had begun. Robert, his son, stood with several others at the head of the bed. He bore himself well, but on two occasions gave way to overpowering grief and sobbed aloud, turning his head and leaning on the shoulder of Senator Sumner. The respiration of the President became suspended at intervals and at last entirely ceased at twenty-two minutes past seven. . . .

On the Avenue in front of the White House were several hundred colored people, mostly women and children, weeping and wailing their loss. This crowd did not appear to diminish through the whole of that cold, wet day; . . . their hopeless grief affected me more than almost anything else, though strong and brave men wept when I met them.

*"To insure health, a man's relation to Nature must
come very near to a personal one . . ."*

Henry David Thoreau

Henry Thoreau (1817–1862), lived a short and uneventful life.
Its substance is preserved as few lives have been in the thirty or
so ledger volumes of a remarkable journal, filled as Thoreau's own
mind was, with immense stores of knowledge and observation. It
is crowded with the raw material from which he shaped almost
everything he ever wrote—drafts of letters, articles and lectures,
personal accounts added up to the penny, things confided to him
privately by insects, animals and birds, complaints of unrequited
love, denunciations of hypocrites and assenters to tyranny, reminders of times and places where wild fruits and berries might
be picked in ripest perfection, notes of pensive tunes to play on
his flute, and data variously zoological, ornithological, botanical,
ecumenical and highly personal.

Thoreau, naturalist, poet and uncommon man, was born in
Concord, Massachusetts, and though his mind ranged ever backward and forward through vast extents of time and space, he
rarely went farther from his birthplace than his feet would take
him. He died in the house where he was born, and lies buried,
as he wanted to be, in Concord's Sleepy Hollow Cemetery near
his friends Emerson and Hawthorne.

Of Scotch and French descent, Thoreau was the son of a none
too prosperous pencil-maker. As a boy he was shy and reserved,
but if he withdrew into himself, as he did all his life, it was because of his impatience with the demands people made on him
rather than a dislike of their company.

After Thoreau's graduation from Harvard at twenty, on Emerson's recommendation he was appointed teacher of the town
school he had himself earlier attended. This job did not last long,
however, for Thoreau stubbornly refused to whip his pupils, a
discipline considered necessary by the school supervisors. With his
brother John, he opened a small academy where he taught

From *The Journals of Thoreau,* by Henry David Thoreau, reprinted by permission
of and arrangement with Houghton Mifflin Company, the authorized publishers.

Greek, Latin, mathematics and nature studies. This second venture also soon came to an end. After he had tried his hand at lecturing (he was not good at it) Emerson invited him to come and live at his rambling white house on the Boston turnpike, there to be family handyman, editorial assistant, baby-sitter and companion. Thoreau was well qualified for all of these tasks. The children loved him, as all children always did; more a scholar than Emerson, he was ready to correct manuscripts and proofs of articles intended for *The Dial,* organ of the transcendentalist movement under Emerson's editorship; he could, and did, paint, plaster and paper, mend roofs, work as a mason and carpenter, and tend to gardens, lawns and orchards so that they thrived as never before or after.

Emerson, fourteen years the elder, was Thoreau's greatest friend, benefactor and guiding influence. When he went to build his famous hut on the pine-slope above Walden pond, it was with Emerson's encouragement and the loan of land he owned there. At Walden Thoreau retired, not to become a recluse as is commonly believed (for he never lacked visitors and walked almost every day into town along the nearby railroad track or the turnpike that ran within three hundred yards of his door) but to find an economical way to live and enough peace and quiet in which to get his writing done. His isolation thus was more intellectual than real, less romantic than practical. The experiment turned out well. In twenty-six months he wrote two of the outstanding books of his century, *Walden* and *A Week on the Concord and Merrimack Rivers,* as well as essays and magazine articles, filled hundreds of journal pages with a running inventory of plants and aphids, the sounds of birds and the rejoinders of animals, the sizes, colours and scents of his stock in trade; transactions with wise ancients who frequented the Concord curb market; the balance, profit or loss, of commerce accomplished on his daily walks with his pockets crammed with pencils (of his own making at his father's shop), paper, magnifying glass, telescope, *The Greek Anthology,* and a hat well stocked with birds' eggs, butterflies and sprigs of plants to examine at leisure and identify.

Except for a few short excursions to Maine or Cape Cod and a journey to Minnesota for the sake of his health (the spectre of tuberculosis, of which he was to die, already confronted him), he lived quietly in the family's Main Street house in Concord. John Brown appeared and fascinated him by his saintly devotion to the abolitionist cause, and a room set aside in Thoreau's home became a busy stop on the underground railway. His refusal to pay his poll tax to a state government whose actions, particularly those in support of the slaveholders, he could not accept, cost him a night of imprisonment in the town jail and resulted in his best known essay, "Civil Disobedience," which for a century set men thinking and stirred them to action.

Thoreau's writing brought him little recognition or reward during his lifetime. Only two of his books were published before his death, and one of them he had to pay to have printed, working for three months as a surveyor to earn the money it cost.

In the spring of 1862 Thoreau's illness forced him to take to his bed under the tender and watchful care of his sister. His friends found it hard to believe that this short, lean man, tough and muscular in body, and with skin tanned and ruddy from a lifetime spent outdoors in wind and sun, had been made so frail by the ravages of tuberculosis that his hands could no longer hold a pen. Thoreau died in May of that year, at the age of 44, just as the first complete reports were being received from the battle of Shiloh, where the ideals he long had cherished were being put to a bloody, hard-fought test.

January 3, 1858.

I see a flock of *F. hyemalis* this afternoon, the weather is hitherto so warm. . . .

The slosh on Walden had so much water in it that it has now frozen perfectly smooth and looks like a semi-transparent marble. Being, however, opaque, it reminds one the more of some vast hall or corridor's floor, yet probably not a human foot has trodden it yet. Only the track-repairers and stokers have cast stones and billets of wood onto it to prove it.

Going to the Andromeda Ponds, I was greeted by the warm brown-red glow of the *Andromeda calyculata* toward the sun. I see where I have been through, the more reddish under sides apparently being turned up. It is long since a human friend has met me with such a glow.

January 4.

The weather still remarkably warm; the ice too soft for skating. I go through by the Andromeda Ponds and down river from Fair Haven. I am encouraged by the sight of men fishing in Fair Haven Pond, for it reminds me that they have animal spirits for such adventures. I am glad to be reminded that any go a-fishing. When I get down near to Cardinal Shore, the sun near setting, its light is wonderfully reflected from a narrow edging of yellowish stubble at the edge of the meadow ice and foot of the hill, an edging only two or three feet wide, and the stubble but a few inches high. . . .

January 5.

I see one of those fuzzy winter caterpillars, black at the two ends and brown-red in middle, crawling on a rock by the Hunt's Bridge causeway.

Mr. Hosmer is loading hay in his barn. It is meadow-hay, and I am interested in it chiefly as a botanist. If meadow-hay is of less worth in the market, it is more interesting to the poet. . . . How completely a load of hay in the winter revives the memory of past summers! Summer in us is only a little dried like it. The rowen in Hosmer's barn has a finer and greener look than the first crop. And so the ferns in coal remind us of summer still longer past.

January 6.

The first snowstorm of much importance. . . .
Up railroad to North River.

The main stream, barely skimmed over with snow, which has sunk the thin ice and is saturated with water, is of a dull-brown color between the white fields.

I . . . derive a certain excitement, not to be refused, even from going through Dennis's Swamp on the opposite side of the railroad, where the poison-dogwood abounds. This simple-stemmed bush is very full of fruit, hanging in loose, dry, pale-green drooping panicles. Some of them are a foot long. . . . I cannot refrain from plucking it and bringing home some pretty sprigs. . . .

I was feeling very cheap, nevertheless, reduced to make the most of dry dogwood berries. Very little evidence of God or man did I see just then, and life not as rich and inviting an enterprise as it should be, when my attention was caught by a snowflake on my coatsleeve. It was one of those perfect, crystalline, star-shaped ones, six-rayed, like a flat wheel with six spokes, only the spokes were perfect little pine trees in shape, arranged around a central spangle. This little object, which, with many of its fellows, rested unmelting on my coat, so perfect and beautiful, reminded me that Nature had not lost her pristine vigor yet, and why should man lose heart? Sometimes the pines were worn and had lost their branches, and again it appeared as if several stars had impinged on one another at various angles, making a somewhat spherical mass. These little wheels came down like the wrecks of chariots from a battle waged in the sky. There were mingled with these starry flakes small downy pellets also. This was at mid-afternoon, and it has not quite ceased snowing yet (at 10 P.M.). We are rained and snowed on with gems. . . .

January 7.

The storm is over, and it is one of those beautiful winter mornings when a vapor is seen hanging in the air between the village and the woods. . . .

I see some tree sparrows feeding on the fine grass seed above the snow, near the road on the hillside below the Dutch hourse. They are flitting along one at a time, their feet commonly sunk in the snow, uttering occasionally a low sweet warble and seemingly as happy there, and with this wintry prospect before them for the night and several months to come, as any man by his fireside. . . .

January 8.

To that small meadow just above the Boaz Brown meadow.
Going through the swamp, the snow balled so as to raise me three inches higher than usual.

January 9.

Snows again.
To Deep Cut. The wind is southwest, and the snow is very moist, with large flakes. Looking toward Trillium Wood, the nearer flakes appear to move quite swiftly, often making the impression of a continuous white line. They are also seen to move directly and nearly horizontally, but the more distant flakes appear to loiter in the air, as if uncertain how they will approach the earth, or even to cross the course of the former, and are always seen as simple and distinct flakes. I think that this difference is simply owing to the fact that the former pass quickly over the field of view, while the latter are much longer in it. . . .
Some chickadees come flitting close to me, and one utters its spring note, *phe-be,* for which I feel under obligations to him.

January 10.

To Goose Pond across Walden.
The north side of Walden is a warm walk in sunny weather. If you are sick and despairing, go forth in winter and see the red alder catkins dangling at the extremities of the twigs, all in the wintry air, like long, hard mulberries, promising a new spring and the fulfillment of all our hopes. We prize any tenderness, any softening in the winter—catkins, birds' nests, insect life, etc., etc. The most I get, perchance, is the sight of a mulberry-like red catkin which I know has a dormant life in it, seemingly greater than my own.

January 11.

Rain, rain—washes off almost every vestige of snow.

January 13.

At Jonathan Buffum's, Lynn. Lecture in John B. Alley's parlor. Mr. J. Buffum describes to me ancient wolf-traps, made probably by the early settlers in Lynn, perhaps after an Indian model; one some two miles from the shore near Saugus, another more northerly; holes say seven feet deep, about as long, and some three feet wide, stoned up very smoothly, and perhaps converging a little, so that the wolf could not get out. Tradition says that a wolf and a squaw were one morning found in the same hole, staring at each other.

January 14.

Mr. Buffum says that in 1817 or 1819 he saw the sea-serpent at Swampscott, and so did several hundred others. He was to be seen off and on for some time. There were many people on the beach the first time, in carriages partly in the water, and the serpent came so near that they, thinking that he might come ashore, involuntarily turned their horses to the shore as with a general consent, and this movement caused him to shear off also . . . Buffum says he has seen him twenty times, once alone, from the rocks at Little Nahant, when he passed along close to the shore just beneath the surface, and within fifty or sixty feet of him, so that he could have touched him with a very long pole, if he had dared to. Buffum is about sixty, and it should be said, as affecting the value of his evidence, that he is a firm believer in Spiritualism. . . .

Saw where one Boyse (if that is the spelling), a miller in old times, got out millstones in a primitive way, so said an old man who was chopping there. He pried or cracked off a piece of the crust of the ledge, lying horizontal, some sixteen or eighteen inches thick, then made a fire on it about its edges, and, pouring on water, cracked or softened it, so that he could break off the edges and make it round with his sledge. Then he picked a hole through the middle and hammered it as smooth as he could, and it was done. But this old man said that he had heard old folks say that the stones were so rough in old times that they made a noise like thunder as they revolved, and much grit was mixed with the meal. . . .

From these rocks and wooded hills three or four miles inland in the northwest edge of Lynn, we had an extensive view of the ocean from Cape Ann to Scituate, and realized how the aborigines, when hunting, berrying, might perchance have looked out thus on the early navigators sailing along the coast—thousands of them—when they little suspected it—how patent to the inhabitants their visit must have been. A vessel could hardly have passed within half a dozen miles of the shore, even—at one place only, in pleasant weather—without being seen by hundreds of savages. . . . Mr. Buffum tells me that they never eat the sea-clams without first taking out "the worm," as it is called, about as large as the small end of a pipestem. He supposes it is the penis.

January 18.

At the Dugan Desert, I notice, under the overhanging or nearly horizontal small white oaks and shrub oaks about the edge, singular little hollows in the sand, evidently made by drops of rain or melting snow falling from the same part of the twig, a foot or two, on the same spot a long time. They are very numerous under every such low horizontal bough, on an average about three quarters of an inch apart or more. They are a third of an inch wide and quarter to even three quarters of an inch deep; made some days ago evidently.

The *F. hyemalis* about. I hear that the Emerson children found ladies'-delights out yesterday.

January 19.

F. *hyemalis.*

January 23.

The wonderfully mild and pleasant weather continues. The ground has been bare since the 11th. . . .

A fine afternoon. There has been but little use for gloves this winter, though I have been surveying a great deal for three months. The sun, and cockcrowing, bare ground, etc., etc., remind me of March.

Standing on the bridge over the Mill Brook on the Turnpike, there being but little ice on the south side, I see several small waterbugs (*Gyrinus*) swimming about, as in the spring. . . .

At Ditch Pond I hear what I suppose to be a fox barking, an exceedingly husky, hoarse, and ragged note, prolonged perhaps by the echo, like a feeble puppy, or even a child endeavoring to scream, but choked with fear, yet it is on a high key. It sounds so through the wood, while I am in the hollow, that I cannot tell from which side it comes. I hear it bark forty or fifty times at least. It is a peculiar sound, quite unlike any other woodland sound that I know.

Walden, I think, begins to crack and boom first on the south side, which is first in the shade, for I hear it cracking there, though it is still in the sun around me. It is not so sonorous and like the jumping of frogs as I have heard it, but more like the cracking of crockery. It suggests the very brittlest material, as if the globe you stood on were a hollow sphere of glass and might fall to pieces on the slightest touch. Most shivering, splintery, screeching cracks these are, as if the ice were no thicker than a tumbler, though it is probably nine or ten inches. . . .

To insure health, a man's relation to Nature must come very near to a personal one; he must be conscious of a friendliness in her; when human friends fail or die, she must stand in the gap to him. I cannot conceive of any life which deserves the name, unless there is a certain tender relation to Nature. This it is which makes winter warm, and supplies society in the desert and wilderness. Unless Nature sympathizes with and speaks to us, as it were, the most fertile and blooming regions are barren and dreary. . . .

I do not see that I can live tolerably without affection for Nature. If I feel no softening toward the rocks, what do they signify?

I do not think much of that chemistry that can extract corn and potatoes out of a barren [soil], but rather of that chemistry that can extract thoughts and sentiments out of the life of a man on any soil. It is in vain to write on the seasons unless you have the seasons in you.

". . . I know now that I have not worked in vain."

John Audubon

Late on Monday afternoon, January 27, 1851, as the setting sun
lingered to light the snow ridges outside a window overlooking the
Hudson, an old man died, his wife, sons and a troop of grandchildren gathered round him. Just how old he was nobody could be
sure, or whether he was born in Santo Domingo, Haiti, or Louisiana, or even who his parents were. It didn't really matter, for
whatever his origins, the artist, ornithologist, naturalist, woods-
man and essayist John Audubon (1772/1785–1851) left behind
him an indelible imprint that time will not erase.

Audubon's early life is not entirely a mystery. His youth was
spent near Nantes in the Loire valley of France. He was the
adopted son of Jean Audubon, a French naval officer who served
under Lafayette in the American Revolutionary war and later became a prosperous merchant planter in the French colonies. The
boy was taught drawing in preparation for an engineering career
and later studied under David, the celebrated French court
painter. But from the earliest times young Audubon's chief interest was in wild life. Ever more at home outdoors than in the
studio, he made more than 200 drawings of French birds while
still a schoolboy.

In 1803 his father packed him off to the United States, under
the charge of a tutor, and gave him the estate he owned called
Mill Grove, near Philadelphia. Audubon not only observed birds
but also his neighbour's daughter, Lucy Bakewell, who became
his wife. Restless, he soon took his bride to Kentucky where he
went into business with a partner who said of him, "Audubon had
no taste for commerce, and was continually in the forest." Audubon admitted that he rarely had time to attend to business, and
added, "I seldom passed a day without drawing a bird. . . ."

Audubon was soon bankrupt and penniless. To provide for his
two young sons and his wife who almost alone had confidence in
him, he took to drawing portraits at $5 a head. Meanwhile his
portfolios were filling up with magnificent representations of

From *Audubon and His Journals*, edited by Marie R. Audubon. Charles Scribner's
Sons, 1897.

American birds, a thousand or more of them, from sketches made in lonely tramps through unexplored stretches of the Missouri, Ohio and Mississippi valleys.

In time Audubon determined to go to England to arrange for the publication of his paintings, and he set about raising funds for the trip. He printed posters announcing that he would teach drawing, music (he played the violin and flute), and dancing. More came to dance than to draw under his tutelage, but at last he had enough, when added to his wife's painfully hoarded savings, to enable him to sail for England with his precious pictures. The portions of his diary given here begin at this point.

The European trip was a success for the unworldly, unpractical Audubon for he came home assured of the future. His *Birds of America* would be published. But in England, far from his "matchless" Lucy and his "two Kentucky lads," homesick for his beloved beach and magnolia woods, made to play the fool at parties by imitating Indian yells and owl hoots, fed too much and at too great length, plied with Scotch which he had no taste for, reduced by social obligations to four hours of sleep to get his day's work done, Audubon felt far from sure of himself. Dreamer that he was, he could scarcely have foreseen then that years later a single water colour half a day in the making would sell in the auction gallery for an amount sufficient to have kept him from all financial concern for a year.

June 30, 1826.

. . . We have at last entered the Atlantic Ocean this morning and with a propitious breeze; the land birds have left us, and I—I leave my beloved America, my wife, my children, my friends. The purpose of this voyage is to visit not only England, but the continent of Europe, with the intention of publishing my work on the "Birds of America." If not sadly disappointed my return to these shores, these happy shores, will be the brightest day I have ever enjoyed. Oh! wife, children, friends, America, farewell! farewell!

July 9. At sea.

My leaving America had for some time the feelings of a dream; I could scarce make up my mind fixedly on the subject. I thought continually I still saw my beloved friends, and my dear wife and children. . . . But now that I have positively been at sea since *fifty-one* days, tossing to and fro, without the sight or the touch of those dear to me, I feel fully convinced, and look forward with an anxiety such as I never felt before. . . .

July 20. St. George's Channel.

. . . From the bow the land of England is plainly distinguishable; the sight around us is a beautiful one, I have counted fifty-six vessels with spreading sails, and on our right are mountains fading into the horizon; my dull thoughts have all abandoned me, I am elated, my heart is filled with hope. To-morrow we shall land at the city of Liverpool. . . .

July 21. Liverpool.

This morning when I landed it was raining, yet the appearance of the city was agreeable; but no sooner had I entered it than the smoke became so oppressive to my lungs that I could hardly breathe; it affected my eyes also. All was new to me. . . . The day was spent in going to the Museum, gazing about, and clearing my brains as much as possible; but how lonely I feel, —not a soul to speak to freely. . . .

July 25.

. . . Took a hackney coach and found Mr. and Mrs. Rathbone with Mr. James Pyke awaiting me, to take me to the home of Mr. Rathbone, Sr., who lives some miles out of Liverpool. Their youngest boy, Basil, a sweet child, took a fancy to me and I to him, and we made friends during our drive. . . . What sensations I had whilst I helped to untie the fastenings of my portfolio! I knew by all around me that these good friends were possessed of both taste and judgment, and I did not know that I should please. I was panting like the winged Pheasant, but ah! these kind people praised *my Birds,* and I felt the praise to be honest; once more I breathed freely. My portfolio thoroughly examined, we returned. . . . Oh! what can I hope, my Lucy, for thee and for us all?

August 6.

When I arrived in this city I felt dejected, miserably so; the uncertainty as to my reception, my doubts as to how my work would be received, all conspired to depress me. Now, how different are my sensations! I am well received everywhere, my works praised and admired, and my poor heart is at last relieved from the great anxiety that has for so many years agitated it, for I know now that I have not worked in vain. This morning I went to church; the sermon was not to my mind, but the young preacher may improve. . . . I went alone to Mr. Roscoe's habitation. It was full of ladies and gentlemen, all his own family, and I knew almost every one. I was asked to imitate the calls of some of the wild birds, and though I did not wish to do so, consented to satisfy the curiosity of the company. . . . Later more guests came in, and more questions were asked; they appeared surprised that I have no wonderful tales to tell, that, for instance, I have not been devoured at least six times by *tigers,* bears, wolves, foxes; no, I never was troubled by any larger animals than ticks and mosquitoes, and that is quite enough.

August 15. Green Bank, three miles from Liverpool.

I am now at this quiet country home; the morning passed in drawing, and this afternoon I took a long walk with Miss Rathbone and her nephew; we were accompanied by a rare dog from Kamschatka. How I did wish I could have conducted them towards the beech woods where we could move wherever fancy led us; but no, it could not be, and we walked between dreary walls, without the privilege of advancing towards any particular object that might attract the eye. Is it not shocking that while in England all is hospitality *within,* all is so different *without?* No one dare *trespass,* as it is called. Signs of *large dogs* are put up; steel traps and spring guns are set up, and even *eyes* are kept out by high walls. Everywhere we meet beggars, for England though rich, has poverty gaping every way you look, and the beggars ask for *bread,*—yes, absolutely for food. I can only pray, May our Heavenly Father have mercy on them.

August 17.

. . . It is dreadful to know of the want of bread here; will it not lead to the horrors of another revolution? The children of the very poor are often forced by their parents to collect daily a certain amount by begging, or perhaps even stealing; failing to obtain this they are cruelly punished on their return home, and the tricks they resort to, to gain their ends, are numberless and curious. The newspapers abound with such accounts, and are besides filled with histories of murders, thefts, hangings, and other abominable acts; I can scarce look at them.

October 2.

. . . Mr. Rathbone sent his servant to drive me in the gig to Green Bank, the night being cold and damp. The man was quite surprised I did not make use of a great coat which had been placed at my disposal. How little he knew how often I had lain down to rest, wet, hungry, harassed and full of sorrow, with millions of mosquitoes buzzing round me as I lay awake listening to the Chuckmill's Widow, the Horned Owl, and the hoarse Bullfrog, impatiently awaiting the return of day to enable me to hunt the forests and feast my eyes on their beautiful inhabitants. I thought of all this and then moved the scene to the hunter's cabin. Again wet, harassed, and hungry, I felt the sudden warmth of the "Welcome, stranger!" saw the busy wife untook dry clothes from the side of the log hut, untie my moccasins, and take my deerskin coat; I saw the athletic husband wipe my gun, clean the locks, hang all over the bright fire; the eldest boy pile on more wood, whilst my ears were greeted with the sound of the handmill crushing the coffee, or the rye, for my evening drink; I saw the little ones, roused by the stranger's arrival, peeping from under the Buffalo robe, and then turn over on the Black Bear skin to resume their slumbers. I *saw* all this, and then arrived at Green Bank to meet the same hearty welcome. The squatter is rough, true, and hospitable; my friends here polished, true, and generous. Both give what they have, freely. . . .

October 21.

. . . I wrote down for Mrs. Rathbone a brief memorandum of the flight of birds, with a few little pencil sketches to make my figures more interesting:

Swallows, two and a half miles a minute; Wild Pigeons, when travelling, two miles per minute; Swans, ditto two miles, Wild Turkeys, one mile and three quarters.

October 25. Edinburgh, Scotland.

. . . For the first time in my life, I tasted Scotch whiskey. It appeared very potent, so after a few sips I put it down, and told Mr. Patison I suspected his son of wishing to make me tipsy; to which he replied that probably it was to try if I would in such a case be as good-natured as I was before. I took this as quite a compliment and forgave the son. The conversation at dinner was very agreeable, several Scotch gentlemen having joined us; some of them drank their native whiskey pure, as if water, but I found it both smoky and fiery. . . .

November 2.

. . . Perhaps even yet fame may be mine, and enable me to provide all that is needful for my Lucy and my children. Wealth I do not crave, but comfort; and for my boys I have the most ardent desire that they may receive the best of education, far above any that I possess; and day by day science advances, new thoughts and new ideas crowd onward, there is always fresh food for enjoyment, study, improvement, and I must place them where all this may be a possession to them.

November 4.

. . . I dined at Mr. Lizars', where were beauties, music, conviviality, and wit. I am working hard withal; I do with four hours' sleep, keep up a great correspondence, keep up my journal, and write many hours on the letter press for my "Birds," which is almost done.

November 5.

. . . With all this I am by no means in spirits to write, I am so alone in this strange land, so far from those I love the best, and the future rises oft-times dark before me.

November 20.

Whilst my breakfast was preparing, and daylight improving, I sat at my little table to write a notice of descriptive import about my painting of the Wild Turkeys that now leaned against the wall of my room, *finished*. My breakfast came in, but my pen carried me along the Arkansas River, and so much did I long for my beloved country that not a morsel could I swallow. . . . The sumptuous dinners of this country are too much for me. They are so long, so long, that I recall briefer meals that I have had, with much more enjoyment than I eat the bountiful fare before me. This is not a *goûter* with friend Bourgeat on the Flat Lake, roasting the orange-fleshed Ibis, and a few

un-perch; neither is it on the heated banks of Thompson's creek, on the
fourth of July, swallowing the roasted eggs of a large Soft-shelled Turtle;
either was I at Henderson, at good Dr. Rankin's, listening to the howlings
f the Wolves, while sitting in security, eating well roasted and jellied veni-
on,—no, alas! it was far from all these dear spots, in Great King Street, No.
2, at Dr. Graham's, a distinguished professor of botany, with a dinner of so
many rich dishes that I cannot remember them.

November 30.

. . . At six we walked in couples to the dining-room; I had the arm of
my good friend Patrick O'Neill, Mr. Lizars sat on my other side, and there was
sumptuous dinner indeed. It at first consisted entirely of Scotch messes of
ld fashion, such as marrow-bones, codfish-heads stuffed with oatmeal and
arlic, black puddings, sheep's-heads smelling of singed wool, and I do not
now what else. Then a *second* dinner was served quite *à l'anglaise*. I fin-
shed with a bit of grouse. Then came on the toasts. Lord Elgin, being presi-
ent and provided with an auctioneer's mallet, brought all the company to
rder by rapping smartly on the table with the instrument. He then rose,
nd simply said: "The King! four times four!" Every one rose to drink to the
monarch's health, and the president saying, "Ip, ip, ip," sixteen cheers were
oudly given. The Dukes of York, Argyle, and many others had their healths
runk, then Sir Walter Scott (who, to my great regret, was not able to be
resent), and so on and on, one and another, until mine was proposed by
Mr. Skene, the first secretary of the society. Whilst he was engaged in a
andsome panegyric the perspiration poured from me, I thought I should
aint; and I was seated in this wretched condition when everybody rose, and
he Earl called out: "Mr. Audubon." I had seen each individual when
oasted, rise, and deliver a speech; that being the case, could I remain speech-
ess like a fool? No! I summoned all my resolution, and for the first time in
my life spoke to a large assembly, saying these few words: "Gentlemen, my
ommand of words in which to reply to your kindness is almost as humble
s that of the birds hanging on the walls of your institution. I am truly obliged
or your favors. Permit me to say, May God bless you all, and may this so-
iety prosper." I felt my hands wet with perspiration. Mr. Lizars poured me
ut a glass of wine and said: "Bravo! take this," which I gladly did. . . .

December 21.

. . . The weather is clear, with a sharp frost. What a number of Wild
Ducks could I shoot on a morning like this, with a little powder and plenty
f shot; but I had other fish to fry. I put up a beautiful male Pheasant, and
utlined it on coarse gray paper to *pounce* it in proper position on my can-
as. . . . My time is so taken up, and daylight so short, that though four
ours is all I allow for sleep, I am behind-hand, and have engaged an
manuensis. I go out so much that I frequently dress three times a day, the
reatest bore in the world to me; why I cannot dine in my blue coat as well
s a black one, I cannot say, but so it seems. . . . The whole morning passed

away, no canvas came for me, and I could not have left my guests to work, if it had. I looked often at the beautiful Pheasant, with longing eyes, but when the canvas came and my guests had gone, daylight went with them, so I had lost a most precious day; that is a vast deal in a man's life-glass. . . .

January 14, 1827.

. . . After receiving many callers I went to Mr. O'Neill's to have a cast taken of my head. My coat and neckcloth were taken off, my shirt collar turned down, I was told to close my eyes; Mr. O'Neill took a large brush and oiled my whole face, the almost liquid plaster of Paris was poured over it, as I sat uprightly till the whole was covered; my nostrils only were exempt. In a few moments the plaster had acquired the needful consistency, when it was taken off by pulling it down gently. The whole operation lasted hardly five minutes; the only inconvenience felt was the weight of the material pulling downward over my sinews and flesh. On my return from the Antiquarian Society that evening, I found *my face* on the table, an excellent cast.

March 4.

. . . I was trundled into a sedan chair to church. I had never been in a sedan chair before, and I like to try, as well as see, all things on the face of this strange world of ours; but so long as I have two legs and feet below them, never will I again enter one of these machines, with their quick, short, up-and-down, swinging motion, resembling the sensations felt during the great earthquake in Kentucky. But Sydney Smith preached. Oh! what a soul there must be in the body of that great man. What sweet yet energetic thoughts, what goodness he must possess. It was a sermon *to me*. He made me smile, and he made me think deeply. He pleased me at times by painting my foibles with due care, and again I felt the color come to my cheeks as he portrayed my sins. I left the church full of veneration not only towards God, but towards the wonderful man who so beautifully illustrates his noblest handiwork. After lunch Mr. Hays and I took a walk towards Portobello, tumbling and pitching in the deep snow. I saw Sky-Larks, poor things, caught in snares as easily—as men are caught. For a wonder I have done no work to-day.

May 1.

This is the day on which last year I left my Lucy and my boys with intention to sail for Europe. How uncertain my hopes at that time were as to the final results of my voyage,—about to leave a country where most of my life had been spent devoted to the study of Nature, to enter one wholly unknown to me, without a friend, nay, not an acquaintance in it. Until I reached Edinburgh I despaired of success; the publication of a work of enormous expense, and the length of time it must necessarily take. . . . Now I feel like beginning a New Year. My work is about to be known, I have made a number f valuable and kind friends, I have been received by men of science on riendly terms, and now I have a hope of success if I continue to be honest, ndustrious, and consistent. My pecuniary means are slender, but I hope to :eep afloat. . . .

". . . life appears to me such a
curious and wonderful thing . . ."

Francis Kilvert

Francis Kilvert (1840–1879), a young curate and son of a clergyman, was educated at Oxford, began his ministry in central Wales
at the age of twenty-five, and died before he was forty. His position was so obscure and his life so uneventful that he could hardly
have expected that he would be remembered beyond his own
village and his own time.

But Kilvert had a special feeling for life and his fellow men.
The commonplace and the astonishing were equally delightful
to him and in his journal he lovingly records the day-to-day
events of country life as he saw it in early Victorian times. Some
twenty notebooks of his diary were recently discovered, and
though two-thirds of the material is still unpublished, Kilvert has
already been ranked with Dorothy Wordsworth and Pepys among
the great diarists.

"Why do I keep this voluminous journal?" Kilvert asks himself,
and he answers: "Because life appears to me such a curious and
wonderful thing." His diary is, indeed, a chronicle of curiosities
and wonders, of an owl named Ruth a-hoot in a London hotel
room, of a bee in his beard, of whippings and laughing gas and
a frog woman, of croquet played in the dark, of the soft haze that
sifts over the people and things and places that only his pen has
saved from oblivion.

February 8, 1870.

. . . Miss Child in great force. She showed me her clever drawings of horses
and told me the adventures of the brown wood owl "Ruth" which she took
home from here last year. She . . . and her sister stranded in London at night
went to London Bridge hotel (having missed the last train) with little money
and no luggage except the owl in a basket. The owl hooted all night in spite
of their putting it up the chimney, before the looking glass, under the bed-

clothes, and in a circle of lighted candles which they hoped it would mistake for the sun. The owl went on hooting, upset the basket, got out and flew about the room. The chambermaid almost frightened to death dared not come inside the door. Miss Child asked the waiter to get some mice for "Ruth" but none could be got.

February 11.

Last night broke the key of my musical box whilst winding the box up. Went down at midnight and tried to turn the broken key barrel with the tongs—unsuccessfully, and the teeth of the comb stuck in the midst of a tune hitched on the spikes all night. Very bad for the box, so I got up early and directly after breakfast ran over to Hay across the fields in a keen white bright frost. Bevan the watchmaker wound up the box, set it right and mended the key. Bought 4 valentines at Herthen's after searching through a tumbled heap for a long time and ordered some cheese at Hadley's. Coming back the hills were lovely . . . stretching away northward dotted with white houses and shining with gleams of green . . . a tender blue haze over the village and woods . . .

February 13.

. . . When I got to the Chapel my beard moustaches and whiskers were so stiff with ice that I could hardly open my mouth and my beard was frozen on my mackintosh. There was a large christening party. . . . The baby was baptized in ice which was broken and swimming about in the Font.

February 20.

Drunk too much port after dinner . . . last night and a splitting headache all today in revenge. Eyes better but not much. Everything in a daze and dazzle and I could hardly see to read. Got through the services somehow, but in the afternoon came to a deadlock in the middle of the 1st Lesson. . . .

May 6.

I set off for Newchurch [vicarage] again . . . and turning the corner of the wain-house I found the two younger ladies assisting at the castration of the lambs, catching and holding the poor little beasts and standing by whilst the operation was performed, seeming to enjoy the spectacle. It was the first time I had seen clergyman's daughters helping to castrate lambs or witnessing that operation and it rather gave me a turn. . . . I don't think the elder members of the family quite expected that the young ladies would be caught by a morning caller castrating lambs, and probably they would have selected some other occupation for them had they foreseen the coming of a guest. However they carried it off uncommonly well.

July 12.

. . . Great fun on the lawn, 6 cross games of croquet and balls flying in all directions. High tea at 7.30 and croquet given up. More than 40 people sat down. Plenty of iced claret cup, and unlimited fruit, very fine, especially the strawberries. After tea we all strolled out into the garden and stood on the high terrace to see the eclipse. It had just begun. The shadow was slowly steadily stretching over the large bright moon and had eaten away a small piece at the lower left side. It was very strange and solemn to see the shadow stealing gradually on till half the moon was obscured. As the eclipse went on . . . all that was left of the moon was a point of brightness like a large three-cornered star. Then it vanished altogether. . . .

July 16.

To-day we heard rumours of war and war itself . . . by France against Prussia, the wickedest, most unreasonable war that ever was entered into to gratify the ambition of one man. . . . After tea Mrs. Bridge took us round into the garden to show us her hives. One bee instantly flew straight at me . . . buzzing about entangled in my beard, having left his sting between my eyes. Consequently I suppose he was in his dying agony. Then we walked round the garden and along the water walk, while the water ran out of my eyes. . . . Then a wild nonsensical game of Croquet in the dark, everyone playing at the same time, and screams of laughter. . . .

September 6.

. . . Saw the reports of Saturday confirmed and that a Republic had been proclaimed in Paris under General Trocher. Crichton sent me 1½ brace of partridges. Really people are very kind in sending me game.

October 3.

How odd, all the news and letters we get from Paris now coming by balloons and carrier pigeons.

October 8.

Heavy rain in the night and in the morning the mists had all wept themselves away. In the night the wind had gone round from the cursed East into the blessed West. All evil things have always come from the East, the plague, cholera, and man.

December 25.

As I lay awake praying in the early morning I thought I heard a sound of distant bells. It was an intense frost. I sat down in my bath upon a sheet of thick ice which broke in the middle into large pieces whilst sharp points and jagged edges stuck all round the sides of the tub . . . not particularly comforting to the naked thighs and loins, for the keen ice cut like broken glass. The ice water stung and scorched like fire. I had to collect the floating pieces of ice and pile them on a chair before I could use the sponge. . . .

May 7, 1871.

. . . Went into the churchyard under the feathering larch which sweeps over the gate. The ivy-grown old church with its noble tower stood beautiful and silent among the elms with its graves at its feet. Everything was still. No one was about or moving and the only sound was the singing of birds. The place was all in a charm of singing, full of peace and quiet sunshine. It seemed to be given up to the birds and their morning hymns. It was the bird church, the church among the birds. . . .

June 29.

Annie Corfield is better but we fear that she and her sisters, the twins Phoebe and Lizzie, are very miserable and badly treated by their father since . . . the neighbours hear the sound of the whip on their naked flesh and the poor girls crying and screaming sadly sometimes when their father comes home late at night. It seems that when he comes home late he makes the girls get out of bed and strip themselves naked and then he flogs them severely or else he pulls the bedclothes off them and whips them all three as they lie in bed together writhing and screaming under the castigation. It is said that sometimes Corfield strips the poor girls naked, holds them face downwards across his knees on a bed or chair and whips their bare bottoms so cruelly that the blood runs down their legs.

July 4.

Hannah Jones told me about the madwoman of Cwmgwanon. They keep her locked up in a bedroom alone, for she will come down amongst them stark naked. She has broken the window and all the crockery in the room, amuses herself by dancing naked round the room and threatens to wring her daughter-in-law's neck. Then she will set to and roar till they can hear her down the dingle at John Williams' house, nearly half a mile.

July 14.

I went to Hereford to see the dentist McAdam. He showed me the apparatus for giving people the new anaesthetic laughing gas which he thinks much safer than chloroform. . . .

July 18.

I went to Wern Vawr. The sun burst fiercely as I climbed the hills but a little breeze crept about the hill tops. Some barbarian—a dissenter no doubt

—probably a Baptist, has cut down the beautiful silver birches on the Little Mountain. . . .

July 22.

. . . Mrs. Nott told me [of] . . . Miss Sylvester, the woman frog. This extraordinary being is partly a woman and partly a frog. Her head and face, her eyes and mouth are those of a frog, and she has a frog's legs and feet. She cannot walk but she hops. She wears very long dresses to cover and conceal her feet which are shod with something like a cow's hoof. She never goes out except to the Primitive Methodist Chapel. Mrs. Nott said she had seen this person's frog feet and had seen her in Presteign hopping to and from the Chapel exactly like a frog. She had never seen her hands. She is a very good person. . . .

September 3.

I went down to Bettws in light rain and preached extempore on the Good Samaritan from the Gospel for the day. A red cow with a foolish white face came up to the window by the desk and stared in while I was preaching.

October 22.

Coming home in the dusk I turned into the school house to tell the schoolmaster I was going out to-morrow for a few days and that I should not be at school this week. The schoolmaster is learning to play the violin. He produced the instrument and began to play upon it. It had a broken string, and there was something wrong with all the rest. . . . "Glory be to Jesus," sang the schoolmaster, loudly and cheerfully sawing away at the cracked and broken strings, while the violin screeched and shrieked and screamed and groaned and actually seemed to writhe and struggle in his arms like a wild animal in agony. There was something so utterly incongruous in the words and the noise, the heart-rending bowel-raking uproar and screams of the tormented violin, that I smiled, I could not help it. Shriek, shriek, scream, groan, yell, howled the violin, as if a spirit in torment were writhing imprisoned within it, and still the schoolmaster sawed away vigorously and sung amid the wailing, screeching uproar. . . .

November 3, 1874.

. . . Why do I keep this voluminous journal? I can hardly tell. Partly because life appears to me such a curious and wonderful thing that it almost seems a pity that even such a humble and uneventful life as mine should pass altogether away without some such record as this, and partly too because I think the record may amuse and interest some who come after me.

December 25.

. . . The churchwarden Jacob Knight was sitting by his sister in front of the roaring fire. We were talking of the death of Major Torrens on the ice at Corsham pond yesterday. Speaking of people slipping and falling on ice the good churchwarden sagely remarked, "Some do fall on their faces and some do fall on their rumps. And they as do hold their selves uncommon stiff do most in generally fall on their rumps." . . .

December 31. New Year's Eve.

Edwin Law told me of an infallible receipt for warming cold and wet feet on a journey. Pour half a glass of brandy into each boot. Also he often carries a large pair of stockings with him to wear over boots and trousers. He has been a long time in Nova Scotia.

My Mother and I sat up by the dining room fire to watch the Old Year out and the New Year in. Soon after eleven o'clock the Chippenham bells began pealing and continued to ring at intervals till after midnight. The wind had veered into the South and brought the sound of the bells to us very distinct and sweet across the river, so that we could plainly hear when they began and paused and all the change-ringing and the firing. . . .

January 12, 1875.

. . . William Ferris told me to-day his reminiscences of the first train that ever came down the Great Western Railway. "I was foddering," he said, "near the line. It was a hot day in May some 34 or 35 years ago, and I heard a roaring in the air. I looked up and thought there was a storm coming down . . . roaring in the tops of the trees, only the day was so fine and hot. Well, the roaring came nigher and nigher, then the train shot along and the dust did flee up."

July 19.

I called on Mrs. Martin. She was busy picking pheasants' feathers to make a pillow. . . . At 7 o'clock came on another terrible storm of rain much worse than the one in the afternoon. I was in my room reading when I heard Fanny screaming to me from the top of the house. Rushing up the back stairs I found that the cistern was overflowing and deluging the water closet, the tank room, and the bathroom and the kitchen. I was obliged to put on a mackintosh and stand in the water closet holding up the handle to relieve the cistern while the water ran down upon my head like a shower bath.

August 12.

I walked across to Kington St. Michael to be present at the school feast. As we were swinging the children under the elms that crown the Tor Hill a girl came up to me with a beseeching look in her eyes and an irresistible request for a swing. . . . I lifted her into the swing and away she went. But about the sixth flight the girl suddenly slipped off the swing seat foremost and still keeping hold of the ropes she hung from the swing helpless. Unfortunately her clothes had got hitched upon the seat of the swing and were all pulled up round her waist and it instantly became apparent that she wore no drawers. A titter and then a shout of laughter ran through the crowd as the girl's plump person was seen naked hanging from the swing. O ye gods, the fall of Hebe was nothing to it. We hustled her out of the swing and her clothes into their proper place as soon as possible and perhaps she did not know what a spectacle she had presented. I believe it was partly my fault. When I lifted the girl into the swing there were many aspirants for the seat and in the struggle and confusion I suppose I set her down with her clothes rumpled up and her bare flesh (poor child) upon the board and as her flesh was plump and smooth and in excellent whipping condition and the board slippery, they managed to part company with this result. . . . She scarcely contemplated the exhibition of herself for the amusement of the spectators. I shall never see the elms on the Tor Hill now without thinking of the fall of Hebe.

August 19.

In the newspapers this morning we saw the account of the Royal M yacht . . . running down, cutting in two and sinking Mr. Heywood's yacht, the *Mistletoe* in Stokes Bay with a loss of three lives . . . the first accident that has ever happened to the Queen in travelling and she is terribly distressed. It is an awkward thing for the Sovereign to destroy her own subjects. . . .

September 4.

This beautiful autumn morning I went out to pray on the sunny common. The luxuriant meadow grass shone green and silver with the hoary webs and sheets of dew. The hills and woods and distances were richly bloomed with azure misty veils, the sweet sudden solitary song of the robin from the hornbeam broke the morning calm, and here and there a yellow leaf, the herald of Autumn, floated silently from the limes. . . .

May 19, 1878.

Yesterday a new wire bird door (the gift of Miss Newton) was hung at the main door. We have been much troubled by the birds in the Church lately, and have been obliged to close the painted East window to keep out the swallows who were darting in and out with mud and building a nest against the wall just over the altar. I was sorry to interfere with them, but it was necessary for they were scattering mud all over the place.

December 17.

Sharp frost again last night. The snow clouds cleared off and the day became cloudless and blue and brilliant. The bridge in the sunshine was most beautiful. . . . As I came down into the sheltered hollow of the Lower CWm in the twilight I heard rising from the cottage in the dingle across the brook a woman's voice addressing a naughty child and uttering that threatening promise which in this form is probably as old as the English language and in some form is probably as old as the world. "I'll whip your bottom!" Were bottoms so formed that they might be whipped? or why since the foundation of the world has this part of the human body been universally chosen to suffer chastisement?

February 4, 1879.

At 7 p.m. the farmers came to dine at the Vicarage. I had ten guests. . . . White soup, roast beef, boiled chickens and ham, curried rabbit, stewed woodpigeons, beaf-steak pie, potatoes and stewed celery, plum pudding, custard, plum tart, mince pies, apricot jam tart.

". . . fried fish and a dash of medicinal whisky . . ."

John Steinbeck

Those who read fiction, go to the theatre or the movies, know John Steinbeck (1902–   ) as one of America's most productive novelists, author of *The Grapes of Wrath, Tortilla Flat, The Red Pony, Of Mice and Men, In Dubious Battle, Cannery Row* and many other widely read books. Comparatively few people know Steinbeck the amateur of science. He has a long-time interest in scientific research and has contributed to a number of important projects. At Stanford University his chief interest was in marine biology; later he was closely associated with Edward F. Ricketts, Director of the Pacific Biological Laboratories, zoologist and an authority in the field of invertebratology. Their collaboration resulted in the expedition to the Gulf of California to collect specimens of marine invertebrates described in their jointly written book, *The Sea of Cortez* (1941). The journal Steinbeck kept of their voyage contains much that is of specialized interest; the portions chosen here combine a little of science with a good deal else—speculative philosophy, fishing, high-spirited adventure and salt-soaked merriment.

When Steinbeck set out with Ricketts in the *Western Flyer* to search the quiet harbours and barren coasts of the California peninsula for new species, he was already world famous. But his success had been anything but easy. His first novels sold only indifferently, and in the early years Steinbeck was often forced to support himself on what he could earn as a hod carrier, fruit picker, surveyor and chemist. Ricketts, who died tragically in an automobile accident in 1948, was a colorful and many-sided personality. He is the thinly disguised biologist, dealer in sponges, tunicates, anemones, sun stars and buttlestars, bivalves, barnacles, nudibranchs and tectibranchs, spiked, nobbed and needly urchins, snails, spiders, cats and rats, honey bees and gila monsters, who was affectionately described in *Cannery Row, Sweet Thursday* and other Steinbeck books and reappeared in the Rodgers and Hammerstein musical comedy *Pipe Dream*.

On March 11, 1940, the marine expedition set forth from Mon-
terey. On board the *Western Flyer* was a crew of seven, armed
with a .22-caliber pistol and a rusty shot-gun. The cargo consisted
of nets, specimen jars and collecting pans, formaldehyde and
pickling alcohol, cameras, binoculars, microscopes, quinine cap-
sules and a store of medicinal whiskey which, taken as a preven-
tive and prophylactic, was soon exhausted. It is at this point that
John Steinbeck begins his log of what is surely one of the least
solemn of scientific voyages . . .

March 12, 1940.

In the morning we had come to the Santa Barbara Channel and the water
was slick and grey, flowing in long smooth swells, and over it, close down,
there hung a little mist so that the sea-birds flew in and out of sight. Then
breaking the water as though they swam in an obscure mirror, the porpoises
surrounded us. They really came to us. We have seen them change course
to join us, these curious animals. The Japanese will eat them, but rarely will
Occidentals touch them. Of our crew Tiny and Sparky [seamen], who loved
to catch every manner of fish, to harpoon any swimming thing, would have
nothing to do with porpoises. "They cry so," Sparky said, "when they are
hurt, they cry to break your heart." This is rather a difficult thing to understand; a dying cow cries too, and a stuck pig raises his protesting voice
piercingly and very few hearts are broken by those cries. But a porpoise cries
like a child in sorrow and pain. And we wonder whether the general seaman's
real affection for porpoises might not be more complicated than the simple
fear of hearing them cry. The nature of the animal might parallel certain
traits in ourselves—the outrageous boastfulness of porpoises, their love of play,
their joy in speed. . . .

In San Diego we filled the fuel tanks and the water tanks. We filled the
icebox and took on the last perishable foods, bread and eggs and fresh meat.
These would not last long, for when the ice was gone only the canned goods
and the foods we could take from the sea would be available. We tied up to
the pier all day and a night; got our last haircuts and ate broiled steaks. . . .
Strangers came to the pier and stared at us and small boys dropped on our
decks like monkeys. Those quiet men who always stand on piers asked where
we were going and when we said "To the Gulf of California," their eyes
melted with longing, they wanted to go so badly. They were like the men
and women who stand about airports and railroad stations; they want to go
away, and most of all they want to go away from themselves. For they do
not know that they would carry their globes of boredom with them wherever
they went. One man on the pier who wanted to participate made sure he
would be allowed to cast us off, and he waited at the bow line for a long
time. Finally he got the call and he cast off the bow line and ran back and
cast off the stern line; then he stood and watched us pull away and he
wanted very badly to go. . . .

March 17.

At two A.M. we passed Point Lazaro, one of the reputedly dangerous places of the world, like Cedros Passage, or like Cape Horn, where the weather is always bad even when it is good elsewhere. There is a sense of relief when one is safely past these half-mythical places, for they are not only stormy but treacherous, and again the atavistic fear arises—the Scylla-Charybdis fear that made our ancestors people such places with monsters and enter them only after prayer and propitiation. . . .

. . . We cleaned ourselves well and shaved while we waited for the Mexican officials to come out and give us the right to land. They were late in coming, for they had to find their official uniforms, and they too had to shave. . . . They come over the side like ambassadors. We shake hands all around. The galley has been prepared: coffee is ready and perhaps a drop of rum. Cigarettes are presented and then comes the ceremonial of the match. In Mexico cigarettes are cheap, but matches are not. If a man wishes to honor you, he lights your cigarette, and if you have given him a cigarette, he must so honor you. . . .

All the time we were indulging in courtliness there had been light gunfire on the cliffs, where several men were shooting at black cormorants; and it developed that everyone in Cape San Lucas hates cormorants. They are the flies in a perfect ecological ointment. The cannery cans tuna; the entrails and cuttings of the tuna are thrown into the water from the end of the pier. This refuse brings in schools of small fish which are netted and used for bait to catch tuna. This closed and tight circle is interfered with by the cormorants, who try to get at the bait-fish. They dive and catch fish, but also they drive the schools away from the pier out of easy reach of the baitmen. Thus they are considered interlopers, radicals, subversive forces against the perfect and God-set balance on Cape San Lucas. And they are rightly slaughtered, as all radicals should be. As one of our number remarked, "Why, pretty soon they'll want to vote." . . .

. . . Six weeks we had, and no more. Was it a wonder that we collected furiously; spent every low-tide moment on the rocks, even at night? . . . When the charter was up we would be through. How different it had been when John Xantus was stationed in this very place . . . in the sixties. Sent down by the United States Government as a tidal observer, but having lots of time, he collected animals for our National Museum. The first fine collections of Gulf forms came from Xantus. . . . Speaking to the manager of the cannery at the Cape we remarked on what a great man Xantus had been. Where another would have kept his tide charts and brooded and wished for the Willard Hotel, Xantus had collected animals widely and carefully. The manager said, "Oh, he was even better than that." Pointing to three little Indian children he said, "Those are Xantus's great-grandchildren," and he continued, "In the town there is a large family of Xantuses, and a few miles back in the hills you'll find a whole tribe of them." There were giants in the earth in those days. We wonder what modern biologist, worried about titles and preferment and the gossip of the Faculty Club, would have the warmth and breadth, or even the fecundity for that matter, to leave a "whole tribe of Xantuses." . . .

March 18.

. . . At Pulmo Reef . . . [a little Indian dugout] canoe put off and came alongside. In it were two men and a woman, very ragged, their old clothes patched with the tatters of older clothes. . . . They sat in the canoe holding to the side of the *Western Flyer* and they held their greasy blankets carefully over their noses and mouths to protect themselves from us. So much evil the white man had brought to their ancestors: his breath was poisonous with the lung disease; to sleep with him was to poison the generations. Where he set down his colonies the indigenous people withered and died. He brought industry and trade but no prosperity, riches but no ease. After four hundred years of him these people have ragged clothes and the shame that forces the wearing of them; iron harpoons for their hands, syphilis and tuberculosis; a few of the white man's less complex neuroses, and a curious devotion to a God who was sacrificed long ago in the white man's country. They know the white man is poisonous and they cover their noses against him. They do find us fascinating. . . .

. . . Sparky worked at the radio and made contact with the fishing fleet that was operating in the region from Cedros Island and around the tip into the Gulf, fishing for tuna. Fishermen are no happier than farmers. It is difficult to see why anyone becomes a farmer or a fisherman. Dreadful things happen to them constantly: they lose their nets; the fish are wild; sea-lions get into the nets and tear their way out; snags are caught; there are no fish, and the price high; there are too many fish, and the price is low; and if some means could be devised so that the fish swam up to a boat, wriggled up a trough, squirmed their way into the fish-hold, and pulled ice over themselves with their own fins, the imprecations would be terrible because they had not removed their own entrails and brought their own ice. There is no happiness for fishermen anywhere. Cries of anguish at the injustice of the elements inundated the short-wave receiver as we lay at anchor. . . .

March 20.

. . . While we were anchored at Espíritu Santo Island a black yacht went by swiftly, and on her awninged after-deck ladies and gentlemen in white clothing sat comfortably. We saw they had tall cool drinks beside them and we hated them a little, for we were out of beer. And Tiny said fiercely, "Nobody but a pansy'd sail on a thing like that." And then more gently, "But I've never been sure I ain't queer." The yacht went down over the horizon, and up over the horizon climbed an old horror of a cargo ship, dirty and staggering. And she stumbled on toward the channel of La Paz; her pumps must have been going wide open. . . . We said to a man on the beach, "She is sinking." And he replied calmly, "She always sinks."

March 27.

. . . When we came back from the early morning collecting we sailed immediately for the port of Loreto. . . . Loreto was asleep in the sunshine, a lovely town, with gardens in every yard and only the streets white and hot. The young males watched us from the safe shade of the *cantina* and passed greetings as we went by, and a covey of young girls grew tight-faced and rushed around a corner and giggled. How strange we were in Loreto! Our trousers were dark, not white; the silly caps we wore were so outlandish that no store in Loreto would think of stocking them . . . the little girls just couldn't take it. We could hear their strangled giggling from around the corner. . . . As usual, a good serious small boy attached himself to us. It would be interesting to see whether a nation governed by the small boys of Mexico would not be a better, happier nation than those ruled by old men whose prejudices may or may not be conditioned by ulcerous stomachs and perhaps a little drying up of the stream of love.

March 29.

. . . At five P.M. . . . we arrived at San Lucas Cove and anchored outside. The cove, a deep salt-water lagoon, guarded by a large sandspit, has an entrance that might have been deep enough for us to enter, but the current is strong and there were no previous soundings available. . . . There was another reason for anchoring outside; in the open Gulf where the breeze moves there are no bugs, while if one anchors in still water near the mangroves little visitors come and spend the night. There is one small, beetle-like fly which crawls down into bed with you and has a liking for very tender places. We had suffered from this fellow when the wind blew over the mangroves to us. This bug hates light, but finds security and happiness under the bedding, nestling over one's kidneys, munching contentedly. His bite leaves a fiery itch; his collective soul is roasting in Hell, if we have any influence in the court of Heaven. . . .

Late, late in the night we recalled that Horace says fried shrimps and African snails will cure a hangover. None was available. And we wonder whether this classical remedy for a time-bridging ailment has been prescribed and tried since classical times. . . . We tore the remedy down to its fundamentals, and decided that it was a good strong dose of proteins and alcohol, so we substituted a new compound—fried fish and a dash of medicinal whisky —and it did the job.

. . . No sooner had we put to sea when it was discovered that each one of us, with the health of the whole party in mind, had laid in auxiliary medicine for emergencies. We had indeed, when the good-will of all was assembled, a medicine chest which would not have profaned a fair-sized bar. And the emergencies did occur. Who is to say that an emergency of the soul is not worse than a bad cold? What was good enough for Li-Po was good enough for us. There have been few enough immortals who did not love wine; offhand we cannot think of any and do not intend to try very hard. The American Indians and the Australian Bushmen are about the only great and intellectual peoples who have not developed an alcoholic liquor and a cult to take care of it. There are, indeed, groups among our own people who have abandoned the use of alcohol, due no doubt to Indian or Bushman blood, but we do not wish to claim affiliation with them. One can imagine such a specimen of Bushman reading this journal and saying, "Why, it was all drinking—beer—and at San Lucas Cove, whisky." So might a night-watchman cry out, "People sleep all the time!" So might a blind man complain, "Among some people there is a pernicious and wicked practice called 'seeing.' This eventually causes death and should be avoided." Actually, with few tribal exceptions, our race has a triumphant alcoholic history and no definite symptoms of degeneracy can be attributed to it. The theory that alcohol is a poison was too easily and too blindly accepted. So it is to some individuals; sugar is poison to others and meat to others. But to the race in general, alcohol has been an anodyne, a warmer of the soul, a strengthener of muscle and spirit. It has given courage to cowards and has made very ugly people attractive. There is a story told of a Swedish tramp, sitting in a ditch on Midsummer Night. He was ragged and dirty and drunk, and he said to himself softly and in wonder, "I am rich and happy and perhaps a little beautiful."

March 31.

. . . Costume on the *Western Flyer* had degenerated completely. Shirts were no longer worn, but the big straw hats were necessary. On board we went barefoot, clad only in hats and trunks. . . . We ate fish nearly every day: bonito, dolphin, sierra, red snappers. We made thousands of big fat biscuits, hot and unhealthful. Twice a week Sparky created his magnificent spaghetti. Unbelievable amounts of coffee were consumed. One of our party made some lemon pies, but the quarreling grew bitter over them; the thievery, the suspicion of favoritism, the vulgar traits of selfishness and perfidy those pies brought out saddened all of us. And when one of us who, from being the most learned should have been the most self-controlled, took to hiding pie in his bed and munching it secretly when the lights were out, we decided there must be no more lemon pie. Character was crumbling, and the law of the fang was too close to us.

April 1.

Without the log we should have lost track of the days of the week, were it not for the fact that Sparky made spaghetti on Thursdays and Sundays. We think he did this by instinct, that he could come out of a profound amnesia, and if he felt an impulse to make spaghetti, it would be found to be either Thursday or Sunday. . . .

April 2.

We started early and moved out through the channel to the Gulf. It was not long before we could make out Sail Rock far ahead. . . . With lots of time, we would have collected at its base, but we were aimed at Puerto

Refugio, at the upper end of Guardian Angel Island. We did take some of our usual moving pictures of Sail Rock, and they were even a little worse than usual, for there was laundry drying on a string and the camera was set up behind it. When developed, the film showed only an occasional glimpse of Sail Rock, but a very lively set of scenes of a pair of Tiny's blue and white shorts snapping in the breeze. It is impossible to say how bad our moving pictures were—one film laboratory has been eager to have a copy of the film, for it embodies in a few thousand feet, so they say, every single thing one should not do with a camera. As an object lesson to beginners they think it would be valuable. If we took close-ups of animals, someone was in the light; the aperture was always too wide or too narrow; we made little jerky pan shots back and forth; we have one of the finest sequences of unadorned sky pictures in existence—but when there was something to take about which we didn't care, we got it perfectly. We dare say there is not on the world a more spirited and beautiful picture of a pair of blue and white shorts than that which we took passing Sail Rock. . . .

April 3.

We sailed around the northern tip of Guardian Angel and down its eastern coast. The water was clear and blue, and a large swell flowed past us. . . . We went down the western coast of Tiburón and watched its high cliffs through the glasses. The cliffs are fairly sheer, and the mountains are higher than those on Guardian Angel Island. This is the island where the Seri Indians come during parts of the year. . . . It is certain that they have killed many strangers, but whether or not they have eaten them does not seem to be documented. Cannibalism is a fascinating subject to most people, and in some way a sin. Possibly the deep feeling is that if people learn to eat one another the food supply would be so generous and so available that no one would be either safe or hungry. . . . We searched the shore for Seris and saw none. In our usual condition of hunger, it would have been a toss-up whether Seris ate us or we ate Seris. The one who got in the first bite would have had the dinner, but we never did see a Seri. . . .

April 4.

The trolling jigs picked up two fine sierras on the way. Our squid jigs had gone to pieces from much use, and had to be repaired with white chicken feathers. We were under way all day, and toward evening began to see the sport-fishing boats of Guaymas with their cargoes of sportsmen out-fitted with equipment to startle the fish into submission. And the sportsmen were mentally on tiptoe to out-think the fish—which they sometimes do. We thought it might be fun some time to engage in this intellectual approach toward fishing, instead of our barbarous method of throwing a line with a chicken-feather jig overboard. These fishermen in their swivel fishing chairs looked comfortable and clean and pink. We had been washing our clothes in salt water, and we felt sticky and salt-crusted; and, being less comfortable and clean than the sportsmen, we built a whole defense of contempt. With no effort at all on their part we had a good deal of dislike for them. It is probable that Sparky and Tiny had a true contempt, uncolored by envy, for they are descended from many generations of fishermen who went out for fish, not splendor. But even they might have liked sitting in a swivel chair holding a rod in one hand and a frosty glass in the other, blaming a poor day on the Democrats, and offering up prayers for good fishing to Calvin Coolidge. . . .

April 5.

We sailed in the morning on the short trip to Guaymas. It was the first stop in a town that had anything like communication since we had left San Diego. The world and the war had become remote to us; all the immediacies of our usual lives had slowed up. Far from welcoming a return, we rather resented going back. . . . We could understand, because we could feel, how the Indians of the Gulf, hearing about the great ant-doings of the north, might shake their heads sadly and say, "But it is crazy. It would be nice to have new Ford cars and running water, but not at the cost of insanity." And in us the factor of time had changed: the low tides were our clock and the throbbing engine our second hand. . . .

April 11.

. . . At last, and with sorrow, Tex started the engine and the anchor came up for the last time. All afternoon we stowed and lashed equipment, set the corks in hundreds of glass tubes and wrapped them in paper toweling, screwed tight the caps of jars, tied down the skiffs, and finally dropped the hatch cover in place. . . . Then we were under way, sailing southward toward the Cape. The swordfish jumped in the afternoon light, flashing like heliographs in the distance. . . . In the morning the tip of the Peninsula was on our right. Behind us the Gulf was sunny and calm, but out in the Pacific a heavy threatening line of clouds hung. Then a crazy literary thing happened. As we came opposite the Point there was one great clap of thunder, and immediately we hit the great swells of the Pacific and the wind freshened against us. The water took on a grey tone.

"The chill of the night, the smell of the swamp,
the feel of mist . . ."

Edwin Way Teale

Edwin Way Teale (1899–   ) has been a naturalist most of
his life. He has won the John Burroughs Medal for distinguished
nature writing, and is a past president of the New York Entomo-
logical Society. His books have been published in half a dozen
foreign countries and have been issued in Braille editions.

Teale was born in Joliet, Illinois and educated at Earlham College and Columbia University. Before devoting himself to writing
nature books, a dozen of which have been published, he was a
magazine staff writer.

From boyhood his interest has been in wild life. He has reproduced it both in words and photographs. His first camera was
earned by picking 20,000 strawberries on his grandfather's Indiana farm, and the first use he made of it was to take a picture
of a rabbit. Since then he has amassed more than 25,000 nature
photographs, many of which have been used to illustrate his
books. His nature writing is valued for its simple, pungent style
as in the excerpts given here, where he describes the homecoming
of the birds to their reed hostelry in Milburn Swamp.

October 15, 1952.

Again, the dawn mist is smoky gray beneath the trees, shining, silver gray
in the open. As I wander through the Insect Garden, I come upon a woolly
bear spangled and starred with droplets of moisture. A little wild cherry beside the trail is adorned like a Christmas tree. Its dead branches are spider-
trimmed with ropes and webs and dew-decorated spangles. Above me, a
cheery "perchicory!" call marks the passage of a goldfinch, invisible in the
vapor. As I approach the swamp stream, out of the autumn fog phragmites
and cattails suddenly seem to step forward.

For a decade and a half now, I have watched the silent battle between
these two. Slowly the phragmites have extended their foothold. These high,
plumed reeds have less food value for wildlife than the cattails. But . . . in

Milburn Swamp, their chief value is as a shelter for blackbirds, grackles and starlings. Each day, at sunset, I see the great starling flocks come in to roost for the night. As I stand in the chill morning vapor, looking into the phragmites—gray and wavering in the gray mist—I begin to imagine what it must be like within that dense stand of canes when the starling hosts pour down from the sky. . . . Tomorrow, before sunset, I will return and secrete myself in the heart of the phragmites and watch homecoming birds descend around me.

October 16.

A little before five P.M., wearing long boots, old army pants, a leather jacket and an ancient felt hat, I push my way into the jungle of the phragmites. The day has been warm for mid-October. But a chill rises early from the swamp. In the heart of the stand, I tramp out a little hollow. Here I await the returning birds and here I set down the following notes:

5:01 P.M. I can see only four or five feet, at most, into the tangle around me. Here and there, by the laws of chance, the stems are arranged into corridors that open for several feet high, thin corridors barred at the end by a maze of upright stems. The interior of the canebrake is so like pictures of bamboo jungles of the Orient that a tiger or cobra would hardly seem out of place. Over my head, eight or nine feet above the floor of the swamp, wave the plumes of the phragmites. Each stem is hardly thicker than my little finger.

5:05 P.M. Each time a breeze sweeps across the swamp, there is a creaking of stems and a dry rustle of leaves. The fall is a time of growing brittleness.

5:07 P.M. The first bird to arrive is a redwing. I hear its monosyllabic "Check! Check!" as it alights in the willow and then flies down to the far side of the phragmites.

5:09 P.M. Birds are assembling in the swampside maples. The sun is going down and the flocks are coming in. I can hear the mingled calling of many birds.

5:12 P.M. After five minutes of this bird bedlam, my ears feel weary and battered and deafened. There are alarm notes, quarreling notes, excitement, discontent, gossiping, the hubbub of hundreds of birds around me.

5:20 P.M. The uproar reaches a crescendo. Then there is, suddenly, silence. A perfect hush falls on the multitude of birds. It is followed by a silken whirring, a mighty fluttering, and the plumes of the phragmites wave in the wing-formed wind as the birds rise in unison into the air. For a moment, all the stems around me rock as in a breeze.

5:22 P.M. Beyond the swamp stream, the birds have alighted in another and larger stand of phragmites where they will spend the night. I hear their confused clamor muted by distance. I also hear the voices of a new concentration of starlings building up in the maples.

5:31 P.M. The chill is growing. Shadows have engulfed the phragmites.

5:42 P.M. Now the second wave breaks over the plumed reeds. The deserted phragmites are again filled with life. The concentration and the vast tumult builds up with each new addition to the flock. A redwing—one of those still to migrate—alights close behind my head. Its surprised "Check!"

rings loud in my ears. There are little pauses, from time to time, in the vast tumult of bird voices beating against my ears. And in one of them a single starling, almost overhead, imitates a snatch of the sweet, plaintive song of the white-throat.

5:51 *P.M.* Again there is the sudden hushing of the din, the sudden mounting "Wooosh!" of wings, the swaying of the plumes above my head. These birds, too, cross the stream to the larger stand of phragmites for the night.

6:07 *P.M.* The individual reed stems are merging together in the gloom. The chill of the night, the smell of the swamp, the feel of mist is in the air.

6:39 *P.M.* No more birds have come. Outside I hear the flutter and splash of two ducks alighting on the swamp stream. The thronging birds in the far phragmites have fallen quiet. Now, even the steely hum of a mosquito sounds large in my ears. . . . Darkness is all around. The homecoming of the birds is over.

"I have been whistling on my wits . . ."

Sir Walter Scott

On September 21, 1832 there was a great crowd in the street outside the window of an Edinburgh newspaper. Men, women, a few children too, were hushed and solemn. Some wept. They stood before a poster bearing an announcement printed within the wide black bands ordinarily used at the death of royalty. A newcomer asked what had happened. "He's passed," was the reply. The poster was headed "Death of Sir Walter Scott."

Sir Walter Scott (1771–1832) was born in College Wynd, Edinburgh, and took great pride in his ancestry. His mother belonged to the ancient Baccleugh family, long famous in Border annals. His father, a lawyer, gave his son a celebrated name. "My father's grandfather," Sir Walter wrote, "was Walter Scott, well known by the name of *Beardie*. He was the second son of Walter Scott, first laird of Raeburn, who was third son of Sir Walter Scott, and the grandson of Walter Scott, commonly called in tradition *Auld Watt* of Harden. I am therefore lineally descended from that ancient chieftain, whose name I have made to ring in many a ditty, and from his fair dame, the Flower of Yarrow—no bad genealogy for a Border minstrel."

After graduation from college, Scott was apprenticed to his father and was called to the bar in 1792, made Sheriff of Selkirk seven years later, and held the post of Clerk of Session for twenty-five years. He married Charlotte Charpentier, daughter of a French *émigré* and was the father of four children. An attack of polio in infancy resulted in injury to one of his legs; like Byron, a poet he admired, he walked with a limp.

As a youth Scott was an insatiable reader and collector of old Scots ballads and romances, and this interest was reflected in most of his work, from *Minstrelsy of the Scottish Border* and *Lay of the Last Minstrel* to *Lady of the Lake*, *Guy Mannering*, *Kenilworth*, and *Ivanhoe*.

Scott wrote prolifically and scores of thousands of avid readers

From *The Journal of Sir Walter Scott*, by Sir Walter Scott. Reprinted by permission of Harper & Brothers.

brought him fame and success. Unfortunately, he invested a substantial part of his newly gained wealth in publishing companies, and when they were driven to bankruptcy by the depression of 1826, Scott felt himself obliged to assume a staggering debt of £130,000 as his personal responsibility.

The rest of Scott's life was devoted to the task of earning the money to repay this debt. Through illness, bereavement, and growing weakness he wrote on and on. When he could no longer hold pen in hand, he called on secretaries to write at his dictation. The first year he earned £40,000, all of which went to the creditors except for the bare expenses of living. His beloved wife died, then his son, and finally his beloved grandson. He suffered apoplectic strokes from which he never recovered. Yet still he kept on, and ultimately all of the creditors were paid to the last penny. But the effort cost Scott his life. Tired, sick and prematurely old, he died in his sixty-first year.

From 1825 until his death, Scott kept a diary. What he wrote in it was quite unlike anything composed for the readers of his widely sold romances. Scott confided to paper his own story—the plain tale of a patient and courageous man.

November 20, 1825.

I have all my life regretted that I did not keep a regular Journal. I have myself lost recollection of much that was interesting, and I have deprived my family and the public of some curious information, by not carrying this resolution into effect. . . .

November 30.

I am come to the time when those who look out of the windows shall be darkened. I must now wear spectacles constantly in reading and writing, though till this winter I have made a shift by using only their occasional assistance. Although my health cannot be better. . . . Well—such things must come, and be received with cheerful submission. My early lameness considered, it was impossible for a man labouring under a bodily impediment to have been stronger or more active than I have been, and that for twenty or thirty years. Seams will slit, and elbows will out, quoth the tailor; and as I was fifty-four on 15th August last, my mortal vestments are none of the newest. . . .

December 7.

. . . Wrote answers to one or two letters which have been lying on my desk like snakes, hissing at me for my dilatoriness. . . . Mighty dark this morning; it is past ten, and I am using my lamp. . . .

December 14.

Affairs very bad in the money-market in London. It must come here, and have far too many engagements not to feel it. To end the matter at once, intend to borrow 10,000. . . . This will enable us to dispense in a great measure with bank assistance, and sleep in spite of thunder. I do not know whether it is this business which makes me a little bilious, or rather the want of exercise during the season of late, and change of the weather to too much heat. . . . But the sun and the moon shall dance on the green ere carelessness, or hope of gain, or facility of getting cash, shall make me go too deep again. . . .

December 18.

. . . My extremity has come. Cadell has received letters from London which all but positively announce the failure of Hurst and Robinson, so that Constable & Co. must follow, and I must go [down] with poor James Ballantyne for company. I suppose it will involve my all. . . . Men will think pride has had a fall. Let them indulge their own pride in thinking that my fall makes them higher, or seems so at least. I have the satisfaction to recollect that my prosperity has been of advantage to many, and that some at least will forgive my transient wealth on account of the innocence of my intentions, and my real wish to do good to the poor. This news will make sad hearts at Darnick, and in the cottages of Abbotsford, which I do not nourish the least hope of preserving. It has been my Delilah, and so I have often termed it; and now the recollection of the extensive woods I planted, and the walks I have formed, from which strangers must derive both the pleasure and profit, will excite feelings likely to sober my gayest moments. I have half resolved never to see the place again. How could I tread my hall with such a dimished crest? How live a poor indebted man where I was once the wealthy, the honoured? My children are provided; thank God for that. I was to have gone there on Saturday in joy and prosperity to receive my friends. My dogs will wait for me in vain. It is foolish—but the thoughts of parting from these dumb creatures have moved me more than any of the painful reflections I have put down. Poor things, I must get them kind masters; there may be yet those who loving me may love my dog because it has been mine. I must end this, or I shall lose the tone of mind with which men should meet distress.

I find my dogs' feet on my knees. I hear them whining and seeking me everywhere—this is nonsense, but it's what they would do could they know how things are. . . . To save Abbotsford I would attempt all that was possible. My heart clings to the place I have created. There is scarce a tree on it that does not owe its being to me, and the pain of leaving it is greater than I can tell. . . .

Half-past Eight . . .

What a life mine has been!—half educated, almost wholly neglected or left to myself, stuffing my head with most nonsensical trash, and undervalued in society for a time by most of my companions, getting forward and held a bold and clever fellow, contrary to the opinion of all who thought me a mere dreamer, broken-hearted for two years, my heart handsomely pieced again, but the crack will remain to my dying day. Rich and poor four or five times, once on the verge of ruin, yet opened new sources of wealth almost overflowing. . . .

December 24.

. . . I was seized with a most violent pain in the right kidney and parts adjacent, which, joined to deadly sickness which it brought on, forced me instantly to go to bed and send for Clarkson. He came and inquired, pronouncing the complaint to be gravel augmented by bile. I was in great agony till about two o'clock, but awoke with the pain gone. . . . I cannot expect that this first will be the last visit of this cruel complaint. . . .

January 1, 1826.

A year has passed—another has commenced. These solemn divisions of time influence our feelings as they recur. Yet there is nothing in it; for every day in the year closes a twelvemonth as well as the 31st of December. . . . To me this new year opens sadly. There are these troublesome pecuniary difficulties. . . .

January 5.

. . . Much alarmed. I had walked till twelve with Skene and Col. Russell, and then sat down to my work. To my horror and surprise I could neither write nor spell, but put down one word for another, and wrote nonsense. I was much overpowered at the same time, and could not conceive the reason. I fell asleep, however, in my chair, and slept for two hours. On waking my head was clearer, and I began to recollect that last night I had taken the anodyne left for the purpose by Clarkson, and being disturbed in the course of the night, I had not slept it off. . . .

January 23.

Slept ill, not having been abroad these eight days. . . . Then a dead sleep in the morning, and when the awakening comes, a strong feeling how well I could dispense with it for once and for ever. This passes away, however, as better and more dutiful thoughts arise in my mind. I know not if my imagination has flagged; probably it has; but at least my powers of labour have not diminished during the last melancholy week. On Monday and Tuesday my exertions were suspended. Since Wednesday inclusive I have written thirty-eight of my close manuscript pages, of which seventy make a volume of the usual Novel size. Wrote till twelve A.M., finishing half of what I call a good day's work—ten pages of print, or rather twelve. . . .

January 26.

. . . Gibson comes with a joyful face announcing all the creditors had unanimously agreed to a private trust. This is handsome and confidential, and must warm my best efforts to get them out of the scrape. I will not doubt —to doubt is to lose. Sir William Forbes took the chair, and behaved as he has ever done, with the generosity of ancient faith and early friendship. They are deeper concerned than most. In what scenes have Sir William and I not borne share together—desperate, and almost bloody affrays, rivalries, deep drinking-matches, and, finally, with the kindest feelings on both sides, somewhat separated by his retiring much within the bosom of his family, and I moving little beyond mine. It is fated our planets should cross though, and that at the periods most interesting for me. Down—down—a hundred thoughts.

Jane Russell drank tea with us.

I hope to sleep better to-night. If I do not I shall get ill, and then I cannot keep my engagements. Is it not odd? I can command my eyes to be awake when toil and weariness sit on my eyelids, but to draw the curtain of oblivion is beyond my power. . . . .

February 3.

. . . From the 19th January to the 2d February inclusive is exactly fifteen days, during which time, with the intervention of some days' idleness, to let imagination brood on the task a little, I have written a volume. I think, for a bet, I could have done it in ten days. Then I must have had no Court of Session to take me up two or three hours every morning, and dissipate my attention and powers of working for the rest of the day. A volume, at cheapest, is worth £1,000. This is working at the rate of £24,000 a year; but then we must not bake buns faster than people have appetite to eat them. They are not essential to the market, like potatoes. . . .

February 14.

. . . I have not seen a creature at dinner since the direful 17th January, except my own family and Mr. Laidlaw. The love of solitude increases by indulgence; I hope it will not diverge into misanthropy. . . .

March 16.

Pleasant days make short Journals, and I have little to say to-day. I wrote in the morning at *Woodstock;* walked from one till four; was down at Huntly Burn and paid my respects to the ladies. The spring seems promising, and everything in great order. . . .

March 17.

. . . I need not have exulted so soon in having attained ease and quiet. I am robbed of both with a vengeance. A letter from Lockhart, with one enclosed from Sophia, announces [that grandson Johnnie Lockhart] . . . is visibly losing strength, that its walking becomes more difficult, and, in short, that the spine seems visibly affected. . . . The child was almost too good for this world; beautiful in features; and, though spoiled by every one, having one of the sweetest tempers, as well as the quickest intellect I ever saw; a sense of humour quite extraordinary in a child, and, owing to the general notice which was taken of him, a great deal more information than suited his years. He was born in the eighth month, and such children are never strong —seldom long-lived. I look on this side and that, and see nothing but protracted misery. . . .

March 18.

Slept indifferently, and under the influence of Queen Mab, seldom auspicious to me, dreamed of reading the tale of the Prince of the Black Marble Islands to little Johnnie, extended on a paralytic chair, and yet telling all his pretty stories about Ha-papa, as he calls me. . . .

March 19.

I have a most melancholy letter from Anne. Lady S., the faithful and true companion of my fortunes, good and bad, for so many years, has, but with difficulty, been prevailed on to see Dr. Abercrombie, and his opinion is far from favourable. Her asthmatic complaints are fast terminating in hydropsy, as I have long suspected; yet the avowal of the truth and its probable consequences are overwhelming. . . .

April 3.

I have from Ballantyne and Gibson the extraordinary and gratifying news that *Woodstock* is sold for £8,228 in all, ready money—a matchless sum for less than three months' work. If *Napoleon* does as well, or near it, it will put the trust affairs in high flourish. Four or five years of leisure and industry would, with [such] success, amply replace my losses, and put me on a steadier footing than ever. I have a curious fancy: I will go set two or three acorns, and judge by their success in growing whether I will succeed in clearing my way or not. I have a little toothache keeps me from working much to-day, besides I sent off, per Blucher, copy for *Napoleon*, as well as the d----d proofs. . . .

April 11.

Wrought out my task, although I have been much affected this morning by the Morbus, as I call it. Aching pain in the back, rendering one posture intolerable, fluttering of the heart, idle fears, gloomy thoughts and anxieties. . . .

April 19.

. . . Two melancholy things. Last night I left my pallet in our family apartment, to make way for a female attendant, and removed to a dressing-room adjoining, when to return, or whether ever, God only can tell. Also my servant cut my hair, which used to be poor Charlotte's personal task. I hope he will not observe it. . . .

May 2.

. . . I wrote and read for three hours, and then walked, the day being soft and delightful; but alas! all my walks are lonely from the absence of my poor companion. She does not suffer, thank God, but strength must fail at last. Since Sunday there has been a gradual change—very gradual—but, alas! to the worse. My hopes are almost gone. But I am determined to stand this grief as I have done others. . . .

May 16.

She died at nine in the morning, after being very ill for two days,—easy at last. . . .

When I contrast what this place now is, with what it has been not long since, I think my heart will break. Lonely, aged, deprived of my family—all but poor Anne, an impoverished and embarrassed man, I am deprived of the sharer of my thoughts and counsels, who could always talk down my sense of the calamitous apprehensions which break the heart that must bear them alone. . . .

Another day, and a bright one to the external world, again opens on us; the air soft, and the flowers smiling, and the leaves glittering. They cannot refresh her to whom mild weather was a natural enjoyment. Cerements of lead and of wood already hold her; cold earth must have her soon. . . . I remembered the last sight of her; she raised herself in bed, and tried to turn her eyes after me, and said, with a sort of smile, "You all have such melancholy faces." They were the last words I ever heard her utter. . . . Oh, my God!

June 8.

Bilious and headache this morning. A dog howl'd all night and left me little sleep. Poor cur! I dare say he had his distresses, as I have mine. . . .

June 17.

. . . Wrought very fair accordingly till two; then walked; after dinner out again with the girls. Smoked two cigars, first time these two months.

August 17.

. . . In the evening we had music from the girls, and the voice of the harp and viol were heard in my halls once more, which have been so long deprived of mirth. It is with a mixed sensation I hear these sounds. I look on my children and am happy; and yet every now and then a pang shoots across my heart. It seems so strange that my poor wife could not be there But enough of this. Colonel Ferguson dined.

October 17.

. . . Thank God, little Johnnie Hoo, as he calls himself, is looking well, though the poor dear child is kept always in a prostrate posture.

November 21.

Breakfasted with Charles in his chambers [at Oxford], where he had everything very neat. How pleasant it is for a father to sit at his child's board! It is like an aged man reclining under the shadow of the oak which he has planted. . . .

December 18.

Almost sick with pain, and it stops everything. I shall tire of my Journal if it is to contain nothing but biles and plasters and unguents. In my better days, I had stories to tell; but death has closed the long dark avenue upon loves and friendships; and I can only look at them as through the grated door of a long burial-place filled with monuments of those who were once dear to me. . . .

December 24.

To add to my other grievances I have this day a proper fit of rheumatism in my best knee. I pushed to Abbotsford, however, after the Court rose, though compelled to howl for pain as they helped me out of the carriage.

January 2, 1827.

I had resolved to mark down no more griefs and groans, but I must needs briefly state that I am nailed to my chair. . . .

January 24.

Visit from Mr. Audubon, who brings some of his birds. The drawings are of the first order—the attitudes of the birds of the most animated character, and the situations appropriate. . . .

February 7.

Wrote six leaves to-day, and am tired—that's all.

July 12.

. . . The urchins are stealing the cherries in the outer garden. But I can spare a thousand larch-trees to put it in order with a good fence for next year. It is not right to leave fruit exposed; for if Adam in the days of innocence fell by an apple, how much may the little *gossoon* Jamie Moffatt be tempted by apples of gold in an age of iron! . . .

August 10.

This is a morning of fidgety, nervous confusion. I sought successively my box of Bramah pens, my proof sheets, and last, not least anxiously, my spectacles. I am convinced I lost a full hour in these various chases. . . .

December 24.

Left Arniston after breakfast and arrived to dinner at Abbotsford. My reflections on entering my own gate were of a very different and more pleasing cast than those with which I left my house about six weeks ago. I was then in doubt whether I should fly my country or become avowedly bankrupt, and surrender my library and household furniture, with the life rent of my estate, to sale. A man of the world will say I had better done so. No doubt had I taken this course at once, I might have employed the £25,000 which I made since the insolvency of Constable and Robinson's houses in compounding my debts. But I could not have slept sound as I now can, under the comfortable impression of receiving the thanks of my creditors and the conscious feeling of discharging my duty like a man of honour and honesty. I see before me a long tedious and dark path, but it leads to true fame and stainless reputation. If I die in the harrows, as is very likely, I shall die with honour. . . .

March 13, 1828.

. . . I found that, like the foolish virgins, the servants had omitted to get oil for my lamp, so I was obliged to be idle all the evening. But though I had a diverting book . . . yet an evening without writing hung heavy on my hands. . . .

March [14 to] 16.

. . . From seven to half-past nine writing—from half-past nine to a quarter past ten a hearty breakfast. From eleven or thereby, to one or two, wrote again, and from one or two ride, drive, or walk till dinnertime—for two or three hours—five till seven, dine and rest yourself—seven till nine, wrote two pages more, from nine to quarter past ten lounge, read the papers, and then

go to bed. If your story is tolerably forward you may, I think, keep at this
rate for twelve days, which would be a volume. But no brain could hold it
out longer. Wrote two additional leaves in the evening.

May 5.

Breakfasted with Haydon, and sat for my head. I hope this artist is on his
legs again. The King has given him a lift by buying his clever picture of the
election in the Fleet prison. . . . He is certainly a clever fellow, but somewhat too enthusiastic, which distress seems to have cured in some degree.
His wife, a pretty woman, looked happy to see me, and that is something.
Yet it was very little I could do to help them. . . .

May 19.

. . . Dined by command with the Duchess of Kent. I was very kindly
recognised by Prince Leopold. I was presented to the little Princess Victoria
—I hope they will change her name,—the heir apparent to the Crown as
things now stand. How strange that so large and fine a family as that of his
late Majesty should have died off and decayed into old age with so few
descendants! Prince George of Cumberland is, they say, a fine boy about nine
years old—a bit of a picle, swears and romps like a brat that has been bred
in a barrack yard. This little lady is educated with much care, and watched
so closely by the Duchess and the principal governess, that no busy maid has
a moment to whisper, "You are heir of England." I suspect if we could dis-
sect the little head, we should find that some pigeon or other bird of the air
had carried the matter. She is fair, like the Royal Family, but does not look
as if she would be pretty. . . .

June 19.

Scribbled away lustily. . . . I am become a sort of writing automaton, and
truly the joints of my knees, especially the left, are so stiff and painful in
rising and sitting down, that I can hardly help screaming—I that was so robust and active; I get into a carriage with great difficulty. My head, too,
is bothered with rheumatic headaches. . . .

June 20.

. . . I have a painful letter from Lockhart, which takes away the last hope
of poor Johnnie's recovery. It is no surprise to me. The poor child, so amiable
in its disposition, and so promising from its talents, was not formed to be
long with us, and I have long expected that it must needs come to this. I
hope I shall not outlive my children in other cases, and I think there is little
chance of it. My father did not long survive the threescore and ten; it will
be wonderful if I reach that goal of ordinary mortality. God send it may
find me prepared; and, whatever I may have been formerly, high spirits are
not now like to carry me away.

June 13, 1829.

. . . My poor Johnnie is . . . so much bent on coming to see Abbotsford and grandpapa, that it would be cruel not to comply with his wish—and if affliction comes, we will bear it best together. . . .

December 20, 1830.

. . . Miss Young, the daughter of Dr. Young, had occasion to call on me on some business, in which I had hopes of serving her. As I endeavoured to explain to her what I had to say, I had the horror to find I could not make myself understood. I stammered, stuttered, said one word in place of another —did all but speak; Miss Young went away frightened enough, poor thing; and Anne and Violet Lockhart were much alarmed. I was bled with cupping-glasses, took medicine, and lived on panada; but in two or three days I was well again. The physicians thought, or said at least, that the evil was from the stomach. It is very certain that I have seemed to speak with an impedi-ment, and I was, or it might be fancied myself, troubled with a mispro-nouncing and hesitation . . . I had for a long time taken only one tumbler of whisky and water without the slightest reinforcement. This night I took a very little drop, not so much as a bumper glass, of whisky altogether. It made no difference on my head that I could discover, but when I went to the dressing-room I sank stupefied on the floor. I lay a minute or two—was not found, luckily, gathered myself up, and got to my bed. I was alarmed at this second warning, consulted Abercrombie and Ross, and got a few restric-tive orders as to diet. I am forced to attend to them; for, as Mrs. Cole says, "Lack-a-day! a thimbleful oversets me." To add to these feelings I have the constant increase of my lameness: the thigh-joint, knee-joint, and ankle-joint.

January 21, 1831.

. . . Am sensible that my fingers begin to stammer—that is, to write one word instead of another very often. I impute this to fancy, the terrible agency of which is too visible in my illness, and it encourages me to hope the fatal warning is yet deferred. . . .

January 31 [to February 9].

. . . The physical folks, Abercrombie and Ross, bled me with cupping-glasses, purged me confoundedly, and restricted me of all creature comforts. But they did me good, as I am sure they meant to do sincerely; and I got rid of a giddy feeling, which I have been plagued with, and have certainly returned much better. I did not neglect my testamentary affairs. I executed my last will. . . . Besides, during the unexpected stay in town, I employed Mr. Fortune, an ingenious artist, to make a machine to assist my lame leg, —an odd enough purchase to be made at this time of day, yet who would not purchase ease? . . .

I wrote a good deal of *Count Robert,* yet I cannot tell why my pen stammers egregiously, and I write horridly incorrect. . . .

March 16.

. . . My ordinary runs thus:—Rise at a quarter before seven; at a quarter after nine breakfast, with eggs, or in the singular number, at least; before breakfast private letters, etc.; after breakfast Mr. Laidlaw comes at ten, and we write together till one. I am greatly helped by this excellent man, who takes pains to write a good hand, and supplies the want of my own fingers as far as another person can. We work seriously at the task of the day till one o'clock, when I sometimes walk—not often, however, having failed in strength, and suffering great pain even from a very short walk. Oftener I take the pony for an hour or two and ride about the doors; the exercise is humbling enough, for I require to be lifted on horseback by two servants, and one goes with me to take care I do not fall off and break my bones, a catastrophe very like to happen. My proud promenade a pied or a cheval, as it happens, concludes by three o'clock. An hour intervenes for making up my Journal and such light work. At four comes dinner,—a plate of broth or soup, much condemned by the doctors, a bit of plain meat, no liquors stronger than small beer, and so I sit quiet to six o'clock, when Mr. Laidlaw returns, and remains with me till nine or three quarters past, as it happens. Then I have a bowl of porridge and milk, which I eat with the appetite of a child. I forgot to say that after dinner I am allowed half a glass of whisky or gin made into weak grog. I never wish for any more, nor do I in my secret soul long for cigars, though once so fond of them. About six hours per day is good working, if I can keep at it.

April 27.

They have cut me off from animal food and fermented liquor of every kind, and would press upon me such trash as panada and the like, which affect my stomach. This I will none of, but quietly wait till my ordinary diet is permitted, and thank God I can fast with any one. I walked out and found the day delightful; the woods are looking charming, just bursting forth to the tune of the birds. I have been whistling on my wits. . . .

May 8.

I have suffered terribly, that is the truth, rather in body than in mind, and I often wish I could lie down and sleep without waking. But I will fight it out if I can. It would argue too great an attachment of consequence to my literary labours to sink under. Did I know how to begin, I would begin this very day, although I knew I should sink at the end. After all, this is but fear and faintness of heart, though of another kind from that which trembleth at a loaded pistol. My bodily strength is terribly gone; perhaps my mental too?

May 9.

The weather uncommonly beautiful and I am very eager to get on thinning woods while the peeling season lasts. We made about £200 off wood last season, and this is a sum worth looking at.

January 16–23, 1832.

. . . Poor Johnnie Lockhart! The boy is gone whom we have made so much of. I could not have borne it better than I now do, and I might have borne it much worse. . . .

"These city dudes from the East . . ."

F. Scott Fitzgerald

Named after the author of "The Star Spangled Banner," whose collateral descendant he was, Francis Scott Key Fitzgerald (1896–1940) experienced in his forty-four years extremes of wealth and poverty, fame and neglect.

Fitzgerald was born in St. Paul, Minnesota, and educated at Princeton. He served in the first world war, afterwards worked briefly in an advertising agency, and then quit his job to seek fulfillment of his boyhood dream of becoming a writer. His first novel, *This Side of Paradise* (1920), was a tremendous success. It described the era, with which his name became associated, of the bobbed-haired, short-skirted flapper; bathtub gin; easy money and soaring stocks; and youth engaged early and late in burning candles at both ends. Other novels that came rapidly from his typewriter, among them *The Beautiful and Damned* and *The Great Gatsby,* rounded out the picture, brought Fitzgerald wealth, and made him an almost legendary figure.

With his wife, Zelda Sayre, painter and novelist from Alabama, Fitzgerald set about living the scenes and plots of his books. His money and ultimately his sureness of literary touch slipped away from him all too soon in madcap pranks and extravagances. A daughter, Zelda, was born. By the time the depression came Fitzgerald was broke, his wife was in a sanitarium following a nervous collapse, and he himself had emotional difficulties which made it almost impossible for him to write. During Fitzgerald's long period of silence readers had forgotten his name. It is at this point that Fitzgerald made the diary entry given here, written at the lowest ebb of his fortunes.

Fitzgerald spoke self-mockingly of "this bankrupt's comedy" but the bitter sting his predicament held for him is pathetically apparent.

Autumn, 1936 [?]. *Undated.*

In Hendersonville [North Carolina]: I am living very cheaply. Today I am

From *The Notebooks,* by F. Scott Fitzgerald. Copyright 1945 by New Directions.

in comparative affluence, but Monday and Tuesday I had two tins of potted meat, three oranges and a box of Uneedas and two cans of beer. For the food, that totalled eighteen cents a day—and when I think of the thousand meals I've sent back untasted in the last two years. It was fun to be poor—especially if you haven't enough liver power for an appetite. But the air is fine here, and I liked what I had—and there was nothing to do about it anyhow because I was afraid to cash any checks, and I had to save enough for postage for the story. But it was funny coming into the hotel and the very deferential clerk not knowing that I was not only thousands, nay tens of thousands in debt, but had less than forty cents cash in the world and probably a defecit in the bank. I gallantly gave Scotty [his daughter at school] my last ten when I left her and of course the Flynns, etc., had no idea and wondered why I didn't just "jump into a taxi" (four dollars and tip) and run over for dinner.

Enough of this bankrupt's comedy—I suppose it has been enacted all over the U.S. in the last four years, plenty of times.

Nevertheless I haven't told . . . the half of it—i.e., my underwear I started with was a pair of pyjama pants—*just that*. It was only today I could replace them with a union suit. I washed my two handkerchiefs and my shirt every night, but the pyjama trousers I had to wear all the time, and I am presenting it to the Hendersonville Museum. My socks would have been equally notorious save there was not enough of them left, for they served double duty as slippers at night. The final irony was when a drunk man in the shop where I bought my can of ale said in a voice obviously intended for me, "These city dudes from the East come down here with their millions. Why don't they support us?"

"The rest is silence."

W. N. P. Barbellion

This is the journal of a man who for many months has lain almost helpless, looking death in the face. Doomed, certain of his fate, feeling neither hope nor despair, sometimes jesting at what is to happen, sometimes enraged, sometimes welcoming, he watches the slow approach of the end. With a skipping rope borrowed from a little girl his jerking legs are tied down to the bed. He counts over and over again the leaves on the wall paper, the bars on a chair; makes out faces in the curtains and in the fire. He thinks of his love for his wife and his little daughter; considers how gruesome he must look, shrunken to a gaunt, white framework of skin and bone, with fingers too benumbed and shaking to hold his pen. He soaks up the sounds outside his ivy-covered cottage—birdsong, the postman's stride, his nurse puffing up the walk. Then, "the rest is silence."

The man who called himself W. N. P. Barbellion (the initials stand for "Wilhelm Nero Pilate") was a young scientist named Bruce Frederick Cummings (1889–1919). He was born in Barnstaple, North Devonshire, the youngest of a family of three sisters and three brothers. His father was a country newspaper reporter whose income probably never exceeded £200 a year. From infancy until his death Barbellion was plagued by illness. As a baby he narrowly survived an attack of influenza; as a youth and a man he had recurrent heart attacks, influenza, eye infections, dyspepsia, muscular tremors, and fits of acute depression. He was puny and under-sized as a child, nervously shy, and too frail to be sent to school at the usual age. He grew to be a man more than six feet tall, very thin, with a large head, brown hair and deep sunk brown eyes. He was largely self-taught and had no college training.

Barbellion was keenly interested in nature and made himself an expert biologist. At eighteen he was a regular contributor to scientific journals, and at twenty he won appointment to the staff of the Plymouth Marine Biological Laboratory. His father's illness

From *A Last Diary*, by W. N. P. Barbellion. Reprinted by permission of Chatto & Windus Ltd.

made it impossible for him to take the low-paid post. A year later, however, he got a better paid position as biologist at the South Kensington Museum of Natural History; he led the list in a competitive examination for the vacancy with 141 points to spare. He worked in the Museum's Insect room, meanwhile writing a number of scientific papers, until ill health compelled him to resign in 1917. He then went to live for the two remaining years of his life with his wife and baby daughter in an old country cottage at Gerrard's Cross, Buckinghamshire. The disease from which he suffered was finally diagnosed as multiple sclerosis in the acute form in which there is a slow, steady, killing disintegration of all bodily functions.

Barbellion left two diaries, both recognized on their publication as being of major importance: *The Journal of a Disappointed Man,* and *Last Diary* from which extracts are given here. The first has been compared, with reason, to the journal kept by Marie Bashkirtseff, for he has her flair for candour and self-revelation. The second is bound to recall the last volume of Amiel's journal when, in 1881, he too was dying, and the journal of Katherine Mansfield (who will be met later in this book). All had fatal ailments and all were greedy for life; but Barbellion, with more physical pain than either of them, spared himself and his readers the exacerbation of self-pity.

On June 3, 1919, Barbellion wrote his last journal entry. He died on October 22. He was thirty-one.

March 25, 1918.

. . . When am I going to die? This is a death in life.

I intended never to write in this diary again. But the relief it affords could not be refused any longer. I was surprised to find I could scribble at all legibly. Yet it is tiring.

March 26.

. . . I must anaesthetise thought and accept without comment. My mind is in an agony of muddle, not only about this world but the next.

June 15.

. . . I sat up in my chair to tea yesterday. It was all very quiet, and two mice crept out of their holes and audaciously ate the crumbs that fell from my plate. It is a very old cottage. In the ivy outside a nest of young starlings keep up a clamour. The Doctor has just been (three days since) and says I may live for thirty years. I trust and believe he is a damned liar. . . .

August 7.

In the cottage alone with E. [his wife] and nurse. Four weeks of happiness with the obvious reservation. I am in love with my wife! Oh! dear woman, what agony of mind, and what happiness you give me. To think of you alone struggling against the world, and you are not strong, you want a protector, someone's strong arm. But we are happy these few weeks—I record it because it's so strange. I am deeply in love. . . .

September 1.

. . . I insist on being left alone, this grotesque disease and I. Meanwhile I must elaborately observe it getting worse by inches. . . . The days creep past shrouded in disappointment; still I cling to my spar—if not to-day, why then to-morrow, perhaps. . . . My thoughts move about my languid brain like caterpillars on a ravaged tree. All the while I am getting worse—and they are all so slow. . . .

September 2.

It was a brilliantly fine day to-day. . . . Suddenly I sprang from my chair, upset it, dumbfounded the nurse, and disappeared thro' the hedge into the woods. I . . . flung myself down on the ground and passionately squeezed the cool soft leaf-mould as a man presses a woman's breasts. I scraped away the surface leaves and, bending down, drew in the intoxicating smell of the earth's naked flesh. It was a splendid dream. . . .

October 5.

Some London neurologist has injected a serum into a woman's spine with beneficial results, and as her disease is the same as mine, they wish me to try it too. I may be able to walk again, to write, etc., my life prolonged! They little know what they ask of me. . . . I have been dead these eighteen months. Death is sweet. All my past life is ashes. . . .

November 26.

My old nurse lapses into bizarre malapropisms. She is afraid the Society for the *Propagation* of Cruelty to Animals will find fault with the way we house our hens; for boiling potatoes she prefers to use the camisole (casserole)! . . . Yesterday, in the long serenity of a dark winter's night, with a view to arouse my interest in life, she went and brought some heirloom treasures from the bottom of her massive trunk—some coins of George I. "Of course, they're all obsolute now," she said. "What! absolutely obsolute?" I enquired in surprise. The answer was in the informative. . . .

December 1.

What I have always feared is coming to pass—love for my little daughter. Only another communication string with life to be cut. I want to hear "the tune of little feet along the floor." I am filled with intolerable sadness at the thought of her. . . .

December 23.

. . . To-day, a faint tremor passes along my palsied limbs—a tremor of lust—lust of life, a desire to be up and mingling in the crowd, to be soaked up by it, to feel a sense of all mankind flooding the heart, and strong masculine youth pulsing at the wrists. . . .

January 4, 1919.

. . . Light, frivolous talk. At the most, such moods are only short lulls between the spasms of agony of suffering; one longs to be free of them as of acute physcial pain, to be unconscious. I look forward to night, to darkness, rest, and sleep. I sleep well between twelve and six and then watch the dawn, from black (and the owl's hoot) to grey (and the barncock's crow) to white (and the blackbirds' whistle). The oak beam on my ceiling, the Japanese print on the wall come slowly into view, and I dread them. I dread the day with my whole soul. Each dawn is hopeless. . . .

January 8.

I lie stiff and contorted till Nurse arrives at eight-thirty. She straightens me out and bolsters me up. Breakfast at nine. Cigarettes while I listen with ravenous ears for the postman. . . . There usually is no letter for me. My chief discovery in sickness and misfortune is the callousness of people to our case—not from hard-heartedness (everyone is kind), but from absence of sympathetic imagination. People don't know the horrors and they can't imagine them—perhaps they are unimaginable. . . .

January 13.

. . . I lie on my back and rest awhile. Then I force myself on to the left side by putting my right arm over the left side of the bed beneath the woodwork and pulling (my right arm is stronger than any of the other limbs). To-night, Nurse had not placed me in the middle of the bed (I was too much over on the right side), so even my long arm could not reach down beneath the wood-work on the left. I cursed Nanny for a scabby old bean, struggled, and at last got over on my left side. The next thing was to get my legs bent up—now out as stiff and straight as ferrules. When lying on the left side I long ago found out that it is useless to get my right leg up first, as it only shoots out again when I come to grapple with the left. So I put my right arm down, seized the left leg just above the knee and pulled! The first result is always a violent spasm in the legs and back. But I hang on and presently it dies away, and the leg begins to move upward a little. Last night Nanny uncrossed my legs, but was not careful to separate them. Consequently, knee stuck side by side to knee, and foot to foot, as if glued, and I found, in pulling at my left, I had the stubborn live weight of both to lift up. I would get them part way, then by a careless movement of the hand on a ticklish spot both would shoot out again. So on for an hour—my only relief to curse Nanny. And thus, any time, any week, these last eighteen months. . . .

January 28.

"The rest is silence"—I should like this inscribed at the end of this garrulous Journal, an inscription for the base of my self-erected monument.

January 30.

. . . There are some days when I give up, surrender voluntarily every earthly desire, when every thread binding me to life is cut. I long to be free, and hack and cut in a frenzy—frenzies in which I curse and swear out loud to myself, alternating with fits of terrible apathy, when I am indifferent to everything and everybody, when the petty routine of my existence, washing, eating, and sitting out, goes on and carries me along with it mechanically. And . . . I am neither one thing nor the other, neither dead nor alive, a nondescript creature in a No-Man's Land, and, like all who keep a middle course, not claimed with any enthusiasm by either side. The living must be tired of me, and the dead don't seem eager for my reception. . . .

February 3.

. . . I have not left my room since November 11th. I eat well, sleep well, am in my possession of all my higher faculties—those for feeling and thinking. But I can't get out.

I think sometimes people do not come to see me because I am such a gruesome object. It is not pleasant to feel you are gruesome. I have outstayed my welcome. I know everyone will be relieved to hear of my death—no doubt for my sake, as they will eagerly point out, but also for their own sake, as I believe. Yet now and then in selfish and ignoble moods, I, being an egotist, fancy I would like some loving hands to clutch at me, in a blind, ineffectual effort to save me in any condition, if only alive.

February 4.

The last part of yesterday's entry was maudlin tosh—*entirely foreign to my nature*. I hereby cancel it.

February 11.

. . . On the wall in front of me is a pattern of ivy-leaves. In odd moments of listlessness I am always counting them: there are 30 perpendicular rows with 47 leaves in each row—that's 1,410 leaves in all. You'd never think there were so many, to look at the wall. I know to nausea that there are 40 little panes of glass in the window on my left—really only 39, as one is broken and stopped with cardboard. There are 7 bars (5 thin and 2 thick) in the back of the wooden chair. There were 17 degrees of frost this morning, and I have to stop constantly to wipe my nose and warm my hands on a water-bottle.

There is also a water-bottle at my feet. KLIM—that is MILK backwards—printed on a wooden box I use as a book-rest and now lying upside down. YLIAD SWEN—this is the *Daily News* backwards. I am forever reading it backwards as it lies about on my bed upside down. Then there are faces on the morris-patterned curtain and in the fire. . . . My hand has gone too cold and stiff to write more.

February 21.

I sometimes fancy I am not weaned from life even now. Pictures in the paper make me agonise. Oh, for a little happiness for her and me together, just a short respite. What agony it is to have a darling woman fling herself into your arms, press you to her dear bosom and ask you desperately to try to get well, when you know it is hopeless. She knows it is hopeless, yet every now and then. . . . She pictures me in a study in her flat (all her own), walking on two sticks. And already the tendons of my right leg are drawing in permanently. . . .

February 27.

A little easier in mind. . . . A load of sadness settled on me this afternoon. As I lay resting down in bed, for no reason I can discover, the memory of the evening prayers my mother taught me flashed over my mind, and because steeped in memory seemed very beautiful. Here they are:

> "Gentle Jesus, meek and mild,
> Look upon a little child,
> Pity my simplicity,
> Suffer me to come to Thee."

Then the Lord's Prayer. Then:

> "Keep us faithful, keep us pure,
> Keep us ever more Thine own,
> Help, O help us to endure,
> Fit us for the promised crown."

Then I hopped into bed and was asleep in a moment. . . .

March 16.

I am getting rapidly worse. One misery adds itself to another as I explore the course of this hideous disease.

April 1.

I love my hair to be combed—it makes one realise what an avenue for self-expression was closed when man lost his tail; I love the benison of hot water for my urticating friends; the tick-tack of our cottage clock; a cigarette—many cigarettes; letters—these are all my pleasures; pills, the air-cushion, hot bottle, a cramped leg straightened—these are my reliefs; sleep—this my refuge.

May 2.

I long to see my little daughter again. Yet I fear it horribly, I am ashamed to meet her gaze. She will be frightened at me. Better she should have no memory of me at all to take through life.

May 16.

On the 14th at 2 p.m. a well-appointed ambulance took me to a nursing home at Eastbourne, where I arrived at 7 p.m., exhausted but cheerful. It was like being raised from the dead. We . . . turned down H. road past my old rooms, across Kensington Road, and down Warwick Gardens, where one dark November night E. and I plighted our troth beneath a lamp-post. We passed the lamp-post! Then . . . at four-thirty we drew up at an inn and a servant-maid put a tray of tea and cakes on the bench beside me, and I ate and smoked while the driver in the road compared notes with the landlord on war adventures. . . . It was so hot, I lay on my couch with my rugs, etc., off. But the street boys were so curious over my pyjama suit, I pulled the blinds. Then they moved round and looked in through the door. Nurse closed it. They moved round to the other side, so Nurse drew these blinds too. Then they capered off.

After that across Crowborough Forest, the car running at an even pace uphill and down. I lay happy and triumphant, and watched the country speeding by. We passed picnic parties . . . the sky was cloudless. . . . Then I became displeased at my mood, on E.'s account, as I recollected the picture of her and the baby in the road waving me good-bye.

May 18.

. . . A beautiful morning. At the bottom of my bed two French windows open out on to the garden, where a blackbird is singing. . . . I listen to him and my withered carcase soaks up his song with a sighing sound, like a dry sponge taking up water.

May 20.

If I could please myself, I should have my coffin made and kept under my bed. Then if I should die they could just pull the old box out and put me in it. . . . I like the idea of William Morris, who was taken to the cemetery in an old farm-cart.

I often laugh loud at the struggles of Nurse with my perfectly ludicrous, impotent body. . . . My right leg is almost completely anaesthetised—curious experience this. You could poke the fire with it, and I shouldn't feel anything out of the way. . . . It is so dead that if you put my body out in the sun, the flies in error would come and lay their eggs on me. . . .

May 24.

My legs have to be tied down to the bed with a rope. A little girl staying here lends me her skipping rope.

. . . This is the end. I am not going to keep a diary any more.

June 3.

To-morrow I go to another nursing home.

The rest is silence.

*"It's like that wherever I go. I wonder
where all the fourteen-year-olds have gone."*

Selma Lagerlöf

Selma Lagerlöf (1858–1940) was born in Varnland, a province in southwestern Sweden, and during her lifetime she made many trips to Stockholm. The proudest visit was in 1909 when as a woman of fifty she went to Stockholm to receive the Nobel Prize for Literature. She was already rich in honours. From the obscurity of a teacher's position in a girls' school, she had risen to membership in many learned societies and held honorary degrees from several leading European universities. Her novels were eagerly awaited in Sweden and translated into many languages. Even then her *Wonderful Adventures of Nils* was well on the way to becoming a world-famous children's classic.

The Nobel Prize winner must have remembered another trip to Stockholm—a trip in 1873 when her family sent her there in the hope that treatments by a famous Stockholm physician might cure her lameness. Her diary reveals that even as a fourteen-year-old she had the perceptive eye and sensitive spirit of the creative child—that even then she had the courage that was later to bring her back to Stockholm as one of the world's great writers.

February 10, 1873. Stockholm.

Every morning at a quarter before eleven I open the gate at Klara Strandgata 7 and step out upon the sidewalk. In accordance with Aunt Georgina's wishes I wear a hat and coat, galoshes and gloves, and carry a muff and umbrella. Then . . . up a short but difficult hill paved with jagged stones, and in through a gate that leads to Klara Churchyard.

In the churchyard there are smooth and even gravel paths where walking is easy. But I'm anxious to get past it as quickly as possible so as not to encounter the schoolboys. Klara School lies at the corner of the churchyard; at recess the boys rush out to the large grave mounds and stone caskets near the church, where they play at war, and I fear that they will knock me down.

From *The Diary of Selma Lagerlöf*, by Selma Lagerlöf, translated by Velma Swanston Howard. Copyright 1936 by Doubleday & Company, Inc.

I feel a little afraid of those schoolboys, but . . . there is one boy in particular. He is poorly clad like the others, but he is not quite so wild. I have often noticed that he stands looking on while his comrades are fighting their hardest. He has beautiful blue eyes and perhaps, when he is full-grown. . . .

One day I saw the quiet boy sitting with head bowed, all alone on the largest of the stone coffins. . . . I stopped in front of him, as I wished to say something comforting—for I felt so well acquainted with that boy! I was waiting until I could think of something really nice to say, when he suddenly raised his head, pulled a wry face and, with a savage look, roared at me:

"Why do you stand there glaring at me, you limping devil's spawn!"

I made no retort, but went on my way. But I wished that the elegant couple who lay in the big stone coffin would raise the lid a trifle and tweak his nose. . . .

February 11.

. . . After I cross Klara Churchyard I come to a fine large building . . . which I enter. For it is there that Professor Herman Sätherberg has his Gymnastic Orthopedic Institute.

As soon as I'm inside the gate I always pause awhile. I fold my hands inside my muff and pray to God that Professor Herman Sätherberg, who is a learned and skilful physician, may soon find some way to cure me so that I won't have to go through life limping.

Then, hurrying up the stairs, I come into a large hall where there are many hangers. There I remove not only my coat and hat, but also my dress and petticoats, and put on bloomers and blouse—for otherwise one can't exercise properly.

After that I go into the gymnasium, which is very large. There, ladders and trapezes and all kinds of gymnastic appliances hang from the walls. . . .

There are always many people exercising in the gymnasium. When they are all here, I think there are about a hundred going back and forth, though of course I've never counted them. All are dressed in bloomers and blouses. Some wear fine embroidered blouses, while others look as if they had jumped into a bag. There are old people and children, but the majority are nineteen or twenty years of age. Nearly all have some fault—uneven hips or a clubfoot or a stiff knee or round shoulders. Some are taking gymnastic exercises as a cure for green-sickness which they contracted by too much dancing at the Stockholm balls. I don't think there is anyone in the Institute but myself who is fourteen years old. It's like that wherever I go. I wonder where all the fourteen-year-olds have gone. At the gymnasium they are either too old to talk to me or else so young that I wouldn't bother to talk to them. . . .

My lame leg has grown stronger already, for which I'm very thankful. Some of the patients who have been exercising all winter are now perfectly well and they say that Professor Sätherberg is a regular wonder-worker.

Sometimes the Professor steps out of his reception room and goes the rounds of the gymnasium to see whether the attendants give us the proper movements, or to speak to some of the patients. When he comes I can't take my eyes off him.

I know that Professor Sätherberg is a poet . . . but perhaps there is no one here but myself who knows this. . . . A slight little man and not at all good-looking. His eyes are always red, and he has a sallow complexion and deep lines around the mouth. His face is sad as though he were ill. I think that a poet should be handsome and proud and radiant like Goethe. When he went skating on the river Main he was the most distinguished-looking gentleman in all the world.

Here in the gymnasium, at least, the Professor speaks only of crooked spines and stiff joints; but I should like to hear him talk a little about poetry. I may never have another opportunity to meet a real poet.

Several days ago, as I stood by the window looking down at Klara Churchyard, Professor Sätherberg came and stood beside me. I thought at first that he wished to ask me something, but he stood there looking out as though he had not seen me. As he was quite near me and no person could hear, I made an attempt to get him to speak about something else than crooked spines. Moving a little nearer, I said as clearly as I could—for I was so nervous over my daring that I could scarcely utter the words:

"Is it a pleasure to write verse?" . . .

"Yes," said the Professor . . . "But it is also a pleasure to straighten crooked backs and make stiff joints flexible." . . .

He had given me a beautiful answer, but I did not think he was right. Now, if I could write poetry I should never care to do anything else.

"Everyone who reads these lines will suffer . . ."

Vaslav Nijinsky

Balletomanes, those irrepressible enthusiasts who put dancing at the summit of the arts, offer rival claims in behalf of the great, and fabled and mighty of ballet. They talk much of Fokine, Massine, Balanchine, Lifar, Karsavina, Markova. But sooner or later two celebrated names always receive special mention—that of the ballerina Anna Pavlova and a young, Polish-born partner of hers, a slim lad, dark-haired, long-lashed with deep-sunk eyes, named Vaslav Nijinsky (1890–1950). Pavlova's *The Dying Swan* has not kept pace with her reputation in recent years, perhaps slandered too long by the tasteless galumphings of two generations of inept dancing school graduates. Meanwhile Nijinsky's *Le Spectre de la Rose, Pétrouchka, Les Sylphides, Schérézade* and *L'Après-midi d'un Faune* have grown ever more glamourous in ballet retrospect.

Nijinsky grew up in a poor family that had come to Leningrad from Warsaw. As a youth he knew bitter poverty, gnawing hunger, a mother's unhappiness, a brother's insanity. His aptitude for dancing, however, won him a place in the city's famous Ballet School and there, after years of rigorous training, he made his début at 17. Two years later he joined Serge Diaghilev's *Ballet Russe* in Paris where, unsophisticated except in the dancer's skills, he was thrust into an intellectual and psychological ferment for which he was unprepared. Gathered around the newly unfolding medium of ballet were such men as the designer Bakst, the poet Cocteau, and the as yet untried composers Ravel, Stravinsky, Prokofiev and Debussy.

The center of this galaxy of genius was Diaghilev, something of a genius himself, but a maladjusted man whose attitude toward his own sex was admittedly abnormal. Nijinsky and Diaghilev soon became intimate. Meanwhile the young dancer went on from one artistic triumph to another until the pair separated on his marriage to Romola Nijinska.

The onset of war produced signs of emotional stress in the dancer that led Nijinsky's wife to take him to her family's home in St. Moritz. Madness crept nearer as the war years stretched on. Late in 1918, Nijinsky began to keep a diary. "For hours and hours, day and night, he wrote and wrote." He poured out a whole torrent of words, spurred by the burden of guilt, urged on by his striving for a sane new world in which there would not loom again the ballet impresario who threatened to come between him and his wife and beloved little daughter.

As fascinating as it is pitiful, this is the terrible diary of an artist at the point of madness, a man haunted by moving figures on stages where he would never dance again.

1918–1919, St. Moritz.

. . . I am not a child prodigy to be exhibited—I am a sensible man. Millions of years have gone by since the creation of man. Men think that God is where technical inventions are most advanced. God was already there when there was no mechanism. Steel is a necessary thing, but it is also a terrible thing. An aeroplane is a terrible thing. I flew in an aeroplane and cried in it. I do not know why, but I felt that aeroplanes destroy birds. All birds fly away at the sight of an aeroplane. An aeroplane is a useful thing but it must not be exaggerated. It is a thing coming from God and therefore I like it, but it must not be used for the purposes of war. An aeroplane should express goodwill. I like aeroplanes and will therefore fly in them where there are no birds. I love birds. I do not want to frighten them. A well-known flyer was flying in Switzerland and flew into an eagle. The eagle is . . . a bird of God and one must not kill tsars, emperors, and kings. I like tsars and the aristocrats, but their deeds are not always good deeds. I will give them a good example, by not destroying them. . . .

. . . I will help people to understand Diaghilev. I worked with him for five years without rest. I know all his sly tricks and habits. I was with Diaghilev. I know him better than he knows himself, his weak and his strong points. I am not afraid of him. . . . The Spaniards spill the blood of bulls and therefore like murder. Even the Church and the Pope cannot put an end to this slaughter. The Spaniards think that a bull is a beast. The toreador weeps before killing the bull. I know many toreadors whose stomachs the bull has split. I hated this slaughter but I was not understood. Diaghilev said . . . that a bullfight is a magnificent art. . . . I understand him and therefore challenge him to a bullfight. I am the bull, a wounded bull. I am God in the bull. I am Apis. I am an Egyptian. I am an Indian. I am a Red Indian. I am a Negro. I am a Chinaman. I am a Japanese. I am a foreigner, a stranger. I am a sea bird. I am a land bird. I am the tree of Tolstoy. I am the roots of Tolstoy—Tolstoy is mine. I am his. . . .

I will remain alone, and cry in my loneliness. I cry a lot, but will not give up writing. I am afraid that Doctor X., my friend, will come in and see my tears, and as I do not want to upset him, I will wipe them away. I cry in such a way as not to interfere with anyone. . . . I do not want people to pity me, but to be loved. . . . I am poor. I have nothing and I want nothing. I am not crying, but have tears in my heart. I do not wish any harm to my wife, I love her more than anyone else, and know that if we parted I would

die. I cry . . . I cannot restrain my tears, and they fall on my left hand and
on my silken tie, but I cannot and do not want to hold them back. I feel
that I am doomed. I do not want to go under. . . .

I went for a walk and thought of Christ. I am a Christian—a Catholic, a
Russian. My daughter does not speak Russian, because the war prevented us
from going to Russia. My little one sings in Russian, because I taught her
Russian songs. I love them and the Russian language. I know many Russians,
who are not really so in their heart, but always use foreign languages. I love
Russia. I love France. I love England. I love America. I love Switzerland.
I love Spain. I love Italy. I love Japan. I love Australia. I love China. I love
Africa. I love the Transvaal. I want to love everyone and therefore I am like
God. . . .

. . . Igor Stravinsky does not know what life is, he does not love me. Igor
thinks that I am against his aims. He seeks riches and glory. I do not want
these. Stravinsky is a good composer, but he does not think about life. His
compositions have no purpose. I do not like works of art that have no moral
aim. . . . Stravinsky smells things out. He is not my friend, but at the bottom of his heart he loves me, because he feels me, but he considers me his
enemy because I am in his way. Diaghilev loves Massine [dancer and ballet
choreographer] and not me and that is awkward for Stravinsky. Stravinsky
forces his wife to carry out all his caprices. . . . He is like an emperor and
his children and wife are the servants and soldiers. . . .

I understood the man Diaghilev loved before me. Diaghilev loved this man
physically, therefore he wanted to be loved in return. Diaghilev developed
in him the passion for works of art. In Massine he developed the love for
glory. I was not passionate either about works of art or glory. . . . We often
quarreled. I used to lock my door—our rooms were communicating—and
would let in no one. I was afraid of him. I knew that all my life was in his
hands. I would not leave the room. . . . I did not like Diaghilev, but lived
with him; I hated Diaghilev from the first days of our acquaintance, because
I knew his power. I was poor and 65 rubles [the monthly salary of the dancers
at the Moscow Imperial Theater] were not enough to keep my mother and
myself from starvation. We rented a flat with two rooms for 35 or 37 rubles
a month. . . .

I loved music. One day I met a Russian prince who introduced me to a
Polish count. I have forgotten his name, because I wanted to. I do not want
to hurt his whole family. This count bought me a piano. I did not love him.
I loved the prince and not the count. Ivor introduced me to Diaghilev, who
asked me to come to the Hotel Europe, where he lived. I disliked him for
his too self-assured voice, but went to seek my luck. I found my luck. At
once I allowed him to make love to me. I trembled like a leaf. I hated him,
but pretended, because I knew that my mother and I would die of hunger
otherwise. I understood Diaghilev from the first moment and pretended to
agree with him at once. One had to live, and therefore it was all the same
to me what sort of sacrifice I had to make. I worked hard at my dancing
and was always tired. But I pretended not to be tired at all in order that
Diaghilev should not be bored with me. I know what he felt, he loved
boys. . . .

Diaghilev cheats people and thinks that no one sees through him. He dyes his hair in order to look young. Diaghilev's hair is white. He buys black dyes and rubs them in. I have seen this dye on Diaghilev's cushions—his pillowcase is blackened by it. I hate dirty linen and therefore was disgusted by this sight. Diaghilev has two false front teeth. When he is nervous he passes his tongue over them. Diaghilev reminds me of an angry old woman, when he moves his two false teeth. His front lock is dyed white. He wants it to be noticed. Lately this lock has grown yellow, because he has bought bad dye. . . .

One day in the streets of Paris I pushed him in order to show him that I was not afraid of him. Diaghilev hit me with his stick as I wanted to go away from him. He felt that I wanted to leave him, and therefore ran after me. I went at a slow trot. I was afraid of being noticed. I saw people were looking. I felt pain in one leg and pushed Diaghilev, not strongly because what I felt was not anger towards Diaghilev, but sorrow. I was crying. Diaghilev was scolding me. He was grinding his teeth and I felt as depressed as if cats were scratching my soul. I could no longer control myself and started walking slowly. Diaghilev also. . . . After this we lived for a long, long time together. I lived sadly, and sorrowed alone. I wept alone. . . .

February 27, 1919.

. . . It is past one o'clock and I am still awake. People ought to work during the day but I work at night; tomorrow my eyes will be red. . . . My wife is not asleep and I am also awake. She thinks and I feel. I am afraid for her. I do not know what to tell her tomorrow. I will talk to no one tomorrow. Tomorrow I will sleep. I want to write but cannot. I think. I am so cold that I cannot write. My fingers are beginning to stiffen. . . . I am so sad. My heart is heavy. I know that people get used to sadness and also I will get used to it, but I am afraid to get used to sadness because I know it is death. . . .

I do not think that timidity and fear are faults. People who are afraid are usually good people. Some people pretend that they are not afraid. Many say that fear is a weakness. People will say that I do not know what fear is because I did not fight in the war—but I fought for life, not in the trenches but at home. I fought with my wife's mother when I was interned in Hungary. People say that I lived very well because I lived in the house of my wife's mother. I lived well—I was not hungry but my soul suffered. I like solitude. I worked on some ballets because I had nothing to do. . . . It was difficult for them to keep us. My mother-in-law had to feed me without being paid for it because I was a relation. Relations usually dislike each other, and so I decided to pretend that I was offended. . . . She . . . thought that I was a poor man and was afraid I would cost money. I know the meaning and the value of money but like to think it is not important. I knew the value of money when I was a child. My mother used to give me fifty kopecks a week for sweets. She used to earn money by letting rooms, and by her doing this we were able to get food. I ate a great deal as I was always hungry, not understanding that I should have been eating less. I used to eat like a grown-up person although I was only twelve years old. . . . [While interned] I was working on a system of notation for dancing and under the table the cats were making a mess. I disliked the cats because of their filth, hating filth. I did not realize that in reality it was not the cats who were making the mess, but the people. I looked after the cats and cared only for my system of dancing. I wanted to forget myself and so started to write down my ballet *Faun* [the *L'Après-midi d'un Faune* of Mallarmé and Debussy] by this system. It was a tough job—it took me two months, and it took only ten minutes to perform this ballet itself. . . .

I do not write for my own pleasure—there can be no pleasure when a man spends all his free time on writing. One has to write a great deal to be able to understand what writing means. It is a difficult occupation—one gets tired of sitting, having the legs cramped, the arm stiff. It spoils the eyes and one does not get enough air; the room gets stuffy. From such a life a man dies sooner. People who write at night spoil their eyes and have to wear glasses, the hypocrites use monocles. I notice that from writing a long time my eyes get bloodshot. People who write a great deal are martyrs. . . .

I am a simple man who has suffered a lot. I believe I suffered more than Christ. I love life and want to live, to cry but cannot—I feel such a pain in my soul—a pain which frightens me. My soul is ill. My soul, not my mind. The doctors do not understand my illness. I know what I need to get well. My illness is too great to be cured quickly. I am incurable. My soul is ill, I am poor, a pauper, miserable. Everyone who reads these lines will suffer—they will understand my feelings. I am a man, not a beast. I love everyone, I have faults, I am a man. . . . I am a part of God, my party is God's party. . . . God is in me. I am in God. I want Him, I seek Him. . . . I am a seeker, for I can feel God. God seeks me and therefore we will find each other.

". . . a very great princess who knows everything . . ."

André Hurault de Maisse

In 1597 Henry IV. of France and Elizabeth of England were nearing the end of their long struggle with Spain. The Armada had been destroyed, and Henry, with much of his invaded land recovered, was eager to bring the wars to an end. To discover whether his ally would join him in peace negotiations, he sent a trusted ambassador, André Hurault de Maisse (1539–1607) to confer secretly with the sixty-four year old Queen.

Keen diplomat and trained observer that he was, de Maisse focused his attention on Elizabeth and her court. The meticulous record he kept of his audiences has left us one of the most undiplomatic and startlingly vivid portraits ever made of the Virgin Queen. As the editors of the first English translation dryly point out, "At times his curiosity savours of Peeping Tom, but he has always a lively sense of character," and particularly when writing about the Queen: "of her fantastic dress; her vanity and shrewdness; her scholarly accomplishments and her love of music and dancing; her digressions."

De Maisse could "value a woman's dress and jewels with the eye of a pawnbroker." But in that month in London those same keen eyes saw far deeper than the outward trappings of royalty.

December 2, 1597.

reached London . . . and was lodged in a house that the Queen had commanded for me wherein Drake had formerly lodged. What I learned of the Queen and of the principal of her Council before I had seen either her or any f them is that when a man speaks to her, and especially when he says something displeasing, she interrupts not seldom. . . . She is a haughty woman, alling easily into rebuke. . . . In her own nature she is very avaricious, and when some expense is necessary her Councillors must deceive her before embarking her on it little by little. She thinks highly of herself and has little

rom *The Journal of André Hurault de Maisse,* reprinted by permission of The Nonesuch Press.

regard for her servants and Council, being of opinion that she is far wiser than they; she mocks them and often cries out upon them. . . .

December 8.

. . . About one hour after noon there came a gentleman from the Queen who said to me that her Majesty was much grieved that she had not given me audience sooner, and that she prayed me to come to her that very hour He brought me in a coach to take me down the river where one of the barges awaited me and we went thence to the gate of the Queen's palace. . . . He led me along a passage somewhat dark, into a chamber that they call the Privy Chamber, at the head of which was the Queen, seated in a low chair by herself, and withdrawn from all the Lords and Ladies that were present they being in one place and she in another. After I had made her my reverence at the entry of the chamber, she rose and came five or six paces towards me, almost into the middle of the chamber. I kissed the fringe of her robe and she embraced me with both hands. She looked at me kindly, and began to excuse herself that . . . the day before she had been very ill with a gathering on the right side of her face, which I should never have thought seeing her eyes and face: but she did not remember ever to have been so ill before She excused herself because I found her attired in her nightgown. . . . She was strangely attired in a dress of silver cloth, white and crimson, or silver "gauze," as they call it. This dress had slashed sleeves lined with red taffeta and was girt about with other little sleeves that hung down to the ground which she was forever twisting and untwisting. She kept the front of her dress open, and one could see the whole of her bosom, and passing low, and often she would open the front of this robe with her hands as if she was too hot The collar of the robe was very high, and the lining of the inner part all adorned with little pendants of rubies and pearls, very many, but quite small She had also a chain of rubies and pearls about her neck. On her head she wore a garland of the same material and beneath it a great reddish coloured wig, with a great number of spangles of gold and silver, and hanging down over her forehead some pearls, but of no great worth. On either side of her ears hung two great curls of hair, almost down to her shoulder and within the collar of her robe, spangled as the top of her head. Her bosom is somewhat wrinkled . . . but lower down her flesh is exceeding white and delicate, so far as one could see.

As for her face, it is and appears to be very aged. It is long and thin, and her teeth are very yellow and unequal. . . . Many of them are missing so that one cannot understand her easily when she speaks quickly. Her figure is fair and tall and graceful in whatever she does; so far as may be she keeps her dignity, yet humbly and graciously withal. . . .

December 12.

. . . When the Queen is served, a great table is set in the Presence Chamber near the Queen's throne. The cloth being laid, a gentleman and a lady come in, walking from the end of the room with the cover, and make three reverences, the one by the door, the next in the middle of the chamber, the

ird by the table. Then they set down the cover and the lady tries the food.
The guards bring in the meat in the same manner; then the lady tries the
ood with a piece of bread and gives it to the guards; thence the meat, such
s the Queen desires, is carried into the Privy Chamber where she dines.
Her service is neither very sumptuous nor delicate. . . .

December 15.

. . . Today she sent her coaches and one of her own gentleman servants
o conduct me . . . to the Privy Chamber where the Queen was standing by
window. She looked in better health than before. She was clad in a dress
of black taffeta, bound with gold lace, and like a robe in the Italian fashion
with open sleeves and lined with crimson taffeta. She had a petticoat of white
damask, girdled, and open in front, as was also her chemise, in such a man-
er that she often opened this dress and one could see all her belly, and even
o her navel. Her head tire was the same as before. She had bracelets of
pearls on her hands, six or seven rows of them. On her head tire she wore
coronet of pearls, of which five or six were marvellously fair. When she
raises her head she has a trick of putting both hands on her gown and open-
ng it insomuch that all her belly can be seen. . . . She often called herself
foolish and old, saying she was sorry to see me there, and that, after having
een so many wise men and great princes, I should at length come to see a
poor woman and a foolish. I was not without an answer, telling her of the
blessings, virtues and perfections that I had heard of her from stranger Princes,
but that was nothing compared with what I saw. With that she was well
contented, as she is when anyone commends her for her judgment and pru-
ence, and she is very glad to speak slightingly of her intelligence and sway
of mind, so that she may give occasion to commend her. . . . When anyone
peaks of her beauty she says that she was never beautiful, although she had
hat reputation thirty years ago. Nevertheless she speaks of her beauty as
ften as she can. As for her natural form and proportion, she is very beauti-
ul; and by chance approaching a door and wishing to raise the tapestry that
ung before it, she said to me laughing that she was as big as a door, meaning
hat she was tall. . . . I departed from her audience at night, and she re-
ired half dancing to her chamber, where is her spinet. . . .

December 24.

. . . I went to see the Queen, and she sent me her coaches. I found her
very well and kindly disposed. She was having the spinet played to her in her
hamber, seeming very attentive to it; and because I surprised her, or at least
he feigned surprise, I apologised to her for diverting her from her pleasure.
he told me that she loved music greatly and that she was having a pavanne
played. I answered her that she was a very good judge, and had the reputa-
ion of being a mistress in the art. She told me that she had meddled with it
ivers times, and still took great pleasure in it. She was clad in a white robe
of cloth of silver, cut very low and her bosom uncovered. . . . My audience
was long, during which she told me many tales of all kinds. . . . Whilst I
was treating with her in the matter of my charge she would often make such

digressions, either expressly to gain time and not to feel pressed by that I asked of her, or because it is her natural way. Then would she excuse herself, saying "Master Ambassador, you will say of the tales that I am telling you that they are mere gullery. See what it is to have to do with old women such as I am." Then she returned to the subject of her talk to which I led her back, pressing her for an answer. She said to me, "I am between Scylla and Charybdis." She knows all the ancient histories, and one can say nothing to her on which she will not make some apt comment. . . . Having told her at some point that she was well advertised of everything that happened in the world, she replied that her hands were very long by nature . . . whereupon she drew off her glove and showed me her hand, which is very long and more than mine by three broad fingers. It was formerly very beautiful, but it is now very thin, although the skin is still most fair. . . . At my departure from the audience I presented to her the secretary Phillips . . . at which she was very pleased and made good cheer to this Phillips, saying that she had seen several of his letters but did not know him. He was on his knees and she began to take him by the hair and made him rise and pretended to give him a box on the ears. It is a strange thing to see how lively she is in body and mind and nimble in everything she does. This day she was in very good humour and gay, and at my departure made me very good cheer, saluting all the gentlemen who were with me altogether. She is a very great princess who knows everything. . . .

January 6, 1598.

. . . After dinner the Queen sent for me . . . and being in the Chamber of the Council a gentleman came to say that very soon the Queen would pass by with her ladies on her way to the dancing, and, that if I wished to see her pass, it was she who had sent him. I went there, and straightway she came out; and seeing me from afar she came towards me saying . . . that she was going to see the dancing, and demanded whether I did not wish to accompany her. I told her that I would do everything she commanded me, and bore her company. She herself sat in the gallery and made me sit by her.

She takes great pleasure in dancing and music. She told me that she entertained at least sixty musicians; in her youth she danced very well, and composed measures and music, and had played them herself and danced them. She takes such pleasure in it that when her Maids dance she follows the cadence with her head, hand and foot. She rebukes them if they do not dance to her liking, and without doubt she is a mistress of the art, having learnt in the Italian manner to dance high. She told me that they called her "the Florentine". . . .

January 10.

. . . I was conducted to her chamber, where I found her attired after her accustomed manner. She made me sit near her. . . . She spoke to me of the languages that she had learned, for she makes digressions very often, telling me that when she came to the Crown she knew six languages better than

er own; and because I told her that it was great virtue in a princess, she
aid that it was no marvel to teach a woman to talk; it were far harder to
each her to hold her tongue. . . . She said several words on the private
natters of His Majesty, and then on mine, telling me that she was very well
leased to know me and well knew my merits. She embraced me twice; and
hen all the gentlemen who were with me made their reverence. She com-
nanded the Admiral who was present to see that a good ship was given me,
nd then laughing said that I might be made a prisoner of the Spanish. I
nswered that marching under her banner I had scarcely need to fear them.
'hat is what was done this day.

anuary 15.

I left London hoping with God's aid to return to France. I arrived at Dover
n the 17th in the evening. . . .

"There have been good and wise kings, but . . ."

Charles Cavendish Fulke Greville

The editor of the Greville diaries chose as a motto for them a remark by the wise Swedish chancellor Oxenstiern. "You do not
know yet, my son, with how little wisdom mankind is governed."
It is appropriate. Charles C. F. Greville (1794–1863) in the
diaries which he kept for forty years relates a tale of dotards thrice
on the English throne—pathetic, deranged George III. who cost
England her American colonies; and his sons; queer George IV.
("a more contemptible, cowardly, selfish, unfeeling dog does not
exist than this king") and "cracked" William IV., Victoria's uncle,
who was popularly known as "Silly Billy." To Greville "the divinity that doth hedge a king was not apparent"; nor did it ever
stay his pen.

Greville, born of a noble family, handsome, and a man of fashion and parts, spent most of his life as clerk to the privy council.
This privileged position gave him intimate views of majesty and
of all the passing great of his time. He was born in Bulstrode,
educated at Eton and Oxford and first introduced to court circles
as a page to George III. His contemporaries, who knew him as
something of a fop with a stable of race horses, never seem to
have suspected that each night he put down in his diary a frank
account of everything that reached his sharp ears and keen eyes.
No matter how he may have dissembled during the day, to his
journal he entrusted the most uncompromising judgments of what
went on around him.

Victoria, born two years before the diary's beginning, was first
seen by Greville at a children's ball. He thought her plain looking, but became her liege. Ten years after Greville's death a
greatly abridged version of his diary appeared and within a single
year five large editions were avidly read by those who long before had guessed that all was not right with the monarchy under
George III. and his sons. But Victoria thought it improper, almost
lèse-majesté, that his journals were published. Ironically, the dis-

From *The Greville Memoirs*, by Charles C. F. Greville, edited by Richard Henry
Stoddard. Scribner, Armstrong. New York 1876.

closure of matters only whispered about before, probably did much to consolidate support for her reign of normalcy.

Diarists have left a fascinating gallery of kings and queens painted at close range, but it is safe to say that none has ever been less inhibited than Greville in his depiction of the follies of the royal scene.

February 7, 1821.

The King [George IV.] went to the play last night (Drury Lane) for the first time, the Dukes of York and Clarence and a great suite with him. He was received with immense acclamations, the whole pit standing up, hurrahing, and waving their hats. . . . A few people called "the Queen," but very few. A man in the gallery called out, "Where's your wife, Georgy?"

May 2.

Lady Conyngham [the King's favourite] lives in one of the houses in Marlborough Row. All the members of her family are . . . supplied with horses, carriages, etc., from the King's stables. . . . They never appear in public together. She dines there every day. . . . She comports herself entirely as mistress of the house . . . has received magnificent presents . . . strings of pearls of enormous value. Madame de Lieven said she had seen the pearls of the Grand Duchesses and the Prussian Princesses, but had never seen any nearly so fine as Lady Conyngham's. The other night . . . the King seized her arm and said with the greatest tenderness, ". . . you cannot please me so much as by doing everything you please, everything to show that you are mistress here."

June 24.

The King dined at Devonshire House last Thursday se'nnight. Lady Conyngham had on her head a sapphire which belonged to the Stuarts, and was given by Cardinal York to the King. . . .

December 18.

. . . I came to town, went to Brighton yesterday se'nnight for a council. I was lodged in the Pavilion and dined with the King. The gaudy splendor of the place amused me for a little and then bored me. The dinner was cold and the evening dull beyond all dullness. They say the King is anxious that form and ceremony should be banished, and if so it not only proves how impossible it is that form and ceremony should not always inhabit a palace. The rooms are not furnished for society, and, in fact, society cannot flourish without ease; and who can feel at ease who is under the eternal constraint which etiquette and respect impose? The King was in good looks and good spirits, and after dinner cut his jokes with all the coarse merriment which is his characteristic. . . I saw nothing very particular in the King's manner to Lady Conyngham. He sat by her on the couch almost the whole evening playing at patience.

. . . I was curious to see the Pavilion and the life they lead there, and I now only hope I may never go there again, for the novelty is past and I should be exposed to the whole weight of the bore of it without the stimulus of curiosity.

August 19, 1822.

. . . The Pavilion is finished. The King has had a subterranean passage made from the house to the stables, which is said to have cost 3,000 *l.* or 5,000 *l.*: I forget which. There is also a bath in his apartment with pipes to conduct water from the sea; these pipes cost 600 *l.* The King has not taken a sea bath for sixteen years.

November 29, 1823.

In the various conversations which I have with the Duke of York [the King's brother] he continually tells me a variety of facts more or less curious . . . concerning the affairs of the royal family. . . . In all these histories the King acted a part, in which his bad temper, bad judgment, falseness, and duplicity were equally conspicuous. I think it is not possible for any man to have a worse opinion of another than the Duke has of the King. From various instances of eccentricities I am persuaded that the King is subject to occasional impressions which produce effects like insanity; that if they continue to increase he will end by being decidedly mad. . . .

June 17, 1827.

I was at the Royal Lodge for one night last Wednesday; about thirty people sat down to dinner, and the company was changed nearly every day. It is a delightful place to live in, but the rooms are too low and too small for very large parties. Nothing can exceed the luxury of the internal arrangements; the King was very well and in excellent spirits, but very weak in his knees and could not walk without difficulty. . . . It is clear that nothing would be more insupportable than to live at this court; the dullness must be excessive, and the people who compose his habitual society are the most insipid and uninteresting that can be found. As for Lady Conyngham, she looks bored to death, and she never speaks, never appears to have one word to say to the King, who, however, talks himself without ceasing. . . .

January 12, 1829.

Lord Mount Charles came to me this morning and . . . talked to me about Knighton [George's private secretary], whom the King abhors with a detestation that could hardly be described. . . . He says that his language about Knighton is sometimes of the most unmeasured violence—wishes he was dead, and one day when the door was open, so that the pages could hear, he said, "I wish to God somebody would assassinate Knighton." . . . Still it appears that there is some secret chain which binds them together, and which compels the King to submit to the presence of a man whom he detests, and induces

Knighton to remain in spite of so much hatred and ill-usage. The King's insolence is so great that it is next to impossible to get him to do even the most ordinary business, and Knighton is still the only man who can prevail on him to sign papers, etc. His greatest delight is to make those who have business to transact with him, or to lay papers before him, wait in his anteroom while he is lounging with Mount Charles or anybody, talking of horses or any trivial matter. . . . He does it on purpose, and likes it. This account corresponds with all I have before heard, and confirms the opinion I have long had that a more contemptible, cowardly, selfish, unfeeling dog does not exist than this king, on whom such flattery is constantly lavished. . . . There have been good and wise kings, but not many of them. Take them one with another they are of an inferior character, and this I believe to be one of the worse of the kind. The littleness of his character prevents his displaying the dangerous faults that belong to great minds, but with vices and weaknesses of the lowest and most contemptible order it would be difficult to find a disposition more abundantly furnished.

March 19.

. . . The King . . . leads a most extraordinary life—never gets up till six in the afternoon. They come to him and open the window curtains at six or seven o'clock in the morning; he breakfasts in bed, does whatever business he can be brought to transact in bed too, he reads every newspaper quite through, dozes three or four hours, gets up in time for dinner, and goes to bed between ten and eleven. He sleeps very ill, and rings his bell forty times in the night; if he wants to know the hour, though a watch hangs close to him, he will have his *valet de chambre* down rather than turn his head to look at it. The same thing if he wants a glass of water; he won't stretch out his hand to get it. His valets are nearly destroyed. . . .

May 14.

. . . The influence of Knighton and that of Lady Conyngham continues as great as ever; nothing can be done but by their permission, and they understand one another and play into each other's hands. Knighton opposes every kind of expense, except that which is lavished on her. The wealth she has accumulated by savings and presents must be enormous. The King continues to heap all kinds of presents upon her, and she lives at his expense; they do not possess a servant; even Lord Conyngham's *valet de chambre* is not properly their servant. They all have situations in the King's household, from which their receive their pay, while they continue in the service of the Conynghams. They dine every day while in London at St. James's, and when they give a dinner it is cooked at St. James's and brought up to Hamilton Place in hackney coaches and in machines made expressly for the purpose; there is merely a fire lit in their kitchen for such things as must be heated on the spot. At Windsor the King sees very little of her except of an evening; he lies in bed half the day or more, sometimes goes out, and sometimes goes to her room for an hour or so in the afternoon. . . . A more despicable scene cannot be exhibited than that which the interior of our court presents—every base, low, and unmanly propensity, with selfishness, avarice, and a life of petty intrigue and mystery.

May 29.

Yesterday the King gave a dinner to the Dukes of Orleans and Chartres and in the evening there was a child's ball. It was pretty enough, and I saw for the first time the Queen of Portugal and our little Victoria. . . . Our little Princess is a short, plain looking child, and not near so good looking as the Portuguese. However, if nature has not done so much, fortune is likely to do great deal more for her. . . .

September 16.

The King has nearly lost his eyesight, and is to be couched as soon as his eyes are in a proper state for the operation. He is in a great fright with his father's fate before him, and indeed nothing is more probable than that he will become blind and mad too; he is already a little of both. . . .

November 20.

. . . The expenses of the civil list [funds allowed the King] exceed the allowance in every branch, every quarter; but nobody can guess how the money is spent, for the King makes no show and never has anybody there My belief is that [certain persons, (?) Knighton and Lady Conyngham] . . plunder him, or rather the country, between them, in certain stipulated proportions. Among other expenses his tailor's bill is said to be 4,000 *l.* or 5,000 *l* a year. He is now employed in devising a new dress for the Guards.

May 7, 1830. Rome.

. . . Everybody here is in great alarm about the King, who I have no doubt is very ill. I am afraid he will die before I get home, and I should like to be in at the death and see all the proceedings of a new reign; but, now am here, I must stay out my time, let what will happen. I shall probably never see Rome again, and "according to the law of probability, so true in general so false in particular," I have a good chance of seeing at least one more king leave us.

July 3. Paris.

Got here last night, after a fierce journey of sixty-three hours from Geneva only stopping for two hours for breakfast. . . . It rained torrents. . . . We heard of the King's death in the middle of the night.

July 16. London.

. . . Nobody thinks any more of the late King than if he had been dead fifty years, unless it be to abuse him and to rake up all his vices and misdeeds

Never was elevation like that of King William IV. His life has been hitherto passed in obscurity and neglect, in miserable poverty, surrounded by a numerous progeny of bastards, without consideration or friends, and he was ridiculous from his grotesque ways and little meddling curiosity. Nobody ever invited him into their house, or thought it necessary to honor him with any mark of attention or respect; and so he went on for forty years.

July 18.

. . . The new King began very well. . . . His first speech to the council was well enough given, but his burlesque character began even then to show itself. Nobody expected from him much real grief, and he does not seem to know how to act it consistently; he spoke of his brother with all the semblance of feeling, and in a tone properly softened and subdued, but just afterwards, when they gave him the pen to sign the declaration, he said in his usual tone, "This is a damned bad pen you have given me." . . . At the late King's funeral he behaved with great indecency. . . . The attendance was not very numerous, and when they had all got together in St. George's Hall a gayer company I never beheld; with the exception of Mount Charles, who was deeply affected, they were all as merry as grigs. The King was chief mourner, and to my astonishment, as he entered the chapel directly behind the body, in a situation in which he should have been apparently, if not really, absorbed in the melancholy duty he was performing, he darted up to Strathaven, who was ranged on one side below the Dean's stall, shook him heartily by the hand, and then went on nodding to the right and left. . . . Altogether he seems a kind-hearted, well-meaning, not stupid, burlesque, bustling old fellow, and if he doesn't go mad may make a very decent king, but he exhibits oddities. He would not have his servants in mourning—that is, not those of his own family and household—but he sent the Duke of Sussex to Mrs. Fitzherbert to desire she would put hers in mourning. . . . Yesterday morning he sent for the officer on guard, and ordered him to take all the muffles off the drums, the scarfs off the regimentals, and so to appear on parade, where he went himself. . . . In the meantime it is said that the bastards [resulting from his long intimacy with the actress Dorothea Jordan] are dissatisfied that more is not done for them, but he cannot do much for them at once and he must have time. He has done all he can; he has made Errol master of the horse, Sidney a Guelph and equerry, George Fitzclarence the same and adjutant-general, and doubtless they will all have their turn. . . .

July 20.

Yesterday was a very busy day with his Majesty, who is going much too fast, and begins to alarm his ministers and astonish the world. In the morning he inspected the Coldstream Guards, dressed (for the first time in his life) in a military uniform and with a great pair of gold spurs half-way up his legs like a game cock, although he was not to ride, for having chalk-stones in his hands he can't hold the reins. The Queen came to Lady Bathurst's to see the review and hold a sort of drawing-room. . . . She is very ugly, with a horrid complexion, but has good manners, and did all this (which she hated) very well. She said the part as if she was acting, and wished the green curtain to drop. . . .

July 24.

. . . Yesterday, after the House of Lords, he drove all over the town in an open *calèche* with the Queen, Princess Augusta, and the King of Würtemberg, and coming home he set down the King (*dropped him*, as he calls it) at Grillon's Hotel. The King of England dropping another king at a tavern!

July 25.

. . . The other night the King had a party, and at eleven o'clock he dismissed them thus: "Now ladies and gentlemen, I wish you a good-night. I will not detain you any longer from your amusements, and shall go to my own, which is to go to bed; so come along, my Queen." . . .

August 3.

. . . I went yesterday to the sale of the late King's wardrobe, which was numberous enough to fill Monmouth Street, and sufficiently various and splendid for the wardrobe of Drury Lane. He hardly ever gave away anything except his linen, which was distributed every year. These clothes are the perquisites of his pages, and will fetch a pretty sum. There are all the coats he has ever had for fifty years, 300 whips, canes without number, every sort of uniform, the costumes of all the orders in Europe, splendid furs, pelisses, hunting-coats and breeches, and among other things a dozen pair of corduroy breeches he had made to hunt in when Don Miguel was here. His profusion in these articles was unbounded, because he never paid for them, and his memory was so accurate that one of his pages told me he recollected every article of dress, no matter how old, and that they were always liable to be called on to produce some particular coat or other article of apparel of years gone by. It is difficult to say whether in great or little things that man was most odious and contemptible.

January 19, 1831.

. . . The King is supposed to be in a bad state of health. . . . He will be a great loss in these times; he knows his business, lets his ministers do as they please, but expects to be informed of everything. He lives a strange life at Brighton, with tagrag and bobtail about him, and always open house. The Queen is a prude, and will not let the ladies come *décolletées* to her parties. George IV., who liked ample expanses of that sort, would not let them be covered.

February 24.

The King went to the play the night before last; was well received in the house, but hooted and pelted coming home, and a stone shivered a window of his coach and fell into Prince George of Cumberland's lap. The King was excessively annoyed, and sent for Baring, who was the officer riding by his coach, and asked him if he knew who had thrown the stone; he said that it terrified the Queen and "was very disagreeable . . .".

September 8.

After dinner I had much talk with the Duke, who told me a good deal about the late King and the Duchess of Kent; talked of his extravagance and love of spending, provided that it was not his own money that he spent. . . . He always had money. When he died, they found 10,000 *l.* in his boxes and money scattered about everywhere, a great deal of gold. There were above 500 pocketbooks, of different dates, and in every one money—guineas, one pound notes, one, two, or three in each. There never was anything like the quantity of trinkets and trash that they found. He had never given away or parted with anything. There was a prodigious quantity of hair—women's hair—of all colors and lengths, some locks with the powder and pomatum still sticking to them, heaps of women's gloves, *gages d'amour* which he had got at balls, and with the perspiration still marked on the fingers. . . .

June 18, 1832.

The government and their people have now found out what a fool the King is, and it is very amusing to hear them on the subject. Formerly, when they thought they had him fast, he was very honest and rather wise; now they find him rather shuffling and exceedingly silly. When Normanby went to take leave of him on going to Jamaica, he pronounced a harangue in favor of the slave trade, of which he has always been a great admirer, and expressed sentiments for which his subjects would tear him to pieces if they heard them. It is one of the great evils of the recent convulsion that the King's imbecility has been exposed to the world, and in his person the regal authority has fallen into contempt. . . . Walter Scott has arrived here, dying. A great mortality among great men; Goethe, Périer, Champollion, Cuvier, Scott, Grant, Macintosh, all died within a few weeks of each other.

May 23, 1834.

There is a very strong impression abroad that the King is cracked, and I dare say there is some truth in it. He gets so very choleric, and is so indecent in his wrath. . . .

November 7, 1836.

. . . He was very angry at King Leopold's coming here, received him very coldly at Windsor, had no conversation with him on business, and on one occasion exhibited a rudeness even to brutality. It seems he hates water-drinkers; God knows why. One day at dinner Leopold called for water, when the King asked, "What's that you are drinking, sir?" "Water, sir." "God damn it!" rejoined the other King; "why don't you drink wine? I never allow anybody to drink water at my table." Leopold only dined there, and went away in the evening. . . .

June 13, 1837.

Bad accounts of the King yesterday. Melbourne desired I would get everything ready *quietly* for a council. . . .

June 16.

On Wednesday the King was desperately bad, yesterday he was better, but not so as to afford any hope. . . . What renders . . . events uncertain is the absolute ignorance of everybody, without exception, of the character, disposition, and capacity of the Princess [Victoria]. She has been kept in such jealous seclusion by her mother (never having slept out of her bedroom, nor been alone with anybody but herself and the Baroness Lehzen), that not one of her acquaintance, none of the attendants at Kensington, not even the Duchess of Northumberland, her governess, have any idea what she is, or what she promises to be. . . .

June 19.

Yesterday the King was sinking fast; the Sacrament was administered to him by the Archbishop of Canterbury. He said, "This is the 18th of June; I should like to live to see the sun of Waterloo set." . . .

June 21.

The King died at twenty minutes after two yesterday morning, and the young Queen met the council at Kensington Palace at eleven. Never was anything like the first impression she produced, or the chorus of praise and admiration which is raised about her manner and behavior, and certainly not without justice. It was very extraordinary, and something far beyond what was looked for. . . . The first thing to be done was to teach her her lesson, which for this purpose Melbourne had himself to learn. I gave him the council papers, and explained all that was to be done, and he went and explained all this to her. . . . She went through the whole ceremony, occasionally looking at Melbourne for instruction when she had any doubt what to do, which hardly ever occurred, and . . . when the business was done she retired as she had entered, and I could see that nobody was in the adjoining room. . . .

No contrast can be greater than that between the personal demeanor of the present and the late sovereigns at their respective accessions. William IV. was a man who, coming to the throne at the mature age of sixty-five, was so excited by the exaltation, that he nearly went mad, and distinguished himself by a thousand extravagances of language and conduct, to the alarm or amusement of all who witnessed his strange freaks; and though he was shortly afterwards sobered down into more becoming habits, he always continued

to be something of a blackguard and something more of a buffoon. . . .
The young Queen, who might well be either dazzled or confounded with
the grandeur and novelty of her situation, seems neither the one nor the other,
and behaves with a decorum and propriety . . . the want of which was so
conspicuous in her uncle.

"I protest I was ready to die."

Fanny Burney

Chased round the palace gardens, caught and kissed twice by England's mad King George III; kissed by Samuel Johnson, too; keeper of Queen Charlotte's lap-dog and snuff-box; wife of a French general; author; playwright, and friend of genius—Fanny Burney (1752–1840) was a noteworthy woman, who came from a noteworthy family.

Dr. Charles Burney, Fanny's father, was a distinguished composer, organist and music historian. Admiral James Burney, Fanny's brother, sailed with Captain Cook on two of his voyages. The Rev. Charles Burney, another brother, became a classical scholar. After the death of her mother when she was nine, Fanny was left to educate herself at home, mainly by reading books she could find in her father's library, and the company of her elders and family guests, among whom were leading men of the time. Almost all of them made much of the little girl.

Fanny was a shy, stiff, prudish child; slight of build, near-sighted and not beautiful. She became less attractive as the years went on, but this never seemed a handicap to her.

Dr. Burney's second wife did not approve of literary young women and to please her step-mother Fanny destroyed most of her early manuscripts. Somehow the manuscript of her diaries escaped the flames. When she came to write her famous *Evelina* (1778) she did it secretly and this much-admired novel of family life was published anonymously; even her father did not know about it until it was clearly a success. Other novels of Fanny's later life are virtually forgotten. Some of her plays have never been printed.

A major event in Fanny's life was her designation as one of Queen Charlotte's court ladies, a post she held for five years until 1791. Intimate attendance upon the Queen was burdensome and humiliating to her, and she was delighted to be allowed to resign. Not long after, she married an impoverished French military

From *The Diary of Fanny Burney*. Reprinted by permission of E. P. Dutton & Co., Inc. and J. M. Dent & Sons, Ltd.

officer, General D'Arblay, former aide to LaFayette, and they lived at first in Paris and then in England, on a small pension she received from the Queen. They had one son. Madame D'Arblay survived the General by twenty-two years.

Fanny's diaries have delighted many and have irritated some. Macaulay did much to recruit for her the devoted following she still retains. But another critic said that the diaries were "nearly the most worthless we have ever waded through." Certainly they are often long-winded, and almost always strewn with little vanities that may either provoke or amuse. Most readers choose to be amused.

August, 1778. Undated.

I have now to write an account of the most consequential day I have spent since my birth; namely my Streatham visit. Our journey to Streatham was the least pleasant part of the day, for the roads were dreadfully dusty, and I was really in the fidgets from thinking what my reception might be, and from fearing they would expect a less awkward and backward kind of person than I was sure they would find.

Mr. Thrale's house is white, and very pleasantly situated, in a fine paddock. Mrs. Thrale . . . took me upstairs, and showed me the house, and . . . at last, she mentioned "Evelina" [Fanny Burney's novel, just published]. "Yesterday at supper," said she, "we talked it all over, and discussed all your characters; but Dr. Johnson's favourite is Mr. Smith. He declares the fine gentleman *manqué* was never better drawn, and he acted him all the evening, saying 'he was all for the ladies'! He repeated whole scenes by heart. I declare I was astonished at him. O, you can't imagine how much he is pleased with the book. . . ."

When we were summoned to dinner . . . this great man entered. I have so true a veneration for him, that the very sight of him inspires me with delight and reverence, notwithstanding the cruel infirmities to which he is subject; for he has almost perpetual convulsive movements, either of his hands, lips, feet, or knees, and sometimes of all together. . . .

August 29.

Dr. Johnson was again all himself and so civil to me!—even admiring how I dressed myself! Indeed, it is well I have so much of his favour; for it seems he always speaks his mind concerning the dress of ladies, and all ladies who are here obey his injunctions implicitly, and alter whatever he disapproves. This is a part of his character that much surprises me: but notwithstanding he is sometimes so absent, and always so near-sighted, he scrutinizes into every part of almost everybody's appearance. . . .

November. Undated.

In the evening the company divided pretty much into parties and almost everybody walked on the gravel walk before the windows. I was going to have joined some of them, when Dr. Johnson stopped me, and asked how I did.

"I was afraid, sir," cried I, "you did not intend to know me again, for you have not spoken to me before since your return from town."

"My dear," cried he, taking both my hands, "I was not sure of you. I am so near-sighted, and I apprehended making some mistake." Then drawing me very unexpectedly towards him, he actually kissed me! . . . Mrs. Thrale laughed heartily, and said she hoped I was contented with his amends for not knowing me sooner. A little after she said she would go and walk with the rest, if she did not fear for my reputation in being left with the doctor. . . .

June 19, 1783.

We heard to-day that Dr. Johnson had been taken ill, in a way that gave a dreadful shock to himself, and a most anxious alarm to his friends. . . . The stroke was confined to his tongue. Mrs. Williams told me a most striking and touching circumstance that attended the attack. It was at about four o'clock in the morning: he found himself with a paralytic affection; he rose, and composed in his own mind a Latin prayer to the Almighty, "that whatever were the sufferings for which he must prepare himself, it would please Him, through the grace and mediation of our blessed Saviour, to spare his intellects, and let them all fall upon his body." When he had composed this, internally, he endeavoured to speak it aloud, but found his voice was gone.

November 28, 1784.

Last Thursday . . . I was anxious to again see poor Dr. Johnson, who has had terrible health since his return from Lichfield. He let me in, though very ill. He was alone, which I much rejoiced at: for I had a longer and more satisfactory conversation with him than I have had for many months. He . . . told me he was going to try what sleeping out of town might do for him.

"I remember," said he, "that my wife, when she was near her end, poor woman, was also advised to sleep out of town; and when she was carried to the lodgings that had been prepared for her, she complained that the staircase was in very bad condition—for the plaster was beaten off the walls in many places: 'Oh,' said the man of the house, 'that's nothing but by the knocks against it of the coffins of the poor souls that have died in the lodgings!'"

He laughed, though not without secret anguish, in telling me this. I felt extremely shocked. . . .

December 20.

This day was the ever-honoured, ever lamented Dr. Johnson committed to the earth. Oh, how sad a day to me! . . . I could not keep my eyes dry all day! Nor can I now in the recollecting it; but let me pass over what to mourn is now so vain. . . .

November 25, 1785. Windsor.

. . . "I do beg of you," said dear Mrs. Delany [with whom Fanny stayed when she first went to Windsor Court as Assistant Keeper of the Robes to Queen Charlotte], "when the Queen or the King speaks to you, not to answer with mere monosyllables. The Queen often complains to me of the difficulty with which she can get any conversation, as she not only always has to start the subjects, but, commonly, entirely to support them: and she says there is nothing she so much loves as conversation, and nothing she finds so hard to get." . . .

December 17.

. . . You would never believe—you, who distant from courts and courtiers, know nothing of their ways—the many things to be studied, for appearing with a proper propriety before crowned heads. . . . I shall give you those instructions I have received myself, that, should you find yourself in the royal presence, you may know how to comport yourself.

Directions for coughing, sneezing or moving, before the King and Queen.

In the first place, you must not cough. If you find a cough tickling in your throat, you must arrest it from making any sound; if you find yourself choking with the forbearance, you must choke—but not cough.

In the second place, you must not sneeze. If you have a vehement cold, you must take no notice of it; if your nose membranes feel a great irritation, you must hold your breath; if a sneeze still insists upon making its way, you must oppose it, by keeping your teeth grinding together; if the violence of the repulse breaks some blood-vessel, you must break the blood-vessel—but not sneeze.

In the third place, you must not, upon any account, stir either hand or foot. If, by any chance, a black pin runs into your head, you must not take it out. If the pain is very great, you must be sure to bear it without wincing. . . . If, however the agony is very great, you may privately, bite the inside of your cheek, or of your lips, for a little relief; taking care, meanwhile to do it so cautiously as to make no apparent dent outwardly. And, with that precaution, if you even gnaw a piece out, it will not be minded, only be sure either to swallow it, or commit it to a corner of the inside of your mouth till they are gone—for you must not spit. . . .

July 24, 1786.

. . . I rise at six o'clock, dress in a morning gown and cap, and wait my first summons, which is at all times from seven to near eight, but commonly in the exact half hour between them. The Queen never sends for me till her hair is dressed. This, in a morning, is always done by her wardrobe woman, Thielky. . . . No maid ever enters the room while the Queen is in it. Mrs. Thielky hands the things to me, and I put them on. 'Tis fortunate for me I have not the handing them! I should never know which to take first, embarrassed as I am, and should run a prodigious risk of giving the gown before the hoop, and the fan before the neckerchief. By eight o'clock, or a little after, for she is extremely expeditious, she is dressed. . . . I then return to my own room to breakfast. I make this meal the most pleasant part of the day; I have a book for my companion, and I allow myself an hour for it. . . . At nine o'clock I send off my breakfast things, and relinquish my book, to make a serious and steady examination of everything I have upon my hands in the way of business—in which preparations for dress are always included, not for the present day alone, but for the court days, which require a particular dress; for the next arriving birthday of any of the Royal Family, every one of which requires new apparel; for Kew, where the dress is plainest. . . .

These times mentioned call me to the irksome and quick-returning labours of the toilette. The hour advanced on the Wednesdays and Saturdays is for curling and craping the hair, which it now requires twice a week. A quarter before one is the usual time for the Queen to begin dressing for the day. . . . We help her off with her gown, and on with her powdering things, and then the hairdresser is admitted. She generally reads the newspapers during that operation. . . . It is commonly three o'clock when I am thus set at large. And I have then two hours quite at my own disposal. . . . At five, we have dinner . . . my little supper at near eleven. Between eleven and twelve my last summons usually takes place, earlier and later occasionally. Twenty minutes is the customary time then spent with the Queen: half an hour, I believe, is seldom exceeded. I then come back . . . and to sleep I fall the moment I have put out my candle and laid down my head. Such is the day. . . .

July 25.

. . . I had this morning, early, for the first time, a little visit from one of the Princesses. I was preparing for my journey, when a little rap at my room door made me call out: "Come in!" and who should enter but the Princess Royal. I apologized for my familiar admittance, by my little expectation of such an honour. She told me she had brought the Queen's snuff-box, to be filled with some snuff which I had been directed to prepare. It is a very fine-scented and mild snuff, but requires being moistened from time to time to revive its smell. The Princess, with a very sweet smile, insisted on holding the box while I filled it; and . . . she had left me but a short time before she again returned. "Miss Burney," cried she, smiling with a look of congratulation, "Mamma says the snuff is extremely well mixed; and she has sent another box to be filled." . . .

October 6.

. . . "How do you like it, ma'am?" he [Colonel Goldsworthy, King George III's equerry] says to me, "though it's hardly fair to ask you yet, because you know almost nothing of the joys of this sort of life. But wait till November and December, and then you'll get a pretty taste of them! Running along in these cold passages; then bursting into rooms fit to bake you; then back again into all these agreeable puffs! Bless us! I believe in my heart there's wind enough in these passages to carry a man of war! And there you'll have your share, ma'am, I promise you that. . . . One thing, however, pray let me caution you about—don't go to early prayers in November; if you do, that will completely kill you! . . . When the Princesses, used to it as they are, get regularly knocked up before this business is over, off they drop, one by one: first the Queen deserts us; then Princess Elizabeth is done for; then Princess Royal begins coughing; then Princess Augusta gets the snuffles; and all the poor attendants, my poor sister at their head, drop off one after another, like so many snuffs of candles: till at last, dwindle, dwindle, dwindle— not a soul goes to the chapel but the King, the parson, and myself; and there we three freeze it out together!"

One evening, when he had been out very late hunting with the King, he . . . gave us more entertainment than ever, by relating his hardships. "After all the labours," cried he, "of the chase, all the riding, the trotting, the galloping, the leaping, the—with your favour, ladies, I beg pardon, I was going to say a strange word, but the—the perspiration—and—and all that—after being wet through over head, and soused through under feet, and popped into ditches, and jerked over gates, what lives we do lead! Well, it's all honour that's my only comfort! Well, after all this, fagging away like mad from eight in the morning to five or six in the afternoon, home we come, looking like so many drowned rats, with not a dry thread about us, nor a morsel within us—sore to the very bone, and forced to smile all the time! and then, after all this, what do you think follows? 'Here, Goldsworthy,' cries his Majesty: so up I comes to him, bowing profoundly, and my hair dripping down to my shoes; 'Goldsworthy,' cries his Majesty. 'Sir,' says I, smiling agreeably, with the rheumatism just creeping all over me! but still, expecting something a little comfortable, I wait patiently to know his gracious pleasure, and then, 'Here, Goldsworthy, I say!' he cries, 'will you have a little barley water?' Barley water in such a plight as that! Fine compensation for a wet jacket, truly!—barley water! I never heard of such a thing in my life! Barley water after a whole day's hard hunting!" . . .

December 25.

. . . Colonel Goldsworthy was in one of his most facetious humours, and . . . ran on, till General Budé reminded him it was time they should appear in the concert room.

"Aye," cried he, "now for the fiddlers! There I go, plant myself against the side of the chimney, stand first on one foot, then on the other, hear over and over again all that fine squeaking, and then fall fast asleep, and escape by mere miracle from flouncing down plump in all their faces!"

"What would the Queen say if you did that?"

"Oh, ma'am, the Queen would know nothing of the matter; she'd only suppose it some old double bass that tumbled. . . . But the worst is, sometimes, when my poor eye-peepers are not quite closed, I look to the music books to see what's coming; and there I read *Chorus of Virgins:* so then, when they begin, I look about me. A chorus of virgins, indeed! Why, there's nothing but ten or a dozen fiddlers!" . . .

December 30.

This morning my dear father carried me to Dr. Herschel [the astronomer]. . . . His immense new telescope, the largest ever constructed, will still, I fear, require a year or two more for finishing, but I hope it will then reward his labour and ingenuity by the new views of the heavenly bodies, and their motions, which he flatters himself will be procured by it. Already, with that he has now in use, he has discovered fifteen hundred universes! How many more he may find who can conjecture? . . . By the invitation of Mr. Herschel, I now took a walk which will sound to you rather strange; it was through his telescope! and it held me quite upright, and without the least inconvenience; so would it have done had I been dressed in feathers and a bell hoop —such is its circumference.

November 1, 1788.

Our King does not advance in amendment; he grows so weak that he walks like a gouty man, yet has such spirits that he has talked away his voice, and is so hoarse it is painful to hear him. . . .

November 3.

The King is better and worse so frequently, and changes so, daily, backwards and forwards, that everything is to be apprehended, if his nerves are not some way quieted. The Queen is almost overpowered with some secret terror. . . .

November 5.

Oh, dreadful day! . . . At noon the King went out in his chaise, with the Princess Royal, for an airing. I looked from my window; he . . . gave so many orders to the postilions, and got in and out of the carriage twice, with such agitation, that again my fear of a great fever hanging over him grew more and more powerful. . . . The King, at dinner, had broken forth into positive delirium, which long had been menacing all who saw him most closely; and the Queen was so overpowered as to fall into violent hysterics. All the princesses were in misery, and the Prince of Wales had burst into tears. . . .

November 6.

I rose at six, dressed in haste by candle light. . . . The King, in the middle of the night, had insisted upon seeing if his Queen was not removed from the house; and he had come into her room, with a candle in his hand, opened the bed-curtains, and satisfied himself she was there. . . . He stayed a full half hour, and the depth of terror during that time no words can paint. . . . "I am nervous," he cried; "I am not ill, but I am nervous: if you would know what is the matter with me, I am nervous. . . ."

February 2, 1789.

What an adventure had I this morning! one that has occasioned me the severest personal terror I ever experienced in my life. . . . I strolled into the gardens. I had proceeded, in my quick way, nearly half the round, when I perceived, through some trees . . . the person of his Majesty! Alarmed past all possible expression, I waited not to know more, but turning back, ran off with all my might. But what was my terror to hear myself pursued! to hear the voice of the King himself loudly and hoarsely calling after me: "Miss Burney! Miss Burney!"

I protest I was ready to die. I knew not in what state he might be at the time. . . . On I ran, too terrified to stop, and in search of some short passage, for the garden is full of little labyrinths, by which I might escape. The steps still pursued me, and . . . Heavens, how I ran! I do not think I should have felt the hot lava from Vesuvius—at least not the hot cinders—had I so run during its eruption. My feet were not sensible that they even touched the ground. . . . I fairly believe no one of the whole party could have overtaken me, if these words, from one of the attendants, had not reached me: "Doctor Willis begs you to stop!" . . . Then, indeed, I stopped—in a state of fear really amounting to agony. I turned round, I saw the two Doctors had got the King between them, and three attendants of Dr. Willis's were hovering about. . . . I fairly think I may reckon it the greatest effort of personal courage I have ever made. The effort answered: I looked up, and met all his wonted benignity of countenance, though something still of wildness in his eyes. Think, however, of my surprise, to feel him put both his hands round my two shoulders, and then kiss my cheek!

I wonder I did not really sink, so exquisite was my affright when I saw him spread out his arms! Involuntarily, I concluded he meant to crush me: but . . . he now spoke in such terms of his pleasure in seeing me, that I soon lost the whole of my terror. . . . What a conversation followed! . . . What did he not say! He opened his whole heart to me—expounded all his sentiments, and acquainted me with all his intentions . . . but ended it more seriously: he suddenly stopped, and held me to stop too, and putting his hand on my breast, in the most solemn manner, he gravely and slowly said: "I will protect you!—I promise you that—and therefore depend upon me!" . . . Finding we now must part, he stopped to take leave, and . . . saluted me again just as at the meeting, and suffered me to go on. . . .

February 18.

The King I have seen again—in the Queen's dressing-room. On opening the door, there he stood! He smiled at my start, and saying he had waited on purpose to see me, added: "I am quite well now—I was nearly so when I saw you before—but I could overtake you better now!"

May 28, 1790.

. . . Three hours' conference with my dearest father—the only conference of that length I have had in four years . . . and he repeated sundry speeches of discontent at my seclusion from the world. . . . I owned the species of life distasteful to me; I was lost to all private comfort, dead to all domestic endearment; I was worn with want of rest, and fatigued with laborious watchfulness and attendance. My time was devoted to official duties; and all that in life was dearest to—my friends, my chosen society, my best affections —lived now in my mind only by recollection, and rested upon that with nothing but bitter regret. . . . "I have long," he cried, "been uneasy, though I have not spoken—but—if you wish to resign—my house, my purse, my arms shall be open to receive you back!"

October. Undated.

I was ill the whole of this month. . . . And now for a scene a little surprising. The beautiful chapel of St. George . . . brought innumerable strangers to Windsor, and, among others, Mr. Boswell. This I heard, in my way to the chapel, from Mr. Turbulent, who overtook me, and mentioned having met Mr. Boswell at the Bishop of Carlisle's the evening before. He proposed bringing him to call upon me; but this I declined, certain how little satisfaction would be given here by the entrance of a man so famous for compiling anecdotes. But yet I really wished to see him again, for old acquaintance sake, and . . . accordingly, at the gate of the choir, Mr. Turbulent brought him to me. We saluted with mutual glee: his comic-serious face and manner have lost nothing of their wonted singularity; nor yet have his mind and language.

"I am extremely glad to see you, indeed," he cried, "but very sorry to see you here. My dear ma'am, why do you stay?—it won't do, ma'am! you must resign! we can put up with it no longer. I told my good host the Bishop so last night; we are all grown quite outrageous!"

Whether I laughed the most, or stared the most, I am at a loss to say; but I hurried away from the cathedral, not to have such treasonable declarations overheard, for we were surrounded by a multitude. He accompanied me, however, not losing one moment in continuing his exhortations:

"I want your help."

"My help?"

"Yes, madam; you must give me some of your choice little notes of the Doctor's; we have seen him long enough upon stilts; I want to show him in a new light. Grave Sam, and great Sam, and solemn Sam, and learned Sam— all these he has appeared over and over. Now I want to entwine a wreath of graces across his brow; I want to show him as gay Sam, agreeable Sam, pleasant Sam: so you must help me with some of his beautiful billets to yourself."

I evaded this by declaring I had not any stores at hand. He proposed a thousand curious expedients to get at them, but I was invincible. . . . He then told me his *Life of Dr. Johnson* was nearly printed, and took a proof sheet out of his pocket to show me; with crowds passing and repassing, knowing me well, and staring well at him: for we were now at the iron rails of the Queen's Lodge.

I stopped; I could not ask him in: I saw he expected it, and was reduced to apologize. . . .

However, I saw him again the next morning, in coming from early prayers, and he again renewed his remonstrances and his petition for my letters of Dr. Johnson. I cannot consent to print private letters, even of a man so justly celebrated, when addressed to myself. . . .

July 7, 1791.

. . . I took, for the last time, the cloak of the Queen, and putting it over her shoulders, slightly ventured to press them earnestly, though in a low voice, saying: "God Almighty bless your Majesty!" She turned round, and, putting her hand upon my ungloved arm, pressed it with the greatest kindness, and said: "May you be happy!" . . .

Here, therefore, end my Court Annals; after having lived in the service of her Majesty five years within ten days—from July 17, 1786, to July 7, 1791.

". . . I bade adieu to Mount Vernon, to private life,
and to domestic felicity . . ."

George Washington

The boy who chopped down the cherry tree, at least in popular
legend, grew up to be the proprietor of cherry trees almost beyond number and vast agricultural riches besides, at Mount
Vernon and its extensive surrounding plantations where he lived
the comfortable life of a bluff, fox-hunting Virginia squire with
his wife and 216 slaves.

As soldier, legislator, commander of the Revolutionary forces,
and first President, George Washington (1732–1799) was often
away from Mount Vernon. But always he looked forward to coming back. Unfortunately, when his grateful countrymen released
him at last from a series of responsibilities greater than any ever
assumed by an American, only a few short years remained to him.
He died at Mount Vernon, however, as he wished, "amid the mild
concerns of ordinary life."

General Washington was a confirmed diarist and the records he
kept of his public life furnish much of the substance of many
biographies. For the most part the excerpts chosen here from the
eighteen hundred or so printed diary pages show glimpses of his
less familiar private life. He is seen as hunter and planter, ranging over his estates; sojourning in Philadelphia at the Constitutional Convention; visiting again the encampments at Valley
Forge; calling at Benjamin Franklin's house to see a machine for
pressing "called a Mangle"; departing to assume the Presidency;
receiving the first federal budget ($551,491.71); choosing places
for the first public buildings in the newly laid out District of
Columbia; and at last writing his final entry only a few hours before his death.

January 28, 1786.

Went out after breakfast with my hounds. Found a Fox in the Branch within

From *The Diaries of George Washington,* edited by John C. Fitzpatrick. Reprinted
by permission of and arrangement with Houghton Mifflin Company, the authorized publishers.

Mr. Thomson Mason's Field and run him sometimes hard and sometimes at cold hunting from 11 o'clock till near two, when I came home and left the huntsmen with them, who followed in the same manner two hours or more longer, and then took the Dogs off without killing. In the course of the chase, and at the upper end of the cover in which the above Fox was found, I see two run out at once, neither of which appear to be the chased Fox. This shows how plenty they are on that side the Creek. . . .

February 10.

This day was remarkably fine and promotive of vegetation. The buds of the lylack were much swelled and seemed ready to unfold. . . . I began to hand weed the drilled Wheat from the Cape behind the stables. The . . . last sowed wheat had, within these few days, vegitated a good deal, and was stooling very prettily. Making up the banks round the Serpentine walks to the front gate.

February 11.

. . . Brought a Goose and Gander of the Chinese breed of Geese, from the Reverend Mr. Griffiths; and also two of the large white (or Portugal) Peach trees. . . .

February 18.

. . . The Bitch Stately was lined by the Dog Vulcan. Jupiter had been put to her and Venus, but never seemed to take the least notice of them; but whether he ever lined either of them is not certain. The contrary is supposed. . . . Took a list to day all my Negroes which are as follow, at Mount Vernon and the plantations around it—viz. . . . Total 216.

April 20.

. . . The Shad began to run to day, having caught 100, 200 and 300 at a draught. My Jack covered a she Mule to day, after which two Mares. . . .

May 18.

. . . John Knowles came here to work at £5 pr. month, and a pint of rum pr. day.

August 29.

Plowed up the Cowpens on the left of the road in order to sow Turneps but was prevented by the rain. Spreading stable dung on the poorest parts of my clover at home.
Thatching the Hay stacks at the same place.
Taken with an Ague about 7 Oclock this morning which being succeeded

by a smart fever confined me to the House till evening. Had a slight fit of both on Sunday last. . . .

November 16.

. . . On my return home, found Mons. Campoint, sent by the Marqs. de la Fayette with the Jack and two She Asses which he had procured for me in the Island of Malta, and which had arrived at Baltimore with the Chinese Pheasants, &ca., had, with my Overseer, &ca., got there before me. These Asses are in good order and appear to be very fine. The Jack is two years old and the She Asses, one three and the other two. The Pheasants and Partridges will come round by Water.

May 7, 1787.

At home preparing for my journey to Philadelphia [to the Constitutional Convention]. . . .

May 9.

Crossed from Mt. Vernon to Mr. Digges a little after Sun rise and pursuing the rout by the way of Baltimore, dined at Mr. Richd. Henderson's in Bladensbg., and lodged at Majr. Snowden's, where, feeling very severely a violent hd.ach and sick stomach, I went to bed early.

May 10.

Very great appearances of rain in the morning, and a little falling, induced me, tho' well recovered to wait till abt. 8 Oclock before I set off. At one Oclock I arrived at Baltimore. Dined at the Fountain, and Supped and lodged at Doctr. McHenry's. Slow rain in the Evening.

May 11.

Set off before breakfast, rid 12 miles to Skerrett's [Tavern] for it; baited there, and proceeded without halting (weather threatning) to the Ferry at Havre de gras, where I dined, but could not cross, the wind being turbulent and squally. Lodged here.

May 12.

With difficulty (on acct. of the Wind) crossed the Susquehanna. . . .

May 13.

About 8 Oclock . . . set out, and dined at Chester (Mrs. Withys), where I was met by the Genls. Mifflin (now Speaker of the Pennsylvania Assembly) Knox and Varnum; the Colonels Humphreys and Minges; and Majors Jackson and Nicholas, with whom after dinner I proceeded to Philada. At Gray's

Ferry the city light horse, commanded by Colo. Miles, met me, and . . .
saluted as I passed. Alighted through a crowd at Mrs. House's [who kept a
boarding-house]; but being again and warmly pressed by Mr. and Mrs. Robt.
Morris to lodge with them, I did so, and had my baggage removed thither.
Waited on the President, Doctr. Franklin, as soon as I got to town. On my
arrival, the Bells were chimed.

May 14.

This being the day appointed for the Convention to meet, such members
as were in town assembled at the State Ho. but only two States being represented viz. Virginia and Philadelphia, agreed to attend at the same place
tomorrow at 11 Oclock. Dined in a family way at Mr. Morris's and drk. Tea
there.

May 16.

No more than two States being yet represented . . . Dined at the President Doctr. Franklin's, and drank Tea, and spent the evening at Mr. Jno.
Penn's.

May 18.

The representation from New York appeared on the floor today. Dined
at a Club at Gray's ferry, over the Schuylkill and drank Tea at Mr. Morris's;
after which accompanied Mrs. and some other ladies to hear a Mrs. O'Connell
read (a charity affair), The lady being reduced in circumstances had had
recourse to this expedient to obtain a little money. Her performance was
tolerable. at the College Hall.

May 22.

The Representation from No. Carolina was compleated, which made a
representation for five States. Dined and drank Tea at Mr. Morris's.

May 25.

Another Delegate coming in from the State of New Jersey gave it a representation and encreased the number to seven, which, forming a quorum of
the 13, the Members present resolved to organize the body; when by a unanimous vote I was called up to the Chair as President of the body. . . .

May 28.

Met in Convention at 10 Oclock. Two States more—viz. Massachusetts and
Connecticut . . . were on the floor today. Established Rules, agreeably to
the plan brot. in by the Comee. for the governmt. of the Convention and adjourned (about 2 Oclock). No Com'ns without doors [i.e., the deliberations

were to be secret]. Dined at home, and drank Tea in a large circle at Francis's.

June 2.

. . . A representation to Maryland; which brought all the States in the Union into Convention, except Rhode Island, which had refused to send delegates thereto. Dined at the City Tavern with the Club and spent the evening at my own quarters.

June 10.

Breakfasted by agreement at Mr. Powell's, and in company with him rid to see the Botanical garden of Mr. Bartram which, tho' stored with many curious plts. shrubs and trees, many of which are exotics, was not laid off with much taste, nor was it large. From hence we rid to the Farm of one Jones, to see the effect of the plaister of Paris, which appeared obviously great . . . for where the Plaister had been spread the white and red clover was luxuriant; and but little of either beyond it, and these thin. The soil of these appeared loamy, slightly mixed with Ising-glass and originally had been good; but according to Jones's account was much exhausted. . . . This manure he put on the 29th of October in a wet or a moist spell, and whilst the Moon was in its increase, which Jone says (though there certainly can be nothing in it) he was directed to attend to (but this must be whimsical) and at the rate of about 5 bushls. to the Acre. . . . Returned to the City abt. dark.

July 27.

In Convention, which adjourned this day, to meet again on Monday the 6th of August, that a Comee. which had been appointed (consisting of 5 Members) might have time to arrange, and draw into method and form the several matters which had been agreed to by the Convention as a Constitution for the United States. Dined at Mr. Morris's, and drank Tea at Mr. Powell's.

July 30.

In company with Mr. Govr. Morris and in his Phaeton with my horses, went up to one, Jane Moore's, (in whose house we lodged) in the vicinity of Valley Forge to get Trout.

July 31.

Whilst Mr. Morris was fishing, I rid over the whole old Cantonment of the American Army of the Winter, 1777 and 8, visited all the Works, wch. were in Ruins; and the Incampments in woods where the grounds had not been cultivated. . . .

September 3.

In Convention. Visited a Machine at Doctr. Franklin's (called a Mangle) for pressing, in place of ironing, clothes from the Wash. Which Machine from the facility with which it dispatches business is well calculated for Table cloths and such articles as have not pleats and irregular foldings and would be very useful. . . .

September 17.

Met in Convention, when the Constitution received the unanimous assent of 11 States . . . and was subscribed to by every Member present except Govr. Randolph and Colo. Mason from Virginia, and Mr. Gerry from Massachusetts. The business being thus closed, the Members adjourned to the City Tavern, dined together and took a cordial leave of each other; after which I returned to my lodgings, did some business with, and received the papers from the Secretary of the Convention, and retired to meditate on the momentous work which had been executed, after not less than five, for a large part of the time Six, and sometimes 7 hours sitting every day, except sundays and the ten days adjournment to give a comee. opportunity and time to arrange the business, for more than four months.

March 31, 1788.

. . . [At home again] Visited all the Plantations. In the Neck, began to sow in the So. Wt. part of the West Cut of No. 2 . . . At Muddy Hole, began to sow Barley and grass-seeds . . . at Dogue run, finished sowing and harrowing Oats . . . began Saturday afternoon to plow for Engh. Barley in the Turnip ground at this place. At French's . . . the Women, in part were filling gullies in No. 3, and . . . the Cart gettg. dung to the gullies which had been levelled in the lower meadow. At the Ferry, harrowing in Oats with one harrow, the . . . Women hoeing in the swamp as before. In my Botanical Garden, next the Necessary House, was sown 3 rows of Grass-seeds sent me from Kentucke by Colo. Marshall, name unknown; and the next 3 rows to these were sown with what this gentleman calls wild Rye but it more resembles Oats. All the other Rows of this were of the painted lady Pease. Put in cuttings of the Weeping Willow, behind the Post and Rail fence along the Road leading to the Gate in the hollow. . . .

November 14.

Mr. Wilming . . . having offered to engage a Gardener for me and to send him in a ship from Bremen, I requested that it might not exceed the following conditions for him and his Wife (if he brings one): viz. Ten pounds sterling for the 1st year, Eleven for the 2d., Twelve for the 3d., and so on, a pound increase, till the sum should amt. to 15, beyond which not to go. That he would be found a comfortable House, or room in one, with bedding, victuals and drink; but no clothes, *these* for *self* and *wife* to be provided at his own expence. That he is to be a compleat Kitchen Gardener with a competent knowledge of Flowers and a Green House. And that he is to come under Articles and firmly bound. His, or their passages to be on as low terms as it can be obtained. The Wife if one comes is to be a Spinner, dairy Woman, or something of that usefulness. . . .

February 2, 1789.

. . . I went up to the election . . . and returned home in the afternoon. On my way home met Mr. George Calvert on his way to Abingdon with the Hounds I had lent him: viz.—Vulcan and Venus, from France; Ragman and two other dogs, from England; Dutchess and Doxey, from Philadelphia. Jupiter and Countess, descended from the French Hounds.

[Thus ends the last page of this volume of the diary and the succeeding volume has been lost containing his record of his election to the Presidency, and his first months in office in New York, then the Capital. The following entry survives from Jared Sparks' *Writings of Washington* (1836):]

April 16.

About ten o'clock I bade adieu to Mount Vernon, to private life, and to domestic felicity, and with a mind oppressed with more anxious and painful sensations than I have words to express, set out for New York . . . with the best disposition to render service to my country in obedience to its calls, but with less hope of answering its expectations.

[The surviving journal resumes in October.]

October 9.

Exercised on horseback between the hours of 9 and 11. . . . The visiters this evening to Mrs. Washington were respectable, both of gentlemen and ladies.

October 10.

. . . I set off about 9 o'clock in my barge to visit Mr. Prince's fruit gardens and shrubberis at Flushing, on Long Island. . . . These gardens, except in the number of young fruit trees, did not answer my expectations. The shrubs were trifling, and the flowers not numerous. The inhabitants of this place shewed us what respect they could, by making the best use of one cannon to salute. On our return we stopped at the seats of General and Mr. Gouvernr. Morris, and viewed a barn, of which I had heard the latter speak much, belonging to his farm—but it was not of a construction to strike my fancy—nor did the conveniences of it at all answer their cost. From hence we proceeded to Harlaem . . . and came home in the evening.

November 15.

Went to St. Paul's Chapel in the forenoon—and after returning from thence . . received an invitation to attend the Funeral of Mrs. Roosevelt, (the wife of a Senator of this State) but declined. . . .

November 26.

Being the day appointed for a thanksgiving, I went to St. Paul's Chapel, though it was most inclement and stormy—but few people at Church.

January 8, 1790.

. . . At 11 o'clock, I set out for the City Hall in my coach . . . followed by . . . the Chief Justice of the United States and Secretary of the Treasury and War Departments, in their respective carriages, and in the order they are named. At the outer door of the hall I was met by the door-keepers of the Senate and House, and conducted to the door of the Senate Chamber; and passing from thence to the Chair through the Senate on the right, and House of Representatives on the left, I took my seat. The gentlemen who attended me followed and took their stand behind the Senators; the whole rising as I entered. After being seated, at which time the members of both Houses also sat, I rose, (as they also did) and made my speech [the first Annual Message to the First Congress] . . . after which, and being a few moments seated, I retired, bowing on each side to the assembly (who stood) as I passed, and descending to the lower hall, attended as before, I returned with them to my house.

In the evening a *great* number of ladies, and many gentlemen visited Mrs. Washington. On this occasion I was dressed in a suit of clothes made at the Woolen Manufactory at Hartford, as the buttons also were.

January 9.

Exercised with Mrs. Washington and the children in the coach the 14 miles round. In the afternoon walked round the Battery.

February 1.

Agreed on Saturday last to take Mr. McCombs' house [on the west side of Broadway, below Trinity Church], lately occupied by the Minister of France, for one year. . . .

February 6.

Walked to my newly engaged lodgings to fix on a spot for a new stable which I was about to build. Agreed . . . to erect one 30 feet square, 16 feet pitch, to contain 12 single stalls; a hay loft, racks, manger, etc., planked floor, and underpinned with stone, with windows between each stall, for £65. . . .

February 23.

. . . After dinner, Mrs. Washington, myself, and children removed, and lodged at our new habitation.

March 16.

. . . Visited (having given permisn.) by a Mr. Warner Miflin, one of the People called Quakers; active in pursuit of the Measures laid before Congress for emancipating the Slaves: after much general conversation . . . he used arguments to show the immorality—injustice—and impolicy of keeping these people in a state of Slavery; with declarations, however, that he did not wish for more than a gradual abolition, or to see any infraction of the Constitution to effect it. To these I replied, that as it was a matter which might come before me for official decision I was not inclined to express any sentimts. on the merits of the question. . . .

March 25.

. . . Received from . . . a Comee. of Congress two Acts—one, for establishing the mode for uniformity in Naturalization of Foreigners [two years' residence required]—the other making appropriations for the support of Government for the year 1790. By this last was granted,

doll'rs	cents	
141.492—	73—	for the Civil list.
155.537—	72—	War Department.
96.979—	72—	Invalid Pensions.
10.000—		President for Contingent Services of Government.
147.169—	54—	For demands enumerated by the Secrety. of the Treas'y on wch. the light Ho. on Cape Henry is includ'd.
120—		To Jehoiakim McToksin [interpreter and guide on an expedition against the Indian peoples]
96—		To James Mathers [Door-keeper of the Senate]
96—		To Gifford Dally [Door-keeper of the House]
551.491—	71.	Total amount.

June 27, 1791.

Left Mount Vernon for Georgetown before Six oclock; and according to appointment met the Commisioners at that place by 9—then calling together the Proprietors of those Lands on which the federal City [i.e., the District of Columbia] was proposed to be built who had agreed to cede them on certain conditions . . . and giving some explanation of the present State of matters and the consequences of delay in this business they readily waved their objections and agd. to convey to the utmost extent of what was required.

June 28.

Whilst the Commissioners were engaged in preparing the Deeds . . . I went out with Majr. L'Enfant and Mr. Ellicot to take a more perfect view of the ground, in order to decide finally on the spots on which to place the public buildings. . . .

February 11, 1799.

Went up to Alexandria to the celebration of my birthday. Many Manoeuvres were performed by the Uniform Corps, and an elegant Ball and Supper at night.

July 4.

Went up to Alexa. and dined with a number of the Citizens there in celebration of the Anniversary of the declaration of American Independe. at Kemps Tavern.

December 13.

Morning Snowing and abt. 3 inches deep. Wind at No. Et. and Mer. at 30. contg. Snowing till 1 O'clock, and abt 4 it became perfectly clear. Wind in the same place but not hard. Mer. 28 at Night.

[These words were the last Washington wrote. "A heavy snow kept him from riding out as usual. He complained of a sore throat, and in the evening (December 13) he was very hoarse. Between two and three o'clock Saturday morning (December 14), he woke Mrs. Washington and told her he was ill. He could scarcely speak; but would not allow her to get up for fear of her catching cold. When daylight came, the household was aroused . . . about one half a pint of blood was taken and . . . various remedies, hot applications, gargles, foot-baths, etc. were tried. It was decided to bleed the General again, which still further weakened him without bringing any improvement. He gradually sank and died about 10 P.M. December 14, 1799. . . ."]

". . . I kept wondering whether the ghost . . .
might not emerge . . ."

Harold L. Ickes

For thirteen years the Secretary of the Interior in the administration of Franklin D. Roosevelt was a man known with varying
degrees of affection as the "Old Curmudgeon." Harold L. Ickes
(1874–1952) liked the epithet. He did not mind in the least being thought irascible; his honesty compelled him to admit that he
was just that—and if things did not always go his way he seemed
almost to enjoy being peppery, peevish and petulant.

These qualities are not often met with in a politician, but then
the United States has had few holders of public office anything
like Ickes. He was remarkable in two further respects. He held his
cabinet seat longer than any predecessor ever had. And he kept
what is quite possibly the most voluminous diary ever written—
one hundred volumes of closely typed manuscript totalling some
six million words, covering slightly more than a dozen years of
his life.

Ickes was born in Frankstown Township, Blair County, Pennsylvania. He showed an interest in politics at an early age. When
he was nine, during the Blaine-Cleveland presidential campaign,
he threw his support to Blaine. The family story has it that he
said, by way of explanation, "Cleveland is no good anyhow; he
can take off his collar without unbuttoning it."

He was educated at the University of Chicago, and from 1907
onwards practiced law and was active in the reform wing of the
Republican party. Ickes switched allegiance to support the Roosevelt ticket in 1932 and, somewhat to his surprise was named to
the new cabinet. As head of the public works program he super-
vised the spending of three and one-third billion dollars, and he
was also Petroleum Administrator.

Both friends and enemies generally agreed about his integrity
and incorruptibility, and both flinched at his outraged bellows
when, in his view, a danger threatened the country's natural re-

sources. He loved a fight, and was expert at roaring down an opponent.

As a diarist Ickes wrote with truculent candour; even in the expurgated version of his journals published shortly after his death, few public figures escaped the lash of his tongue. But accompanying his rude comments on the bureaucratic great, there is relish for the company of the famous and the well known. Perhaps there is no more revealing episode than that in which the ex-country boy from Pennsylvania entertains, with the aid of butlers, candlelight, song, and carefully selected wines, the President of the United States on his back lawn.

July 11, 1933.

I had an appointment with the President at nine thirty this morning. I was shown into his bedroom just as his breakfast tray was being brought out. He was sitting up in bed and received me with his usual charm. His bedroom is just to the right of the Oval Room on the second floor which he makes his White House office. I noticed that he had a telephone right at hand and in a nearby corner stood the apparatus that he has to wear to support his crippled legs. Near his bed stood his wheel chair. . . .

July 27.

There was a meeting of the Special Board for Public Works at two o'clock and . . . I had asked Chief of Staff MacArthur to come in on some Army projects. He had presented a very large list running into the hundreds of millions, out of which the President allowed him $6 million for coast defenses in the Canal Zone and Hawaii, in addition to $6 million previously allowed for ammunition. MacArthur is the type of man who thinks that when he gets to heaven, God will step down from the great white throne and bow him into His vacated seat, and it gave me a great kick to have him in and break the news to him. While he was here though, two or three of the members foolishly asked him some questions which gave him a chance to deliver a lecture on the subject of the necessity for the little old peanut Army posts that we have scattered around the country.

August 8.

At five o'clock I went to the home of Secretary of Commerce Roper for some watermelon and it was the best watermelon I have ever eaten—a special variety that is grown in only one county in South Carolina. Secretary of State Hull and Mrs. Hull were there, and Secretary Hull was quite frank in what he said about Dr. [Raymond] Moley at the London Economic Conference. . . . According to Hull, the impression at London was that Moley was going to come over and solve all the international economic difficulties. For several days preceding Moley's arrival he was heralded in all the newspapers and the conference practically ceased to do business in expectation of his arrival. The British sent airplanes out to meet him and hundreds of newspapermen in London flocked down to Liverpool or wherever it was that Moley landed. He was escorted in great state to London with all the Premiers and dignitaries from the attending nations doing him reverence. . . . Two prior proposals for a temporary stabilization of the dollar had been rejected by President Roosevelt but notwithstanding this, Moley undertook, at the instance of the gold countries, to negotiate a third settlement. . . . After it was approved he called Hull and told him that the agreement was ready and for him to come down and sign it as Secretary of State. . . . Hull refused to go and refused to sign. Hull was then told that on a certain morning Moley would be at 10 Downing Street with the assembled statesmen to receive the approval of President Roosevelt to the stabilization agreement. According to Mr. Hull, 10 Downing Street had a crowd in front of it such as hadn't been seen since the war. The visiting statesmen of the various nations entered at intervals and when they were all there and the stage well set, Moley appeared, the cynosure of all eyes, and entered the residence of the Prime Minister. . . . Moley and the other statesmen of the world sat there expectantly while the clock ticked on. After two or three hours had passed, Moley began to have some feeling of uncertainty. . . . The President subsequently turned down the proposition hard . . . a cold and hard turndown. Of course, from that time on, Moley's balloon was punctured.

I had dinner with Henry Morgenthau after I left the Ropers', at Olney Inn, a delightful place at Olney, Maryland. Here I heard some more dirt about the London Conference. I was told that a certain prominent United States Senator who was a member of the commission didn't attend a single meeting; that he was drunk practically all the time he was in London. . . .

August 21.

. . . Harry F. Sinclair was in to see me today. . . . This is the first time I had ever met Sinclair and I kept wondering whether the ghost of Albert B. Fall, carrying a little black satchel, might not emerge from one of the gloomy corners of this office.

August 29.

Yesterday morning at nine o'clock I started off for Hyde Park. . . . A picnic was planned for the evening at the instance of the newspaper correspondents. We all drove about two miles to a cottage where Mrs. Roosevelt and two women friends carry on their furniture-making industry, and where Mrs. Roosevelt has her office when she and the President are at Hyde Park. Here on a flat stretch of ground, well drained, we had a very satisfactory supper, cooked in the open, consisting of steak, roast Virginia ham, golden bantam corn, and a salad, followed by ice cream and chocolate cake. There was an enormous fireplace built at one end, in which a big fire was crackling. The newspaper men put on some stunts, mostly songs . . . and we had a very enjoyable evening. We got back to the President's home about ten o'clock . . . long and rambling and apparently containing many rooms, with an enormous living room at one end. It is situated on a high bluff overlooking the Hudson and in all directions could be seen running water and tree-covered heights. It is a perfectly charming place, such a place as I would dearly love to live in myself.

October 12.

At five o'clock I went to the White House for an interview with the President. It was the President's day for officially receiving the members of the Supreme Court. We waited in the parlor until this reception was over. On our way to the second floor the President remarked that whenever he saw a certain member of the Supreme Court he thought of that musical comedy— *Of Thee I Sing.* I told him I had the same feeling; that I didn't see why the member of the court in question hadn't shaved off his whiskers after that play. . . .

November 22.

Last night Anna [Mrs. Ickes] and I went to dinner at the Turkish Embassy. There were twenty-two guests present. . . . The house is a large one, richly furnished and beautiful. The appointments were magnificent in every respect, but when I got through dinner I was no longer surprised at what Mrs. Hiram Johnson told me on one occasion. I happened to drop in there about dinner time once and found that she and the Senator were having dinner although they were going out to an official dinner later. She explained that they always did that because at official dinners they gave you very little to eat and if you happened to turn your head to talk to a neighbor, when you looked around again you were likely to find that the butler had grabbed your plate from in front of you. There wasn't much to eat at the Turkish Minister's and it was a race against time to consume what you had before the butler disappeared with your plate. The result was that I actually got up from the table hungry. . . .

November 29.

Saturday afternoon at four forty-five I took the train for . . . Warm Springs, where I was the personal guest of the President. He has a small cottage beautifully located on the edge of a well-wooded ravine just a little way out of Warm Springs. He has only three bedrooms but Mrs. Roosevelt was not there and I occupied her room. A common bathroom connected the President's room and mine. Miss Le Hand, his personal secretary, had the other bedroom. Meals are served in the living room and the President works there. The President is always charming but he was delightful at Warm Springs. Everyone there loves him, and crowds hang outside the gate, especially on Sundays, just to see him and cheer him as he drives in and out occasionally. They stay there literally all day long, hour after hour. He didn't leave the house on Sunday until about three o'clock in the afternoon and there they still were, men, women, and children. He drives his own car at Warm Springs, an open Plymouth, so arranged with some contraption on the steering wheel that he can operate it without having to use his feet which are helpless. . . .

October 12, 1934.

I didn't get to sleep until about half past one, and then only after taking a pretty stiff drink of whisky. The result has been that all day I have been tired and sleepy, and yet I know that if I should go to bed I couldn't sleep. I lunched with the President today. I told him about the latest from the *Chicago Tribune,* and he agreed with me that it was the rottenest newspaper in the whole United States.

December 19.

. . . The President and Mrs. Roosevelt gave their annual official dinner to the Cabinet last night. There were about eighty at table. I am bound to confess that the White House dinners are neither inspiring nor do they stand out as Lucullan repasts. I am not very fussy about my food and I suppose one ought to be satisfied with dining on and with a solid-gold service, but it does seem a little out of proportion to use a solid-gold knife and fork on ordinary roast mutton. Besides which, I never did like carrots.

Wine was served officially at dinner for the first time since prohibition went into effect back in President Wilson's administration. Mrs. Roosevelt had announced that she would serve one glass each of two domestic wines and she kept her word. The sherry was passable, but the champagne was undrinkable. I hopefully took one drink and then set my glass down with a final gesture. Mrs. Farley almost made a face when she tasted the champagne. She was quite indignant but consoled herself with the reflection that she had had some real champagne before she went to the White House and that more would be awaiting her on her return to the Mayflower. She seems to be quite fussy about the quality and quantity of her wines, although Jim never touches a drop. I am bound to say, however, that probably on only one other occasion have I ever tasted worse champagne, and it does seem to me that if decent champagne can't be made in the United States, it ought to be permissible, even for the White House to serve imported champagne. . . . The dinner was followed by a musicale in the East Room. It wasn't a particularly good one and I found my chair as uncomfortable as I did last season. . . .

July 16, 1935.

I went down to Jefferson Island in Chesapeake Bay on Sunday as a guest of the Jefferson Club, which is almost exclusively a Democratic Club. The officers and directors, almost without exception, are Democratic members of the Senate. . . . We arrived at the island about eleven o'clock. The President, with a party, of which the Vice President was a member, had gone down on Saturday. His party was just getting up when we arrived, as the result of a poker game the night before which had lasted until four o'clock Sunday morning. The Vice President is supposed to be the best poker player in Washington, but the President took him into camp. He told me with great delight later how on one hand, when there was a big jackpot, he had outbluffed the Vice President, inducing him to lay down two pairs topped by kings, whereas the President had only 7's and 4's. According to reports, this just about broke the heart of the Vice President. During the game Senator Pittman remarked of the Vice President that when he bet ten cents, it wasn't merely ten cents but the interest on $2 for a year. . . .

There was a plentiful cold lunch and abundant liquid refreshments. There was a little card playing, some clay pigeon shooting, and some crabbing, but generally people just sat around and talked and had a good time. . . .

July 22.

I had an exceptionally bad night last night. I hardly slept at all, in spite of liberal libations of whisky, which usually puts me to sleep. . . .

August 23.

I had a ten-thirty appointment with the President this morning. . . . When I got up to his study, his valet ushered me into his bedroom, telling me that the President was shaving. He waved toward the bathroom and the President called out to me to come in. There he was, sitting before a mirror in front of the washstand, shaving. He invited me to sit on the toilet seat while we talked. When he was through shaving he was wheeled back to his room where he reclined on his bed again while his valet proceeded to help him dress. . . .

August 27.

. . . After dinner I went to the Senate Chamber. The expectation was that Congress would adjourn not later than midnight. . . . While the motion was being debated in the Senate and the House, Huey Long took advantage of the situation to deliver one of his typical speeches. I had never really seen him at his best, and he was at his best Saturday night. He waved his arms, he contorted, he swayed, and at all times he talked in a very loud voice. I must admit, however, that he was clever. Any Senator who ventured to cross swords with him was usually discomfited. He has a sharp quick wit, even though he is a blatant and unconscionable demagogue.

The Vice President had apparently had enough whisky to pep him up because he presided in a very sprightly manner. I do not mean to imply that he was under the influence of liquor because he didn't appear to be. But he was on his toes. Senator Clark also evidently had had one or two drinks too many because he tried to engage in a physical brawl with Senator Tydings when Tydings referred to a statement by Clark as not being the truth. . . . I didn't get home until half past twelve.

September 13.

. . . Frank Walker [later Postmaster General] had reached Hyde Park Wednesday morning and he and I roomed together. He confided to me that his wife said he was a terrible snorer and he warned me that I ought to go to sleep before he went to bed. I wasn't able to do that and I don't think it would have done me any good anyhow. All I can say about Frank is that he fully lived up to the advance notices of his prowess in that direction. I have never heard anyone snore worse but there were intermissions and when he was going it the strongest, I would turn promptly over onto my good ear. It seemed strange to room with a man that I know as slightly as I know Frank. I confess that it seemed even stranger to see him sink to his knees for a long prayer. I had hardly realized how far in the past that sort of thing was with me, and it all goes to show that religion has a much firmer grip on a Catholic than it has on a Protestant. At any rate, I admired his sincerity. . . .

July 10, 1936.

After dinner Tuesday I had a call from Miss Le Hand, who said that the President would like to come out to my house for dinner on Wednesday night. Several months ago the President had remarked to Miss Le Hand that he wished he knew some place in the country where he could go and have a quiet and undisturbed evening and she told him that my place was just right for that sort of thing, she just having been there for dinner. I got in some extra help on Wednesday and invited the following persons at the suggestion of Miss Le Hand: Miss Grace Tully [assistant secretary to President Roosevelt], Mr. and Mrs. C. R. Larrabee [government official], Tom Corcoran [RFC counsel], Alfred Hobson, Assistant Secretary of RFC, and Miss Le Hand herself.

The President got out [to Ickes' country home] about a quarter to seven. The dining table was set on the lawn, since it was a warm, clear day with no wind. Fortunately, the President's car could bring him within a very few feet of the place where the table was by coming round the house and the garage. From the car he was carried to my own favorite chair which I had had taken out on the lawn for him. After cocktails and cocktail sandwiches, we moved him over to the table where the eight of us sat down. We started with honeydew melon, then had cold salmon with mayonnaise dressing, as well as cucumbers and tomatoes, bread and butter, then squab with peas and potatoes. Then followed a green salad with a choice of cream, Swiss, or Roquefort cheese. For dessert there was my own special ice cream, black raspberry, with cookies and coffee to finish with. For wines, I served Château Yquem, a good claret, and a good vintage champagne. We had liqueurs afterward and when the dining table had been removed, the butlers brought out and put on a table, with a supply of cracked ice, Scotch, rye and bourbon whisky, gin and Bacardi rum. To go with these we had White Rock and ginger ale.

The party was a great success, although personally I did not contribute anything to it. I have been very much out of sorts lately. I have been sleeping worse than I have been sleeping for years, with the result that I have been taking soporifics practically every night. I have been very tired and depressed and even the honor of this occasion, graced as it was with the President, was not sufficient to shift the load that I have been carrying.

Tom Corcoran had brought his accordion with him and he played and sang practically the whole evening. Hobson sang two or three times and a few stories were told. The President seemed to enjoy himself hugely and he entered into the fun very naturally and spontaneously. I kept them all supplied with their favorite highballs. The President certainly carries his liquor well. He must have had five highballs after dinner. He drank gin and ginger ale but he never showed the slightest effect. I am glad to say that nobody showed any signs of having had too much to drink although everyone had all that he wanted. He must have had a good time because he didn't leave until half past twelve and then only after Miss Le Hand prodded him two or three times and insisted that he must go home and to bed. . . . It was lovely out on the lawn with almost an entire absence of insect life. Just before dessert we had candles lighted on the table and we kept them burning throughout the rest of the evening. This was all the light that we had, except what came from the house, until the late moon came up. Although the weather was warm, it was quite tolerable and no one suffered from the heat, while at the same time no one had to put on anything extra to keep warm. It was difficult to realize that this man who was so friendly and delightful and who entered into the affair so wholeheartedly was the President of the United States. . . .

> "... immobilized ... in old human dreams that
> have almost disappeared from the earth."

Pierre Loti

Pierre Loti (1850–1923) spent most of his life as a French naval
officer, and yet he was elected to the French Academy (the
"academy of the immortals") and is numbered among the important French writers of the late nineteenth century.

He was born Louis Marie Julien Viaud in Rochefort of an old
Presbyterian family. His naval career began at seventeen, and he
rose to the rank of Captain before his retirement. He was called
back to active service during the first World War, largely because
of his expert knowledge of Pacific waters where he had spent
most of his years at sea. He was married to Judith Gautier, poet
and orientalist, the daughter of Théophile Gautier.

Not much given to books, study or writing in early years, the
dozens of books signed with the pseudonym "Loti" were written in his maturity. The best known of them are *Madame
Chrysanthème*, an account of Japanese life, and *Pêcheur d'Islande*,
a tale of Breton fishermen in Iceland—his first great success.

In 1889, Loti was named a member of a French diplomatic
mission sent to Fez, ancient capital of the sultanate of Morocco.
Among other things, the mission carried with it on its difficult
overland journey an electric-powered boat, a present to the Sultan
from the French government. In the journal Loti kept, published
as *Au Maroc*, the Sultan's boat keeps appearing and reappearing
as it is borne along on the shoulders of forty perspiring Arabs,
an absurdly incongruous object in a dusty, cruel, almost unim-
aginably remote and primitive scene.

March 26, 1889.

. . . I experience, as I land today on this quay of Tangier in the bright noon
sunshine, a sense of translation. . . . Here, it is as if a white shroud impended
over everything, shutting out the sounds that exist elsewhere, stilling all the
modern activities of life: the old shroud of Islam. . . . And I am yet only on

From *Morocco* by Pierre Loti, translated by W. P. Baines. Reprinted by permission
of J. B. Lippincott Company.

the threshold . . . Fez, which is the goal of our journey, is far away, under
the burning sun, in the heart of this closed, unchanging country, where life
remains the same today as it was a thousand years ago.

April 3.

Eight days of waiting, of preparations, of delays. . . . The departure is
fixed at last for tomorrow morning. . . .

April 4.

. . . Before sunrise the din has become a thing infernal: shrill cries, such
as monkeys utter; a savage hurly-burly that might well strike terror. As I lie
half-awake I could imagine, if I were not used to these uproars of Africa,
that a fight, and one of a most barbarous kind, was proceeding under my
window; that throats were being cut, that destruction was afoot. But I tell
myself, simply: "Our beasts are arriving and the muleteers are beginning to
load them." It is an awkward business, truly, to load some five score obstinate
mules and stupid camels, in little streets that are barely two yards across. . . .
Our mission consists of fifteen persons, of whom seven of us are officers; our
uniforms, also, contribute to this picture of departure a note of diversity, of
colour, of gold. Five blue-cloaked African guards accompany us. . . .

We have camped for the night. . . . My bed, which is very light, is
placed comfortably on my two cases, which uplift it sufficiently from the
ground, the crickets and the ants; my saddle, in guise of a pillow, raises it at
the head, and I am wrapped in a Moroccan blanket. . . . At midnight the
hail rattles outside and a mighty wind shakes the canvas of my tent. Then I
hear . . . men of the watch, come, by direction of the kaid [Sultan's func-
tionary sent to aid the mission], to tighten, by blows of mallet, the pegs of
my tent, so that the wind may not carry it away. I understand that when
the Sultan is on his travels, in his great tent of state, which needs for its transport sixty mules, if by chance a storm arise during the night, use is not made
of mallets for fear of disturbing the slumbers of the master and of the fair
ladies of the harem. Instead, they call up a regiment of men who crouch in
circle around the nomad palace and remain there till daybreak, holding in
innumerable fingers all the ropes of the wall. . . .

April 6.

. . . An extraordinary object which has accompanied us from Tangier and
which we have grown used to seeing, sometimes ahead of us, sometimes behind us, in the distance, is an electric launch, [a self-powered boat] some
twenty feet in length, which we are taking as a present to his Majesty the
Sultan. It is enclosed in a shell of greyish wood and has the appearance of a
block of granite; and it proceeds slowly, through the ravines, over the mountains, borne on the shoulders of two score Arabs. One may see huge things
of the kind in the Egyptian bas-reliefs, carried, like this, by trains of white-
robed, bare-legged men. We camp tonight at a place called Tlata-Raissana,

where, I am told, an immense market of beasts and slaves is held every month. . . .

April 7.

. . . And still it rains, rains in torrents. . . . The water streams from us all. And the Sultan's launch, always like some accessory of an Egyptian procession, advances with the utmost difficulty, the feet of its forty bearers sinking at each step into the sodden ground.

After travelling for two hours . . . we notice something like a very long fissure serpentining in the plain, something that bids fair to be a river with very steep banks. It is the Oued M'Cazen, reputed difficult to cross, and on its banks is an assemblage of unhappy augury: laden mules in hundreds, camels, horsemen, pedestrians, all brought to a stop there, evidently because the river is not fordable. The Oued, swollen by rains, is turbulent, rapid, rolls noisily its muddy waters. . . . With our European notions of travel, it would seem to us practically impossible, without some sort of bridge, to get our men, our baggage and tents across it. Our kaids, however, are of a different opinion, and are going to make the attempt, venturing first that which is of least consequence. First our serving men, who, in a trice, take off their bournouses, all their handsome draperies of grey wool, bare their graceful brown bodies and plunge into the cold and tormented water. . . . Let us try now some lightly burdened mules. Encouraged by blows, they enter the water and swim towards the middle; are bewildered for a minute in the current, which sweeps them along; then quickly feel their feet on the mud of the farther bank, with their load complete, though soaked with muddy water.

But how are we to cross, whose ambassadorial dignity prevents us from disrobing? And our mattresses? And our elegant uniforms with their facings of gold, which are to figure before the Sultan at the presentation? On the height of the opposite bank a small troop of horsemen arrives at a gallop, shouting lustily, and making signs to us. We are saved! It is one Shaoush of Czar-el-Kebir (a town we are approaching), who has come to our assistance, with a numerous suite, bringing a *mahàdia* constructed in haste against our need . . . a kind of sheaf, an enormous bundle of reeds, bound together in such a manner as to float. . . . As for the rest of our column, men and beasts, they have to swim, all of them, and as quickly as may be. . . . Resignedly, the handsome Arab horsemen disrobe, then unharness their horses too, and remount them, holding them forked between their strong limbs as in a vice of bronze. On their own heads they place in a monumental pile their caftans and their bournouses; above that again, their enormous high-peaked saddle, their gaily coloured harness; and then raise their arms, like the handles of a Grecian amphora, to support the whole. . . . The horses neigh with fear; slide, like one who skates, like one who toboggans, some still upright on their legs, others on their haunches, and, all covered with a sticky mud, plunge into the Oued with a great splashing of water; then swim in midstream and, on the hither bank, climb like goats. Out of the quantity there are a few that fall, that struggle, that kick; there are horsemen who are thrown into the river, with their bright folded bournouses, their handsome saddles, which in their top-heaviness drag them down. Some of the mules falter in distress in the mud: they are urged on by cries and blows, horribly wrung by the girths and pack-saddles, their flesh all raw; and the tents they carry, so white at the setting out, are now smothered in mud. . . . Towards the finish, the clayey earth of the banks is polished like a veritable mirror by the successive slippings. Then the crossing becomes a kind of catastrophe, a general downfall, to the accompaniment of furious cries; an immense confusion of maddened beasts, of naked men, of baggage of every sort, of red saddles, of packages wrapped in gaudy coverings. . . . At length . . . we are all, with our baggage, on the farther bank without drownings, without loss; our cases, our mattresses, soaked and covered with mud; our mules sore and breathless; ourselves, wet with rain only. And the desert of daffodils and irises begins again, tranquil and mournful, for another hour. . . .

April 10.

I am awakened by cries—horrible cries—quite near me; a kind of vile belching which seems to issue from some monstrous gullet suffocating with fury. . . . Rays of the rising sun outline in fantastic shadow on my [tent] wall the form of the beast responsible for these hideous cries: a long, long neck that twists like a caterpillar, and, at its extremity, a small, flattened head with hanging lips: a camel. I knew it indeed at once from the horrible voice: a fool of a camel, restive or in distress. I watch the movement of its silhouette with the greatest uneasiness. Confusion! What I feared has happened; the beast has caught its feet in the ropes of my tent, and struggles now, and bellows its hardest, shaking the whole tent, which threatens momentarily to collapse upon my head. Then I hear the camel-driver running up calling: "Ts! Ts! Ts!" (That is what is said to the camels to calm them. . . .)

April 12.

. . . The chief of the region in which we now are has not come to meet us, which is an extraordinary circumstance. For the first time we are without escort, alone. . . . At last our dilatory chief arrives with his troop. He is full of excuses; he was in pursuit of three Zemur brigands very dreaded in the country; he has succeeded in capturing them with their horses. They are now confined in safe custody in his house, whence they will be taken to Fez to undergo the "punishment of salt," as ordained by law. . . .

The Sultan's barber, it appears, is charged with it. The culprit, tightly bound, is brought to some public place, preferably to the market place. With a razor, lengthwise in the palm of each hand, four slits are cut to the bone. By stretching the palm, the lips of these four bleeding cuts are made to gape as much as possible and are filled with salt. The hands thus slashed are then closed, the tips of the fingers being inserted into the several slits, and in order that this atrocious arrangement may last till death, the hand is enclosed in a kind of tight glove, made of wet ox-hide, which shrinks as it dries. The cutting finished, the culprit is taken back to his cell, where, in exceptional cases, he is fed, in order to prolong his agony. From the first moment, in addition to the indescribable suffering, he has the anguish of knowing that this horrible glove will never be removed, that his fingers embedded in the quivering wounds will never be released, that no one in the world will take pity on him, that neither day nor night will bring a respite to his writhings and his shrieks of suffering. But the worst, so I am told, does not come till some days later —when the nails, growing into the hand, dig ever deeper into the cloven flesh. Then the end is near; some die of tetanus, others are driven to dash their head against the wall. . . .

April 15.

. . . I dwell in Fez-Bali (Old Fez), so called in contradistinction to Fez-Djedid (New Fez); and New Fez has been a nest of owls for the last six or eight hundred years. This Fez-Bali is a labyrinth of dark and hidden streets, which wind in all directions between high blackish walls. And . . . of all these little intersecting streets, the narrowest, I think, and the darkest, is mine. One enters it . . . to find there the darkness almost of night in high noon; it is strewn with refuse, with dead mice, dead dogs; the ground is channelled in the middle in the form of a stream, and one sinks to above the ankles in liquid mud. It has a width of one yard, neither more nor less. . . .

April 17.

We are to be presented to the Sultan this morning. . . . Issue now some fifty little Negro slaves, in red robes and muslin surplices, for all the world like choir-boys. They advance clumsily, huddled together like a flock of sheep. Then six magnificent white horses, all saddled and harnessed in silk, are led out, rearing and prancing. Then a gilt coach, in the style of Louis Quinze, unlooked for in such a setting, quaintly incongruous, ridiculous even amid all this rude grandeur (the solitary carriage, be it said, existing in Fez, a present to the Sultan from Queen Victoria). Some minutes more of waiting and silence. Suddenly, a tremor of religious awe passes along the line of soldiers. The band, with its drums and huge brass instruments, strikes up a deafening, mournful air. The fifty little black slaves start running, running, seized by a sudden madness, spreading out fanwise like a flight of birds, like a swarm of bees. And . . . mounted on a superb white horse led by four slaves, appears a tall, white, brown-faced mummy, completely veiled in muslin. Above his head is borne a red parasol of ancient shape, such as might have belonged to the Queen of Sheba, and two huge Negroes, one in a pink robe, the other in a blue, wave fly-flaps before the august countenance. . . . And here now, come to a stop quite near us, is the last authentic descendant of Mohammed. . . . What good purpose can be served by a mission to such a sovereign, immobilized, like his people, in old human dreams that have almost disappeared from the earth? We are absolutely incapable of understanding one another; the distance between us is almost as great as that which would separate us from a caliph of Cordova or Baghdad, come suddenly to life again after a thousand years of sleep. . . .

April 18.

. . . The state dinners will not commence till next week; so far there are only luncheons, but luncheons worthy of Pantagruel, such as were those of our ancestors in the Middle Ages. On tables, or on the ground, are set large tubs of European or Japanese porcelain, heaped with fruits, shelled nuts, almonds, "gazelles' hoofs," preserves, dates, saffroned sweetmeats. Gauze veils, highly coloured and sequined with gold, cover these mountains of things, which would suffice for a couple of hundred people. Blue and rose-coloured decanters, richly painted and overlaid with gildings, contain a detestable water, earthy and fetid, which it behoves one not to drink. We sit down on carpets, on broidered cushions . . . and are waited on . . . by kinds of janissaries armed with long, curved sabres, and coiffed in pointed tarbushes. Never any coffee or cigarettes, for the Sultan has forbidden their use . . . nothing but tea, and the odorous, and a little intoxicating, smoke of that precious Indian wood, which is burnt before us in silver brasiers. Everywhere, the tall Russian samovars, and the same tea, flavoured with mint, with citron, and sweetened to excess. Good form requires that one should partake of it three times, and the custom is a grievous one; for at each turn of the tray the cups used by the different guests become hopelessly mixed, and the dregs remaining in each are poured ruthlessly back into the tea-urn. . . .

April 20.

. . . We have all to go to the palace . . . and we set out at half-past eight, from the Minister's house, on restive mules. The inevitable red soldiers, their bayonets fixed, escort us with large lanterns . . . through a neighbourhood of gardens, zigzagging in the darkness . . . then through a corner of a covered bazaar; through winding streets, paved in breakneck fashion, where a few lights are still glimmering in the little, sleeping shops . . . then at length the gates of the first enclosures of the palace . . . and we cross, by lantern-light, the immense courtyards already known to us; the deserted spaces with their sinks and quagmires, bounded by the gigantic walls which outline, against the starry sky, all their pointed battlements, like rows of black combs. . . . Beyond, in the far background, are other lanterns perforated like our own, and towards these we direct our steps. They illuminate grave, white-robed personages who are awaiting us: the viziers and kaids of the palace.

We are going to display before them the presents we have brought for the ladies of the seraglio: clusters of electric flowers, electric jewels, stars and crescents, to be worn in the hair of the invisible fair ones. We are warned that the Sultan himself is roaming around us, in the great darkness that envelops us, in order to see without being seen; that perhaps, if he be interested, he may go so far as to show himself. We watch, therefore, the few rare torches that move about in the distances of the courtyard, expecting every minute his saintly apparition. But it is not to be; the Caliph, insufficiently interested no doubt, shows himself not.

The batteries take a long time to get ready; they seem to be actuated by a spirit of perverseness. And all these little playthings of the nineteenth century which we have brought hither light up with difficulty, shine no more brightly than so many glow-worms, in the immense, age-old darkness that surrounds us.

May 4.

After another long day's march, under a burning sun, we see, towards evening, Tangier the White appearing in the distance; above it, the blue line of the Mediterranean. . . . We experience a first impression of constraint, almost of surprise, in passing between the European villas of the outskirts. And our constraint becomes confusion when, on entering the garden of the hotel, with our travel-stained faces, our bournouses and bare legs, our following of muleteers and bales, our paraphernalia of nomad Bedouins, we find ourselves in the midst of a swarm of young English misses on the way to play lawn tennis. And, truly, Tangier seems to us the height of civilisation, of modern refinement. A hotel, where we are given to eat without being required to produce the letter of ransom signed by the Sultan . . . and ugly things and convenient things. The town everywhere open and safe; no longer need of guards in passing through the streets; no longer need of personal watchfulness . . . and in the pause that now is given us, we realise how oppressing, despite its charm, was this deep plunge we have just made into anterior ages. Nevertheless . . . may Allah preserve to the Sultan his unconquered territories, and his solitudes carpeted with flowers, his deserts of daffodils and irises, that he may exercise there the agility of his cavaliers and the muscles of his horses; that he may wage war there as once the paladins, and reap there his harvest of rebel heads. May Allah preserve to the Arab people its mystical dreams, its disdainful immobility and its grey rags. May he preserve to the Bedouin bagpipes their mournful, harrowing sound; to the old mosques their inviolable mystery—and the shroud of white chalk to the ruins. . . .

11.   ALONE, WITH OTHER WORLDS OUTSIDE

"Where dat old man?"

Herman Melville

Herman Melville (1819–1891) was never really happy far from the sea. The salt and the smell of the ocean flavour the books which have put him in the first rank of American novelists.

Melville was born within sight of the New York wharves, and when he was eighteen he ran away to sea. He rounded the Horn on a whaler, jumped ship in the South Seas, was captured by a tribe of cannibals, served as a seaman in the United States Navy until October, 1844.

Within five years of his discharge from the Navy, Melville had published four books: *Typee* (1846), *Omoo* (1847), and *Mardi* and *Redburn* (1849), all summoned from recollections of the sailing years. On the whole the novels were well received, and won him considerable fame but they failed to earn Melville money enough to meet his debts and provide for a growing family. He had married his wife Elizabeth in 1847 and twenty months later his son Malcolm was born.

Nevertheless Melville continued to write, and it was as something of a literary celebrity that he boarded the packet-ship *Southampton* one stormy October day in 1849, bound for London, and taking with him the manuscript of a fifth novel, *White Jacket,* which he hoped to sell to a British publisher. ·

This was a new rôle for Melville. He had last seen England a dozen years before under vastly different circumstances, then an unhappy, mistreated ship's boy newly gone to sea. Understandably he was a little uneasy to find himself in a luxurious stateroom, a little uncomfortable separated from the sailors before the mast. Troubled and lonely, he thought of his wife and little son whose baby-phrase, "Where dat old man?" came often to his mind as he wrote his shipboard journal.

There was more than time enough to ponder the past and the

future through days melancholy or sunny, evenings in talk of philosophy with a knowledgeable shipmate, hours aloft in the rigging under the sounding sails. And someplace within him there must have been shaping the outlines of that extravagant voyage of the soul which Melville began to put on paper just eight months later—the greatest of all American novels, *Moby Dick*.

October 11, 1849.

After a detention of three or four days, owing to wind & weather, with the rest of the passengers I went on board the tugboat Goliath about 12½ P.M. during a cold violent storm from the West. The "Southampton" (a regular London liner) lay in the North River. We transferred ourselves aboard with some confusion, hove up our anchor, & were off. Our pilot, a large, beefy-looking fellow, resembled an oysterman more than a sailor. We got outside the "Narrows" about 2 o'clock; shortly after, the "tug" left us & the Pilot. At half past 5 P.M. saw the last of the land, with our yards square, & in half a gale.

As the ship dashed on, under double-reefed topsails, I walked the deck, thinking of what they might be doing at home, & of the last familiar faces I saw on the wharf. . . . To my great delight, the promise that the Captain had given me at an early day, he now made good; & I find myself in the undivided occupancy of a large stateroom. It is as big almost as my own room at home; it has a spacious berth, a large washstand, a sofa, glass &c. &c. I am the only person on board who is thus honored with a room to himself. I have plenty of light, & a little thick glass window in the side, which in fine weather I may open to the air. I have looked out upon the sea from it, often, though not yet 24 hours on board.

October 12.

Walked the deck last night till about eight o'clock; then made up a whist party & played—till one of the number had to visit his room from sickness. Retired early & had a sound sleep. Was up betimes, & aloft, to recall the old emotions of being at the masthead. Found that the ocean looked the same as ever. Have tried to read, but found it hard work. However, there are some very pleasant passengers on board with whom to converse. Chief among these is a Mr. Adler, a German scholar . . . author of a formidable lexicon, (German & English); in compiling which he almost ruined his health. He was almost crazy, he tells me, for a time. He is full of the German metaphysics, & discourses of Kant, Swedenborg, &c. He has been my principal companion thus far. There is also a Mr. Taylor among the passengers . . . full of fun— or rather *was* full of it. Just at this moment I hear his mysterious noises from the stateroom next to mine. Poor fellow! he is seasick. As yet there have been but few thus troubled, owing to pleasant weather. There is a Scotch artist on board, a painter, with a most unpoetical-looking child, a young one all cheeks & forehead, the former preponderating . . . [McCurdy] a lisping youth of genteel capacity, but quite disposed to be sociable . . . several Frenchmen &

Englishmen . . . also, a middle-aged English woman, who sturdily walks the deck, & prides herself upon her sea legs, & being an old tar.

October 13.

. . . Rose early this morning, opened my bull's-eye window, & looked out to the East. The sun was just rising, the horizon was red; a familiar sight to me, reminding me of old times. Before breakfast went up to the masthead, by way of gymnastics. About 10 o'clock A.M. the wind rose, the rain fell, & the deck looked dismally enough. By dinner time, it blew half a gale, & the passengers mostly retired to their rooms, seasick. After dinner, the rain ceased, but it still blew stiffly, & we were slowly forging along under close-reefed top-sails—mainsail furled. I was walking the deck, when I perceived one of the steerage passengers looking over the side; I looked too, & saw a man in the water, his head completely lifted above the waves,—about twelve feet from the ship, right abreast the gangway. For an instant, I thought I was dreaming; for no one else seemed to see what I did. Next moment, I shouted "Man overboard!" & turned to go aft. The Captain ran forward, greatly confused. I dropped overboard the tackle fall of the quarter-boat, & swung it towards the man, who was now drifting close to the ship. He did not get hold of it, & I got over the side, within a foot or two of the sea, & again swung the rope towards him. He now got hold of it. By this time, a crowd of people—sailors & others— were clustering about the bulwarks; but none seemed very anxious to save him. They warned *me,* however, not to fall overboard. After holding on to the rope about a quarter of a minute, the man let go of it, & drifted astern under the mizzen chains. Four or five of the seamen jumped over into the chains & swung him more ropes. But his conduct was unaccountable; he could have saved himself, had he been so minded. I was struck by the expression of his face in the water. It was merry. At last he drifted off under the ship's counter, & all hands cried "He's gone!" Running to the taffrail, we saw him again, floating off—saw a few bubbles & never saw him again. No boat was lowered, no sail was shortened, hardly any noise was made. The man drowned like a bullock. It afterwards turned out, that he was crazy, & had jumped overboard . . . his wife . . . miserably sick in her berth. The Captain said that this was the fourth or fifth instance he had known of people jumping overboard. He told a story of a man who did so, with his wife on deck at the time. As they were trying to save him, the wife said it was no use; & when he was drowned, she said "there were plenty more men to be had." Amiable creature! By night it blew a terrific gale, & we hove to.

Miserable time! nearly every one sick, & the ship rolling & pitching in an amazing manner. It was blowing horribly—pitch dark, & raining. The Captain was in the cuddy, & directed my attention "to those fellows" as he called them,—meaning several "Corposant balls" [St. Elmo's fire] on the yardarms & mastheads. They were the first I had ever seen, & resembled large, dim stars in the sky.

October 14.

A regular blue devil day. A gale of wind, & every one sick. Saloons deserted, & all sorts of nausea noise heard from the staterooms . . . & I alone am left to tell the tale of their misery. . . . Managed to get through the day somehow, by reading & walking the deck, though the last was almost as much as my neck was worth. I forgot to say that shortly after the loss of the crazy man (a Dutchman by the way) some of the steerage passengers came aft & told the Captain that there was another crazy man, an Englishman in the steerage. This morning . . . this poor fellow was on deck, crying out at steamers, boats &c &c. I thought that his mad feelings found something congenial in the riot of the raging sea. In the evening, he forced his way into the dining saloon, & struck the Steward. . . . The crazy man turns out to be afflicted with delirium tremens, consequent upon keeping drunk for the last two months. . . .

Saw a lady with a copy of *Omoo* [the diarist's second novel] in her hand two days ago. Now & then she would look up at me, as if comparing notes. . . .

October 15.

The gale has gone down, & we have fine weather. By noon the passengers were pretty nearly all on deck, convalescent. They seem to regard me as a hero, proof against wind & weather. My occasional feats in the rigging are regarded as a species of tight-rope dancing. . . . The wind is not fair yet, & there is much growling consequently. Drank a small bottle of London Stout today for dinner, & think it did me good. I wonder how much they charge for it? I must find out. . . .

October 16.

Beautiful weather, but wind against us. . . . Read little or nothing, but lounged about. The sea has produced a temporary effect upon me, which makes me for the time incapable of anything but vegetating. What's little Barney about? Where's Orianna? [familiar names for his son Malcolm, his wife Elizabeth].

October 17.

Fine weather, quite warm & sunny. The decks lively, the ladies lively, the Captain lively, & the ship now going her course. Spent a good part of the day aloft. . . .

October 19.

No events; spent the morning in lounging & reading; and after a hand at cards, retired.

October 20.

Newfoundland weather—foggy, rainy &c. . . . In the evening for the first time went into the Ladies' Saloon, & heard Mrs. Gould, the opera lady, sing.

There was quite a party—the saloon is gilt & brilliant, & as the ship was going on quietly, it seemed as if I were ashore in a little parlor or cabinet. Where's Orianna? How's little Barney? Read a chapter in Pickwick & retired pretty early. Towards morning was annoyed by a crying baby adjoining.

October 21.

Rainy—near the Banks. Can not remember what happened today. It came to an end somehow.

October 22.

Clear & cold; wind not favorable. I forgot to mention, that *last night* about 9½ P.M. Adler & Taylor came into my room, & it was proposed to have whisky punches, which we *did* have, accordingly. Adler drank about three table-spoons full—Taylor 4 or five tumblers &c. We had an extraordinary time and did not break up till after two in the morning. We talked metaphysics continually, & Hegel, Schlegel, Kant &c were discussed under the influence of the whisky. . . . After Adler retired Taylor & I went out on the bowsprit—splendid spectacle. It came on calm in the evening, & we await a favorable shift of wind.

October 23.

On gaining the deck this morning, was delighted to find a fair wind. It soon blew stiff, & we scudded before it under double-reefed topsails, & main-sail hauled up. Running about 14 knots all day. Every one in high spirits. . . .

October 24.

Fair wind still holds on; at 12 M. supposed to be half way over. Saw several land birds—very tame, lighted on deck—caught one.

October 25.

A fair wind—good deal of rain. About noon saw a ship on the other tack. She showed her colors & proved a Yankee. The first vessel that we had seen so near. She excited much interest. By evening blew a very stiff breeze, & we dashed on in magnificent style. Fine moonlight night, & we rushed on through snow-banks of foam. . . . I never saw such sailing before.

October 26.

Fair wind still. Towards noon came on calm, with a gawky sea. The ship rolled violently, & many comical scenes ensued among the passengers. Breezed up again in the afternoon, & we went on finely. . . .

October 27.

Steered our course on a wind. I played Shuffleboard for the first time. Ran about aloft a good deal. McCurdy invited Adler, Taylor & I to partake of some *mulled wine* with him, which we did, in my room . . . sat down to whist, & separated at about 3 in the morning.

October 28.

Came on a strong breeze & lasted all day. Ship going about 12 miles an hour—began to talk of port. Decks very wet, & hard work to take exercise. ("Where dat old man?"). Read a little, dozed a little, & to bed early.

October 29.

Wet & foggy, but a fair fresh breeze—12 knots an hour. Some of the passengers sick again. . . . In the evening . . . after chat & Stout . . . went on deck, & found it a moonlight midnight. Wind astern. Retired at 1 A.M.

October 30.

Glorious day—Capital cakes for breakfast. ("Where dat old man?") Saw a land bird. Weather beautifully clear. For the first time in five days got our observation. Find ourselves heading right into the Channel—the Scilly Islands out of sight to the North. Played Shuffleboard with Taylor & the ladies. Had a superb dinner, which we all relished amazingly. Drawing near port with a fine fair wind makes passengers feel generous. A good deal of wine and porter on the table. A magnificent night—but turned in very early.

October 31.

Fair, fresh wind still holds. Coming on deck in the morning saw a brig close to—& two or three ships. If the wind holds we shall make the Lizzard Light this evening, probably. May be in Portsmouth tomorrow night. All hands in high spirits. Had some mulled Sherry in the evening from McCurdy. Up late, expecting it to be the last night.

November 1.

Just three weeks from home, and made the land—Start Point—about 3 P.M. —well up Channel—past the Lizzard. Very fine day—great number of ships in sight. Through these waters Blake's & Nelson's ships once sailed. Taylor suggested that he & I should return McCurdy's civilities. We did, and Captain Griswold joined and ordered a pitcher of his own. The Captain is a very intelligent & gentlemanly man—converses well & understands himself. . . . Taylor played a rare joke upon McCurdy this evening, passing himself off as Miss Wilbur, having borrowed her cloak &c. They walked together. Shall see Portsmouth tomorrow morning.

November 2.

Wind from the East—ahead. Clear & beautiful day but every one grievously disappointed. . . . Melancholy looking voyage, white cliffs indeed! In the evening played chess, & talked metaphysics . . . till midnight.

November 3.

Woke about 6 o'clock with an insane idea that we were going before the wind, & would be in Portsmouth in an hour's time. Soon found out my mistake. . . . Devilish dull, & too bad altogether. Continued tacking all day with a light wind from West. . . . In the evening all hands in high spirits—Played chess in the ladies' saloon—another party at cards; good deal of singing in the gentlemen's cabin & drinking—very hilarious & noisy. . . .

November 4.

Looked out of my window first thing upon rising & saw the Isle of Wight again—very near—ploughed fields &c. Light wind ahead—expected to be in a little after breakfast time.

About 10 A.M. rounded the Eastern end of the Isle, when it fell flat calm. The town in sight by telescope. Were becalmed about three or four hours. Foggy, drizzly; long faces at dinner—no porter bottles. Wind came from the West at last. Squared the yards & struck away for Dover—distant 60 miles. At 6 o'clock (evening) passed Dungeness—then saw the Beachy Head light. Close reefed the topsails so as not to run too fast. . . .

It is now eight o'clock in the evening. I am alone in my stateroom. . . . This time tomorrow I shall be on land, & press English earth after the lapse of ten years—*then* a sailor, *now* H. M. author. . . . ("Where dat old man?— Where books?")

". . . and I prayed God to keep us all together."

Louisa May Alcott

On the best-seller lists of 1868 there first appeared a book called *Little Women* which to this day still remains perhaps the most-loved of all stories for girls. Its author was Louisa May Alcott (1832–1888), daughter of Bronson Alcott, philosopher, educational reformer, and friend of Emerson, Thoreau and Hawthorne. The book is based in part on nostalgic, somewhat glossed over memories of Fruitlands, an unsuccessful experiment in cooperative community-living, founded by her father in 1843 in an old red farmhouse near the village of Harvard, Massachusetts. This "New Eden" lasted through a single summer and autumn only to founder on discord, hunger and poverty when winter came. The world was not yet ready for Utopia, especially one that lacked (as Louisa later remembered) milk, butter, cheese, tea and meat, with salt considered a useless luxury. "Unleavened bread, porridge, and water for breakfast; bread, vegetables, and water for dinner; bread, fruit and water for supper was the bill of fare ordained by the elders."

At Fruitlands Alcott's four young daughters were "little women" before their time with burdens beyond their years. There were moments of fun and cheer, as those who grew up on Louisa's books will remember. But from between the lines of the diary kept that summer and autumn by the ten-year-old Louisa there emerges more than a hint of a slightly different story, a gnawing nameless fear that troubled a child's heart.

September 1, 1843.

I rose at five and had my bath. I love cold water! Then we had our singing-lesson with Mr. Lane. After breakfast I washed dishes, and ran on the hill till nine and had some thoughts,—it was so beautiful up there. Did my lessons, —wrote and spelt and did sums; and Mr. Lane read a story, "The Judicious Father." How a rich girl told a poor girl not to look over the fence at the

From *Bronson Alcott's Fruitlands*, compiled by Clara Endicott Sears, reprinted by permission of and arrangement with Houghton Mifflin Company, the authorized publishers.

flowers, and was cross to her because she was unhappy. The Father heard her do it, and made the girls change clothes. The poor one was glad to do it, and he told her to keep them. But the rich one was very sad; for she had to wear the old ones a week, and after that she was good to shabby girls. I liked it very much, and I shall be kind to poor people.

Father asked us what was God's noblest work. Anna said *men*, but I said *babies*. Men are often bad; babies never are. We had a long talk, and I felt better after it, and *cleared up*.

We had bread and fruit for dinner. I read and walked and played till supper-time. We sung in the evening. As I went to bed the moon came up very brightly and looked at me. I felt sad because I have been cross to-day, and did not mind Mother. I cried, and then I felt better, and said that piece from Mrs. Sigourney, "I must not tease my mother." I get to sleep saying poetry,—I know a great deal.

September 14.

Mr. Parker Pillsbury came, and we talked about the poor slaves. I had a music lesson with Miss P. I hate her, she is so fussy. I ran in the wind and played be a horse, and had a lovely time in the woods with Anna and Lizzie. We were fairies, and made gowns and paper wings. I "flied" the highest of all. . . .

It rained when I went to bed and made a pretty noise on the roof.

September 24.

Father and Mr. Lane have gone to N. H. to preach. . . . Anna and I got supper. In the eve I read "Vicar of Wakefield." I was cross to-day, and I cried when I went to bed. I made good resolutions, and felt better in my heart. If I only *kept* all I make, I should be the best girl in the world. But I don't, and so am very bad. . . .

October 8.

When I woke up, the first thought I got was, "It's Mother's birthday: I must be very good." I ran and wished her a happy birthday, and gave her my kiss. After breakfast we gave her our presents. I had a moss cross and a piece of poetry for her.

We did not have any school, and played in the woods and got red leaves. In the evening we danced and sung, and I read a story about "Contentment." I wish I was rich, I was good, and we were all a happy family this day. . . .

October 12.

After lessons I ironed. We all went to the barn and husked corn. It was good fun. We worked till eight o'clock and had lamps. Mr. Russell came. Mother and Lizzie are going to Boston. I shall be very lonely without dear little Betty, and no one will be as good to me as Mother. I read in Plutarch. I made a verse about sunset:—

> "Softly doth the sun descend
> To his couch behind the hill,
> Then, oh, then, I love to sit
> On mossy banks beside the rill."

Anna thought it was very fine; but I didn't like it very well.

November 2.

Anna and I did the work. In the evening Mr. Lane asked us, "What is man?" These were our answers: A human being; an animal with a mind; a creature; a body; a soul and a mind. After a long talk we went to bed very tired. . . .

November 20.

I rose at five, and after breakfast washed the dishes, and then helped mother work. Miss P. is gone, and Anna in Boston with Cousin Louisa. I took care of Abba (May) in the afternoon. In the evening I made some pretty things for my dolly. . . .

November 29. Eleven years old.

It was Father's and my birthday. We had some nice presents. We played in the snow before school. Mother read "Rosamond" when we sewed. Father asked us in the eve what fault troubled us most. I said my bad temper.

I told mother I liked to have her write in my book. She said she would put in more, and she wrote this to help me:—

"DEAR LOUEY,—Your handwriting improves very fast. Take pains and do not be in a hurry. I like to have you make observations about our conversations and your own thoughts. It helps you to express them and to understand your little self. Remember, dear girl, that a diary should be an epitome of your life. May it be a record of pure thought and good actions, then you will indeed be the precious child of your loving mother."

December 10.

I did my lessons, and walked in the afternoon. Father read to us in dear "Pilgrim's Progress." Mr. L. was in Boston and we were glad. In the eve father and mother and Anna and I had a long talk. I was very unhappy, and we all cried. Anna and I cried in bed, and I prayed God to keep us all together.

"I feel happy—deep down."

Katherine Mansfield

Katherine Mansfield (1888–1923) was perhaps the greatest short story writer of her generation. Her achievement is the more remarkable because her brief thirty-four years of life were filled with ill-health, lack of recognition, unhappy loves, loneliness, hardship, and constant bad luck.

She was born Kathleen Beauchamp in Wellington, New Zealand. At thirteen she was separated from her brother and sisters and sent half way round the world to be educated at a girls' school in England. She had considerable musical ability and in England became a promising cellist. But the roots she put down during five years at school were torn away when her family required her to return to New Zealand. There she found herself alienated from a way of life that by her new standards seemed constricted and barren. Two years of rebellion followed before she was permitted to go back to London on a small allowance.

Katherine Mansfield had been writing since childhood (her first story was published when she was nine) and in London she quickly abandoned music for a literary career. From then on her life was crowded with misfortune. Editors were uninterested in what she wrote, and she was soon forced to return to music to support herself. After an unhappy marriage she suffered the first of a series of illnesses that were to beset her the rest of her life. Her beloved brother, to whom she was devoted, was tragically killed in the war. The publisher of the book she had written during her convalescence, *In a German Pension,* went bankrupt before she received the royalties due her for the three editions that were sold. The magazines that did occasionally buy her stories had a habit of going out of business after two or three issues. In the four years after 1915 she managed to sell only three stories. In 1918 after she was finally able to obtain a divorce from her first husband, she married the critic J. Middleton Murry, but he was as short of money as was she. As a final blow, shortly after

Reprinted from *The Journal of Katherine Mansfield,* by Katherine Mansfield, by permission of Alfred A. Knopf, Inc. and John Middleton Murray. Copyright 1927 by Alfred A. Knopf, Inc.

her marriage she discovered that she had contracted tuberculosis. For the remaining five years of her life she wandered about France, Italy, and Switzerland seeking a cure. Meanwhile she went on writing from her sick bed the pure, clear and shining stories that were collected in *Bliss, The Garden Party* and *The Dove's Nest.*

For years Katherine Mansfield kept a journal whose pages are deeply affecting when read against the background of her life. The passage given here, one of the last she wrote, was torn out to be sent to her husband. "I found it among her papers," he says, "with this inscription: 'These pages from my journal. Don't let them distress you. The story *has* a happy ending, really and truly.'"

October 10, 1922.

I have been thinking this morning until it seems I may get things straightened out if I try to write . . . where I am.

Ever since I came to Paris I have been as ill as ever. In fact yesterday I thought I was dying. It is not imagination. My heart is so exhausted and so tied up I can only walk to the taxi and back. I get up at midi, and go to bed at 5:30. I try to "work" by fits and starts, but the time has gone by. I cannot work. Ever since April I have done practically nothing. But why? Because, although M.'s treatment improved my blood and made me look well and did have a good effect on my lungs, it made my heart not a snap better, and I only won that improvement by living the life of a corpse in the Victoria Palace Hotel.

My spirit is nearly dead. My spring of life is so starved that it's just not dry. Nearly all my improved health is pretence—acting. What does it amount to? Can I walk? Only creep. Can I do anything with my hands or body? Nothing at all. I am an absolutely helpless invalid. What is my life? It is the existence of a parasite. And five years have passed now, and I am in straighter bonds than ever.

Ah, I feel a little calmer already to be writing. Thank God for writing! I am so terrified of what I am going to do. All of the voices out of the "Past" say "Don't do it." J. says "M. is a scientist. He does his part. It's up to you to do yours." But that is no good at all. I can no more cure my psyche than my body. Less it seems to me. Isn't J. himself, perfectly fresh and well, utterly depressed by boils on his neck? Think of five years imprisonment. Someone has got to help me to get out. If that is a confession of weakness—it is. But it is only lack of imagination that calls it so. And who is going to help me? Remember Switzerland: "I am helpless." Of course he is. One prisoner cannot help another. Do I believe in medicine alone? No, never. It seems to me childish and ridiculous to suppose one can be cured like a cow *if one is not a cow.* And here all these years I have been looking for someone who agreed with me. I have heard of G. who seems not only to agree but to know infinitely more about it. Why hesitate?

Fear? Fear of what? Doesn't it come down to fear of losing J.? I believe it does. But, good Heavens! Face things. What have you of him now? What s your relationship? He talks to you—sometimes—and then goes off. He thinks of you tenderly. He dreams of a life with you *some day* when the miracle has happened. You are important to him as a dream. Not as a living reality. For you are not one. What do you share? Almost nothing. Yet there is a deep, sweet, tender flooding of feeling in my heart which is love for him and longing for him. But what is the good of it as things stand? Life together, with me ill, is simply torture with happy moments. But it's not life. . . . You do know that J. and you are only a kind of dream of what might be. And that might-be never, never can be true unless you are well. And you won't get well by "imagining" or "waiting" or trying to bring off that miracle yourself.

Therefore if the Grand Lama of Thibet promised to help you—how can you hesitate? Risk! Risk anything! Care no more for the opinions of others, for those voices. Do the hardest thing on earth for you. Act for yourself. Face the truth. . . .

But perhaps to people who are not ill, all this is nonsense. They have never travelled this road. How can they see where I am? All the more reason to go boldly forward alone. Life is not simple. In spite of all we say about the mystery of Life, when we get down to it we want to treat it as though it were a child's tale?

Now, Katherine, what do you mean by health? And what do you want it for?

Answer: By health I mean the power to live a full, adult, living, breathing life in close contact with what I love—the earth and the wonders thereof—the sea—the sun. All that we mean when we speak of the external world. I want to enter into it, to be part of it, to live in it, to learn from it, to lose all that is superficial and acquired in me and to become a conscious direct human being. I want, by understanding myself, to understand others. I want to be all that I am capable of becoming so that I may be (and here I have stopped and waited and waited and it's no good—there's only one phrase that will do) *a child of the sun*. About helping others, about carrying a light and so on, it seems false to say a single word. Let it be at that, *a child of the sun*.

Then I want to *work*. At what? I want so to live that I work with my hands and my feeling and my brain. I want a garden, a small house, grass, animals, books, pictures, music. And out of this, the expression of this, I want to be writing. (Though I may write about cabmen. That's no matter.)

But warm, eager, living life—to be rooted in life—to learn, to desire to know, to feel, to think, to act. That is what I want. And nothing less. That is what I must try for.

I wrote this for myself. I shall now risk sending it to J. He may do with it what he likes. He must see how much I love him.

And when I say "I fear"—don't let it disturb you, dearest heart. We all fear when we are in waiting rooms. Yet we must pass beyond them, and if the other can keep calm, it is all the help we can give each other. . . . And all this sounds very strenuous and serious. But now that I have wrestled with it, it's no longer so. I feel happy—deep down. *All is well.*

[J. Middleton Murry added this:

"With those words Katherine Mansfield's Journal comes to a fitting close. Thenceforward the conviction that "All was well" never left her. She entered a kind of spiritual brotherhood at Fountainbleau. The object of this brotherhood, at least as she understood it, was to help its members achieve a spiritual regeneration.

"After some three months, at the beginning of 1923, she invited me to stay with her for a week. I arrived early in the afternoon of January 9. I have never seen, nor shall I ever see, anyone so beautiful as she was on that day; it was as though the exquisite perfection which was always hers had taken possession of her completely. To use her own words, the last grain of 'sediment,' the last 'traces of earthly degradation' were departed for ever. But she had lost her life to save it.

"As she came up the stairs to her room at 10 p.m. she was seized by a fit of coughing which culminated in a violent haemorrhage. At 10:30 she was dead."]

*". . . we live without a future . . . with our noses pressed
to a closed door . . ."*

Virginia Woolf

Virginia Woolf (1882–1941) was a casualty of the second world
war. Its impact on her sensitive being destroyed her as surely as
if she had fallen under enemy fire. With her beloved London in
flames, and almost all that she valued rapidly slipping away, her
footsteps took her in March, 1941, to the river where, by mischance or design, her life came to an end.

Adeline Virginia Stephen belonged to one of England's sprawling literary families. Her father was Sir Leslie Stephen, critic and
editor of the multi-volumed Dictionary of National Biography.
His first wife was Thackeray's daughter. For generations preceding him, literature had been a family pursuit. His grandfather,
James Stephen, was the celebrated English abolitionist and writer
of tracts against slavery; his father, Sir James Stephen, wrote many
historical works; his brother, Sir James Fitzjames Stephen, was
the celebrated legal scholar and author; his nephew was James
Stephen the poet. The mother of Virginia, her sister Vanessa, and
her brothers Thoby and Adrian, was Julia Jackson, Sir Leslie's
second wife, granddaughter of a French nobleman who was page
to Marie Antoinette. Vanessa married the critic Clive Bell, and
her daughter married the novelist, David Garnett. Virginia married Leonard Woolf, writer, teacher, publisher and socialist, who
was one of the founders of the Labour Party. Although possessed
of nieces, nephews, cousins and aunts almost beyond count, Virginia Woolf had no children of her own.

With her husband, Virginia Woolf became the center of London's "Bloomsbury Circle," a group made up of younger writers
ranging from Aldous Huxley to Lytton Strachey, who were setting new trends in literature. Soon they became publishers to this
group, too, establishing the famous Hogarth Press in the basement of their house. Virginia Woolf set most of the type herself

and helped to print on a hand-press books that launched such writers as T. S. Eliot into literary fame.

Virginia Woolf's first novel, *The Voyage Out,* appeared in 1915 and was followed by *Mrs. Dalloway, The Waves, The Years,* and *To the Lighthouse,* and by a number of books of criticism. Readers responded slowly at first, finding her "stream of conscious-ness" technique difficult to master. By the time of her death, how-ever, she was generally acknowledged to be in the first rank of contemporary novelists.

From 1915 onwards Virginia Woolf regularly wrote a diary on large sheets of blank white paper which were bound together at the end of the year. From the twenty-six volumes of these, Leonard Woolf made the selection published as *A Writer's Diary* (1953).

The extracts given here come from the last fourteen months or so of Virginia Woolf's life as the mounting intensity of the war together with its meaning struck home to her susceptive mind. With each new horror viewed or imagined, the diary entries can be seen advancing to their inevitable conclusion.

February 2, 1940.

Only the fire sets me dreaming—of all the things I mean to write. The break in our lives from London to country is a far more complete one than any change in house. Yes, but I haven't got the hang of it altogether. The im-mense space suddenly becomes vacant: then illuminated. And London, in nips, is cramped and creased. Odd how often I think with what is love I suppose of the City: of the walk to the Tower: that is my England: I mean, if a bomb destroyed one of those little alleys with the brass bound curtains and the river smell and the old woman reading, I should feel—well, what the patriots feel.

May 13.

I admit to some content, some closing of a chapter and peace that comes with it, from posting my proofs today. I admit—because we're in the third day of "the greatest battle in history." It began (here) with the 8 o'clock wireless announcing as I lay half asleep the invasion of Holland and Belgium. The third day of the Battle of Waterloo. Apple blossom snowing the garden. A bowl lost in the pond. Churchill exhorting all men to stand together. "I have nothing to offer but blood and tears and sweat." . . . Duncan saw an air battle over Charleston—a silver pencil and a puff of smoke. Percy has seen the wounded arriving in their boots. So my little moment of peace comes in a yawning hollow. But though L. [Leonard, her husband] says he has petrol in the garage for suicide should Hitler win, we go on. . . .

May 20.

. . . The war is like a desperate illness. For a day it entirely obsesses: then

he feeling faculty gives out; next day one is disembodied, in the air. Then
he battery is re-charged again—what? Well, the bomb terror. Going to Lon-
lon to be bombed. And the catastrophe—if they break through: Channel
his morning said to be their objective. Last night Churchill asked us to re-
lect, when being bombed, that we were at least drawing fire from the sol-
liers. . . . A fine windy morning.

May 25.

Then we went up to what has been so far the worst week in the war. And
;o remains. On Tuesday evening . . . the B.B.C. announced the taking of
Amiens and Arras. The French P.M. told the truth and knocked all our
"holding" to atoms. On Monday they broke through. It's tedious picking up
letails. It seems they raid with tanks and parachutists: roads crammed with
efugees can't be bombed. They crash on. Now are at Boulogne. . . . The
`eeling is we're outwitted. They're agile and fearless and up to any new
lodge. The French forgot to blow up bridges. The Germans seem youthful,
:resh, inventive. We plod behind. . . . Are we to be bombed, evacuated?
Guns that shake the windows. Hospital ships sunk. So it comes our way. To-
lay's rumour is the Nun in the bus who pays her fare with a man's hand.

May 28.

And today at 8, the French P.M. broadcast the treachery of the Belgian
King. The Belgians have capitulated. The Government is not capitulating.
Churchill to broadcast at 4. A wet dull day.

May 29.

But hope revives. I don't know why. A desperate battle. The Allies hold-
ng. . . . A great thunderstorm. I was walking on the marsh and thought it
vas the guns on the channel ports. Then, as they swerved, I conceived a
`aid on London; turned on the wireless; heard some prattler; and then the
guns began to lighten; then it rained. . . .

May 30.

Walking today . . . by Kingfisher pool saw my first hospital train—laden,
1ot funereal but weighty, as if not to shake bones: something—what is the
vord I want—grieving and tender and heavy laden and private—bringing our
vounded back carefully through the green fields at which I suppose some
looked . . . I can't catch it when I come home—the slowness, cadaverousness,
;rief of the long heavy train, taking its burden through the trees. Very quietly
t slid into the cutting at Lewes. Instantly wild duck flights of aeroplanes
:ame over head; manoeuvered; took up positions and passed over. . . .

May 31.

. . . Percy weeding: "I shall conquer 'em in the end. If I was sure of our

winning the other battle . . ." Raid, said to be warned, last night. All the
searchlights in extreme continual vibration: they have blots of light, like bead
of dew on a stalk. . . . "Any waste paper?" Here I was interrupted by the
jangling bell. Small boy in white sweater come, I suppose, for Scouts, and
Mabel [the cook] says they pester us daily. . . . Desperate fighting. The
same perorations. Coming through Southease I saw Mrs. Cockell in old gar
den hat weeding. Out comes a maid in muslin apron and cap tied with blue
riband. Why? To keep up standards of civilisation?

June 22.

Waterloo I suppose. And the fighting goes on in France; and the term:
[of surrender] aren't yet public; and it's a heavy grey day, and I've been
beaten at bowls, feel depressed and irritated and vow I'll play no more . .
oughtn't I to finish something by way of an end? The end gives its vividness
even its gaiety and recklessness to the random daily life. This, I thought yes
terday, may be my last walk. On the down above Baydean I found some
green glass tubes. The corn was glowing with poppies in it. And I read my
Shelley at night. How delicate and pure and musical and uncorrupt he and
Coleridge read . . . and how they sing; and how they compact; and fuse
and deepen. . . . And now dinner to cook. A rôle. Nightly raids in the eas
and south coast. 6, 3, 22 people killed nightly.

A high wind was blowing: Mabel, Louie picking currants and gooseberries
Then a visit to Charleston, threw another stone into the pond. And at the
moment . . . I'm loosely anchored. Further, the war—our waiting while the
knives sharpen for the operation—has taken away the outer wall of security
No echo comes back. . . . Those familiar circumvolutions—those standard:
—which have for so many years given back an echo and so thickened my
identity are all wide and wild as the desert now. I mean, there is no "autumn,"
no winter. We pour to the edge of a precipice . . . and then? I can't con
ceive that there will be a 27th June 1941. . . .

July 24.

. . . All the walls, the protecting and reflecting walls, wear so terribly thin
in this war. There's no standard to write for: no public to echo back; even
the "tradition" has become transparent. Hence a certain energy and recklessness—part good part bad I daresay. But it's the only line to take. And perhaps
the walls, if violently beaten against, will finally contain me. I feel tonight
still veiled. The veil will be lifted tomorrow when my book comes out. That's
what may be painful: may be cordial. And then I may feel once more round
me the wall I've missed—or vacancy? or chill? . . .

August 16.

. . . Many air raids. One as I walked. A haystack was handy. But walked
on, and so home. All clear. Then sirens again. Then Judith and Leslie. Bowls
Then Mrs. Ebbs etc. to borrow table. All clear. . . .

They came very close. We lay down under the tree. The sound was like

meone sawing in the air just above us. We lay flat on our faces, hands
ehind head. Don't close your teeth, said L. They seemed to be sawing at
mething stationary. Bombs shook the windows of my lodge. Will it drop I
sked? If so, we shall be broken together. I thought, I think, of nothingness—
atness, my mood being flat. Some fear I suppose. Should we take Mabel to
arage. Too risky to cross the garden, L. said. Then another came from New-
aven. Hum and saw and buzz all round us. A horse neighed in the marsh.
'ery sultry. Is it thunder? I said. No, guns, said L., from Ringmer, from
harleston way. Then slowly the sound lessened. Mabel in kitchen said the
indows shook. Air raid still on: distant planes. . . .

eptember 5.

. . . All writers are unhappy. The picture of the world in books is thus
o dark. The wordless are the happy. . . .

eptember 16.

Well, we're alone in our ship. A very wet stormy day. Mabel stumped off,
ith her bunions, carrying her bags at 10. Thank you for all your kindness;
he said the same to us both. Also would I give her a reference? "I hope we
hall meet again," I said. She said "Oh no doubt" thinking I referred to death.
o that 5 years' uneasy mute but very passive and calm relation is over: a
eavy unsunned pear dropped from a twig. . . .

eptember 29.

A bomb dropped so close I cursed L. for slamming the window. I was
riting to Hugh, and the pen jumped from my finger. Raid still on. It's like
sheep dog, chasing a fox out of the fold. You see them yapping and biting
nd then the marauder, dropping a bone, a bomb towards Newhaven, flies.
ll clear. Bowls. Villagers at their doors. Cold. All now become familiar. . . .

ctober 2.

Ought I not to look at the sunset rather than write this? A flush of red
 the blue; the haystack on the marsh catches the glow; behind me, the
pples are red in the trees. L. is gathering them. Now a plume of smoke goes
om the train under Caburn. And all the air a solemn stillness holds. Till
:30 when the cadaverous twanging in the sky begins; the planes going to
ondon. Well it's an hour still to that. Cows feeding. The elm tree sprinkling
s little leaves against the sky. Our pear tree swagged with pears; and the
eathercock above the triangular church tower above it. Why try again to
ake the familiar catalogue, from which something escapes. Should I think
f death? Last night a great heavy plunge of bomb under the window. So
ear we both started. A plane had passed dropping this fruit. We went on to
he terrace. Trinkets of stars sprinkled and glittering. All quiet. The bombs
ropped on Itford Hill. There are two by the river, marked with white wooden
rosses, still unburst. I said to L.: I don't want to die yet. The chances are

against it. But . . . they get closer every time. Caburn was crowned wit
what looked like a settled moth, wings extended—a Messerschmitt it was, sho
down on Sunday. . . . Oh I try to imagine how one's killed by a bomb. I'v
got it fairly vivid—the sensation: but can't see anything but suffocating nor
entity following after. I shall think—oh I wanted another 10 years—not this
and shan't, for once, be able to describe it. It—I mean death; no, the scrunch
ing and scrambling, the crushing of my bone shade in on my very active ey
and brain: the process of putting out the light—painful? Yes. Terrifying. I sup
pose so. Then a swoon; a drain; two or three gulps attempting consciousnes
—and then dot dot dot.

October 12.

I would like to pack my day rather fuller: most reading must be munching
If it were not treasonable to say so, a day like this is almost too—I won't sa
happy: but amenable. The tune varies, from one nice melody to another
All is played (today) in such a theatre. Hills and fields; I can't stop looking
October blooms; brown plough; and the fading and freshening of the marsh
Now the mist comes up. And one thing's "pleasant" after another: breakfas
writing, walking, tea, bowls, reading, sweets, bed. . . . L. gathering apples
Sally barks. I imagine a village invasion. Queer the contraction of life to th
village radius. Wood bought enough to stock many winters. All our friend
are isolated over winter fires. Chance of interruption small now. No cars. N
petrol. Trains uncertain. And we on our lovely free autumn island. . . .

December 29.

There are moments when the sail flaps. Then, being a great amateur o
the art of life, determined to suck my orange, off, like a wasp if the blossor
I'm on fades, as it did yesterday—I ride across the downs to the cliffs. A ro
of barbed wire is hooped on the edge. I rubbed my mind brisk along th
Newhaven road. Shabby old maids buying groceries, in that desert road wit
the villas; in the wet. And Newhaven gashed. But tire the body and th
mind sleeps. All desire to write diary here has flagged. What is the righ
antidote? I must sniff round. I think Mme. de Sévigné. Writing to be a dail
pleasure. I detest the hardness of old age—I feel it. I rasp. I'm tart. . . .

January 1, 1941.

On Sunday night, as I was reading about the Great fire [in Pepys' diary
. . . London was burning. Eight of my city churches destroyed, and th
Guildhall. . . .

January 9.

A blank. All frost. Still frost. Burning white. Burning blue. The elms red.
did not mean to describe, once more, the downs in snow; but it came. An
I can't help even now turning to look at Asheham down, red, purple, dov
blue grey, with the cross so melodramatically against it. What is the phras

always remember—or forget. Look your last on all things lovely. Yesterday
Mrs. X was buried upside down. A mishap. Such a heavy woman, as Louie
put it, feasting spontaneously upon the grave. . . .

January 15.

. . . We were in London on Monday. I went to London Bridge. I looked
at the river; very misty; some tufts of smoke, perhaps from burning houses.
There was another fire on Saturday. Then I saw a cliff of wall, eaten out, at
one corner; a great corner all smashed; a Bank; the Monument erect: tried to
get a bus; but such a block I dismounted; and the second bus advised me
to walk. A complete jam of traffic; for streets were being blown up. So by
tube to the Temple; and there wandered in the desolate ruins of my old
squares: gashed; dismantled; the old red bricks all white powder, something
like a builder's yard. Grey dirt and broken windows . . . all that completeness
ravished and demolished.

January 26.

A battle against depression. . . . This trough of despair shall not, I swear,
engulf me. The solitude is great. Rodmell life is very small beer. The house
is damp. The house is untidy. But there is no alternative. Also days will
lengthen. What I need is the old spurt. "Your true life, like mine, is in ideas"
Desmond said to me once. But one must remember one can't pump ideas. I
begin to dislike introspection: sleep and slackness; musing; reading; cooking;
cycling: oh and a good hard rather rocky book . . . This is my prescription.
There's a lull in the war. Six nights without raids. But Garvin says the
greatest struggle is about to come—say in three weeks—and every man,
woman, dog, cat, even weevil must girt their arms, their faith—and so on. It's
the cold hour, this: before the lights go up. A few snowdrops in the garden.
Yes, I was thinking: we live without a future. That's what's queer: with our
noses pressed to a closed door. . . .

February 7.

Why was I depressed? I cannot remember. We have been to Charlie
Chaplin. . . . A week of broken water impends.

February 16.

In the wild grey water after last week's turmoil. . . . Perhaps I shall re-
enter one of my higher lives. But not yet.

March 8.

. . . Brighton. Like a foreign town: the first spring day. Women sitting
on seats. A pretty hat in a teashop—how fashion revives the eye! And the
shell encrusted old women, rouged, decked, cadaverous at the teashop. The
waitress in checked cotton. No: I intend no introspection. I mark Henry

James' sentence: observe perpetually. Observe the oncome of age. Observe greed. Observe my own despondency. By that means it becomes serviceable. Or so I hope. I insist upon spending this time to the best advantage. I will go down with my colours flying. This I see verges on introspection; but doesn't quite fall in. Suppose I bought a ticket at the Museum; biked in daily and read history. . . . Occupation is essential. And now with some pleasure I find that it's seven; and must cook dinner. Haddock and sausage meat. I think it is true that one gains a certain hold on sausage and haddock by writing them down.

[With these words the published diary ends. Later the body of Virginia Woolf was found floating in the "wild grey water" near her country home.]

"For God's sake look after our people."

Robert Falcon Scott

The polar regions, like other areas at the edges of the map, were explored at the cost of infinite struggle and suffering, sometimes at the cost of life itself. And the suffering was not always confined to the explorers alone. Their anxious families, thousands of miles away from the dangers and rigours of the voyages underwent a different kind of misery—the torture of interminable years of waiting with no word. Like the families of soldiers in battle, they too made their sacrifice. Seldom if ever has this double trial been more clearly or more movingly expressed than in the two diaries that follow—the first by one of the most heroic antarctic explorers, and the other written in the lonely years of his absence by his wife.

Captain Robert Falcon Scott (1868–1912) was born in Devenport, England. He entered the British navy as a youth, and at the age of thirty-two became a commander and was put in charge of the National Antarctic Expedition of 1900–1904. Ernest Shackleton, who later led his own expedition, was one of those who sailed with Scott in the *Discovery*. The voyage was a great success, resulting in the discovery of King Edward VII. Land, the determination of the southern magnetic pole, and the charting of large areas of the antarctic continent and its surrounding waters. Scott was primarily interested in scientific work rather than in reaching the pole, but on one notable sledge journey he came closer to it than any before him.

After his return, Scott wrote the classic *Voyage of the Discovery*, married Kathleen Bruce, a sculptor, and became the father of a son, Peter, who later was famous as a painter of birds. He also began to organize a second polar expedition. To raise the large amount of money necessary, he announced his determination to reach the pole, a feat that Shackleton had just failed to accomplish. The funds were collected and the *Terra Nova* sailed in 1910.

Scott began the final stage of the southern sledge journey with four companions in November, 1911. The excitement of Scott's dash to the pole was heightened by the fact that the Norwegian explorer, Roald Amundsen, meanwhile had undertaken a race to be the first to reach the southern tip of the world. He had a head start, for he had at first pretended that his destination was the North Pole. He also chose a better base, and benefited greatly from his arctic experience with the use of dogs and Eskimo food and clothing. As Scott's party neared their goal they discovered the first signs that Amundsen was well ahead of them. Scott noted in his diary: "All the day dreams must go; it will be a wearisome return."

Dauntlessly the English explorers pressed on. They reached the South Pole on January 18, 1912, only to find that Amundsen had preceded them by thirty-four days. Looking about him at the dreary wastes over which flew the Norwegian flag, Scott could only say: "Great God! This is an awful place."

The trip back was a tragic one. Bad luck, shortages of food, frost-bite, illness and bitter storms followed Scott's party. Two died along the way. The final ordeal came in a blizzard that raged so furiously for eight days that Scott and his two remaining companions could not leave their tent and with food and fuel gone (their depot just eleven miles away) they faced death. Scott kept his diary through the last hours of privation. It was found, with his notes and treasured geological specimens, by a relief expedition eight months later. Among the papers was a message: "Had we lived, I should have had a tale to tell of hardihood, endurance, and courage of my companions which would have stirred the heart of every Englishman. These rough notes and our dead bodies must tell the tale. . . ."

February 22, 1912.

. . . There is little doubt we are in for a rotten critical time going home, and the lateness of the season may make it really serious. . . . In the afternoon, Bowers being sure we were too far to the west, steered out. Result, we have passed another pony camp without seeing it. Looking at the map tonight, there is no doubt we are too far to the east. With clear weather we ought to be able to correct the mistake, but will the weather get clear?

March 11.

Titus Oates is very near the end, one feels. What he or we will do, God only knows. We discussed the matter after breakfast; he is a brave, fine fellow and understands the situation, but he practically asked for advice. Nothing could be said but to urge him to march as long as he could. One satisfactory result to the discussion; I practically ordered Wilson to hand over the means of ending our troubles to us, so that any one of us may know what to do. Wilson had no choice between doing so and our ransacking the medicine case.

We have thirty opium tabloids apiece and he is left with a tube of morphine. So far the tragical side of our story.

The sky completely overcast when we started this morning. We could see nothing, lost the tracks, and doubtless have been swaying a good deal since— 3.1 miles for the forenoon—terribly heavy dragging—expected it. Know that six miles is about the limit of our endurance now, if we get no help from wind or surfaces. We have seven days food and should be about 55 miles from One Ton Camp tonight.

March 14.

No doubt about going down hill, but everything going wrong for us. Yesterday we woke to a strong northerly wind with temperature −37°. Couldn't face it, so remained in camp till 2, then did 5¼ miles. Wanted to march later, but party feeling the cold badly as the breeze (N) never took off entirely, and as the sun sank the temp. fell. Long time getting supper in dark.

This morning started with southerly breeze, set sail and passed another cairn at good speed; half way, however, the wind shifted to W by S or WSW, blew through our wind clothes and into our mits. Poor Wilson horribly cold, could [not] get off skis for some time. Bowers and I practically made camp, and when we got into the tent at last we were all deadly cold. We *must* go on, but now the making of every camp must be more difficult and dangerous. It must be near the end, but a pretty merciful end. Poor Oates got it again in the foot. I shudder to think what it will be like tomorrow. It is only with greatest pains rest of us keep off frostbites. No idea there could be temperatures like this at this time of year with such winds. Truly awful outside the tent. Must fight it out to the last biscuit, but can't reduce rations.

March 16 or 17.

Lost track of dates, but think the last correct. Tragedy all along the line. At lunch, the day before yesterday, poor Titus Oates said he couldn't go on; he proposed we should leave him in his sleeping bag. That we could not do, and we induced him to come on, on the afternoon march. In spite of its awful nature for him, he struggled on and we made a few miles. At night he was worse and we knew the end had come.

Should this be found I want these facts recorded. Oates' last thoughts were of his mother, but immediately before he took pride in thinking that his regiment would be pleased with the bold way in which he met his death. We can testify to his bravery. He has borne intense suffering for weeks without complaint and to the very last was able and willing to discuss outside subjects. He did not—would not—give up hope till the very end. He was a brave soul. This was the end. He slept through the night before last—hoping not to wake; but he woke in the morning—yesterday. It was blowing a blizzard. He said, "I am just going outside and may be some time." He went out into the blizzard and we have not seen him since. . . .

. . . We knew that poor Oates was walking to his death, but though we tried to dissuade him, we knew it was the act of a brave man and an English gentleman. We all hope to meet the end with a similar spirit, and assuredly the end is not far.

I can only write at lunch and then only occasionally. The cold is intense, −40° at midday. My companions are unendingly careful, but we are all on the verge of serious frostbites, and though we constantly talk of fetching through, I don't think any of us believes it in his heart.

We are cold on the march now, and at all times except meals. Yesterday we had to lay up for a blizzard and today we move dreadfully slowly. We are at Number 14 pony camp, only two pony marches from One Ton depot. We leave here our theodolite, a camera, and Oates' sleeping bags. Diaries, etc., and geographical specimens carried at Wilson's special request will be found with us or on our sledge.

March 18.

Today, lunch, we are 21 miles from the depot. Ill fortune presses, but better may come. We have had more wind and drift from ahead yesterday; had to stop marching; wind northwest, force 4, temp. −35°. No human being could face it, and we are worn out *nearly*.

My right foot has gone, nearly all the toes—two days ago I was proud possessor of best feet. These are the steps of my downfall. Like an ass, I mixed a small spoonful of curry powder with my melted pemmican—it gave me violent indigestion. I lay awake and in pain all night; woke and fell down on the march; foot went and I didn't know it. A very small measure of neglect and have a foot which is not pleasant to contemplate. Bowers takes first place in condition, but there is not much to choose after all. The others are still confident of getting through—or pretend to be. I don't know! We have the last *half* fill of oil in our primus and a very small quantity of spirit—this alone between us and thirst. The wind is fair for the moment, and that is perhaps a fact to help. The mileage would have seemed ridiculously small on our outward journey.

March 19. Lunch.

We camped with difficulty last night, and were dreadfully cold till after our supper of cold pemmican and biscuit and a half a pannikin of cocoa cooked over the spirit. Then, contrary to expectation, we got warm and all slept well. Today we start in the usual dragging manner. Sledge dreadfully heavy. We are 15½ miles from the depot and ought to get there in three days. What progress! We have two days' food but barely a day's fuel. All our feet are getting bad—Wilson's best, my right foot worse, left all right. There is no chance to nurse one's feet till we can get hot food into us. Amputation is the least I can hope for now, but will the trouble spread? That is the serious question. The weather doesn't give us a chance—the wind from N to NW and −40° temp. today.

March 21.

Got within 11 miles of depot Monday night; had to lay up all yesterday in severe blizzard. Today forlorn hope, Wilson and Bowers going to depot for fuel.

March 22 and 23.

Blizzard bad as ever—Wilson and Bowers unable to start—tomorrow last chance—no fuel and only one or two of food left—must be near the end. We shall march for the depot with or without our effects and die in our tracks.

[Six days passed before the next entry.]

March 29.

Since the 21st we have had a continuous gale from WSW and SW. We had fuel to make two cups of tea apiece and bare food for two days on the 20th. Every day we have been ready to start for our depot 11 *miles* away, but outside the door of the tent it remains a scene of whirling drift, I do not think we can hope for better things now. We shall stick it out to the end, but we are getting weaker of course, and the end cannot be far. It seems a pity, but I do not think I can write more.

[*Last entry, undated.*]

For God's sake look after our people.

*"If he . . . could face it with such sublime fortitude,
how dare I possibly whine."*

Kathleen, Lady Scott

Captain Scott's wife has left two memorials of him, a statue she shaped that stands among other monuments to British heroes in Waterloo Place, London, and her moving diary kept through his long absence until at last she had to face the realization he would never come home.

She received the title of Lady Scott in recognition of the intention to confer knighthood on her husband when he returned. Ten years after his death, during which she continued her career as sculptor, she married again, becoming the wife of Baron Kennet, a financial and political figure.

Half a world apart from him Lady Scott was often sensitively, almost uncannily, attuned to her husband's moments of crisis. The diary's last entries are an extraordinary record of a noble grief.

September 3, 1911.

Tonight I went a long walk along the beach, to where you and I once went. You won't remember—right along to where the river flows into the sea; and I saw the very tuft of grass on the sand that we sat down upon to light your pipe. That was a long time ago. It was more beautiful weather today than then, for there was an exquisite sunset, and over the marshes the moon was rising, and not a sound but my own bare toes on the sand. I wonder if you will be here with me next year? You should love it as I do.

September 20.

I had rather a horrid day today. I woke up having a bad dream about you, and then Peter [aged 2] came very close to me and said emphatically, "Daddy won't come back," as though in answer to my silly thoughts. By the time you read this, you will probably be comfortably lounging in a deckchair on a P. and O. near Colombo and will say contentedly, "Silly little maid," and you'll be quite right. Happily, I am not often silly.

From *Self Portrait of an Artist,* by Lady Kennet. Reprinted by permission of John Murray Ltd.

February 18, 1912.

I was very taken up with you all evening. I wonder if anything special is happening to you. Something odd happened to the clocks and watches between nine and ten p.m.

[On February 18 Captain Scott's party started across the Barrier Ice. On February 19 the Polar party was struggling with severe conditions on the Barrier, and Captain Scott wrote in his own diary, "I wonder what is in store for us."]

February 19.

I was still rather taken up by you and a wee bit depressed. As you ought about now to be returning to ship I see no reason for depression. I wonder.

[On February 4, 1913, Lady Scott sailed for New Zealand to meet the explorers who were to return on the *Terra Nova*. When her ship was eight days out from San Francisco, the *Terra Nova* reached New Zealand on February 12 with the first news of the death of Captain Scott and the Polar party eleven months before. For the next week efforts were made to inform Lady Scott by wireless, but signals in those early days of wireless were too weak to be heard so far away.]

February 17, 1913.
We arrived at Tahiti.

[The news of Captain Scott's death finally reached her on the ship between Tahiti and Rarotonga.]

February 19.

I got my wireless. I was sitting on deck after breakfast, not feeling very well. The captain came and said he wanted to speak to me in his cabin. It did not occur to me in the slightest what he wanted, but I went. The poor old chap's hands were trembling when he said, "I've got some news for you, but I don't see how I can tell you." I said, "The Expedition?" And he said, "Yes." "Well," I said, "let's have it," and he showed me the message which came, "Captain Scott and six others perished in blizzard after reaching South Pole January 18."

I remember I said, without the least truth, "Oh, well, never mind! I expected that. Thanks very much. I will go and think about it," and I went downstairs. It was the hour at which I sometimes have a Spanish lesson. I had my Spanish lesson for an hour and a half and acquitted myself well. I went down to lunch and discussed American politics. I had asked the captain not to tell the passengers; the officers already knew. I read a book on the wreck of the *Titanic,* and determined to keep my mind off the whole subject until I was sure I could control myself. It was too hot to go to my cabin; I therefore stayed on the deck the whole day. My god is godly. I need not touch him to know that. Let me maintain a high, adoring exaltation, and not let the contamination of sorrow touch me. Within I shall be exultant. My god is glorious and could never become less so. Loneliness is a fear that I have never known. Had he died before I had known his gloriousness, or before he had been the father of my son, I might have felt a loss. Now I have felt none for myself. Won't anybody understand that?—probably nobody. So I must go on and on with the tedious business of discretion. Must even the greatest visions of the heart be blurred by discretions?

February 20.

We arrived at Rarotonga in the morning. There was no further news there, but what there was, was posted up at the Postoffice, and the passengers, of course, saw it. There were two cables, one from Wilfred [her brother with the expedition] saying he would meet me at Wellington, and one from the *Terra Nova,* of sympathy. I stayed on the boat and wrote letters. Late in the afternoon I went ashore with a young South American. As he speaks no language I understand, but just quietly devotes himself, he does not worry. We sat on coral rocks in the rain and watched the breakers curl in over the reef. We returned by moonlight, wet to the skin. He did not know.

February 21.

It is too hot to stay in my cabin and there is absolutely no privacy on the ship. If only I could go away somewhere, or even have some human, understanding person to talk to. The Third Officer is a dear, clean boy, but only 23, and almost always on duty. I played five games of deck golf and read violently. Anything to get the awful, haunting picture out of my head. It is good that I do not believe firmly in life after death, or surely, I would have gone overboard today. But I am afraid my Con has gone altogether, except in the great, stirring influence he must have left on everyone who had knowledge of him. I think he made me twice the man I am. Certainly I couldn't have faced this with complete self-control before his teaching. Ever since I knew him I have worked, striven, and strained that he might applaud ever so little, though I shall never have the applause. Perhaps it has become so much a habit that one will go on. I have always recognized how much he has been my god and my conscience, but now it grows more evident. He has been my motive-power all this while. I feel as though even now it will not give out. I wonder. He's raised my standard anyhow, shown me what men can be, and what he expects me to be. Can I keep to it without the hope of his applause.

All these long, weary days with no more news. Always only his pain, his mental agony, boring into my brain. I sleep, or don't, on the top deck and the nights are beautiful with the moon, and all the different aspects of it come to me one by one. How one hopes his brain soon got numbed and the weight of his responsibility left him; for I think never was there a man with such sense of responsibility and duty, and the agony of leaving his job undone, losing the other lives, and leaving us uncared for, must have been unspeakable.

February 23.

These have been the strangest nights. At about 11 or 12 midnight the wireless messages begin and go on till about 3 A.M. I sit in the Wireless Room, watching the moving pencil of the operator. It is like a planchette. A few words come and then a stop at the most critical moment. Messages of condolence, lovely messages, keep coming through, coming and coming without ceasing, but thus blocking the line and preventing me getting press news. It is of course necessary for the operators to send through paid messages before sending press news, and so without knowing it my kind friends, and so kind, are balking my news and keeping me absolutely in ignorance except of the main fact. Through these long nights of anxiety the young Third Officer is the only human whom I have to turn to. He understands very little, but he is healthy and sane, and always ready to be with me when I can't sleep. He is the only person I can talk to at all, and he understands very little; but like a big dog he sits by me and is sorry.

February 24.

All night the messages came. I sat a long while in the Wireless Room and then went up on the upper deck as usual to bed, and from 12 to 3 the Third Officer went backwards and forwards bringing me the messages. They were none of them what I wanted, none of them news, just condolences from governments, from Asquith, Marconi, Arty and Muriel Paget, Lord Liverpool, etc. One from Mrs. Wilson crossed mine. One came yesterday, sent by Marconi, to say Peter is well.

February 25.

Last night there came through the last words of Con's diary, at least the appeal that the country should take care of us. We were alone, the wireless operator and I. I had come back after undressing, just to see if anything was coming. It was my first knowledge that it was starvation that had killed them. I thought it was exposure. The operator is an Irishman; we have never had any conversation. He just hands me the papers as he has finished writing them. I took my papers and went to bed; I didn't want to hear any more.

That was a glorious, courageous note, and a great inspiration to me. If he in his weakness could face it with such sublime fortitude, how dare I possibly whine. I will *not*. I regret nothing but his suffering.

[The British public did not fail to heed Scott's appeal for aid to the families of those who had bravely perished. A fund of £100,000 was quickly raised.]

"Upon my soul, not a bad specimen of a man . . ."

James Boswell

A young man of twenty-two, called Bozzy by his friends, set off from his native Edinburgh in a post-chaise on November 15, 1762, to spend a year or so in London. The days ahead were important ones for the traveller and scarcely less so for literature. It was just six months later that James Boswell (1740–1795) met Dr. Samuel Johnson, and began to write down in his *London Journal* the notes of their walks and talks on which he based what is generally regarded as the greatest of all biographies.

Boswell came from an old and prosperous Scotch family linked to nobility. He could boast that he was a cousin of George III. The family profession was law; his grandfather was a lawyer, his father was Lord Auchinleck, justice of the highest Scotch courts, and it was for a legal career that Boswell was trained when he entered the University of Edinburgh at thirteen, and later the University of Glasgow. Law was not to his liking, however, for he was interested in writing, the theatre, society, and the company of women. After a sickly youth, he was at twenty-two a robust, fairly handsome young man, of average height, plump, with very dark hair and eyes and a dark-hued complexion. He was not unattractive to women and to the alarm of his family was much given to casual love affairs, one of which resulted in the birth of an illegitimate son.

Perhaps it was this particular scrape that persuaded his father to give him an allowance of £200 a year and permit him to go off to London to seek a commission in the Footguards, the personal bodyguard of the King.

From his first day in England, Boswell began to keep a diary of daily happenings, written with remarkable neatness on folded sheets of paper about the size of this book. "In this way," he said, "I shall preserve many things that would otherwise be lost in oblivion. I shall find daily employment for myself, which will

Reprinted by permission from *Boswell's London Journal*, 1762–1763, edited by Frederick A. Pottle, published by McGraw-Hill Book Company, Inc. Copyright, 1950, by Yale University.

save me from indolence and help to keep off the spleen, and I shall lay up a store of entertainment for my after life."

After Boswell's death, the diary and many of his other papers were neglected or suppressed by members of his family who were shocked by its candid, uninhibited revelations. Only after a hundred and fifty years did the lost manuscripts come to light again, thanks to the enterprise and detective work of American scholars, notably Lieutenant-Colonel Ralph Heyward Isham who, with others, patiently recovered them from bags, chests, bean sacks, an old croquet box, a cabinet, and closets and attics of several old country houses. Col. Isham succeeded in coaxing Boswell's descendants to sell the papers to him and ultimately this great treasure was acquired by Yale University for preservation and publication.

The *London Journal* was first printed in 1950. Frank, self-analytical, confessional, the diary was immediately recognized as one of the finest in the English language. With engaging candour Boswell describes his wandering thoughts and roving eyes directed at fair ladies in church; his tears over the story of Joseph and his brethren; his glee in counting and fingering the golden guineas of his quarterly allowance; his delight in his lodgings where he slept late in a luxurious tent bed; his preoccupation with erotic adventures. He brings alive the noisy, crowded London streets, the chop houses and taverns where he ate and drank, the theatres, the cock fights, the sound of the night watchman calling outside the window. And then, of course, there is the first appearance of Dr. Samuel Johnson. . . .

November 15, 1762.

Elated with the thoughts of my journey to London, I got up . . . had a long serious conversation with my father and mother. They were very kind to me. I felt parental affection was very strong towards me; and I felt a very warm filial regard for them. The scene of being a son setting out from home for the wide world and the idea of being my own master, pleased me very much. . . . At ten I got into my chaise, and away I went. . . .

November 19.

. . . When we came upon Highgate hill and had a view of London, I was all life and joy. I . . . made the boy drive me to Mr. Hayward's, at the Black Lion, Water Lane, Fleet Street. The noise, the crowd, the glare of shops and signs agreeably confused me. I was rather more wildly struck than when I first came to London. . . . I then had a bit of dinner, got myself shaved and cleaned, and had my landlord, a civil jolly man, to take a glass of wine with me. I was all in a flutter at having at last got to the place which I was so madly fond of, and being restrained, had formed so many wild schemes to get back to. I had recourse to philosophy, and so rendered myself calm.

I . . . went to Covent Garden—*Every Man in His Humour* [by Ben Jonson]. Woodward played Bobadil finely. He entertained me much. It was fine after the fatigues of my journey to find myself snug in a theatre, my body warm and my mind elegantly amused. I went to my inn, had some negus, and went comfortably to bed.

November 20.

. . . I strolled about all the forenoon calling for different people, but found nobody in. I went and saw a collection of wild beasts. I felt myself bold, easy, and happy. . . .

November 21.

I got up well and enjoyed my good situation. I had a handsome dining-room and bed-chamber, just in Pall Mall, the finest part of the town; I was in pursuit of my commission [in the Guards], which I was vastly fond of; and I had money enough to live like a gentleman.

I went to Mayfair Chapel and heard prayers and an excellent sermon from the Book of Job on the comforts of piety. I was in a fine frame. And I thought that God really designed us to be happy. I shall certainly be a religious old man. I was much so in my youth. I have now and then flashes of devotion, and it will one day burn with a steady flame. . . .

November 26.

. . . I was much difficulted about lodgings. A variety I am sure I saw, I dare say fifty. At last I fixed in Downing Street, Westminster. I took a lodging up two pair of stairs with the use of a handsome parlour all the forenoon, for which I agreed to pay forty guineas a year, but I took it for a fortnight first, by way of a trial. I also made a bargain that I should dine with the family whenever I pleased, at a shilling a time. . . .

November 28.

. . . Went to St. James's Church and heard service and a good sermon on "By what means shall a young man learn to order his ways," in which the advantages of early piety were well displayed. What a curious, inconsistent thing is the mind of man. In the midst of divine service I was laying plans for having women. . . . I have a warm heart and a vivacious fancy. I am therefore given to love, and also to piety or gratitude to God, and to the most brilliant and showy method of public worship.

I then walked in the Park and went home to dinner, which was just a good joint of veal and a pudding. This they told me was the usual fare, which I approved of. I found my landlord rather too free. Therefore I carried myself with reserve and something of state. . . .

December 2.

. . . Went to Leicester Street, where Lady Betty had a house taken. I pitied Macfarlane, who is very narrow, and had now house and footmen and coach and dress and entertainment of all kinds to pay. . . . What an absurd thing it was for this old clumsy dotard to marry a strong young woman of quality. It was certainly vanity, for which he has paid very heavily. Her marrying him was just to support herself and her sisters; and yet to a woman of delicacy, poverty is better than sacrificing her person to a greasy, rotten, nauseous carcass and a narrow vulgar soul. She certainly wants feeling who can submit to the loathed embraces of a monster. She appears to me unclean: as I said to Miss Dempster, like a dirty table-cloth. I am sure no man can have the gentle passion of love for so defiled a person as hers—O my stomach rises at it!

December 3.

I began now to be much at home in my lodgings and to get into a regular method. I resolved to want a servant for my first year and in every respect to be frugal, that I might learn the value of money, see what I could afford to do with my allowance, and rather live within than exceed my income. I am really surprised at the coolness and moderation with which I am proceeding. . . .

I now received a card of invitation to the rout on Tuesday the 7. This raised my spirits, gave me notions of my consequence, and filled me with grandeur. Fain would I have got rich laced clothes, but I commanded my inclination and got just a plain suit of a pink colour, with a gold button. . . .

December 4.

. . . At night, Erskine and I strolled through the streets and St. James's Park. We were accosted there by several ladies of the town. Erskine was very humorous and said some very wild things to them. There was one in a red cloak of a good buxom person and comely face whom I marked as a future piece, in case of exigency.

December 5.

. . . Went to St. George's Church, where I heard a good sermon on the prophets testifying of Jesus Christ. I was upon honour much disposed to be a Christian. Yet I was rather cold in my devotion. The Duchess of Grafton attracted my eyes rather too much. . . .

Dempster, talking of *Irene*, a tragedy written by Mr. Samuel Johnson, said it was as frigid as the regions of Nova Zembla; that now and then you felt a little heat like what is produced by touching ice.

December 8.

. . . At night I went to Covent Garden and saw *Love in a Village,* a new comic opera, for the first night. I liked it much. I saw it from the gallery, but I was first in the pit. Just before the overture began to be played, two Highland officers came in. The mob in the upper gallery roared out, "No Scots! No Scots! Out with them!," hissed and pelted them with apples. My heart warmed to my countrymen, my Scotch blood boiled with indignation. I jumped up on the benches, roared out, "Damn you, you rascals!," hissed and was in the greatest rage. I am very sure at that time I should have been the most distinguished of heroes. I hated the English; I wished from my soul that the Union was broke and that we might give them another battle of Bannockburn. . . .

December 11.

. . . I am pushing to get into the Guards, where to distinguish myself as a good officer and to get promotion will be my favourite objects. If that does not succeed, I am at least living happily, I am seeing the world, studying men and manners, and fitting myself for a pleasing, quiet life in old age, by laying up agreeable ideas to feast upon in recollection. . . . O happy situation of mind which I now have! All things look well. . . . I have an honest mind and a warm friendship. Upon my soul, not a bad specimen of a man. . . .

December 12.

I took a whim of dining at home every day last week, which I kept exactly to. The pleasure of gratifying whim is very great. It is known only by those who are whimsical. This day I was in a pleasing indolent humour. I sat at home writing till three, and then . . . went and heard prayers in St. Margaret's Church, Westminster. I dined at home very comfortably. I really am very well situated in lodgings. My landlord is a jolly, civil man. His wife a quiet, well-behaved woman, and his sister a neat-handed, clever girl. They do everything to serve me. Mr. Terrie is in a public office, so that he supplies me with paper and all materials for writing in great abundance, for nothing. Mrs. Terrie gets all things that I want bought for me, and Miss sews the laced ruffles on my shirts. . . . I sat in all this evening calm and indulgent. I had a fire in both my rooms above-stairs. I drank tea by myself for a long time. I had my feet washed with milk-warm water, I had my bed warmed, and went to sleep soft and contented.

December 14.

It is very curious to think that I have now been in London several weeks without ever enjoying the delightful sex, although I am surrounded with numbers of free-hearted ladies of all kinds: from the splendid Madam at fifty guineas a night, down to the civil nymph with white-thread stockings who tramps along the Strand and will resign her engaging person to your honour for a pint of wine and a shilling. Manifold are the reasons for this my present wonderful continence. I am upon a plan of economy, and therefore cannot be at the expense of first-rate dames. I have suffered severely from the loathsome distemper, and therefore shudder at the thoughts of running any risk of having it again. Besides, the surgeons' fees in this city come very high. But the greatest reason of all is that fortune, or rather benignant Venus, has smiled upon me and favoured me so far that I have had the most delicious intrigues with women of beauty, sentiment, and spirit, perfectly suited to my romantic genius.

Indeed, in my mind, there cannot be higher felicity on earth enjoyed by man than the participation of genuine reciprocal amorous affection with an amiable woman. There he has a full indulgence of all the delicate feelings and pleasures both of body and mind, while at the same time in this enchanting union he exults with a consciousness that he is the superior person. The dignity of his sex is kept up. These paradisial scenes of gallantry have exalted my ideas and refined my taste, so that I really cannot think of stooping so far as to make a most intimate companion of a groveling-minded, ill-bred, worthless creature, nor can my delicacy be pleased with the gross voluptuousness of the stews. I am therefore walking about with a healthful stout body and a cheerful mind, in search of a woman worthy of my love, and who thinks me worthy of hers, without any interested views, which is the only sure way to find out if a woman really loves a man. If I should be a single man for the whole winter, I will be satisfied. . . .

December 15.

The enemies of the people of England who would have them considered in the worst light represent them as selfish, beef-eaters, and cruel. In this view I resolved today to be a true-born Old Englishman. I went into the City to Dolly's Steak-house in Paternoster Row and swallowed my dinner by myself to fulfill the charge of selfishness; I had a large fat beefsteak to fulfill the charge of beef-eating; and I went at five o'clock to the Royal Cockpit in St. James's Park and saw cock-fighting for about five hours to fulfill the charge of cruelty. A beefsteak-house is a most excellent place to dine at. You come in there to a warm, comfortable, large room, where a number of people are sitting at table. You take whatever place you find empty; call for what you like, which you get well and cleverly dressed. You may either chat or not as you like. Nobody minds you, and you pay very reasonably. My dinner (beef, bread and beer and waiter) was only a shilling. . . . At five I filled my pockets with gingerbread and apples (quite the method), put on my old clothes and laced hat, laid by my watch, purse, and pocket-book, and with oaken stick in my hand sallied to the pit. I was too soon there. So I went into a low inn, sat down amongst a parcel of arrant blackguards, and drank some beer. . . .

I then went to the Cockpit, which is a circular room in the middle of which the cocks fight. It is seated round with rows gradually rising. The pit and the seats are all covered with mat. The cocks, nicely cut and dressed and armed with silver heels, are set down and fight with amazing bitterness and resolution. Some of them were quickly dispatched. One pair fought three quarters of an hour. The uproar and noise of betting is prodigious. A great deal of money made a very quick circulation from hand to hand. . . . I was sorry for the poor cocks. I looked round to see if any of the spectators pitied them when mangled and torn in a most cruel manner, but I could not observe the smallest relenting sign in any countenance. I was therefore not ill pleased to see them endure mental torment. Thus did I complete my true English day, and came home pretty much fatigued and pretty much confounded at the strange turn of this people.

January 11, 1763.

I am amazed how I have neglected last Friday to mention a circumstance so very material to me as the payment of my allowance, which indeed elevated me to a most extraordinary pitch. Many a time did I lay the lovely shining pieces upon my table, count them over, put them in rank and file like the Guards, and place them in many different sorts of figures. In short, a boy at school could not be more childishly fond of sugar plums than I was of golden guineas. . . .

January 13.

. . . At night went to Covent Garden gallery and saw *The Jovial Crew.* . . . The songs revived in my mind many gay ideas, and recalled in the most lively colours to my imagination the time when I was first in London, when all was new to me, when I felt the warm glow of youthful feeling and was full of curiosity and wonder. I then had at times a degree of ecstasy of feeling that the experience which I have since had in some measure cooled and abated. But then my ignorance at that time is infinitely excelled by the knowledge and moderation and government of myself which I have now acquired. After the play I came home, eat a Bath cake and a sweet orange, and went comfortably to bed.

January 20.

. . . Called at Drury Lane for Mr. Garrick. He was vastly good to me. "Sir," said he, "you will be a very great man. And when you are so, remember the year 1763. I want to contribute my part towards saving you. And pray, will you fix a day when I shall have the pleasure of treating you with tea?" I fixed next day. "Then, Sir," said he, "the cups shall dance and the saucers skip."

What he meant by my being a great man I can understand. For really, to speak seriously, I think there is a blossom about me of something more distinguished than the generality of mankind. But I am much afraid that this blossom will never swell into fruit, but will be nipped and destroyed by many a blighting heat and chilling frost. Indeed, I sometimes indulge noble reveries of having a regiment, of getting into Parliament, making a figure, and becoming a man of consequence in the state. But these are checked by dispiriting reflections on my melancholy temper and imbecility of mind. Yet I may probably become sounder and stronger as I grow up. Heaven knows, I am resigned. I trust to Providence. . . .

February 9.

I got up excellently well. My present life is most curious, and very fortunately is become agreeable. My affairs are conducted with the greatest regularity and exactness. I move like very clock-work. At eight in the morning Molly lights the fire, sweeps and dresses my dining-room. Then she calls me up and lets me know what o'clock it is. I lie some time in bed indulging indolence, which in that way, when the mind is easy and cheerful, is most pleasing. I then slip on my clothes loosely, easily, and quickly, and come into my dining-room. I pull my bell. The maid lays a milk-white napkin upon the table and sets the things for breakfast. I then take some light amusing book and breakfast and read for an hour or more, gently pleasing both my palate and my mental taste. Breakfast over, I feel myself gay and lively. I go to the window, and am entertained with the people passing by, all intent on different schemes. . . . My day is in general diversified with reading of different kinds, playing on the violin, writing, chatting with friends. Even the taking of medicines serves to make time go on with less heaviness. I have a sort of genius for physic. . . .

How easily and cleverly do I write just now! I am really pleased with myself; words come skipping to me like lambs upon Moffat Hill; and I turn my periods smoothly and imperceptibly like a skilful wheelwright turning tops in a turning-loom. There's fancy! There's simile! In short, I am at present a genius. . . .

February 14.

. . . This night my new tent-bed was put up. I liked it much. It gave a snug yet genteel look to my room, and had a military air which amused my fancy and made me happy.

February 20.

. . . This forenoon I read the history of Joseph and his brethren, which melted my heart and drew tears from my eyes. It is simply and beautifully told in the Sacred Writings. It is a strange thing that the Bible is so little read. I am reading it regularly through at present. I dare say there are many people of distinction in London who know nothing about it. Were the history of Joseph published by some genteel bookseller as an Eastern fragment and circulated amongst the gay world, I am persuaded that those who have any genuine taste might be taken in to admire it exceedingly and so by degrees have a due value for the oracles of God. I have a great mind to make the experiment. . . .

March 21.

. . . When I went home in the evening, I felt myself quite dissipated by running about so much. I was indolent and careless and could not fix to anything. Even this my journal was in danger of being neglected. Near a whole week had elapsed without my writing a single page of it. By way of penance for my idleness, and by way of making up for the time lost and bring up my business, I determined to sit up all this night; which I accordingly did, and wrote a great deal. About two o'clock in the morning I inadvertently snuffed out my candle, and as my fire was long before that black and cold, I was in a great dilemma how to proceed. Downstairs did I softly and silently step to the kitchen. But, alas, there was as little fire there as upon the icy mountains of Greenland. With a tinder-box is a light struck every morning to kindle the fire, which is put out at night. But this tinder-box I could not see, nor knew where to find. I was now filled with gloomy ideas of the terrors of the night. I was also apprehensive that my landlord, who always keeps a pair of loaded pistols by him, might fire at me as a thief. I went up to my room, sat quietly till I heard the watchman calling, "Past three o'clock." I then called to him to knock at the door of the house where I lodged. He did so, and I opened it to him and got my candle relumed without danger. Thus was I relieved and continued busy till eight next day.

May 16.

. . . I drank tea at Davies's in Russell Street, and about seven came in the great Mr. Samuel Johnson, whom I have so long wished to see. Mr. Davies introduced me to him. As I knew his mortal antipathy at the Scotch, I cried to Davies, "Don't tell where I come from." However, he said, "From Scotland." "Mr. Johnson," said I, "indeed I come from Scotland, but I cannot help it." "Sir," replied he, "that, I find, is what a very great many of your countrymen cannot help." Mr. Johnson is a man of a most dreadful appearance. He is a very big man, is troubled with sore eyes, the palsy, and the king's evil. He is very slovenly in his dress and speaks with a most uncouth voice. Yet his great knowledge and strength of expression command vast respect and render him very excellent company. He has great humour and is a worthy man. But his dogmatical roughness of manners is disagreeable. . . .

May 19.

. . . Sallied forth to the Piazzas in rich flow of animal spirits and burning with fierce desire. I met two very pretty little girls who asked me to take them with me. "My dear girls," said I, "I am a poor fellow. I can give you no money. But if you choose to have a glass of wine and my company and let us be gay and obliging to each other without money, I am your man." They agreed with great good humour. So back to the Shakespeare I went. "Waiter," said I, "I have got here a couple of human beings; I don't know how they'll do." "I'll look, your Honour," cried he, and with inimitable effrontery stared them in the face and then cried, "They'll do very well." "What," said I, "are they good fellow-creatures? Bring them up, then." We were shown into a good room and had a bottle of sherry before us in a minute. . . . I was quite *raised*, as the phrase is: thought I was in a London tavern, the Shakespeare's head, enjoying high debauchery after my sober winter. I parted with my ladies politely and came home in a glow of spirits.

May 24.

. . . I went and waited upon Mr. Samuel Johnson, who received me very courteously. He has chambers in the Inner Temple, where he lives in literary state, very solemn and very slovenly. He had some people with him, and when they left him, I rose too. But he cried, "No, don't go away." "Sir," said I, "I am afraid that I intrude upon you. It is benevolent to allow me to sit and hear you." He was pleased with this compliment, which I sincerely paid him, and he said he was obliged to any man who visited him. I was proud to sit in such company. . . .

I begged that he would favour me with his company at my lodgings some evening. He promised that he would. I then left him, and he shook me cordially by the hand. Upon my word, I am very fortunate. I shall cultivate this acquaintance. . . .

June 4.

. . . It was the King's birthnight, and I resolved to be a blackguard and to see all that was to be seen. I dressed myself in my second mourning suit, in which I had been powdered many months, dirty buckskin breeches and black stockings, a shirt of Lord Eglinton's which I had worn two days, and little round hat with tarnished silver lace belonging to a disbanded officer of the Royal Volunteers. I had in my hand an old oaken stick battered against the pavement. And was I not a complete blackguard? I went to the Park, picked up a low brimstone, called myself a barber and agreed with her for sixpence. . . . I then went as far as St. Paul's Church-yard, roaring along, and then came to Ashley's Punch-house and drank three threepenny bowls. In the Strand I picked up a little profligate wretch and gave her sixpence. . . . At Whitehall I picked up another girl to whom I called myself a high-wayman and told her I had no money and begged she would trust me. But she would not. My vanity was somewhat gratified tonight that, notwithstanding of my dress, I was always taken for a gentleman in disguise. I came home about two o'clock, much fatigued.

June 7.

I just read, eat, drank, and walked.

July 5.

. . . At night Temple and his brother sat with me at my lodgings over some negus, and as they were in a frolicsome humour, and were tickling me and jumping about, we made a good deal of noise. Mr. Terrie, my landlord . . . took it into his head that we had the maid with us, and came and rapped furiously at the parlour door, calling my name. I went out and asked him what he meant. He bawled out that he would be in, and would turn us every one out. He then called the watch, desired him at his peril to bring more of his brethren, and said he charged us with a riot, and would send us to the roundhouse. However, when the watch returned, he began to dread the consequence of false imprisonment, and desisted. . . .

July 6.

. . . We talked of Scotland. Ogilvie, who is a rank Scot, defended his native land with all the powers he could muster up . . . said that Scotland had a great many noble wild prospects. "Sir," said Johnson, "I believe you have a great many noble wild prospects. Norway too has some noble wild prospects; and Lapland is remarkable for prodigious noble wild prospects. But, Sir, I believe the noblest prospect that a Scotsman ever sees is the road which leads him to England!" . . .

July 10.

. . . Some days ago I went to the old printing-office in Bow Church-yard kept by Dicey, whose family have kept it fourscore years. There are ushered into the world of literature *Jack and the Giants, The Seven Wise Men of Gotham,* and other story-books which in my dawning years amused me as much as *Rasselas* does now. I saw the whole scheme with a kind of pleasing romantic feeling to find myself really where all my old darlings were printed. . . .

July 14.

Mr. Johnson and I met at the Mitre by ourselves. He was in most excellent humour, though the night was very rainy. I said it was good for the vegetable part of the creation. "Ay, Sir," said he, "and for the animals who eat those vegetables, and for the animals who eat those animals." We had a good supper, which made us very comfortable. . . . Mr. Johnson said, "We will not drink two bottles of port." When one was drank, he called for another pint; and when we had got to the bottom of that, and I was distributing it equally, "Come," said he, "you need not measure it so exactly." "Sir," said I, "it is done." "Well, Sir," said he, "are you satisfied? or would you choose another?" "Would you, Sir?" said I. "Yes," said he, "I think I would. I think two bottles would seem to be the quantity for us." Accordingly we made them out. . . . He took me cordially by the hand and said, "My dear Boswell! I do love you very much." —I *will* be vain, there's enough.

July 16.

. . . At my last meeting with Mr. Johnson, he said that when he came first to London and was upon his shifts, he was told by a very clever man who understood perfectly the common affairs of life that £30 a year was enough to make a man live without being contemptible; that is to say, you might be always clean. He allowed £10 for clothes and linen. He said you might live in a garret at eighteen-pence a week, as few people would inquire where you lodge; and if they do, it is easy to say, "Sir, I am to be found at such a place." For spending threepence in a coffee-house, you may be for hours in very good company. You may dine for sixpence, you may breakfast on bread and milk, and you may want supper.

He advised me to keep a journal of my life, fair and undisguised. He said it would be a very good exercise, and would yield me infinite satisfaction when the ideas were faded from my remembrance. . . . He said indeed that I should keep it in private, and that I might surely have a friend who would burn it in case of my death. For my own part, I have at present such an affection for this my journal that it shocks me to think of burning it. I rather encourage the idea of having it carefully laid up among the archives of Auchinleck. However, I cannot judge fairly of it now. Some years hence I may. I told Mr. Johnson that I put down all sorts of little incidents in it. "Sir," said he, "there is nothing too little for so little a creature as man. . . ."

July 26.

. . . We talked of the education of children and what was best to teach them first. "Sir," said he, "there is no matter what you teach them first, any more than what leg you shall put into your breeches first. Sir, you may stand disputing which is best to put in first, but in the meantime your backside is bare. Sir, while you are considering which of two things you should teach your child first, another boy has learnt 'em both." . . .

July 28.

. . . As we walked along the Strand tonight, arm in arm, a woman of the town came enticingly near us. "No," said Mr. Johnson, "no, my girl, it won't do." . . . And here I must record perhaps the most curious singularity that ever a man had. When Mr. Johnson's wife was alive, she brought into the house as a companion Miss Williams, an amiable, ingenious woman who had attained a remarkable knowledge of the modern languages. This lady's eyes were tender. The disorder increased and ended at last in a gutta serena, so that she became stone-blind. Mrs. Johnson died, and while Mr. Johnson continued to keep house, Miss Williams remained with him. When he took to chambers in the Temple, Miss Williams then went to a lodging of her own. But Mr. Johnson is never a night without seeing her. Let him be never so late in company, Miss Williams sits up till he comes and drinks tea with her. I believe Miss Williams is supported chiefly by Mr. Johnson's generosity, and I believe nobody has ever had the folly or the malice to suspect anything criminal between them. . . .

July 30.

Mr. Johnson and I took a boat and sailed down the silver Thames. I asked him if a knowledge of the Greek and Roman languages was necessary. He said, "By all means. . . ." "And yet," said I, "people will go through the world very well and do their business very well without them." "Why," said he, "that may be true where they could not possibly be of any use; for instance, this boy rows us as well without literature as if he could sing the song which Orpheus sang to the Argonauts, who were the first sailors of the world." He then said to the boy, "What would you give, Sir, to know about the Argonauts?" "Sir," said he, "I would give what I have." The reply pleased Mr. Johnson much, and we gave him a double fare. . . .

July 31.

In the forenoon I was at a Quaker's meeting in Lombard Street, and in the afternoon at St. Paul's, where I was very devout and very happy. After service, I stood in the center and took leave of the church, bowing to every quarter. I cannot help having a reverence for it. Mr. Johnson says the same. Mr. Johnson said today that a woman's preaching was like a dog's walking on his hinder legs. It was not done well, but you were surprised to find it done at all.

August 3.

I should have mentioned that on Monday night, coming up the Strand, I was tapped on the shoulder by a fine fresh lass. I went home with her. She was an officer's daughter, and born at Gibraltar. I could not resist indulging myself. . . . Surely, in such a situation, when the woman is already abandoned, the crime must be alleviated, though in strict morality, illicit love is always wrong. . . .

August 4.

This is now my last day in London before I set out upon my travels, and makes a very important period in my journal. Let me recollect my life since this journal began. Has it not passed like a dream? Yes, but I have been attaining a knowledge of the world. I came to town to go into the Guards. How different is my scheme now! I am now on a less pleasurable but a more rational and lasting plan. Let me pursue it with steadiness and I may be a man of dignity. My mind is strangely agitated. I am happy to think of going upon my travels and seeing the diversity of foreign parts; and yet my feeble mind shrinks somewhat at the idea of leaving Britain in so very short a time from the moment in which I now make this remark. How strange must I feel in foreign parts. . . .

> *"I walk slow, make short steps,*
> *and never tread on my heel."*

Jonathan Swift

In the same tomb in St. Patrick's Cathedral in Dublin lie two figures whose relationship to each other still remains a mystery. The enigma is posed by Esther Johnson (1681–1728), known to posterity as "Stella," and her friend Jonathan Swift (1667–1745), former dean of St. Patrick's and author of the extraordinary "Journal to Stella."

Swift, who came of an English family, was born in Dublin and educated there at Kilkenny School and Trinity College. He was the cousin of John Dryden, poet and dramatist. When he left school Swift went to England to become literary secretary to Sir William Temple, a distant kinsman, at Moor Park, near Farnham, Surrey. Then twenty-two, he became attached to the daughter of a Temple family retainer, a girl named Esther Johnson, who at eight, with dark hair, bright eyes and quick intelligence, promised to be something of a beauty. Swift taught the child to write and chose books for her to read. They were much in each other's company.

Swift returned to Ireland to take holy orders, then he came back to Moor Park again. Esther was now fifteen. Their close association was renewed. Until his restlessness took him off to London, Swift continued to guide the child's education.

In the capital Swift soon made a name for himself as a keen pamphleteer whose stinging pen was always ready to serve a political cause. He became the friend of Pope, Addison, Steele, and Congreve. Everybody liked him except Dr. Samuel Johnson who thought London would benefit by his return to Ireland. Swift's facility at writing and flair for satire presently led him to write some of his memorable books, among them *The Tale of a Tub*, *The Battle of the Books* and, some years later, his immortal *Gulliver's Travels*, all aimed at the foibles of his time and noteworthy for their clear, direct style, with effective use of plain, colloquial speech.

From *Journal to Stella.*

In 1710 Swift began his famous journal in which he minutely recorded for himself and for Stella the incidents of his daily life. He became Dean of St. Patrick's in 1713 after lesser clerical responsibilities (in the parish of Laracor he preached to a congregation of fifteen persons, "all simple"). After some initial hostility, he won great popular favour in Ireland for his support of grievances against the government. He gave a third of his income to charity, and was loved for this.

Meanwhile, Swift continued his journal. The Stella he had known at eight and fifteen was now in her twenties. He still sent her his journal pages with their diffident overtures of affection and scribbled caresses. What claim did these two have on each other? Nobody knows. One story has it that they were married in 1716. Certainly each had rejected other possibilities of marriage, and the strange dean and his loyal pupil always remained devoted to each other.

The end of Swift's life was haunted by the fear of insanity. The fear became reality when a long illness finally cost him his reason. Two ironies remained. Quite mad when he died, in the years of his sanity Swift had willed his fortune to endow a hospital for treatment of the mentally ill. And, though there was apparently no precedent in life for such an intimacy, he was interred snugly by Stella's side thirteen years after her death.

November 24, 1710.

. . . I have had no fit since the first: I drink brandy every morning, and take pills every night. . . .

January 18, 1711.

I was this morning with Mr. Secretary St. John, and we were to dine at Mr. Harley's alone, about some business of importance, but there were two or three gentlemen there. Mr. Secretary and I went together from his office to Mr. Harley's, and thought to have been very wise; but the deuce a bit: the company stayed, and more came, and Harley went away at seven, and the Secretary and I stayed with the rest of the company till eleven. . . . I wonder at the civility of these people; when he saw I would drink no more, he would always pass the bottle by me, and yet I could not keep the toad from drinking himself, nor he would not let me go neither. . . . I go earlier to bed than formerly; and have not been out so late these two months; but the Secretary was in a drinking humour. . . .

January 19.

. . . This was an insipid snowy day, no walking day, and I dined gravely with Mrs. Vanhomrigh, and came home, and am now got to bed a little after ten; I remember old Culpepper's maxim:

> Would you have a settled head,
> You must early go to bed:
> I tell you, and I tell't again,
> You must be in bed at ten.

January 21.

It has snowed terribly all night, and is vengeance cold. I am not yet up, but cannot write long; my hands will freeze. . . . I write on the dark side of my bedchamber, and am forced to have a candle till I rise, for the bed stands between me and the window, and I keep the curtains shut this cold weather. . . . —At night. We are now here in high frost and snow, the largest fire can hardly keep us warm. It is very ugly walking; a baker's boy broke his thigh yesterday. I walk slow, make short steps, and never tread on my heel. 'Tis a good proverb the Devonshire people have:

> Walk fast in snow,
> In frost walk slow,
> And still as you go,
> Tread on your toe:
> When frost and snow are both together,
> Sit by the fire and spare shoe leather.

I dined to-day with Dr. Cockburn, but will not do so again in haste, he has generally such a parcel of Scots with him.

October 24.

I called at Lord-Treasurer's to-day at noon; he was eating some broth in his bed-chamber, undressed, with a thousand papers about him. He has a little fever upon him, and his eye terribly blood-shot; yet he dressed himself and went out to the Treasury. . . . I had a little turn in my head this morning; which, though it did not last above a moment, yet being of the true sort, has made me as weak as a dog all this day. 'Tis the first I have had this half year. I shall take my pills if I hear of it again. . . .

October 26.

I dined with Mrs. Van; for the weather is so bad, and I am so busy, that I can't dine with great folks: and besides I dare eat but little, to keep my head in order, which is better. Lord-Treasurer is very ill, but I hope in no danger. We have no quiet with the Whigs, they are so violent against a peace; but I'll cool them, with a vengeance very soon. . . .

October 27.

I forgot to go about some business this morning, which cost me double the time; and I was forced to be at the Secretary's office till four, and lose my dinner; so I went to Mrs. Van's, and made them get me three herrings, which I am very fond of, and they are light victuals: besides, I was to have supped at Lady Ashburnham's; but the drab did not call for us in her coach, as she promised, but sent for us, and so I sent my excuses. It has been a terrible rainy day, but so flattering in the morning, that I would needs go out in my new hat. . . .

October 29.

I was all this terrible rainy day with my friend Lewis upon business of importance; and I dined with him, and came home about seven, and thought I would amuse myself a little, after the pains I had taken. I saw a volume of Congreve's plays in my room . . . and I looked into it, and in mere loitering read in it till twelve, like an owl and a fool: if ever I do so again; never saw the like. . . .

October 30.

. . . Few of this generation can remember any thing but war and taxes, and they think it is as it should be; whereas 'tis certain we are the most un-done people in Europe, as I am afraid I shall make appear beyond all con-tradiction. . . .

November 1.

I went to-day into the city to settle some business with Stratford, and to dine with him; but he was engaged, and I was so angry I would not dine with any other merchant, but went to my printer, and ate a bit, and did busi-ness of mischief with him. . . . A fine day always makes me go into the city, if I can spare time, because it is exercise; and that does me more good than any thing. I have heard nothing since of my head, but a little, I don't know how, sometimes: but I am very temperate, especially now the Treasurer is ill, and the ministers often at Hampton Court, and the Secretary not yet fixed in his house, and I hate dining with many of my old acquaintance. Here has been a fellow discovered going out of the East India House with sixteen thousand pounds in money and bills; he would have escaped, if he had not been so uneasy with thirst, that he stole out before his time, and was caught. . . . I wish we had the money, provided the East India Company was never the worse; you know we must not covet, &c. Our weather, for this fortnight past, is chequered, a fair and a rainy day; this was very fine, and I have walked four miles. . . .

November 2.

It has rained all day with a *continuendo,* and I went in a chair to dine with Mrs. Van; always there in a very rainy day. But I made a shift to come back afoot. I live a very retired life, pay very few visits, and keep but very little company; I read no newspapers. . . . The Queen has the gout a little; I hoped the Lord-Treasurer would have had it too, but Radcliffe told me yes-terday it was the rheumatism in his knee and foot; however, he mends, and I hope will be abroad in a short time. . . .

November 3.

. . . If I grow worse, I will; otherwise I will trust to temperance and ex ercise: your fall of the leaf; what care I when the leaves fall? I am sorry to see them fall with all my heart; but why should I take physic because leave fall off from trees? that won't hinder them from falling. If a man falls from a horse, must I take physic for that? —This arguing makes you mad; but i is true right reason, not to be disproved.—I am glad at heart to hear poor Stella is better; use exercise and walk, spend pattens and spare potions, wear out clogs and waste claret. . . .

November 17.

. . . I have been visiting Lady Oglethorpe and Lady Worsley; the latter is lately come to town for the winter, and with child. . . . This is Queer Elizabeth's birth-day, usually kept in this town by apprentices, &c.; but the Whigs designed a mighty procession by midnight, and had laid out a thou sand pounds to dress up the Pope, Devil, cardinals, Sacheverell, &c and carry them with torches about, and burn them. . . . But they were seized las night. . . . They had some very foolish and mischievous designs; and it was thought they would have put the rabble upon assaulting my Lord-Treasurer's house, and the Secretary's; and other violences. The militia was raised to prevent it, and now, I suppose, all will be quiet. The figures are now at the Secretary's office at Whitehall. I design to see them if I can.

November 18.

I was this morning with Mr. Secretary, who just came from Hampton Court. He was telling me more particulars about this business of burning the Pope. It cost a great deal of money, and had it gone on, would have cos three times as much: but the town is full of it, and half a dozen Grub Street papers already. The Secretary and I dined at Brigadier Britton's, but I lef them at six, upon an appointment with some sober company of men and ladies, to drink punch at Sir Andrew Fountaine's. We were not very merry and I don't love rack punch, I love it better with brandy. . . .

November 23.

. . . I saw Leigh last night; he gives a terrible account of Sterne; he reckons he is seduced by some wench; he is over head and ears in debt and has pawned several things. . . .

December 1.

. . . Find I make many mistakes of leaving out words; so 'tis impossible to find my meaning. . . . I will take more care for the future, and read over every day just what I have written that day, which will take up no time to speak of.

". . . twas great odds between handling a dead Goat,
and a living Lady."

Samuel Sewall

Samuel Sewall (1652–1730) was a practical, if uxorious, man.
He was much absorbed with his own material and connubial
comfort so long as it could be had on properly prudent terms. A
complex man he was in many respects, but in his private life
he had a single-minded regard for the felicities of marriage.
Whenever he became a widower, he lost little time in seeking the
restoration of domestic bliss.

Sewall was an experienced husband and those with whom he
was engaged were experienced wives. Abigail, who died to his
astonishment after a "rising of Flegm," was *his* second wife; he
was *her* third husband. Madame Katherine Winthrop, the object
of his attentions in the diary entries given below, had already out-
lived two of *her* husbands. When, two years later, Sewall married Mary Gibbs, he was *her* second husband and she was *his*
third wife. It should not be thought that these matrimonial ven-
turings were those of giddy youth.

Samuel Sewall was born at Horton, Bishopstoke, Hampshire,
England and brought to Newbury, Massachusetts by his family at
the age of nine. He was the son of a merchant and the grandson
of a linen-draper. Educated at Harvard where he studied divinity,
he became a fellow and keeper of the College library. He abandoned the ministry (although not his life-long preoccupation with
theology) to become a printer and later sought public office as
a judge, serving in various Massachusetts courts for thirty-eight
years. A justice of the Massachusetts supreme court at the time
he wooed Madame Winthrop, he later rose to become its chief
justice. He was one of those who presided over the Salem witchcraft trials of 1692 in which nineteen persons were condemned to
death. When the hysteria subsided, Sewall was moved to stand
up in Boston's Old South Church to confess his blame and guilt
in those ignoble proceedings and beg for pardon. The rest of his

From *The Diary of Samuel Sewall*, published by the Massachusetts Historical
Society 1878–1882.

life he fasted and prayed for a day each year in repentance for his part in the miscarriage of justice.

Sewall gave time and money (by thrift and shrewd investments he had become wealthy) to the cause of the Indian missions and he wrote in 1700 the first anti-slavery tract published in America. Joseph, his son and the pastor of the Old South Church, preached his father's views, while another descendant, Samuel Edward, took an active rôle in the abolitionist movement and acted as counsel without fee for fugitive slaves.

Samuel Sewall wrote one of the liveliest of American diaries. It is treasured for its artless candour about all things great or small that caught his attention. Its amatory passages are best known, probably because they neatly comprehend the man.

If despite blandishments of cake, ginger-bread, sermons, news letters and sugared almonds, Sewall was unsuccessful in his suit for Madame Winthrop's hand, he did in time gain another less reluctant bride. And had true love run smoother the diary-reader's delight would have been far less.

May 26, 1720.

. . . Went to Bed after Ten: about 11 or before, my dear wife was opress'd with a rising of Flegm that obstructed her Breathing. I arose and lighted a Candle, made Scipio give me a Bason of Water (he was asleep by the fire) Call'd Philadelphia, Mr. Cooper, Mayhew. About midnight my dear wife expired to our great astonishment, especially mine. . . .

May 31.

Buried my dear Wife. . . . had a Comfortable day; though threatened with Rain. . . .

September 5.

. . . Going to Son Sewall's I there meet with Madam Winthrop, told her I was glad to meet her there, had not seen her a great while; gave her Mr Homes's Sermon. . . .

September 30.

. . . Daughter Sewall acquaints Madam Winthrop that if she pleas'd to be within at 3 p.m. I would wait on her. She answer'd she would be at home

October 1.

Satterday. I dine at Mr. Stoddard's: from thence I went to Madam Winthrop's just at 3. Spake to her, saying, my loving wife died so soon and suddenly, 'twas hardly convenient for me to think of Marrying again; however came to this Resolution that I would not make my Court to any person without first Consulting with her. Had a pleasant discourse. . . .

October 3.

Waited on Madam Winthrop again; twas a little while before she came. . . Then I usher'd in Discourse . . . at last I pray'd that . . . [she] might be the person assign'd for me. She instantly took it up in the way of Denyal, as if she had catch'd at an Opportunity to do it, saying she could not do it before she was asked. Said that was her mind unless she should Change it, which she believed she should not; could not leave her Children. I express'd my Sorrow that she should do it so Speedily, pray'd her Consideration, and ask'd her when I should wait on her agen. She setting no time, I mention'd that day Se'nnight. . . .

October 6.

A little after 6 p.m. I went to Madam Winthrop's . . . Madam seemed to harp upon the same string. Must take care of her Children; could not leave that House and Neighbourhood where she had dwelt so long. . . . I gave her a piece of Mr. Belcher's Cake and Ginger-Bread wrapped up in a clean sheet of Paper. . . .

October 10.

. . . I visited Madam Winthrop, who treated me with a great deal of Curtesy; Wine, Marmalade. I gave her a News-Letter about the Thanksgiving; Proposals, for sale of the verses for David Jeffries. She tells me Dr. Increase Mather visited her this day. . . .

October 12.

. . . Madam Winthrop was within . . . the little Room, where she was full of work behind a Stand; Mrs. Cotton came in and stood. Madam Winthrop pointed to her to set me a Chair. Madam Winthrop's Countenance was much changed from what twas on Monday, look'd dark and lowering. At last, the work, (black stuff or silk) was taken away, I got my Chair in place, had some Converse, but very Cold and indifferent to what 'twas before. Ask'd her to acquit me of rudeness if I drew off her Glove. Enquiring the reason, I told her twas great odds between handling a dead Goat, and a living Lady. Got it off. I told her I had one Petition to ask of her, that was, that she would take off the Negative she laid on me the third of October; She readily answer'd she could not, and enlarg'd upon it; She told me of it so soon as she could; could not leave her house, children, neighbours, business. I told her she might do som Good to help and suport me. Mentioning Mrs. Gookin, Nath, the widow Weld was spoken of; said I had visited Mrs. Denison. I told her Yes! Afterward I said, If after a first and second Vagary she would Accept of me returning, Her Victorious Kindness and Good Will would be very Obliging. . . . Told her the reason why I came every other night was lest I should drink too deep draughts of Pleasure. She had talk'd of Canary, her Kisses were to me better than the best Canary. . . .

October 17.

. . . I visited Madam Winthrop, who Treated me Courteously, but not in Clean Linen as sometimes. . . .

October 19.

Visited Madam Winthrop . . . Was Courteous to me; but took occasion to speak pretty earnestly about my keeping a Coach: I said 'twould cost £100. per anum: she said 'twould cost but £40. Spake much against John Winthrop, his false-heartedness. . . .

October 20.

. . . Madam Winthrop not being at Lecture, I went thither first; found her very Serene. . . . She took one of the Candles and went into the best Room, clos'd the shutters, sat down upon the couch. She told me Madam Usher had been there, and said the Coach must be set on Wheels, and not by Rusting. She spake something of my needing a Wigg. . . . Asked her if she would be within tomorrow, for we had had but a running Feat. She said she could not tell whether she should, or no. I took Leave. As were drinking at the Governour's, he said: In England the Ladies minded little more than that they might have Money, and Coaches to ride in. I said, And New-England brooks its Name. . . .

October 21.

. . . About 6. a-clock I go to Madam Winthrop's; Sarah told me her Mistress was gon out, but did not tell me whither she went. . . . After a good while and Claping the Garden door twice or thrice, she came in. I mention'd something of the lateness; she bantered me, and said I was later. She receiv'd me Courteously. I ask'd when our proceedings should be made publick: She said They were like to be no more publick than they were already. Offer'd me no Wine that I remember. I rose up at 11 a-clock to come away, saying I would put on my Coat. She offer'd not to help me. I pray'd her that Juno might light me home, she open'd the Shutter, and said twas pretty light abroad; Juno was weary and gon to bed. So I came home by Star-light as well as I could. . . .

October 24.

I went in the Hackny Coach through the Comon, stop'd at Madam Winthrop's (had told her I would take my departure from thence). . . . I told her . . . I was come to enquire whether she could find it in her heart to

ave that House and Neighbourhood, and go and dwell with me at the
outh-End [of Boston]; I think she said softly, Not yet. I told her it did not
in my Lands to keep a Coach. If I should, I should be in danger to be
rought to keep company with her Neighbour Brooker (he was a little before
nt to prison for Debt). . . . As to a Perriwig, My best and greatest Friend,
could not possibly have a greater, began to find me with Hair before I was
orn, and had continued to do so ever since; and I could not find it in my
eart to go to another. . . . She gave me a dram of Black-Cherry Brandy,
nd gave me a lump of the Sugar that was in it. She wish'd me a good Journy.
pray'd God to keep her, and came away. Had a very pleasant Journy to
alem.

November 1.

I was so taken up that I could not go if I would.

November 2.

Went again, and found Mrs. Alden there, who quickly went out. Gave
er about ½ pound of Sugar Almonds, cost 3s. per £. Carried them on Mon-
ay. She seem'd pleas'd with them, ask'd what they cost. Spake of giving her
Hundred pounds per anum if I dy'd before her. Ask'd her what sum she
vould give me, if she should dy first? Said I would give her time to Consider
f it. She said she heard as if I had given all to my Children by Deeds of Gift.
told her 'twas a mistake . . . I think when I seem'd to excuse pressing this,
he seemed to think 'twas best to speak of it; a long winter was coming on.
ave me a Glass or two of Canary.

November 4.

Went again about 7. a-clock. . . . I ask'd Madam what fashioned Neck-
ace I should present her with. She said, None at all. I ask'd her Whereabout
ve left off last time; mention'd what I had offer'd to give her; Ask'd her what
he would give me; She said she would not Change her Condition. . . . Said
he had not pleasure in things of that nature as formerly. . . .

November 7.

. . . I went to Mad. Winthrop; found her rocking her little Katee in the
radle. I excus'd my Coming so late (near Eight). She set me an arm'd
hair and Cusheon; and so the Cradle was between her arm'd Chair and
ine. Gave her the remnant of my Almonds; She did not eat of them as be-
ore; but laid them away. . . . I did not bid her draw off her glove as some-
ime I had done. Her Dress was not so clean as somtime it had been. Jehovah
reh!

November 9.

Dine at Bro^r Stoddards: were so kind as to enquire of me if they invite

M^m Winthrop; I answer'd No. . . . At night our Meeting was at the Widow Belknap's. . . . She sent her servant home with me with a Lantern. Madam Winthrop's Shutters were open as I pass'd by.

November 11.

Went not to M^m Winthrop's. This is the 2^d Withdraw.

"Wine is a mocker, strong drink is raging . . ."

Thomas Turner

Strange goings-on in the Sussex village of East Hoathly and
morning-after recriminations over excesses of drink and merriment
fill the pages of Thomas Turner's diary. Beyond these vivid
glimpses we know little about the man. He was born in 1729,
married twice, and apparently lived in perpetual conflict with his
conscience. Much of his diary and even the date of his death
have been lost.

These key-hole glimpses of a month's robust carousing reveal
Turner, his friends and his times more intimately than a volume
of formal history. It is easier to marvel at Turner's stamina than
to judge him as harshly as he did himself in this record of eager
folly and pious regret.

February 2, 1757.

We supped at Mr. Fuller's and spent the evening with a great deal of mirth,
till between one and two. Tho. Fuller brought my wife home upon his back.
I cannot say I came home sober, though I was far from being bad company.
I think we spent the evening with a great deal of pleasure.

February 17.

This being the day appointed for a general fast and humiliation, myself,
the boys, and servant was at church this morning. This fast day hath, to all
outward appearance, been observed in this parish with a great deal of decorum—the church in the morning being more thronged than I have seen it
lately. Oh! may religion once more rear up her head in this wicked and im-
pious nation.

February 22.

About four p.m. I walked down to Whyly. We played at bragg the first
part of the even. After ten we went to supper on four boiled chickens, four

From *The Diary of Thomas Turner.* Reprinted by permission of the Sussex
Archaeological Society.

boiled ducks, minced veal, sausages, cold roast goose, chicken pasty, an
ham. Our company, Mr. and Mrs. Porter, Mr. and Mrs. Coates, Mrs. Atkin
Mrs. Hicks, Mr. Piper and wife, Joseph Fuller and wife, and Mr. French
family. After supper our behaviour was far from that of serious, harmle
mirth; it was downright obstreperous, mixed with a great deal of folly an
stupidity. Our diversion was dancing or jumping about, without a violin c
any music, singing of foolish healths, and drinking all the time as fast as
could be well poured down; and the parson of the parish [Mr. Porter] wa
one among the mixed multitude. . . . About three o'clock, finding myself
have about as much liquor as would do me good, I slipt away unobserved
leaving my wife to make my excuse. Though I was very far from sober,
came home, thank God, very safe and well, without even tumbling; and M
French's servant brought my wife home at ten minutes past five.

February 25.

This morning about six oclock [i.e., the morning after the night before
for Turner was not surprisingly fuddled about his dates] as my wife was go
to bed, we was awakened by Mrs. Porter, who pretended she wanted som
cream of tartar; but as soon as my wife got out of bed, she vowed she shoul
come down. She found Mr. Porter, Mr. Fuller and his wife, with a lighte
candle, and part of a bottle of wine and a glass. The next thing was to hav
me down stairs, which being apprized of, I fastened my door. Up stairs the
came, and threatened to break it open; so I ordered the boys to open it, whe
they poured into my room; and as modesty forbid me to get out of bed, s
I refrained; but their immodesty permitted them to draw me out of bed, a
the common phrase is, topsy turvey; but, however, at the intercession of M
Porter, they permitted me to put on my *******, and instead of my uppe
cloaths, they gave me time to put on my wife's petticoats; and in this manne
they made me dance, without shoes and stockings, until they had emptie
the bottle of wine, and also a bottle of my beer.

About three o'clock in the afternoon, they found their way to their re
spective homes, beginning to be a little serious, and, in my opinion, ashame
of their stupid enterprise and drunken perambulation. Now, let any one ca
in reason to his assistance, and seriously reflect on what I have before recite
and they will join with me in thinking that the precepts delivered from th
pulpit on Sunday, tho' delivered with the greatest ardour, must lose a grea
deal of their efficacy by such examples.

March 3. (Sunday).

We had as good a sermon as I ever heard Mr. Porter preach, it bein
against swearing.

March 7.

We continued drinking like horses, as the vulgar phrase is, and singing ti
many of us were very drunk, and then we went to dancing and pulling wig
caps, and hats; and thus we continued in this frantic manner, behaving mor

like mad people than they that profess the name of Christians. Whether this is consistent to the wise saying of Solomon, let any one judge. Wine is a mocker, strong drink is raging, and he that is deceived thereby is not wise.

March 10.

Supped at Mr. Porter's, where the same scene took place, with the exception that there was no swearing and no ill words, by reason of which Mr. Porter calls it innocent mirth, but I in opinion differ much therefrom.

March 11.

At home all day. Very piteous.

*"But whatever I undertake I must reach
an eminence in"*

Lady Charlotte Elizabeth Guest

Remarkable even in a century of remarkable women, Lady Charlotte Guest (1812–1895) was the daughter of the ninth Earl of Lindsey and the granddaughter of the Dean of Bristol. Largely through her own efforts she acquired the education denied women of her day, and taught herself French, Italian, German, Greek, Latin, Hebrew and Persian. She learnt Welsh so that she could translate from ancient manuscripts the collection of medieval Welsh tales called *Mabinogion,* held by scholars to have opened a new era of Romance studies and used by her friend Lord Tennyson as the source for his *Idylls of the King.*

She was an accomplished etcher and played the piano and harp. She was proficient at billiards and whist, was fond of hunting and amateur dramatics, and excelled as a horsewoman. She supported the archaeological researches of her cousin, later her son-in-law, Henry Layard, the discoverer of Nineveh. Her collection of China was the most celebrated of her day. She read every new book and was an indefatigable hostess and party-goer. And until the end of her life she busied herself with knitting red woollen comforters which she gave to London cabmen.

At 21, Lady Charlotte married Sir John Guest, a man of more than twice her age who was the proprietor of a growing iron works in Wales and a Member of Parliament. They had met through an acquaintance, Benjamin Disraeli.

Society looked down on Guest's humble origin and connection with trade and Lady Charlotte immediately began a campaign to win him social acceptance. At the same time she aided her husband in his expanding business affairs. She had her own office adjoining his, an innovation almost without precedent in Victorian times. Soon she became in a real sense her husband's partner in conducting what was then the largest industrial enterprise in the world. Their Dowlais works alone had more than 7,000 employees and supplied most of the iron and steel that were the sinews of

From *Lady Charlotte Guest: Extracts from her Journal,* edited by the Earl of Bessborough. Reprinted by permission of John Murray Ltd.

the industrial revolution. Great wealth became theirs, one evidence of which was the purchase of the vast estate of Canford in Dorsetshire for the equivalent of almost two million dollars.

Her energy unflagging, Lady Charlotte added to her other interests that of improving the living and working conditions of employees. She founded six schools, organized nursing services, and vigorously supported the cause of social legislation. Somehow, too, she found time to become the mother of ten children within thirteen years. The regular appearance of new sons and daughters, whose arrival could scarcely have been more casual, punctuate the mid-years of the journal Lady Charlotte kept from the age of ten until blindness compelled her to stop when she was 79.

The portion of the diary sampled here begins with her wedding and ends twenty years later with Sir John's death. It is a tremendous record, in which is crowded a lifetime of achievement. And yet Lady Charlotte was only 41 at the time and more than half her life still lay before her.

uly 29, 1833.

A Journal! Again I dare commence a journal, and with what hope of continuing it? How, indeed, can I even now expect to recover the last three weeks? . . . Not now, as in the winter, can I say that the only friend I had to confide in was my journal. Now, every care and every joy, every sorrow and every delight is shared and sympathized with, and henceforth my only friend, my only confidant, is my husband. . . . In writing up the last three weeks I fill it with three weeks of the most unbroken peace, the most unclouded happiness. . . . To begin at the beginning:—I draw a veil over much confusion and much arrangement and disarrangement. On Monday the 29th at 10 in the morning I left my room, all being then prepared as fully as could be. The carriage was not yet come, and for the last time I made my way into the back drawing-room of Eaton Place. There were workmen there, and had to scramble over tables and chairs to reach the window where once my friends the gold-fish stood. There I sat down, and surrounded by noise calmly went over the ceremony that was within an hour to seal my fate for ever. The situation struck me as singular, and of 19, Eaton Place it is one of my last reminiscences. Startled by a notice that the carriage had come I went down stairs. Mamma and I proceeded together, the rest following. Nearly all my friends and relatives were in the vestry when we arrived. . . . All proceeded according to order, and the ceremony was performed by the Bishop of Gloucester. I mumbled very slightly at the commencement, but I soon surmounted this, and I believe in the responses my voice was perfectly steady, clear and audible. . . .

March 19, 1834.

. . . I drove with dear Merthyr [the name by which Lady Charlotte always called her husband] to the House. He was very wild, and did not behave with propriety; so I here record my resolution that if he in future insists upon kissing me in the middle of Regent Street, in broad daylight, I will not take him down to the House again after dinner. . . . I was very well pleased with him too for coming home tonight as early as nine o'clock.

June 13.

. . . I was very well contented with the success of my concert. The singing was certainly admirable; nothing could surpass Rubini and Grisi. All the people I wished came, and several of those I merely asked perforce were prevented coming. The supper was very pretty. At the beginning of the evening I attempted to sit down, but I was soon expelled from my seat by the crowd, and obliged to stand at the top of the staircase. From ten to about one o'clock the house was full. All being over as to music, my friends made a grand eating and drinking and left me very tired at about 2 o'clock. . . .

July 3.

. . . I had written home, and had got half through a long letter at twelve o'clock, when I was taken ill. At two my dear child [Maria] was born. I was soon pretty well. Merthyr had gone to the House soon after eleven, and did not return till past three. No one had told him of the little one till he reached the top of the stairs, when Mamma met him and told him that he had a little girl. He was quite overcome when he entered my room immediately after, and he kissed me and our dear infant. It was a very happy meeting. . . .

August 2.

. . . Bertie [her younger brother] had come from the Tower to spend the day with us, and after dinner he accompanied us in the open carriage. The route was by Tottenham Court Road to Pentonville. The evening was very warm and lovely, and we were disposed to enjoy a ramble. Accordingly we got out, and sending the carriage on a little way, we walked. The neat houses in that vicinity have some enclosed grounds and some gardens in front of them. Before one of these gardens we stopped. It evidently fronted a house of entertainment, for under its trees sat various jovial groups enjoying the good things of this life, and indulging in mirthful conversation. They appeared to consist of lower tradesmen, and tolerably respectable, and there were two or three gigs waiting for them near the entrance. We next stopped near a similar garden, where, however, we found a very different description of persons. They appeared to belong to the class of least respectable mechanics. They had all their pots of porter before them, and their mirth was noisy. Four or five musicians were playing on different instruments the while. One man, as we passed, was parleying with his wife, who endeavoured to persuade him to return home. He was promising to do so after the next draught, and then he went back unconcerned with his pipe in his mouth, and she turned away, perhaps to bewail, in her miserable and solitary dwelling, the wretched poverty and loneliness which his sad propensity inflicted upon her. My greatest ambition was to go inside a gin shop, and the view of several very gay ones renewed my curiosity. At last we made for one, but thought it prudent to reconnoitre ere we entered it. We looked in accordingly through the half-open doors; such a collection of debased squalid-looking wretches I never saw. They sat in two rows, all drinking, and many of them had the laugh of drunkenness on their brow. From their appearance, the very best of them must have been a common street-beggar. In this alone of all the resorts of drinking which we passed, I did not see a single woman. To enter such a place was revolting, and indeed impossible, dressed as we were. We crossed to another gin shop, nearly opposite, and again found a different rank of society. This one was crowded with labourers, and was of a much more respectable stamp. We should have entered it, had not the carriage been waiting for us close by. Life is altogether different at that end of town. . . .

December 3.

. . . I have had a Welsh lesson, and have been all the afternoon translating . . . a French pamphlet of the advantage of using hot air in the manufacture of iron. . . .

March 10, 1836.

. . . We went to Lansdowne House. It was a small party and to me the opening of it was rather disastrous. I did not know Lord Lansdowne and my remarks to him came rather mal à propos, and while scarce recovered from my confusion my dress in the crowd caught in Lord Melbourne's coat (he also an utter stranger), and we stood making bows to each other for some time before we could be disentangled. It was ridiculous. . . .

March 17, 1837.

. . . Yesterday I gave Mr. Marsh, the agent, authority to enquire the terms of Lord Wilton's House in Grosvenor Square, which we were disposed to give about £10,000 for. We dined early after hurrying over Mr. Fullarton's House in Stanhope Street which has been for a long time for sale. It was very melancholy to me to see its desolate appearance without an atom of furniture within it, and to recollect the different aspect it bore on the only other occasion on which I was ever there. Mr. Fullarton then at the height of his prosperity gave a sumptuous ball, which, in those fine rooms, seemed almost like a scene of Fairyland. At that time I was perfectly wretched. I danced at his ball with a heavy heart and hated my partner, a mutilated being to whom I dreaded that I might be sacrificed for his wealth. . . . The year succeeding this, Mr. Fullarton, owing to failures of banks in India left England—a beggar —and I, at the distance of only five years, with very different feelings and prospects, am debating whether I shall purchase his splendid home! . . .

June 2.

. . . I contemplate a history of the Iron Trade, but materials are scanty and my occupations at home leave now but little leisure. . . .

June 20.

Merthyr came into my room while I was dressing and announced that the King [William IV, uncle of Victoria] had expired at 2 that morning. Everybody seemed in great excitement at the news. . . . The Queen received the Privy Council with great firmness this morning and read her speech extremely well. They say she has put herself entirely in Lord Melbourne's hands, but I cannot help thinking there is much Toryism at heart in some of those high quarters. . . .

July 16.

. . . After the Post came in Merthyr, Thomas Evans [her husband's assistant] and I went in a tram to the Castle Quarry which Merthyr thought would do him good. He was playful as a child the whole way, spite of the grave matters he is immersed in, and amused himself in throwing grapes to the children. When we had drove as far as the tram and our very unskilful conductor could take us, we got out and walked to the lane, where Merthyr sat down and dictated a fresh version of his Poor Law address to Thomas Evans. The scene was quite beautiful but not in unison with the subject. To think that with such a view of the lovely Vaynor Valley at our feet, and with the lofty Beacons rising proud and free before us, we could ever consider with common patience the Law by which our fellow creatures are to be immured in a Workhouse for no other sin than that of being poor and afflicted! . . .

August 4.

. . . I am now going down to the village [to observe the voting in the General Election]. . . . Everything was going on sadly at this Polling place. The Tory landlords brought their Tenants up themselves like flocks of sheep, and made them break their pledge-words. They absolutely dragged them to the Poll, threatening to turn them out of their farms unless they voted plumpers for Lord Adare. One man shed tears on being forced to this. Although they had just been voting against us by compulsion the poor farmers received me enthusiastically, and wanted to drag my carriage up the Hill, but this I would not allow. . . .

August 9.

I walked to the Works with Merthyr. He took me to the top of the Yard and to look at the new Blast Engine which is still not finished. Having no door, I was obliged to enter it by a ladder put against a window, and as the flooring was still wanting, my only way of going over it was by climbing along the rafters and machinery, and in one instance walking along the arm of a fly-wheel. Blind as I am, I thought the experiment rather perilous, but Merthyr wished it, and I suppose my neck is at his disposal. . . .

May 21, 1838.

This evening I went to the Cambrian Ball in my regular Welsh peasant's dress. . . . Such a thing I believe had never been seen before in London and it caused quite a sensation. . . .

May 30.

. . . In the evening we went to the Duke of Sussex's, where there was an immense crowd and so tremendous a string of carriages that we were two hours getting there. The low and crowded rooms were very hot and there was nothing very agreeable in the party, but all trouble and inconvenience were fully repaid by the pleasure of seeing the Queen receive. Her manner was so perfect, so self-possessed and so courteous, that it was more like one sees in very good acting on the stage than anything else. . . .

July 3.

. . . In to-day's gazette my dear Merthyr was elevated, if so I must call it, to the rank of Baronet. I consider it a paltry distinction. . . .

March 28, 1839. London.

. . . I was all day quite well but woke about 3 o'clock the next morning (Good Friday) in a little pain. And within half an hour had the pleasure of giving birth to my fifth child and third boy [Montague], with less suffering than I believed possible. Even with less pain and in a shorter time than with dear little Merthyr last year. This baby was born some little while before Dr. Locock arrived, and when they were all quiet I went to sleep again. . . .

April 27.

. . . I went for the first time to see the new Office in the City, 42, Lothbury, it is well situated and very commodious. They have paid me the compliment of fitting up a room for me there, and I think it is a retreat that I shall often be tempted to resort to from the gaieties and interruptions of Grosvenor Square. I have so schooled myself into habits of business that it is now more congenial to me to calculate the advantage of half per cent commission on a cargo of iron than to go to the finest Ball in the world. But whatever I undertake I must reach an eminence in. I cannot endure anything in a second grade. I am happy to see that we are at the head of the iron trade. Otherwise I could not take pride in my house in the City and my Works at Dowlais, and glory (playfully) in being (in some sort) a tradeswoman. Then again, my blood is of the noblest and most princely in the Kingdom, and if I go into Society, it must be the very best and first. I can brook no other. If I occupy myself in writing, my book must be splendidly got up and must be, as far at least as decoration and typography are concerned, at the head of literature, and I delight in the contrast of musty antiquarian researches, and the brilliant fêtes and plodding counting house, from all of which I seem to derive almost equal amusement. . . .

May 24.

To-night we went to the Queen's ball, which I quite enjoyed . . . and was amused at seeing the old Duchess of Somerset dance a Scotch reel and the Grand Duke dance the Mazourka. The dear little Queen looked pretty and pleased. I was not home till past three o'clock.

February 10, 1840.

[Having been given tickets for St. James's Palace for the Queen's wedding] . . . we proceeded by the Green Park to the Palace. Our places were in Queen Anne's room, where we saw everything remarkably well. After waiting some time the groupe, composed of the Prince, his family and suite, came through from the inner rooms. I had never seen him before but I thought him very handsome. He has a particularly pleasing countenance. The Queen's procession followed almost immediately afterwards. . . . Her dress was very simple and very rich. White satin, and a Honiton lace veil fastened to back of her head by a small circle of large diamonds. I thought her looking well but anxious. . . . The bridesmaids, twelve in number, who held her train, might have been of the highest rank, but with one or two exceptions they were not of the greatest beauty of the kingdom. Their dress was simple in the extreme. The Duchess of Sutherland looked much the best of all the ladies of the suite. She wore white and diamonds, without, I think, any admixture of colour. She had three rows of large single diamonds standing out like three diadems from her head. The Duchess of Bedford was one mass of scarlet and gold, in very curious taste. The others I had hardly time to observe. They were not long absent in the chapel. On the return Prince Albert . . . walked by the side of the Queen holding her left hand. They both looked more composed than on first going through. . . .

April 26, 1842.

We were tonight at a magnificent Ball at Lady Londonderry's which Mary exceedingly enjoyed. Splendid as it was there are no particular details relative to it in my memory and nothing to record. I always feel so solitary at all these gay things. I am shy and proud, or rather from extreme sensitiveness I seem so, and almost all the people I am acquainted with appear, as it were, strangers to me. A great deal of it is owing to me not having lived amongst them young. But I do not care, uncongenial as this kind of visiting is; it is sufficient to enable me to place my children on that footing with theirs, that they may never feel the disadvantages of want of fellowship. For myself I have occupations and resource enough never to feel dependent on *Society* for amusement. . . . [Lady Charlotte continues in this vein on May 7:] Though my husband is peculiarly formed to shine and rise, and is infinitely more elegant than half of the Lordlings I meet, and though I have my own rank [her father and brother were the ninth and tenth Earls of Lindsey] which is high enough to assist me, the consciousness frequently obtrudes itself that in this aristocratic nation the word trade conveys a taint. . . . I am determined to overcome the prejudice; I will force them, whether they will or no, to disguise, if they do not forget, its existence in my case. . . . The children shall never feel that there live any on the earth who dare to look down upon them, and their own feelings on this head will go far in giving the tone to those of others toward them. . . .

July 1.

Dear Ivor had strewed my room with the toys his father had bought for them all at Cardiff, and with the acquisition of which he was delighted. I let him stay a little while, then got him and my dear husband to go to luncheon, without however giving any hint that I was otherwise than quite well. However I went to bed as soon as they had left me, and in a very few minutes Merthyr came up again to see why I had not followed them down. I tranquillized him as well as I could and he again went out of the room, but only to be recalled almost immediately to see the eighth child to which, thank God, I had given birth with as little pain as I suppose it is possible to suffer on such occasions. . . .

March 12, 1846.

. . . My dear husband and I went to our new home [Canford, in Dorset, purchased for £335,000] on foot. It was a most delicious evening. The western sky was bathed in gold, and the air was mild, and everything looked beautiful. We walked on, arm in arm, from the turn of the road, all through the village to the front door, both in quiet, subdued spirits, but not unhappy. When we entered the house, Merthyr hung up his hat, and I put down my basket, and it might have seemed as though we had been settled here for ages and had only been out to take an evening's walk. . . . The church bells rang for our arrival and made me quite melancholy. There was a fine bright moonlight succeeding the glorious day, and certainly Canford looked so beautiful. . . .

August 25.

This day I did not come down. At night I had rather suspected I might soon be confined, but I went to sleep and forgot it. In the morning when I woke I became pretty sure the event was not far distant. I merely told Merthyr I would breakfast upstairs, which I did. I suffered scarcely at all, and at half past 10 gave birth to another little girl, our 5th daughter and 10th child. . . .

December 28, 1850.

. . . I had a nice large piece of worsted work to occupy me when sitting waiting . . . and I filled up any chance intervals by reading a singular novel,

Jane Eyre, written with force but coarseness, and not of the best tone. I am glad no unmarried daughter of mine wrote it. Yet it is a striking book.

November 26, 1852.

. . . It is all over! I am bereaved, but I cannot help sitting down at once to record it all in order. Not that *I* can ever forget, but to refresh the memory of my poor children hereafter. . . .

January 18, 1853.

. . . We reached Wimborne in due time. The open carriage met us there, and soon we were at Canford. It was a cold bright night. . . . When we stopped at the door, I got out silently, and leaving them all went straight to the Library, where luckily there was a light. A slight veil had been thrown over his bust, which at once I removed and then I flung my arms around it, and remained clasping it for some minutes, kissing the cold lips—not colder than his own when I kissed them last—and shedding torrents of passionate tears. And this cold marble is now all that is left me!

*"I shall have been a failure unless
I do something great! . . ."*

Henry James

Born in New York City, Henry James (1843–1916) was early
sent abroad to be educated and there acquired the taste for European life and manners that set an example for two generations
of American literary expatriates. He came home to study law at
Harvard, but having a greater interest in writing and concluding
that the American atmosphere was uncongenial to the artist, he
soon returned to Europe. For him England came closest to being
a congenial spiritual home and he lived there for nearly forty
unbroken years, becoming a British subject in 1915.

The James family was cosmopolitan, although of New England
origin, and accustomed to go abroad as casually as contemporaries
ventured from Cambridge to New York. Modest inherited wealth,
too, provided the means to follow literary and scholarly pursuits.
The senior Henry James, a follower of Swedenborg, was the author of half a dozen books on theology and social philosophy. A
younger brother William James, was professor of philosophy at
Harvard, developed the theory of pragmatism, and was a founder
of modern psychology. After half a century, his books remain
classics in their field.

James himself was devoted to fiction. He began writing at
twenty-two when still at Harvard, and through the years novels
and stories came steadily from his pen, thirty-five volumes of them
in the collected edition. *The Turn of the Screw* is one of the most
famous of American short stories, and some of his best known
novels are *Daisy Miller, Washington Square, The Portrait of a
Lady, The Ambassadors, What Maisie Knew, The Bostonians* and
The Golden Bowl. Besides, he wrote plays, dramatic criticism,
biographies, and contributed regularly to magazines.

Influenced by Zola, Maupassant, Flaubert and other leaders of
the French Realist movement he met in Paris, and perhaps also
by the family preoccupation with psychology, James perfected
the technique of psychological realism, an approach primarily

concerned with the inner life, the motives and processes of thought.

This probing of the internal world is reflected especially in the notebook-journals James kept for thirty years, and never more clearly than in the following passages, written when James was thirty-nine and making one of his rare visits to the United States. Here it is James himself who is scrutinized by that remarkably perceptive and sensitive mind.

November 25, 1881. Boston.

. . . I ought to endeavour to keep, to a certain extent, a record of passing impressions, of all that comes, that I see, and feel, and observe. To catch and keep something of life—that's what I mean. Here I am back in America, for instance, after six years of absence, and likely while here to see and learn a great deal that ought not to become mere waste material. Here I am . . . likely to be for the next five months. I am glad I have come—it was a wise thing to do. I needed to see again *les miens* [my own people], to revive my relations with them, and my sense of the consequences that these relations entail. Such relations, such consequences, are a part of one's life, and the best life, the most complete, is the one that takes full account of such things. One can only do this by seeing one's people from time to time, by being with them, by entering into their lives. Apart from this I hold it was not necessary I should come to this country. I am 37 years old, I have made my choice, and God knows that I have now no time to waste. My choice is the old world—my choice, my need, my life. . . .

December 20. New York.

I had to break off the other day in Boston—the interruptions in the *morning* here are intolerable. That period of the day has none of the social sanctity here that it [has] in England, and which keeps it singularly free from intrusion. People—by which I mean ladies—think nothing of asking you to come and see them before lunch. Of course one can decline, but when many propositions of that kind come, a certain number stick. Besides, I have had all sorts of things to do, chiefly not profitable to recall. I have been three weeks in New York, and all my time has slipped away in mere movement. I try as usual to console myself with the reflection that I am getting impressions. This is very true; I have got a great many. . . .

December 26. Cambridge.

I came here on the 23d, to spend Xmas. . . . Here I sit writing in the old back sitting room which William and I used to occupy and which I now occupy alone. . . . The long interval of years drops away, and the edges of the chasm "piece together" again, after a fashion. The feeling of that younger time comes back to me in which I sat here scribbling, dreaming, planning, gazing out upon the world in which my fortune was to seek, and suffering tortures from my damnable state of health. It was a time of suffering so keen that that fact might [claim] to give its dark colour to the whole period; but this is not what I think of today. . . . What comes back to me freely, delightfully, is the vision of those untried years. Never did a poor fellow have more; never was an ingenuous youth more passionately and yet more patiently eager for what life might bring. Now that life has brought something, brought a measurable part of what I dreamed of then, it is touching enough to look back. I knew at least what I wanted then—to see something of the world. I have seen a good deal of it, and I look at the past in the light of this knowledge. What strikes me is the definiteness, the unerringness of those longings. I wanted to do very much what I have done, and success, if I may say so, stretches back a tender hand to its younger brother, desire. I remember the days, the hours, the books, the seasons, the winter skies and darkened rooms of summer. I remember the old walks, the old efforts, the old exaltations and depressions. I remember more than I can say here today. . . .

February 9, 1882. Boston.

When I began to make these rather ineffectual records I had no idea that I should have in a few weeks to write such a tale of sadness as today. I came back from Washington on the 30th of last month (reached Cambridge the next day), to find that I should never again see my dear mother. On Sunday, Jan. 29th, as Aunt Kate sat with her in the closing dusk (she had been ill with an attack of bronchial asthma, but was apparently recovering happily), she passed away. It makes a great difference to me! I knew that I loved her—but I didn't know how tenderly till I saw her lying in her shroud in that cold North Room, with a dreary snowstorm outside, and looking as sweet and tranquil and noble as in life. These are hours of exquisite pain; thank Heaven this particular pang comes to us but once. . . . We buried her on Wednesday, Feb. 1st . . . it was a splendid winter's day—the snow lay deep and high. We placed her, for the present, in a temporary vault in the Cambridge cemetery—the part that lies near the river. When the spring comes on we shall go and choose a burial place. I have often walked there in the old years—in those long, lonely rambles that I used to take about Cambridge, and I had, I suppose, a vague idea that some of us would some day lie there, but I didn't see just that scene.

It is impossible for me to say—to begin to say—all that has gone down into the grave with her. She was our life, she was the house, she was the keystone of the arch. She held us all together, and without her we are scattered reeds. She was patience, she was wisdom, she was exquisite maternity. Her sweetness, her mildness, her great natural beneficence were unspeakable, and it is infinitely touching to me to write about her as one that *was*. . . .

August 3d. London.

From time to time one feels the need of summing-up. I have done it little in the past, but it will be a good thing to do it more in the future. . . . I sailed from America on the date I had in mind when I went home—May 10th. Father and Alice [sister] . . . had moved into Boston and were settled very comfortably in a small, pretty house (101 Mt. Vernon St.). Besides, their cottage at Manchester was rapidly being finished; shortly before sailing I went down to see it. Very pretty—bating the American scragginess; with the sea close to the piazzas, and the smell of bayberries in the air. Rest, coolness, peace, society enough, charming drives; they will have all that.

Very soon after I had got back here my American episode began to fade away, to seem like a dream; a very painful dream, much of it. While I was there, it was Europe, it was England, that was dreamlike—but now all this is real enough. . . .

November 11. Paris.

. . . I had meant to write some account of my last months in America, but I fear the chance for this has already passed away. I look back at them, however, with a great deal of tenderness. Boston is absolutely nothing to me —I don't even dislike it. I like it, on the contrary; I only dislike to live there. But all those weeks I spent there, after Mother's death, had an exquisite stillness and solemnity. My rooms in Mt. Vernon St. were bare and ugly; but they were comfortable—were, in a certain way, pleasant. I used to walk out, and across the Common, every morning, and take my breakfast at Parker's. Then I walked back to my lodgings and sat writing till four or five o'clock; after which I walked out to Cambridge over that dreary bridge whose length I had measured so often in the past, and, four or five days in the week, dined in Quincy St. with Father and Alice. In the evening, I walked back in the clear American starlight. I got in this way plenty of exercise.

It was a simple, serious, wholesome time. Mother's death appeared to have left behind it a soft beneficent hush in which we lived for weeks, for months, and which was full of rest and sweetness. I thought of her constantly, as I walked to Boston at night along those dark vacant roads, where, in the winter air, one met nothing but the coloured lamps and the far-heard jingle of the Cambridge horse-cars. My work at this time, interested me, too . . . even more than the importance of it would explain—or than the success of it has justified. . . .

If I can only *concentrate* myself: this is the great lesson of life. I have hours of unspeakable reaction against my smallness of production; my wretched habits of work—or of un-work; my levity, my vagueness of mind, my perpetual failure to focus my attention, to absorb myself, to look things in the face, to invent, to produce, in a word. I shall be 40 years old in April next: it's a horrible fact! I believe however that I have learned how to work and that it is in moments of forced idleness, almost alone, that these melancholy reflections seize me. When I am really at work, I'm happy, I feel strong, I see many opportunities ahead. It is the only thing that makes life endurable. I must make some great efforts during the next few years, however, if I wish not to have been on the whole a failure. I shall have been a failure unless I do something *great!* . . .

"I do believe I have a big bump for cookies"

Thomas Alva Edison

Every schoolboy knows the success story of Thomas Alva Edison (1847–1931), the ex-newsboy whose knack for the practical application of scientific principles led to more than a thousand inventions, many of which have since become everyday necessities. Among these, of course, are the incandescent electric light, the motion picture machine, the phonograph, the microphone, the mimeograph. His achievements are all the more remarkable because this mechanical genius, born in Milan, Ohio, had only a few months of schooling. He worked prodigiously in his New Jersey laboratory, surrounded for years by scientists with many degrees —but the walls of his own office lacked even a framed grammar school diploma.

But what sort of man was this Edison, this creative giant? A brief diary he kept at mid-point in his career, when fame and success had already come his way, gives us a candid close-up of him during a week or so of July, 1885. Borrowing the movie technique that his inventions made possible, the camera dollies closer and closer until the image, perhaps in unexpected outline and detail, fills the screen . . .

July 12, 1885. Menlo Park, New Jersey.

. . . Awakened at 8.15 A.M. Powerful itching of my head, lots of white dry dandruff—what is this d-mnable material. Perhaps it's the dust from the dry literary matter I've crowded into my noodle lately. It's nomadic. Gets all over my coat; must read about it in the Encyclopedia.

Smoking too much makes me nervous—must lasso my natural tendency to acquire such habits—holding heavy cigar constantly in my mouth has deformed my upper lip, it has a sort of Havana curl.

Arose at 9 o'clock; came downstairs expecting 'twas too late for breakfast—'twasn't. Couldn't eat much, nerves of stomach too nicotinny. The root of tobacco plants must go clear through to hell. Satan's principal agent Dyspepsia must have charge of this branch of the vegetable kingdom. It has just

From *The Diary and Sundry Observations of Thomas Alva Edison,* edited by Dagobert D. Runes. Copyright 1948 by Philosophical Library.

occured to me that the brain may digest certain portions of food, say the etherial part, as well as the stomach—perhaps dandruff is the excreta of the mind—the quantity of this material being directly proportional to the amount of reading one indulges in.

A book on German metaphysics would thus easily ruin a dress suit. After breakfast started reading Hawthorne's English Note Book, don't think much of it—perhaps I'm a literary barbarian and am not yet educated up to the point of appreciating fine writing. . . .

Two fine things in the book were these: Hawthorne showing to little Rose Hawthorne a big live lobster, told her it was a very ugly thing and would bite everybody, whereupon she asked, "if the first one God made bit him—" Again "Ghostland is beyond the jurisdiction of veracity."—

I think freckles on the skin are due to some salt of Iron, sunlight brings them out by reducing them from high to low state of oxidation—perhaps with a powerful magnet applied for some time, and then with proper chemicals, these mud holes of beauty might be removed. . . .

Had dinner at 3 P.M. Ruins of a chicken, rice pudding. I eat too quick. . . . Returned from drive at 5 P.M. Commenced reading short sketches of life's Macauley, Sidney Smith, Dickens and Charlotte Bronte. . . . Charlotte Bronte was like DeQuincy. What a nice married couple they would have been. I must read Jane Eyre. Played a little on the piano; it's badly out of tune. Two keys have lost their voice. . . .

Holzer [brother-in-law and research associate] is going to use the old laboratory for the purpose of hatching chickens artificially by an electric incubator. He is very enthusiastic. Gave me full details. He is a very patient and careful experimenter. Think he will succeed. Everything succeeded in that old laboratory. . . . Suggested to H that he vaccinate his hens with chicken-pox virus. Then the eggs would have their embryo heriditarily inoculated and none of the chickens would have the disease. For economy's sake he could start with one hen and rooster. He being a scientific man with no farm experience, I explained the necessity of having a rooster. He saw the force of this suggestion at once.

The sun has left us on time. Am going to read from the Encyclopedia Brittanica to steady my nerves, and go to bed early. I will shut my eyes and imagine a terraced abyss, each terrace occupied by a beautiful maiden. To the first I will deliver my mind and they will pass it down to the uttermost depths of silence and oblivion. Went to bed. Worked my imagination for a supply of maidens. . . .

July 14. Woodside Villa, Massachusetts.

. . . In the evening went out on sea wall. Noticed a strange phosphorescent light in the west, probably caused by a baby moon just going down Chinaward. Thought at first the Aurora Borealis has moved out west. Went to bed early, dreamed of a Demon with eyes four hundred feet apart.

July 15.

Slept well. Breakfasted clear up to my adam's apple. Took shawl strap and went to Boston with . . . things to get. Lavater on the human face, Miss Cleveland's book, Heloise by Rosseau, short neckties, Wilhelm Meister, basket fruit, Sorrows of Werther, Madame Recamier's works, Diary books, pencils, telephone documents, Mark Twain's gummed Potentiality of Literature, i.e., scrap book. Also book called "How Success Is Won," containing . . . something in it about . . . your humble servitor. . . .

July 16.

I find on waking up this morning that I went to bed last night with the curtains up in my room. Glad the family next door retire early. I blushed retroactively to think of it. Slept well. Weather clear, warm. Day so fine that barometer anaethized. Breakfasted. Diaried a lot of nonsense. Read some of Longfellow's Hyperion . . . account of two murders in morning *Herald* to keep up my interest in human affairs. Built an air castle or two. Took my new shoes out on a trial trip. Read some of Miss Cleveland's book where she goes for George Eliot for not having a heavenly streak of imaginative twaddle in her poetry. . . .

July 19.

. . . Went into a drug store and bought some alleged candy, asked the gilded youth with the usual vacuous expression if he had any nitric peroxide. He gave a wild stare of incomprehensibility. Then I simplified the name to nitric acid, which I hoped was within the scope of his understanding. A faint gleam of intelligence crept over his face, whereupon . . . he returned with the remark that he didn't keep nitric acid. Fancy a drug store without nitric acid. A drug store nowadays seems to consist of a frontage of red, blue and green demijohns, a soda fountain, case with candy and toothbrushes, a lot of almost empty bottles with death and stomachatic destruction written in Latin on them, all in charge of a young man with a hatchet-shaped head, hair laid out by a civil engineer, and a blank stare. . . .

July 21.

Slept splendid. . . . After supper, weather being cool but rather windy . . . on the yacht and all hands sailed out on the bay. Had to round an arm of the bay to get coal. Water splashed so I got dashed wet. . . . Afterwards Mrs. and Mr. G. hospitabalized by firing off several champagne bottles and some of those delightful cookies. I do believe I have a big bump for cookies. The first entry made by the recording angel on my behalf was for stealing my mother's cookies. Eleven o'clock came and the pattering of many footsteps on the stairs signalled the coming birth of silence, only to be disturbed by the sonorous snore . . . the demonic laughter of the amatory family cat.

*"My instinct is to multiply books
and articles and plays."*

Arnold Bennett

Arnold Bennett (1867–1931) set himself to write, and he clung to
his purpose with tenacity, achieving in his sixty-four years more
even than had been his intention. He was a successful novelist,
playwright, public figure, man of wealth and position, father,
yachtsman, and intimate of the great. The story of how a young
man from the provinces, a naïve country boy, made all this happen, can be traced in the million-word journal that was published
the year after his death.

Bennett was born in Shelton, North Staffordshire, one of the
"Five Towns" of the pottery-manufacturing region about which
he wrote in many of his novels. He was educated in Newcastle
Middle School and thereafter went to work in his father's law
office. Later he went to London to study law, but before long
turned to journalism. A staff job on *Woman*, which he obtained
when he was twenty-five, led in time to his being named editor
of the magazine. At thirty-three he resigned to devote his full
time to writing. He was not discouraged when his first novel
earned him only one pound. He went on to write *Old Wives' Tale*,
the trilogy made up of *Clayhanger, Hilda Lessways* and *These
Twain;* also *Riceyman Steps, Lord Raingo, Imperial Palace* and
many other successful plays and novels.

As a boy Bennett suffered a severe shock when his hand was
caught in a mangle, the ironing machine of Benjamin Franklin's
invention; this led to a stammer which nothing ever cured. Perhaps because of his speech difficulty, of which he was tremendously self-conscious, he was shy and sensitive in talking to people
he did not know well; with children he got along famously with
never a trace of his stammer. He was stout, of medium height,
and always carried himself stiffly erect as if he wore a corset—
and some thought he did. His eyes were brown, sheathed with
heavy lids; his mouth and teeth were irregular; his voice was

harsh and high-pitched. He was fascinated by the grand, the rich and titled, well-cut clothes, good food taken in smart restaurants. He was sincere in the older sense of that word; modest, and easily shocked although he affected an air of sophistication.

Bennett's literary success was in part based on his diligent application to the mechanics of creation; he kept office hours at his desk, writing regularly and steadily as an artisan practices his craft, regardless of late hours, chronic insomnia, and twinges of pain he attributed to an unruly liver. He loved money for what it bought. But he loved more the words that earned it. He delighted to count them as measures of achievement, striking monthly and annual word balances much as Pepys liked to reckon at intervals his mounting worth in gold coins. "I constantly gloat," Bennett admitted, "over the number of words I have written in a given period. . . ."

Henry James once said that Bennett was one of those who regarded life as a giant orange that could be squeezed at will to provide literary nourishment. In a sense he was right, as Bennett's journal shows; he was a transcriber rather than a creator. However in the journal entries selected here it is Bennett himself who is focussed upon. He appears at the time his first novel is being completed; he savours a tale of literary intrigue involving a lady barber; his liver annoys him and he places bets at Monte Carlo with unsettling results; he has misgivings about chastising a dog and sliding down an ice slope on a toboggan; he watches Pavlova dance; he goes to dancing school; he gives his infant daughter, Virginia, her bottle ("I kept the creature 'very good.'"). Here, in short, is a bit of the prodigiously prolific Arnold Bennett, a figure more complex than any he ever created in his novels.

May 11, 1896.

I read through in the typewritten copy some of the later chapters of my novel, and they seemed to be ineffective and sketchy. Which severely depressed me, and to recover myself I had to read certain other chapters which I knew would not come out badly. . . .

May 15.

At noon precisely I finished my first novel [*In the Shadow*], which was begun about the middle of April last year; but five-sixths of the work at least has been performed since the 1st October. Yesterday, I sat down at 3 P.M. to write, and, with slight interruptions for meals etc. kept at it till 1 A.M. this morning. The concluding chapter was written between 9 and 12 today. . . .

September 21.

A not unknown journalist, finding himself prospering with an income of from £8 to £10 a week, took for paramour a lady barber out of Chancery Lane. Then he wrote a book, and having decided upon the publisher who he thought ought to take it, sought a personal introduction to the man of his choice, who happened to be Mr. John Lane. Only one person of his acquaintance knew Mr. Lane at all well, and he, after some parleying, agreed to give the introduction—for a consideration. It was arranged: the journalist got his introduction, and the acquaintance was allowed to take the lady barber for a week's holiday.

The book was refused.

February 1, 1897.

. . . If I could spend every day as I have spent today, happiness would almost be within grasp. A couple of hours' editorial work at the office in the morning. After dinner I read myself to sleep with d'Annunzio's *Annales d'Anne,* and when I awoke I went to pay some money into the bank. Then I schemed out in my head the next chapter of my novel. Before tea, Mrs. Sharpe came upstairs for a talk, a talk which continued till some time after tea was over. From 6 to 9 I worked fairly easily at my novel, drafting 2,300 words—a complete chapter. After supper, I opened a new copy of Arnold's *Essays in Criticism* (second series) and read the essay on Tolstoy. I shall read myself to sleep (for the second time today) with Maria Edgeworth's *Belinda.* In spite of the laziest liver in the world, I am well-nigh content with myself tonight.

October 5.

To wake up at midnight, after an hour's sleep, with a headache, slight but certainly indicative of the coming attack; to hear the clock strike, every note drilling a separate hole into your skull; to spend the rest of the night uneasily between sleeping and waking, always turning over the pillow, and tormented intermittently by idiotic nightmares, crowded with action, which fatigue the brain: this is a disturbed liver. Towards morning comes the hope, caused by the irregularity of the pain, that the headache will pass away on getting up. But it never does so. Then one comes downstairs, eyes as it were in red-hot sockets, and gulps some effervescing saline. One rises from breakfast with a mouth full of reminiscences—butter, cocoa, porridge; and the headache remains. One walks to the office in the fresh autumn air; the headache remains. Towards noon, one seeks the last remedy, a draught which weakens the action of the heart. It is effective, and after half an hour's somnolence in a chair, one recovers, half dazed, but without the headache; weak, silly, nerveless, but without the headache. The impulse to work is alive again, and one accomplishes an hour. But after lunch and dinner one has a consciousness that a new headache is lying in wait, and, one's resolves worn away by the constant sense of fatigue in the eyes and of rapid pulsation round the back of the head, one weakly lapses into idleness, trusting that to-morrow will be different. . . .

January 2, 1899.

If I gained nothing else last year, I gained facility. In the writing of sensational fiction I made great strides during the last few months, and with ordinary luck I could now turn out a complete instalment (about 4,000 words) after 3 o'clock in an afternoon. For critical work too, I have become much faster and more adroit. . . .

August 10.

I have just remembered a saying of Mrs. Dunmer, our new housekeeper at Witley. She said to me: "There's a lot of old maids in this village, sir, as wants men. There was 3 of 'em after a curate as we had here; a very nice young gentleman he was, sir. No matter how often the church was opened those women would be there, sir, even if it was 5 times a day. It's a sign of a hard winter, sir, when the hay begins to run after the horse."

November 2.

. . . A young couple, married 3 or 4 years, have had no children. They are probably rather more than average amorous, and their reasons for dispensing with offspring are no doubt sternly practical. The husband is the only son of his mother, who, having had one child, requested, from religious motives of purity, to be relieved of any further conjugal duties. The request was granted, her spouse possibly sympathizing with the motives. Now this mother, discussing with her daughter-in-law the fact that the latter has had no children, expresses the opinion that doubtless her son is like herself, has a distaste for the impurity of sexual intercourse, and that this explains why her son is not a father.

Secret wild laughter of the son and his wife. . . .

January 1, 1901. Bedfordshire.

Last year I wrote 3 plays.
The Postmistress (1 act).
Children of the Mist (4 acts—in collaboration with Eden Phillpotts).
The Chancellor (4 acts—in collaboration with Arthur Hooley).
Also a serial, *The Grand Babylon Hotel,* of 70,000 words.
Also the draft of my Staffordshire novel, *Anna Tellwright,* 80,000 words, and part of the final writing.
Also half a dozen short stories.
I also wrote and published 196 articles of various length.
I also collected, revised, and wrote a preface for a series of my articles from the *Academy,* to be called *Fame and Fiction, an Inquiry into Certain Popularities.*
I also edited *Woman* till 30th Sept.—when I resigned, and came to live in the country. . . .
I also advised Pearsons on 50 MS. books. . . .

On the completion of *The Chancellor*, I vowed never again to work so hard, but in future to find time to read poetry regularly, to gather materials for a work on the fiction of the nineteenth century, and—?—to study Latin.

I made £620 last year; more than ever I made in any previous year. . . .

February 2.

This morning I saw what I could, over the heads of a vast crowd, of the funeral procession of the Queen [Victoria]. The people were not, on the whole, deeply moved, whatever journalists may say, but rather serene and cheerful. . . .

May 17.

I finished *Anna Tellwright* [*Anna of the Five Towns*] this morning at 2.45 A.M., after 17 hours' continuous work, save for meals, on the last 5,000 words. I was very pleased with it; slept well for 4 hours, got up with a frightful headache, and cycled through Hemel Hempstead to St. Albans, lunched at the George, and home—42 miles. A.T. is 74,000 in length.

January 26, 1904.

The first visit to Monte Carlo must be a sort of an event in the life of any one with imagination. . . .

Inside the gaming-saloons (4 o'clock) I found a large crowd and many tables in full work. The crowd not so distinguished in appearance as I had (foolishly) expected. Scores and scores of prostitutes, and of course a number of really "classy" people. I saw few signs at the tables of suppressed or *e*xpressed excitement, though quite a large proportion of the people seemed to be gambling seriously. I had no intention of betting, but after I had watched several tables and grasped the details of roulette (30 and 40 I didn't attempt to grasp) I remained at one table as if hypnotized; without knowing it I began to finger a 5-franc piece in my pocket, and then I became aware that I was going to bet. I knew I should bet some seconds before I formally decided to. I staked a 5-franc piece on an even chance and won. Like a provincial up from the country, who has heard tales of metropolitan rascality, I stood close to a croupier and kept a careful eye on my coin, and picked up the winnings without an instant's delay. I kept on playing, carefully, and always on even chances, for some time, and stopped when I had made a little money, and went and had some tea. I didn't play again. . . .

January 31.

. . . My interest in this journal is not what it was. Monte Carlo and other things have disturbed it.

May 27.

Today I am 37. I have lived longer than I shall live. My new series begins to appear today in the *Windsor*. My name is not on the cover. Anthony Hope's stands there alone. And I am 37. Comment is needless. I . . . shall get married before I am 40.

July 17.

Yesterday at 7 P.M., after a week of slogging, I finished *Hugo*, which I think is my eighth novel. I have got that off my mind and now this morning I lose a front tooth, just to be supplied with a new worry.

July 21.

Last night Dr. Mackenzie brought Robert Barr to the Chat Blanc. I had not seen him for several years.

Barr has known most people, including Mark Twain. He said Mark told him that his average expenditure was $35,000 a year, and that once when they got short he and his wife went through all the accounts and found the only things on which they could economize were *Harper's Magazine* and a cheaper close-paper. . . .

October 7.

In chastising my little dog, I find it is quite easy to lose control of myself momentarily and to treat the little brute cruelly. I did this once this afternoon and was so disgusted at myself that my hand trembled afterwards so that I could scarcely write my letter to the Mater.

December 10.

X—described the general sensations of being well drunk as magnificent, splendid. "But," he says, "you mustn't set out to get drunk. It must take you unawares." He told me that when sober he frequently lost umbrellas, but when drunk never. He made a special point of retaining his umbrella then in his hand; it became his chief concern in life. Once he got badly drunk at Maxim's. He just had sense enough to take a cab to the rooms of a mistress he had then. She received him and undressed him and put him to bed. But he would not "leave go" of his umbrella during the process. He passed it from hand to hand as she divested him of his coat, waistcoat, and shirt, and he took it to bed. And he said, "She became very angry with that umbrella." . . .
. . . During 1905 I published 3 books. *Tales of the Five Towns, The Loot of Cities,* and *Sacred and Profane Love.* . . .

I wrote:

1. The second and third parts of *Sacred and Profane Love.*
2. *The City of Pleasure,* a 60,000 serial for Tillotsons.
3. The first 30,000 words of *Whom God Hath Joined.*
4. Eight or 10 short stories, all about the Five Towns.
5. A new series of *Savoir Vivre* articles for T.P.'s *Weekly,* which began on December 1. Also some articles for the *New Tribune.*

6. A little French play in 2 acts, translated by Davray. Title: *Que Faire?*

My total of words was slightly over 200,000 much less than usual, but then I took two months' clear holiday in the summer. On the whole not a satisfactory year. Genuine success seemed, as usual, to delay and postpone itself. But I find that I am much less interested in money than Phillpotts and Wells.

May 13, 1906.

. . . I came down to Les Sablons yesterday. It is summer. The garden full of sun and flowers, the roads humming with insects. The chestnuts in front of the house "snowing" all the time. Bright blue sky, with a border of "capricious towering" white clouds. I walked up to the "grand entrance" to the forest this morning, and it was so beautiful and so imposing that even Henry Ward Beecher's silly remark about a tree being finer than a cathedral seemed for the moment to be not so idiotic and meaningless after all.

July 19, 1907.

. . . Talking about eating, Mme. Bergeret said that in the Midi (neighborhood of Toulouse specially) there used to be men who prided themselves on enormous powers of eating. They did not usually eat a great deal, but on occasions, when put to it, they would perform terrible feats such as consuming a whole turkey. The result sometimes was that they were very ill. The method of curing them was to dig a hole in the muck-heap, strip the sufferer naked, put him in the hole, and pack him tightly with manure up to his neck. The people who did this did it with gusto, telling the sufferer what an odious glutton he was. The heat generated promoted digestion in a manner almost miraculous, and next day the sufferer was perfectly restored.

August 10.

. . . Yesterday I seemed to pass an entirely satisfactory day: Italian, piano, my play, writing finely, excursion with my wife, good meals, and reading my own stories at night in the garden to the Marriotts, who laughed continually as people ought to laugh at such stories. . . .

September 26.

All day the drone of a threshing machine near by, rising and falling, with an occasional high shriek of a whistle to signal a stopping or a starting. A hot heavy day, with undecided hints of a storm. . . .

After lunch I stood at my open window and watched two bees visit every flower on a bush, entering completely hidden into each blossom and emerging after a few seconds. I was surprised at the certainty, rapidity, and thoroughness with which they exhausted the bush of perhaps a hundred flowers. Then I sat down and wrote the first of 12 articles for the *Evening News*—1,000 words in 1¼ hours. M. was asleep all the time.

October 26.

. . . The sound of voices is very clear in the forest in this mushroom weather. I have learnt a little about mushrooms. I have tremendously enjoyed my morning exercise in the mist or rain. But mushrooming only interests me when the sport is good.

In general, slightly too much work. 18,000 words of *Old Wives' Tale* in 2 weeks 4 days.

Much tempted to throw up my Italian and my piano, on account of stress of work, but I still stick to both of them.

January 2, 1908.

. . . I began *The Case of Leek* yesterday, according to programme, and continued it today. But yesterday I was cold and today I had a headache. 1,600 words in 2 days. Chief observation in London: that it is a city of very rich and very poor. The vastness of this rich quarter is astonishing. In Bond Street this morning the main thing to be seen was the well-groomed, physically fit male animal: a sort of physical arrogance with it.

January 4.

I continue to walk about and to have the richness of London forced into my head. It is almost disconcerting to think that all this vast idle class has to "go" one day. The idlers in this hotel make an imposing array. Offensive, many of them. . . .

April 5.

. . . Habit of work is growing on me. I could get into the way of going to my desk as a man goes to whiskey, or rather to chloral. Now that I have finished all my odd jobs and have nothing to do but 10,000 words of novel a week and two articles a week, I feel quite lost, and at once begin to think, without effort, of ideas for a new novel. My instinct is to multiply books and articles and plays. I constantly gloat over the number of words I have written in a given period. . . .

December 31.

Dance. Games. "God save the Queen," and varied songs at the hotel. "God save the Queen" (or King) in various languages. Servants watching eagerly at nothing from behind a curtained window.

I have never worked so hard as this year, and I have not earned less for several years. But I have done fewer silly things than usual. . . . Total words, 423,500.

January 10, 1909.

Miss Sains related stories of a young woman well known to her who had charge of a crèche of 30 infants, and amused herself one day by changing all their clothes so that at night they could not be identified, "and many of them never *were* identified," said Miss Sains. "I knew all her brothers and sisters too. She wanted to go into a sisterhood, and she did, for a month. The only thing she did there was one day she went into the laundry and taught all the laundry-maids to polka. She was *such* a merry girl," said Miss Sains simply.

January 27.

. . . Although I now do more work, more regularly than ever I did, I feel tired more definitely and more consciously than I did 4 or 5 years ago. I remember when I was writing *Leonora* at the Hotel du Quai Voltaire, I used to go out into the Rue de Rivoli (towards the end of the book) with a sensation as if the top of my head would come off. But I did not recognize it as fatigue, simply as the result of worry, a nuisance. I can now work hard all morning and I feel tired, and I know that if I kept on after lunch I should probably be ill. But by consciously refusing to think of my work, by vegetating, I can be sure that by tea-time I shall be restored, and can work again for a bit without letting myself in for a bilious attack. . . .

February 9.

Keen frost and bright sunshine. I went to toboggan down a steep slope, but when it came to the point I was afraid and started halfway down, and rolled over. Afterwards I would not try from the top, though twice I climbed to the top meaning to do it. Curious. No danger, as snow is thick. But I had the *trac.*

April 21, 1911.

London. Palace Theatre. Pavlova dancing the dying swan. Feather falls off her dress. Two silent Englishmen. One says, "Moulting." That is all they say. . . .

October 13. New York.

. . . Called at 2 hotels (free lunch-counter, etc.) and had . . . views of Broadway, 14th Street, 5th Avenue, etc. Lots of sky signs. Roads up. Not very many people, but a sensation of grandness, immensity, lights, heights. Streets full of holes. The Elevated, on a forest of pillars. Cable cars long and noisy, but fewer at that time of night. . . .

October 14.

Going down change at 155th on to Elevated.
No crush. First view of baseball ground.
The effect of millions of staircased windows of apartment houses, with glimpses every now and then of complicated lines of washing.
Street after street, dirty streets, untidy, littered.
Baseball game. Giants v. Athletics, N.Y. v. Phila.
Again cigarettes, chewing-gum, programmes. . . .
Pitcher lifting left leg high. Tip on right toe. . . .

October 17.

. . . Arrival at fine station at Washington.
Apparently a long drive to Shoreham Hotel, across avenue after avenue. Still, all the air of a provincial town. Had to get out of bed to extinguish final light, otherwise good hotel.
Congress chamber.
Old Congress chamber is a sort of rule-chamber. Its astounding collection of ugly statues. Whispering point, where Adams fell. I was exhausted after this. Declined to visit Library of Congress. Saw Washington monument. Phallic. Appalling. A national catastrophe—only equalled by Albert Memorial. Tiny doll-like people waiting to go into it. . . .
General effect of Washington. A plantation of public edifices amid a rather unkempt undergrowth of streets. Pennsylvania Avenue the great street. Cheapness of its buildings (old private houses turned into business) as the thoroughfare approaches the Capitol.
The White House very nice architecture. Rather small. Distinguished Overflow of Capitol into huge buildings at either side rather to front of Capitol. Dome too big for sub-structure. The wings rather fine.
Badness of saddle of mutton at bkfst. Finger bowls after every damn snack.

April 14, 1913.

Advance of age. I now sit down to brush my hair and put my collar and tie on. I also take a decided pleasure in forming habits, and reforming old ones. . . .
Net earnings received during 1913: Books, £6924 18s. 1d. Plays, £8524 19s. 0d. Total, £15,449 17s. 1d. The gross sum (before paying agents' fees) was £17,166 10s. 1d. In addition, interest on investments, £405, 11s. 3d. All this handsomely beats last year's record.

November 12, 1918.

In Sunday's papers we saw the abdication of the Kaiser. Returned to town yesterday morning. In Lower Regent Street first news that armistice was signed—a paper boy calling out in a subdued tone. 10.45. . . .
Raining now. An excellent thing to damp hysteria and Bolshevism. Great

struggling to cross Piccadilly Circus twice. No buses. (It was rumoured that tubes stopped. I believe they were stopped for a time.) It stopped raining. Then cold mire in streets. Vehicles passed, festooned with shouting human beings. Others, dark, with only one or two occupants. Much light in Piccadilly up to Ritz corner, and in Piccadilly Circus. It seemed most brilliant. Some theatres had lights on their façades too. The enterprising Trocadero had hung a row of temporary lights under one of its porticoes. Shouting. But nothing terrible or memorable. Yet this morning Brayley, my valet, said to me the usual phrases: "You wondered where the people came from. You could walk on their heads at Charing Cross, and you couldn't cross Picc. Circus at all." When he came in with my tea I said, "Well, Brayley, it's all over." He smiled and said something. That was all our conversation about the end of the war. Characteristic. . . .

April 19, 1920.

. . . Robert Nichols gave me Henry James's copy of the Fowler translation of Lucian in 4 vols. Looking through these volumes in bed last night, I found that the only part of which the leaves were cut was the Dialogues of Courtesans. Swinnerton and I agreed this morning that it was a very pretty problem whether these leaves were cut by Henry James or by Robert. . . .

March 14, 1924.

Yesterday, Reform lunch. Talking about gambling. It was defended by James Currie and even by Lord Buckmaster. Stated to be the one distraction of the people. There is, however, fornication. Lord R. said that 40 years ago, walking up St. James's Street he used to be accosted by 6 or 7 prostitutes and by 2 at once. Certainly the change on the streets is tremendous. I said there was, however, just as much fornication as ever, and must be, and I think this is so. Nevertheless, I agree sometimes with R.D.'s old assertion that copulation is largely a matter of habit. She ought to know. . . .

March 25.

. . . Last night I had what I call a goodish night for me. 12.30 a.m. to about 2.55 a.m. Then about 3.15 a.m. to 5.45 a.m. Then a few short snoozes, totalling perhaps 40 minutes at the very most. In all 5½ hours. I don't think I have ever had to be called, certainly not for 20 or 30 years, even for the most urgent or early occasions. I can always be sure of being awake for anything in reason.

October 8.

Walking in Fulham Road yesterday morning I saw in a slatternly chemist's shop a section of window given to "Yeast is life. Vitamines mean health. X——Yeast Tablets. . . . A lightning pick-me-up" guaranteed (or money back) to aid headaches, etc. in 5 minutes, flatulence, etc. in 5 to 10, stomach trouble in 10 to 15, flu, cold in 24 hours. I went in and bought some—

probably because I used to take yeast and it may have done me a certain amount of good. I didn't know what was in the tablets (beyond yeast). I knew that for many years I had tried all sorts of remedies, and that not one of them had succeeded with me. Yet, as usual, I had hope again. I believed again, etc., etc. I took stuff blind again. This indestructible (though often destroyed) faith in quack medicine advertisements is a very interesting and perhaps almost universal trait. I took a tablet. Felt nothing. But about tea time I felt a rather wonderful change in my organism. After tea I took two more tablets—or was it before tea? Anyhow I felt very much better. I took two on going to bed, and I have had the best night for many weeks. In fact I slept 5¾ hours, of which 3¼ at a stretch. . . .

October 13.

On Saturday night I dined with T. and his fiancée, an American widow with 2 children and some money. She had that American feminine way of implicitly or explicitly expecting a sort of homage from men, and of putting them gently in their place at intervals. . . . I said that Englishmen had points and she said: "Oh! I am sure they must have." American women are metallic. They may tinkle sweetly or harshly, but they are metallic.

February 24, 1925.

. . . Fjellsted told me on Saturday a story of how trouble may be caused by indiscretion. The story was told to him by a patient, a Justice of the Peace, and it happened to two of the J.P.'s friends. One of these two had a splendid car, and the two went out for a drive. They overtook two nurses from a nursing home, and offered them a lift, which was accepted. They came to London (I think). The four met again in the evening. Later one of the nurses found herself pregnant. She did not even know the name of her lover; but he had told her that a well-known surgeon had performed a rather peculiar operation on him. She went to the surgeon and actually got the man's name and address. She then wrote to her lover, and mentioned the other man and the other girl sufficiently for people who knew the circle to identify them, and told him of her condition. The letter to the lover was opened by the lover's daughter (one of those careless go-as-you-please households where everybody casually opens everybody else's letters). The daughter showed the letter to her mother. The mother identified the friend and went and told the friend's wife. Finally she went to the nursing home and denounced the second girl, who was dismissed. Only it happened that she denounced the wrong girl, and the wrong girl brought an action for damages, and damages had to be paid. Also of course the lover had to pay for his illegitimate child— £1 a week. To say nothing of the horrid mess in the two homes. The moral is, don't pick up girls when you are motoring, and, if you are a girl, don't be picked up. Also if you let a man seduce you, get at any rate his name and address. But chiefly, have an absolute rule in your home that your letters are to be opened by nobody but yourself.

March 12.

The head of the little dancing school, where I am daily being taught to dance, came in to watch me being taught yesterday. He said to me: "What you want is courage, decision. Don't be afraid of 'em (women). Remember they have to do what you want. You've *got* 'em. And it's the only time you *have* got 'em."

March 21.

We were at Lady Colefax's supper to meet John Barrymore on Thursday night. . . . Barrymore, at the supper (where he arrived after 1 A.M.) seemed to be partly exhausted. He looked distinguished but didn't talk distinguished. During songs he closed his eyes and seemed to sleep. Then he exclaimed: "Oh, for some Cointreau!" very urgently, and it was brought quickly to him. . . .

September 4.

The big new French clock was on the floor in the box-room. She [Dorothy] said: "I put it away there because it stuck out on the mantelpiece, and all the curves of the ornament, leaves and twigs and things, seemed to be the same as the curves of my nausea. So I put it away till the nausea has gone."

She saw two nice-looking little boys in the restaurant at Harvey Nichols, and kept on referring to the extraordinary niceness of the face of one of them. At last she said: "I should like my boy to have a face like that." The secret was out.

September 11.

She said: "I've never enjoyed things so much. The sky. The mind. He is a happy creature (note "he is" not "he will be"—less than two months gone). This does not mean that I'm happy. But he is. Also he is adventurous. I have a much stronger feeling of the adventure of life than ever I had before. (But she always had it.) When I take a taxi, I'm apt to think of the danger in the traffic, to him and to me. But when I think it over I say: 'This is life. This is adventure.'" . . .

February 7, 1926. Rome.

As I passed across the end of the hotel lounge tonight the noise of the American accent everywhere was simply awful. The American tourists will overrun Europe like the Goths soon. It is positively frightening.

May 31.

. . . I nursed Virginia for 20 minutes, while D. played a Bach-Tausig Fugue etc. It is very interesting nursing the baby for a short time; but the narrowness of the baby's interests must make it tedious quite soon. I kept the creature very "good."

June 1.

Tremendous morning's work. In the afternoon we drove . . . to Littlehampton. Littlehampton scarcely coincided at all with my memories of it— about thirty years ago. . . . I slept there one night, and heard a Norwegian crew singing some songs. Most romantic. And I remembered the softness of the ebb tide, and craft coming down it swirling, and being kept straight by all hands and then dropping a stern anchor on which they could swing themselves straight; then the anchor hiked up again.

September 22.

. . . I fear for my projected average of 1000 words a day for the year. I am already a day behind it.

Last evening, we listened extensively to the wireless. It soon gets boring, in fact as soon as one has got used to the marvel of it. All sounds are somewhat falsified—thickened. Still, it is all very marvellous.

October 31.

At 12 Dorothy and I went for our Sunday morning walk in Hyde Park. . . . Dorothy wanted to know whether I felt that it was "undignified" for me to walk by the perambulator in the crowded Sunday morning Park! I did, however, refuse to push the vehicle myself.

November 29.

I didn't finally wake up till 7.58, very rare occurrence, as I had had very few breaks during the night. *Daily Mail* article by Birkenhead on me, in which he practically accused me of lying.

I went downstairs and wrote my reply to Birkenhead in the form of a letter to the *Mail*. When I took it to Miss Nerney, she said that the *Mail* had telephoned for an article: so I crossed out the Sir, and Yours truly, and called it an article and charged £60 for it.

January 1, 1927.

I wrote 378,100 words last year, having contracted with myself to write, at first 300,000, and then 365,000. I make no contract with myself for 1927. I published 28 articles during 1926 and, apparently, only four short stories. I know I wrote more than four—I should think, seven, eight, or ten.

Very feeble this morning, after the New Year's Eve carousing, and bed at 2.30. . . .

March 20.

. . . I didn't spend one penny of petty cash all day. . . .

January 2, 1928.

It is now difficult for me to begin "writing" before 11 o'clock. Chores seem to increase. Tea with Dorothy. The infant Virginia continues to make a devil of a fuss if the gramophone is not started for her. She lies down on the floor and sobs or weeps quietly. When the music begins she puts up her arms to be carried about with rhythmic motions of the carrier's feet. Strange! Dorothy keeps insisting that she is no ordinary child. . . .

January 17.

Formerly in my life I was always preoccupied by my insomnia and my digestion. I only rarely think about my digestion now—it is so good—but I am still terribly preoccupied with my sleeping. . . .

April 13.

. . . Walked to Dent's in Cockspur Street, where yesterday I had seen a bed-table watch, which I had the notion of giving to Dorothy. The price £15, annoyed and repelled me, but in the end I yielded to the d . . . d thing and bought it. . . .

April 29.

I wore my new house-suit from Sulka's. As I wanted to wear it all morning, I decided not to go out. It is so magnificent that I felt rather shy about showing it to the nurses. However, they gave no sign of stupefaction. I wrote my *Evening Standard* article, finishing it at just 1 o'clock; but before that I had done chores. Virginia came down to lunch with me. I am told that Virginia now strongly objects to being put in her pen. She made a fantastic noise this morning. . . .

December 3.

. . . Dined at home, and we dashed off to see Tallulah Bankhead in *Her Cardboard Lover,* a French farce by Deval, anglicized by P. G. Wodehouse and another. This was quite a good boulevard farce in the traditional manner, well played by Tallulah and Leslie Howard. The rest very mediocre. Wodehouse had handled it with some skill. Tallulah has great resource, and so has Leslie Howard. We got home by 11.15, after learning that the King was *slightly* better. Crowds continually in front of the Palace. I read some of J. W. N. Sullivan's *Beethoven,* and wasn't much struck by it. Then 100 pages of *Alice in Wonderland.* Quite readable, though confined to one set of fanciful invention. Tenniel's pictures very ugly.

December 16.

Terrific day. The best I have done for years. Nearly 5000 words. I dined at the Savoy. The millionaire owner of a number of papers . . . wanted some *really* good stuff for X. . . . I said I didn't know whether I could think of any subjects; I had too much to do. He said he worked harder than I did. I said: "You don't!" "Don't?" said he. "Don't," said I. "Don't?" said he. "Don't," said I. I gazed at him. His eyes fell.

December 31.

This year I have written 304,000 words; 1 play, 2 films, 1 small book on religion, and about 80 or 81 articles. Also I lost a full month in rehearsals, and a full month, no, six weeks, on holidays.

"Be disinterested; that is what really matters."

William Ralph Inge

Following his education at Cambridge and more than a score of
years of teaching there and at Oxford, the Very Reverend
W. R. Inge (1860–1954) became Dean of St. Paul's Cathedral,
London in 1911. For nearly twenty-five years he was one of England's ranking clergymen, and certainly one of the best known.

Dean Inge had an almost pessimistic disposition, and because
of his melancholy manner and tartness of tongue and pen he was
popularly—and rather fondly—known as "the Gloomy Dean."

Inge's diary of a quarter-century in the Deanery begins with
the first faint rumblings of the first World War and ends with
the premonitory sounds of the second. But his account is far from
somber. Inge had an inquiring and lively mind, firm convictions,
and a disconcertingly quick wit. Because he believed that "the
diary allows the repressed self to stretch his legs," he used his to
"let off steam at my surroundings." In the privacy of his diary he
lays about him with fine gusto belaboring the foolishness of the
world where he finds it—whether it be the quirks of the Royal
Family or the foibles of the Gloomy Dean himself.

May 2, 1912.

. . . I dined with the Royal College of Surgeons. My neighbour Sir John
Dwelly was interesting about faith-healing. He thinks it not impossible that a
hopeful mind may help to cure microbic diseases. He also spoke of the growing evil of taking cocaine and morphia by hypodermic injections. After dinner
we inspected the pickles, including part of the intestines of Napoleon, showing small malignant growths. . . .

January 20, 1913.

A most interesting meeting of the Clerical and Medical Committee. . . .
The impression is growing upon me that the medical dogma, that no organic

disease can be cured by suggestion, needs careful scrutiny. . . . A scientific man, whose case had been diagnosed as cerebrospinal meningitis, as tumour on the brain, and as locomotor ataxy, was cured by suggestion, and a few months later he was climbing the Alps. There was another story of a doctor's wife who could not sleep unless she was tied by the leg to her husband. . . . She was cured by suggestion. . . .

December 2.

We dined with Lord and Lady Ferrers. I talked to Mr. Thomson, head of the detective department of Scotland Yard. He thinks that *Trent's Last Case* [by E. C. Bentley] is the best detective novel; "but of course," he said, "we go by information, not by deduction, or we should have run in an archbishop before now." His father was Archbishop of York! . . .

April 20, 1917.

The great service at St. Paul's went off very well. The Star-Spangled Banner is a vulgar thing, but the Battle Hymn of the Republic, to the tune of "John Brown," was magnificent. Bishop Brent preached an aggressively democratic sermon, which made me a little uneasy, with all the royalties present. But the King said to me, "I thought it an admirable sermon, quite excellent." So if he was pleased it is all right. It was a strange sight to see the American flag waving over the Houses of Parliament. I pictured to myself George III., saying "What, what, what, Mr. Washington; have they made you King of England?"

May 15.

A long walk with [Bishop] Barnes, who told me very interesting stories about German spies, which he had heard from Justice Sankey. An Englishman, who had married early, was deserted by his wife. He did not know whether she was alive or not. In middle life he fell in love with the sister of his German correspondent—he was in business—and explained matters to her. She was willing to take the risk, and they were married. When the war broke out a private enemy informed the police that he was living with an alien who was not his wife. The police with many apologies asked for proof which he could not give. After reflection he sent for the oldest man in his employment, and said "Jones, would you like to earn an extra pound a week as long as you live?" "That would suit me very well, sir." "Well, you will come up to London tomorrow, and go through the form of marriage with a lady whom you will never see again." So he married his wife to Jones, and defied the Defence of the Realm Act to do its worst. He was prosecuted for fraud, and Sankey was about to pass sentence when the culprit said, "My Lord, may I ask you a question?" "Yes." "If you had been in my place, what would you have done?" . . .

December 8.

A Mirfield monk came to stay and preach for me. He ate up all the food in the house.

December 14.

A meeting of the "League for Promoting International Friendship through the Churches." I took the opportunity to tell them some unpopular truths. "We cherish three impossible hopes: (1) that we can destroy German militarism. We cannot; they will only live for revenge. (2) A restoration of the balance of power. This means a mad competition in armaments and the suicide of Europe. (3) That we can force Germany to adopt our democratic system. They do not want government by mass-bribery, and will prefer a military dictatorship." I do not want to be unduly discouraging. There is a real horror of war among the peoples; but in spite of the proverb it takes only one to make a quarrel. . . .

June 4, 1920.

Opening of a new Eugenics Branch at University College. The speaking was very bad. . . . Nothing was said about eugenics by anybody. . . .

June 13, 1921.

The Haldanes asked us to dinner to meet Einstein . . . and found a crowd of distinguished people—the Davidsons, Gosse, the Bernard Shaws, J. J. Thomson, the Ranee of Sarawak, and Whitehead. I cannot understand Einstein's theory, and I doubt whether Haldane does either.

> We thought that lines were straight and Euclid true;
> God said, "Let Einstein be," and all's askew.

April 11, 1925.

Kitty [his wife] and I started for America on the *Mauretania.* . . . We were treated with great consideration when we landed in New York. The unlucky Americans had to show innumerable papers, and every bit of luggage was ransacked. If anything that looked new was found, the owner was hauled off to an office and smartly fined. My bags were passed through unexamined. Before I left the ship . . . I found myself in the midst of about twenty reporters, with whom I amused myself. "Well, Dr. Inge, what do you think about prohibition?" "I am quite willing to stick it for three weeks, but, since you ask me, I think cold water, with which the Psalmist says wild asses quench their thirst, is a poor beverage to offer to a human being." "Well, Dr. Inge, what do you think of the morals of the modern flapper as compared with those of her grandmother?" "The early indiscretions of the flapper's grandmother I neither witnessed nor shared." Then the whole gang photographed me again and again, and the chief reporter said to Kitty, "The Dean will be most popular over here. . . ."

October 15, 1929.

We dined with Sir Lawrence and Paula Jones. We discussed the tragedy of the passing of the old-fashioned hospitality. Servants are now impossible to find. We shall soon have to do all our own housework, and shall have no time to improve our minds. . . .

December 17.

We dined at Lambeth. The pictures have been rearranged. The Archbishop . . . told me that at his audience with the King after his appointment the only thing the King had to say was that he hoped the Archbishop would stop the clergy from wearing moustaches. Terribly characteristic of our Royal Family.

December 24.

My pocket has been picked in a tube lift, and I bought a new watch from Bennett, explaining my misfortune. The shopman said, "That is much like what happened to the late Sir John Bennett. He was dining at the Mansion House, where he sat between the Chancellor of the Exchequer and the Bishop of London. His gold watch was taken."

December 31, 1930.

. . . Like other people who are in the public eye I have enemies. There is G. K. Chesterton, who certainly hates me, and is reported to have said that one of his reasons for becoming a Papist was that he could not remain in the same Church as the Dean of St. Paul's. I retaliated in my diary by hoping that the public would soon get tired of the elephantine capers of an obese mountebank. These flowers of speech happily did not find their way into print. . . .

January 15, 1931.

I gave an address at Birmingham on Lippmann's *Preface to Morals* which seems to me a valuable and interesting book. Some Americans, like Lippmann, Santayana, and Thornton Wilder, have an excellent English style; others give us on every other page words which we have never heard before and do not wish to hear again. The main argument of Lippmann's book is that "disinterestedness" is the vital part of higher religion. Aldous Huxley has since said the same, calling it less happily, nonattachment. When I was ordained . . . the only thing that the Bishop said to me was "Be disinterested; that is what really matters." Perhaps no wiser counsel could be given to a young man who might be suspected of being ambitious. I have always remembered it; though I have taken occasion to say, "Don't fancy yourself disinterested when you are only uninterested, and don't fancy yourself attracted by God when you are only repelled by man."

November 7.

We lunched with Lady Mary Glyn, who was very interesting about the King's part in the recent crisis. "Ramsey MacDonald came to the palace one evening and said to the King, 'It is all over with me. My party will not follow me. All that I have tried to do has failed. There is nothing for your Majesty to do except to send for Mr. Baldwin and ask him to try to form a Government.' The King replied, 'I don't want to do that. You are overwrought now. Go home and go to bed. . . .'" Archbishop Lang afterwards told me his version of the story, which agreed in every particular with Lady Mary's. The Archbishop added, "That 'Go to Bed' saved the country."

13. THIS DAY, THIS ENTRY FOR A LATER TIME

"I undertook to kiss no more."

Samuel Pepys

Out of the more than 2000 pages of what is undoubtedly the most remarkable diary ever written there steps a man. Short, plump, bewigged and powdered, he advances in mincing steps with his gold-headed cane in hand, his thick sensual lips slightly parted. He stops and turns upon the reader his warm, disarming smile. This is Samuel Pepys (1633–1703).

The fifth child in a large family, Pepys was the son of a London tailor. He had the good fortune to attend Magdalene College, Cambridge, and also to have a well placed relative, Sir Edward Montague (later the Earl of Sandwich), who helped him obtain a clerkship in the naval offices. He diligently improved his position, becoming wealthy in the process, until he was named Secretrary of the Admiralty. He married Elizabeth St. Michel, daughter of a Huguenot refugee. They had no children.

Pepys lived a life of modest achievement. His friend John Evelyn thought him "a very worthy industrious and curious person . . . universally beloved, hospitable, generous, learned in many things, skilled in music, a very great cherisher of learned men of whom he had the conversation." It is doubtful, however, if he would be remembered had he not kept his great diary. Most of his career was spent in naval affairs. He wrote *Memoirs of the Royal Navy* (1690), a work still consulted by historians, sat briefly in Parliament as the member from Harwich, and was briefly imprisoned on the suspicion that he was involved in the Popish Plot and had given naval secrets to France. He died, honoured by all who knew him, at his house in Clapham.

Pepys' books and manuscripts were left to Magdalene College. Among them was his diary, six bound manuscript volumes of some 3000 pages covering the years between 1660 and 1669. It was written in Thomas Shelton's shorthand and was made still more difficult to read by cyphers of Pepys' own invention and phrases in dog-Latin and French. The diary lay entirely unread

From *The Diary of Samuel Pepys*, edited by Henry B. Wheatley. Reprinted by permission of Random House, Inc.

until the early nineteenth century, and it was not until 1825 that extracts first appeared in print.

In the pages of the diary there was a self-portrait—a picture done with such frankness, honesty, and detail that it has never been equaled. Here *is* Pepys; his peccadillos and his pettiness, his generosity and his penuriousness, his frivolity, venality, and self-indulgence. He never flinched from the truth. He never forgot when he had too much to drink or trifled with a casual love, and he remembered in painful detail the way he felt the morning afterward. Sometimes he was cruel and exacting, sometimes he was absurdly generous. He was libidinous himself, but almost madly jealous of any attentions paid his wife. All eyes and ears, he wrote down everything—sometimes so plainly that his editors still expurgate him. Nobody who ever kept a diary has told more of himself, whether of things in general or of the trivia of personal life. He was a convivial man who relished food and drink. The theatre was a passion. He remembered and celebrated as a feast day each year the anniversary of a successful operation for the removal of a kidney stone. He went regularly to church—more to be seen than to listen to the sermon. He was devoted to music, sang, composed and played several instruments. He loved life with a zest that is reflected in almost every entry in his diary.

Here, then, is a fragment of Pepys—the Shakespeare of all diarists.

January 1, 1659–60.

Blessed be God [so Pepys' diary begins], at the end of the last year I was in very good health, without any sense of my old pain, but upon taking of cold. I lived in Axe Yard, having my wife, and servant Jane, and no more in family than us three. . . . My own private condition very handsome, and esteemed rich, but indeed very poor; besides my goods of my house, and my office, which at present is somewhat uncertain. . . .

January 15.

Having been exceedingly disturbed in the night with the barking of a dog of one of our neighbours that I could not sleep for an hour or two, I slept late, and then in the morning took physic, and so staid within all day. . . . My wife and I in pleasant discourse till night, then I went to supper, and after that to make an end of this week's notes in this book, and so to bed. It being a cold day and a great snow my physic did not work so well as it should have done.

January 16.

. . . To the Green Dragon, on Lambeth Hill, both the Mr. Pinkney's, Smith, Harrison, Morrice, that sang the bass, Sheply and I, and there we sang of all sorts of things . . . and staid there till nine o'clock, very merry and drawn on with one song after another till it came to be so late . . . and thence home, where I found my wife and maid a-washing. I staid up till the bell-man came by with his bell just under my window as I was writing this very line, and cried, "Past one of the clock, and a cold, frosty, windy morning." I then went to bed and left my wife and the maid a-washing still.

January 30.

. . . I came back by water playing on my flageolette and not finding my wife come home again from her father's I went and sat awhile and played at cards with Mrs. Jem, whose maid had newly got an ague and was ill thereupon. So homewards again, having great need to do my business, and so pretending to meet Mr. Shott the wood monger of Whitehall, I went and eased myself at the Harp and Ball, and thence home where I sat writing till bed-time and so to bed. . . . Spent a little time this night in knocking up nails for my hat and cloaks in my chamber.

March 26.

This day it is two years since it pleased God that I was cut of the stone at Mrs. Turner's in Salisbury Court. And did resolve while I live to keep it a festival, as I did the last year at my house, and for ever to have Mrs. Turner and her company with me. . . .

September 5.

. . . In the evening my wife being a little impatient I went along with her to buy her a necklace of pearl, which will cost £4 10*s*., which I am willing to comply with her in for her encouragement, and because I have lately got money, having now above £200 in cash beforehand in the world. Home, and having in our way bought a rabbit and two little lobsters, my wife and I did sup late, and so to bed. . . .

October 13.

. . . I went out to Charing Cross, to see Major-general Harrison hanged, drawn, and quartered; which was done there, he looking as cheerful as any man could do in that condition. He was presently cut down, and his head and heart shown to the people, at which there was great shouts of joy. . . . Thus it was my chance to see the King [Charles I.] beheaded at White Hall, and to see the first blood shed in revenge for the blood of the King at Charing Cross. From thence to my Lord's, and took Captain Cuttance and Mr. Sheply to the Sun Tavern, and did give them some oysters. After that I went by water home, where I was angry with my wife for her things lying about, and in my passion kicked the little fine basket, which I bought her in Holland, and broke it, which troubled me after I had done it. Within all the afternoon setting up shelves in my study. At night to bed.

October 20.

This morning one came to me to advise with me where to make me a window into my cellar in lieu of one which Sir W. Batten had stopped up, and going down into my cellar to look I stepped into a great heap of ——, by which I found that Mr. Turner's house of office is full and comes into my cellar, which do trouble me, but I shall have it helped. . . . This afternoon, going through London, and calling at Crowe's the upholster's, in Saint Bartholomew's, I saw the limbs of some of our new traitors set upon Aldersgate, which was a sad sight to see; and a bloody week this and the last have been, there being ten hanged, drawn, and quartered. Home, and after writing a letter to my uncle by the post, I went to bed.

December 16.

. . . In discourse I learnt a pretty trick 'to try whether a woman be a maid or no, by a string going around her head to meet at the end of her nose, which if she be not will come a great way beyond. . . .

January 1, 1660–61.

At the end of the last and the beginning of this year, I do live in one of the houses belonging to the Navy Office as one of the principal officers, and have done now about half a year. After much trouble with workmen I am now almost settled; my family being, myself, my wife, Jane, Will. Hewer, and Wayneman, my girle's brother. Myself in constant good health, and in a most handsome and thriving condition. Blessed be Almighty God for it. . . . I take myself now to be worth £300 clear in money, and all my goods and all manner of debts paid, which are none at all.

January 3.

This day I first begun to go forth in my coat and sword, as the manner now among gentlemen is. To Whitehall . . . where I staid to hear the trumpets and kettle-drums, and then the other drums, which are much cried up, though I think it dull, vulgar musique. . . .

February 10.

Took physique all day, and, God forgive me, did spend it in reading of some little French romances. . . .

April 10.

. . . To Rochester, and there saw the Cathedrall, which is now fitting for use, and the organ then a-tuning. Then away thence, observing the great doors of the church, which, they say, was covered with the skins of the Danes,

and also had much mirth at . . . the Salutacion tavern, where Mr. Alcock
and many of the town came and entertained us with wine and oysters and
other things . . . but I was a little troubled to stay too long, because of
going to Hempson's, which afterwards we did, and found it in all things a
most pretty house, and rarely furnished, only it had a most ill access on all
sides to it, which is a greatest fault that I think can be in a house. Here we
had, for my sake, two fiddles, the one a base viall, on which he that played,
played well some lyra lessons, but both together made the worst musique
that ever I heard. We had a fine collacion, but I took little pleasure in that,
for the illness of the musique and for the intentness of my mind upon Mrs.
Rebecca Allen. After we had done eating, the ladies went to dance, and
among the men we had, I was forced to dance too; and did make an ugly
shift. Mrs. R. Allen danced very well, and seems the best humoured woman
that ever I saw . . . and so broke up very pleasant and merry, and so walked
home, I leading Mrs. Rebecca, who seemed, I know not why, in that and
other things, to be desirous of my favours and would in all things show me
respects. Going home, she would needs have me sing, and I did pretty well
and was highly esteemed by them . . . and I staid there till 2 o'clock in the
morning and was most exceeding merry, and I had the opportunity of kissing
Mrs. Rebecca very often. Among other things Captain Pett was saying that
he thought he had got his wife with child since I came thither. Which I took
hold of and was merrily asking him what he would take to have it said for
my honour that it was of my getting? He merrily answered that he would if
I would promise to be godfather to it if it did come within the time just, and
I said that I would. So that I must remember to compute it when the time
comes.

April 23.

About 4 [on the coronation day of Charles II] I rose and got to the Abbey
. . . and with much ado . . . did get up into a great scaffold across the North
end of the Abbey, where with a great deal of patience I sat from past 4 till 11
before the King came in. And a great pleasure it was to see . . . but so great
a noise that I could make but little of the musique; and indeed, it was lost to
every body. . . . I went out a little while before the King had done all his
ceremonies, and went round the Abbey to Westminster Hall, all the way
within rayles, and 10,000 people, with the ground covered with blue cloth;
and scaffolds all the way. Into the Hall I got, where it was very fine with
hangings and scaffolds one upon another full of brave ladies; and my wife
in one little one, on the right hand. Here I staid walking up and down, and
at last upon one of the side stalls I stood and saw the King come in . . . with
his crown on, and his sceptre in his hand, under a canopy borne up by six
silver staves, carried by Barons of the Cinque Ports, and little bells at every
end. . . . I went from table to table to see the Bishops and all others at
their dinner, and was infinitely pleased with it. And at the Lords' table, I met
with William Howe, and he spoke to my Lord for me, and he did give me
four rabbits and a pullet, and so I got it and Mr. Creed and I got Mr. Michell
to give us some bread, and so we at a stall eat it, as every body else did what

they could get. I took a great deal of pleasure to go up and down, and look upon the ladies, and to hear the musique of all sorts, but above all, the 24 violins. About six at night they had dined, and I . . . to Axe-yard, in which at the further end there were three great bonfires, and a great many gallants, men and women; and they laid hold of us, and would have us drink the King's health upon our knees, kneeling upon a faggot, which we all did, they drinking to us one after another. Which we thought a strange frolique; but these gallants continued thus a great while, and I wondered to see how the ladies did tipple. At last I sent my wife and her bedfellow to bed, and Mr. Hunt and I went in with Mr. Thornbury . . . to his house; and there, with his wife and two of his sisters, and some gallant sparks that were there, we drank the King's health, and nothing else, till one of the gentlemen fell down stark drunk, and there lay spewing; and I went to my Lord's pretty well. But no sooner a-bed with Mr. Shepley, but my head began to hum, and I to vomit, and if ever I was foxed it was now, which I cannot say yet, because I fell asleep and slept till morning. Only when I waked I found myself wet with my spewing. Thus did the day end with joy every where; and blessed be God, I have not heard of any mischance to any body through it all, but only to Serj^t. Glynne, whose horse fell upon him yesterday, and is like to kill him. . . . There was also this night in King street, a woman had her eye put out by a boy's flinging a firebrand into the coach. Now, after all this, I can say that, besides the pleasure of the sight of these glorious things, I may now shut my eyes against any other objects, nor for the future trouble myself to see things of state and show, as being sure never to see the like again in this world.

June 5.

This morning did give my wife £4 to lay out upon lace and other things for herself. . . . After dinner to the office, where we sat and did business, and Sir W. Pen and I went home with Sir R. Slingsby to bowls in his ally, and there had good sport, and afterwards went in and drank and talked. So home Sir William and I, and it being very hot weather I took my flageolette and played upon the leads in the garden, where Sir W. Pen came out in his shirt into his leads, and there we staid talking and singing, and drinking great drafts of claret, and eating botargo [dried fish roe] and bread and butter till 12 at night, it being moonshine; and so to bed, very nearly fuddled.

June 30.

. . . To Graye's Inn Walk, all alone and with great pleasure seeing the fine ladies walk there. Myself humming to myself (which now-a-days is my constant practice since I begun to learn to sing) the trillo, and found by use that it do come upon me. . . . Myself in good health, but mighty apt to take cold, so that this hot weather I am fain to wear a cloth before my belly.

July 6.

Waked this morning with news, brought me by a messenger on purpose, that my uncle Robert is dead, and died yesterday; so . . . to the Post House and set out about eleven and twelve o'clock, taking the messenger with me that came to me, and so we rode and got well by nine o'clock to Brampton, where I found my father well. My uncle's corps in a coffin standing upon joynt-stools in the chimney in the hall; but it begun to smell, and so I caused it to be set forth in the yard all night, and watched by two men. My aunt I found in bed in a most nasty ugly pickle, made me sick to see it. My father and I lay together to-night, I greedy to see the will, but did not ask to see it until to-morrow.

August 30.

. . . At Court things are in very ill condition, there being so much emulacion, poverty, and the vices of drinking, swearing, and loose amours, that I know not what will be the end of it, but confusion. And the Clergy so high, that all people that I meet with do protest against their practice. . . . The season very sickly every where of strange and fatal fevers.

September 23.

. . . And so away to Stevenage, and staid till a showre was over, and so rode easily to Welling, where we supped well, and had two beds in the room and so lay single, and still remember it that of all the nights that ever I slept in my life I never did pass a night with more epicurism of sleep; there being now and then a noise of people stirring that waked me, and then it was a very rainy night, and then I was a little weary, that what between waking and then sleeping again, one after the other, I never had so much content in all my life, and so my wife says it was with her.

February 3, 1861–2.

After musique practice I went to the office, and there with the two Sir Williams all the morning about business, and at noon I dined with Sir W. Batten with many friends more, it being his wedding day, and among other froliques, it being their third year, they had three pyes, whereof the middlemost was made of an ovall form, in an ovall hole within the other two, which made much mirth, and was called the middle piece; and above all the rest, we had great striving to steal a spoonful out of it; and I remember Mrs. Mills, the minister's wife, did steal one for me and did give it me; and to end all, Mrs. Shippman did fill the pye full of white wine, it holding at least a pint and a half, and did drink it off for a health to Sir William and my Lady, it being the greatest draft that ever I did see a woman drink in my life. . . .

March 26.

Up early. This being, by God's great blessing, the fourth solemn day of my cutting for the stone this day four years, and am by God's mercy in very good health, and like to do well, the Lord's name be praised for it. . . . At noon come my good guests, Madame Turner, The., and Cozen Norton, and a gentleman, one Mr. Lewin of the King's Life Guard; by the same token he told us of one of his fellows killed this morning in a duel. I had a pretty dinner for them, viz., a brace of stewed carps, six roasted chickens, and a jowl of salmon, hot, for the first course; a tanzy and two neats' tongues, and cheese the second; and were very merry all the afternoon, talking and singing and piping upon the flageolette. In the evening they went with great pleasure away, and I with great content and my wife walked half an hour in the garden, and so home to supper and to bed. . . .

May 25.

To trimming myself, which I have this week done every morning, with a pumice stone, which I learnt of Mr. Marsh, when I was last at Portsmouth; and I find it very easy, speedy, and cleanly, and shall continue the practice of it. . . .

May 31.

. . . And so home, and had Sarah to comb my head clean, which I found so foul with powdering and other troubles, that I am resolved to try how I can keep my head dry without powder; and I did also in a suddaine fit cut off all my beard, which I had been a great while bringing up, only that I may with my pumice-stone do my whole face, as now I do my chin, and to save time, which I find a very easy way and gentile. So she also washed my feet in a bath of herbs, and so to bed. This month ends with very fair weather for a great while together. My health pretty well, but only wind do now and then torment me. . . .

June 21.

. . . Hearing from my wife and the maids' complaints made of the boy, I called him up, and with my whip did whip him till I was not able to stir, and yet I could not make him confess any of the lies that they tax him with. At last, not willing to let him go away a conqueror, I took him in task again, and pulled off his frock to his shirt, and whipped him till he did confess that he did drink the whey, which he had denied, and pulled a pink, and above all did lay the candlestick upon the ground in his chamber, which he had denied this quarter of a year. I confess it is one of the greatest wonders that ever I met with that such a little boy as he could possibly be able to suffer half so much as he did to maintain a lie. I think I must be forced to put him away. So to bed, with my arm very weary.

June 30.

Up betimes, and to my office, where I found Griffin's girl making it clean, but God forgive me! what a mind I had to her, but did not meddle with her. She being gone, I fell upon boring holes for me to see from my closet into the great office, without going forth, wherein I please myself much. . . .

November 2.

Lay long with pleasure talking with my wife, in whom I never had greater content, blessed be God! than now, she continuing with the same care and thrift and innocence, so long as I keep her from occasions of being otherwise, as ever she was in her life, and keeps the house as well. To church, where . . . there being a lazy preacher I slept out the sermon . . . and so home and to bed, with some pain, . . . having taken cold this morning in sitting too long bare-legged to pare my corns. . . .

December 1.

. . . Over to the Parke (where I first in my life, it being a great frost, did see people sliding with their skeates, which is a very pretty art). . . .

January 9, 1662–63.

Waking in the morning, my wife I found also awake, and begun to speak to me with great trouble and tears . . . and called for Jane to reach her out of her trunk, giving her the keys to that purpose, a bundle of papers, and pulls out a paper, a copy of what, a pretty while since, she had wrote in a discontent to me, which I would not read, but burnt. She now read it, and it was so piquant, and wrote in English, and most of it true, of the retiredness of her life, and how unpleasant it was; that being wrote in English, and so in danger of being met with and read by others, I was vexed at it, and desired her and then commanded her to tear it. When she desired to be excused of it, I forced it from her, and leapt out of the bed and in my shirt clapped them into the pocket of my breeches, that she might not get them from me, and having got on my stockings and breeches and gown, I pulled them out one by one and tore them all before her face, though it went against my heart to do it, she crying and desiring me not to do it, but such was my passion and trouble to see the letters of my love to her, and my Will wherein I had given her all I have in the world, when I went to sea with my Lord Sandwich, to be joyned with a paper of so much disgrace and dishonour, if it should have been found by any body. Having torn them all, saving a bond of my uncle Robert's, which she hath long had in her hands, and our marriage license, and the first letter that ever I sent her when I was her servant, I took up the pieces and carried them into my chamber, and there, after many disputes with myself whether I should burn them or no, and having picked up the pieces of the paper she read to-day, and of my Will which I tore, I burnt all the rest, and so went out to my office troubled in mind. . . .

January 19.

. . . By coach to Mr. Povy's, being invited thither . . . where really he made a most excellent and large dinner, of their variety, even to admiration, he bidding us, in a frolique, to call for what we had a mind, and he would undertake to give it us: and we did for prawns, swan, venison, after I had thought the dinner was quite done, and he did immediately produce it, which I thought great plenty, and he seems to set off his rest in this plenty and the neatness of his house, which he after dinner showed me, from room to room, so beset with delicate pictures, and above all, a piece of perspective in his closett in the low parler; his stable, where was some most delicate horses, and the very racks painted, and mangers, with a neat leaden painted cistern, and the walls done with Dutch tiles, like my chimnies. But still, about all things, he bid me go down into his wine-cellar, where upon several shelves there stood bottles of all sorts of wine, new and old, with labells pasted upon each bottle, and in the order and plenty as I never saw books in a bookseller's shop; and herein, I observe, he puts his highest content, and will accordingly commend all that he hath, but still they deserve to be so. . . .

May 4.

. . . By and by the dancing-master came, whom standing by, seeing him instructing my wife, when he had done with her, he would needs have me try the steps of a coranto, and what with his desire and my wife's importunity, I did begin . . . and am become his choller. The truth is, I think it a thing very useful for a gentleman, and sometimes I may have occasion of using it, and though it cost me what I am heartily sorry it should, and . . . though it be against my stomach yet I will try it a little while; if I see it comes to any great inconvenience or charge I will fling it off. . . .

May 15.

. . . Home, where I found it almost night, and my wife and the dancing-master alone above, not dancing but talking. Now so deadly full of jealousy I am that my heart and head did so cast about and fret that I could not do any business possibly, but . . . I am ashamed to think what a course I did take by lying to see whether my wife did wear drawers to-day as she used to do, and other things to rouse my suspicion of her, but I found no true cause of doing it.

May 26.

Lay long in bed talking and pleasing myself with my wife. So up and to my office a while and then home, where I found Pembleton [the dancing-master], and by many circumstances I am led to conclude that there is something more than ordinary between my wife and him, which do so trouble me that I know not at this very minute that I now write this almost what either I write or am doing. . . . This is my devilish jealousy, which I pray God may be false, but it makes a very hell in my mind, which the God of heaven remove, or I shall be very unhappy. So to the office, where we sat awhile. By and by my mind being in great trouble I went home to see how things were, and there I found as I doubted Mr. Pembleton with my wife, and nobody else in the house, which made me almost mad, and . . . so up to my chamber, and as I think if they had any intention of hurt I did prevent doing anything at that time, but Lord! to see how my jealousy wrought so far that I went softly up to see whether any of the beds were out of order or no, which I found not. . . .

May 27.

So I waked by 3 o'clock, my mind being troubled, and so took occasion by making water to wake my wife, and after having lain till past 4 o'clock seemed going to rise, though I did it only to see what she would do, and so going out of the bed she took hold of me and would know what ailed me, and after many kind and some cross words I began to tax her discretion in yesterday's business, but she quickly told me my own, knowing well enough that it was my old disease of jealousy, which I denied, but to no purpose. After an hour's discourse, sometimes high and sometimes kind, I found very good reason to think that her freedom with him is very great and more than was convenient, but with no evil intent, and so after awhile I caressed her and parted seeming friends, but she crying in a great discontent. . . .

June 4.

Up betimes . . . and I did so watch to see my wife put on drawers, which poor soul she did, and yet I could not get off my suspicions, she having a mind to go into Fenchurch Street before she went out for good and all with me, which I must needs construe to be to meet Pembleton, when she afterwards told me it was to buy a fan that she had not a mind that I should know of, and I believe it is so. Specially I did by a wile get out of my boy that he did not yesterday go to Pembleton's or thereabouts, but only was sent all that time for some starch, and I did see him bringing home some, and yet all this cannot make my mind quiet. . . .

July 18.

. . . To Westminster Hall, where I expected some bands made me by Mrs. Lane, and while she went to the starchers for them, I staid at Mrs. Howlett's, who with her husband were abroad, and only their daughter (which I call my wife) was in the shop, and I took occasion to buy a pair of gloves to talk to her, and I find her a pretty spoken girl, and will prove a mighty handsome wench. I could love her very well. By and by Mrs. Lane comes, and my bands not being done she and I posted and met at the Crown in the Palace Yard, where we eat a chicken I sent for, and drank, and were mighty merry, and I had my full liberty of towzing her and doing what I would, but the last thing of all. . . . Of which I am heartily ashamed, but I do resolve never to do more so . . . and so I by water to the Temple, and thence walked home, all in a sweat with my tumbling of her and walking, and so a little supper and to bed, fearful of having taken cold.

September 27.

. . . Home to dinner, being a little troubled to see Pembleton out again, but I do not discern in my wife the least memory of him. Dined, and so to my office a little, and then to church again, where a drowsy sermon, and so home to spend the evening with my poor wife, consulting about her closett, clothes, and other things. At night to supper, though with little comfort, I finding myself both head and breast in great pain, and what troubles me most my right ear is almost deaf. It is a cold, which God Almighty in justice did give me while I sat lewdly sporting with Mrs. Lane the other day with the broken window in my neck. I went to bed with a posset, being very melancholy in consideration of the loss of my hearing.

October 31.

. . . To the office, where busy till night, and then to prepare my monthly account, about which I staid till 10 or 11 o'clock at night, and to my great sorrow find myself £43 worse than I was the last month, which was then £760, and now it is but £717. But it hath chiefly arisen from my layings-out in clothes for myself and wife; viz., for her about £12, and for myself £55, or thereabouts; having made myself a velvet cloake, two new cloth suits, black, plain both; a new shagg gowne, trimmed with gold buttons and twist, with a new hat, and silk tops for my legs, and many other things, being resolved henceforward to go like myself. And also two perriwiggs, one whereof costs me £3, and the other 40 s. I have worn neither yet, but will begin next week, God willing. So that I hope I shall not need now to lay out more money a great while . . . but I hope I shall with more comfort labour to get more, and with better successe than when, for want of clothes, I was forced to sneake like a beggar. . . .

November 6.

This morning waking, my wife was mighty earnest with me to persuade me that she should prove with child since last night, which, if it be, let it come, and welcome. . . .

January 21, 1663–64.

. . . Seeing people flock in the City, I enquired, and found that Turner was not yet hanged. And so I went among them to Leadenhall Street, at the end of Lyme Street, near where the robbery was done; and to St. Mary Axe, where he lived. And there I got for a shilling to stand upon the wheel of a cart, in great pain, above an houre before the execution was done; he delaying the time by long discourses and prayers one after another, in hopes of a reprieve; but none came, and at last was flung off the ladder in his cloake. A comely-looked man he was, and kept his countenance to the end: I was sorry to see him. It was believed there were at least 12 or 14,000 people in the street. So I home all in a sweat. . . .

February 3.

. . . This night late coming in my coach, coming up Ludgate Hill, I saw two gallants and their footmen taking a pretty wench, which I have much eyed, lately set up shop upon the hill, a seller of riband and gloves. They seek to drag her by some force, but the wench went, and I believe had her turn served, but God forgive me! what thoughts and wishes I had of being in their place. In Covent Garden to-night, going to fetch home my wife, I stopped at the great Coffee-house there, where I never was before; where Dryden the poet (I knew at Cambridge), and all the wits of the town. . . .

March 8.

Up with some little discontent with my wife upon her saying that she had got and used some puppy-dog water, being put upon it by a desire of my aunt Wight to get some for her, who hath a mind, unknown to her husband, to get some for her ugly face. . . .

August 7.

. . . Came by several poor creatures carried by, by constables, for being at a conventicle [secret religious meeting]. They go like lambs, without any resistance. I would to God they would either conform, or be more wise, and not be catched!

February 21, 1664–65.

. . . Busy till noon, and then my wife being busy in going with her woman to a hot-house to bathe herself, after her long being within doors in the dirt, so that she now pretends to a resolution of being hereafter very clean. How long it will hold I can guess. . . .

August 15.

Up by 4 o'clock and walked to Greenwich, where . . . something put my last night's dream into my head, which I think is the best that ever was dreamt, which was that I had my Lady Castlemayne in my armes and was admitted to use all the dalliance I desired with her, and then dreamt that this could not be awake, but that it was only a dream; but that since it was a dream, and that I took so much real pleasure in it, what a happy thing it would be if when we are in our graves (as Shakespeere resembles it) we could dream, and dream but such dreams as this, that then we should not need to be so fearful of death, as we are this plague time. . . .

August 31.

. . . This month ends with great sadness upon the publick, through the greatness of the plague every where through the kingdom almost. Every day sadder and sadder news of its encrease. In the City died this week 7,496, and of them 6,102 of the plague. But it is feared that the true number of the dead this week is near 10,000; partly from the poor that cannot be taken notice of, and partly from the Quakers and others that will not have any bell ring for them. . . .

September 3.

. . . Among other stories, one was very passionate, methought, of a complaint brought against a man in the towne for taking a child from London from an infected house. Alderman Hooker told us it was the child of a very able citizen in Gracious Street, a saddler, who had buried all the rest of his children of the plague, and himself and wife now being shut up and in despair of escaping, did desire only to save the life of this little child; and so prevailed to have it received stark naked into the arms of a friend, who brought it (having put it into new fresh clothes) to Greenwich; where upon hearing the story, we did agree it should be permitted to be received and kept in the towne. . . .

December 25.

(Christmas-day). To church in the morning, and there saw a wedding in the church, which I have not seen many a day; and the young people so merry one with another, and strange to see what delight we married people have to see these poor fools decoyed into our condition, every man and woman gazing and smiling at them. . . .

July 1, 1666.

. . . To the Tower several times, about the business of the pressed men, and late at it till twelve at night, shipping of them. But Lord! how some poor women did cry; and in my life I never did see such natural expression of passion as I did here on some women's bewailing themselves, and running to every parcel of men that were brought, one after another, to look for their husbands, and wept over every vessel that went off, thinking they might be there, and looking after the ship as far as ever they could by moone-light, that it grieved me to the heart to hear them. Besides, to see poor patient labouring men and housekeepers, leaving poor wives and families, taking up on a sudden by strangers, was very hard, and that without press-money, but forced against all law to be gone. It is a great tyranny. . . .

August 14.

. . . In the evening our company come to supper. We had invited to a
venison pasty Mr. Batelier and his sister Mary, Mrs. Mercer, her daughter
Anne, Mr. Le Brun, and W. Hewer; and so we supped, and very merry. And
then about nine o'clock to Mrs. Mercer's gate, where the fire and boys expected us, and her son had provided abundance of serpents and rockets; and
there mighty merry (My Lady Pen and Pegg going thither with us, and Nan
Wright), till about twelve at night, flinging our fireworks, and burning one
another and the people over the way. And at last our businesses being most
spent, we went into Mrs. Mercer's, and there mighty merry, smutting one
another with candle grease and soot, till most of us were like devils. And that
being done, then we broke up, and to my house; and there I made them
drink, and upstairs we went, and then fell to dancing (W. Batelier dancing
well), and dressing, him and I and one Mr. Banister (who with his wife come
over also with us) like women; and Mercer put on a suit of Tom's, like a boy,
and mighty mirth we had, and Mercer danced a jigg; and Nan Wright and
my wife and Pegg Pen put on perriwigs. Thus we spent till three or four in
the morning, mighty merry; and then parted, and to bed.

September 2.

(Lord's Day). Some of our mayds sitting up late last night to get things
ready against our feast to-day, Jane called us up about three in the morning,
to tell us of a great fire they saw in the City. So I rose and slipped on my
night-gowne, and went to her window, and thought it to be on the backside of Marke-Lane at the farthest; but, being unused to such fires as followed,
I thought it far enough off; and so went to bed again and to sleep. About
seven rose again to dress myself, and there looke at the window, and saw
the fire not so much as it was and further off. So to my closett to set things
to rights after yesterday's cleaning. By and by Jane comes and tells me that
she hears that above 300 houses have been burned down to-night by the fire
we saw, and that it is now burning down all Fish-street, by London Bridge.
So I made myself ready presently, and walked to the Tower, and there got
up on one of the high places, Sir J. Robinson's little son going up with me;
and there I did see the houses at that end of the bridge all on fire, and an
infinite great fire on this and the other side of the bridge. . . . So down, with
my heart full of trouble, to the Lieutenant of the Tower, who tells me that it
begun this morning in the King's baker's house in Pudding-lane, and that it
hath burned St. Magnus's Church and most part of Fish-street already. So
I down to the water-side, and there got a boat and through bridge, and
there saw . . . everybody endeavouring to remove their goods, and flinging
into the river or bringing them to lighters that lay off; poor people staying
in their houses as long as till the very fire touched them, and then running
into boats, or clambering from one pair of stairs by the water-side to another.
And among other things, the poor pigeons, I perceive, were loath to leave
their houses, but hovered about the windows and balconys till they were,
some of them burned, their wings, and fell down. . . . Having seen as much

as I could now, I away to . . . my boat; and there upon the water again, and to the fire up and down, it still encreasing, and the wind great. So near the fire as we could for smoke; and all over the Thames, with one's face in the wind, you were almost burned with a shower of fire-drops. This is very true; so as houses were burned by these drops and flakes of fire, three or four, nay, five or six houses, one from another. When we could endure no more upon the water, we to a little ale-house on the Bankside, over against the Three Cranes, and there staid till it was dark almost, and saw the fire grow; and, as it grew darker, churches and houses, as far as we could see up the hill of the City, in a most horrid malicious bloody flame . . . one entire arch of fire from this to the other side the bridge, and in a bow up the hill for an arch of about a mile long: it made me weep to see it . . . and a horrid noise the flames made, and the cracking of houses at their ruins. So home with a sad heart, and there . . . forced to begin to pack up our owne goods, and prepare for their removal; and did by moonshine (it being brave, dry, and moonshine, and warm weather) carry much of my goods into the garden, and Mr. Hater and I did remove my money and iron chests into my cellar, as thinking that the safest place. And got my bags of gold into my office, ready to carry away, and my chief papers of accounts also. . . .

September 3.

About four o'clock in the morning, my Lady Batten sent me a cart to carry away all my money, and plate, and best things, to Sir W. Rider's at Bednall-greene. Which I did, riding myself in my night-gowne in the cart; and, Lord! to see how the streets and the highways are crowded with people running and riding, and getting of carts at any rate to fetch away things. . . .

September 4.

Up by break of day . . . and I to Tower-streete, and there met the fire burning three or four doors beyond Mr. Howell's, whose goods, poor man, his trayes, and dishes, shovells, &c., were flung all along Tower-streete in the kennels, and people working therewith from one end to another; the fire coming on in that narrow streete, on both sides, with infinite fury. Sir W. Batten not knowing how to remove his wine, did dig a pit in the garden, and laid it in there; and I took the opportunity of laying all the papers of my office that I could not otherwise dispose of. And in the evening Sir W. Pen and I did dig another, and put our wine in it; and I my Parmazan cheese. . . . Now begins the practice of blowing up of houses in Tower-streete, which at first did frighten people more than any thing; but it stopped the fire where it was done, bringing down the houses to the ground in the same places they stood, and then it was easy to quench. . . .

September 5.

. . . About two in the morning my wife calls me up and tells me of new cryes of fire, it being come to Barkeing Church, which is the bottom of our lane. I up, and finding it so, resolved presently to take her away, and did, and took my gold which was about £2,350 . . . to Woolwich; but, Lord! what a sad sight it was by moone-light to see the whole City almost on fire, that you might see it plain at Woolwich, as if you were by it. . . .

September 7.

Up by five o'clock; and, blessed be God! find all well; and by water to Paul's Wharfe. Walked thence, and saw all the towne burned, and a miserable sight of Paul's church, with all the roofs fallen, and the body of the quire fallen into St. Fayth's; Paul's school also, Ludgate, and Fleet-street, my father's house, and the church, and a good part of the Temple the like. So to Creed's lodging . . . borrowed a shirt of him, and washed. To Sir W. Coventry, at St. James's, who . . . hopes we shall have no publique distractions upon this fire, which is what everybody fears, because . . . it is a proper time for discontents; but all men's minds are full of care to protect themselves, and save their goods: the militia is in armes every where. . . . Late to Sir W. Pen's, who did give me a bed; but without curtains or hangings, all being down. So here I went the first time into a naked bed, only my drawers on; and did sleep pretty well: but still both sleeping and waking had a fear of fire in my heart, that I took little rest. . . .

November 22.

. . . At noon home to dinner, where my wife and I fell out, I being displeased with her cutting away a lace handkercher sewed about her neck down to her breasts almost, out of a belief, but without reason, that it is the fashion. Here we did give one another the lie too much, but were presently friends, and then I to my office, where very late and did much business. . . .

December 24.

. . . I do truly find that I have overwrought my eyes, so that now they are become weak and apt to be tired, and all excess of light makes them sore, so that now to the candlelight I am forced to sit by, adding, the snow upon the ground all day, my eyes are very bad, and will be worse if not helped. . . .

December 25.

(Christmas day). Lay pretty long in bed, and then rose, leaving my wife desirous to sleep, having sat up till four this morning seeing her mayds make mince-pies. I to church, where our parson Mills made a good sermon. Then home, and dined well on some good ribbs of beef roasted and mince pies . . . plenty of good wine of my owne, and my heart full of true joy; and thanks to God Almighty for the goodness of my condition at this day. . . .

January 24, 1667.

. . . Away with all my company down to the office, and there fell to
dancing, and continued at it an hour or two . . . then to supper in the office,
a cold, good supper, and wondrous merry. Here . . . after supper to dancing
again and singing, and so continued till almost three in the morning, and then,
with extraordinary pleasure, broke up—only towards morning, Knipp fell a little ill, and so my wife home with her to put her to bed, and we continued
dancing and singing; and, among other things, our Mercer unexpectedly did
happen to sing an Italian song I know not of, of which they two sung the
other two parts to, that did almost ravish me, and made me in love with
her more than ever with her singing. As late as it was, yet Rolt and Harris
would go home to-night, and walked it, though I had a bed for them; and
it proved dark, and a misly night, and very windy. The company being all
gone to their homes, I up with Mrs. Pierce to Knipp, who was in bed; and
we waked her, and there I handled her breasts and did baiser la, and sing a
song, lying by her on the bed, and then left my wife to see Mrs. Pierce in
bed to her, in our best chamber, and so to bed myself, my mind mightily
satisfied with all this evening's work, and thinking it to be one of the merriest enjoyment I must look for in the world, and did content myself therefore
with the thoughts of it, and so to bed. . . .

February 25.

Lay long in bed, talking with pleasure with my poor wife, how she used
to make coal fires, and wash my foul clothes with her own hand for me,
poor wretch! in our little room at my Lord Sandwich's; for which I ought for
ever to love and admire her, and do; and persuade myself she would do the
same thing again, if God should reduce us to it. . . .

August 18.

. . . Walked towards White Hall, but, being wearied, turned into St.
Dunstan's Church, where I heard an able sermon of the minister of the place;
and stood by a pretty, modest maid, whom I did labour to take by the hand
and the body; but she would not, but got further and further from me; and,
at last, I could perceive her to take pins out of her pocket to prick me if I
should touch her again—which seeing I did forbear, and was glad I did spy
her design. And then I fell to gaze upon another pretty maid in a pew close
to me, and she on me; and I did go about to take her hand, which she suffered
a little and then withdrew. So the sermon ended, and the church broke up,
and my amours ended also, and so took coach and home. . . .

September 27.

Up, and to the office, where very busy all the morning. While I was busy
at the Office, my wife sends for me to come home, and what was it but to
see the pretty girl [Deb. Willet] which she is taking to wait upon her: and

though she seems not altogether so great a beauty as she had before told me, yet indeed she is mighty pretty; and so pretty, that I find I shall be too much pleased with it, and therefore could be contented as to my judgement, though not to my passion, that she might not come, lest I may be found too much minding her, to the discontent of my wife. . . .

February 8, 1667–68.

Up, and at my chamber all the morning and the office doing business, and also reading a little of "L'escholle des filles," which is a mighty lewd book, but yet not amiss for a sober man once to read over to inform himself in the villainy of the world. . . . And after I had done it I burned it, that it might not be among my books to my shame, and so at night to supper and to bed.

February 27.

All the morning at the Office, and at noon home to dinner, and thence with my wife and Deb. to the King's House, to see "The Virgin Martyr," the first time it hath been acted a great while: and it is mighty pleasant; not that the play is worth much, but it is finely acted by Becke Marshal. But that which did please me beyond anything in the whole world was the wind-musique when the angel comes down, which is so sweet that it ravished me, and indeed, in a word, did wrap up my soul so that it made me really sick, just as I have formerly been when in love with my wife; that neither then, nor all the evening going home, and at home, I was able to think of any thing, but remained all night transported, so as I could not believe that ever any musick hath that real command over the soul of a man as this did upon me. . . .

July 31.

Up, and at my office all the morning. About noon with Mr. Ashburnham to the new Excise Office, and there discoursed about our business, and I made him admire my drawing a thing presently in shorthand [such as that in which Pepys kept his diary]: but, God knows! I have paid dear for it, in my eyes. . . . The month ends mighty sadly with me, my eyes being now past all use almost. . . .

October 25.

. . . After dinner all the afternoon got my wife and boy to read to me, and at night W. Batelier comes and sups with us; and after supper, to have my head combed by Deb., which occasioned the greatest sorrow to me that ever I knew in this world, for my wife, coming up suddenly, did find me embracing the girl. . . . I was at a wonderful loss upon it, and the girle also, and I endeavoured to put it off, but my wife was struck mute and grew angry, and so her voice come to her, grew quite out of order, and I to say little, but to bed, and my wife said little also, but could not sleep all night, but about two in the morning waked me and cried, and . . . went on from one thing to another till at last it appeared plainly her trouble was at what she saw, but yet I did not know how much she saw, and therefore said nothing to her. But after her much crying and reproaching me with inconstancy and preferring a sorry girl before her, I did give her no provocation, but did promise all fair usage to her and love. . . .

October 26.

Rose, and up and by water to White Hall, but with my mind mightily troubled for the poor girle, whom I fear I have undone by this. . . . I all the evening busy, and my wife full of trouble in her looks, and anon to bed, where about midnight she wakes me, and there falls foul of me again. . . .

October 27.

In the morning up, but my mind troubled for the poor girle, with whom I could not get opportunity to speak, but to the office, my mind mighty full of sorrow for her. . . . My wife did towards bedtime begin to be in a mighty rage from some new matter that she had got in her head, and did most part of the night in bed rant at me in most high terms of threats of publishing my shame, and when I offered to rise would have rose too, and caused a candle to be light to burn by her all night in the chimney while she ranted, while the knowing myself to have given some grounds for it, did make it my business to appease her all I could possibly, and by good words and fair promises did make her very quiet. . . .

November 8.

. . . At my chamber again to work all the afternoon till night, when Pelling comes, who wonders to find my wife so dull and melancholy, but God knows she hath too much cause. However, as pleasant as we can, we supped together, and so made the boy read to me, the poor girle not appearing at supper, but hid herself in her chamber. So that I could wish in that respect that she was out of the house, for our peace is broke to all of us while she is here, and so to bed, where my wife mighty unquiet all night, so as my bed is become burdensome to me.

November 10.

Up, and my wife still every day as ill as she is all night, will rise to see me out doors, telling me plainly that she dares not let me see the girle . . . and so I to my office, and there late, and so home to supper with her, and so to bed, where after half-an-hour's slumber she wakes me and cries out that she should never sleep more, and so kept raving till past midnight, that made me cry and weep heartily all the while for her, and troubled for what she reproached me with as before. . . .

November 13.

. . . Home, and there to talk, with great pleasure all the evening, with my wife, who tells me that Deb. has been abroad to-day, and is come home and says she has got a place to go to, so as she will be gone to-morrow morning. This troubled me, and the truth is, I have a good mind to have the maidenhead of this girl, which I should not doubt to have if je could get time para be con her. . . .

November 19.

. . . Before it was late, there was, beyond my hopes as well as desert, a durable peace; and so to supper, and pretty kind words, and to bed, and here je did hazer con ell to her content, and so with some rest spent the night in bed, being most absolutely resolved, if ever I can master this bout, never to give her occasion while I live of more trouble of this or any other kind, there being no curse in the world so great as this of the differences between myself and her, and therefore I do, by the grace of God, promise never to offend her more, and did this night begin to pray to God upon my knees alone in my chamber, which God knows I cannot yet do heartily; but I hope God will give me the grace more and more every day to fear Him, and to be true to my poor wife. This night the upholsters did finish the hanging of my best chamber. . . .

November 20.

. . . When I come home, hoping for a further degree of peace and quiet, I find my wife upon her bed in a horrible rage afresh, calling me all the bitter names, and, rising, did fall to revile me in the bitterest manner in the world, and could not refrain to strike me and pull my hair, which I resolved to bear with, and had good reason to bear it. So I by silence and weeping did prevail with her a little to be quiet, and she would not eat her dinner without me; but yet by and by into a raging fit she fell again, worse than before, that she would slit the girl's nose . . . and at last it come to this, that if I would call Deb. whore under my hand and write to her that I hated her, and would never see her more, she would believe me and trust in me, which I did agree to, only as to the name of whore I would have excused, and therefore wrote to her sparing that word, which my wife thereupon tore it, and would not be satisfied till . . . I did write so with the name of a whore as that I did fear she might too probably have been prevailed upon to have been a whore by her carriage to me, and therefore as such I did resolve never to see her more. This pleased my wife . . . and so spent the evening with very great joy, and the night also with good sleep and rest, my wife only troubled in her rest, but less than usual, for which the God of Heaven be praised. I did this night promise to my wife never to go to bed without calling upon God upon my knees by prayer, and I begun this night, and hope I shall never forget to do the like all my life; for I do find that it is much the best for my soul and body to live pleasing to God and my poor wife, and will ease me of much care as well as much expense.

March 9, 1668–69.

. . . I drank a glass, of a pint, I believe, at one draught, of the juice of oranges, of whose peel they make comfits; and here they drink the juice as wine, with sugar, and it is very fine drink; but, it being new, I was doubtful whether it might not do me hurt. . . .

May 1.

Up betimes. Called up by my tailor, and there first put on a summer suit this year; but it was not my fine one of flowered tabby vest, and coloured camelott tunique, because it was too fine with the gold lace at the hands, that I was afeard to be seen in it; but put on the stuff suit I made the last year, which is now repaired. . . . At noon home to dinner, and there find my wife extraordinary fine, with her flowered tabby gown that she made two years ago, now laced exceedingly pretty; and, indeed, was fine all over; and mighty earnest to go, though the day was very lowering; and she would have me put on my fine suit, which I did. And so anon we went alone through the towne with our new liveries of serge, and the horses' manes and tails tied with red ribbons, and the standards there gilt with varnish, and all clean, and green reines, that people did mightily look upon us; and, the truth is, I did not see any coach more pretty, though more gay, than ours, all the day. But . . . there were so many hackney-coaches as spoiled the sight of the gentleman's; and so we had little pleasure. . . . My wife . . . was out of humour all the evening, and I vexed at her for it, and she did not rest almost all the night, so as in the night I was forced to take her and hug her to put her to rest. So home, and after a little supper, to bed.

May 31.

Up very betimes, and . . . in the afternoon by water to White Hall, calling by the way at Michell's, where I have not been many a day till just the other day, and now I met her mother there and knew her husband to be out of town. And here je did baiser elle, but had not opportunity para hazer some with her as I would have offered if je had had it. And thence . . . to "The World's End," a drinking-house by the Park; and there merry, and so home late.

And thus ends all that I doubt I shall ever be able to do with my own eyes in the keeping of my Journal, I being not able to do it any longer, having done now so long as to undo my eyes almost every time that I take a pen in my hand; and, therefore, whatever comes of it, I must forbear: and, therefore, resolve, from this time forward, to have it kept by my people in longhand, and must therefore be contented to set down no more than is fit for them and all the world to know; or, if there be any thing, which cannot be much, now my amours to Deb. are past, and my eyes hindering me in almost all other pleasures, I must endeavour to keep a margin in my book open, to add, here and there, a note in short-hand with my own hand.

And so I betake myself to that course, which is almost as much as to see myself go into my grave: for which, and all the discomforts that will accompany my being blind, the good God prepare me!

". . . conspiracies . . . parleaments, wars, plagues,
fires, comets, revolutions abroad . . ."

John Evelyn

John Evelyn (1620–1706) was, as his friend Samuel Pepys said,
"a most excellent person . . . a man so much above others." He
was, indeed, one of the most favoured of men—gifted, rich, well-
born, long-lived, learned, tolerant and wise.

Evelyn was born near Dorking, Surrey, one of five children of
a large estate-owner, the High Sheriff of Surrey and Sussex. The
family wealth came from the manufacture of gunpowder. He was
educated informally, but later attended Oxford and read law. He
travelled extensively as a young man and his early diary entries
note some of the strange sights then to be seen in Europe. It was
there he met Mary Browne, daughter of an English diplomat, to
whom he was married when she was twelve. He was fortunate
in marriage as in other things. His wife was beautiful, well read,
talented, and in time proved to be a good mother. John and Mary
Evelyn had nine children, all but one of whom died young. A
daughter and a son, Richard, proved to be remarkably precocious;
Evelyn has given a moving tribute to his little boy, who did not
survive his fifth year.

Spared the necessity of earning a living, Evelyn devoted himself to public service and to writing. He was commissioner for the
improvement of London streets, the examination of affairs of
charitable institutions, the manufacture of saltpetre, the administration of foreign plantations, the regulation of hackney coaches,
the repair of St. Paul's and the care of wounded or disabled veterans of the Dutch war. He was a generous art patron, linguist
and scientist. He wrote on widely varying subjects, his thirty
books being devoted to such topics as numismatics, sculpture,
forestry, Jesuitism, the Navy, architecture, politics, education,
landscape gardening, engraving, painting, and commerce. He was
a founder and prominent member of the Royal Society.

Evelyn began his journal when he was twenty-one and kept it
for almost sixty-five years. His account covers a half century filled

From *The Diary of John Evelyn*, edited by William Bray. W. W. Gibbings, London,
1890.

with many remarkable scenes and events, most of which he had
seen at first-hand. Evelyn's diary is often compared to that of
Samuel Pepys. Actually their diaries are quite different. No matter what Pepys wrote about, the central figure was always Pepys
himself; Evelyn chose to stand modestly at one side and to ex-
hibit impersonally things he saw and did. There is, fortunately,
no need to choose between them for each, in his own way, left
rich gifts to mankind.

October 7, 1644.

We had a most delicious journey to Marseilles, thro' a country sweetly de-
clining to the South and Mediterranean coasts, full of vine-yards and olive
yards, orange trees, myrtils, pomegranads, and the like sweete plantations . . .
[and when there] we went to visite the Gallys, being about 25; the Captaine
of the Gally Royal gave us most courteous entertainment in his cabine, the
slaves in the interim playing both loud and soft musiq very rarely. Then he
shew'd us how he commanded their motions with a nod and his whistle, making them row out. The spectacle was to me new and strange, to see so many
hundreds of miserably naked persons, having their heads shaven close and
having onely high red bonnets, a payre of course canvas drawers, their whole
backs and leggs naked, doubly chayn'd about their middle and leggs, in couples, and made fast to their seates, and all commanded in a trise by an im-
perious and cruell seaman. One Turk he much favor'd, who waited on him
in his cabin, but with no other dress than the rest, and a chayne lock'd about
his leg but not coupled. This gally was richly carv'd and gilded, and most
of the rest were very beautifull. After bestowing something on the slaves,
the captain sent a band of them to give us musiq at dinner where we lodged.
I was amaz'd to contemplate how these miserable catyfs lie in their gally
crowded together, yet there was hardly one but had some occupation by
which, as leisure and calmes permitted, they gat some little monye, insomuch as some of them have, after many years of cruel servitude, been able
to purchase their liberty. Their rising forward and falling back at their oare
is a miserable spectacle, and the noyse of their chaines with the roaring of
the beaten waters has something of strange and fearfull to one unaccustom'd
to it. . . .

January 25, 1645.

. . . We went to see Dr. Gibbs, a famous poet and countryman of ours,
who had some intendency in an Hospital built on the Via Triumphalis, called
Christ's Hospital, which he shew'd us. . . . The beds are very faire; in the
middle is a stately cupola, under which is an altar decked with divers marble
statues, all in sight of the sick, who may both see and heare masse as they
lye in their beds. The organs are very fine, and frequently play'd on to
recreate the people in pain. To this joyns an apartment destined for the or-
phans; and there is a schoole; the children weare blew like ours in London
at an Hospital of the same appellation. Here are 40 nurses who give suck to
such children as are accidentally found expos'd and abandon'd. In another

quarter are children of bigger growth, 450 in number, who are taught letters. In another, 500 girles under the tuition of divers religious matrons, in a Monastry, as it were, by itselfe. I was assur'd there were at least 2000 more maintain'd in other places. I think one appartiment had in it neere 1000 beds; these are in a very long rome having an inner passage for those who attend, with as much care, sweetnesse, and conveniency as can be imagin'd. . . .

February 6.

[In Naples] we went by coach to take the ayre, and see the diversions or rather maddnesse of the Carnival; the courtisans (who swarme in this Citty to the number, as we are told, of 30,000, registred and paying a tax to the State) flinging eggs of sweete water into our coach as we passed by the houses and windows. Indeed the town is so pester'd with these cattell, that there needes no small mortification to preserve from their enchantment, whilst they display all their naturall and artificiall beauty, play, sing, feigne compliment, and by a thousand studied devices seeke to inveigle foolish young men.

April 17, 1649.

I fell dangerously ill of my head; was blistered and let blood behind the eares and forehead; on the 23rd began to have ease by using the fumes of cammomile on embers applied to my eares after all the physitians had don their best.

March 11, 1651.

I went to the Châtelet or Prison [in Paris], where a malefactor was to have the question of torture given to him, he refusing to confess the robbery with which he was charg'd, which was thus: they first bound his wrist with a strong rope or small cable, and one end of it to an iron ring made fast to the wall about 4 foote from the floore, and then his feete with another cable, fastned about 5 foote farther than his uttmost length to another ring on the floore of the roome: thus suspended and yet lying but aslant, they slid an horse of wood under the rope which bound his feete, which so exceedingly stiffened it, as sever'd the fellow's joynts in miserable sort, drawing him out at length in an extraordinary manner, he having onely a paire of linnen drawers on his naked body: then they questioned him of a robbery (the Lieutenant Criminal being present, and a clearke that wrote), which not confessing, they put an higher horse under the rope, to increase the torture and extension. In this agonie, confessing nothing, the Executioner with a horne (just such as they drench horses with) stuck the end of it into his mouth, and poured the quantity of two bouketts of water downe his throat and over him, which so prodigiously swelled him, as would have pittied and affrighted any one to see it; for all this, he denied all that was charged to him. They then let him downe, and carried him before a warme fire to bring him to himselfe, being now to all appearance dead with paine. . . . There was another Malefactor to succeede, but the spectacle was so uncomfortable, that I was not able to stay the sight of another. . . .

March 29, 1652.

Was that celebrated eclipse of the sun so much threatened by the astrologers, and which had so exceedingly alarm'd the whole Nation that hardly any one would worke, nor stir out of their houses. So ridiculously were they abus'd by knavish and ignorant star-gazers. . . .

June 11.

. . . The weather being hot, and having sent my man on before, I rod negligently under favour of the shade, till within three miles of Bromley, at a place call'd the Procession Oake, two cut-throates started out, and striking with long staves at the horse and taking hold of the reines threw me down, took my sword, and haled me into a deepe thickett some quarter of a mile from the highway, where they might securely rob me, as they soone did. What they got of money was not considerable, but they took two rings, the one an emerald with diamonds, the other an onyx, and a pair of bouckles set with rubies and diamonds, which were of value, and after all bound my hands behind me, and my feete, having before pull'd off my bootes; then they set me up against an oake, with most bloudy threats to cutt my throat if I offer'd to crie out or make any noise, for they should be within hearing; I not being the person they looked for. I told them if they had not basely surpriz'd me they should not have had so easy a prize, and that it would teach me never to ride neere an hedge, since had I ben in the mid-way they durst not have adventur'd on me; at which they cock'd their pistols, and told me they had long guns too, and were 14 companions. I begg'd for my onyx, and told them it being engraven with my armes would betray them, but nothing prevail'd. My horse's bridle they slipt, and search'd the saddle, which they pulled off, but let the horse graze, and then turning againe bridl'd him and tied him to a tree, yet so as he might graze, and thus left me bound. My horse was perhaps not taken because he was mark'd and cropt on both eares, and well known on that roade. Left in this manner grievously was I tormented with flies, ants, and the sunn, nor was my anxiety little how I should get loose in that solitary place, where I could neither heare or see any creature but my poore horse and a few sheep stragling in the copse. After neare two houres attempting I got my hands to turn palm to palm, having been tied back to back, and then it was long before I could slip the cord over my wrists to my thumb, which at last I did, and then soone unbound my feete, and saddling my horse and roaming awhile about I at last perceiv'd dust to rise, and soone after heard the rattling of a cart, towards which I made, and by the help of two country men I got back into the high way. I rode to Coll. Blount's, a greate justiciarie of the times, who sent out hue and cry immediately. . . .

September 15, 1657.

Going to London with some company, we stept in to see . . . the hairy woman, 20 years old, whom I had before seen when a child. She was borne at Augsburg in Germany. Her very eye-browes were comb'd upwards, and all her forehead as thick and even as growes on any woman's head, neatly dress'd; a very long lock of haire out of each eare; she had also a most prolix beard, and mustachios, with long locks growing on the middle of her nose, like an Iceland dog exactly, the colour of a bright browne, fine as well-dress'd flax. She was now married, and told me she had one child that was not hairy, nor were any of her parents and relations. She was very well shap'd, and plaied well on the harpsichord. . . .

January 27, 1658.

After six fits of a quartan ague with which it pleased God to visit him, died my deare son Richard, to our inexpressible griefe and affliction, 5 yeares and 3 days old onely, but at that tender age a prodigy for witt and understanding; for beauty of body a very angel; for endowment of mind incredible and rare hopes. To give onely a little taste of some of them . . . at 2 yeares and halfe old he could perfectly read any of the English, Latine, French, or Gottic letters, pronouncing the first three letters exactly. He had before the 5th yeare, or in that yeare, not onely skill to reade most written hands, but to decline all the nouns, conjugate the verbs regular, and most of the irregular; learn'd out Puerilis, got by heart almost the entire vocabularie of Latin and French primitives and words, could make congruous syntax, turne English into Latine, and *vice versa,* construe and prove what he read, and did the government and use of relatives, verbs, substantives, elipses, and many figures and tropes, and made a considerable progress in Comenius's Janua; began himself to write legibly, and had a stronge passion for Greeke . . . a wonderful disposition to mathematics, having by heart divers propositions of Euclid that were read to him in play, and he would make lines and demonstrate them. . . .

March 7.

. . . This had ben the severest winter that any man alive had known in England. The crowes feete were frozen to their prey. Islands of ice inclos'd both fish and fowl frozen, and some persons in their boates.

September 3.

Died that arch rebell Oliver Cromwell, cal'd Protector.

October 22.

. . . It was the joyfullest funerall I ever saw, for there were none that cried but dogs, which the soldiers hooted away with a barbarous noise, drinking and taking tobacco in the streetes as they went. . . .

April 23, 1661.

Was the Coronation of his Majesty Charles II. in the Abby . . . in this order: First went the Duke of York's Horse Guards. Messengers of the Chamber. 136 Esquires to the Knights of the Bath, each of whom had two, most richly habited. The Knight Harbinger. Serjeant Porter. Sewers of the Chamber. Quarter Waiters. Six Clearks of Chancery. Clearke of the Signet. Clearke of the Privy Seale. Clearks of the Council, of the Parliament, and of the Crowne. Chaplains in ordinary having dignitaries 10. Kings Advocats and Remembrancer. Council at Law. Members of the Chancery. Puisne Serjeants. Kings Attorney and Solicitor. Kings eldest Serjeant. Secretaries of the French and Latine tongue. Gent. Ushers, Daily Waiters, Sewers, Carvers, and Cupbearers in ordinary. Esquires of the Body 4. Masters of standing offices being no Councellors, *viz.* of the Tents, Revels, Ceremonies, Armorie, Wardrobe, Ordnance, Requests. Chamberlaine of the Exchequer. Barons of the Exchequer. Judges. Lord Chiefe Baron. Lord C. Justice of the Common Pleas. Master of the Rolls. Lord C. Justice of England. Trumpets. Gentlemen of the Privy Chamber. Knights of the Bath, 68, in crimson robes exceeding rich. . . . Knt. Marshall. Treasurer of the Chamber. Master of the Jewells, Lords of the Privy Council. Comptroller of the Household. Treasurer of the Household. Trumpets. Serjeant Trumpet. Two Pursuivants at Armes. Barons. Two Pursuivants at Armes. Vicounts. Two Heraulds. Earles. Lord Chamberlaine of the Household. Two Heraulds. Marquisses. Dukes. Heralds Clarencieux and Norroy. Lord Chancellor. Lord High Steward of England. Two persons representing the Dukes of Normandy and Aquitain, *viz.* Sir Richard Fanshawe and Sir Herbert Price, in fantastiq habits of the time. Gentlemen Ushers. Garter. Lord Maior of London. The Duke of York alone (the rest by two's). Lord High Constable of England. Lord Great Chamberlaine of England. The Sword borne by the Earle Marshal of England. The KING in royal robes and equipage. Afterwards follow'd Equerries, Footmen, Gent. Pensioners. Master of the Horse leading a horse richly caprison'd. Vice Chamberlaine. Captain of the Pensioners. Captain of the Guard. The Guard. The Horse Guard. The Troope of Volunteers with many other Officers and Gentlemen.

This magnificent traine on horseback, as rich as embroidery, velvet, cloth of gold and silver, and jewells, could make them and their pransing horses, proceed'd thro' the streetes strew'd with flowers, houses hung with rich tapessry, windoes and balconies full of ladies; the London Militia lining the ways, and the severall Companies with their banners and loud musiq rank'd in their orders; the fountaines running wine, bells ringing, with speeches made at the severall triumphal arches; at that of the Temple Barr (neere which I stood). . . . Bonfires at night. . . .

February 17, 1662.

. . . This night and the next day fell such a storm of hail, thunder and lightning, as never was seene the like in any man's memorie, especialy the tempest of wind, being South West, which subverted besides huge trees, many houses, innumerable chimnies (amongst others that of my parlour at Sayes Court), and made such havoc at land and sea that several perish'd on both. Divers lamentable fires were also kindl'd at this time. . . .

December 21.

One of his Majesty's Chaplains preach'd, after which, instead of the ancient, grave, and solemn wind musiq accompanying the organ, was introduced a concert of 24 violins betweene every pause, after the French fantastical light way, better suiting a tavern or playhouse than a church. This was the first time of change, and now we no more heard the cornet which gave life to the organ, that instrument quite left off in which the English were so skillfull.

March 26, 1663.

It pleas'd God to take away my sonn Richard, being now a moneth old, yet without any sicknesse of danger perceivably, being to all appearance a most likely child; we suspected much the nurse had overlayne him; to our extreame sorrow, being now againe reduced to one; but God's will be done!

July 16, 1665.

There died of the plague in London this weeke 1100, and in the weeke following above 2000. . . .

August 8.

. . . Died this week in London 4000.

August 15.

There perished this week 5000.

September 7.

Came home, there perishing neere 10,000 poore creatures weekly; however I went all along the Citty and suburbs from Kent Streete to St. James's, a dismal passage, and dangerous to see so many coffines expos'd in the streetes, now thin of people; the shops shut up, and all in mournefull silence, as not knowing whose turn might be next. I went to the Duke of Albemarle for a pest-ship. . . .

March 18, 1669.

I went with Lord Howard of Norfolk to visit Sir William Ducie at Charlton, where we din'd; the servants made our coachmen so drunk that they both fell off their boxes on the heath, where we were fain to leave them, and were driven to London by two servants of my Lord's. This barbarous custom of making the masters welcome by intoxicating the servants had now the second time happen'd to my coachmen. . . .

June 10.

. . . I went this evening to London, to carry Mr. Pepys to my brother Richard, now exceedingly afflicted with the stone, who had ben successfully cut, and carried the stone as big as a tennis-ball, to shew him and encourage his resolution to go thro' the operation.

June 16, 1670.

I went with some friends to the Bear Garden, where was cock-fighting, beare and bull baiting, it being a famous day for all these butcherly sports, or rather barbarous cruelties. The bulls did exceeding well, but the Irish wolfe-dog exceeded, which was a tall greyhound, a stately creature indeede, who beate a cruell mastiff. One of the bulls toss'd a dog full into a *lady's lap*, as she sate in one of the boxes at a considerable height from the arena. Two poore dogs were kill'd, and so all ended with the ape on horseback, and I most heartily weary of the rude and dirty pastime. . . .

October 9, 1671.

. . . To Euston, a palace of Lord Arlington's, where . . . his Majesty came almost every second day with the Duke, who commonly return'd to Newmarket, but the King often lay here, during which time I had twice the honor to sit at dinner with him, with all freedome. It was universally reported that the faire Lady —— was bedded one of these nights, and the stocking flung, after the manner of a married bride; I acknowledge she was for the most part in her undresse all day, and that there was fondnesse and toying with that young wanton. . . . 'Twas with confidence believed she was first made *a Misse,* as they call these unhappy creatures, with all solemnity at this time.

August 1, 1672.

I was at the marriage of Lord Arlington's onely daughter (a sweete child if ever there was any [then *five* years old]) to the Duke of Grafton, the King's natural son by the Dutchesse of Cleaveland. The Abp. of Canterbury officiating, the King and all the grandees being present. I . . . tooke no greate joy at the thing for many reasons.

November 6, 1679.

. . . Was this evening at the re-marriage of the Dutchesse of Grafton to the Duke (his Majesty's natural sonn) she being now 12 years old. The ceremonie was performed . . . at White-hall by the Bishop of Rochester, his Majesty being present. . . . I was privately invited by my Lady, her mother, to be present. I confesse I could give her little joy, and so I plainely told her, but she said the King would have it so, and there was no going back.

This sweetest, hopefullest, most beautifull child, and most vertuous too, was sacrific'd to a boy that had ben rudely bred . . . and the sweete child made me behold all this with regret. . . .

February 7, 1682.

. . . Having had several violent fits of an ague, recourse was had to bathing my legs in milk up to the knees, made as hot as I could endure it; and sitting so in it in a deepe churn or vessell cover'd with blankets, and drinking carduus posset, then going to bed and sweating, I not onely miss'd that expected fit, but had no more, only continued weak. . . .

July 13, 1683.

. . . The astonishing newes was brought to us of the Earle of Essex having cut his throat, having ben but three days a prisoner in the Tower, and this happening on the very day and instant that Lord Russell was on his trial, and had sentence of death. . . . It is certaine the King and Duke were at the Tower, and pass'd by his window about the same time this morning, when my Lord asking for a razor shut himselfe into a closet and perpetrated the horrid act. Yet it was wondred by some how it was possible he should do it in the manner he was found, for the wound was so deepe and wide, that being cut through the gullet, wind-pipe, and both the jugulars, it reach'd to the very vertebrae of the neck, so that the head held to it by a very little skin as it were; the gapping too of the rasor, and cutting his owne fingers, was a little strange; but more, that having pass'd the jugulars he should have strength to proceed so far, that an executioner could hardly have don more with an axe. There were odd reflections upon it. . . .

October 4.

. . . Following his Majesty this morning thro' the gallerie, I went, with the few who attended him, into the Dutchesse of Portsmouth's *dressing roome* within her bed-chamber, where she was in her morning loose garment, her maids combing her, newly out of her bed, his Majesty and the gallants standing about her; but that which engag'd my curiosity was the rich and splendid furniture of this woman's apartment, now twice or thrice pull'd down and rebuilt to satisfie her prodigal and expensive pleasures, whilst her Majestys dos not exceede some gentlemen's ladies in furniture and accomodation. Here I saw the new fabriq of French tapissry, for designe, tendernesse of worke, and incomparable imitation of the best paintings, beyond any thing I had ever beheld . . . purchas'd with vice and dishonour!

January 1, 1684.

The weather continuing intolerably severe, streetes of booths were set upon the Thames; the aire was so very cold and thick, as of many yeares there had not ben the like. The small pox was very mortal.

January 24.

The frost continuing more and more severe, the Thames before London was still planted with boothes in formal streetes, all sorts of trades and shops furnish'd and full of commodities, even to a printing presse, where the people and ladyes tooke a fancy to have their names printed, and the day and the yeare set down when printed on the Thames; this humour tooke so universally, that 'twas estimated the printer gain'd £5. a day, for printing a line onely, at sixpence a name, besides what he got by ballads, &c. Coaches plied from Westminster to the Temple, and from several other staires to and fro, as in the streetes, sleds, sliding with skeetes, a bull-baiting, horse and coach races, puppet plays and interludes, cookes, tipling, and other lewd places, so that it seem'd to be a baccanalian triumph, or carnival on the water, whilst it was a severe judgment on the land, the trees not onely splitting as if by lightning-struck, but men and cattle perishing in divers places, and the very seas so lock'd up with ice, that no vessells could stir out or come in. The fowles, fish, and birds, and all our exotiq plants and greenes universally perishing. Many parkes of deer were destroied, and all sorts of fuell so deare that there were greate contributions to preserve the poore alive. Nor was this severe weather much less intense in most parts of Europe, even as far as Spaine and the most Southern tracts. London, by reason of the excessive coldnesse of the aire hindering the ascent of the smoke, was so fill'd with the fuliginous steame of the sea-coale, that hardly could one see crosse the streetes, and this filling the lungs with its grosse particles, exceedingly obstructed the breast, so as one could scarcely breath. Here was no water to be had from the pipes and engines, nor could the brewers and divers other tradesmen worke, and every moment was full of disastrous accidents.

January 25, 1685.

. . . I saw this evening such a scene of profuse gaming, and the King in the midst of his three concubines, as I had never before seen. Luxurious dallying and prophaneness.

February 4.

I went to London, hearing his Majesty had ben the Monday before (2 Feb.) surpriz'd in his bed-chamber with an apoplectic fit, so that if, by God's providence, Dr. King (that excellent chirurgeon as well as physitian) had not ben accidentally present to let him blood (having his lancet in his pocket) his Majesty had certainly died that moment. . . . This rescu'd his Majesty for the instant, but it was only a short reprieve. He still complain'd, and was relapsing, often fainting, with sometimes epileptic symptoms, till Wednesday, for which he was cupp'd, let bloud in both jugulars, had both vomit and purges, which so reliev'd him that on Thursday hopes of recovery were signified in the publiq Gazette, but that day, about noone, the physitians . . . prescrib'd the famous Jesuits powder [quinine]: but it made him worse, and . . . the effect of his frequent bleeding and other sharp operations us'd by them about his head, so that probably the powder might stop the circulation, and renew his former fits, which now made him very weake. Thus he pass'd Thursday night with greate difficulty, when complaining of a paine in his side, they drew 12 ounces more of blood from him . . . and after some conflicts, the physitians despairing of him, he gave up the ghost at halfe an houre after eleven in the morning. . . .

Thus died King Charles II. . . . a Prince of many virtues, and many greate imperfections; debonnaire, easy of accesse, not bloudy nor cruel; his countenance fierce, his voice greate, proper of person, every motion became him; a lover of the sea, and skillfull in shipping; not affecting other studies, yet he had a laboratory, and knew of many empirical medicines, and the easier mechanical mathematics; he lov'd planting and building, and brought in a politer way of living, which pass'd to luxury and intolerable expense. He had a particular talent in telling a story, and facetious passages, of which he had innumerable; this made some buffoons and vitious wretches too presumptuous and familiar, not worthy the favour they abus'd. He tooke delight in having a number of little spaniels follow him and lie in his bed-chamber, where he often suffer'd the bitches to puppy and give suck, which render'd it very offensive, and indeede made the whole Court nasty and stinking. He would doubtlesse have ben an excellent Prince, had he ben less addicted to women, who made him uneasy, and allways in want to supply their unmeasurable profusion, to the detriment of many indigent persons who had signaly serv'd both him and his father. He frequently and easily chang'd favorites, to his greate prejudice. . . . The history of his reigne will certainly be the most wonderfull for the variety of matter and accidents, above any extant in former ages: the sad tragical death of his father, his banishment and hardships, his miraculous restauration, conspiracies against him, parleaments, wars, plagues, fires, comets, revolutions abroad happening in his time . . . inexpressible luxury and prophanenesse, gaming and all dissoluteness, as it were total forgetfullnesse of God . . . I was witnesse of, the King sitting and toying with his concubines, Portsmouth, Cleaveland, and Mazarine, &c. a French boy singing love songs, in that glorious gallery, whilst about 20 of the greate courtiers and other dissolute persons were at Basset round a large table, a bank of at least 2000 in gold before them, upon which two gentlemen who were with me made reflexions with astonishment. Six days after was all in the dust!

*". . . the enterprising Yankees, who run faster, fly higher,
and dig deeper than any people under the sun . . ."*

Philip Hone

At the age of twenty, Philip Hone (1780–1851) was a successful
New York auctioneer, and at forty he had acquired a fortune
and retired from business. Thereafter he led a full and busy life
judged either by the standards of his day or the more frantic ones
of our own.

Hone watched New York grow from a town of 20,000 to a
metropolis of half a million. His home, one of the great mansions
of the city, was frequented by such eminent Americans as Webster, Clay, John Quincy Adams and Washington Irving, and over-
seas celebrities such as Captain Marryat, Fanny Kemble and
Charles Dickens. In 1824 Hone was elected assistant alderman
and in 1825 he became mayor of New York. During his long life
he was active in many philanthropic organizations; he was president of the city's first savings bank, and at one time or another
was founder, governor, officer or director of a score of institutions
including New York Hospital, Columbia College, the Delaware
and Hudson Canal Company, and several insurance companies.
He still found time to be active in the Whig party, to which he
gave its name. He was an avid reader, a great theatre-goer, a
patron of the arts.

This tall, thin, spare man of distinguished bearing and courtly
manners had a wide-ranging mind and an insatiable curiosity.
Whatever was and whatever happened keenly interested Hone,
and what he saw and felt he noted in the diary which he con-
scientiously kept up for more than twenty years, almost to the
day of his death at seventy-one.

Hone's diary is important to the historian and a delight to the
casual reader. Shrewd, opinionated, conservative, knowledgeable,
Philip Hone introduces us at first-hand, sometimes reluctantly, to
the dangers of the speeding railroad and the transatlantic steamer,

From *The Diary of Philip Hone, 1826–1851.* Edited by Bayard Tuckerman. Published by Dodd, Mead & Company, Inc. 1889.

the marvels of the daguerreotype, and the gas light—but more than that, he reintroduces us to America in its adolescence.

November 27, 1830.

Yesterday took place the New York celebration of the late revolution in France. The procession, divided into sixteen divisions, was . . . so long that when the right entered Broadway from Broome street, the military, who formed an unusually splendid array, had not yet left Canal street, and when we arrived at the parade-ground, the whole were not yet in motion. The whole route must have been two miles and a half. The ex-President, Monroe, drove in his carriage, as did Mr. Gallatin and the orator and reader of the address. . . . The president, faculty, and students of Columbia College were conspicuous in the procession, and the citizens of France, with their splendid banner, made a proud display. Their banner was formally presented on the ground to the first division of artillery. Among the trades and societies the most prominent were the fire department, with their beautiful engines, badges, and other decorations, to the number of fifteen hundred persons; the printers, who were employed at two places in striking off and distributing among the multitude copies of the ode, etc.; the butchers on horseback, to the number of three hundred, in leg-of-mutton sleeves; the cartmen on horseback in white frocks; a steamboat with her steam up and machinery in motion; the famous Whitehall boat, carried by the pilots and watermen; and a great many stages, displaying the emblems of various trades, and on which mechanical operations were carried on during the march. The procession was closed by the military, who formed on the grounds north of the [Washington] square and fired a *feu-de-joie* after the civic ceremonies were concluded.

March 19, 1832. Washington.

Mr. Hamilton and I had an agreeable visit this afternoon from Mr. Webster, who came in after dinner to drink a glass of wine with us. He was in a fine talking humour, and of course we were pleased and instructed. We went this evening to a ball at Mrs. Bankhead's. It is a delightful house to visit, but the New Yorkers say we have better evening parties at home. There were many great folk, some clever folk, and a fair proportion of queer folk.

June 18.

Prayers were offered up yesterday in all the churches to avert the threatened visit of the cholera, and sermons preached to prepare the minds of the people for the affliction, which seems now to be considered inevitable. The weather is warm, but clear and pleasant; recent showers have refreshed the earth, and have been succeeded by pleasant southerly winds and a bright atmosphere. The reports of the day are that the disease has increased in Montreal and Quebec. The number of deaths in the former place is said to be two hundred and fifty. . . .

July 4.

It is a lovely day, but very different from all previous anniversaries of independence. The alarm about the cholera has prevented all the usual jollification under the public authority. There are no booths in Broadway, the parade which was ordered has been countermanded, no corporation dinner, and no ringing of bells. Some troops are marching about the street, "upon their own hook," I suppose. Most of the stores are closed, and there is a pretty smart cannonade of crackers by the boys; but it is not a regular Fourth of July. The disease is here in all its violence, and will increase. God grant that its ravages may be confined and its visit short!

April 1, 1833.

Mr. Audubon, the celebrated ornithologist, called upon me a day or two since. . . . He is about setting out on one of his enterprising excursions to the coast of Labrador, in pursuit of information to illustrate his favorite science, to which he is devoted with the ardour of a lover to his mistress. He is an interesting man of about fifty-five years of age, modest in his deportment, possessing general intelligence, an acute mind, and great enthusiasm. His work on the birds of North America, on which he is now engaged, is probably the most splendid book ever published. I have seen several of the numbers in the library of Congress. It will require nine years to complete it, and will cost eight hundred dollars; all the drawings are executed by himself or under his special superintendence. . . .

June 13.

The President [Jackson] is certainly the most popular man we have ever known. Washington was not so much so. His acts were popular, because all descriptions of men were ready to acknowledge him the Father of his Country; but he was superior to the homage of the populace,—too dignified, too grave for their liking; and men could not approach him with familiarity. Here is a man who suits them exactly. He has a kind expression for each,— the same to all, no doubt, but each thinks it intended for himself. His manners are certainly good, and he makes the most of them. He is a *gourmand* of adulation, and by the assistance of the populace has persuaded himself that no man ever lived in the country to whom the country was so much indebted. Talk of him as the second Washington! It won't do now. Washington was only the first Jackson. Poor Adams used to visit New York during his presidency. The papers, to be sure, announced his arrival; but he was welcomed by no shouts, no crowd thronged around his portals, no huzzas rent the air when he made his appearance, and yet posterity, more just than ourselves, will acknowledge him to have been, in all the qualifications which constitute his fitness to fill the office of a ruler of this great Republic, twenty times superior to Jackson. . . .

December 27.

The holidays are gloomy; the weather is bad; the times are bad; stocks are falling; and a panic prevails which will result in bankruptcies and ruin in many quarters where, a few short weeks since, the sun of prosperity shone with unusual brightness. It will be worse before it is better.

December 3, 1834.

Yesterday at noon the President's message was communicated to both Houses, and it was in New York at two o'clock this morning, having been brought on by express, in little more than twelve hours, two hundred and thirty miles. This is a great performance, and shows what money can do; but *cui bono?* the game is not worth the candle. There is not one reader of the daily papers out of a hundred who would give sixpence to read this document four hours earlier than he otherwise might, and the express in this instance is said to have cost seven hundred dollars. The message is, as usual, too long; but the people have become accustomed to take these annual outpourings of executive wet-nurses in pretty large doses, and rely more upon the efficacy of a bottle of Congress water than on the concentrated virtue of a Seidlitz-powder; and so Dr. Jackson, who can make his patients swallow anything, has, by the aid of his regular-bred practitioners in the study, and the green-apron boys below, managed to give the body politic enough to insure tolerable regularity until his next regular visit. . . .

January 1, 1835.

The new year commences auspiciously so far as the weather is concerned. There has never been a finer New Year's Day; the air is clear and pleasant, and just cool enough to preserve the snow, which gives facility to the visiting part of the population. I went out in the sleigh at twelve o'clock, and visited until four, leaving several of my visits unpaid, which delinquency my wife and I made up in the evening. Broadway, from morning until night, and in the night too, was crowded with pedestrians, and the music of sleigh bells was heard without the least intermission. . . .

April 25.

A man named Clayton made an ascension [by balloon] a few days since from Cincinnati in a style of adventure more splendid than any hitherto attempted. He gave notice that he meant to remain in the air as long as his supply of gas continued. He started at five o'clock P.M., went to sleep at a good regular hour in his car, travelled four hundred miles, made fast his balloon at two o'clock to the top of a tree on one of the mountains of Virginia, and then returned leisurely home to relate his adventures. We run faster, sail smarter, dive deeper, and fly farther than any other people on the face of the earth.

October 25.

My birthday. I am fifty-five years of age. My health is tolerably good, my faculties unimpaired, my mind capable, I believe, as ever it was, but less disposed to exertion; my temper, I fear, a little more irritable than it should be, and I cannot jump so high, nor run so fast, as I did twenty years ago; but, on the whole, I have not much reason to complain, and am better off in all respects than I deserve to be.

November 27.

. . . Living in New York is exorbitantly dear, and it falls pretty hard upon persons like me, who live upon their income, and harder still upon that large and respectable class consisting of the officers and clerks in public institutions whose support is derived from fixed salaries. I can raise my rents, if the tenants are able and willing to pay; but the increase of their pay depends upon others, who in their turn are precluded from the exercise of liberality by the fact of their being the stewards of others. . . . Marketing of all kinds, with the exception of apples and potatoes, is higher than I ever knew it. The sweat of the brow of New York all runs into the pockets of the farmers. I paid to-day $30 a ton for hay, and not an old fashioned ton of 2,240 pounds, but a newfangled ton, invented to cheat the consumer, of 2,000 lbs. I paid also for my winter butter, 400 to 500 lbs, $2.14 per pound. In the long course of thirty-four years' housekeeping I never buttered my bread at so extravagant a rate. Good butter is almost an indispensable article in the family; but there are many persons in New York as good as myself who must be content to eat dry bread this winter, or at least to spread the children's slices confoundedly thin.

December 17.

How shall I record the events of last night, or how attempt to describe the most awful calamity which has ever visited these United States? The greatest loss by fire that has ever been known, with the exception perhaps of the conflagration of Moscow, and that was an incidental concomitant of war. I am fatigued in body, disturbed in mind, and my fancy filled with images of horror which my pen is inadequate to describe. Nearly one-half of the first ward is in ashes, five hundred to seven hundred stores, which with their contents are valued at $20,000,000 to $40,000,000, are now lying in an indistinguishable mass of ruins. There is not, perhaps, in the world the same space of ground covered by so great an amount of real and personal property as the scene of this dreadful conflagration. The fire broke out at nine o'clock last evening. I was writing in the library when the alarm was given, and went immediately down. The night was intensely cold, which was one cause of the unprecedented progress of the flames, for the water froze in the hydrants, and the engines and their hose could not be worked without great difficulty. The firemen, too, had been on duty all night, and were almost incapable of performing their usual services. The fire originated in the store of Comstock &

Adams, in Merchant street, a narrow, crooked street, filled with high stores lately erected and occupied by dry-goods and hardware merchants, which led from Hanover to Pearl street. When I arrived at the spot the scene exceeded all description; the progress of the flames, like flashes of lightning, communicated in every direction, and a few minutes sufficed to level the lofty edifices on every side. It crossed the block to Pearl street. I perceived that the store of my son was in danger, and made the best of my way, by Front street around the old Slip, to the spot. We succeeded in getting out the stock of valuable dry goods, but they were put in the square, and in the course of the night our labours were rendered unavailing, for the fire reached and destroyed them, with a great part of all which were saved from the neighbouring stores; this part of Pearl street consisted of dry-goods stores, with stocks of immense value, of which little or nothing was saved. At this period the flames were unmanageable, and the crowd, including the firemen, appeared to look on with the apathy of despair, and the destruction continued until it reached Coenties Slip, in that direction and Wall street down to the river, including all South street and Water street; while to the west Exchange street, including all Post's stores, Lord's beautiful row, William street, Beaver and Stone streets, were destroyed. The splendid edifice erected a few years ago by the liberality of the merchants, known as the Merchants' Exchange, and one of the ornaments of the city, took fire in the rear, and is now a heap of ruins. The facade and magnificent marble columns fronting on Wall street are all that remain of this noble building, and resemble the ruins of an ancient temple rather than the new and beautiful resort of the merchants. When the dome of this edifice fell in, the sight was awfully grand; in its fall it demolished the statue of Hamilton, executed by Ball Hughes, which was erected in the rotunda only eight months ago, by the public spirit of the merchants. . . .

The buildings covered an area of a quarter of a mile square, closely built up . . . the number of buildings burned is 570 . . . the whole loss is something over $15,000,000. The insurance offices are all, of course, bankrupt, their collective capitals amount to $11,750,000; but those down-town have a large proportion of the risks, and will not be able to pay fifty per cent. of the losses. The unfortunate stockholders lose all. In this way I suffer directly, and in others indirectly, to a large amount. The Mayor, who has exerted himself greatly in this fearful emergency, called the Common Council together this afternoon for the purpose of establishing private patrols for the protection of the city; for if another fire should break out before the firemen have recovered from the fatigues of the last two nights, and the engines and hose be repaired from the effects of the frost, it would be impossible to arrest its progress. Several companies of uniformed militia and a company of United States marines are under arms, to protect the property scattered over the lower part of the city.

I have been alarmed by some of the signs of the times which this calamity has brought forth; the miserable wretches who prowled about the ruins and became beastly drunk on the champagnes and other wines and liquors with which the streets and wharves were lined, seemed to exult in the misfortune, and such expressions were heard as, "Ah! they'll make no more than five per cent. dividends," and "This will make the aristocracy haul in their horns."

Poor, deluded wretches!—little do they know. . . . This cant is the very text from which their leaders teach their deluded followers. It forms part of the warfare of the poor against the rich. . . .

December 30.

I went this evening to a party at Mrs. Charles H. Russell's. . . . The splendid apartments of this fine house are well adapted to an evening party, and everything was very handsome on this occasion. The house is lighted with gas, and the quantity consumed being greater than common, it gave out suddenly in the midst of a cotillon. This accident occasioned great merriment to the company, and some embarrassment to the host and hostess, but a fresh supply of gas was obtained, and in a short time the fair dancers were again "tripping it on the light fantastic toe." Gas is a handsome light, in a large room like Mr. Russell's, on an occasion of this kind, but liable (I should think) at all times to give the company the slip, and illy calculated for the ordinary uses of a family.

April 10, 1837.

. . . Markets continue extravagantly high; meat of all kinds and poultry are as dear as ever. The farmers (or rather the market speculators) tell us this is owing to the scarcity of corn; but the shad, the cheapness of which in ordinary seasons makes them, as long as they last, a great resource for the poor, are not to be bought under seventy-five cents and a dollar. Is this owing to the scarcity of corn, or are the fish afraid to come into our waters lest they may be caught in the vortex of Wall street? Brooms, the price of which, time out of mind, has been twenty-five cents, are now sold at half a dollar; but corn is scarce. Poor New York!

May 22.

The loss of life by steamboats in this country, and especially on the Western waters, is shocking in the extreme, and a stigma on our country; for these accidents (as they are called) seldom occur in Europe, where they do not understand the art and mystery of steam devices, or, indeed, of shipbuilding, better than we do. But we have become the most careless, reckless, headlong people on the face of the earth. "Go ahead!" is our maxim and pass-word; and we do go ahead with a vengeance, regardless of consequences and indifferent about the value of human life. What are a few hundred persons, more or less? There are plenty in this country, and more coming every day; and a few years in the life of a man makes very little difference in comparison with the disgrace of a steamboat being beaten in her voyage by a rival craft.

April 23, 1838.

. . . The "Great Western" . . . came up from Sandy Hook about two o'clock . . . the largest vessel propelled by steam which has yet made her appearance in the waters of Europe. Her . . . voyage, under the disadvantages of new machinery and a prevalence of head-winds, in fifteen days.

The city was in a ferment during the day. . . . The Battery and adjacent streets were crowded with curious spectators, and the water covered with boats conveying obtrusive visitors on board. The passengers on board . . . speak in the highest terms of the convenience, steadiness, and apparent safety of the new mode of conveyance across the ocean. Everybody is so enamoured of it, that for a while . . . our countrymen, "studious of change, and pleased with novelty," will rush forward to visit the shores of Europe instead of resorting to Virginia or Saratoga Springs; and steamers will continue to be the fashion until some more dashing adventurer of the go-ahead tribe shall demonstrate the practicability of balloon navigation, and gratify their impatience by a voyage *over*, and not *upon*, the blue waters in two days, instead of as many weeks, thereby escaping the rocks and shoals and headlands which continue yet to fright the minds of timid passengers and cautious navigators. Then they may soar above the dangers of icebergs, and look down with contempt upon the Goodwin sands or Hempstead beach. As for me, I am still skeptical on this subject. It would be presumptuous in this age of mechanical and scientific miracles to doubt the success of any startling experiment, or even to hint the possible difficulty of a contrivance by which a man might bite off his own nose; but . . . I should hesitate to trust to the powers of the air or the fire-god for my transportation and safe-conduct over this rivulet of blue water of three thousand miles in width, which separates us from the land of our fathers.

May 1, 1839.

May day is fine, pleasant weather, much to the comfort of jaded wives and fretting husbands. There is a great deal of moving in the streets out of Broadway, in the upper part of the city, but less, I think, than usual amongst the tenants of good houses. But the pulling down of houses and stores in the lower parts is awful. Brickbats, rafters, and slates are showering down in every direction. There is no safety on the sidewalks, and the head must be saved at the expense of soiling the boots. . . . The spirit of pulling down and building up is abroad. The whole of New York is rebuilt about once in ten years.

July 19.

An extract from a St. Louis newspaper states that the hunters had come in with twenty-four thousand buffalo-robes and a quantity of beaver, worth altogether $100,000. Twenty-four thousand buffaloes! . . . the imagination cannot keep pace with the magnificent scale on which the works of nature are represented in the regions of the great West. . . .

December 4.

I went this morning . . . to see a collection of the views made by the wonderful process lately discovered in France by Monsieur Daguerre, which is called by his name. . . . The pictures he has are extremely beautiful,—

they consist of views in Paris, and exquisite collections of the objects of still life. The manner of producing them constitutes one of the wonders of modern times, and, like other miracles, one may almost be excused for disbelieving it without seeing the very process by which it is created. It . . . is nothing less than the palpable effect of light occasioning a reproduction of sensible objects. . . . Every object, however minute, is a perfect transcript of the thing itself; the hair of the human head, the gravel on the roadside, the texture of a silk curtain, or the shadow of the smaller leaf reflected upon the wall, are all imprinted as carefully as nature or art has created them in the objects transferred; and those things which are invisible to the naked eye are rendered apparent by the help of a magnifying glass. . . . Who knows whether, in this age of inventions and discoveries, we may not be called upon to marvel at the exhibition of a tree, a horse, or a ship produced by the human voice muttering over a metal plate, prepared in the same or some other manner, the words "tree," "horse," and "ship." How greatly ashamed of their ignorance the by-gone generations of mankind ought to be!

April 10, 1840.

The Whigs are more ardent and active, and, they say, better organized than usual, for the charter election, which is to be held on Tuesday. Immense meetings take place every night at the general and ward places of rendezvous. Processions parade the streets at night with music, torches, and banners; the prevailing device for the latter is the *log-cabin;* and we had hard cider, which has become the fountain of Whig inspiration. In an evil hour the Loco-focos taunted the Harrison men with having selected a candidate who lived in a log-cabin and drank hard-cider, which the Whigs, with more adroitness than they usually display, appropriated to their own use, and now on all their banners and transparencies the temple of Liberty is transformed into a hovel of unhewn logs; the military garb of the general, into the frock and the shirt-sleeves of a labouring farmer. The American eagle has taken his flight, which is supplied by a cider-barrel, and the long-established emblem of the ship has given place to the plough. Hurrah for Tippecanoe! is heard more frequently than Hurrah for the Constitution! "Behold old things are passed away, and all things have become new." . . .

February 15, 1842.

"The agony is over"; the "Boz" ball, the greatest affair in modern times, the tallest compliment ever paid to a little man, the fullest libation ever poured upon the altar of the muses, came off last evening in fine style; everything answered the public expectation, and no untoward circumstances occurred to make anybody sorry he went.

The theatre was prepared for the occasion with great splendour and taste. The whole area of the stage and pit was floored over, and formed an immense saloon. The decorations and ornaments were all "Pickwickian." Shields with scenes painted from several stories of Dickens, the titles of his works on others surrounded with wreaths, the dome formed of flags, and the side walls in fresco, representing the panels of an ancient oaken hall. A small stage was erected at the extreme end, opposite the main entrance, before which a curtain was suspended, exhibiting the portly proportions of the immortal Pickwick, his prince of valets, and his body-guard of choice cronies. This curtain was raised in the intervals between the cotillons and waltzes, to disclose a stage on which were exhibited a series of *tableaux vivants*, forming groups of the characters. . . .

The company began to assemble at half-past seven o'clock, and at nine, when the committee introduced Mr. and Mrs. Dickens, the crowd was immense; a little upward of two thousand tickets were handed in at the door. . . . Everybody was there, and every lady was dressed well and in good taste, and decorum and good order were preserved during the whole evening. Refreshments were provided in the saloons on the several floors, and in the green room, which was kept for the members of the committees and their families. This branch of the business was farmed out to Downing, the great man of the oysters, who received $2,200. On the arrival of the "observed of all observers" a lane was opened through the crowd, through which he and his lady were marched to the upper end, where the committee of reception were stationed. Here I, as chairman of that committee, received him, and made a short speech, after which they joined in the dancing.

The author of the "Pickwick Papers" is a small, bright-eyed, intelligent-looking young fellow, thirty years of age, somewhat of a dandy in his dress . . . brisk in his manner, and of a lively conversation. If he does not get his little head turned by all this, I shall wonder at it. Mrs. Dickens is a little, fat, English-looking woman, of an agreeable countenance, and, I should think, "a nice person."

November 24, 1846.

The honourable John Quincy Adams was stricken by paralysis on Thursday last, whilst walking from his son's house in Boston. The last accounts state that he had partially recovered, his consciousness having returned and his speech being restored. . . . The country cannot afford to lose such a man. With all his eccentricities, prejudices, and want of tact, we have not his equal in this country for the most minute information on all subjects, technical, statistical, artistical, historical and diplomatical. No man knows so much, nor so accurately. He has probed deeply into the arcana of all the sciences, understands and can explain all subjects, from the solar system down to the construction of a toothpick. He has the Holy Scriptures at his fingers' ends, knows every line of Shakespeare, can recite Homer in the original Greek; could name, if he had a mind to do it, the author of "Junius," and knows all about Jack the Giant Killer. He speaks on all subjects, overthrows his opponents, and bothers his friends; and, in short, does more work than any day-labourer, and this, too, under some physical disabilities. He is so nervous that his pen has to be tied to his fingers. This prodigious amount of labour is accomplished by early rising, exact method, and the most untiring industry.

But Mr. Adams cannot last forever. He is eighty years of age, and it is greatly to be feared that the warning voice has come to him in this recent visitation. What a pity it is that on his decease he cannot leave his knowledge behind him; it would, indeed, be a rich inheritance.

February 24, 1847.

. . . John Quincy Adams is no more. Full of age . . . he died, as he must have wished to die, breathing his last in the capitol, stricken down by the angel of death on the field of his civil glory,—employed in the service of the people, in the people's Senate house, standing by the Constitution at the side of its altar and administering in the temple of liberty the rites which he had assisted in establishing. At twenty minutes past one o'clock, on Monday, the 21st, Mr. Adams, being in his seat in the House of Representatives (from which he was never absent during its session), attempted to rise (as was supposed, to speak), but sank back upon his seat and fell upon his side. Those nearest caught him in their arms. Mr. Grinnell bathed his temples with ice-water, when he rallied for an instant. The House immediately adjourned, in the utmost consternation, as did the Senate, when informed of the melancholy event. His last words were characterized by that concise eloquence for which he was remarkable: *"This is the last of earth; I am content."* Dr. Fries of Ohio, a member, raised him in his arms and bore him to the Speaker's room, where he lay, with occasional indications of consciousness, until last evening. The intelligence of his death came to Albany by the telegraph. Thus has "a great man fallen in Israel,"—in many respects the most wonderful man of the age. . . . Equal to the highest, the planetary system was not above his grasp. Familiar with the lowest, he could explain the mysteries of a mousetrap. . . . I listened once, with Mr. Webster, for an hour, at Mr. Adams's breakfast-table in Washington, to a disquisition on the subject of *dancing girls;* from those who danced before the ark and the daughter of Jairus, whose premature appearance caused so melancholy a termination to her graceful movements in the dance, through the fascinating exhibition of the odalisques of the harem down to the present times. . . . He was ignorant on no subject. . . .

December 16, 1848.

Now that the election is over, and General Taylor President past peradventure, California gold and the cholera are the exciting topics of the day. . . . Our newly acquired territory of California, having passed from the hands of Spaniards and Indians into those of the enterprising Yankees, who run faster, fly higher, and dig deeper than any people under the sun, has now developed its riches. The region of country watered by the river Sacramento is found to abound in pure gold; the shining tempter of mankind is found in the land and crevices of the rocks, and all the world have become diggers and delvers. The towns are deserted by all but the women; business is neglected; houses stand empty; vessels are laid up for want of hands; the necessaries of life cannot be obtained, and the people are starving with their pockets full of gold. . . .

June 1, 1849.

The cholera increases, the weather is foggy, murky, and damp,—just such weather as produces and propagates this dreadful disease. A panic is created; vegetables and fish, oysters and clams, generous wine and nourishing porter, are repudiated; foolish people run from one extreme to another; let them live well and temperately, wear flannel, and think less of cholera, and defy the foul fiend.

September 3, 1850.

"Sing a song of sixpence," at the rate of a thousand dollars a night. Our good city is in a new excitement. . . . Nothing else is heard in our streets, nothing seen in the papers, but the advent of the "Swedish Nightingale." Jenny Lind arrived on Sunday, in the "Atlantic." This noble steamer was a most fitting fiddle-case, a suitable cage for such a bird. The wharf was thronged with anxious expectants of her landing.

September 9.

There is rejoicing over the land; the bone of contention is removed; disunion, fanaticism, violence, insurrection, are defeated. These horrible slavery questions, which have suspended the public business for more than eight months, are settled; but how? The lovers of peace, the friends of the Union, good men, conservatives, have sacrificed sectional prejudices, given up personal predilections, given up everything, for Union and peace; and for this sacrifice the Lord be good to them! But, although all good men rejoice that the affair is settled, none are satisfied. It all comes of that crowning curse of national legislation, the annexation of Texas; and did not Daniel Webster warn the Loco-focos of all this? Did not Henry Clay sound his admonishing trumpet? Did not every Whig orator previous to General Harrison's election prophesy what would be the effects of this unnatural connection? And did not I, even I, in my harangues, portray the evils to result from this idle assumption of gratuitous trouble and vexation?

But the question is settled: we have made war upon Mexico, gaining glory by the gallantry of our warriors; conquered them all, and then, as in the case of Dr. Franklin's Frenchman, agreed to pay for heating the poker. But all is well. The House of Representatives on Saturday got rid of all the vexation in a bunch. The Texas boundary bill was passed, California was admitted as a State, Utah and New Mexico came in as Territories; all obstructions were removed, all amendments rejected. They came into the House, determined to cast all political differences, all sectional jealousy, all party violence, upon the altar of Union, harmony, and the Constitution; and I presume the rest of the nation's business will be hurried through head over heels, and the people's representatives will go forthwith to their wives and children, their farms and merchandise.

September 17.

Another of those dreadful railroad disasters which every mail brings us, and the news-packets transmit on their paper wings to every corner of the country, occurred one day last week on the Western railroad between Albany and Boston. The train ran off the track, the cars were demolished, several persons were injured, and three passengers killed. . . . So much for railroad travelling. Give me the post-coach and seven miles to an hour. I enjoyed it lately, and travelled for once again like a gentleman and man of sense.

September 24.

The Knickerbockers are crowing . . . at the great voyage of the "Pacific," . . . the shortest yet; she went to and returned from England in less than thirty days. What wondrous changes have occurred in our day and generation! The summer after I married I was nine days going in a sloop from New York to Albany,—this voyage which is now made in as many hours; then it occupied one day less than is now required to make a European passage. We fly through the air, glide over the bosom of the ocean, and dive beneath its waters with the speed of lightning; speed is the ruling principle of mankind; the wind is a laggard, and the shooting star comparatively slow in its movements.

April 10, 1851.

Dr. Francis will not let me go to the office, and my migrations are confined to the sofa and the large easy-chair. I eat no breakfast and very little dinner. . . . The doctor plies me with brandy-toddy, milk-punch, and other buttresses to my feeble frame-work.

April 30.

This volume of my journal, which has only four vacant leaves to be completed, has been suspended during nearly the whole month by continued unmitigated illness and incapacity to perform any act of mental or physical ability. Feeble beyond description, utterly destitute of appetite, with no strength in my limbs, and no flesh upon my bones, shall this journal be resumed? During this illness I have gone occasionally to my office for a short time, and performed a little *pro forma* business; but it could have been performed by deputy. To-morrow will be the first of May. Volume 29 lies ready on my desk. Shall it go on?

[Philip Hone made no entries in Volume 29. Four days later he died in his seventy-first year.]

"Who can paint the depression . . .
the blackness of the crowds . . ."

Edmond and Jules de Goncourt

One of the most remarkable journals ever written was that of two
French brothers, Edmond (1827–1896) and Jules (1830–1870)
de Goncourt. There exists no other example of a similarly successful collaboration in diary keeping. The de Goncourts were so
closely linked in life and writing that they seemed to have merged
into a single personality. "This journal," said Edmond de Goncourt, "is our nightly confession—the confession of two lives in-
separable in pleasure, travail and pain."

The brothers were sons of an artillery officer who had won
honours in the Napoleonic campaigns; Edmond was born in
Nancy, Jules in Paris. The younger de Goncourt began a career
in the Ministry of Finance, but he soon abandoned his post to
join his brother on a sketching tour of France. This journey convinced them that it was necessary to make a new approach to
the writing of art criticism and history. They set new directions in
this field, as they did later when they introduced Japanese art to
France, and influenced a whole generation of writers and painters.
When the brothers turned to novel writing success came slowly;
their first book sold only sixty copies. Undiscouraged they continued to write. Their *Renée Mauperin* is probably best known to
English readers. Despite extravagances of style, their many literary innovations (they were among the first to experiment with
realism, naturalism and symbolism, each of which produced
schools of followers) significantly affected other writers of the
time. Zola said of Edmond de Goncourt at a memorial service, "I
was his pupil before I became his rival."

The most important of the de Goncourt originations was the
"human documentary"—indeed, this term for a device now familiar in books, radio broadcasts, and motion pictures, was of their
own coinage. By means of it the de Goncourts sought to present
in minute detail the infinitely varied bits and pieces which life,

From *The Journals of the de Goncourts,* edited by Julius West. Reprinted by
permission of Thomas Nelson and Sons, Ltd.

as in the patterns of a kaleidoscope, offers at any single moment. They used "documentation" in some of their novels and art histories, and particularly in their journal. Theirs were "scrapbooks on a glorious scale," as one critic put it.

The de Goncourts always went about with notebooks in their pockets to be sure nothing that was worthy of recording escaped them. Some of these gleanings were used for other literary purposes, but most of them went into the journal—some 900,000 words filling nine printed volumes. The death of Jules, a month before the outbreak of the Franco-German war, brought an end to their collaboration, but not to the journal. Edmond continued it. The passages given here preserve indelibly the drama of a city being strangled, of Paris prostrate under an ever-tightening siege and its people strained by emotion and mounting physical trials and tensions . . .

August 6, 1870.

From the gallery of Engravings of the National Library I saw people running in the rue Vivienne. Instinctively I put down the volume of reproductions and, soon outside, I began to run behind the runners. At the Bourse, from one end to the other, all heads are bared, hats are waving in the air, and every one is singing a mighty Marseillaise, the deafening waves of which swamp the buzzing within. I have never seen any enthusiasm like this. One passes men pale from emotion, children skipping from excitement, and women making intoxicating movements. . . .

August 7.

A frightful silence fills the Boulevard. There is not a carriage to be heard, not a child's cry of joy, and on the horizon is a Paris where sound itself seems dead.

August 21.

In the Bois de Boulogne. To see all these great trees fall under the axe, with the quiverings of men wounded to death; to see these, where a green curtain was spread, this mass of sharpened stakes, shining whitely, this sinister harrow—you feel a hatred of the Prussians rising in your heart. . . .

August 26.

At the East Station. In the middle of cases, baskets, parcels of old linen, bottles, mattresses, quilts, tied together with great ropes, there is now a little crowd shaking and tumbling down among all this variety of objects, of keen-eyed countrymen, buried and sunk in the holes and interstices. Here is an old woman of Lorraine, with a hunting dog at her feet and a crutch at her side, in a pointed brown bonnet, who draws from time to time from a basket some of the black grapes of her country, which she passes over to her grand-children.

August 30.

From the top of the Auteuil omnibus, going down from the Trocadéro, I saw, on the large grey open space of the Champ-de-Mars, in the sun-filled clearness, a mass of little red dots, of little blue dots—the men of the line.

I got down, and here I am in the middle of gleaming bundles; in the middle of little kitchens, where tin-pots are boiling; in the middle of open-air toilets, which are being made by men in their shirt-sleeves; in the middle of tents, in a triangle of shadow, in which may be seen the tan-coloured head of a pot-soldier, lying near his water-bottle in the straw. Some soldiers are filling their cans from bottles, sold by a wine-seller from a barrow; others are kissing a laughing woman who is selling green apples. I walk about in this movement, this animation, this gaiety of French soldiers about to start for death, when the broken voice of a little bandy-legged old man . . . cries out: "Pens and writing paper!" A cry which was almost a funereal memento, a sort of discreetly formulated piece of advice, which really meant, "Gentle-men, have you made your wills?"

August 31.

This morning at daybreak the demolition of houses on the military zone has been commenced. . . . One sees queer corners of half-demolished houses, with the remains of fantastic pieces of furniture. . . .

September 2.

I caught hold of Chennevières coming out of the Louvre, who tells me he is going to Brest tomorrow to escort the third consignment of pictures from the Louvre, which have been taken out of their frames, rolled up, and sent away, to be saved from the Prussians . . . now mere luggage, protected against the accidents of removal only by the word "Fragile."

September 3.

. . . What a sight Paris was this evening, under the blow of the news of the defeat of MacMahon and the capture of the Emperor! Who can paint the depression on all faces, the comings and goings of people walking aim-lessly about, the blackness of the crowds around the municipal offices, the assaults on the newspaper sellers' stands, the triple line of readers under ev-ery gas-lamp, . . . and on the chairs in the back shops the overcome attitudes of the women, who are alone, without their men. . . .

September 4.

This morning there is a fearful silence everywhere, under a grey sky which saddens everything. Towards four o'clock . . . outside of the *Chambre* . . . a multitude has accumulated, a world of men whose blouses make blue and white spots . . . the majority of whom have boughs in their hands or bouquets of green leaves fastened to their hats. Suddenly a hand raises itself above all the heads . . . "The Republic is Proclaimed." Then shouts of applause, hats in the air, people climbing up the pedestals of the statues, a man in a blouse who calmly begins to smoke his pipe. . . . Above the pediment, a man takes the blue and the white away from the tricolour flag, and leaves only the red waving. On the railings of the Tuileries, the gilt N's are hidden away under old newspapers, and crowns of everlasting flowers hang in the place of the absent eagles. . . . On the benches, against the kitchens, women are sitting about, cockades in their hair; and a young mother is quietly nursing a quite small infant in white swaddling-clothes. . . . Pavements and roadways are full, covered with men and women who behave as if they were entirely at home, a sort of holiday in the great city; yes, a million creatures who seem to have forgotten that the Prussians are only three or four days from Paris. . . . All along the rue de Rivoli troops are marching, singing the Marseillaise. Outside the Hôtel de Ville is an enormous crowd. From time to time little papers fall from the windows, which the crowd collects and throws back into the air, and which seem like snowflakes above the heads. . . . Returning by the rue Saint-Honoré, I found myself walking over pieces of gilt plaster which were, two hours ago, the shields bearing the imperial arms of purveyors to His Majesty [Napoleon III] that was. . . . This evening, right along the boulevards, the flower-sellers are only selling red button-holes.

September 7.

Between the Barrière de l'Étoile and Neuilly. It has rained all night. The tents have pailfuls of water in their folds, and damp straw is coming out, showing inside the tents pieces of red, which are soldiers sleeping rolled up. Sentries, like sick men in a hospital, are standing on guard, wrapped up in a covering, and with their heads swathed in handkerchiefs with blue squares. They all show, both by their faces and by the slackness of their movements, the bad effects of the cold night. . . .

September 17.

At Boulogne-sur-Seine only the butcher, the wine-merchant, and the hairdresser are open. . . . Here and there a few old women sitting in the sun, before the entrances to obscure alleys, refuse to go away, determined to die where they have lived. In the little side streets, deserted and inanimate, pigeons walk about the sidewalks, on which no human being disturbs them. The brilliant flowers, and the corners of the gardens in flower, contrast strangely with this absence of human life. As far as Saint-Cloud the road goes on between houses with blinds down, closed shops, catching the eye of the passer-by on account of the quantity of lost goods, sown broadcast on the pavements in the hurry of the retreat to Paris. A little child's sock, quite a new sock, tells me a whole story. Saint-Cloud, with its terraces of houses, on the finest day of the year, frightens one by its silence. It might almost be a dead city, under the implacable blue of a beautiful cholera sky.

September 22.

On the top of the Trocadéro, in the quickly moving air, all sonorous with the incessant drumming in the Champ-du-Mars, there are groups of sightseers, in the midst of whom are correctly-dressed Englishmen, with race-glass cases hanging behind them, holding in their gloved hands enormous binoculars. . . .

September 24.

It is really ironical to see Parisians, of all people those who most like their meat fresh and their vegetables new, consulting one another in front of the tinned provisions of cosmopolitan grocers. . . . Restaurant menus are contracting. Yesterday the last oysters were eaten, and the only fish now left are eels and gudgeons. . . .

September 25.

Both banks of the Seine are lined with cavalry horses. . . . The windows of the galleries of the Louvre are closed up with bags of sand. In the rue Saint-Jacques women in groups of two or three are plaintively talking of the rise in the price of food. . . . In the Luxembourg Gardens thousands of sheep, tightly packed and restless, are rumbling about in their narrow enclosure like maggots in a box.

September 30.

Awakened by cannons. A red dawn. The hollow rumbling in the distance. . . .

October 1.

Horseflesh has entered on the sly into the diet of Paris. . . . Yesterday, at Péters, they brought me a roast beef of a blackish red of which my artist's eyes made me suspicious. The waiter merely assured me quite peacefully that this horse is beef.

October 10.

This morning I went out to get a card for an allowance of meat. . . . I took away a blue paper. . . . It gives me the right to buy every day, for myself and my servant, two rations of meat or four portions of other food, prepared in the national canteens. There are coupons up to 14th November.

October 13.

It is a strange feeling, closer akin to mournful humiliation than to fear, to know that those hills, so near you, are no longer French; that those woods are no longer the places in which one's friends walk; that those houses, bathing so beautifully in the sunshine, no longer shelter your friends and acquaintances; and to look through binoculars at men in busbies and with black and white flags on that Parisian soil, and to feel those men we conquered at Jena hidden on the green horizon, only just over a couple of miles away. . . . From the Place d'Italie to the Jardin des Plantes . . . everywhere are men in blouses going through military drill, and who are being imitated by swarms of slatternly little girls with frizzled hair and the bright eyes of Bohemians, armed with laths. Night has come, little bats are zigzagging on the dense violet of the towers of Notre-Dame, against the pale sky, underlined, as it were, by the bayonets of the armed multitude marching on the embankments.

October 17.

All day long I hear the thundering from Mont-Valérien, the rolling and prolonged echo like that of a pop-gun on the rising ground about Sèvres and Meudon, and the snapping noise of the Mortemart battery.

October 18.

The cannonade attracts me to the Bois de Boulogne, to the Mortemart battery. There is something solemn in the serious gravity and the thoughtful slowness with which the artillerymen do their work. They load; they stand immovable on each side; a few lean in fine sculpture-like attitudes on their ramrods. An artilleryman in shirt-sleeves standing on the right holds the cord. There are a few moments of stillness, of silence—I should almost say of emotion; then the cord is pulled; there is a thunder, a flame, a cloud of smoke in which the bunch of trees which mask the battery is lost. For a long time there is a white cloud, which slowly disappears, and once more reveals the yellow of the sanded embrasure, furrowed by the charge, the grey of sacks of earth, of which two or three are broken open by the recoil of the gun, the red of the artillerymen's caps, and the white of the shirt of the man who drew the cord.

This thing which kills from afar is a real entertainment for Paris, which comes in barouches and landaus up to the firing-point, where women mingle with the soldiers, and get as near to the formidable noise as they can. . . .

October 20.

. . . The windows of the food shops begin to take on a sinister appearance, on account of the absence of exhibits. The cook-shops have nothing more to show than the soiled table-napkins of their customers. . . . The Grand Market is curious. Where fish used to be sold, only horseflesh is now to be had; and instead of butter the grease of unspecified animals is offered, looking like large squares of white soap. . . .

October 28.

The astonishing, the marvellous, the incredible thing is the absence of all communication with the outside world. There is not a single inhabitant who has received news of his relatives during the last forty days. If a copy of a Rouen newspaper manages, by hook or by crook, to gain admittance, it is reproduced in facsimile, as if it were the most wonderful of rarities. Never before have two million men been shut up in such a coop. . . .

November 12.

I hope posterity will not talk to future generations about the heroism of the Parisians in 1870. All their heroism will have consisted in eating nasty butter with their haricots, and horse steaks instead of beef, and that without taking too much notice: the Parisian has hardly the discernment of the animal he eats.

November 24.

The rag-picker of our boulevard, who at the moment keeps a place in the queue at the market for a low eating-house keeper, told Pélagie [the household servant] that he was buying, for his employer, cats at six francs, rats at one franc, and dog-flesh at one franc fifty, the pound.

December 25.

It is Christmas Day. I heard a soldier say, "When we called the réveillé we found five men frozen in their tents!"

What an extraordinary transformation has taken place in our shops. A jeweller in the rue de Clichy is now exhibiting in jewel-cases fresh eggs, wrapped up in cotton wool.

The mortality rate in Paris is high. It is not altogether due to starvation. And the dead do not merely consist of sick and sickly people, finished off by the hardships and continual privations. This mortality is largely due to depression, to enforced removals, to home-sickness, for that corner in the sun which people used to have outside Paris. . . .

December 26.

A new eatable has been discovered for the unsatisfied appetite of Parisians; it is arsenic. Newspapers cheerfully describe the energy this poison gives to Styrian chamois hunters, and offer you, for lunch, an arsenical globule of some doctor or other. . . .

This cold, this frost, the lack of fuel to cook the little ration of meat one is given has exasperated the feminine population, which throws itself upon trellises, wooden shutters, and snatches at all that comes to its angry hands. These women are helped in their work of destruction by the terrible children, who mount on each other's shoulders and break down all they can . . . and go away dragging fagots behind them by means of a little string which they hold in their hands buried in their pockets. If this terrible winter continues, all the trees in Paris will fall under the pressing need of fuel.

December 31.

I had the curiosity to call on Roos, the English butcher of the Boulevard Haussmann. I saw all sorts of strange relics. On the wall, hanging in a place of honour, is the trunk of young Pollux, the elephant from the Jardin d'Acclamation; and in the midst of nameless meats, and of unusual horns, a boy is offering camel kidneys.

The master butcher is holding forth, surrounded by a circle of women: "It's forty francs the pound for the fillet, and for the trunk . . . yes, forty francs . . . You find that dear? . . . Well, really, I don't see what I am going to get out of it. . . . I reckoned on 3,000 pounds, and I've only got 2,300. . . . The feet, you want to know how much the feet are? They are twenty francs. Other parts go from eight to forty francs. . . . Yes, I can recommend those sausages; elephant's blood, you know, is most nourishing . . . his heart weighs twenty-five pounds . . . Yes, there's some onion in the sausage. . . ." I buy two larks for my tomorrow's lunch. . . .

January 8, 1871.

This night I asked myself, behind my curtains, if there was a hurricane going on. I got up and opened the window. The hurricane was the incessant and continuous whistling of the howitzer shells passing over my house. . . .

January 24.

. . . On the boulevard, outside the Opéra-Comique, I meet a crowd stretching across the roadway, and preventing the omnibuses from going on. I asked myself if it was another riot. No; all these heads in the air, these arms pointing out something, all these women's parasols, all this anxious and hopeful waiting is on account of a pigeon—perhaps the bearer of dispatches—who rests on the tile of one of the chimneys of the theatre. In this crowd I meet the sculptor Christophe, who tells me that negotiations for an armistice have been entered upon. . . .

At Brébant's [restaurant] . . . we speak in hushed, sickroom voices of the sad events of the day and the day that awaits us. . . . A shoulder of mutton is brought along. "Oh!" says Hébrard, "we shall be eating the shepherd at our next dinner." In fact, it is a very nice shoulder of dog. . . . Coming out of Brébant's, on to the boulevard, the word surrender, which might have been dangerous to pronounce a few days ago, is on everybody's lips.

January 26.

It is drawing near. New batteries seem to have been unmasked. Shells burst every minute on the railway lines, and our Boulevard Montmorency is crossed by people walking on all fours. Everybody is filled with a sorrow which induces one to consider the shame of surrender. It is, however, the women who still resist the idea. This very morning there were poor women who stood in the lines outside the bakers' shops and cried: "Let them cut down our rations still more, but don't let them surrender!"

[Two days later Paris capitulated. The war dragged on for a few more weeks. On March 1, 1871 the German army entered Paris in triumph.]

"Where am I to begin, where am I to stop,
what am I to write? . . ."

Odd Nansen

Fridtjof Nansen, the father of Odd Nansen (1901–   ), was a
Norwegian arctic explorer and statesman who won the Nobel
Prize for his work for prisoners' welfare at the time of the first
world war. Just twelve years after his death his son was himself
a German political prisoner in the second war.

It was Nazi policy to treat Norwegian captives with comparative leniency lest the position of their Quisling allies be imperilled.
Thus Nansen and his compatriots fared relatively well behind the
barbed wire of the concentration camps. From this vantage point
of limited privilege Nansen was able to describe the horror of
the scenes before him with some detachment. He did not have to
fear each morning that he would not live to see another night.
Nansen's concentration camp diary is in a sense more persuasive
of the truth of things than had it been written in desperation by
one less favoured. He had moments in which to ask himself searching questions. If his hungry, verminous, degraded existence was
the best, the *de luxe* treatment the Nazis could offer, what then
was the worst?

Nansen kept his diary undetected through all the days of his
imprisonment, writing it in a microscopic hand on the thinnest of
tracing paper. The words of his manuscript are so minute that it
requires a magnifying glass to make them legible. Assigned to
work at a joinery, he made a number of breadboards with cun-
ningly hollowed-out centers cut just the size of the diary pages
and carefully glued together again to conceal the precious enclosures. The breadboards (they served as plates for camp meals)
he confided to trusted friends and in these knife-scratched, grease-
stained depositories the diary was ultimately smuggled into Norway. Only one section was lost.

Nansen lives today in Oslo. He is a practicing architect, but,
following the interests of his father, devotes much of his time to
the work of providing relief for political prisoners and displaced
people.

From *Day to Day* by Odd Nansen, copyright, 1949, G. P. Putnam's Sons.

The passages of the diary given here chronicle the days of hope and despair wearing wretchedly away after two endless concentration camp years. The pace of Gestapo brutality has quickened. Nothing seems to be happening to shorten the ordeal. But then . . .

January 13, 1944.

Today it's two years since I was arrested. Two everlasting, senseless years. What's become of them? I daren't look back on them. My optimism is paling, too—in spite of good news from the east. When on earth are the *decisive* events coming? . . .

January 21.

They were back again last night, that is yesterday evening—a big raid. It started after evening roll call. Just another raid. We've gotten so used to it that we've ceased to take much notice. . . .

There's almost nothing happening, except that the Russians are advancing steadily and surely, while the English and Americans jabber and appoint generals and commanders-in-chief—for what?

February 24.

. . . Yesterday as we were marching in from work there stood by the gate a curious piece of furniture that produced a disagreeable impression at once, even if one didn't know what it was for. It looked much like an ordinary gymnasium horse, only that it was equipped with a great variety of straps. At evening roll call we learned why the horse had been produced. A prisoner was to be publicly flogged. . . .

First the victim was harnessed firmly to the horse. His legs were lashed to the horse's legs, and then the man was doubled over the horse on his belly, and his arms secured. A sack was fastened down over his head and shoulders and a cloth stuffed into his mouth, to prevent his screams from being heard. None the less those who were nearest heard at every blow a heart-rending groan, rising finally to one long roar that pierced through all muffling layers. First he was given thirteen blows with "the big stick," a baton in a leather sheath with lead in it. This is wielded by a stout hangman, a hulking fellow whose job it is. He is a prisoner too—and a political prisoner. Then the man was given twelve blows with a smaller stick, no doubt of the same type; this one is wielded by a second hangman—also a prisoner. When the five and twenty had been reached the Commandant announced that he would now get five more as a special bonus from himself. It was then he bawled so loud that it could be heard all over the camp. . . .

Now, after the thirty blows, he's going into the SK, which means a slow form of capital punishment. . . .

February 25.

. . . The smoke rises from the crematory chimney without a pause, day and night. Many, many people are being shot or otherwise put to death. . . .

May 31.

So May has gone too, just like that—and midsummer is drawing near. Light summer nights—flowery dresses—warmth and fragrance in the air. The mere thought of violets and lilies of the valley and all the other flowers at home calls up the most wonderful pictures—and memories. But this is Sachsenhausen—nothing, nothing but dusty, filthy, ghastly Sachsenhausen. And nothing happens.

June 6.

The invasion started this morning! In Normandy. From both sides there were bulletins at noon about heavy fighting. Large forces are said to have been landed from the early hours onward. Also a great number of parachute troops, of course. There is no report of whether they've succeeded in establishing a bridgehead.

It came like thunder from a clear sky. I'd almost given up the idea of that everlasting invasion, that second front that has been haunting our minds for almost three years, and now it's really started! . . .

June 7.

Yes, one can talk of a festive atmosphere this seventh of June, cynical as it may appear in view of the horrors now being enacted in the West. But there's no denying it, the camp is as though bewitched. People are whistling, singing, smiling, joking; a mood of gaiety has completely gotten the upper hand, and from now on the days will no longer be gray and endless. The decision is approaching, perhaps with giant strides.

August 14.

. . . This morning, as we marched out to work after the first straitened night, a dismal sight met our eyes on the main road from Sachsenhausen. An endless train of women, children, and men. They had been standing there, lined up five and five under guard, for five hours, it's said. . . . There were supposed to be three thousand people there, all told; there were babies among them, in their mothers' arms, and young girls and boys. . . .

August 15.

The 3,500 people on the road yesterday were refugees from Warsaw. Warsaw is burning. The Germans did it. Completely! One can imagine what is going on there! . . .

August 31.

Yesterday two men were hanged at once on the same gallows at evening roll call. A Pole and a Russian. They had stolen some food in a cellar where they worked. That was all. Again there was something wrong with the "technical apparatus." The ropes were too long. Their feet touched the ground after the drop. One of them was not dead; people ran up and tried to get off his wooden shoes, and when they didn't succeed the hangman lifted his legs off the ground. The victim turned blue in the face, and it looked as though he were suffering the most frightful agonies before he died.

Nor did these two know that they were going to be hanged until they came marching up with their guards and saw the gallows. One exclaimed in Polish, "My God! my God!" The other in Russian, "So long, comrades," looking across and down the ranks, where they stood in silence, thousands of comrades. Both mounted the scaffold bravely, and went calmly to their deaths. . . . Both young lads. Anonymous to most. Two less among many, many hundreds of thousands. . . . If only one could sleep into another age!

September 18.

. . . The other day I had punishment gymnastics. I had been "reported" one morning at roll call for turning round and talking to Erik. That of course is highly improper. As I was made to feel. For punishment gymnastics are no joke. It's now three days ago, and even yet I have the greatest difficulty in moving, let alone bending, sitting down, or getting up again.

The gymnastics lasted about an hour and were conducted by one of the greatest brutes in camp. . . . And ultra-brutal they were. Three times from Block Fourteen to the *Revier* and back, that is, three times the diameter of the parade ground in a frog jump—squatting low with one's arms stretched up in front of one, and jumping along in that posture. . . .

Reeling I got to my feet again when that exercise was over—but alas— only to start another just as hard. Walking in the same doubled-up attitude, that is waddling like a duck. Up and down again the full length of the parade ground. I managed that, too. Then there was running—running on and on. I was reeling and my head swam and I swallowed dust; but I managed. I came through, but many fell and didn't get up. The SK bandit flew at them with boots and stick. Most took no further notice of him. They were carried off.

We had knee-bendings—up and down—ten times, twenty times, thirty times—God knows how many times; and God knows how I got through them. . . .

November 16.

. . . Railway cars drew up to the crematory buildings, with their tragic loads of people mostly condemned to death. Transport after transport from Hungary, from Slovakia, Bohemia, Moravia, Germany, Belgium, Holland, Norway, France, Yugoslavia, the Ukraine, with thousands upon thousands more Jews came rolling in to that ramp. When the trucks had been emptied, the Jews were lined up five and five on the ramp, and a selection was made. All the healthy and able-bodied were picked out; the rest were for the "baths."

All the small children went into the "bath." Every woman with a child in her arms went the same way, and all the old and feeble. . . .

When those who were to die had been separated from those who were to live—the death cortege moved off to the crematories. These contained, besides the gas chambers and the furnaces, which could burn forty-eight corpses at a time, a big dressing room, where they were taken on the pretext that they were to have a bath. They undressed without suspicion and went into the "bath," which was next door. There gas came out of the showers instead of water. . . . The road from the bath to the furnace was short. This process has now been going on several years without a break, and in spite of that the five crematories have been inadequate. They also had to burn corpses out in the open. . . .

February 2, 1945.

Yesterday, after we got back to camp at night, was indescribable. It was almost as though we were already free. All were in smiling spirits, rubbing their hands and breathing deeply. At last! Now it was only a question of hours. The Russians were just yonder in the cutting. Several wouldn't go to bed, at least not to sleep. . . .

February 3.

From the brightest and wildest optimism we've been plunged into gloomy pessimism. When we got back from the job last night, we were met by the sinister announcement that the camp is to be evacuated. We're all to start off on a trek. To the great majority the news was thunder from a clear sky, and many still refuse to believe it, such an utterly outrageous impossibility and insanity does it seem. Forty thousand men on the tramp south, southwest or west, miserably clad, with nothing to eat. . . .

February 9.

The evacuation continues. Now almost ten thousand must have gone, but no Norwegians, except for a small transport of those newly discharged from the *Revier*, and a few others who had no working squad. The transport was going to Bergen-Belsen near Hanover. Activity in the crematory is undiminished; the burning goes on day and night. . . .

February 12.

The language is exhausted. I've exhausted it myself. There are no words left to describe the horrors I've seen with my own eyes. How am I to give even a reflection of the hell I was plunged in yesterday?

It was in the isolation area between Blocks Thirteen and Fourteen, which was filled with Jews from Liberose. . . . It was appalling. Dante's inferno couldn't be worse. There were more than a thousand Jews; that is, they had once been Jews and human beings, now they were living skeletons, beastlike in their mad hunger. They flung themselves on the dustbins, or rather plunged into them, head and shoulders, several at a time; they scratched up everything, absolutely everything that was lying in them, potato peel, garbage, rottenness of every kind. They didn't see what they were eating, simply shoved it into their faces, clawed and tore at it, fought over it. They stuck fast in the dustbins, taking them along when they straightened up again, and off they went like that, two or three skeletons combined into a strange walking caryatid sculpture. But the worst was that the whole time, without a break, the blows from rubber truncheons were hailing down on them. Young lads (SAW lads) thrashed away at them to their hearts' content. But they took no notice. The instant the tormentors turned away to hit out in another direction, they plunged into the dustbins again. The blood was pouring off them, from their faces and hands and legs. Most were barefoot, and the clothes hung round them in shreds; more great wounds from blows shone through rents and openings in the clothes on their bodies.

The tormentors were indescribable. They were only boys, but the act of striking intoxicated them and drove them wild. I followed them, I saw their faces as they struck, they were no longer human, they were living devils, possessed, transported with ecstasy. They struck whatever they saw, not merely those they saw in the dustbins. They hurled themselves on the crowds like roaring lions, and struck out right and left. The wretched victims went down round them by dozens; that only inspired them, and they went on striking at them as they lay, trod upon them, kicked them, while the blood was streaming from mouths, ears, and wounds. Every time they needed a rest, they turned exultantly to their laughing and smiling comrades, laughed back, and gave the truncheon a limber, playful swing round their heads. Then they flew at it again.

A Jew who had been struck ten or twenty times tottered and fell down at my feet. He lay motionless, the blood was running out of his mouth and trickling from one ear. His eyes were bloody and the cheekbones swollen and cracked with blows. One of his lips was cleft and some teeth knocked out. He was barefoot, and his feet covered with frostbite. His trousers had slipped down, so that his matchstick thighs were visible, and through a rent in his shirt one could see his ribs. . . .

[They] dragged the Jew to the wall and managed to prop him up against it, and he came to again. He looked at me with such eyes—oh God, such eyes; all the white was red, and the red was running down his cheeks—the brown pupils were dull, as though a film had been drawn over them, and the big eyelids hung over them heavily. Some gurgling noises came from him, I thought he had difficulty in breathing, I tried to straighten him up; still the gurgling noises came, more regularly, it sounded as though he were being choked—but he was crying, crying like a child. . . .

February 13.

From the Tub section of the *Revier* men are constantly being picked out who go direct to the crematory. Yes, *direct!* Not into the gas chamber first.

They get a knock on the head, that's usually enough. One hears screams and single shots when a detachment has gone there. . . .

February 14.

Yesterday the total of deaths in camp (for the previous twenty-four hours) was given as: 150 men in the *Revier*, 46 in the blocks, 14 of the Jews from Liberose, 1,542 men in transports. A day's harvest. Yesterday (the next twenty-four hours) 110 men were "picked out" from the Tub and taken "round the corner," that is, to the crematory. . . .

March 21.

. . . On Monday evening (the day before yesterday) a list was called over that got part of the way through N. Then came packing and goodbys, and at eleven o'clock, in pitch darkness, but under a starry sky, we were stumbling across the square to the bathhouse. A lovely night, "worthy" to be the last in Sachsenhausen. We got cold standing still, and began walking about between the huts for the last time. Deserted "streets," lit only by a pale and slightly veiled young half-moon. The outlines of the camp loomed dark and sinister against the night sky; from the square the hut gables looked like the teeth of a gigantic semi-circular saw; one felt it could only be the dark that prevented one from seeing the blood running down them. I stood a long time on the square, and let my gaze pass from tooth to tooth. Cleanliness—honesty—obedience—truthfulness—and love of the Fatherland! And the blood ran down and dripped onto the sand of Sachsenhausen, as it has done for many years without stopping.

About one o'clock we got into the bathhouse, and there we stayed, packed like herrings in a barrel, until four. Then we had to fall in outside. Obviously the cars had come. Just as we were marching off, there was an alert. Back into the bathhouse! Another hour in the crush, then the all clear sounded, and out we went again. This time out through the gate, on through the furthest gate; it was as though we sprouted wings and flew out, to where the row of white busses stood. . . .

March 22.

. . . The trains—or caravans—of refugees covered all the roads. It looked as though the whole country were full of gipsy gangs. Everything gave the impression of disintegration and confusion, hopelessness, misery, and disaster. . . .

At last we turned down a side road, and immediately afterward all eleven busses drew up before the entrance to Neuengamme concentration camp.

The first thing we encountered as we got out of the busses and stretched our stiff legs was a stink of garbage and unadulterated sewer. A stink that has pursued us ever since, only we've got more used to it. . . .

We came out on a middle-sized concrete square surrounded by huts, which again were surrounded with barbed-wire fences, behind which we caught a glimpse of friends from the previous transports. We were called over, lined

up five and five, and at length marched through the barbed-wire enclosure
and thence into a hut. But what a hut! The filth was positively sticking out
of it, and it smelled of everything that smells bad. The hut was a single open
room, eight meters wide and fifty or sixty meters long; the floor was divided
up into hutches filled with straw, and on the straw were blankets. One got
the feeling that the straw and blankets were alive with lice, though we
couldn't see them yet. We were to be better acquainted! . . .

The whole yard was pretty much an open sewer, which stank even worse
than the inside of the huts. Although the weather was dry and had been
for a long time, puddles filled the holes in the concrete, and the grooves and
cracks. What they were puddles of, the smell betrayed, and the condition of
the gully holes and the drain they were supposed to lead to was also beyond
all doubt. The filth was everywhere, in thick layers; it was worse than a pigsty.
The hut was the stall where the beasts were kept at night, the courtyard the
outer sty. . . .

March 24.

. . . There is already typhus in the camp. The dungheaps lie open, sewage
and filth are afloat everywhere. Lousy, sick, and dying mussulmen drag themselves around and hang begging on the barbed-wire fences round our yards.
One has a sense of wading in and swallowing bacteria and bacilli. Every day
a hundred or a hundred and fifty men are dying in the camp, which contains
eight thousand prisoners altogether, or possibly twelve thousand. The figure
varies, for fresh transports keep arriving. . . .

March 25.

. . . One sight I saw yesterday afternoon is in my mind the whole time;
it is like a permanent background, a kind of horizon to all that passes on the
stage in front of me. The sight of hundreds of corpses, piled on top of one
another in the mortuary, as high as houses. Arvid and I went there. I wanted
to see. It was appalling. There might have been three or four hundred skeletons; they reminded one of lean, plucked chickens; these weren't human beings—so small and miserable. The numbers, the overwhelming numbers, I
suppose completely threw out one's sense of scale. But the faces and those
ghastly hundreds of pairs of staring eyes, those gaping mouths and pain-
distorted features—they were human. Those of human beings who had lived,
suffered, and died. And all those hundreds were only three days' harvest! . . .

March 28.

. . . Orders came for a number of us, about twelve hundred Norwegians
and Danes, to move into the *Schonungsblock*, a two-story brick building that
looks quite grand from outside, but the inside of which no one could forget
in a hurry, after one look at it. The misery passed all bounds and baffled all
conception. In every bed there were three or four, indeed sometimes five or
six men. It sounds incredible, but I saw them. Certainly they were lying on

top of each other, but most of them were nothing but skeletons and didn't take up much room. And they lay quiet; they hadn't the strength to move. *They were there to die!* and many were already dead! The whole interior of the building was one inferno, a waiting room of death worse than could be conjured up in the wildest fantasies. With no attendance those poor creatures lay in their beds; some had tuberculosis, others dysentery and typhus, others open wounds and running venereal diseases and all conceivable and inconceivable sufferings of every kind. Those . . . who lacked the strength to hoist themselves out of their bunks, which were in three tiers, and they were the majority, relieved themselves where they lay. . . . In the passages, in the washroom, in the well of the staircase, inside the wards, and in the beds corpses lay around.

And now these people were to clear out, to make room for more Norwegians in the camp. And we were to move in after them. The SS intended us to move into the house and get into the mussulmen's beds just as they were. Into the cakes of ordure and the filth, into the same straw that has lain in the bunks for years, collecting every known species of bacterium and bacillus and every variety of human excrement! Here we have German *Sauberkeit* in a nutshell; that's what it is. The covers must be smooth and the edges flush like rulers in a row, there must be nothing on the blankets, nothing under the beds; what the blankets are concealing, though it were a dungheap, is of no interest, provided it's as smooth as a dance floor. Yes, even if there are corpses under the blankets, rotting away, that's quite in order so long as they are invisible. I mention this last because in the cleaning that followed, dead bodies actually were found, hidden in the straw of the bunks. Their bedmates "kept" the bodies there so as to get an extra helping of soup or an extra bread ration. . . .

April 18.

The front is drawing nearer. . . .

Huge transports of prisoners are leaving here every day. Whither no one knows. We merely suspect the very worst. The smoke from the crematory chimney, which on certain days rolls out black and thick and settles with a loathsome stench over the camp, is a reminder that the "harvest" here is still in full swing. . . .

April 20.

I am writing in the bus. The bus to freedom. We're going northward through Germany, over the North German plain. We're not far from Lubeck, but our destination is farther north. . . .

April 28.

What on earth am I to write? It's as impossible today as on all the other days that have passed in one long whirl of unreality and fairy tale. I am no longer in Germany! I am in Denmark, at a country house; Mogelkaer is its

name, outside Horsens, and I've already been here more than a week! It's unbelievable. And what have I not experienced in that week? Only it seems so
hopelessly impossible to describe. Where am I to begin, where am I to stop,
what am I to write? . . .

"War here is pure madness; obscene, arrogant madness."

Harry Levin

When David united the tribes of Judah and Israel and made
Jerusalem his capital some 2,900 years ago, the city was already
three or four times as old as New York is now, and even then it
was much coveted and contended for. In the first four centuries
after King David, the citadel on the hills commanding the mountains of Judea was seized and sacked by Egypt, Philistia, Arabia,
Syria, Egypt again, and Babylon. Then came conquering Greeks,
Romans, Persians, the Crusaders, Tartars, and finally the Turks.
When Turkey was defeated in the first world war Jerusalem was
put under British mandate and Jews, left out so long, hoped that
a turn had come for them again to regain their homeland.
"L'shana haba'a b-Yerushalaim," "next year in Jerusalem," a Jewish aspiration for centuries, seemed possible of realization. On
May 15, 1947 the British mandate ended, and on the same day
the independent state of Israel was born with a provisional capital
at Tel-Aviv. As usual, Jerusalem was under siege, this time by
Arab forces.

Harry Levin's diary tells the story of the suffering and privations of the 100,000 persons trapped in the ancient city by Arab
fire.

"It is told," he says, "as I, a Jew, experienced it. It is coloured
inevitably by my attitude. . . . It is necessarily incomplete, as
the narration is a personal one. Every man, woman and child lived
through his own experiences. These are mine, as they were recorded at the time."

Levin was born and educated in South Africa. Journalist, editor, and war correspondent, he reported the ill-fated British campaign in Burma in the second war for an American radio network.
During the battle of Jerusalem he conducted the English language
broadcasts that brought what news was available of the conflict
under the shadow of Mount Scopus. He is now in the Israel diplomatic service.

Here then, dateline the Bible lands, are rams' horns and Sten guns sounding anachronously in sacred places while the oldest testament was being once again rewritten.

March 25, 1948. Tel-Aviv.

The stars were going out when Ruth [his wife] and I left the Tel-Aviv hotel. The clock said 5.15. Shooting was sporadic now, after the savage night. Double-barrelled mortar blasts and the spasms of machine-guns diminished and renewed themselves since early evening like the unwinding of an endless chain. From our balcony we watched the red-and-purple tracer bullets knifing their way upwards and flares splashing fiery globes of light into the sky. The sounds of a dance party floated across from a nearby flat. Lorries filled with young Jews rushed through the street below, heading for the Jaffa border, about half a mile away. . . . The city's bulk was still dark against the dawn when we reached our starting point. There were 26 buses drawn up in a line. . . . The last to board our bus was a frowsy, bearded man with a lot of small packages. Before him came an elderly German Jew. He was very timid, kept wiping his glasses gently, and tried to make himself as small as possible. The seats and racks had been removed and we were tightly squeezed together on three narrow, backless, lateral benches running the length of the bus. Seven or eight young men stood in the aisles. . . . A young man in khaki shorts looked in.

"Not enough women here," he said. A few minutes he returned with two girls. They seated themselves on the floor in the narrow aisle behind the driver. One carried a box wrapped in newspaper, handling it gently. "Cakes," she said, smiling to the driver. . . .

Six fellows and a girl formed our Haganah [Jewish self-defence organiza-tion] escort. . . . A tall dark lad they called Boaz was in charge. He had the head of a Greek God and eyes that sparkled. . . . A small saloon car scouted on ahead of the convoy. We drove through the narrow-meshed back streets of the city. Daytime sounds were stealing on the stillness of the early morn-ing. . . . To avoid Arab Yazour, where a Jewish patrol car and its ten occu-pants were wiped out yesterday, we turned off along narrow tracks between the orange groves. The milky languorousness of the early morning sky was changing to the provocative blue of a bright Mediterranean day. The sun sifted its way through the closely-growing trees, gilding the shiny young leaves and diapering the yellow earth with dark patterns. A pleasant smiling land, this Sharon, and the white blossoms and pigeons and humming bees made our steel-plated buses, creaking beneath their weighted clumsiness, look monstrously unreal.

At 8 we pulled into Rehovoth. . . . Beyond the township we stopped again and some heavy sacks were handed in to Boaz. "Here it comes, girls," he grinned, and began pulling out the dismantled parts of sub-machine guns and pistols, and hand-grenades and ammunition. The women hid them about their bodies. Ruth had a revolver under an armpit and a sten-gun barrel under her skirt. The old woman who looked like a swaddled lump of flesh called out . . . "Aren't you going to give me something?"

"All right, Granny. Here's a piece for you too." Gingerly the old woman laid hands on the sten-gun magazine, hesitated for a second, then slipped it into her bosom. She closed her eyes and shuddered as the cold metal touched her flesh, then wriggled in discomfort. We moved on.

The search several minutes later was a desultory affair. Two British soldiers fumbled casually under the benches and ran their fingers over the pockets of the younger men. The women, most of them now very pregnant-looking, stared stonily at them. Flustered by the stares, the soldiers left off suddenly.

"Nothing 'ere," we heard one of them report outside. The second added: "Least as 'ow nothing we could find." . . .

We bumped and tossed along a rough track, the relics of a Roman road. At 11 we stopped near Hulda and all of us tumbled out. . . .

It is 3 o'clock now and we are still here. I am writing this seated on the ground, leaning against a boulder. Young grain, dotted with anemones, sways over the undulating plain. Our convoy passengers lie sprawled about the fields. . . . Boaz has been pointing out the historic associations of the landscape with an air of passing on something he witnessed yesterday.

"See where our scout is posted on that hillock? Samson probably posted some of his scouts about there when he went raiding with his 'Foxes.' . . . Over there David met Goliath. . . . Saul and Jonathan drove the Philistines that way. . . . The Pharaohs came up along there in their invasion" . . .

Night. After 11, and I am utterly exhausted. But I must put this down while the memory of it, the way things happened and the way they looked, are still so fresh. . . .

It was dark and breathless inside the bus. The boys stood with their arms cocked near the peep-holes. Everybody silent, but you felt the tenseness . . . when a dull crackling rang out. In a minute it came sweeping down on us from all sides. The first shots sounded surprisingly like pebbles against our steel sides. . . . No longer the sound of pebbles. The bus quaked beneath the impact. The ratatat, whistling and thuds merged into an unbroken uproar. . . . A shot hit our engine. Then two more pierced our roof. One of them struck the back wall of our bus; the other hit the paper-covered package which one of the girls had described as cakes (a wireless transmitter). For those of us who were not handling guns the only thing was to sit quiet and sweat. Some crouched on the floor wherever there was an inch of space. Most bent low where they sat. During a brief lull I heard the bearded man murmuring psalms. . . . Suddenly, a low cry from the freckled student, who was standing near me. His hand rose slowly, then he slumped down on top of a man crouching on the floor. The girl of the escort pushed her way forward, torch in hand. She was very business-like now. She took out a battle-dressing from its pouch and gave crisp directions. He had been hit in the side of the head, a chance shot through the peep-hole. In a few minutes he died. . . . Just then another bullet crashed through our roof and grazed Boaz's leg. The roof seemed to be our most vulnerable part; I wondered why more shots weren't penetrating. Boaz ignored his leg, keeping his eyes on his gun-sight. We heard the bus beside us moving off. We moved after it, our engine gurgling irregularly. . . . Jerusalem lay darkly outlined against the sky. Fireflies were shining out across the road. . . . Our journey ended behind the Egged bus terminus, finishing quietly, like the anti-climax of a play.

March 29.

Ruth was out early, shopping, and returned despondent. Four hours of tramping and cajoling yielded only 9 tins—nothing of it very substantial—2 packets of candles, and some dried fruit. The only things in plenty are tea, expensive canned fruit, and Australian asparagus soup that nobody seems to want. We decided to lay in asparagus soup in a big way. . . .

. . . I had to step in to T.'s. They were waiting for Dalia, who had been out since midday. Only 16, so she is still in an auxiliary unit. She came in after 10 and you felt everyone breathe more freely. She said casually that they had been out in the hills . . . and her young brother tried to question her, but she brushed him aside. "I've got to go to school to-morrow, and haven't done my homework yet."

April 10.

. . . Woke up this morning to the sound of renewed firing, which continued all day. Michael was horrified to see families, with children, taking their *Shabbath* morning stroll in Rehavia (can't go further southward) while snipers' bullets were crackling out only a few hundred yards away.

April 15.

. . . A minute ago a company of Haganah boys passed my window. Some in knitted caps, some bare-headed; one wore over-alls and another grey flannels; most carried rifles or sten-guns and a few had machine-guns. Nurses marched with the men. Motley in appearance, but . . . the deep roughness of their voices and metallic beat of their tramp echo in the air for anyone to hear. Almost imperceptibly Haganah has emerged at last from its 40-year-old hide-out . . . its leaders known only to the few, moving about as farmers from the settlements engaged on special duties, as members of innocuous public institutions or committees; the Government clerks, engineers, policemen who are also officers of Haganah; the labour organizers, teachers, taxi-drivers and its other contact men; the men and women of every sphere who form its rank and file . . . fitting like pieces into the vast jigsaw pattern. If you happen to know their personal identities, here you forget them. At H.Q. everyone is still anonymous; no one has a surname, the Biblical first names pinned up on their doors are all assumed. . . .

April 16.

This evening Don brought me some pipefuls of tobacco; exquisite. . . . Spoke also about the other fellows in his unit, an oddly assorted crowd, hailing from seven different countries; some of the men didn't know one end of a rifle from the other. "It's crazy the way we're armed," he said. "We've only one weapon for two or three men, and those we have are of all kinds. When we go out on a *peula* [military operation] they bring us enough to go round, but some are still hot from the last *peula*. As soon as we get back, half the stuff is taken away for some other bunch. . . .

Sixth day to-day that we have no water. The reserve tank we set up in the kitchen is getting low. The lavatory smells, and I feel itchy. . . .

April 21.

. . . It goes on and on; simply a question of which ends first, the shooting or I. Every day, by the law of proportion, my chances grow slimmer. I go to my office or into town, run across open spaces, duck as the shells and shots whizz overhead, and feel all the while the helplessness of the individual, the futility of trying to avoid death or maiming here when it may be waiting for you as you turn the corner. At night I listen to the implacable accent of finality of every shot and shell and think of those for whom this night is their last. M. asked me yesterday if she could name me executor in her will. I made mine weeks ago. Everyone is writing his will. That is the only legal work lawyers are doing these days. . . .

May 1.

Two hours ago, at 20 past 1, we had our first direct shell hit. It struck the house like the blow of a colossal fist, crashing into B.'s bedroom. . . . No whistle, no shriek, just a monstrous shock. . . .

May 2.

. . . Ration to-day: olives, about 8 per person, and 1½ oz. of jam. Supper to-night: asparagus soup and half a dried herring (imported from Turkey; used to be food of the poorest of the poor, sometimes also given as animal feed). Ruth's latest "shopping" expedition yielded 2 packets of bran flakes and 2 tins of asparagus soup. If life were not so full, I would try to plumb the bottom of the Great Asparagus Soup Mystery. How do tins of it still show up when everything else has vanished? . . .

May 6.

Shooting stiffened to-night. Coming out of the "news-room," we found ourselves in the midst of a hiss of bullets. We edged low along the outer wall, then took cover behind the new defence wall before Yeshurun Synagogue. (Similar walls erected to cover the entrances to public buildings all over town.) We got on the air four minutes late. . . .

May 8.

It really is cease-fire, and the tormented city is catching its breath. . . . Not a shot all day. Makes one feel almost uneasy, like a toothache that persists even after removal of an aching tooth. . . .

This morning I heard a woman across the road send her young children out to play. They were not to go far out of call; if there were shots, they must hurry in at once. . . .

May 10.

. . . No water in the taps yet, and our reserve running low. In some quarters a black market has sprung up in branches and twigs for cooking; the papers are telling people how to make fireless cookers. . . . Worried about Ruth; noticed again to-day how much weight she is losing. She is nervy and irritable. Everyone is thinner; some look gaunt. . . .

May 11.

. . . Yesterday Ben-Gurion said in Tel-Aviv: "I believe that the Jewish State will arise in a few days, after an interval of over 1,900 years." It will seem incredible when it happens . . . on the 15th. . . .

May 12.

. . . Water rationing started to-day. We have had none for six days. . . . The daily ration, two bucketfuls per person. . . . I passed two queues in town, one waiting to take part in the £5,000,000 national loan; the other, on the opposite pavement, waiting for water. . . .

May 14.

Morning. It is dawn of Friday. To-day the British leave Palestine. One can still barely comprehend it. It was ominously still during the night, and I slept fitfully . . . in the distance, a dull, indistinct, receding noise, like the rumour of a river. The British Army stealing through the night, as though in complicity with the darkness.

The sun is low over the Mountains of Moab. Its first rays are lighting up the slopes of Scopus and Mount of Olives. It is going to be a hot day, perhaps *hamseen* again. From the window a few minutes ago I watched a young boy furtively break branches in the avenue, then run with them to the stove made of stones and tin-piping in the backyard of his house. . . . I am writing these lines now because I don't know if I shall be able to write anything more to-day. For the moment time hangs suspended. Any minute it may break into violent motion. . . .

Ruth is out, working on maps. Haven't seen her since early morning, but found a note from her, saying: "Please, please, don't get yourself killed to-day of all days." . . .

May 15.

First day of Israel. A radiant day. . . . What will that new life, independence, freedom, mean? . . .

Sounds so simple: Haganah into Army of Israel. Who can stop to think of it now, but what a tale! The 40-year, illegal building up of an underground self-defence; years of exhausting struggle against the Ottoman Turks; the cold, frustrating struggle against the British; the secret assembling through the years of light equipment, armoured cars, a few heavy guns, some light planes, getting it wherever they could, paying fantastic prices, stealing it where they couldn't buy it, smuggling it into the country by every ruse. (Remember stumbling once upon a consignment of meat imported from Syria that had machine-gun parts in the carcases; learning on another occasion, that lorry-loads of bee-hives, all menacingly a-buzz, held ammunition); manufacturing bits of equipment in under-cover workshops; training its men (from a score of countries) in cellars, caves, farm settlements; half their energies given to maintaining secrecy. Now . . . it is challenged by regular armies, squadrons of planes, tanks, cannon. How much the iron of their wills must make up in the balance! . . .

In the midst of it all, this morning, a boatload of 500 Jewish refugees from the D.P. camps land in Tel-Aviv. Yesterday they would have been called "illegal immigrants" and deported. To-day flags wave in their honour.

May 22.

. . . A mortar has been set up on a roof not far from us. Every night the gunner fires a lone shot or two as if to say: "Just to prove to you that I'm here"; occasionally, he fires one or two shells also by day. People say, with bitter irony, that the gunner makes the shells himself and it takes him all day to make two. We hear them tearing the air to pieces, wait eagerly to hear the echo of the distant crash six or seven seconds later. . . .

May 30.

Another day of merciless shelling. . . . A city loses its character in war, it becomes a snare; death and survival alone have meaning. But Jerusalem is not just another city. War here is pure madness; obscene, arrogant madness. And as *they* wage it, this is not war. They are not fighting for it . . . they sit on the hills, pump shells into it, into every street and corner, and mangle it. The city the world calls Holy!

June 2.

The Arabs have accepted the cease-fire, conditionally. . . . The broadcast of the news of the Arab acceptance was almost drowned by cannon fire, earlier this morning than usual. . . .

June 3.

. . . We are cut off, absolutely. . . .

I sit here by the pin-point light of a small candle, that seems designed to throw up dark shadows rather than illumine, and think of us, buried in night, and the world there, vast and self-absorbed. Out there people walk across fields, saunter home in the evening shadows. Lights are lit in homes and halls. Music played, books read . . . people go to their appointed work, are busy with it, know the purpose it serves. They eat a square meal and don't give a thought to what there'll be to-morrow. In some places they are even feeding corn to the cattle; use milk to fatten pigs, having no other use for it. They stay at home or go out, as they wish. They talk about all things under the sun. They sleep in a bed and take a shower. Their children play in the parks. . . . The whine of a shell stabs me into life. And then everything changes. I feel it is the world that is drained away. There is no other city, no other people, no other sky, no other light, but these I know here.

June 10.

Last day before cease-fire; 27th day of consecutive shelling, and the bitterest. For the first time they are firing hundred-pounders. . . . Three shells exploded in quick succession somewhere near us. I was thinking how stupid it would be to get killed now, a few hours before the truce, and . . . suddenly, in the brief lull that followed, a boy's shout split the silence. It came from about a block away. The cry was more terrible even than the shells: "*Ima* [Mother] . . . *Ima* . . . *Ima* . . ." each call louder and more horror-stricken than the last, and the third broke down in sobs. An abominable day. . . .

June 18

The first week of the truce is gone. . . . The dead are buried, and the maimed and wounded are still out of sight. How quickly the dead of yesterday are forgotten—unless they be your very own. Life strives to take shape again, closing up its gaps. We watch the moon rise quietly, silvering the old stones . . . impatient . . . hungry. There are a thousand things we want daily and can't get, a match, a cigarette, a book, a Tel-Aviv newspaper, a sound of music, a bath, contact with the world. . . . Still no water except the ration. Nor electricity, except for a few rare hours a week. . . . People are irritable, full of bitter retrospects. You feel the sagging of their will. Ruth says: "Everything is angular; people and their tempers. Nothing is round or smooth any more." It is hot, and bodies smell, and the toilet is more horrible than ever. . . .

July 2. Tel-Aviv.

Two days in Tel-Aviv. After Jerusalem, it is like emerging from a nightmare into the brilliant light of the sun. Everywhere delirious enthusiasm . . . immense assurance . . . surging movement. . . . The streets are crowded, people eat well, sit at ease in the packed cafés, patronize beauty parlours, cake-shops, gift-shops, stand window-shopping amidst the endless clatter of traffic, queue up for seats at concerts, theatres, opera, cinemas, lectures. They jump on buses, order taxis, switch on lights, turn on water without giving it a thought. They . . . take unashamed delight in every new feature and trapping of independence. *Our own* Cabinet Ministers, diplomats, officials, police; our own stamps. . . .

For hours yesterday Ruth and I just walked, allowing ourselves to be carried away by the dream come true. We looked at . . . the food-shops stacked high with provisions, at the fruiterers' crates overflowing with abundance, at the smart clothes in the windows. Suddenly Ruth, bethinking herself that she looked thin, pale and ugly, made straight for a hairdresser. It didn't help her much, because her hair, the hairdresser said, was brittle; she could not, he thought, be having enough vitamins. . . .

We are sitting on a café terrace by the sea. This evening . . . the Mediterranean is indescribably beautiful in the last rays of the sun. Laughing children, brown as nuts, are still playing in the sand. . . . A little while ago I heard an immigrant, speaking in Yiddish, at the table behind us, tell his companion that before he came he dreamed only of Tel-Aviv; but now he wanted to go on the land.

"I was a book-keeper in Budapest," he said, "but in the camps they taught me what labour is. I want to start life anew, like Israel, for myself now. I want to dig my hands into the earth and know that it is mine and that I'll never have to leave it."

14. AND THEN AN END—OR A NEW BEGINNING

"The sun had gone down . . ."

Michihiko Hachiya

In the early days of August 1945 every diarist in the world recorded what was literally the most earth-shaking event of the century—the explosion of an atomic bomb over the small Japanese city of Hiroshima.

The story was told on six continents, in every language spoken by man. Within seconds, it was said, a hundred thousand lives had been snuffed out, as many more had been doomed to invalidism and lingering death from radiation. The homes of a quarter million people had been destroyed instantly "as if ground into dust by a giant foot," as one American airman described it. The flash of the bomb was clearly visible 170 miles away. The mushroom cloud towered 20,000 feet above Hiroshima, bearing the pulverized remains of trees, motor cars and human beings.

That flash marked not only the greatest planned catastrophe in history. It was also the birth of a new dimension in the world—of bombs incomprehensibly destructive, of an unlocked energy of which the ancient alchemists had dreamed, of a chain reaction that might end in a miracle world of ease and prosperity.

But in Hiroshima that morning of August 6th there lived one diarist with another story to tell—a modest, compassionate, middle-aged physician named Michihiko Hachiya. Dr. Hachiya was born and educated in Okayoma. He was director of the Hiroshima Communications Hospital, serving civil service employees of the area, the hospital in whose gutted remains many of the victims were to be treated. And he was himself among the first patients, for the bomb did not spare him.

As the night of that long day came on, Dr. Hachiya began his journal on odds and ends of salvaged, scorched paper. Here are the words of a man who had just felt the blast that shook the world. "The hour was early; the morning still, warm, and beautiful . . ."

From *Hiroshima Diary*, by Michihiko Hachiya, M.D., translated and edited by Warner Wells, M.D. Copyright 1955 by The University of North Carolina Press.

August 6, 1945.

The hour was early; the morning still, warm, and beautiful. Shimmering leaves, reflecting sunlight from a cloudless sky, made a pleasant contrast with shadows in my garden as I gazed absently through wide-flung doors opening to the south.

Clad in drawers and undershirt, I was sprawled on the living room floor exhausted because I had just spent a sleepless night on duty as an air warden in my hospital.

Suddenly, a strong flash of light startled me—and then another. So well does one recall little things that I remember vividly how a stone lantern in the garden became brilliantly lit and I debated whether this light was caused by a magnesium flare or sparks from a passing trolley.

Garden shadows disappeared. The view where a moment before all had been so bright and sunny was now dark and hazy. Through swirling dust I could barely discern a wooden column that had supported one corner of my house. It was leaning crazily and the roof sagged dangerously.

Moving instinctively, I tried to escape, but rubble and fallen timbers barred the way. By picking my way cautiously I managed to reach the *rōka* and stepped down into my garden. A profound weakness overcame me, so I stopped to regain my strength. To my surprise I discovered that I was completely naked. How odd! Where were my drawers and undershirt?

What had happened?

All over the right side of my body I was cut and bleeding. A large splinter was protruding from a mangled wound in my thigh, and something warm trickled into my mouth. My cheek was torn, I discovered as I felt it gingerly, with the lower lip laid wide open. Embedded in my neck was a sizable fragment of glass which I matter-of-factly dislodged, and with the detachment of one stunned and shocked I studied it and my blood-stained hand.

Where was my wife?

Suddenly thoroughly alarmed, I began to yell for her: "Yecko-san! Yecko-san! Where are you?"

Blood began to spurt. Had my carotid artery been cut? Would I bleed to death? Frightened and irrational, I called out again: "It's a five-hundred-ton bomb! Yecko-san, where are you? A five-hundred-ton bomb has fallen!"

Yecko-san, pale and frightened, her clothes torn and blood-stained, emerged from the ruins of our house holding her elbow. Seeing her, I was reassured. My own panic assuaged, I tried to reassure her.

"We'll be all right," I exclaimed. "Only let's get out of here as fast as we can."

She nodded, and I motioned for her to follow me.

The shortest path to the street lay through the house next door so through the house we went—running, stumbling, falling, and then running again until in headlong flight we tripped over something and fell sprawling into the street. Getting to my feet, I discovered that I had tripped over a man's head.

"Excuse me! Excuse me, please!" I cried hysterically.

There was no answer. The man was dead. The head had belonged to a young officer whose body was crushed beneath a massive gate.

We stood in the street, uncertain and afraid, until a house across from us began to sway and then with a rending motion fell almost at our feet. Our own house began to sway, and in a minute it, too, collapsed in a cloud of dust. Other buildings caved in or toppled. Fires sprang up and whipped by a vicious wind began to spread.

It finally dawned on us that we could not stay there in the street, so we turned our steps towards the hospital [a few hundred yards away]. Our home was gone; we were wounded and needed treatment; and after all, it was my duty to be with my staff. This latter was an irrational thought—what good could I be to anyone, hurt as I was.

We started out, but after twenty or thirty steps I had to stop. My breath became short, my heart pounded, and my legs gave way under me. An over-powering thirst seized me and I begged Yecko-san to find me some water. But there was no water to be found. After a little my strength somewhat returned and we were able to go on.

I was still naked, and although I did not feel the least bit of shame, I was disturbed to realize that modesty had deserted me. On rounding a corner we came upon a soldier standing idly in the street. He had a towel draped across his shoulder, and I asked if he would give it to me to cover my naked-ness. The soldier surrendered the towel quite willingly but said not a word. A little later I lost the towel, and Yecko-san took off her apron and tied it around my loins.

Our progress towards the hospital was interminably slow, until finally, my legs, stiff from drying blood, refused to carry me farther. The strength, even the will, to go on deserted me, so I told my wife, who was almost as badly hurt as I, to go on alone. This she objected to, but there was no choice. She had to go ahead and try to find someone to come back for me.

Yecko-san looked into my face for a moment, and then, without saying a word, turned away and began running towards the hospital. Once, she looked back and waved and in a moment she was swallowed up in the gloom. It was quite dark now, and with my wife gone, a feeling of dreadful loneliness overcame me.

I must have gone out of my head lying there in the road because the thing I recall was discovering that the clot on my thigh had been dislodged and blood was again spurting from the wound. I pressed my hand to the bleeding area and after a while the bleeding stopped and I felt better.

Could I go on?

I tried. It was all a nightmare—my wounds, the darkness, the road ahead. My movements were ever so slow; only my mind was running at top speed.

In time I came to an open space where the houses had been removed to make a fire lane. Through the dim light I could make out ahead of me the hazy outlines of the Communications Bureau's big concrete building, and be-yond it the hospital. My spirits rose because I knew that now someone would find me; and if I should die, at least my body would be found.

I paused to rest. Gradually things around me came into focus. There were the shadowy forms of people, some of whom looked like walking ghosts. Others moved as though in pain, like scarecrows, their arms held out from their bodies with forearms and hands dangling. These people puzzled me un-til I suddenly realized that they had been burned and were holding their arms out to prevent the painful friction of raw surfaces rubbing together. A naked woman carrying a naked baby came into view. I averted my gaze. Perhaps they had been in the bath. But then I saw a naked man, and it occurred to me that, like myself, some strange thing had deprived them of their clothes. An old woman lay near me with an expression of suffering on her face; but she made no sound. Indeed, one thing was common to everyone I saw—complete silence.

All who could were moving in the direction of the hospital. I joined in the dismal parade when my strength was somewhat recovered, and at last reached the gates of the Communications Bureau.

Familiar surroundings, familiar faces. There was Mr. Iguchi and Mr. Yoshihiro and my old friend, Mr. Sera, the head of the business office. They hastened to give me a hand, their expressions of pleasure changing to alarm when they saw that I was hurt. I was too happy to see them to share their concern.

No time was lost over greetings. They eased me onto a stretcher and carried me into the Communications Building, ignoring my protests that I could walk. Later, I learned that the hospital was so overrun that the Communications Bureau had to be used as an emergency hospital. The rooms and corridors were crowded with people, many of whom I recognized as neighbors. To me it seemed that the whole community was there.

My friends passed me through an open window into a janitor's room recently converted to an emergency first-aid station. The room was a shambles; fallen plaster, broken furniture, and debris littered the floor; the walls were cracked; and a heavy steel window casement was twisted and almost wrenched from its seating. What a place to dress the wounds of the injured.

To my great surprise who should appear but my private nurse, Miss Kado, and Mr. Mizoguchi, and old Mrs. Saeki. Miss Kado set about examining my wounds without speaking a word. No one spoke. I asked for a shirt and pajamas. They got them for me, but still no one spoke. Why was everyone so quiet?

Miss Kado finished the examination, and in a moment it felt as if my chest was on fire. She had begun to paint my wounds with iodine and no amount of entreaty would make her stop. With no alternative but to endure the iodine, I tried to divert myself by looking out the window.

The hospital lay directly opposite with part of the roof and the third floor sunroom in plain view, and as I looked up, I witnessed a sight which made me forget my smarting wounds. Smoke was pouring out of the sunroom windows. The hospital was afire!

"Fire!" I shouted. "Fire! Fire! The hospital is on fire!"

My friends looked up. It was true. The hospital *was* on fire.

The alarm was given and from all sides people took up the cry. The high-pitched voice of Mr. Sera, the business officer, rose above the others, and it seemed as if his was the first voice I had heard that day. The uncanny stillness was broken. Our little world was now in pandemonium.

I remember that Dr. Sasada, chief of the Pediatric Service, came in and tried to reassure me, but I could scarcely hear him above the din. I heard Dr. Hinoi's voice and then Dr. Koyama's. Both were shouting orders to evacuate the hospital and with such vigor that it sounded as though the sheer strength of their voices could hasten those who were slow to obey.

The sky became bright as flames from the hospital mounted. Soon the Bureau was threatened and Mr. Sera gave the order to evacuate. My stretcher was moved into a rear garden and placed beneath an old cherry tree. Other patients limped into the garden or were carried until soon the entire area became so crowded that only the very ill had room to lie down. No one talked, and the ominous silence was relieved only by a subdued rustle among so many people, restless, in pain, anxious, and afraid, waiting for something else to happen.

The sky filled with black smoke and glowing sparks. Flames rose and the heat set currents of air in motion. Updrafts became so violent that sheets of zinc roofing were hurled aloft and released, humming and twirling, in erratic flight. Pieces of flaming wood soared and fell like fiery swallows. While I was trying to beat out the flames, a hot ember seared my ankle. It was all I could do to keep from being burned alive.

The Bureau started to burn, and window after window became a square of flame until the whole structure was converted into a crackling, hissing inferno.

Scorching winds howled around us, whipping dust and ashes into our eyes and up our noses. Our mouths became dry, our throats raw and sore from the biting smoke pulled into our lungs. Coughing was uncontrollable. We would have moved back, but a group of wooden barracks behind us caught fire and began to burn like tinder.

The heat finally became too intense to endure, and we were left no choice but to abandon the garden. Those who could fled; those who could not perished. Had it not been for my devoted friends, I would have died, but again, they came to the rescue and carried my stretcher to the main gate on the other side of the Bureau.

Here, a small group of people were already clustered, and here I found my wife. Dr. Sasada and Miss Kado joined us.

Fires sprang up on every side as violent winds fanned flames from one building to another. Soon, we were surrounded. The ground we held in front of the Communications Bureau became an oasis in a desert of fire. As the flames came closer the heat became more intense, and if someone in our group had not had the presence of mind to drench us with water from a fire hose, I doubt if anyone could have survived.

Hot as it was, I began to shiver. The drenching was too much. My heart pounded; things began to whirl until all before me blurred.

"*Kurushii*," I murmured weakly. "I am done."

The sound of voices reached my ears as though from a great distance and finally became louder as if close at hand. I opened my eyes; Dr. Sasada was feeling my pulse. What had happened? Miss Kado gave me an injection. My strength gradually returned. I must have fainted.

Huge raindrops began to fall. Some thought a thunderstorm was beginning and would extinguish the fires. But these drops were capricious. A few fell and then a few more and that was all the rain we saw.

The first floor of the Bureau was now ablaze and flames were spreading rapidly towards our little oasis by the gate. Right then, I could hardly understand the situation, much less do anything about it.

An iron window frame, loosened by fire, crashed to the ground behind us. A ball of fire whizzed by me, setting my clothes ablaze. They drenched me with water again. From then on I am confused as to what happened.

I do remember Dr. Hinoi because of the pain, the pain I felt when he jerked me to my feet. I remember being moved or rather dragged, and my whole spirit rebelling against the torment I was made to endure.

My next memory is of an open area. The fires must have receded. I was alive. My friends had somehow managed to rescue me again. . . . The entire northern side of the city was completely burned. The sky was still dark, but whether it was evening or midday I could not tell. It might even have been the next day. Time had no meaning. What I had experienced might have been crowded into a moment or been endured through the monotony of eternity. . . .

The streets were deserted except for the dead. Some looked as if they had been frozen by death while in the full action of flight; others lay sprawled as though some giant had flung them to their death from a great height.

Hiroshima was no longer a city, but a burnt-over prairie. To the east and to the west everything was flattened. The distant mountains seemed nearer than I could ever remember. The hills of Ushita and the woods of Nigitsu loomed out of the haze and smoke like the nose and eyes on a face. How small Hiroshima was with its houses gone.

The wind changed and the sky again darkened with smoke.

Suddenly, I heard someone shout: "Planes! Enemy planes!"

Could that be possible after what had already happened? What was there left to bomb? My thoughts were interrupted by the . . . [coming of Dr. Katsube the hospital's head surgeon, and being carried to an operating room]. . . . The distance was only a hundred meters, but it was enough to cause my heart to pound and make me sick and faint.

I recall the hard table and the pain when my face and lip were sutured, but I have no recollection of the forty or more other wounds Dr. Katsube closed before night.

They removed me to an adjoining room, and I remember feeling relaxed and sleepy. The sun had gone down, leaving a dark red sky. The red flames of the burning city had scorched the heavens. I gazed at the sky until sleep overtook me.